AF605873

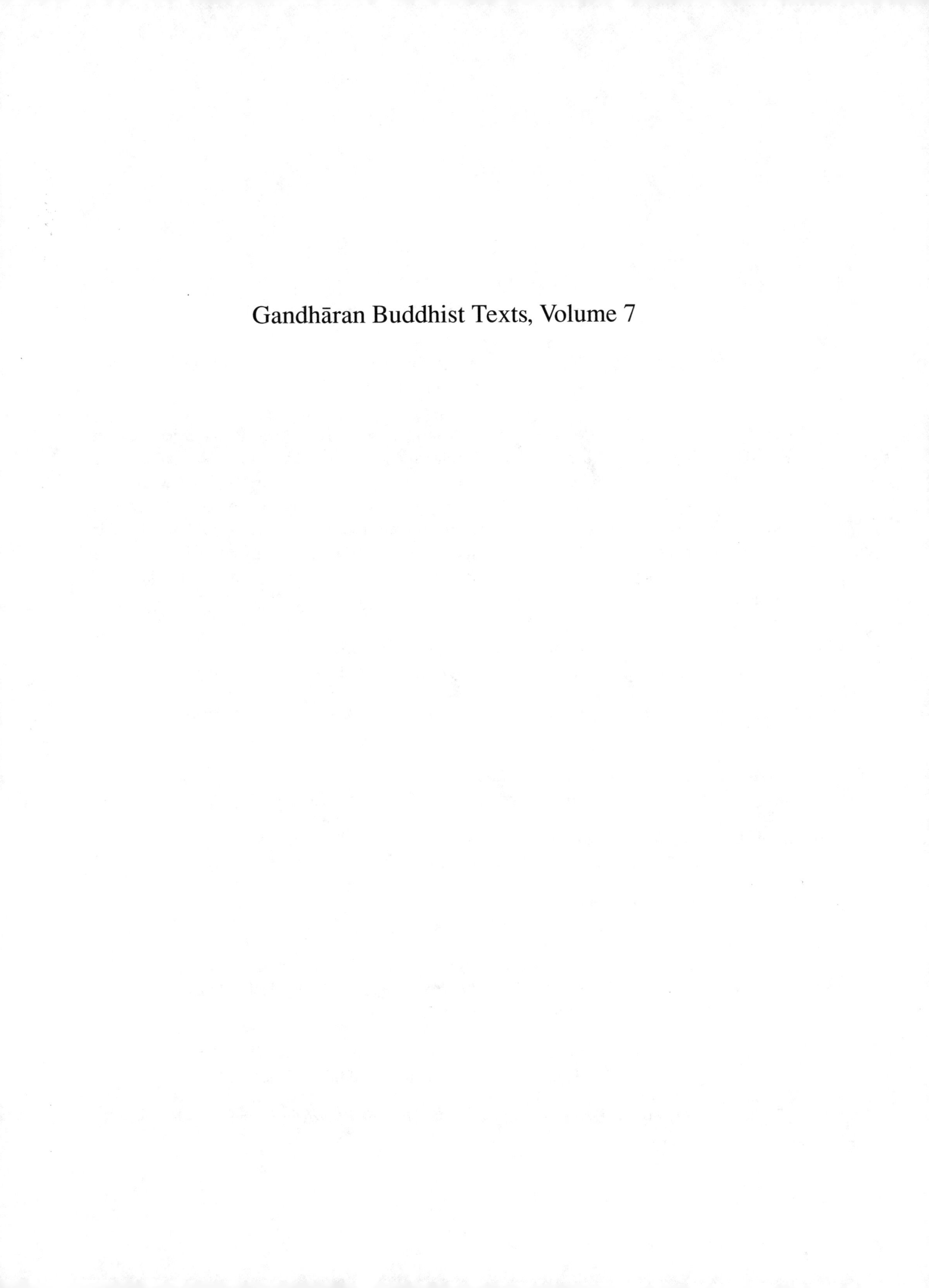

Gandhāran Buddhist Texts, Volume 7

Gandhāran Buddhist Texts

Editor-in-chief: Richard Salomon
Co-editors: Stefan Baums and Ingo Strauch

The present volume is the seventh in the Gandhāran Buddhist Texts series. This series presents text editions and studies of early Buddhist birch-bark scrolls in the Gāndhārī language, dating from about the first century BCE to the third century CE. These manuscripts, discovered in the ancient region of Gandhāra (modern Pakistan and Afghanistan), provide unprecedented insight into the early history of Buddhism as it was transmitted from India to Central Asia and China on its way to becoming a world religion. At the same time, as the earliest preserved manuscripts from South Asia, they are invaluable primary sources for the linguistic and literary history of the region.

Ancient Buddhist Scrolls from Gandhāra: The British Library Kharoṣṭhī Fragments, by Richard Salomon (1999)

A Gāndhārī Version of the Rhinoceros Sūtra: British Library Kharoṣṭhī Fragment 5B, by Richard Salomon, Gandhāran Buddhist Texts, vol. 1 (2000)

Three Gāndhārī Ekottarikāgama-Type Sūtras: British Library Kharoṣṭhī Fragments 12 and 14, by Mark Allon, Gandhāran Buddhist Texts, vol. 2 (2001)

A New Version of the Gāndhārī Dharmapada and a Collection of Previous-Birth Stories: British Library Kharoṣṭhī Fragments 16 + 25, by Timothy Lenz, Gandhāran Buddhist Texts, vol. 3 (2003)

Four Gāndhārī Saṃyuktāgama Sūtras: Senior Kharoṣṭhī Fragment 5, by Andrew Glass, Gandhāran Buddhist Texts, vol. 4 (2007)

Two Gāndhārī Manuscripts of the Songs of Lake Anavatapta (Anavatapta-gāthā): British Library Kharoṣṭhī Fragment 1 and Senior Scroll 14, by Richard Salomon, Gandhāran Buddhist Texts, vol. 5 (2008)

Gandhāran Avadānas: British Library Kharoṣṭhī Fragments 1–3 and 21 and Supplementary Fragments A–C, by Timothy Lenz, Gandhāran Buddhist Texts, vol. 6 (2010)

Three Early Mahāyāna Treatises from Gandhāra: Bajaur Kharoṣṭhī Fragments 4, 6, and 11, by Andrea Schlosser, Gandhāran Buddhist Texts, vol. 7 (2021)

Three Early Mahāyāna Treatises from Gandhāra

Bajaur Kharoṣṭhī Fragments 4, 6, and 11

Andrea Schlosser

UNIVERSITY OF WASHINGTON PRESS
Seattle

Copyright © 2022 by Andrea Schlosser

Printed and bound in the United States of America

This work may be used under the terms of the Creative Commons Attribution-NonCommercial 2.0 Generic (CC BY-NC 2.0) license for a duration of five years after date of initial publication, thereafter under a Creative Commons Attribution 2.0 Generic (CC BY 2.0) license.
DOI 10.6069/9780295750750

Published for the Bavarian Academy of Sciences and Humanities
Project: Buddhist Manuscripts from Gandhāra

UNIVERSITY OF WASHINGTON PRESS
uwapress.uw.edu

LIBRARY OF CONGRESS CONTROL NUMBER: 2022930193
Cataloging information available at https://lccn.loc.gov/2022930193
ISBN 9780295750736 (hardcover)
ISBN 9780295750750 (e-book)

∞ This paper meets the requirements of ANSI/NISO Z39.48-1992 (Permanence of Paper).

atvahidae ca parahidae ca sarvasatvahidae ca

Contents

Illustrations and Tables

Figures

Tables

Plates

Series Editors' Preface

This seventh volume in the Gandhāran Buddhist Texts series marks a new departure in several respects. It is the first text of the Mahāyāna tradition presented in the series; the discovery in recent years of this and several other Gandhāran Mahāyāna texts is having a profound effect on our understanding of the history of Buddhism. It is also the first text from the Bajaur Collection to be published in book form, joining the manuscripts from the British Library and Robert Senior collections that were presented in previous volumes. Finally, it is the first of several editions to be produced under the auspices of the Buddhist Manuscripts from Gandhāra project at the Bavarian Academy of Sciences and Humanities.

The series editors are aware of the long gap since the publication of the sixth volume of the series in 2010, and wish to make it clear that this interval was not a fallow period. It was rather a time of intensive activity on other aspects of Gandhāran manuscript studies, including the discovery and evaluation of new manuscripts and the development of new tools that are expected to accelerate the production of future volumes.

Author's Preface

This volume contains the edition and translation of fragments 4, 6, and 11 of the Bajaur Collection of Kharoṣṭhī manuscripts. Fragments 4 and 11 were first edited in my dissertation, which was submitted in 2014 and published online in 2016 under the title *On the Bodhisattva Path in Gandhāra*. While the entire edition has been thoroughly revised, most of the major problems and uncertain passages still remain unsolved. However, one new fragment was found among the scans of the Bajaur Collection, which is now included and the reconstruction updated. Since the fragment belongs to the first part of BC 11, most of the line numbers on the recto have changed, that is, 11r4 is now 11r6 and so on. The recto side now contains 53 lines instead of 51.

In this volume, also fragment 6 has been reconstructed and translated as far as possible. All three fragments belong together in that they refer to each other through certain phrases and terms. BC 4 seems to be the base text. BC 11 refers to parts of BC 4 and discusses certain aspects of the latter. And BC 6 refers to both BC 4 and BC 11. Based on this relationship the sequence of the fragments within this volume is BC 4, BC 11, and then BC 6 (and not BC 4, BC 6, BC 11).

The three manuscripts were categorized as non-canonical scholastic texts, group A, in Ingo Strauch's preliminary survey of the Bajaur Collection published in 2008 in the journal *Studien zur Indologie und Iranistik*. The second group, B, consists of the fragments 14, 16, and 18. Another two manuscripts, numbered 12 and 19, were left unassigned.[1]

Most of the scholastic texts (BC 4, 6, 11, 12, 14, 16, 18, and 19) may have been written by the same scribe, since the letter forms are in general the same. One of the scholastic texts, however, written on BC 9 verso, is clearly in another hand. The manuscripts in groups A and B could all be part of the same text corpus, because the general topic in all of them is non-attachment to the sense bases in order to proceed on the path to awakening and prevent further rebirth. BC 14, 16, and 18 are related to each other through the formula *yadi atva / jive / dhama bhaveadi*. Also, certain phrases in passages labeled with the same number are identical. The exact interrelations between these manuscripts as well as the relationship between group A and B has yet to be established. For example, certain words used in group A are also used in group

---

1 Fragment 19 was previously part 3 of fragment 6, but was later renamed. In the publication Nasim Khan 2008, which reproduces Ingo Strauch's preliminary transliteration from 2006 together with the original scans, a different numbering system is used: BC 4 = fragment 11 (frames 24, 25), BC 6 = fragment 12, part 1 and 3 (frames 26, 28), BC 11 = fragment 13 (frames 29, 30), BC 19 = fragment 12, part 2 (frame 27).

B (*ahara*, *divacakṣu*, *paralogo*, *pradibhavo*, *bhaṭarae*, *baleṇa*, *matra*, *loia*, *loutarea*, *vaïraga*, *śala*, *hura*). Moreover, in both groups the same syntactical structure is found, namely questions (G *aha*) and answers (G *ta vucadi*). BC 19 has been included in this volume in the appendix, since it was formerly part of BC 6. It might be another free commentary on BC 4, but its relationship to BC 4, 6, or 11 cannot be established, as most of the readings are unclear.

For the history and contents of the Bajaur Collection in general the reader is referred to earlier publications dealing with the collection as a whole (Strauch 2007/2008, 2008, Falk and Strauch 2014).

Over the years, the editing of these manuscripts has been supported by various institutions. To begin, I received financial support through the Elsa Neumann Scholarship of the state of Berlin. Further, the generous support of the Dhammachai International Research Institute enabled me, during a stay in Seattle, to discuss the contents of the manuscripts in the "Kharoṣṭhī Klub." Finally, in 2014, I was honored with the Ernst-Waldschmidt-Preis of the Stiftung Preussischer Kulturbesitz for my dissertation on two of the manuscripts presented in this volume.

With respect to the reconstruction and translation of the texts, I received help from many scholars and colleagues who I would like to thank for their suggestions and words of advice (in alphabetical order): Mark Allon, Stefan Baums, Daniel Boucher, Johannes Bronkhorst, Collett Cox, Harry Falk, Andrew Glass, Paul Harrison, Jens-Uwe Hartmann, Oskar von Hinüber, Seishi Karashima, Timothy Lenz, Joseph Marino, Gudrun Melzer, Jason Neelis, Richard Salomon, Cristina Scherrer-Schaub, Jonathan Silk, Blair Silverlock, Ingo Strauch, Vincent Tournier, and Klaus Wille. In addition, Henry Albery, Kelsey Martini, Britta Schneider, Gleb Sharygin, and Elisabeth Steinbrückner helped me with proofreading. To all of them I am grateful, and I thank everyone for his or her time and attention.

Special thanks go to Cynthia Peck-Kubaczek, the new editor of the GBT series. She has been an invaluable help in finalizing this publication and making the content more comprehensible to the reader. It has been a great joy to discuss various unclear passages with her, and I admire her patience, curiosity, and enthusiasm, as well as, of course, her editing skills.

Finally, I am indebted to the University of Washington Press for their support in publishing this book as part of the Gandhāran Buddhist Texts series. In particular I would like to thank Lorri Hagman.

My sincere apologies to everyone I forgot to mention, as well as for every mistake and misunderstanding that is still left in the following edition and translation.

Conventions

The transliteration conventions are modeled on those used in the previous volumes of the Gandhāran Buddhist Texts series and in the *Dictionary of Gāndhārī* (Baums and Glass 2002–a) with minor modifications. The following symbols are used in this volume:

[ ]	An unclear or partially preserved akṣara whose reading is less than certain.
(*)	A lost or illegible akṣara that has been conjecturally restored on the basis of context, parallel texts, or other evidence.
⟨* ⟩	An akṣara or a component thereof that was omitted by the scribe and has been conjecturally restored by the editor.
《 》	An akṣara or a component thereof that was added by the scribe as an interlinear insertion.
{ }	A superfluous akṣara that was written in error.
{{ }}	An akṣara or a component thereof that was deleted by the scribe.
.	The missing portion of a partially legible akṣara.
?	A visible or partially visible but illegible akṣara.
+	A presumably missing akṣara that would have appeared on a lost or obscured portion of the scroll.
///	Beginning or end of an incomplete line where it is uncertain how many akṣaras are missing.
·	A small dot marking the end of a minor syntactic unit.
∘	A small circle marking the end of a syntactic unit.
○	A larger circle sporadically used to mark the end of a section.
◎	Two concentric circles sporadically used to mark the end of a section.
⊗	An ×-shape enclosed in a circle sporadically used to mark the end of a section.
=	In the diplomatic transliteration, a word division within an akṣara, used in phrases such as *sarvam=eva* in which the final *m* of the preceding word and the initial vowel of the following word are written together as a single syllable.
◊	In the diplomatic transliteration, a space left empty on purpose.
◈	In the diplomatic transliteration, a space left empty due to the uneven surface of the birch bark.
∘	In the annotations, the symbol ∘ before or after a sequence of letters replaces previously cited word segments.

Abbreviations

Gāndhārī text citations follow the abbreviation system of the *Dictionary of Gāndhārī* (Baums and Glass 2002–a). Pali texts are cited by their standard title or abbreviation as given in the *Critical Pāli Dictionary* (Trenckner et al. 1924–). Citations of other Indian Buddhist texts are referred to by their abbreviation in the *Abkürzungsverzeichnis zur buddhistischen Literatur in Indien und Südostasien* (Bechert 1990).

abl.	ablative
abs.	absolutive
acc.	accusative
adj.	adjective
adv.	adverb
Anav^{L}	Gāndhārī *Anavataptagāthā* (BL 1, line 1–126, ed. Salomon 2008a)
Anav^{S}	Gāndhārī *Anavataptagāthā* (RS 14, ed. Salomon 2008a)
AN	*Aṅguttaranikāya*
AsP	*Aṣṭasāhasrikā Prajñāpāramitā* (ed. Mitra 1888)
AsP^{Sp}	Gāndhārī (*Aṣṭasāhasrikā*) *Prajñāpāramitā* (SC 5, ed. Falk and Karashima 2012, 2013)
Av^{L1}	Gāndhārī avadāna (BL 1, line 127–213, ed. Lenz 2010: 33)
Av^{L2}	Gāndhārī avadāna (BL 2, ed. Lenz 2010: 95–104)
Av^{L4}	Gāndhārī avadāna (BL 4.2)
Av^{L6}	Gāndhārī pūrvayoga texts (BL 16+25, line 15–61, ed. Lenz 2003, part II)
BC	Bajaur Collection
BCE	Before the Common Era
B^{e}	Burmese edition (in citations from CSCD)
BHS	Buddhist Hybrid Sanskrit
BHSD	*Buddhist Hybrid Sanskrit Dictionary* (Edgerton 1953)
BHSG	*Buddhist Hybrid Sanskrit Grammar* (Edgerton 1953)
BL	British Library [Collection]
bv.	bahuvrīhi
ca.	circa
card.	cardinal number
cf.	confer

caus.	causative
CDIAL	*A Comparative Dictionary of the Indo-Aryan Languages* (Turner 1966–85)
CE	Common Era
ch.	chapter
CKD	*Corpus of Kharoṣṭhī Documents* (see Baums and Glass 2002–b)
CKI	*Corpus of Kharoṣṭhī Inscriptions* (see Baums and Glass 2002–b)
cm	centimeter(s)
Cp-a	*Paramatthadīpanī* on *Cariyāpiṭaka* (ed. Barua 1979)
cpd.	compound
CPD	*A Critical Pāli Dictionary* (Trenckner et al. 1924–)
CSCD	*Chaṭṭha Saṅgāyanā CD-ROM*. Pali Tipiṭaka in 216 volumes with Aṭṭhakathā, Ṭīkā, Anuṭīkā, and other works; published by the Vipassana Research Institute, Dhammagiri, Igatpuri, India (www.tipitaka.org)
dat.	dative
DDB	*Digital Dictionary of Buddhism* (www.buddhism-dict.net/ddb)
dem. pron.	demonstrative pronoun
denom.	denominative
Dhp	*Dhammapada* (ed. von Hinüber and Norman 1995)
Dhp-a	*Dhammapada* commentary (ed. H. C. Norman 1906)
Dhp^{K}	Gāndhārī *Dharmapada* from Khotan (ed. Brough 1962)
Dhp^{L}	Gāndhārī *Dharmapada* in London (BL 16+25, line 1–15, ed. Lenz 2003, part I)
Dhp^{P}	Buddhist Hybrid Sanskrit *Dharmapada* from Patna (ed. Shukla 1979)
Dhp^{Sp}	Gāndhārī *Dharmapada* of the Split Collection (SC 3, ed. Falk 2015)
Dhs	*Dhammasaṅgaṇī* (ed. Müller 1885)
DN	*Dīghanikāya*
DP	*A Dictionary of Pāli* (Cone 2001), 1 volume to date
EĀ^{L}	Gāndhārī *Ekottarikāgama*-type sūtras (BL 12+14, line 1–73, ed. Allon 2001)
ed.	edited by / editor
e.g.	exempli gratia
f.	feminine
fig.	figure
fut.	future
G	Gāndhārī
GD	*A Dictionary of Gāndhārī* (Baums and Glass 2002–a)
GNAI	Gilgit Manuscripts in the National Archives of India, Fascimile Edition (Soka University)
gdv.	gerundive
gen.	genitive
ibid.	ibidem
i.e.	id est
impv.	imperative

ind.	indeclinable
instr.	instrumental
interr. pron.	interrogative pronoun
It	*Itivuttaka* (ed. Windisch 1889)
Jā	*Jātaka*, together with *Jātakatthavaṇṇanā* (ed. Fausbøll 1877–96)
Khvs^{L}	Gāndhārī **Khargaviṣaṇasutra* (BL 5B, ed. Salomon 2000)
KN	*Khuddakanikāya*
Kv	*Kathāvatthu* (ed. Taylor 1894–97, 2 vols.)
Bbs	Gāndhārī **Bahubuddhasutra* (Library of Congress scroll)
lit.	literally
loc.	locative
LPG	*Larger Prajñāpāramitā* from Gilgit (ed. Conze 1962, 1974, cf. Zacchetti 2005)
m.	masculine
MIA	Middle Indo-Aryan
Mil	*Milindapañha* (ed. Trenckner 1880)
MN	*Majjhimanikāya*
MPPŚ	*Mahāprajñāpāramitopadeśaśāstra* (ed. Lamotte 1944–80)
MS	Martin Schøyen [Collection]
Mvu	*Mahāvastu* (ed. Senart 1882–97)
Mvy	*Mahāvyutpatti* (ed. Sakaki 1926)
MW	*A Sanskrit-English Dictionary* (Monier-Williams 1899)
n.	neuter
n.	note
neg.	negative
Nett	*Nettippakaraṇa* (ed. Hardy 1902)
Nird^{L1}	Gāndhārī Verse Nirdeśa (BL 4.1)
Nird^{L2}	Gāndhārī Verse Nirdeśa (BL 7, 9, 18, and 13 up to line 90, ed. Baums 2009)
Nird^{L3}	Gāndhārī Verse Nirdeśa (BL 13 from line 91, see Baums 2009, appendix 1)
Nidd I	*Mahāniddesa* (ed. de La Vallée Poussin and Thomas 1916–17)
no.	number
nom.	nominative
NWS	*Nachtragswörterbuch des Sanskrit* (http://nws.uzi.uni-halle.de, 2013–16)
OIA	Old Indo-Aryan
opt.	optative
P	Pali
p.	page
pass.	passive
Paṭis	*Paṭisambhidāmagga* (ed. Taylor 1905–07)
pers.	person
pers. pron.	personal pronoun

Peṭ	*Peṭakopadesa* (ed. Barua 1982)
Pkt.	Prakrit
pl.	plural
pp.	past participle
pres.	present
pres. part.	present participle
pret.	preterite
pron.	pronoun
PTS	Pali Text Society
PTSD	*Pali Text Society's Pali-English Dictionary* (Rhys Davids and Stede 1921–25)
PvsP	*Pañcaviṃśatisāhasrikā Prajñāpāramitā* (ed. Kimura 1986–2009)
PW	*Sanskrit-Wörterbuch* (Böhtlingk and Roth 1855–75)
r	recto
RE	Rock Edict
rel. pron.	relative pronoun
RS	Robert Senior [Collection]
SĀ^{S1}	Gāndhārī *Saṃyuktāgama* sūtras (RS 5, ed. Glass 2007)
SĀ^{S6}	Gāndhārī **Mahaparaḍahasutra* (RS 20, ed. Marino 2017)
SaṅgCm^{L}	Gāndhārī *Saṅgītisūtra* commentary (BL 15)
SC	Split Collection
sg.	singular
SHT	*Sanskrithandschriften aus den Turfanfunden* (ed. Waldschmidt et al. 1965–)
Skt.	Sanskrit
SN	*Saṃyuttanikāya*
Sn	*Suttanipāta* (ed. Andersen and Smith 1913)
Sn-a	*Suttanipāta* commentary / *Paramatthajotikā* II (ed. Smith 1916–18)
s.v.	sub verbo
SWTF	*Sanskrit-Wörterbuch der buddhistischen Texte aus den Turfan-Funden* (ed. Bechert, Röhrborn, and Hartmann 1994–)
T	*Taishō shinshū daizōkyō* 大正新脩大藏經 (ed. Takakusu and Watanabe 1924–32)
Th	*Theragāthā* (ed. Oldenberg and Pischel 1966)
Thī	*Therīgāthā* (ed. Oldenberg and Pischel 1966)
Tib.	Tibetan
tr.	translated by / translator
Ud-a	*Udāna* commentary / *Paramatthadīpanī* (ed. Woodward 1926)
v	verso
v.l.	varia lectio
Vism	*Visuddhimagga* (ed. Rhys Davids 1920–21)
Vism^{W}	*Visuddhimagga* (ed. Warren and Kosambi 1950)

Three Early Mahāyāna Treatises from Gandhāra

Bajaur Kharoṣṭhī Fragments 4, 6, and 11

Chapter 1

Introduction

1.1 General Remarks and the Topic of the Manuscripts

The three manuscripts, apparently found in the late 1990s in the district of Bajaur in modern Northwest Pakistan, offer us a valuable and rare insight into Buddhist thinking during the early centuries of the Common Era, a time when the Mahāyāna movement was at its inception. They are written in a Kharoṣṭhī script datable to the second century, all by the same scribe. As the birch bark on which they were written is only preserved in fragments, the Gāndhārī texts are not complete and thus not always fully comprehensible. In addition, since there are no parallel texts, sometimes words are clearly legible but remain unclear as to their meaning. Nevertheless, large parts of the preserved texts are coherent and show us an interesting picture of a scholastic approach to the Buddhist way towards awakening and liberation from suffering.

The unifying element between all three manuscripts is the knowledge of what is painful and useless (G *dukhañaṇaṇisamarthañaṇa* = Skt. *duḥkhajñāna* and *niḥsāmarthyajñāna*). However, it is not directly explained what this knowledge is. In BC 4 it is said to be the Dharma, which one should teach other beings, and thus establish them on the path to awakening. One should abandon what is painful and useless, empty, and like a dream. In BC 11 this is more specific: it is the inner and outer sense bases that are painful and useless, as they are the seed of suffering. Any happiness based on them would be useless, because it is transitory. In BC 6 dharmas in general are said to be painful and useless. Accepting and fully understanding this, one should not become passionate or hateful. The proper mind set to overcome this kind of attachment to the dharmas (by way of passion or hatred) is apparently to stop every agitation of the mind. Then, a notion of happiness will arise, a happiness that does not depend on anything. In short, if one abandons what is useless and painful (which seems to be the perception of any dharma by way of the senses), inevitably a special kind of joy will arise that does not decay and does not lead to rebirth.

All three manuscripts deal more or less with the same topic, namely abandoning attachment to sense experiences and the five aggregates of existence—a process which will finally lead to the bliss of liberation (*mokṣasukha*). In BC 4 this is expressed by being "dispassionate with regard to the triple world" or by the "benefit of dispassion" (BHS *virāgānuśaṃsa*). In BC 11 the same is called "benefit of release" (*avasargānuśaṃsa*). The theme and background is essentially the *śūnyatā*/*prajñāpāramitā* doctrine, through which one realizes that in ultimate reality everything is void of inherent existence and one is encouraged to not have attachment to it. The proposed practice of the bodhisattva path is: thoroughly understanding (*parijñā*) the origins of suffering, abandoning (*prahāṇa*) these origins, and attaining sustained joy and happiness by realizing the emptiness of all dharmas. While on the path, only good states will be gained and one will lead other beings to awakening.

1.2 Summary of the Texts and Their Interrelation to Each Other

Each of the three manuscripts is written on a separate scroll. Regarding their internal structure and style they are all somewhat different. BC 4 is a coherent text dealing with the practice of a bodhisattva. It is predominantly written from the first-person perspective, giving the impression that the author is sharing his experience. BC 11 seems more like a scholastic comment on certain passages of BC 4, although not directly citing them but discussing aspects of the same issues, especially the bliss experienced on the path to awakening. Likewise, BC 6 refers to passages in BC 4 as well as BC 11, focusing on the process of becoming passionate and hateful. BC 4 thus appears to be the basic text.[1]

1.2.1 BC 4

At the beginning of BC 4 (§ 1), the author of the text advertises detachment and presents the prospect of every kind of fortune (*sampatti*), contrasting these fortunes to their opposites. The benefits (BHS *anuśaṃsa*) are exemplified and enumerated in two lists, of which the first is related to states and experiences in this life and the next (*sāṃdr̥ṣṭika* / *dr̥ṣṭadhārmika* and *sāmparāyika*), and the second refers to meditation or physical issues during the development of the path (see table 1).[2] The prospects are a good destination (*sugati*), meetings with worthy men (*satpuruṣa-darśana*), and liberation (*mokṣa*). While reborn as a human, one will experience only good things: physical ease and mental happiness (*sukha*), as well as pleasant (*śubha*) and wholesome (*kuśala*) states.[3] During practice one will be mentally and physically alert (*jāgaryā*, *laghūtthāna*), one will know what to do and do it [with words, thoughts, and deeds] (*kr̥tya*, *karman*), and one will achieve states of comfort and health (BHS *spr̥śana*, *ārogya*). By relinquishing attachment to the *skandha*s that constitute existence, one will finally attain liberation from rebirth (§ 2). The knowledge helping one let go of everything [relating to the triple world] is the knowledge of what is useless and painful. This is indirectly equated with the *prajñāpāramitā* (§ 3–6), the realization of the emptiness of all dharmas,[4] which is obtained in this lifetime after one has formed the intention to attain awakening for the first time (*prathamacittotpāda*).[5]

---

1 Interrelationships between BC 4, BC 6, and BC 11 have been marked in the edition by cross-references in the margins.

2 I have not found any similar listings in other Buddhist texts, whether in Pali or Sanskrit.

3 In BC 11 the stereotypic G *hakṣati* of BC 4 ("will exist") is replaced by G *anubhaviea* ("would experience") in the case of *śubha* and *kuśala*, and by G *gachiea* ("would go to") in the case of *gati*s (11r15). In general, the items of the lists are characterized by "relating to this and the next life" or "relating to body and mind" (11r10–11).

4 In § 3 the *bodhimaṇḍa* is said to be void, thus indicating an understanding of emptiness that is not only related to the self but to everything, as is common in *prajñāpāramitā* literature and Madhyamaka philosophy.

5 That the *prajñāpāramitā* was esteemed as a shortcut to awakening is indicated in the *Aṣṭasāhasrikā* in a passage also (partly) preserved in the Gāndhārī version; cf. AsP^{Sp} 5-55 (Falk and Karashima 2013: 162–63).

Table 1. Summary of the miseries and fortunes enumerated in BC 4.

	droaca / doṣa	Skt. *daurgatya / doṣa*	***sapati / aṇuśaśa***	Skt. *sampatti* / BHS *ānuśaṃsa*
list 1	***drogadi***	Skt. *durgati*	***sugadi***	Skt. *sugati*
§ 1A2 § 1B2 § 7A2a § 7B2a	***as̱apuruṣa / drugaṇa***	Skt. *asatpuruṣa / durgaṇa*	***sapuruṣa* (*darśaṇa*)**	Skt. *satpuruṣa* (*darśana*)
	(*saṃsara*) *badhaṇa*	Skt. (*saṃsāra*) *bandhana*	**(*saparaïa*) *mokṣa***	Skt. (*sāmpārayika*) *mokṣa*
	(*kaïacedas̱ia*) *dukha*	Skt. (*kāyikacaitāsika*) *duḥkha*	**(*sadriṭhia*) *suha***	Skt. (*sāṃdṛṣṭika*) *sukha*
	aśuha	Skt. *aśubha*	***śuha***	Skt. *śubha*
	akuśala	Skt. *akuśala*	***kuśala***	Skt. *kuśala*
list 2	***midha***	Skt. *middha*	***jagaria***	Skt. *jāgaryā*
§ 7A2b § 7B2b	***alas̱ia***	Skt. *ālasya*	***lahuṭhaṇa***	Skt. *laghūtthāna*
	akica	Skt. *akṛtya*	***kica***	Skt. *kṛtya*
	akarma	Skt. *akarman*	***karma***	Skt. *karman*
	aśpris̱aṇa	BHS *aspṛśana*	***śpris̱aṇa***	BHS *spṛśana*
	gelaña	BHS *glānya*	***aroga***	Skt. *ārogya*

One of the most important parts of BC 4 is its section 6, since due to its contextual and structural elements, it can be compared to a *praṇidhāna*, i.e., the resolution of a bodhisattva to strive for awakening for the sake of others.[6] If we compare this passage to other *praṇidhāna*s (cf. Binz 1980: 88 ff.), all essential parts are included:

(1) the intention to become a Buddha,
(2) the duties of a bodhisattva (*kuśalamūla*, "wholesome roots"),
(3) the dedication.

BC 4 (1) *edeṇa dukhañaṇaṇisamarthañaṇeṇa*
sarve dukha uadiṇae as̱ivas̱idae hakṣadi uekṣidae hakṣadi
sarve suhe paricatae as̱ivasidae hakṣadi
*ta par⟨*i⟩ṇirvahido log̱ado cariśe*
(2) *akuśalo varjamaṇa kuśalo karamaṇa*
*(*sarva)g̱areṇa b(*u)dhadharmasagho puyamaṇa*
satvaṇa ca artho karamaṇa
*dharme ca edam io ṇis̱ama(*r)thadukhañaṇo des̱amaṇa*
satva ya bos̱a praïṭhavamaṇa

---

[6] *Praṇidhāna*s as such mainly occur in Mahāyana contexts, even though they are not totally unknown in Śrāvakayāna texts (cf. Binz 1980: 1, 78, 161). One of the few is the vow of the bodhisattva Sumedha (later to become Buddha Śākyamuni) in the presence of Dīpaṃkara, even though this is called *adhikāra* or *abhinīhāra* (Binz 1980: 79–80). The identification of § 6 in BC 4 with a *praṇidhāna* was first suggested by Vincent Tournier during a workshop in Lausanne (2013).

(3) *ṇa ciri ve (*sa)rvasapati ca me ha(*kṣa)di sarvadroaca ca ṇa hakṣadi atvahida ca parahida ca sarvasatvahida ca hakṣadi*

(1) By this knowledge of [what is] painful and this knowledge of [what is] useless, every suffering [that will be] taken up will be accepted [and] looked at with an even mind. Every happiness [that will be] given up will be accepted. In this way, having reached complete extinction, I will leave this world.

(2) Avoiding [what is] unwholesome, doing [what is] wholesome, honoring Buddha, Dharma, and Sangha in (*every) respect, acting for the profit of [all] living beings, teaching this Dharma, which is the knowledge of [what is] useless and painful, and establishing [all] beings in awakening,

(3) [then] certainly before long every fortune will exist for me and every misery will not exist; [there] will be welfare for myself, welfare for others, and welfare for every living being.

The intention (1) is expressed by "… I will leave this world" (G *logado cariśe*). The duties of a bodhisattva (2) are: doing good, honoring Buddha, Dharma, and Sangha (i.e., the founder, the doctrine, and the community in the name of the Buddha), acting for the profit of other beings, teaching the Dharma (which is the knowledge of what is useless and painful), and leading others to awakening. The dedication or aim (3) is the wish to achieve good states for oneself, as well as welfare for oneself and others. Although the passage contains all the common elements, the differences from other known Buddhist sources are quite sizable, and none of the standard formulations mentioned by Binz (1980: 91) are found.[7]

An interesting difference is also that the passage describes a resolution rather than an earnest wish, indicated by the use of the future instead of the usual optative,[8] and accordingly, there is no prediction (*vyākaraṇa*) by a presiding Buddha. Nonetheless, a slight difference in style may be justified. Similarly, in the *Sukhāvatīvyūha* the *praṇidhāna*s are not expressed as wishes but as demands (cf. Binz 1980: 131 for references). Another difference in BC 4 to usual *praṇidhāna* passages (cf. Binz 1980: 4) is that the term itself is not mentioned anywhere. However, this could also be due to the fact that the *praṇidhāna*s examined by Binz are always embedded in a narrative, whereas in BC 4 the passage rather seems to represent some kind of invocatory recitation, perhaps for a ritual or meditation. Such a resolution might also be called a "self proficiency of a bodhisattva."

The position of a *praṇidhāna* within a bodhisattva career is principally at its beginning, together with the *cittotpāda*. This is followed by a long period of practicing the *pāramitā*s until one finally reaches buddhahood. In comparison to the bodhisattva career as found in other

---

7 Hence, it may be assumed that BC 4 is to be dated to a time before stereotypes had been formulated, that is, before the fixing of wording evident in such texts as the *Mahāvastu*, *Divyāvadāna*, etc. as they have come down to us (cf. Binz 1980: 91 and 96–120 in general for the development of *praṇidhāna*s).

8 One could argue that the future may be interpreted as carrying an optative sense, but other *praṇidhāna*s are unambiguous in their use of an optative verb (cf. Binz 1980: 5).

Mahāyāna texts, BC 4 comes closest to the system presented in the *Daśabhūmikasūtra*, where the *bodhisattvacaryā* begins with the resolve to attain awakening (*bodhicittotpāda*) and not give up, after which the adept is to practice the *pāramitā*s while ascending the ten stages to buddhahood.[9] In BC 4, however, the concept of ten stages is not referred to, and nothing more is said about the bodhisattva's career.[10] The main issue concerns the performance of good and the avoidance of bad things. The duration of such practice seems to be considered joyful and pleasant. Similar statements can be found in other texts, as for example, in the *Ratnāvalī*, where the fruits of following the Mahāyāna are not only future awakening, but all kinds of comfort or happiness during the journey, both in this life and the next (verses 126–27, 222, 285, 398). One of the duties is also quite simply avoiding unwholesome actions and striving for wholesome ones (verses 22, 222, 227, 230), as well as practicing non-attachment due to realizing the truth as it really is (verses 290, 230). Likewise, in the *Pratyutpannabuddhasaṃmukhāvasthitasamādhisūtra*, happiness is concomitant to the realization of truth, i.e., understanding and accepting that all dharmas are in fact unarisen and empty (cf. Harrison 1998: 103, T 13 no. 418 p. 919b6).

The last section of BC 4 (§ 7) is not yet clear, because too many as yet unclarified but crucial words make this section almost incomprehensible (G *aloa* / *aloṇea* and *aride kerea* / *aṇaride kerea*, cf. p. 176). It could possibly be connected with some sort of ritual of repentance regarding one's negative actions and of rejoicing in meritorious acts. Paul Harrison has suggested that the passage might deal in some way with the *triskandhaka* ritual.[11] According to Jan Nattier, the *triskandhakadharma* must be recited three times during the day and three times at night (Nattier 2003: 117 and 259–60). It has not been exactly defined what is meant by "three sections" (*triskandhaka*), but one of the more favored suggestions is: repenting for bad deeds, rejoicing in future merits, and requesting the Buddhas to teach. Other suggestions brought forward by Jan Nattier have been repentance regarding *rāga*, *dveṣa*, and *moha*, or repentance of the body, speech, and mind. She has argued that not all three items (repentance, rejoicing, requesting) are attested in the earliest version of the *Ugraparipṛcchā*, "which lacks any mention of requesting

---

9 The beginning of the bodhisattva career is also referred to this way in the *Abhisamayālaṃkārālokā* (1. *bodhipraṇidhicitta*, 2. *bodhiprasthānacitta*). Cf. Binz 1980: 123–27 and 148 for other examples. In the earliest Chinese translations of Mahāyāna texts by Lokakṣema at the end of the second century CE, the *cittotpāda* is followed by three key stages: (1) the *anutpattikadharmakṣānti* (the realization of the fact that *dharma*s are unarisen); (2) the attainment of the stage of non-regression, whereupon a bodhisattva is assured of reaching his or her goal (*avaivartika*); and (3) the prediction (*vyākaraṇa*); cf. Harrison 1993: 171 and also Strauch 2010a: 43.

10 Likewise, in the *Ugraparipṛcchā* the *pāramitā*s are not associated with particular stages (Nattier 2003: 154).

11 Personal communication. Cf. also Skilling 2004: 151: "The aspiration to full awakening is called 'giving birth to *bodhicitta*.' This is something more than a dry doctrine: it was, and is, a public ritual act, a social performance. The earliest text we know for this is the *triskandhaka*, to which reference is made in several early Mahāyāna sūtras, for example the *Ugraparipṛcchā*." Cf. Pagel 1995: 24–26 for potential texts and references: "In the *Vimaladattaparipṛcchā*, a *triskandhaka* is cited alongside the *Bodhisattvapiṭaka* as a treatise (*dharmaparyāya*) the bodhisattva should retain and memorise" (Pagel 1995: 25, italics adjusted in both citations).

the Buddhas to teach." Additionally, "in all extant versions of the sūtra the practice of rejoicing in the merit of others is said to precede the recitation of the *triskandhaka*, rather than being contained within it" (Nattier 2003: 121).

Likewise, in BC 4 the invocation of Buddhas is not indicated. The text begins with a contemplation on the benefits of freedom from all desires, which could point to the act of rejoicing before reciting the *triskandhaka*. The ritual itself could be represented by section 7, where on the one hand a person should admonish and exhort something or someone (*paribhāṣ*), and on the other hand one should praise/salute something or someone and recommend the opposite (*abhivad*). In the first half of the paragraph (§ 7A1), the verbs have negative connotations and could refer to the bad deeds to be confessed and repented (*svadoṣa*, leading to *svadaurgatya*); in the second half (§ 7B1) they are positive in meaning and could refer to the good deeds to be rejoiced at (BHS *svayamānuśāṃsa*, leading to *svasampatti*). If this is done, all the fortunes that have been enumerated will come into existence, and finally the states of intrinsic nature will disappear and not rise anew.

The repeated attribute "three" for all nouns in the lists is interpreted as referring to the three times, i.e., past, present, and future (see p. 157), since the times are also named in the instructions preceding the lists (§§ 7A1 and 7B1). Thus, if BC 4 is indeed connected to a *triskandhaka* intended for recitation, or if parts represent it, the prefix *tri-* would most probably refer to the three periods of time. This being the case, the term *trikoḏi* in § 7A1 (4r24), translated as "three points of time," might refer to the three points of time during the day or night when, according to the *Ugraparipṛcchā*, the *triskandhaka* is said to be performed. The following G *uhae vatave* (Skt. *ubhaye vaktavyam*, "both should be spoken") in addition to other verbs related to speech indicates the oral character of this (proposed) ritual. However, it is not clear what exactly is to be done. The pronominal adjective "both" seems to point to the phrases G *satahi aloehi / asatiade ca aloneade ca aride kerea* and *sata aloa / asatia ca alonea ca anaride kerea*. Unfortunately, all these uncertain words are the basis of a mystery, and as long as they are not satisfyingly identified, nothing definite can be said.

Nevertheless, it becomes clear that the text deals in general with the starting point of bodhisattva practice, describing in particular a certain ritual that must be performed. This ritual resembles the *triskandhaka*,[12] as well as, in part, the seven-membered prayer consisting of verses about regretting past negative acts, rejoicing in positive deeds, and dedicating accumulated virtue to the welfare of all beings. Even though BC 4 does not contain the otherwise usual invocation of Buddhas, common steps are the confession of unwholesome deeds and the rejoicing in wholesome ones. A similar confession and repentance practice is also known from early Chinese Buddhist texts commonly categorized as *bodhisattvaprātimokṣa*, such as the *Vinayaviniścayopāliparipṛcchāsūtra*.[13]

---

12 According to the *Ugraparipṛcchā*, the *triskandhaka* ritual is performed by a lay bodhisattva who is still a beginner on the path to expiate his faults and overcome possessiveness and attachment [to the world], if no Buddha or member of the *āryasaṅgha* is "at hand" (Barnes 2012: 213).

13 決定毘尼經, *Juédìng píní jīng*, T 12 no. 325 pp. 37b1–42c10, cf. Barnes 2012 for this text and others related to the *triskandhaka* ritual, as well as Martini 2013.

1.2.2 BC 11

It is difficult to find a structure in the text of BC 11. The author seems to be loosely examining various topics found in BC 4, discussing them at length. The main focus, however, is a discussion of different types of happiness (*sukha*).

The highest forms of happiness are *avasargasukha* ("happiness of release") and *parijñāsukha* ("happiness of thorough understanding"). Elsewhere also *viveka-* and *virāgasukha* ("happiness of detachment and dispassion") are named as being the most important. Other types of happiness that are mentioned include: *aparādhīnasukha*, *avijñaptisukha*, [*indriya*]*antargatasukha*, *mokṣasukha* ("happiness that is not dependent on anything else, happiness due to non-cognition, inner happiness or happiness [with the senses] turned inwards, happiness of liberation"). Thus, the highest forms are any kind of bliss not based on something else, whether in the realm of desire, forms or something formless (*kāma-*, *rūpa-*, or *ārūpyadhātu*).

Opposed to this is the happiness that is mixed with suffering due to sense experiences or desires (summarized as *kāmasukha*), as well as happiness due to a remedy (*pratikārasukha*) and happiness due to a cause (BHS *upaniṣatsukha*). However, as long as one abides in *saṃsāra* it seems impossible to experience *viveka-*/*virāgasukha* without traces of happiness arising from sensual pleasures.[14] Only *lokottarabhūtajñāna* (superworldly true knowledge, i.e., knowing phenomena as they really are) enables the experience of sustained happiness or contentment. Given this perspective, the joy attained does not then lead to rebirth, and therefore does not need to be relinquished. Thus, it is important to abide in knowledge while experiencing *sukha*. The *lokottarabhūtajñāna* is not explicitly equated to the realization of *śūnyatā*, but it is circumscribed as a way to look at all phenomena as being impermanent, having no self, being empty, being like a dream, not coming from anywhere or going anywhere, etc., common expressions to describe the illusionary character of the perceived world, which is nothing other than *śūnyatā*.

In general, the aim is not the total elimination of feelings, but achieving or maintaining a state of bliss (comparable to that of an "arhat monk who, free from the fever of desire has entered the third stage of contemplation"[15]). This might involve first a shift from rather negative or neutral aims to a more positive aim concentrating on *sukha*, finally leading to imagining pure lands like Sukhāvatī or Abhirati, where only happiness prevails and one is reborn in order to strive for buddhahood under the best circumstances (cf., e.g., Gómez 1999: 74, 90). This ideal is similar to the future prospect of all kinds of prosperities presented in BC 4. It may be noted, however, that aiming for bliss does not contradict the principles of Śrāvakayāna affiliated texts, where *nirvāṇa* is also sometimes described as a state of bliss or supreme joy.[16]

---

14 Cf. Drewes 2010a: 62, where he states that the *Śūraṃgasamādhisūtra* "repeatedly makes the point that avoidance of sensual pleasures is not important for bodhisattvas" (cf. also Drewes 2011: 356). Drewes refers to a passage in the *Aṣṭasāhasrikā*, where the listener is instructed that "we should not be surprised if a *dharmabhāṇaka* turns out to be devoted to the pursuit of wealth and sensual pleasures […] Given that Buddhist monks are traditionally not supposed to engage in the pursuit of sensual pleasure, it seems that this advice can only be an attempt to justify behavior that actual followers of the *Aṣṭasāhasrikā*'s *dharmabhāṇaka*s were likely to encounter."

15 Larger *Sukhāvatīvyūha* § 28(38), tr. Gómez 1999: 74. Similarly: "comparable to that of a monk who in meditation has attained the state of cessation," Larger *Sukhāvatīvyūha* § 82, tr. Gómez 1999: 90.

16 Cf., e.g., Giustarini 2006: 170.

1.2.3 BC 6

The preserved text of BC 6 is often incomplete or difficult to understand. Therefore, the following statements are partly based on my own interpretation. The text first places what is painful and useless in relation to the aggregates, elements, and sense bases (*skandhadhātvāyatana*). It seems to be said that if one considers these aggregates to be permanent, that is, if one views dharmas as arising and ceasing, and considers them to exist, then this causes suffering (§ 1). If one views dharmas as neither arising nor ceasing, and considers them as being like a dream and thus non-existent, that is, if one understands that it is useless to hold on to them, then suffering does not arise (§ 2). Thus, one should not long for the existence of aggregates, elements, and sense bases. If one understands that dharmas are, by their very nature, painful and useless, then one ultimately does not become passionate or hateful towards them. Even though at this point the manuscript is fragmentary (§ 3), the text seems to say that one should not be attached to any view at all: neither a non-existential one, whereby dharmas are without boils, thorns, etc., nor an existential one, whereby dharmas are permanent, etc. On the contrary, the correct mind set seems to be a concentrated state of mind in which notions are reduced to a minimum. Finally, there should be no mental agitation at all; then the "master's notion of happiness" arises (§§ 4–5). It seems to be discussed whether there is an exception with respect to *paligodha*; apparently this form of desire had a special status. However, the author of our text is of the opinion that any form of passion (as well as, of course, any form of hatred) is to be avoided.

1.3 Genre of the Texts

1.3.1 Elements of Mahāyāna

Based on the *praṇidhāna* section, the *cittotpāda* and, above all, the *prajñāpāramitā* as the most important of the six *pāramitā*s, BC 4 can be classified as Mahāyāna,[17] or more cautiously as proto-Mahāyāna, since the designation Mahāyāna is not mentioned in the text itself and most probably at the time of its composition was not yet established or widely used.[18] The

---

17 Cf., e.g., Skilling (2004: 151) for the distinctive indications for Mahāyāna. These are essentially the reading of (or listening to) Mahāyāna sūtras and the practice of the six (or ten) perfections within the Mahāyāna doctrine. According to Lethcoe (1977: 265, referring to the *Aṣṭasāhasrikā*), aiming for the *prajñāpāramitā* is a necessary condition for being on the bodhisattva path. Cf. also Murakami 2004: 8. However, as the evidence of BC 2 shows, the term *prajñāpāramitā* does not need to be included to make a text Mahāyāna. More important is the common basic understanding and calm acceptance of the fact that all dharmas are without arising (*anutpattikadharmakṣānti*). It seems that only in a second stage of development did the term *prajñāpāramitā* become equivalent to this realization of emptiness.

18 The earliest written evidence in Indic languages is from the third or fourth centuries onwards: (1) A Schøyen fragment, ca. fourth century CE (Gupta Brāhmī), mentioning the king Huviṣka having "set out on the Mahāyāna path," G (**mahā)yānasamprasthito huveṣko nā*(**ma rājā*); Salomon 2002: 256. (2) Correspondingly, the Mathurā/Govindnagar pedestal inscription documents the ritual establishment of an image of Amitābha in the year 26 [of Kaniṣka I] during the reign of Huviṣka, i.e., 153 CE (cf. Schopen 1987). (3) Further, the Endere site stone inscription characterizes the king of Shanshan/Kroraina, who is most likely Aṃgoka of the middle of the third century CE, as one who had "set out on the Mahāyāna path," G *mahayanasaṃprastida-*; Salomon 1999b: 3. (4) Another secular document on a wooden tablet from Niya (document no. 390) with the epithet *mahāyānasaṃprastita-*

prajñāpāramitā is nothing other than the concept of *śūnyatā* and the denial of any *svabhāva*, also expressed as "superworldly true knowledge" (*lokottarabhūtajñāna*) in BC 11. Further, while an altruistic orientation is indicated (by the statements "establish [all] beings in awakening" and "welfare for myself, welfare for others, and welfare for every living being"), it is not stressed as such. Additionally, the author uses typical exaggerations like "world systems [as numerous] as the sands of the river Gaṅgā," which are so familiar from Mahāyāna texts.

The mention of a bodhisattva (BC 4) does not conclusively prove a Mahāyāna orientation, since this term was already used in non-Mahāyāna texts as an epithet of the Buddha, and "there is evidence that the term 'bodhisattva' originally meant only 'a *śrāvaka* who truly understands the Dharma' rather than [someone] of a separate group" (Rawlinson 1977: 8–9). In fact, there seem to have been two "true" bodhisattvas in the early first centuries, both claiming that they represented the prototype of someone striving for awakening (cf. Fujita 2009: 144, who differentiates between the two by the designations "Nikāya bodhisattva" and "Mahāyāna bodhisattva," with respect to the texts they are based on). Thus, the "Nikāya bodhisattva" relies only on the *tripiṭaka* and the avadānas (also called the *śrāvakadharma*), while the "Mahāyāna bodhisattva" adds the *prajñāpāramitā* sūtras, claiming that the *tripiṭaka* is not enough.[19] In due course of time, the latter came to designate themselves as *bodhisattva mahāsattva* to make their position clear (cf. Williams 2009: 55). Thus, BC 4 and, based thereon, also BC 6 and BC 11 seem to stand somewhere in the middle, being grounded in the Śrāvakayāna tradition but incorporating ideas that were later central to Mahāyāna texts.

1.3.2 Elements of Abhidharma

In addition to these Mahāyāna features, scholastic elements are evident in the texts, as for example, the lists of contrastive pairs as well as the summaries and categories in BC 4.[20] A more scholastic approach in general can be observed in BC 11, where logical conclusions are drawn in the process of argumentation (G *yadi … ta avaśi …*, *keṇa karaṇeṇa …*, *ṇa ida ṭ́haṇo vijadi*) and instructions are given. In all three texts, the literary technique of dialogue has been used

---

is dated to the third or fourth century CE (cf. Salomon 1999b: 6, 10). For all of these instances, see Allon and Salomon 2010: 3–4. One of the earliest attestations in Chinese (possibly the earliest) is the translation of the *Pratyutpannabuddhasaṃmukhāvasthitasamādhisūtra* by Lokakṣema, 179 CE (see Harrison 1998: 12, for one example). Deleanu (2000: 66) dated the proto-Mahāyāna period to ca. 100 BCE–100 CE and the early Mahāyāna period to between the first century BCE and the fifth century CE.

19 In this context, of particular interest is a passage in the *Mahāprajñāpāramitopadeśaśāstra* (cf. Fujita 2009: 102), where "some other bodhisattvas" ask what is lacking in the *śrāvakadharma* and equate each part of their *śrāvakadharma* to the six *pāramitā*s. Since the Abhidharma is described as "six-limbed," it is assumed that reference is being made to the Sarvāstivāda Abhidharma (Fujita 2009: 102 n. 7). Furthermore, this Abhidharma is equated to *prajñā* and *dhyāna*, thus providing a connection between scholasticism and insight/meditation.

20 A typical feature for (early) Abhidharma texts are listings or summaries called *mātṛkā* / P *mātikā*. Normally, these texts begin with a certain list which is then explained. In the *Pātimokkhasutta*, the sequence *dhammadhara*, *vinayadhara*, *mātikādhara* is repeatedly mentioned, making the *mātikā* equivalent to the Abhidharma category (cf. Gethin 1992b).

for rhetorical and argumentative purposes, whereby *aha* (Skt. *āha*) introduces an objection or possible question ("Someone / an objector says" in the sense of "someone might say …") and *ta vucadi* (Skt. *tad ucyate*) introduces the answer or explanation ("it is said [in answer]" in the sense of "then I would say / answer …").[21] Furthermore, the dialectic style is supported by direct addresses (second person pronouns and verbs).

Another possible scholastic feature is the term *traidhātuka* (BC 4), corresponding to *kāma- / rūpa- / ārūpyadhātu* (BC 11), as well as the categorizations *laukika / alaukika / lokottara* (BC 11). Similarly, the concept of *svabhāva* (BC 4) was a development of Abhidharma scholars (Williams 2009: 68). As Johannes Bronkhorst has pointed out (2013), the emphasis on non-substantiality (*niḥsvabhāvatā*) or non-existence of dharmas in—*prajñāpāramitā* related—Mahāyāna texts only makes sense if simultaneously there were convictions about the existence of dharmas. This was the case in the Sarvāstivāda Abhidharma, which is thought to have originated in Gandhāra and Kashmir (cf. Willemen et al. 1998: 57, 70, 73). According to Bronkhorst (2013) a scholastic "intellectual revolution" ("new Abhidharma") took place around 150 BCE, possibly "inspired by the interaction between Buddhist and Indo-Greeks" that gave rise to a new perspective on the doctrinal material and ontological background, resulting in the concept of the emptiness of all dharmas,[22] a key term for (at least one group of) Mahāyāna literature.[23]

It is indeed striking that early Mahāyāna texts show such a strong influence of scholasticism.[24] In the case of BC 4 / 6 / 11 this is observed in the style and application of terms. The same is quite obvious in another text of the Bajaur Collection, namely BC 2, where there are long passages filled with listings of categories and terms revolving around the idea of the non-perception of dharmas, thereby circumscribing the *śūnyatā* doctrine (cf. Schlosser and Strauch 2016). This indeed suggests that (Sarvāstivāda) Abhidharma was one essential precondition for the emergence of Mahāyāna.[25] In this early proto-Mahāyāna literature, this may be more visible than in later texts, where other features became prevalent.

1.4 Context

1.4.1 Prajñāpāramitā and Mahāyāna

Despite some clear commonalities with what later came to be labeled Mahāyāna, the general appearance and wording of the texts is very similar to those associated with basic Nikāya or mainstream Buddhism, suggesting a gradual reform within the traditional Sangha that "can

---

21 Cf. Tubb and Boose 2007: 245–46 § 2.49.6 and § 2.50.1.

22 Bronkhorst 2013: "Indeed, these scholiasts may have been the first to call themselves *śūnyavādins*."

23 There could, however, also be other reasons for the development of new aspects or methods, such as, for example, influence from Brahmanical institutions that were restored by Puṣyamitra in the middle of the second century BCE (cf. Willemen et al. 1998: 102–3).

24 Skilling (2004: 148): "Mahāyāna sūtras may be read as records of debates and negotiations, as attempts to resolve contradictions and tensions in Buddhist doctrine and practice. Debates about dharmas and the path are reflected in the *prajñāpāramitā* sūtras." Cf. Deleanu 2000: 69 for the "new hermeneutic approach" in *prajñāpāramitā* literature, or also Gómez 1999: 117.

25 Cf. von Rospatt 1977: 165, Willemen et al. 1998: 278.

explain the doctrinal continuities between the two movements" (Deleanu 2000: 81).[26] What seems to be the crucial distinguishing element is often the practice of the teaching of *prajñā-pāramitā*, "characterized by emptiness (*śūnyatā*) and essencelessness or nonsubstantiality (*niḥ-svabhāvatā*)" (Fujita 2009: 100). This is realized in meditation, which in the *Aṣṭasāhasrikā*, for example, is indicated by the *samādhi* called *sarvadharma-aparigṛhīta* or *dharma-anupādāna*, the non-appropriation of or non-grasping at dharmas. Also BC 4/6/11 indicate that the proto-Mahāyāna bodhisattva path in the early first centuries—at least in the place in Gandhāra where these texts were produced—was primarily concerned with meditation and withdrawal from the senses. The path, as illustrated in these scrolls, is the practice of *prajñāpāramitā* as a means to let go, in the sense of giving up any attachments to the world.[27]

Likewise, in BC 2 it is repeatedly stated that nothing can or should be perceived (G *ṇa samaṇupaśati*) or conceived (G *prañayadi*): no *ātman*, no *sattva*, etc.[28] Through this non-perception of or non-attachment to any dharma, the practitioner attains the *dharmakṣānti* and becomes non-retrogressive. In BC 4, this analytic process is not described (since it is not the topic of the text), but it is included in terms like *prajñāpāramitā* or *śūnya*, or the disappearance of *svabhāvatā*. In BC 6, terms and formulations like *amaṇas̱iara* (Skt. *amanasikāraḥ*), *ṇa spuramaṇas̱a* (Skt. *na sphuranmānasaḥ*), *taṇua saña* (Skt. *tanukā saṃjñā*), or *vovas̱ama* (Skt. *vyupaśamaḥ*) suggest that the practice mainly consisted of bringing the mind to rest and reducing notions of the outside world.

Based on some of the insights gained from BC 4/6/11, as well as from BC 2, it seems likely that the starting point for Mahāyāna in Gandhāra was the concept of *śūnyatā*, an understanding that all dharmas are essentially unarisen and without inherent existence, which is gained through mental analysis and (physical) experience during absorptive states in meditation. At some point the *prajñāpāramitā* became a key term for this insight. Early Mahāyāna texts, as rightly observed by John Thompson (2008: 53–54), "offer little step-by-step instruction on how to perfect *prajñā*," but rather treat it in a theoretical/philosophical manner. "Perhaps the most common description of *prajñā* in the *prajñāpāramitā*s is non-attachment to objects and ideas" (Thompson 2008: 53–54, cf., e.g., AsP 235), thus inserting *śūnyatā* into the practice of the Buddhist path as a means to an end. The same is true for the Gāndhārī manuscripts edited here.

---

26 Cf. also Rawlinson 1977: 15. Most scholars agree that early Mahāyāna, in principle, was not distinct from mainstream Buddhism (for example, Yamada 1957, 1959, Bechert, e.g., 1973, Silk 2002, Murakami 2004, Sasaki 2009, Fujita 2009).

27 Cf. Deleanu (2000: 88): "Becoming a Buddha oneself means the transcendence of all attachments whatsoever, [...] The early *arhat* ideal is not so different from this but what gives Mahāyāna its distinctive flavour is pushing the non-attachment, emotional and cognitive, to its utmost logical consequences. [...] A discursive mode of thinking can no longer serve the basic purpose of attainment without attainment. It is here that meditative states, super-normal powers, and Buddha's inspiration come to play a crucial role."

28 This is reminiscent of P *passan na passati* in the teaching of Uddaka Rāmaputta (Wynne 2007: 46). Furthermore, the non-perception of the elements (earth, water, fire, air, space) in BC 2 suggests a relation of this kind of meditation to the element meditation of early Brahmanism (cf. Wynne 2007: 29–31).

1.4.2 Prajñāpāramitā and Bodhisattvayāna

The *prajñāpāramitā* teaching or practice and the ideal of a bodhisattva path are not necessarily linked to each other, as for instance was shown by Tilmann Vetter using examples from passages of the *Mūlamadhyamakakārikā*, where the bodhisattva path is not recommended but only the *prajñāpāramitā*, "albeit not under this name," as a kind of absorption method to "experience […] *nirvāṇa* here and now" (Vetter 2001: 82).[29] Moreover, "the method for buddhahood called *prajñāpāramitā* is likely to have been formed after a new method of monks for a direct experience of release" (Vetter 1994: 1259), emphasizing a speedy attainment of awakening in contrast to the more difficult bodhisattva way, which was "probably regarded as taking too much time."[30] It appears as if the meditation on *śūnyatā* was voluntary among bodhisattvas,[31] which explains the co-existence of Śrāvakayāna and Mahāyāna, sometimes also in one and the same monastery.[32] Hence, a Mahāyāna adherent could and most probably had to be a member of a mainstream monastery / Vinaya tradition,[33] but whoever was interested could practice the *prajñāpāramitā*, independent of his traditional *nikāya* affiliation.[34] More important than his status was the mental attitude of the practitioner (cf. Tsai 2014: 266).

If we accept the reconstruction of *tribodhi* in BC 4 and its explanation as referring to the three ways to awakening of a śrāvaka, a pratyekabuddha, or a samyaksaṃbuddha (see p. 164), this could show that the instructions given in BC 4 are addressed to each of the three groups. If so, this scroll would be another piece of evidence for the *prajñāpāramitā* having been used by anyone who wished to follow this sort of method, which was praised as some kind of shortcut to awakening or simply as a method to experience *nirvāṇa*, that is, the contentment and appeasement associated with it, here in this lifetime. This would categorize BC 4 as a representative of

---

29 Cf. also Fujita (2009: 114): "This means that at least in the *Prajñāparamitā-sūtra* the notion of 'Mahāyāna' was not equivalent to that of 'bodhisattva vehicle.'"

30 Vetter 1994: 1257 referring to a paragraph in the *Aṣṭasāhasrikā*, represented in the first Chinese translation (T 8 no. 224 pp. 426c20–21 and 428b17–25).

31 Cf. Nattier (2003: 197 ff.) regarding the "absence of the rhetoric of absence" in the *Ugraparipṛcchā*, thus being an example for a Mahāyāna text not being grounded on the *śūnyatā* doctrine.

32 Strauch 2007/2008: 66: "[…] early Mahāyāna texts like the *Ugraparipṛcchā* clearly show that monks following the newly introduced Bodhisattvayāna lived together with those adherent to the traditional Śrāvakayāna (Nattier 2003: 81–89). Similar is the situation which can be deduced from the *Pratyutpannabuddhasaṃmukhāvasthitasamādhi-sūtra*, which 'suggests that in some monasteries adherents of different movements lived together, avoiding discussing their differences (between mainstream and Mahāyāna, and within Mahāyāna itself) openly' (Vetter 1994: 1265)." Cf. also Drewes 2010b: 71 and Allon and Salomon 2010: 13 n. 45 for further references.

33 Cf. Strauch 2007/2008: 67: "Xuanzang [600–664 CE] is reporting about the Mahāyāna monks in Udyāna (Swāt) […]: 'The schools of the Vinaya traditions traditionally known among them are the Sarvāstivādins, the Dharmaguptas, the Mahīśāsakas, the Kāśyapīyas, and the Mahāsāṃghikas: these five' (Beal 1884,1: 120–121)."

34 Cf. also Skilling 2004: 151 regarding the differences between Mahāyāna and Śrāvakayāna. A significant difference was the reading of Mahāyāna sūtras, in addition to the classical *tripiṭaka*. Skilling 2004: 142–43: "available scriptures of the eighteen schools allow all three options [of *yāna*s]: it is one's own decision" which one to take.

a "weak form" of Mahāyāna universalism,[35] that "retains the traditional scenario of the three vehicles," agreeing with the other vehicles in destination but not in the path (Nattier 2003: 175).[36] In the beginning, both *śūnyatā* adherents and others would have called themselves bodhisattvas to express their striving after buddhahood, but probably in the course of time, more and more distinctive and distinguishing aspects came up that finally lead to a separation, generating the designation Mahāyāna (as well as the more specific appellation *bodhisattva mahāsattva*) in contrast to Hīnayāna (*bodhisattva*). This is likely to have taken place in the second century at the latest, since the term Mahāyāna is already found in the earliest Chinese translations (cf. Nattier 2003: 193–97). Furthermore, there are texts such as the *Ratnāvalī* attributed to Nāgārjuna (second century) that discuss the differences between both parties, encouraging the reader to see their similarities (verse 386) and refrain from condemning the Mahāyāna if one is unable to accept it (verses 388, 389, 397). The need to discuss this and plead for the Mahāyāna might indicate that it was being differentiated and separated from mainstream Śrāvakayāna circles at this time.

1.4.3 Mahāyāna in the Earliest Chinese Translations

Many of the earliest translations of Mahāyāna texts into Chinese by the Yuezhi Lokakṣema at the end of the second century CE[37] display an emphasis on meditation and absorption (*samādhi*) as well as on ascetic practices and forest dwelling (Williams 2009: 30, based on Harrison 1995: 65–66). Lokakṣema stayed in Luoyang between 168 or 178 and 189 CE, translating at this time, most prominently, the *Aṣṭasāhasrikā*, known as the "Practice of the Path" (道行般若經, *Dàoxíng bānruò jīng*, T 8 no. 224).[38] While Ān Shìgāo 安世高, a native from Parthia, was the first translator of Buddhist texts named in Chinese sources (having arrived in Luoyang

---

35 For the universalism of the *prajñāpāramitā* teaching, cf. Rawlinson 1977: 15 referring to the *Aṣṭasāhasrikā*, where it is labeled as "beneficial for all [three] vehicles" (*prajñāpāramitā sārvayānikī*) or another passage where it is stated that "(Those who) want to learn the Dharma of the arhan(t) [...]. (Those who) want to learn the Dharma of the *pratyekabuddhas* [...]. (Those who) want to learn the Dharma of the bodhisattvas, should listen to the Prajñāpāramitā, should study it, should bear it (in mind), should cultivate it" (Falk and Karashima 2012: 38–39, with regard to AsP^{Sp} 1-25 *ṣavagabhumie va śikṣamaṇeṇa ayam eva prañaparamida śodava*). Also in BC 2, all three paths are mentioned side by side without explicitly favoring or degrading any one of them.

36 Nattier (2003: 175) further: "Thus even as they [i.e. early Mahāyāna sūtras] instruct the bodhisattva on the specifics of his or her chosen path [...] they also treat the path of the *śrāvaka* as entirely legitimate. [...] this nonuniversalist position was actually quite widespread, especially in the early stages of the production of Mahāyāna literature."

37 Active ca. 168–89 CE (Harrison 1987: 68). Zürcher (1991: 283): ca. 170–90 CE; Nattier (2008: 73): 178–89 CE.

38 Lokakṣema is reported to have translated fourteen texts, but not all have come down to us. The ones accepted as genuine by Harrison (1987, 1993: 137, 1995: 53) and Zürcher (1991) are the following, with those underlined for which parallels in Gāndhārī manuscripts have already been identified: T 8 no. 224 (*Aṣṭasāhasrikāprajñāpāramitāsūtra*), T 10 no. 280 (part of the *Avataṃsaka*), T 11 no. 313 (*Akṣobhyatathāgatasyavyūha*), T 12 no. 350 (*Kāśyapaparivarta*), T 13 no. 418 (*Pratyutpannabuddhasammukhāvasthitasamādhisūtra*), T 14 no. 458 (*Wénshūshīlì wèn púsà shǔ jīng* with affinity to the *Vimalakīrtinirdeśa*), T 15 no. 626 (*Ajātaśatrukaukṛtyavinodanāsūtra*), T 17 no. 807 (*Lokānu-*

in 148/149 CE), he did not translate any Mahāyāna affiliated texts.[39] His compatriot Ān Xuán 安玄 came to Luoyang in 181 CE and translated the *Ugraparipṛcchā* (T 12 no. 322),[40] a Mahāyāna sūtra that was especially concerned with the bodhisattva path. Another Yuezhi monk and one of Lokakṣema's students was Zhī Yaò 支曜, who, like his teacher, is said to have translated a Mahāyāna text, the "Sūtra on the Completion of Brightness" (成具光明經, *Chéngjù guāngmíng jīng*, T 15 no. 630). It was quite popular even two hundred years later as an authority on the philosophy of *prajñā*, together with, according to Thompson (2008: 96), the *Pañcaviṃśatisāhasrikā* (T 4 no. 211, translated by *Mokṣala) and the *Aṣṭasāhasrikā* (T 8 no. 224, translated by Lokakṣema).[41] Thus, it appears that while the *Ugraparipṛcchā* that was translated by a Parthian (Ān Xuán 安玄) focused on the bodhisattva path and on the *dānapāramitā* as the foremost of the six *pāramitā*s, other texts that were translated by Yuezhi (Lokakṣema, Zhī Yaò 支曜) focused on *prajñā*/*samādhi* (cf. Thompson 2008: 61–81). Thus, not (only) temporal but (also) geographical or ideological reasons might have played a role in the co-existence of different strands of the bodhisattva path, with emphasis either on the bodhisattva ideal or on *śūnyatā*/*prajñā*. Johannes Bronkhorst (2013) has suggested that first the bodhisattva path emerged, with the *prajñāpāramitā* philosophy then added later in Gandhāra.

1.4.4 Mahāyāna in Manuscripts Written in Gāndhārī

It is assumed that the earliest Chinese translations of Mahāyāna texts were made on the basis of manuscripts written in Kharoṣṭhī and composed in Gāndhārī or another similar Prakrit dialect other than pure Sanskrit,[42] suggesting the origin or at least a stronghold of Mahāyāna in the northwest.[43] The so far earliest testimonies to Mahāyāna Buddhism among Gāndhārī manu-

---

vartanāsūtra). Another one, T 15 no. 624 (*Drumakinnararājaparipṛcchāsūtra*) is accepted only by Harrison (1993: 141); cf. Nattier 2008: 76–89 for a discussion.

39 Ān Shìgāo 安世高 translated sixteen texts according to Zürcher 1991, all of them between ca. 150 and 170 CE (T nos. 13, 14, 31, 32, 36, 48, 57, 98, 112, 150, 602, 603, 605, 607, 792, 1508). There is some uncertainty regarding the last; cf. Nattier 2008, also with regard to additional uncertain text attributions.

40 In 181 CE according to Zürcher (1959: 34). Nattier (2003: 44) dates the *Ugraparipṛcchā* to between 180 and 190 CE.

41 Zhī Yaò 支曜 (active in the late second century) was also listed by Harrison in 1987, but cf. Nattier 2008: 94–102.

42 For the Gāndhārī hypothesis, see Boucher 1998 and cf. Allon 2008: 170, 177; Salomon 2006: 144; Salomon 2008b; Salomon 2010: xxxiii. The designation of a manuscript as 胡本 *húběn* as opposed to 梵書 *fànshū* / 梵文 *fànwén* (Brāhmī/Sanskrit) could indicate that it was written in Kharoṣṭhī. For example, the manuscripts from which Dharmarakṣa translated the *Lalitavistara* (with its Arapacana formulary) were labeled 胡本 *húběn* (cf. Boucher 1998: 499–502).

43 Cf. Glass 2004: 138 and also Salomon 2010: xxxiii. Already Lamotte (1954: 392) and Conze (1978: 4) observed that the *prajñāpāramitā* "had a great success in the North-West at the Kushāṇa period, and that […] that region may well be the 'fortress and heart', though not necessarily the 'cradle' of the Mahāyānistic movement. The *Mañjuśrīmūlakalpa* (LIII v. 575) says that under Kaniṣka the *prajñāpāramitā* was 'established' (*pratiṣṭhitā*) in the North-West, but not that it originated there" (Conze 1978: 4). Cf. hereto Dessein (2009: 53), who says: "As the Bahuśrutīyas were the only Mahāsāṃghika subgroup that resided both in the north and in the south, it is not unlikely that they served as an intermediary in a general process in which Mahayanistic ideas that were developed

scripts are a *prajñāpāramitā* text parallel to the *Aṣṭasāhasrikā Prajñāpāramitā*[44] (Falk and Karashima 2012, 2013), the "Bajaur Mahāyāna Sūtra" with partial parallels to the *Akṣobhya-vyūha* (Schlosser and Strauch forthcoming), the **Sucintisūtra* similar to and presupposing the *Vimalakīrtinirdeśa* with parallels to three Chinese translations (T 14 nos. 477–79, cf. Allon and Salomon 2010: 11, Harrison, Lenz, and Salomon 2018: 118), as well as fragments of the *Pratyutpannabuddhasaṃmukhāvasthitasamādhisūtra* (Harrison, Lenz, and Salomon 2018) and the *Samādhirārajasūtra* (cf. Harrison, Lenz, and Salomon 2018: 118), all dated to the first or second century CE.[45] Furthermore, there are several small palm leaf fragments from Bamiyan with text passages familiar from the *Bhadrakalpikasūtra*[46] (Baums, Glass, and Matsuda 2016), the *Bodhisattvapiṭakasūtra* (Baums et al. 2016), the *Sarvapuṇyasamuccayasamādhisūtra* (Harrison et al. 2016), the *Vīradattaparipṛcchā* (Melzer and Schlosser forthcoming), as well as another as yet unidentified Mahāyāna sūtra (Matsuda 2013), all dated to the third or fourth century CE.

The earliest texts are all presumed to have come from Gandhāra, more precisely the Bajaur district or its neighborhood, and they all lay stress on the *śūnyatā* doctrine. Additionally, some of them include visualization techniques, such as imagining a buddhafield. The group of six *pāramitā*s is mentioned in the *prajñāpāramitā* text, in BC 11, and in the fragments of the *Bhadrakalpikasūtra* from Bamiyan. In BC 4 only the *prajñāpāramitā* is mentioned. The notion of the group of six *pāramitā*s does not coincide with the emphasis on *śūnyatā*, but rather represents a universal concept suitable for any bodhisattva path (cf. Nattier 2003: 153).[47]

1.5 Similar Texts

As no direct parallel has been found for the Gāndhārī manuscripts under consideration, the following statements are merely references to texts that are vaguely similar with regard to their overall content, title, special terms, or stylistic features.

With respect to their "background philosophy," BC 4, BC 6, and BC 11 are connected to *prajñāpāramitā* texts. Hence, similar phrases in other Indic languages (Sanskrit/Pali) frequently occur in *prajñāpāramitā* affiliated literature, especially in commentaries on such literature.

---

and matured in the north were transmitted to the south and vice versa. More precisely, it appears that it was in the north that early Mahayanistic ideas were fitted into the framework of Sarvāstivāda abhidharmic developments."

44 The *Aṣṭasāhasrikā Prajñāpāramitā* is also the earliest preserved Mahāyāna manuscript in Brāhmī, composed in (Buddhist Hybrid) Sanskrit. It is written on several palm leaf fragments found in Bamiyan that have been dated to the second half of the third century CE based on paleography (late Kuṣāṇa Brāhmī, cf. Sander 2000b: 1 and Hartmann 2011: 31). The language and orthography point to a northwestern origin of the manuscript and a Gāndhārī influence (Sander 2000a: 97).

45 There is another unidentified Mahāyāna sūtra with an unusually extensive *paścime kāle* formula (cf. Harrison, Lenz, and Salomon 2018: 118), but no more details are known.

46 "The Tibetan and Chinese traditions regard the *Bhadrakalpikāsūtra* as a Mahāyāna text. Therefore these fragments may be part of the oldest known manuscript of a Mahāyāna sūtra. However, some care must be taken before making this connection, as it is not certain that this text would have been considered a Mahāyāna work at this time" (Glass 2004: 141; cf. also Allon and Salomon 2010: 7).

47 A passage in the *Vibhāṣā* (T 27 no. 1545 p. 892a24) claims that the group of six *pāramitā*s were peculiar to the west of Kashmir (cf. Qing 2001: 23).

With respect to categories, terms, and phrases, partial parallels can be found in the commentaries on the *Aṅguttara-* and *Khuddakanikāya* of the Pali canon and in scholastic texts (*Abhidharmakośabhāṣya* and *-vyākhyā*). Sometimes the parallels are not directly obvious, but can be seen in synonyms.

Among canonical or para-canonical Pali literature discussing the proposed meditation practice, similarities can be observed in the techniques described in the *Pārāyanavagga* in the dialogue with the Brahmin Upasīva.[48] This meditation is based on nothingness; apparently a co-product of it is calm joy or delight. According to Wynne (2007: 75), it has its origin in Brahminic methods of absorption, with the difference that in the Buddhist adaptation, mindfulness and insight are included. The result is liberation in life, although the liberated sage, as well as the liberation itself, is beyond conceptual dualities and not expressible (cf. Wynne 2007: 109). Wynne points to the fact that the Upasīva dialogue is quite unlike other texts in the *Suttapiṭaka*.[49] Moreover, the *Pārāyanavagga* (Sn V) together with the *Aṭṭhakavagga* (Sn IV) and the *Khaggavisāṇasutta* (Sn I 35–75) are thought to have existed independently before they were incorporated into the *Suttanipāta* (Wynne 2007: 73). The Gāndhārī manuscripts show that these texts were also known in Gandhāra in the first centuries CE, separately or as a group (cf. Salomon 2000: 14–18). So far, parallels to the *Khaggavisāṇasutta* (G **Khargaviṣaṇasutra*), preserved in BL 5B, and to parts of the *Aṭṭhakavagga* (G **Arthapada*), preserved both in the Split Collection and another private collection,[50] have been identified. Also a verse commentary (Nird[L2]) edited by Stefan Baums (2009) comments on verses known from the *Aṭṭhakavagga* and the *Pārāyanavagga*, among others from a *Dharmapada* or *Udāna*. Thus, possibly also BC 4 might stand in some connection to the *Pārāyanavagga* or at least the meditation form proposed in it. Already in 1976, Luis Gómez suggested that the *Aṭṭhakavagga* and *Pārāyanavagga* might be proto-Madhyamaka; there are also some indications in the Gāndhārī *Saṅgītisūtra* commentary (SaṅgCm[L]) suggesting that at the time of its composition, categorical systems existed that bore similarities to those in *prajñāpāramitā* texts (cf. Baums 2009: 23, 52). But, again, since Mahāyāna seems to have gradually developed within a Śrāvakayāna environment, the classification into the one or the other vehicle is often not easy to determine, and there are several peculiarities/terms shared by both parties.[51]

---

48 The *Pārāyanavagga* contains three short dialogues with Upasīva, Udaya, and Posāla showing that the Buddha taught a form of meditative practice based on the goal of Āḷāra Kālāma "that was thought to lead to a non-intellectual sort of insight" (Wynne 2007: 75). Among these dialogues, the one with Upasīva is particularly similar to the overall picture emerging from BC 4/6/11.

49 Cf. also Bronkhorst 2011: 171–72: "nothing in the teaching of the B. as traditionally handed down suggests that ordinary reality does not exist. This idea was introduced later into the Buddhist tradition." Especially the *Pārāyanavagga* deals with forms of meditation which are unusual for Buddhism. They are described as meditations that had been taught to Brahmins. Also stylistic features make them different from common texts in the Pali canon (e.g., the unusual beginning "I ask").

50 SC 1, recto: Sn 841–44; private collection: Sn 862–909; SC 1, verso: Sn 966–68.

51 Within the Gāndhārī manuscripts, also some of those that have been assigned to mainstream Buddhism contain possible indications of Mahāyāna, or at least references to *śūnyatā* and *prajñā*. One example is BL 10 (cf. Salomon 1999a: 178). For problems in identifying early Mahāyāna texts, cf. Nattier 2003: 171–97, Ruegg 2004, Schopen 2005, and Pagel 2006.

With regard to its application of the six *pāramitās* as prerequisites to buddhahood as well as its apparent intermediate state between Śrāvakayāna and Mahāyāna, BC 4 is quite similar to the *Cariyāpiṭaka* of the *Khuddakanikāya*.[52] The *Cariyāpiṭaka* is divided into three *vaggas* based on the first three *pāramīs*, i.e., *dāna*, *sīla*, *nekkhamma*, while the other perfections are included in the last *vagga* and in the last stanza (note that also in BC 4, only three *pāramitās* are named specifically as examples, but are otherwise referred to as part of a group of six). Regarding the *Cariyāpiṭaka*, Bhikkhu Bodhi (1996) has emphasized the universalism of the *pāramī* practice, stating that "the work remains well within the bounds of Theravāda orthodoxy" and that its "section on the perfection of wisdom has nothing more in common with the *prajñāpāramitā* literature than the core of Buddhist doctrine shared by all schools." He adds that it "should be noted that in established Theravāda tradition the pāramīs are not regarded as a discipline peculiar to candidates for buddhahood alone but as practices which must be fulfilled by all aspirants to awakening and deliverance, whether as Buddhas, paccekabuddhas, or disciples."[53]

Among texts that can be clearly attributed to the Mahāyāna, a similar work with respect to the *pāramitās* being requisites or provisions for awakening is the *Bodhisambhāra*, ascribed to Nāgārjuna, although it includes more mature Mahāyāna ideas.[54] Judging merely from the title, another text that may resemble BC 4 is the **Bodhisattvanidānasūtra* mentioned in the *Mahāprajñāpāramitopadeśaśāstra* (fascicle 38),[55] but neither the original nor any translation of this work is extant (cf. Kimura R. 1927: 415). As already mentioned above, other works, such as the *Ratnāvalī* commonly attributed to Nāgārjuna, contain statements similar to ones made in BC 4 (as well as BC 6 and BC 11) regarding the practice of a bodhisattva.

Based on Pagel (1995: 91), also some parts of the *Bodhisattvapiṭakasūtra* are similar in their content. Above all, this is the case for section 7.3, which mentions the factors impeding moral conduct and singles out passion (*rāga*) as the most devastating force. It is argued that the best way to overcome this peril is to see its manifestation from the perspective of emptiness (*śūnyatā*). The whole text is much more elaborate than BC 4/6/11 and is surely to be dated later (the earliest material evidence are the Schøyen fragments from the third or fourth century CE). Chapter 11 is about the bodhisattva path, with an emphasis on meditation and *prajñāpāramitā*, also similar to the Gāndhārī texts.

With regard to certain special terms, most notably the twenty kinds of joy (*viṃśati prīti*, BC 4 § 1), there is a Chinese text that contains analogies to the stages of a bodhisattva and to what a bodhisattva must do to help other beings attain awakening: the "Sūtra of the Garland of a

---

52 The *Cariyāpiṭaka* is believed to be a late addition (Horner 1975, II: vi) and has been described as hagiographical (von Hinüber 1996: 43).

53 "What distinguishes the supreme bodhisattva from aspirants in the other two vehicles is the degree to which the pāramīs must be cultivated and the length of time they must be pursued. But the qualities themselves are universal requisites for deliverance, which all must fulfill to at least a minimal degree to merit the fruits of the liberating path" (Bodhi 1996).

54 T 32 no. 1660, being a translation of the South Indian monk Dharmagupta (ca. 609 CE) together with the commentary of Bhikṣu *Vaśitva, who apparently lived not long after Nāgārjuna sometime during the first quarter of the first millennium.

55 For a discussion of the author being Nāgārjuna or Kumārajīva, who was responsible for the only extant Chinese version, produced in 406 CE, cf. Takeda 2000 and also Deleanu 2000: 68.

Bodhisattva's Primary Karmas"[56] (菩薩瓔珞本業經, *Púsà yīngluò běnyè jíng*, T 24 no. 1485).[57] A commentary on it is preserved in T 85 no. 2798 (本業瓔珞經疏, *Běnyè yīngluò jíng shù*). According to Mochizuki (1946), this was considered an apocryphal Chinese composition and not a translation, although it was apparently composed making use of various Central Asian sources.[58] For example, it shows similarities to the *Brahmajālasūtra* and elements in the *Gaṇḍavyūha*, using exaggerations as a typical feature (e.g., *gaṅgānadīvālikāsama*…). T 10 no. 281 (菩薩本業經, *Púsà běnyè jíng*) is purported to be an older version of (parts of) a text with a similar name,[59] although some essential keywords are missing there, as for example the twenty *prīti*s, which constitute the crucial link to BC 4. Apparently T 24 no. 1485 is the only parallel to this group of twenty kinds of joy. Unfortunately, the two texts do not match exactly, but they do examine similar topics and contain wordings in the same sequence. Another parallel is that both are structured with numbers, although the Chinese text is far more elaborate and detailed. It may have originally had the same basis—whether in text form or merely regarding the contents in general—and then grew gradually over the years or centuries, including material from other (Central Asian) sources.

Among the earliest Chinese translations of the late second century CE, there is none with any striking similarities to BC 4 (or BC 6 or BC 11). Based on the overview of texts on Buddhist philosophy from 100 to 350 CE given in Potter 1999 (Vol. VIII), similar or relevant contemporary texts might be T 15 no. 630, 成具光明定意經, *Chéngjù guāngmíng dìngyì jīng*, "Sūtra on the Completion of Brightness" (translated by Zhī Yaò 支曜, ca. 185 CE)[60] or T 17 no. 778, 菩薩內習六波羅蜜經, *Púsà neìxí liù bōluómì jīng* (**Ṣaṭpāramitāsūtra*),[61] with both appearing likely to contain elements congruent to at least BC 4. However, the Gāndhārī manuscripts do not explain the six *pāramitā*s in detail, but simply refer to them without paying much attention to the set as such. Thus, it is unlikely that either of the two Chinese texts forms a direct parallel.

As an example for a similar background or intention behind composing a text, the **Mahāyānaśraddhotpādaśāstra*, "The Awakening of Faith [in the Mahāyāna/suchness]" (T 32 no. 1666, 大乘起信論, *Dàchéng qǐxìn lùn*, tr. Hakeda 1967), may be named. According to Hakeda (1967: 25–26) the reason for the production of this text was to convince men to free themselves from

---

56 "The *Pusa yingluo benye jing* is often rendered as 'Scripture of the Original Acts that Serve as Necklaces for the Bodhisattvas.' A different English translation such as the 'Scripture of the Original Acts as Adornments of Bodhisattvas' may also be possible" (Funayama 2013: 15 n. 1).

57 I owe this information to Abdurishid Yakup, who helped me search for several keywords from BC 4 in the Chinese canon (2011, Berlin). Later (2012, Munich), Hiromi Habata helped me to read the text and compare it to the Gāndhārī manuscript. Cf. also Funayama 2013.

58 Funayama 2013: 17; personal communication of Hiromi Habata (2012).

59 For more information about T 10 no. 281, cf. Nattier 2008: 138, and accordingly, especially Nattier 2005.

60 A treatise on the six perfections and the "Mental Concentration on Integral Illumination. The second part contains a description of the moral and religious duties of various classes of lay devotees" (Zürcher 1991: 299, cf. Potter 1999: 95).

61 Ascribed to Yán Fótiào 嚴佛調 (i.e., late second century CE) according to DDB (s.v. 佛說菩薩內習六波羅蜜經); cf. also Kimura R. 1927: 413, Hirakawa 1990: 276, Pagel 1995: 31 for cross-references to other Buddhist texts.

all suffering and to gain final bliss, and further, to point out the advantages [of studying the treatise] and to encourage them to make an effort [to attain awakening]. The focus is on suchness / one mind only, and it is stated that there are ten advantages gained by the practice of cessation (Hakeda 1967: 99). Due to the inclusion of particularly mature Mahāyāna ideas akin to Yogācāra philosophy (cf. Hubbard 1994), this is by no means a direct parallel, but it may be a further elucidation of the same topic.[62]

1.6 Authorship and Purpose

1.6.1 Oral/Aural Features

Based on some phonological and orthographic observations (p. 71), I argue that certain features point to an oral original, whether this was a speech, lecture or dictation of a second person that was written down by a scribe simultaneously or from memory, or whether it was an independent composition, in which case the oral features would indicate a process of writing while speaking aloud or of noting an inner speech.[63] The linguistic similarities to Niya documents (p. 99) suggest that BC 4, BC 6, and BC 11 are not translations, but texts that were originally produced in Gāndhārī.

Rhetorical elements such as repetitions and summaries at the end of the lists make BC 4 suitable for being presented out loud. Parallel structures, rhythmic patterns, as well as a minimized vocabulary facilitate understanding and make the text catchy and easy to remember. Exhortations, instructions, and the use of first and second person pronouns ("I," "we," or "you") suggest that the text addresses an audience. Also in BC 6 and BC 11 there are direct addresses (as for example: 6r9 "If you too understand it thus," and 11r39 "We should become content by not obtaining something"). These direct addresses function as literary devices, as do the questions and answers, to address the reader, whether real or fictitious, listening or reading. Since *paṇḍitas* are named twice as foremost figures, they may be the target group of the texts. Once they are mentioned as undertaking the right practice (11r7), and once the author appears to regard himself as a *paṇḍita* (6v9). In addition, there seems to be some opposition towards *pravrajitas*, since they are apparently not doing the right practice (11r31).

---

62 It is interesting to note in this context that this text is traditionally believed to have been written by Aśvaghoṣa (ca. 80–150 CE) and, allegedly, translated by Paramārtha in 553 CE. Modern scholars, however, consider it to have been composed in Chinese or even written by Paramārtha himself (cf., e.g., Nattier 1992: 180–81, Buswell 1990: 1–29, Ching 2009). However, the arguments brought forth by Jan Nattier, referring to Waley 1952: 53, are based on the single account of a story, whereby "during his stay at Nālandā University Hsüan-tsang [Xuánzàng 玄奘] discovered that this important text was unknown to his Indian coreligionists. And his response, we are told, was to translate the text into Sanskrit." This of course does not exclude the possibility of it having been renowned somewhere else prior to the seventh century CE.

63 Cf, e.g., Balogh 1927: 212–20, 232 on the act of reading aloud in antiquity (*paginalis locutio*). Cf. also Falk (2011: 14) with regard to SC 1 (*Arthapada*) and the use of different graphemes for *sa* or *ta*: "The scribe obviously tried to differentiate the sounds he uttered when reciting the text. He found variants in pronunciation and tried to assign to them diacritic forms to express the differences he heard in writing." For questions regarding orality and composition, cf. also Skilling 2014: 501, 511, 515.

In another passage in 6v6, reference is made to the "master's notion of happiness" (G *bhaṭareasa suhasaña* = Skt. *bhaṭṭārakasya sukhasaṃjñā*), which suggests that the manuscript was produced after having listened to the teaching of a spiritual person (*bhaṭṭāraka*) and his instructions on the notion and development of happiness.

1.6.2 Material-Based Features

The *scriptio continua* suggests the prevalence of an oral culture ("literate orality").[64] A minor addition to this statement is that in BC 4 the lines are written out in full, whereas in BC 11 sometimes the ends of lines have been left blank on purpose, apparently indicating a sort of conceptual junction with the beginning of the new line. In BC 6 sometimes the lines are written out in full, while other times the end of a line has been left blank on purpose. This could indicate that BC 4 was the result of an oral dictation or represents written notes on a speech given orally, whereas BC 6 and BC 11 were written at a later stage by the scribe himself, as a commentary on BC 4.

Indications of the birch-bark scrolls having been the original medium for the texts are the numbered sections and punctuation marks (though this is not conclusive), as well as instructions with relation to the reading process.

1.6.3 Instructions Referring to Reading the Text

There are two statements in BC 4 and BC 6 that can be understood as instructions to the reader. These are:

> 4r28 *maje ca ṇ(*i)s̱amarth(*e) purve dukhe paca̱ dukhe ma(*je ca ṇi)samarthe purve aśuha pa(*c̱a a)śuha maja ṇisamartha sarvatra ithu kaṭave*
> "In the middle useless, before painful, afterwards painful; in the middle useless, before unpleasant, afterwards unpleasant. '[In the] middle useless,'—[when this is written,] in every case it should be done thus."

> 6v7 *yahi aji tahi sava pada kaṭava yava …*
> "Now every word should be done [as above]—up to …"
> (lit.: "When today / now, then every word / sentence has to be done—up to …")

In 4r28, first the full sequence is given, then an abbreviation (which is added as an interlinear gloss throughout the text), followed by the explanation that every time one comes across the phrase "in the middle useless" one should add "before painful, afterwards painful" as well as "before unpleasant, afterwards unpleasant," as in the full sequence.

In 6v7, the instruction points to a previous passage in the text (cf. the discussion of this phrase on p. 258).

The inclusion of the word *aji* for Skt. *adya* is also known from avadānas and pūrvayoga texts in the British Library Collection:

---

64 Cf. Kim 2013: 28, and also Nattier 2008: 22–23.

Av^{L1} 173 *likhidago aco sarvo*, "Now, all is written."

Av^{L2} 8a *sarva ime avadana aca (*likhidaga)*, "Now, all these avadānas are written."

Av^{L6} 18 *likhidage aca avadane*, "Now the avadānas have been written."

The meaning and significance of these phrases have been discussed in Salomon 1999: 71–76 and Lenz 2003: 102–5 (§ 7.8). In summary, remarks like this suggest "that their scribes are probably the authors of the texts rather than the copyists of previously written documents" (Lenz 2003: 102). In consequence, the dialect of such texts "provides us with examples of more colloquial Gāndhārī" (Lenz 2003: 105). The same seems to hold true for BC 4/6/11 with respect to the language, as well as to the writer being the author.

1.6.4 References to Writing

So far, the pūrvayoga and avadāna texts of the British Library, the Khotan *Dharmapada*, as well as some Niya documents have been the only known Gāndhārī manuscripts containing *likhida* or *likhidaga* notations.[65] Now, in BC 6 similar remarks are found. At several places and in various contexts, reference is made to the writing process by using the word *likhida* or *likhidae* (Skt. *likhita* or BHS *likhitaka*), "has been written":

6r6 *yas̱a aji hi de likhida*, "as it has just been written," probably referring to a longer passage in the previous section, similar to today's note "see above."[66]

6r11 *śeṣ̱a patade likhidae*, "the remainder has been written on the reserve [side of the scroll]," referring to the continuation of the text on the verso.

6v8 *likhide ithu*, "thus it is written," probably referring to the following statement.

In the second example (6r11), reference is being made not only to the process of writing but to the writing material itself, the reader being instructed to turn over the scroll to continue reading the text. Almost the same phrase, at least the beginning of it, is found in BC 4:

4r28 *śeṣ̱ae patade hi vivaryaeṇa matra ca idara ca ahi(*va)d(*i)dava* …
"For the remainder, on the reverse [side of the scroll] inversely the full measure [of seven] as well as the other [group] should be saluted …"

In BC 4, the remark is found in the last line of the recto and embedded directly in the text (it starts in the middle of the line). In BC 6, it is also located at the bottom of the recto, but in a

---

[65] G *likhita* is also used in the Gāndhārī *Prajñāpāramitā* of the Split Collection, but within the narrative. For the reading *Dharmaśraveṇa likhida*, "it has been written by Dharmaśrava," in the uddāna of the Khotan *Dharmapada*, cf. Baums 2014: 204.

[66] Cf. also, for example, the note *yatha upari lihita[ga]* in Niya document no. 345.

separate line. In addition, the script looks a little different than the rest and is smaller, and there is very little space left below it on the scroll. It thus seems to have been added later, after the birch bark was already cut into form. The embedding of the statement "on the reverse [side] …" in BC 4 with reference to the content on the verso presupposes that the scribe knew what was about to follow, and that he also knew the physical position of his writing on the birch bark. This suggests that the scribe was the author of the text. (It is of course also possible that only the "turn the page" note was added later and that the rest was a direct transcript of an oral speech. This, however, seems unlikely since the statement starts in the middle of the line.)

Based on the considerations above, it seems likely that the texts were meant to be read. First of all, this is because statements like the instructions are not the sort of text that would be read out loud. Also, in BC 6 the wording is "as it has just been written" or "thus it is written," and not "thus it is said" or "as it has been said earlier," which would be more reasonable if the text was meant to be recited, or if it was a draft for presentation.

Moreover, the direct addresses in the second person (see above) and cross-references within the text (such as "see above") suggest that the texts were meant to be read by someone other than the author himself. Thus, the texts appear to have been written for an audience, and more precisely, an audience of readers, not listeners.

It might even be possible that the manuscripts are letters, since at the beginning of BC 6 the word *karitava* may have been used as some kind of opening formula to a letter. This, however, is very uncertain (cf. annotations on 6r1 *karitava*, p. 238).

1.6.5 Purpose

It is imaginable that a Buddhist scholar (*paṇḍita*) produced these texts promoting the *prajñāpāramitā* or *śūnyatā* doctrine to motivate and convince others about this new perspective. It has occasionally been suggested that the rise of Mahāyāna was primarily connected with the cultural tool of writing.[67] In the case of our three Bajaur manuscripts, it was not a *dharmabhāṇaka* producing new Mahāyānā sūtras, but rather a Buddhist practitioner writing scholastic treatises, possibly training for debate, either in the form of independent works in their own right or as part of letters.

Another explanation for the use of scriptures, especially for Mahāyāna texts, is that some teachings were initially not accepted widely and thus had to be handed down in written form.[68] This may have been another (additional) reason for writing being the chosen medium for transmitting the Bajaur texts.

---

[67] Drewes 2010b: 70: "What seems more likely is that early Indian Mahāyāna was, at root, a textual movement that developed in Buddhist preaching circles and centered on the production and use of Mahāyāna sūtras. At some point, drawing on a range of ideas and theoretical perspectives that had been developing for some time, and also developing many new ideas of their own, certain preachers began to compose a new type of text […] Mahāyāna preachers gave their imaginations free rein to expand the old Buddhist world and locate it within an infinitely more vast and glorious Buddhist universe with new religious possibilities for all."

[68] Cf., for example, an instruction in the *Aṣṭasāhasrikā* (AsP 221) according to which one should hurry to copy the sūtra and write it down as quickly as possible, because there are so many difficulties and

Still another suggestion for why early texts were written is their relevance for liturgic or ritual purposes.[69] In BC 4, some paragraphs, such as § 6 and parts of § 7, are suitable for recitation, either on a daily basis or on a single occasion, such as an inauguration ceremony at the beginning of a bodhisattva career. Moreover, the *praṇidhāna* in § 6 was perhaps not verbalized only once at the beginning of a bodhisattva career, but also at a later point in time to keep the vow alive. And § 7 may be connected to some sort of ritual of repentance and rejoicing (see p. 7). Through its oral performance the practitioner would confess his misconduct and "get back on the right track."[70] Thus, it could very well be that the Bajaur texts have preserved rituals that were the basis of a (Mahāyāna) bodhisattva's training, also called the *bodhisattvaprātimokṣa*. As such, they should contain most if not all of the foundational practices of Mahāyāna, which Peter Skilling has summarized as "refuge (*śaraṇa*), confession of misdeeds (*pāpadeśanā*), rejoicing in other's merit (*puṇyānumodanā*), [and] liturgical aspiration to awakening (*bodhicitta*)" (Skilling 2018: 124).

Regardless of whether the scrolls were letters or scholastic treatises addressed to a larger audience, I consider BC 4 (as well as BC 6 and BC 11) to be the product of a person wishing to praise detachment through the perspective of *śūnyatā* as the essential prerequisite for a path to awakening. By following the given instructions, it would be possible for practitioners to acquire every possible fortune and gain the ultimate bliss of liberation. This praise appears to be a sort of motivational guide for the practice of letting go. The new aspect or speciality of this method is superworldly true knowledge (*lokottarabhūtajñāna*), through which nothing must be given up, especially not happiness or contentment. There are several indications suggesting that this endeavor is a task for the individual.[71] Although detachment is primarily related to the senses, it may have also involved physical solitude to facilitate the meditation process. As such, it seems more than appropriate if the author wrote these texts in seclusion, later handing them to others in written form.

1.7 Conclusion

The Gāndhārī manuscripts BC 4, BC 6, and BC 11 may be characterized as autographic treatises written by and addressed to a practitioner on the bodhisattva path based on the *prajñāpāramitā* doctrine of the emptiness of all dharmas. This knowledge would enable the practitioner to let

---

obstacles in the way of doing this. In another passage (AsP 328), the opponent claims that the sūtra is poetry and not the word of the Buddha.

69 E.g., Steinkellner 2012: "Dennoch ist dabei noch weniger an das Vorhandensein eines geschriebenen Kanons, etwa des Saṃyuktāgama zu denken, als zunächst an Formen der schriftlichen Niederlegung der oralen Überlieferung zu verschiedenen praktischen oder rituellen Zwecken."

70 A similarity to confessions in the Vinaya corpus is found in § 1B3, which begins with *ya mama ta sakṣitena* (= Skt. *yad mama tad saṃkṣiptena*), i.e., a pronoun in the first person and the operator *saṃkṣiptena* (suggested by Richard Salomon, personal communication).

71 In BC 4, these are the sections §§ 1B3, 3, 4, 5, 6, where there are references to the first person singular being the protagonist, as well as the imperative "establish [yourself]" at the end of the scroll. In BC 11, such indications include the phrase "I am released" (or perhaps "I release [myself]") and terms referring to solitude (*asaṃganikā* and, in this context, also *vivekagata*).

go and become detached from the world of the senses and thus to reach liberation, which is described as a state of permanent bliss not leading to rebirth.

If we think of Mahāyāna having evolved as a slow and silent reform within a Śrāvakayāna environment, with a different approach to or focus on certain topics in the Buddhist doctrine, the first step may have been meditative techniques in which concentrating on emptiness was a means for secluding oneself from the world and for developing new ways of experiencing liberation and happiness in this life. The process was an individualized task of renunciation, possibly, but not necessarily, in physical seclusion. In this respect, the bodhisattva path was a solitary and ascetic endeavor. The altruistic element was confined to the aim of leading other beings on the same way to awakening by teaching them the new doctrine, namely the knowledge of what is useless and painful (and like a dream).

The universal application of the *śūnyatā* concept may have evolved on the basis of the analytic methods of (Sarvāstivāda) Abhidharma, and this scholastic approach is still visible in all three of the manuscripts under consideration. In practice, the realization of emptiness was accomplished by insight meditation aimed at non-perception of anything whatsoever. Among the several theories proposed to date on the origin of Mahāyāna,[72] those explaining it as a concentration on meditative practices combined with new ways to liberation and new ideas about the reality of things are confirmed by BC 4, BC 6, and BC 11. This new approach was to experience the bliss of *nirvāṇa* and liberation "here in this lifetime," with *nirvāṇa* as the end of suffering due to attachment to the world, resulting in a deep happiness and a serene state of mind beyond words.

---

72 The most recent summaries are: Shimoda 2009, Drewes 2010a, Allon and Salomon 2010.

CHAPTER 2

Physical Description

2.1 BC 4

2.1.1 Preservation Status

The fragments of BC 4 are stored in two parts, in frames 10 and 18. The manuscript is heavily damaged and split into several pieces of medium and small size. There is writing on both sides in the same hand and the fragments contain a single text.

2.1.2 Reconstruction of the Scroll

It has been possible to reconstruct the original location of most of the fragments. The connection between the right and left halves of the manuscript is certain in lines 4r11, 4r20, 4r21, and 4r26. Of slight uncertainty are the upper loose fragments from 4r1 up to 4r10. However, the transition from line 4r10 to 4r11, *kaïace-dasia*, is more than likely, which makes lines 4r7 and following quite probable. Moreover, the blank reverse side of those fragments leaves almost no other choice regarding their arrangement. It is uncertain how 4r6 and 4r7 belong to each other exactly, or whether even one or more lines are missing here. Furthermore, a few fragments are placed with a little uncertainty, but their form and/or content make it highly probable that their location is correct in the current reconstruction. These are fragments 4.2 C+P (4r5), S (4r8), and X (4r14), see fig. 6. Fragment 4.1 Q consists of four layers of birch bark, of which one (labeled Q4, see fig. 23) is not easy to allocate, because the four incomplete akṣaras written on it do not connect to any adjoining fragment.

The reconstruction of BC 4 made it clear that physically it does not belong to BC 11, as was presumed by Ingo Strauch in his preliminary survey (2007/2008: 9). BC 4 is a "short format" scroll that was folded once in the middle. In contrast, BC 11 is a "long format" scroll that was folded twice.

2.1.3 Format and Layout

The reconstruction process of BC 4 resulted in a scroll of about 24 cm width and 23 cm height (the safely reconstructed part of the scroll is 24 × 17 cm with an upper part of at least 6 cm).[1] Unfortunately, the beginning of the manuscript is—as usual—lost; we do not know exactly how

1 It is not possible to give any dimensions with absolute certainty, since the available scans do not include any scale for orientation. The size has been calculated on the basis of the information Ingo Strauch gave in his catalogue after measuring the fragments in Pakistan. The fragments were scanned at 600 dpi and 100% scale, so the rulers in the image editing software should give quite exact data.

much is missing. Luckily under the circumstances, the first paragraph is repeated, so a possibility would be to count the number of akṣaras at the beginning of the repetition up to where the text matches the beginning of the preserved manuscript. But the scroll is very fragmentary at this point, making it uncertain where the repetition exactly begins. There are, ultimately, two alternatives:

1. The repetition starts after the small dot · in 4r5 and begins with *vado ṇidaṇa*, meaning about three lines would be missing (green + blue bar in fig. 1).
2. The repetition starts after the bigger circle ○ in 4r7 and begins with *ki hakṣadi*, meaning about one line would be missing (blue bar in fig. 1).

In option (1) the second section (§ 1B) as well as the text itself would begin with *vado ṇidaṇa*. Since this would be repeated, *nidāna* cannot refer here to some kind of introduction (although it is still possible that there was a textual variation in the beginning and not exactly the same wording as in the repetition). The small dot before *vado* could indicate a new train of thought. In option (2) the second section as well as the text itself would begin with *ki hakṣadi* or something similar. In light of bigger circles serving principally as punctuation marks, especially preceding new paragraphs, this seems more likely. Thus, a bit more than one line would be missing, corresponding to about 1 cm and an original scroll of 24 × 25 cm, including a margin of 1 cm. It is also conceivable that the original measurements were 24 × 24 cm since in the digital reconstruction not every fragment could be vertically joined without a gap to the next due to the sometimes strongly warped birch bark strips.

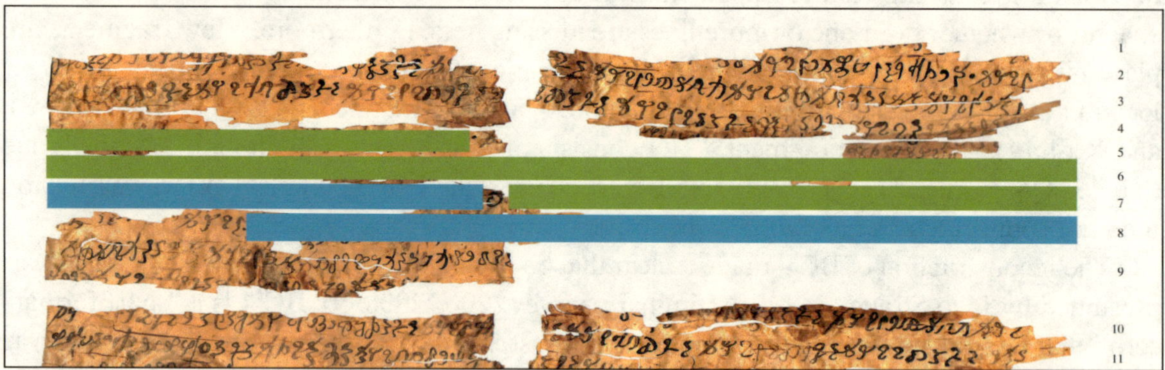

Fig. 1. Reconstruction of the missing lines at the beginning of BC 4.

Based on the measurements and the format, the scroll can be defined as a "short format." It was folded once in the middle at a ratio of approximately 11.50 : 12.50 cm—thus not exactly in the middle of the manuscript. This made it easy to allocate single strips to one side or the other. As is to be expected with short format scrolls, there is no evidence of any overlapping parts that have been glued together (as is the case with longer scrolls produced from shorter strips). Likewise, there are no signs of needle holes indicating stitching along the margins. The margins are ca. 1 cm at the top (seen on the verso, corresponding to the height of one line), 1 cm at the right, i.e., the beginning of the line (corresponding to three akṣaras), 0–0.7 cm at the left end of the lines, and 1.7–2 cm at the bottom (seen on the recto, the lower half of the verso having been left blank). It can be assumed that on the recto the same upper margin was observed. Also at the left end of each line a margin of 1 cm may have been intended, but the scribe usually wrote to the very end of the birch bark.

On the recto, there were presumably 28 lines of writing (depending on how much is missing at the top). On the verso, definitely only 12 lines were written, the rest of the birch bark remaining blank. Each line contains an average of 67 akṣaras. The presumed total number of (all preserved, reconstructed and missing) akṣaras is 2797, of which 2491 (including illegible but still visible akṣaras) = 89% have survived.

In the last line of the recto, an instruction is given that refers to the continuation of the text on the verso (G *śeṣ̱ae patade*). The same remark can be seen at the bottom of the recto of BC 6.

2.1.4 Additional/Unlocated Fragments

In addition to the fragments in frames 10 and 18, some pieces collected in the "debris" frame (no. 35) of the Bajaur Collection could be matched to the scroll (35r l → 4r4, 35r o → 4r5). Judging from content and script, also other fragments, namely 35r m and 35r n, belong to BC 4 (or BC 11), but I was unable to reposition them with certainty (see fig. 22).

On the other hand, a few fragments from BC 4 still await their positioning (4.2 D, O, R, AA, DD). Their "type face" and the words contained suggest that they belong to the top right of the reconstructed manuscript, since the verso is blank in each case and all the other fragments of the same frame 18 (part 2) have exclusively been placed in this area (see fig. 8). In addition, as already mentioned, the little fragment labeled 4.2 Q4 could not be positioned. In part 1 (frame 10) only two very small fragments resisted repositioning. These are 4.1 W and 4.1 K, but nothing is written on them.

Fragment V in frame 18 clearly belongs to another scroll, since the surface of the birch bark and the content are different, and both script and format are slightly larger (fig. 2).

Fig. 2. Fragment V stored in frame 18 together with the fragments of BC 4 (scale 100%).

The transliteration of fragment V is:
V.1 ///
V.2 /// *bhagavado pada śiras̱a vadita egadamate aṭha[e]* ///
V.3 /// *? [ma] sa trisahasae mahasahasae lo(*gadhadue)* ///
V.4 /// *? t[r]i ? ? ? + ? ? ?* ////

The same wording occurs in BC 2 [341] *yavado imasvi tris̱ahas̱ee mahas̱ahas̱ae log̱adhadue* and [343] *(*bha)[g̱a]vato pada śiras̱a vadita ekamaṃte aṭ́has̱a · as̱a yavada imasvi mahas̱ahas̱ae log̱adhadue.* However, the script of fragment 4.2 V is different from that in BC 2. Further, the orthography is dissimilar (*eg̱adamate* vs. *ekamaṃte*), although this is not a sufficient criterion since even in one and the same manuscript, several spelling variations can occur. Also in BC 3 a similar phrase is used (r4 *(*bhag̱ava)[do śiras̱a] pada vadadi bhag̱avado śiras̱a pada va[di](*ta)*), but the script and birch bark do not allow the fragment to be placed there either.

2.2 BC 11

2.2.1 Preservation Status

The manuscript is relatively well preserved. Only at some isolated spots along the right margin are parts of the birch bark broken off, presumably due to the folding of the manuscript, which was folded twice in equal intervals after having been rolled up. The manuscript is conserved in two frames (frames 20 and 21), which were labeled part 1 and 2 during the reconstruction process. Part 1 is a little smaller and better preserved than part 2. There are only a few small fragments alongside the bigger parts. Unfortunately, the bigger sections were not placed in the correct sequence. Both sides contain a single text written by the same scribe.

2.2.2 Reconstruction of the Scroll

The fragments are in five sections with no discernible physical connection to each other. Although the reconstruction status of the manuscript looks satisfying, the arrangement is not the only one possible. The contents do not allow any definitive sequence, since similar keywords are found in the different parts, and thus theoretically any individual section could be linked to any other. Sections 1–3 are blank on the verso, hence their placement may be fixed. While sections 1 and 2 could be interchanged, the first is shorter and more damaged and should most probably be placed at the beginning. This leaves only sections 4 and 5 truly interchangeable. Judging only from the contents, the sequence 3r–5r–4r–4v–5v–3v might be preferred, but the physical form of the fragments and the texture of the birch bark supports the current reconstruction.

Apparently, at the time of writing these different parts were separate, that is, not glued together. At the ends of part 2, 4, and 5 this is especially easy to discern. Either the letters get smaller and smaller in order to still fit onto the piece of birch bark (2r, 5v), or the slanting lines reach the bottom of the birch bark before they reach its end, but the writing is not continued on the next piece (4r, 5r). It is also conceivable that BC 11 consisted of separate sheets that had never been glued together. If so, then all parts (with part 1 and 2 possibly belonging together) would each have to be read first on the recto and second on the verso before continuing with the next sheet.

Symmetrical ink blots on the recto of part 3 (in lines 17/18 and 21/22) suggest that this part of the birch bark (up to and including line 23) was temporarily folded after being written. This could have happened in both scenarios. If BC 11 is one long scroll, the scribe may have folded or bunched up the section he had just written to facilitate writing the remainder on the recto. If BC 11 is a loose-leaf collection, the scribe may have folded the lower part of the birch bark to continue writing on the verso.

2.2.3 Format and Layout

Because of the just mentioned peculiarities, it is uncertain if BC 11 was one long scroll, or if it was made up of separate pieces of birch bark. All the different pieces show an identical vertical folding, which speaks in favor of them having been joined before being rolled up. If all parts are put together, the measurements of the reconstructed manuscript BC 11 are ca. 15 × 40 cm.[2] The width is in accordance with the original format, which is known since there is at least one line whose left and right edges are preserved completely. A width between 10 cm and 20 cm further suggests that the manuscript can be considered a so-called "long-format" scroll (cf. Schlosser 2016: 3 and Baums 2014: 193) with several sheets being glued together.

The margin at the start of each line corresponds to about two akṣara*s*. At the end of each line this surely was also intended, but the space here varies in width between one and four akṣaras. There is no vertical line indicating the text boundaries.[3] In the right margin of the reserve side of part 4, the scribe added some letters vertically. This is most probably an addendum, since it takes up the same phrases used in part 4v. The gloss does not seem to have been continued on (the currently following) part 3v, but is rather squeezed onto part 4v, which would be another argument for the parts having been separate at the time of writing.

In its present condition the manuscript contains altogether 83 lines—53 on the recto, 30 on the verso—with approximately 40 akṣaras per line. The presumed total number of akṣaras is ca. 3240 akṣaras, of which 2887 = 89% have survived. There is no evidence of any notations indicating a pre-planned layout, and the ends of lines are repeatedly left blank on purpose.

2.2.4 Additional/Unlocated Fragments

Two fragments have been added from the "debris" frame: 35 dd + ee → 11r35–36/11v15–16. Among the fragments labeled as BC 14 (frame 33), one larger fragment originally belonged to BC 11 at the beginning of the recto, making line 11r3 complete and adding another two lines. In the same frame 33, another small fragment seems to belong to BC 11 or even BC 4, but it was not possible to find its original place, which should be somewhere in 11r1–21 or 4r1–18, since the verso side is blank (see fig. 24).

There are only a few unlocated fragments left in frame 20 (part 1). One of them, fragment I, appears to belong to BC 11 but could not be allocated with certainty (see fig. 24).[4] Four more fragments (F, G, H, J) most probably belong to BC 2 based on the hand and content (see fig. 25).

---

2 The height of the reconstructed scroll has changed since the first publication discussing it (Schlosser 2016), because in the meantime another fragment of BC 11 was found in a different frame of the Bajaur Collection (frame 33, BC 14).

3 Such lines call to mind the threads running from top to bottom that were sometimes used to hold the strips of birch bark together. For example, in the long-format scrolls BC 3 and BC 5, such a line can be seen, although there are no traces of needle holes. Vertical stitches at the edge of the margins are discernable in the Dhp^{K} scroll and also in BL 1, 3A, 9, 13, and 12+14 (Salomon 1999a: 96, Allon 2001: 44, Salomon 2008a: 86, Baums 2009: 62, 68, 609); horizontal stitches at the overlapping joints of two birch bark parts can be seen (at least) in BL 9 and 13 (Baums 2009: 68), although normally at such joints, the component sheets would have only been glued together.

4 In Schlosser 2016, also fragment K was not positioned. It is now part of the first line on the recto, where it seems to fit both physically and textually.

2.3 BC 6

2.3.1 Preservation Status

Manuscript no. 6 of the Bajaur Collection is in a quite poor state of preservation, above of all because the ink is sometimes very faint, making the letters hardly legible. In the first survey of the Bajaur Collection (Strauch 2007/2008), BC 6 consisted of three parts. In his revised survey (2008) the third part was labeled as BC 19 (frame 32), since due its different width it cannot belong to BC 6. The two remaining parts (frames 29 and 30) are the left and right half of a single manuscript.

2.3.2 Reconstruction of the Scroll

The left, right, and bottom margins of the scroll are preserved. It seems that also the top margin of the scroll is preserved, but it cannot be said with absolute certainty whether another piece of birch bark was originally attached to the top (adding more text at the beginning and end). However, the two preserved edges at the top left and right, the dog-ear at the top right, as well as a quite horizontal upper border suggest that the manuscript is complete as it is.

The reconstruction of the preserved fragments is fairly certain. Although the connection between lines 2 and 3 on the recto (corresponding to lines 7 and 8 on the verso) is not absolutely clear, it looks as if there are some joint letters on both the recto and the verso. Moreover, the imprints of two little chips from 6v5 on 6r1 ensure that the scroll was once folded in accordance with the current reconstruction. The sequence of the rest is evident from one continuous piece of birch bark on the right-hand side. The left half of the manuscript is a little more damaged, but here the contents confirm the current reconstruction. In two cases, the left half of the lines are lost, and in two other cases the left half of the lines are so badly damaged that almost nothing can be read anymore. There is no physical connection between the two halves, but the distance can be estimated with some certainty in 6r8 based on internal textual evidence.

2.3.3 Format and Layout

The original scroll was a "short format" type, measuring about 30 × 10 cm. It was folded quite exactly in the middle (the maximum width of the preserved halves is 14.7 cm on both sides).

The margin on the right edge of the recto is about 0.8 cm (corresponding to two or three akṣaras). At the top it is about 0.5 cm. The margins on the verso are a little wider, measuring 1–1.20 cm on the right (corresponding to three akṣaras) and circa 0.6 cm at the top.

On the recto, there are eleven lines of writing, on the verso there are nine, making twenty lines altogether. Each line contains more or less 68 akṣaras. In total there would have been 1287 akṣaras, of which 1095 survive (fully or partly), which is 85 % of the presumed original text.

The text is structured into paragraphs by different types of circles, however without any numbering. At the end of the recto side there is a note, most likely added later, which says that the rest has been written on the reverse side (G *śeṣa patade likhidae*). The same remark can be found at the bottom of the recto side of BC 4, although there the remark is a little more detailed and embedded in the text with relation to the content.

2.3.4 Additional / Unlocated Fragments

There are no unlocated fragments and also no fragments from other frames. Only in one case is the exact horizontal position of a small fragment (C) in the left half of the manuscript uncertain, which affects the transliteration of line 6r1, as well as lines 6v8 and 6v9.

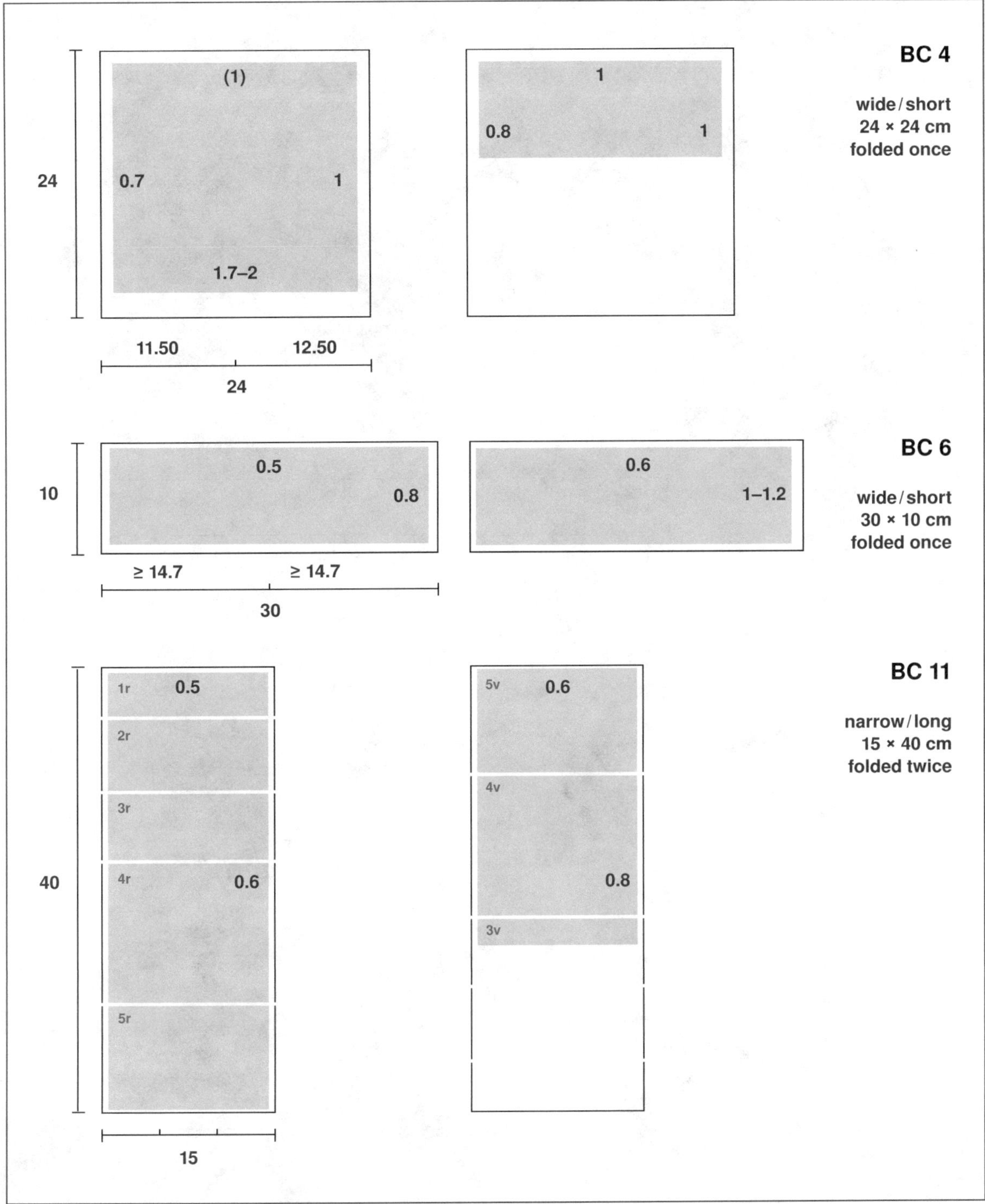

Fig. 3. Illustration of the original format of BC 4, BC 6, and BC 11.

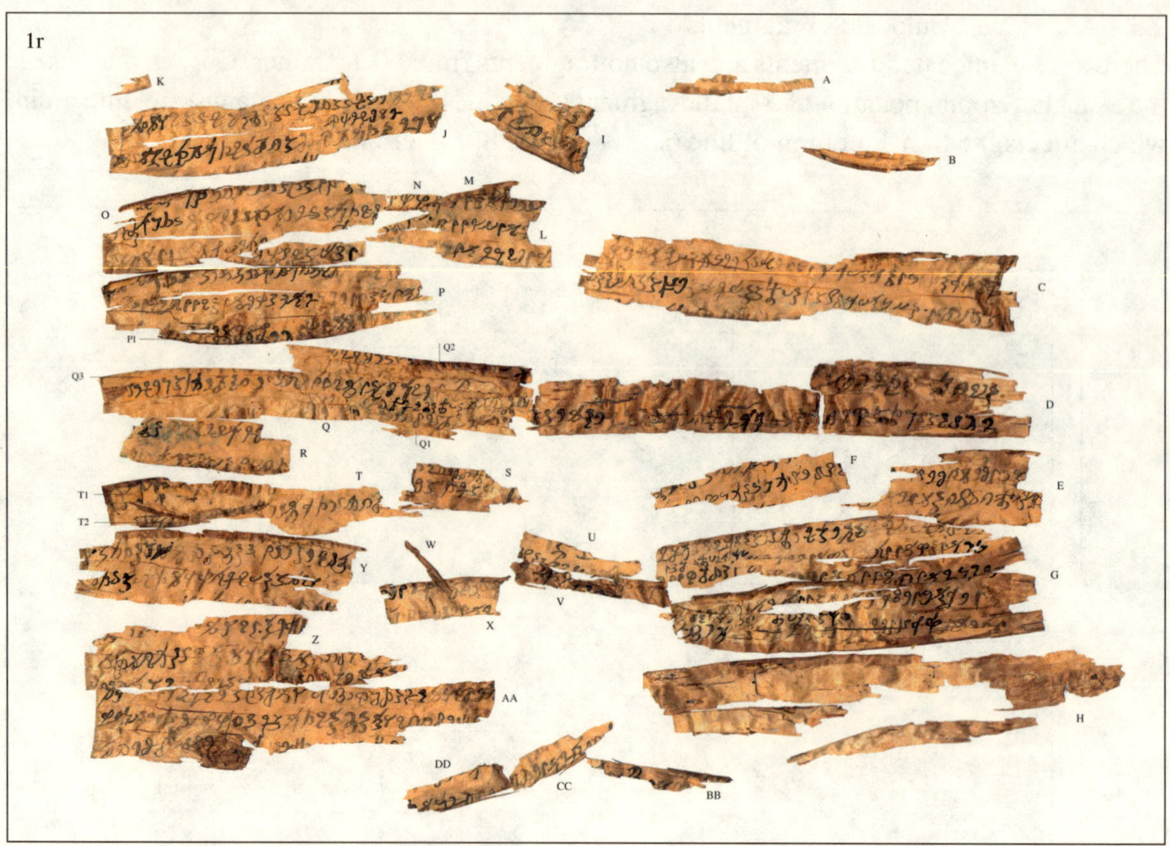

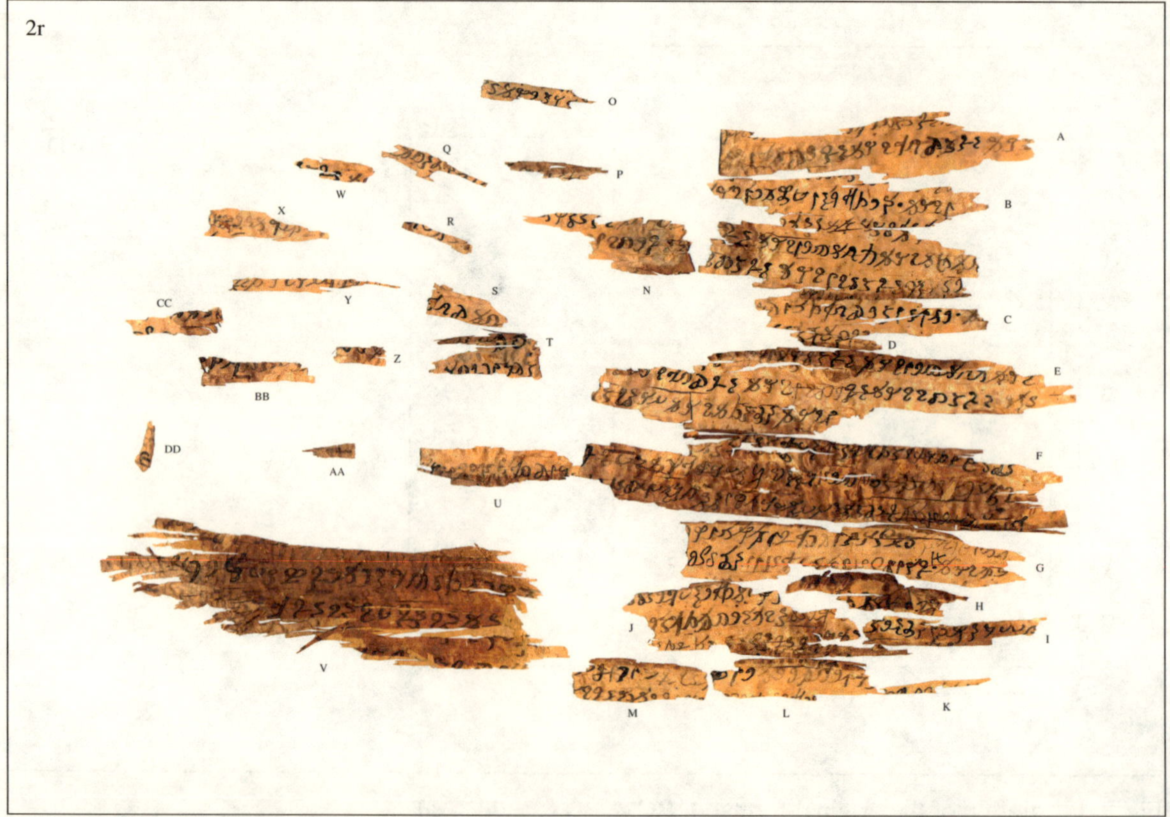

Fig. 4. BC 4, unreconstructed preservation status of the manuscript after unrolling (scale 50%). Part 1 (frame 10) and part 2 (frame 18), recto.

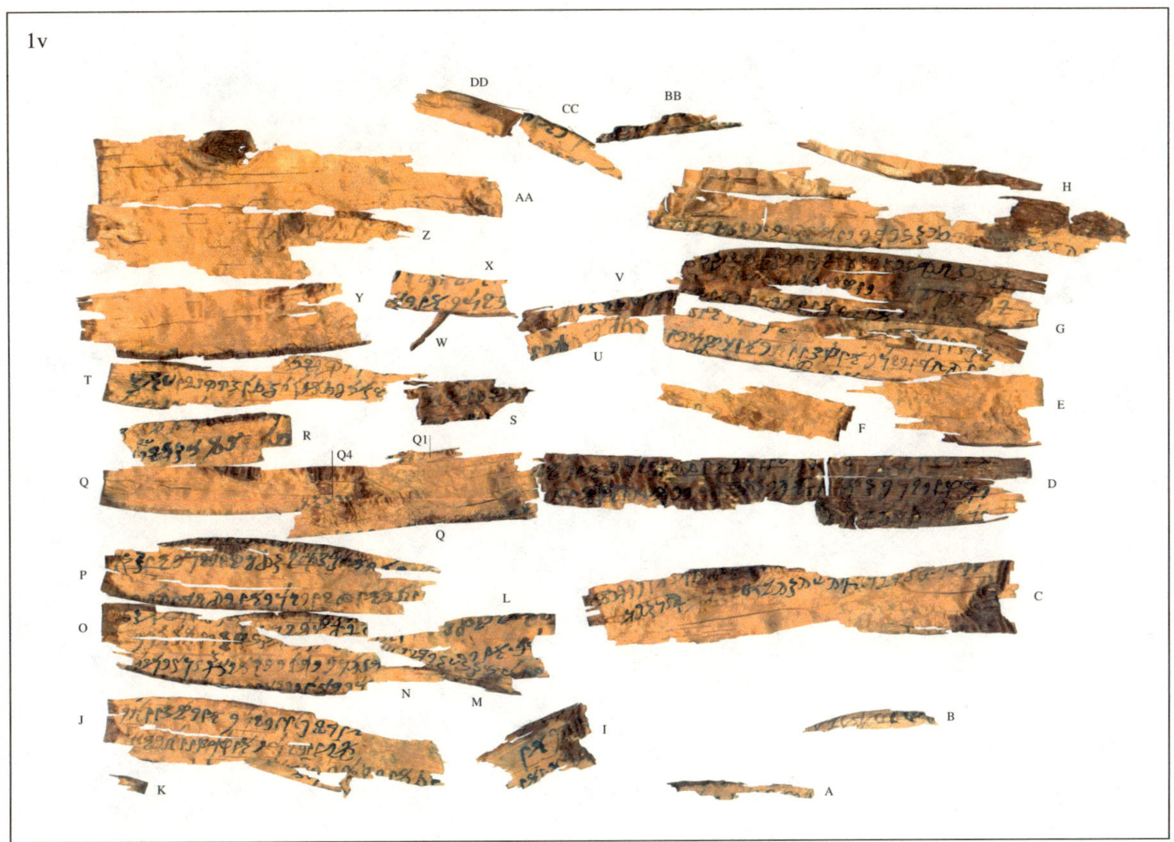

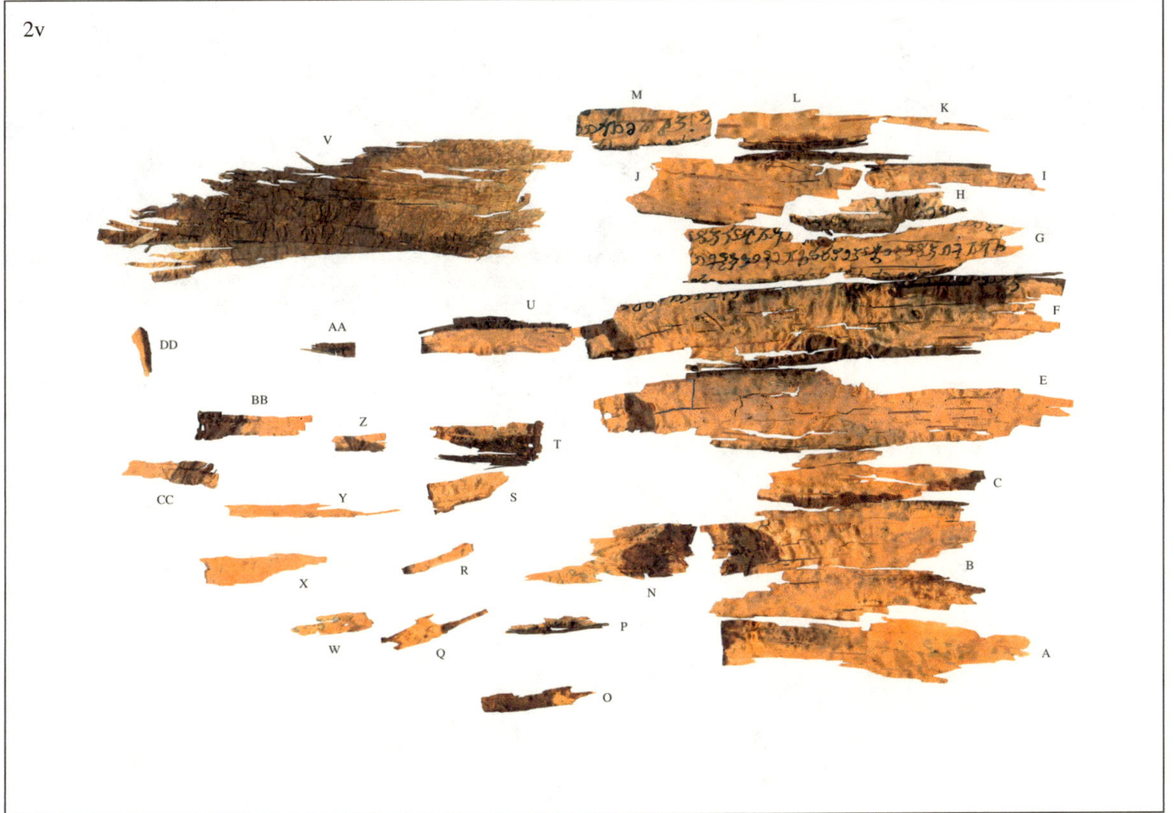

Fig. 5. BC 4, unreconstructed preservation status of the manuscript after unrolling (scale 50%). Part 1 (frame 10) and part 2 (frame 18), verso.

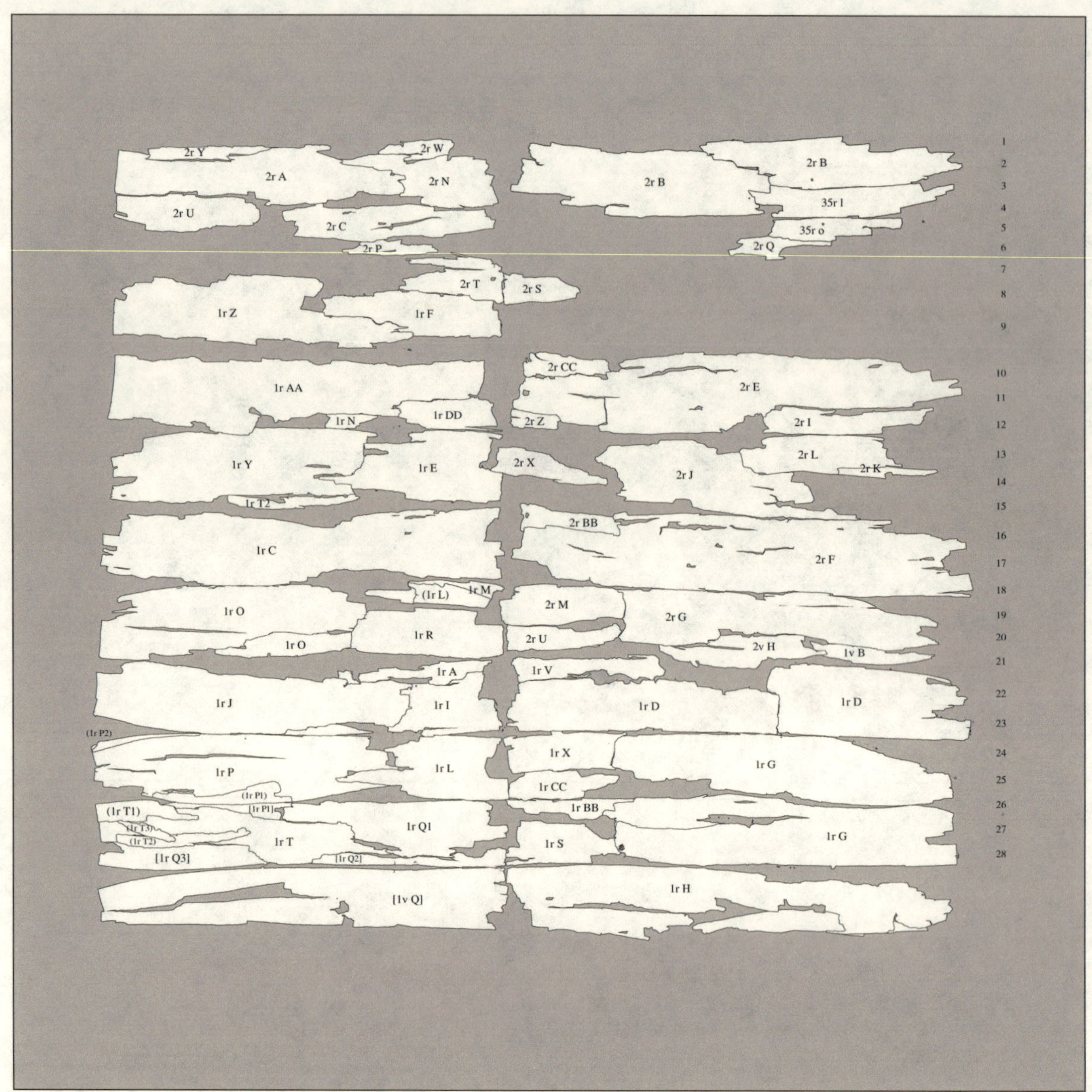

Fig. 6. BC 4, key to the reconstructed manuscript, recto (scale 50%). 1r = BC 4, part 1, recto (frame 10), 2r = BC 4, part 2, recto (frame 18), 35r = frame 35, recto. Designations in round brackets signify overlying fragments. Designations in square brackets label the reverse sides of fragments of which only one side was visible in the scan.

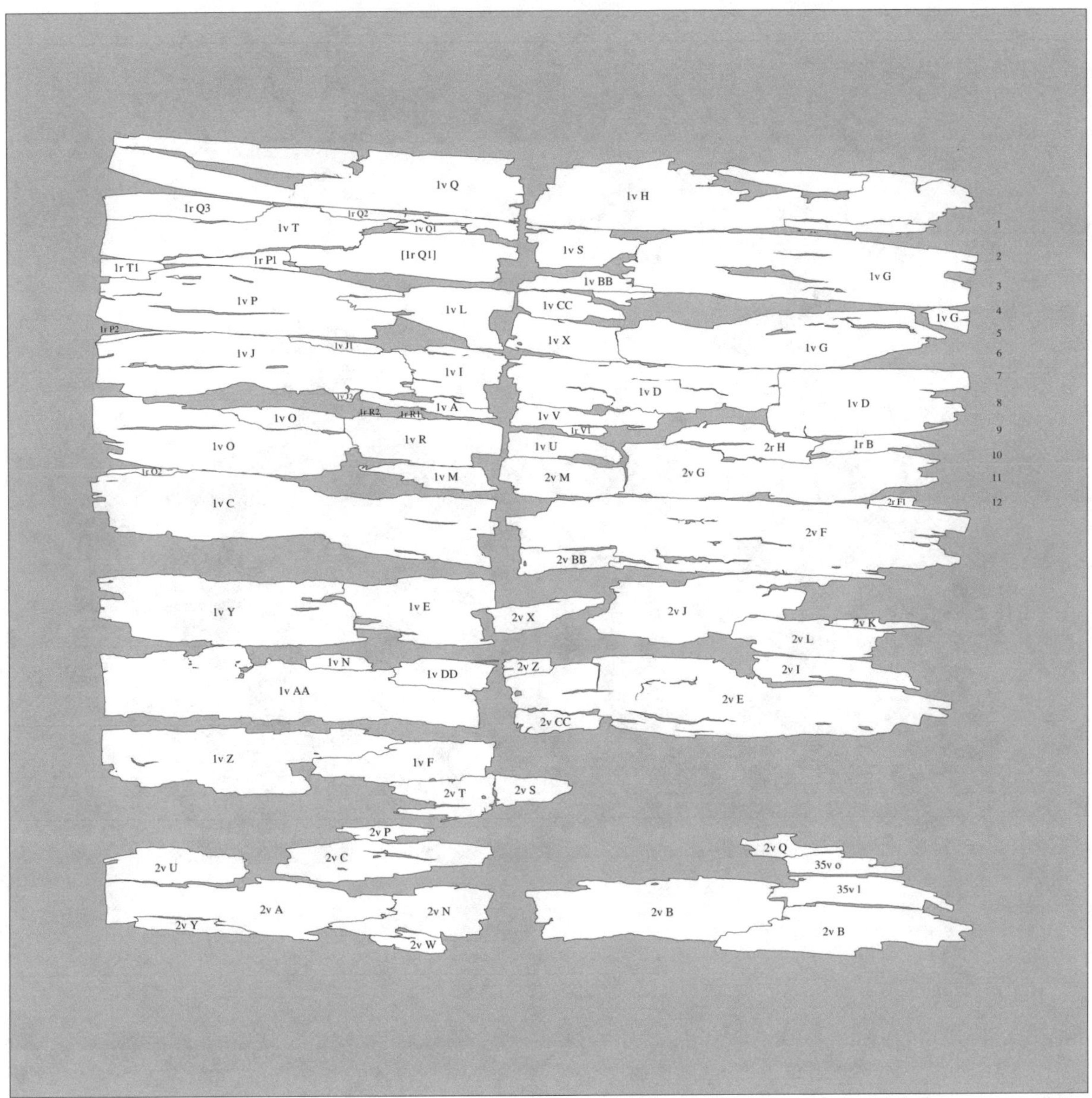

Fig. 7. BC 4, key to the reconstructed manuscript, verso (scale 50%). 1v = BC 4, part 1, verso (frame 10), 2v = BC 4, part 2, verso (frame 18), 35v = frame 35, verso. Designations in round brackets signify overlying fragments. Designations in square brackets label the reverse sides of fragments of which only one side was visible in the scan.

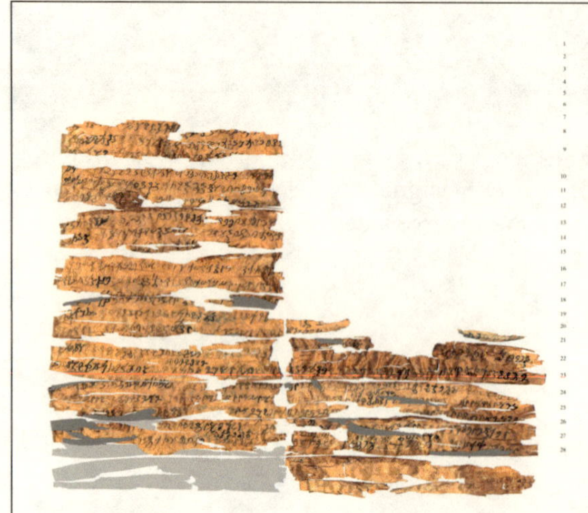

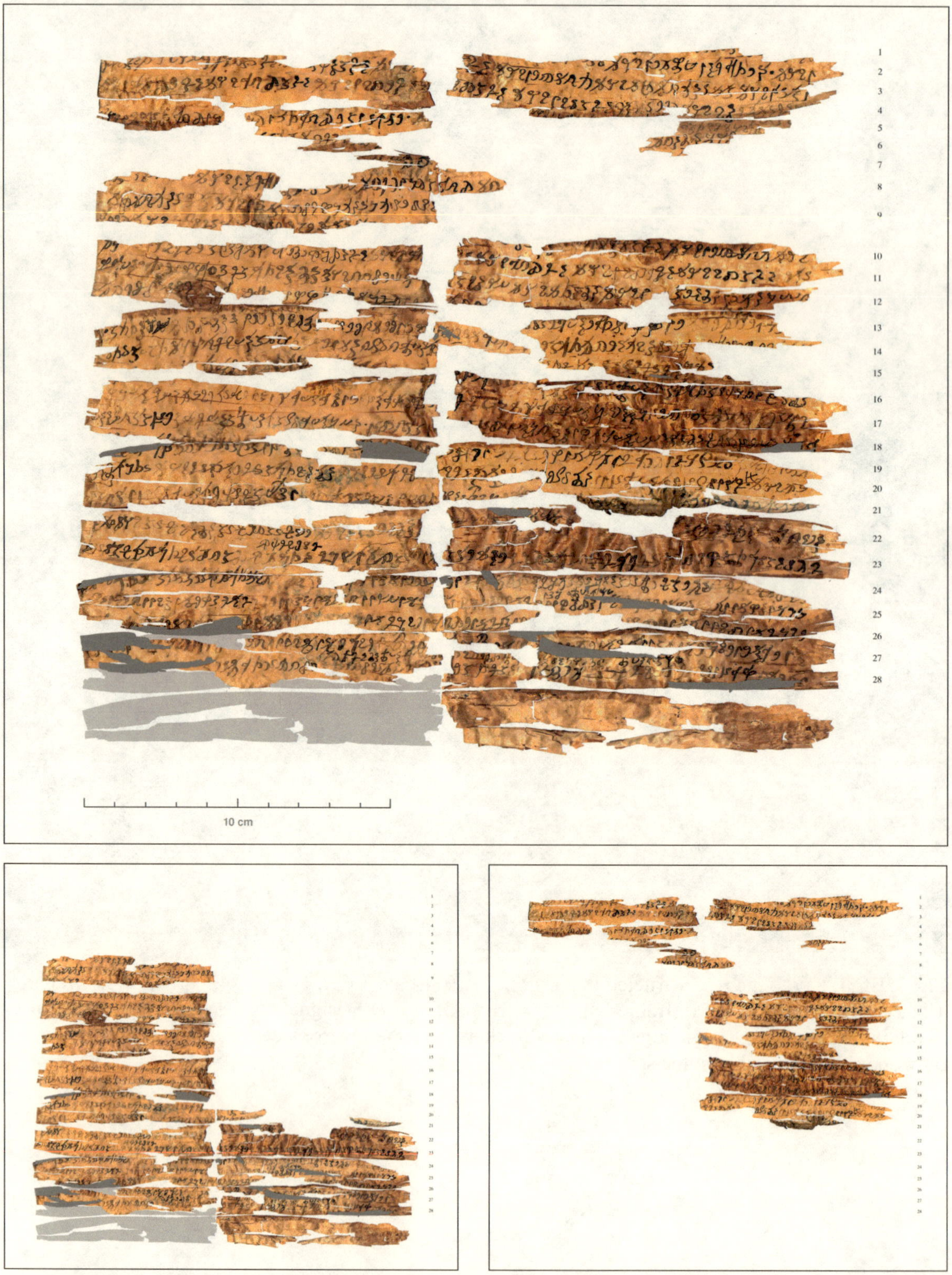

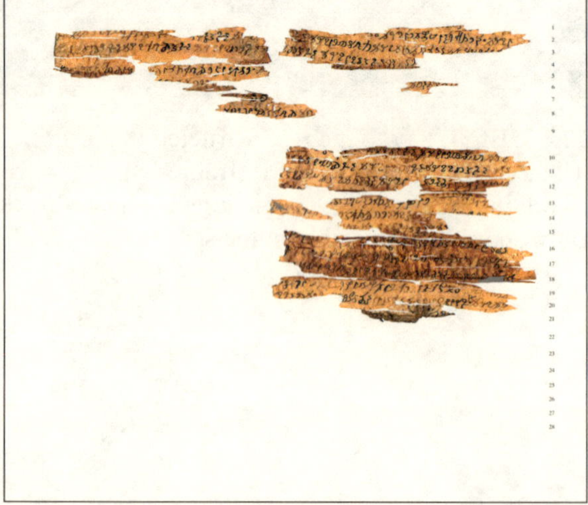

Fig. 8. BC 4, reconstructed manuscript, recto (scale 50%). Dark grey areas represent overlying fragments. Light grey areas represent the reverse sides of reconstructed fragments of which only one side is visible (in the scanned image). Below are the reconstructed fragments of part 1 (frame 10) on the left and part 2 (frame 18) on the right.

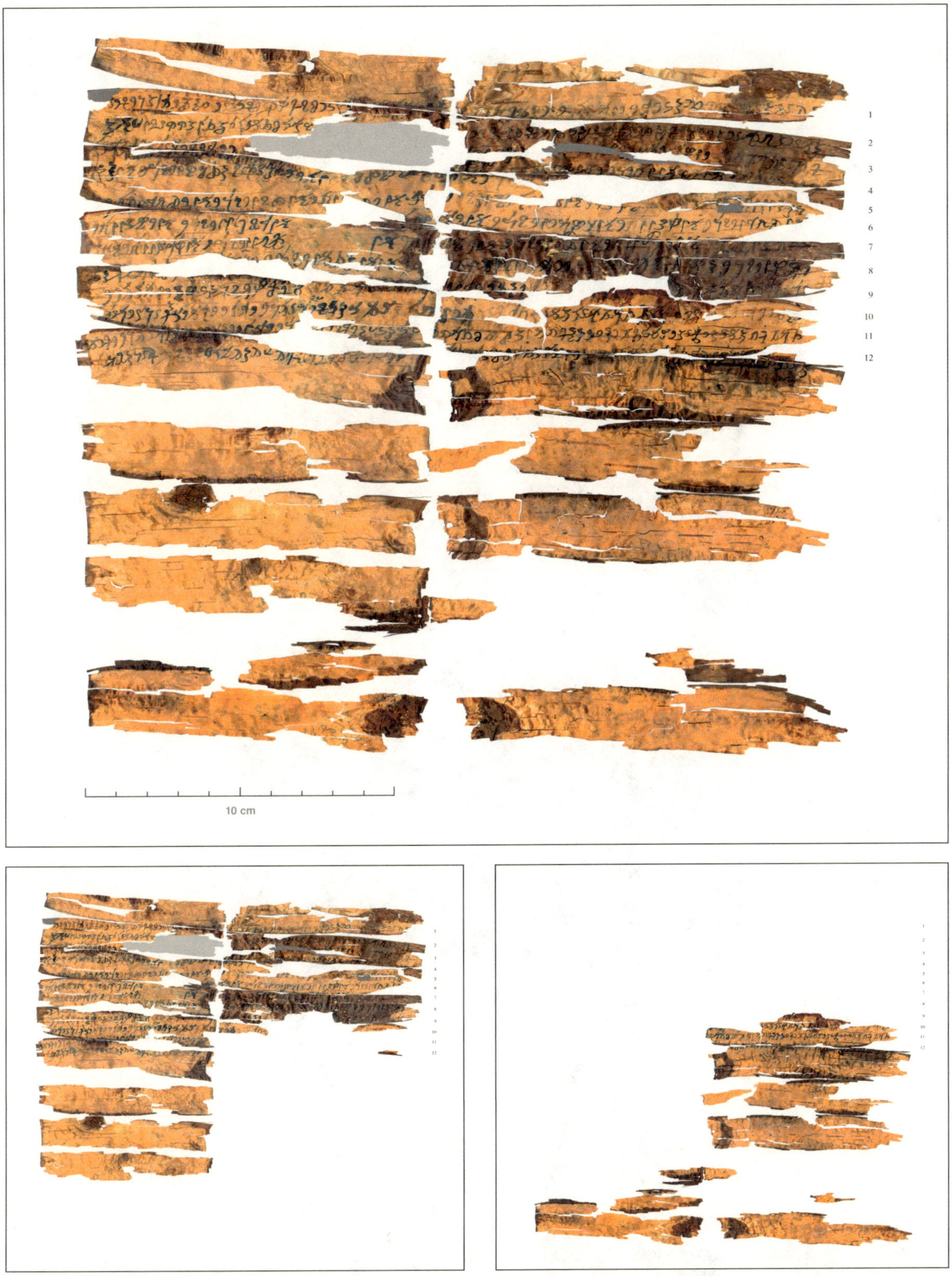

Fig. 9. BC 4, reconstructed manuscript, verso (scale 50%). Dark grey areas represent overlying fragments. Light grey areas represent the reverse sides of reconstructed fragments of which only one side is visible (in the scanned image). Below are the reconstructed fragments of part 1 (frame 10) on the left and part 2 (frame 18) on the right.

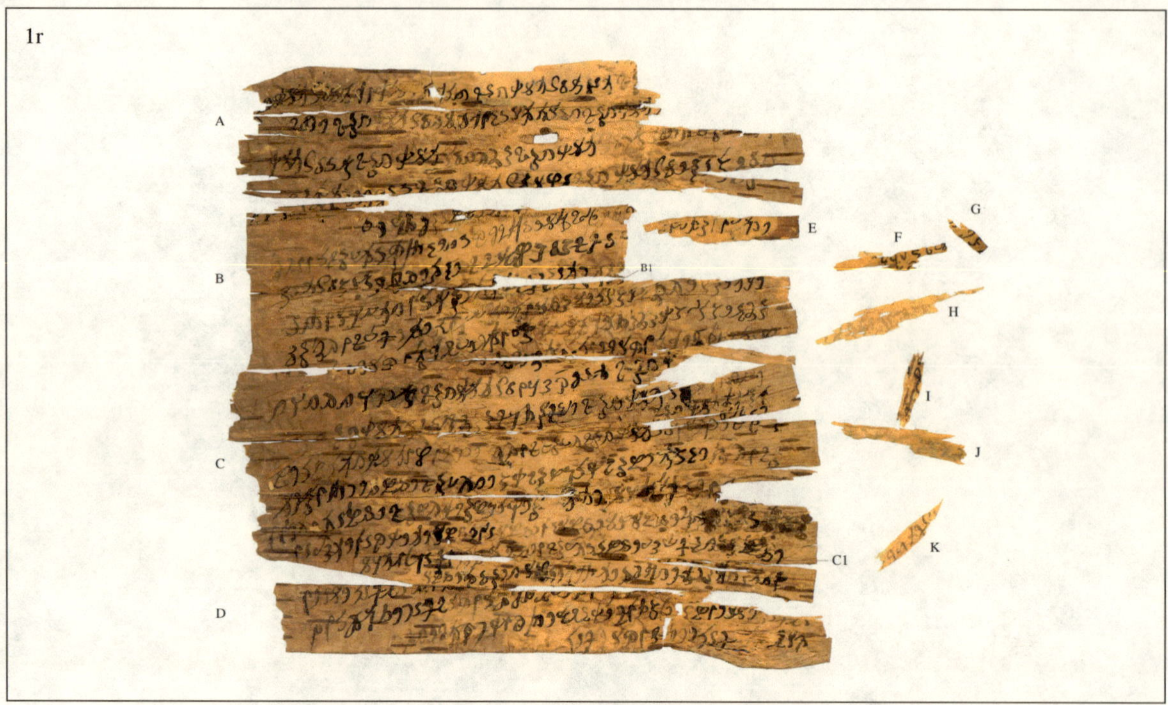

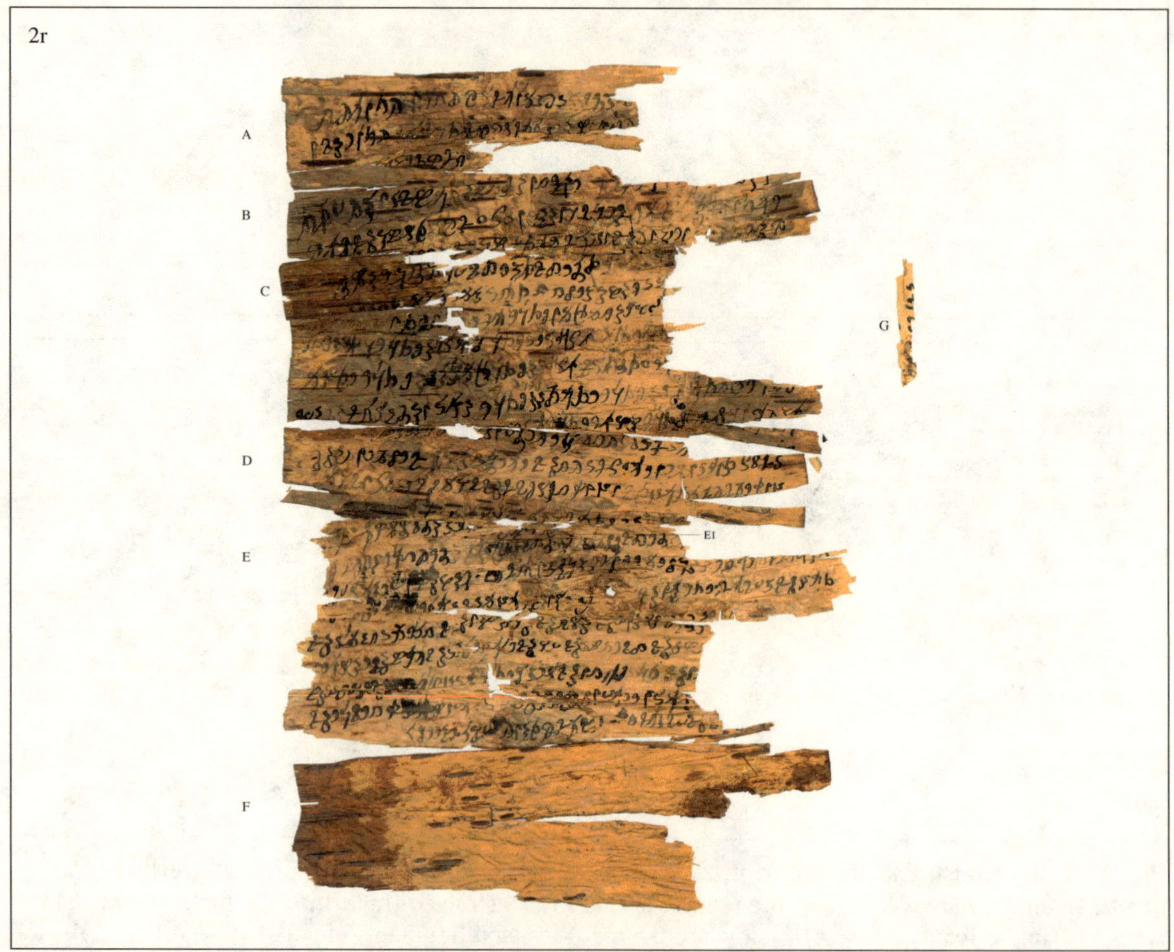

Fig. 10. BC 11, unreconstructed preservation status of the manuscript after unrolling (scale 50%). Part 1 (frame 20) and part 2 (frame 21), recto.

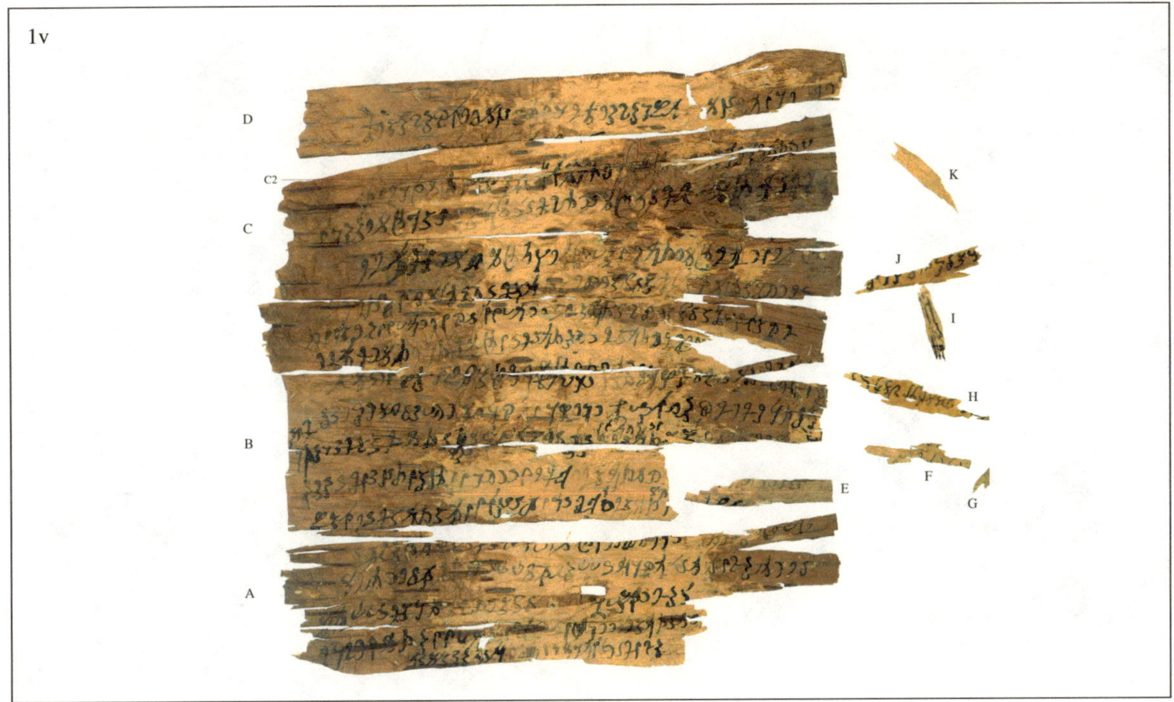

Fig. 11. BC 11, unreconstructed preservation status of the manuscript after unrolling (scale 50%). Part 1 (frame 20) and part 2 (frame 21), verso.

Fig. 12. BC 11, key to the reconstructed manuscript, recto (scale 50%).

Fig. 13. BC 11, key to the reconstructed manuscript, verso (scale 50%).

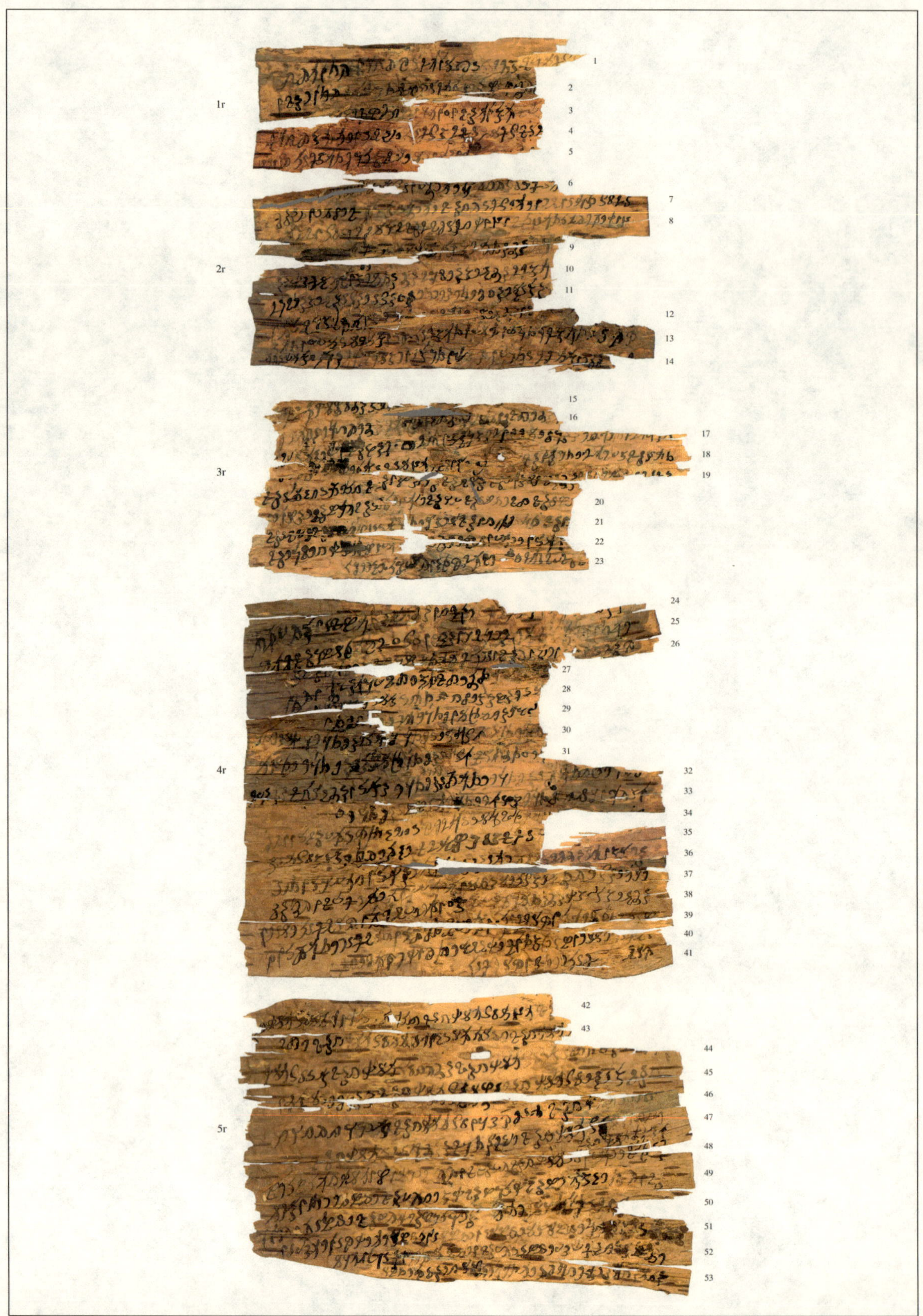

Fig. 14. BC 11, reconstructed manuscript with line and section numbers, recto (scale 50%). Dark grey areas represent overlying fragments.

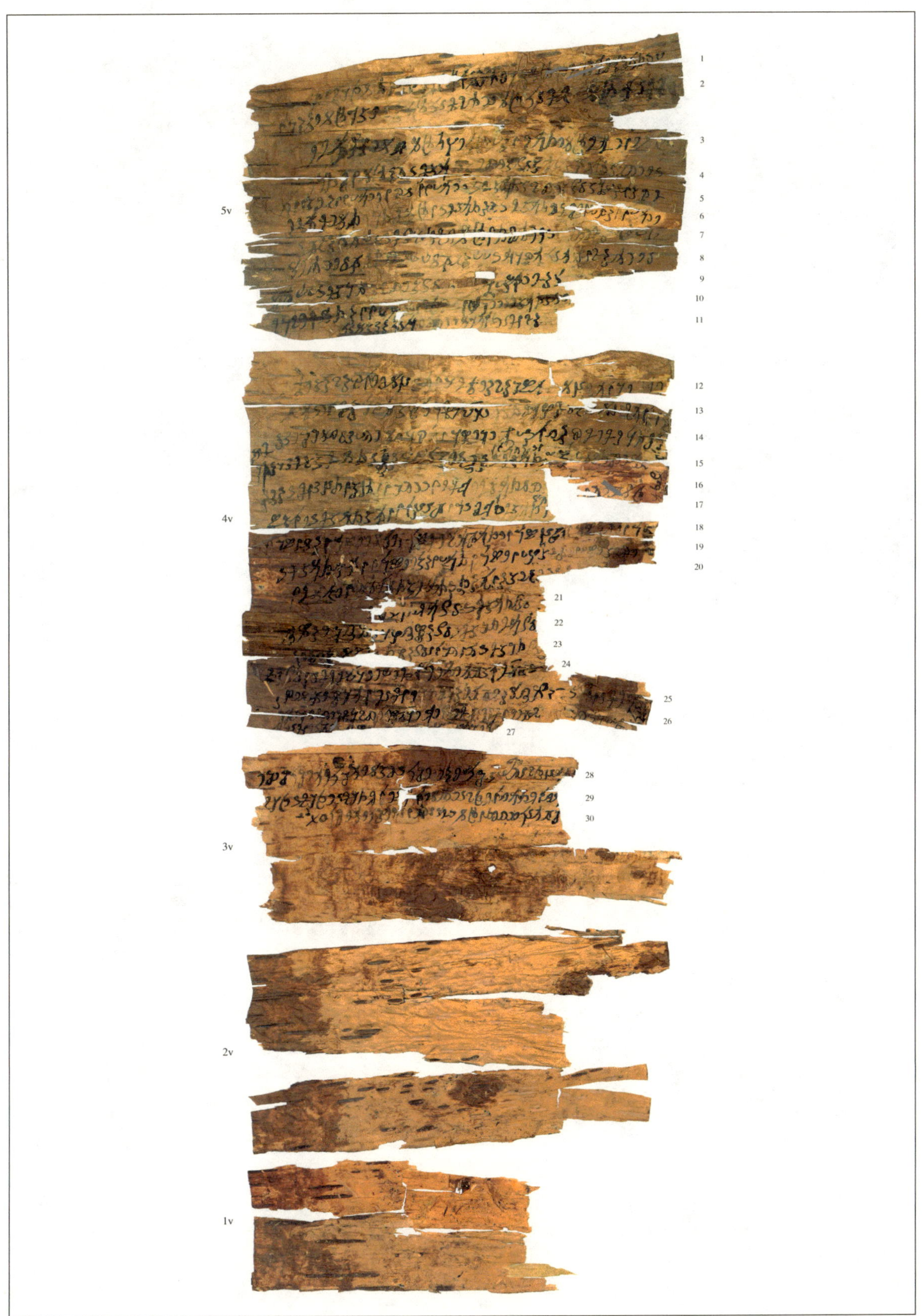

Fig. 15. BC 11, reconstructed manuscript with line and section numbers, verso (scale 50%). Dark grey areas represent overlying fragments.

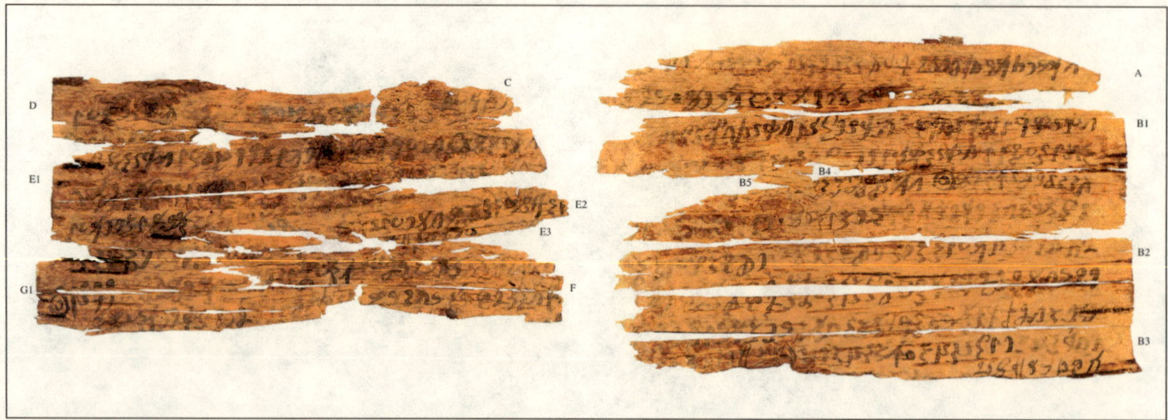

Fig. 16. BC 6, unreconstructed preservation status of the manuscript after unrolling, recto (scale 47%).

Fig. 18. BC 6, key to the reconstructed manuscript, recto (scale 47%).

Fig. 20. BC 6, reconstructed manuscript with line and section numbers, recto (scale 47%). Dark grey areas represent overlying fragments. Light grey areas represent the reverse sides of reconstructed fragments of which only one side is visible (in the scanned image).

Fig. 17. BC 6, unreconstructed preservation status of the manuscript after unrolling, verso (scale 47%).

Fig. 19. BC 6, key to the reconstructed manuscript, verso (scale 47%).

Fig. 21. BC 6, reconstructed manuscript with line and section numbers, verso (scale 47%). Dark grey areas represent overlying fragments. Light grey areas represent the reverse sides of reconstructed fragments of which only one side is visible (in the scanned image).

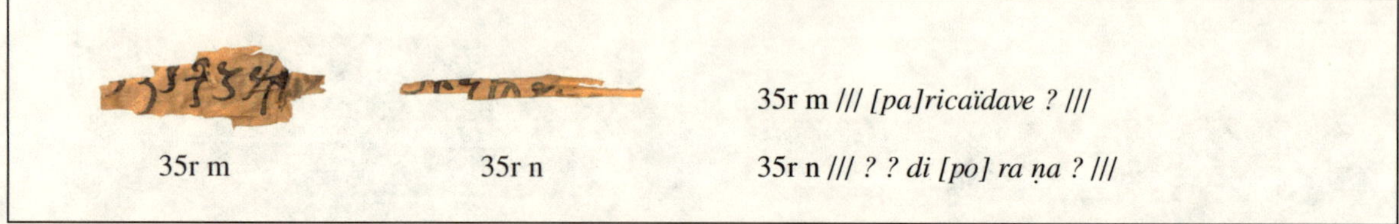

Fig. 22. Fragments from the “debris” frame 35 of the Bajaur Collection, possibly belonging to either BC 4 or BC 11 (scale 100%); the verso is blank in each case.

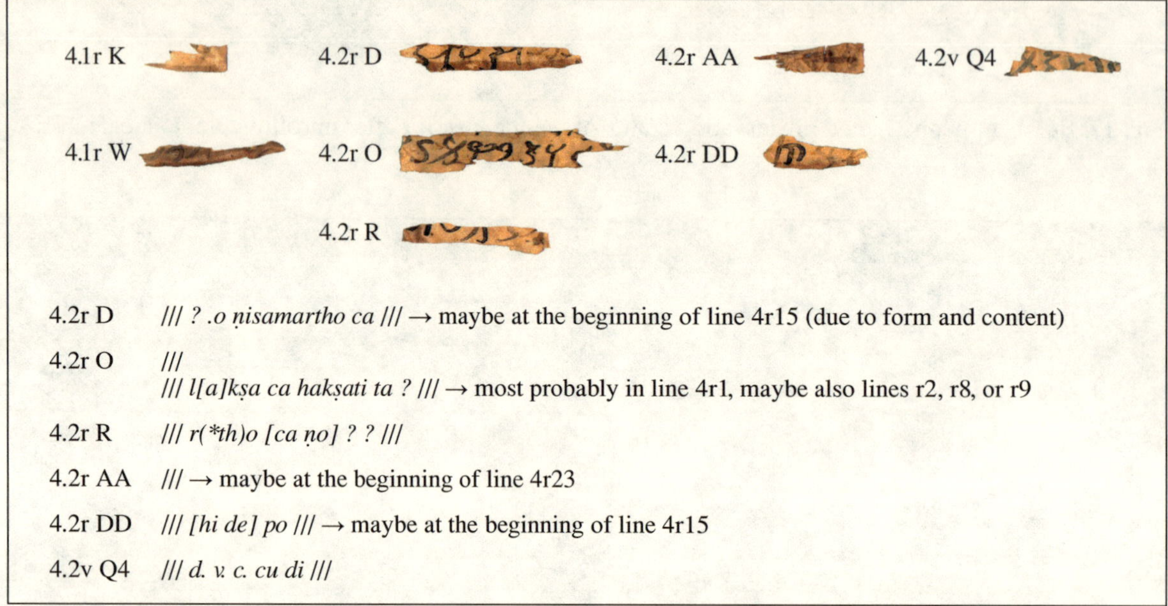

Fig. 23. Unlocated fragments from BC 4 (scale 100%); the verso is blank in each case.

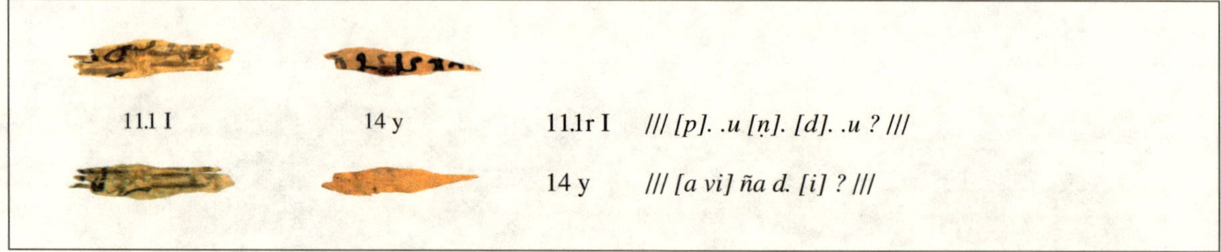

Fig. 24. Unlocated fragments from BC 11 (scale 100%).

Fig. 25. Unlocated fragments from BC 11, probably belonging to BC 2 (scale 100%).

Chapter 3

Paleography

3.1 Writing Instrument

The common writing tool in Gandhāra was probably something like a reed pen (*calamus*, cf. Bühler 1896: 92, Glass 2000: 28–29). Two pens made of copper and dating to the first or second century CE have been discovered in Sirkap (Taxila) and it is assumed that they were modeled on contemporary pens made out of more perishable material (Marshall 1951, II: 598, plate 173, no. 340 and 341; for the dating, cf. Erdosy 1990). When pressed onto a writing surface, such a pen leaves a small linear indentation within the ink stroke. In BC 4 and BC 11 this indentation is not exactly in the middle but to the left side of the strokes (see fig. 26). In BC 6 there are no signs of such indentations.

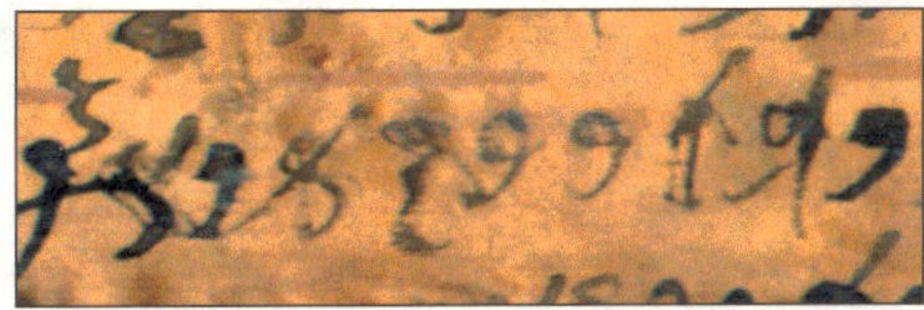
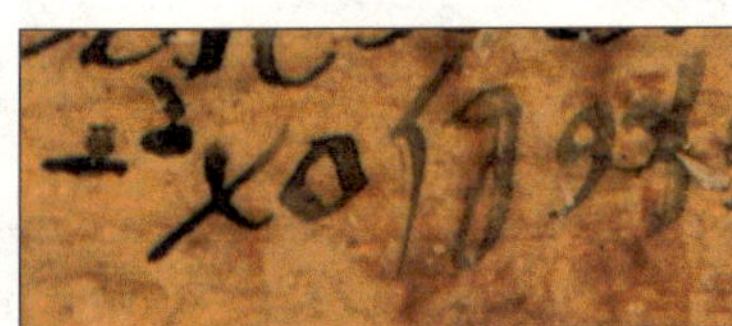

Fig. 26: Split letter strokes as examples for the use of a reed-like pen as writing instrument, (a, b) BC 4 and (c) BC 11.

A further indication that such a writing utensil was used can be seen in the scribe's need to re-ink every few characters. This is visible in a decrease of ink intensity at regular intervals (BC 4: every 15 akṣaras, BC 11: every 12–14 akṣaras, BC 6: every 16–20 akṣaras or even more). In BC 4 and BC 6 the darkness of the ink is quite uniform, and hence the places where the pen was recharged with ink are not as easily discernible. In general, BC 4 is the most carefully written. In BC 11 several ink blots spoil the manuscript (see fig. 28).

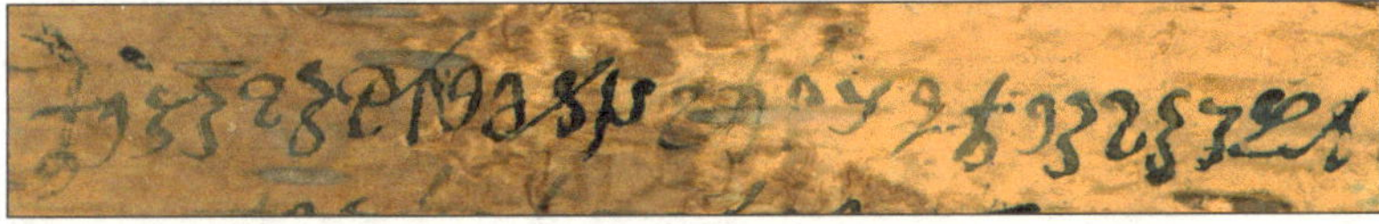

Fig. 27: Decrease of ink intensity, BC 11.

Fig. 28. Ink blots, BC 11.

Every now and then the pen's nib seems to have been re-sharpened, because some letters have variable stroke widths (indicating a sharpened nib), while the strokes of others have relatively equal width and rounded edges (indicating a softer nib). It is remarkable that the direction of the strokes is not always the same, with there being some indications of upward strokes. This would hardly have been possible with a sharpened pen; it was most likely only feasible when the nib was soft and thus had an edge similar to a brush (cf. Glass 2007: 85).

3.2 General Features of the Hand

In his preliminary catalogue, Ingo Strauch characterized the script of BC 4 and BC 11 as a "small, flowing hand with a tendency towards cursivity, sometimes letters are connected" (scribe 5). The same scribe is believed to have also written BC 18. But the letter forms of scribe 5 are also similar to those of other manuscripts in the Bajaur Collection, listed in the following overview based on Strauch 2007/2008.[1]

Table 2. Scribes of the scholastic texts of the Bajaur Collection.

scribe	5	5	5	12	18 = 5?	18 = 5?	19 = 5	19 = 5
BC	4	11	18	12	14	16	6	19

Since all of these manuscripts are scholastic texts, it might be asked whether in fact one person was responsible for all of them. While the letters in BC 12 (scribe 12) are written more carefully and upright compared to BC 4/11, this alone does not necessarily imply a different scribe. Nevertheless, the form of *ka* is quite different in BC 12, and thus it does seem to have been written by a different hand. The scripts of BC 6 and BC 19 (scribe 19 in Strauch 2007/2008) look very similar to BC 4/11, as do the glyphs in BC 14 and BC 16 (scribe 18 in Strauch 2007/2008), although here, when compared to BC 4/11, the letters are a little more elongated. Still, all of the manuscripts could have been written by the same scribe, if we consider that the writing surface and implement also have an impact on the appearance of a hand. Moreover, an individual's handwriting is not necessarily the same from one day to the next. The future study of the remaining scholastic texts (BC 14, 16, 18) will elucidate this matter further, and also help to sort the fragments more reliably according to their content.

In general, the hand of BC 4 and BC 11 has a somewhat ragged appearance due to slightly inconsistent letter dimensions, interlinear insertions and varying amounts of ink. Despite this, the writing is mostly legible, even though some letters, or rather ligatures, are difficult to differentiate. Uncertain readings remain only where the manuscript itself is no longer intact. In BC 6 the letter forms are a bit more consistent in size, and there are no interlinear additions.

The whole scroll BC 4 seems to have been written rather quickly, judging by the cursive and often combined letters. In a revision process, it seems that the same scribe added some numbers (namely 1, 3, 5) and the interlinear notes.

---

1 Strauch (2007/2008: 14) describes the hands briefly as follows: Scribe 12 (BC 12): Flowing, slanting hand with a developed tendency towards cursivity, very similar and possibly identical with scribe 4 (BC 3). Scribe 18 (BC 14, 16): Flowing hand with relatively high, prolonged letters, and a tendency towards cursivity. Very similar to, but obviously different from scribe 5. Scribe 19 (BC 6, 19): Bold, upright and flowing hand, similar to, but obviously different from scribe 12.

The lines in BC 4 are relatively horizontal, the slant of verticals is ca. -20°, and the pen angle (i.e., the angle of the nib to the base line of the writing) is ca. 10°–22°. The natural pen angle for a right-handed person using a square nib is normally 30°–45°, but the manuscript itself may have been rotated, making the angle about 10°–20° softer (Glass 2007: 87). This seems to correspond to our manuscript, and therefore the nib does not seem to have been cut on an angle (as in the case of the scribe of RS 5, studied by Andrew Glass), which was a later scribal practice in India (see Lambert 1953: 5 and Johnston 1971: 71–72, according to Glass 2007: 87).

In BC 11, the lines of writing arc downward as they progress leftwards—especially on the recto side, where the difference in level between the start and end is almost two lines. According to Andrew Glass (2006: 90), this shows that the scribe wrote with his right hand. The slant of verticals is here between -20° and -15°. Together with the downward slanting orientation of the lines, this suggests that the manuscript was rotated slightly to the left for comfort. The pen angle is ca. 15°–30°, and rather than the nib having been cut on a different angle, if compared to BC 4, it might also be assumed here that this was due to rotation of the manuscript.

The lines in BC 6 are relatively horizontal, but still arc downward somewhat. The pen angle is approximately 35°, though here the pen nib seems to have been blunt, since most of the edges of the letter forms are round.

3.3 Foot Marks

In general, there are no "foot marks" as are commonly observed in the British Library Collection (cf. table 12 in Glass 2007: 89), although in one or two instances of the initial letter *e*, a remnant of a foot mark seems to have survived.[2] Normally, the downstroke stems end straight or have a slight curve to the left. When a letter is written with a curve to the right, this is marked by an underbar in the transliteration, e.g., *g̱*, *ḏ*, *ś̱*, *ṣ̱*, *s̱*. Phonetically, this additional diacritic indicates an intervocalic consonant that was pronounced, it is assumed, differently. Additionally, there are a few instances of unusual foot marks in glyphs for *ṇ*- without any apparent phonetic significance.

3.4 Analysis of Selected Letters

For an overall survey of the hand used in all three edited manuscripts, see table 8 at the end of this chapter. In the following, only those letters with differing, ambiguous or unusual notation will be described. They are ordered according to the traditional (Sanskrit) *varṇamālā*.

3.4.1 Vowel Diacritics

-*e*. This vowel mark is normally written as a straight or slightly bent downstroke above a base sign. In some cases (initial *e*, *ñe*, *he*), however, it can be attached horizontally to the stem of the downstroke instead of diagonally at the top. The only clear occurrence of *ñe* is found in BC 4 (4r12 *añe*); another incomplete one is found in 4r18 *śuñe*. Within the Bajaur Collection, another variant also occurs: BC 2, BC 7. The *ñe* with a horizontal stroke is known as well

---

2 "The use of footmarks seems to be restricted to scribes of group A" (Strauch 2007/2008: 13). Group A refers here to the division of the scripts "depending on their relationship to cursivity": A "prefers the older, archaic *ka*"; B "use[s] the younger shape of the *ka*."

from BL 5B (Anav^{L}, cf. Salomon 2000: 58, table 2) and BL 9 (Nird^{L2}, cf. Baums 2009: 92 and 104), and similarly (but written with only one stroke) from Niya document no. 310.

-u. In BC 11, the word *sudhu* is found three times, twice with the *-u* written in the normal form (11r14, 11r37) and once with an additional semicircle below (11v11). This could be interpreted as an anusvāra, but since the other two are clearly written as °*dhu* and the scribe does not use an anusvāra very often, this has been transliterated as *sudhu*. In combination with *ṇ-* there is one unusual vowel marker in 11r16 (*aṇubhaviea*).

3.4.2 Basic Signs

a. The head of the initial *a* usually forms a curve. This can be open or closed. When it is open, it is sometimes difficult to tell whether *a* or *va* was intended. Ideally, the *a* is rather round at the top and curved downwards, in contrast, the *va* more straight. This difference can be seen in the writing of *valia* in BC 4 (4r12, 4r13).

e. Throughout both BC 4 and BC 11, different forms of writing initial *e* are applied, ranging from archaic (with or without foot mark) to cursive: / > / > . No difference in meaning, relationship to the content, or position within a word can be observed. The single-stroke version tends to be used more often, and this is also the only variant used in BC 6. The first documented occurrence of this is in Takht-i Bahi (CKI 53, year 103 [Azes] = 56/57 CE), according to Glass 2000: 46.

i. Initial *i* is written with either two strokes or one. The one-stroke version is used three times in BC 4, once in BC 11, and twice in BC 6.

o. Initial *o* is written with two strokes or only one. The single-stroke version is already known from the BL fragments.

k-. This akṣara is written in a cursive style, being relatively round at the top and similar to *ṣ* , which makes it sometimes difficult to differentiate between the two.

kṣ-. Principally, this character consists of two strokes with or without a slight bend to the left of the downstroke . Rarely the scribe wrote it in one step (4r25); in 4v11 it is very similar to *g-*.

kh/*k̲h̲-*. In addition to normal *kh*, a variant with a stroke to the bottom right is used when writing *ak̲h̲ata* for Skt. *āghāta*. This has so far been documented for Skt. *kh* in *veś̲ak̲h̲a* (Skt. *Vaiśākha*, P *Vesākha*) in the reliquary inscriptions of Menandros and Vijayamitra (CKI 176, Baums 2012: 202, 8/7 BCE), as well as in *danamuk̲h̲a* (CKI 653, Fussman 2011 no. 49, 50–100 CE, see plate; CKI 655, Fussman 2011 no. 50, 50–200 CE, see plate). The same variant is used in the name of a monastery on potsherd inscriptions from Kara-Tepe: *k̲h̲adeka-* (CKI 744, Fussman 2011 no. 11, 50 CE), *k̲h̲adevaka-* (CKI 630, 635, 651, Fussman 2011 nos. 43, 55, 74, all 50–200 CE), *k̲h̲adeuka-viha[ra]* (CKI 762, Fussman 2011 no. 56, 50–200 CE).

g/g̱-. Three forms of *ga/g̱a* are applied: (1) with a straight downstroke, (2) with a curved downstroke open to the left, or (3) with an additional stroke at the bottom to the right, attached at an acute angle.

(1) The *ga* with a straight downstroke is used very rarely: only twice in BC 11 (11v25 *gada* and 11r15 *gachae*, although already slightly bent) and possibly once in BC 4 (4r12 *gaga*—if at all, as the ink here might just be blurred and it may also have had a curved downstroke). This rather archaic form is moreover used when vowel markers for *-i*, *-e*, and *-o* are added. The only exception is *ag̱icaṇa* (4v6), which is written in the third variant.

(2) The *ga* with a curved downstroke is normally used at the beginning of words (BC 11 *gaḍa*, *gachae*, BC 6 *gaḍeṇa*) or in compound elements (BC 11 *a-sa-gaṇia*, *-gamaṇa*, *sa-gaṇia*, BC 4 *su-gadiṇa*, BC 6 *-gamaṇa*). After a negative prefix, however, it is written with *g̱*, as in *a-g̱amaṇa* or *a-g̱icaṇa*; see (3) below. Further, the form with a curved downstroke is applied when corresponding to Skt. *ṅg* (BC 4 *gaga*) or *gn* (BC 4 *ṇagao*).

(3) The *g̱a* with an attached rightward stroke at the bottom denotes a voiced velar in intervocalic position. The spellings are: BC 4 *ag̱icaṇa*, *aṇag̱ada-*, *ahig̱akṣidave*, *jag̱ariaṇa*, *-log̱a-*, *(*sarva)g̱areṇa*. BC 11 *atog̱ada-*, *adidaaṇag̱adapracupaṇehi*, *ag̱amaṇa*, *pradig̱arasuhe*, *-ag̱areṇa*. BC 6 *(a)kuhicaag̱amaṇa*, *rag̱a*, *arog̱a-*, *eg̱agracita-*, *(*e)grag̱acita-*. In one instance of *veragra* (11r48), the *gr* is a mixture between *gra* and *g̱a*, looking very similar to the preceding *viveg̱a-*, but since the other instances of *veragra* (11r49, 11r50) are more clearly written with *gra*, it is consistently transliterated as such. In BC 6 the same sign is written in *agra* as well as in *eg̱agracita*, making this even more likely.

gh-. The *gh* is written in a cursive style, i.e., the first stroke forms the upper loop and the right arm. The second stroke builds the stem.

c̱/c̱̄-. The modified *ca* in *pac̱̄a* = Skt. *paścāt* is written with a horizontal line above it and with a stroke at the bottom bent to the right. In 4r28 the superscript line is not visible, since the manuscript is broken off above, but I assume it was also there. For reasons of consistency it has been transliterated as *c̱̄*, as in 11r27. In BC 6 it is written only with a rightward stroke at the bottom (6v8 *pac̱i* = Skt. *paścāt*). According to Glass (2000: 62), the modified form of *ca* with a line written above it "has been observed only in later materials, such [as] the Niya documents and the Schøyen collection." Since his publication, however, several other attestations in earlier material have been found.[3] In the Bajaur Collection it is abundantly used for Skt. *śc* but

3 The letter *c̄* is used for Skt. *-śc-* in the Library of Congress scroll (*ac̄aria*, personal communication Richard Salomon, cf. also Baums 2009: 198), in the British Library Collection (BL 4 *pac̄a-mukho*, personal communication Timothy Lenz) and in the Senior Collection (RS 4A *ac̄aria*, personal communication Mark Allon; RS 12 *pac̄i*, Silverlock 2015: § 6.4.6.2). It is written as *c̱* for Skt. *-śc-* in BL 15 (*ac̱aria*, cf. Baums 2009: 198, with the suggested transliteration as *aĉaria*). In the Senior Collection the underbarred *c̱* (without superscript line) is also used in the position of initial singular *c-* (e.g., *c̱aḏoṇa* RS 7, *c̱ito* RS 10, *c̱eḏas̱a* RS 24, personal communication Mark Allon). Moreover, in this collection *c̄* is inconsistently used in addition to *c* and *j̄* for Skt. *-jv-* (RS 20 *sapac̄iliḏa*, *sapacaliḏa*, *sapaj̄aliḏa* = Skt. *saṃprajvalita*, personal communication Joe Marino).

also for normal *c*. The foot at the bottom is thereby sometimes distinctly extended to the right, sometimes applied only as a small hook or not written at all (see table 3).

Table 3. Forms of *c̱̄a* / *c̄a* in the Bajaur Collection.

with rightward extension				with small hook		without foot mark		

BC 11	BC 8	BC 5	BC 9	BC 9	BC 9	BC 1	BC 2	BC 9

In BC 1, BC 2, and BC 9 we find the superscript form (BC 2), as familiar from the Niya documents and the Schøyen Collection (cf. Glass 2000: 62). In BC 5, BC 8, BC 11, and perhaps also BC 4 we have the superscript + underbarred form (BC 5, 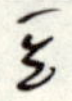 BC 8). BC 9 has both () but in its application, *ca* and *c̱̄a*/*c̄a* are interchangeable. Since in an earlier document, namely BL 1, pre-consonantal *r* is written in cases where a superscript line is later used (G *parce* = Skt. *paścāt*), it seems plausible that the underbarred form may have developed graphically from this pre-consonantal *r*.[4] At a later point in time, this seems to have been replaced by a general superscript line, which could be universally applied to other signs (cf. Baums 2009: 200). Thus, forms with both—a superscript line and an underbar—are reminiscent of characters with only an underbar after the introduction of the universal superscript stroke, suggesting the development *c̱* > *c̱̄* > *c̄*.

j-. This character is written without lifting the pen, sometimes resulting in a loop at the top  . The downstroke is sometimes straight, sometimes bent to the left . The difference between *ja* and *ḍa* is occasionally hard to distinguish, and also *kṣ* can look very similar when it is written in one stroke (for examples, see table 4).

j̄-. The glyph with superscript line is only used for Skt. *-dhy-* / P *-jjh-* in *aj̄atvia* (BC 11); *maje* (Skt. *madhya-* / P *majjha-*) is written with normal *j*.

---

4 There is, however, one instance in the texts written by this scribe (BL scribe 1) where he already uses the superscript line: *vioj̄ita* = Skt. **vibudhyitvā* (Salomon 2008a: 97). Cf. also Baums 2009: 197–200 regarding graphic devices marking long consonants and consonant clusters. The superscript line is, for example, used for *c̄* < *śc*, *j̄* < *dhy*, *s̄* < *ṣṇ* or *s̄* < *sn* (in the British Library fragments and the Library of Congress scroll). Other markers for consonant clusters are pre-consonantal *r* (*rc* < *śc*, *rṇ* < *ṣṇ*, *rñ* < *śn* / P *ñh* in the BL Collection and the Khotan *Dharmapada*), as well as post-consonantal *v*, which is essentially an underbarred form and perhaps better transliterated as *d̲h̲* or *s̱* in the following examples: *idhvivisa* or *id̲h̲ivisa* < *r̥ddhividhā* (Nird[L2] 9·198) and *adhva* or *ad̲h̲a* < *addhā* (SC 1, Falk 2011: 14, and Khvs[L] 27, though the identically written letter is transliterated here as *ardha*; cf. Salomon 2000: 161 and Baums 2009: 197 n. 48). Likewise, for example, *kriṣ̄a*, listed under post-consontal *-v* in Baums 2009: 198, would be transliterated here as *kriṣ̱̄a*.

Table 4. Comparison of *ja*, *ḍa*, and *kṣa* in BC 4, BC 6, and BC 11.

4r15 *jadi*	11v12 *jaṇe*	6r9 *jaṇas̱i*	6r9 *rajas̱i*	6v1 *upajati*		11v22 *gaḍa*	11v14 *gaḍa*	11v13 *gaḍa*		11v15 *mokṣe*	4v11 *akṣati*

ṭ-. Originally, this letter was written with three strokes (compare the forms in BC 7 and BC 5). In BC 4/6/11 (and likewise in BC 2, 16, and 17) it is written with one stroke, resulting in two acute angles at top and bottom: 4v12, 11r8, 6v7.

ṭh-/*ṭ́h*-. This character is written in the usual way as *ṭh* for Skt. *ṣṭ(h)* and *ṭ́h* for Skt. *sth*. There is one exception where *ṭ́h* is written for original retroflex: BC 4 *pad̲itiṭ́ha* = Skt. *pratitiṣṭha*, but apparently derivatives of √*sthā* can be written with *ṭ́h* as well (cf. Anav[L] 60 *vaṭ́hasa* = BHS *upatiṣṭhatha* / P **upaṭṭhātha*, Salomon 2008a: 126).

ḍ/*d̲*-. There are three variants. The first two (*ḍ*) only differ in a straight or slightly bent downstroke . Both are used for the same phoneme going back to Skt./P *ṇḍ*.[5] The third variant (*d̲*) has the bottom curved to the right , corresponding to Skt./P *prati* / *paṭi*, *ṭ*, *ḍ(ḍ)*, *ḍh* / *ḷh*.[6]

ḍh-. This character, , looks similar to *ṭ* or *d̲* , but the bottom is clearly rounded and the top stroke horizontal rather than slanted. The same form can be seen in BC 13 corresponding to Skt. *kaṭhina* and *ūḍha*. In bending the foot to the right, it is further distinguished from its original form, which can still be seen in BC 9 . There, the stem is attached to the middle of the top stroke and the bottom is bent slightly to the left. In BC 5 the bottom is still open to the left , but the top is already in a cursive form, with the downstroke starting at the right of the top-stroke.

ṇ-. As in most other Gāndhārī manuscripts, no distinction is made between original retroflex and dental nasals. In BC 4/6/11 only the glyph which originally denoted retroflex *ṇ* is used. There are a few peculiar foot marks added to *ṇa*, all in final position: *ṇa* 4r8, *triṇa* 4v6, *śpris̱aṇaṇa* (last akṣara) 4v7.

t/*d*-. Often the glyphs for *ta* and *da* are difficult to differentiate, especially when an *i*-diacritic is added. In uncertain cases the transliterations have been based on etymological grounds rather than on their mere outward appearance. Nevertheless, they tend to be interchangeable and their

---

[5] BC 4 *bos̱imaḍa* / *mos̱imaḍa*, BC 11 *gaḍa*, *paṃḍida*, BC 6 *gaḍa*, *pad̲ide*.

[6] *prati*/*paṭi*: BC 4 *pad̲iladha*, BC 6 *vipad̲is̱ara*. *ṭ*: BC 4 *trikod̲i*, BC 6 *kud̲ae*, *kud̲eami*. *ḍ(ḍ)*: BC 4 *praod̲idave*. *ḍh*: BC 11 -*hod̲e*-. *ḍh*/*ḷh*: BC 11 *amud̲a*-, *mud̲easa* (perhaps also BC 4 + + *d̲a cite*). BC 11 *caduragud̲iehi* is uncertain, either corresponding to Skt. *caturguḍaka* or *caturaṅgulika* (cf. annotations on 11r35, p. 216).

phonetic value may have already merged. There is one instance, in BC 4, where a modified *t* is written (*hakṣaṯi* 4r12 = Skt. *bhaviṣyanti*). In BC 11 there is a similar modified *d* in *aparibhuḏasa* (11r32) = Skt. *aparibhuktasya*, and possibly also in the preceding *paribhuḏasa* (11r32), but the ink is faded here. In BC 6, four akṣaras that are understood as corresponding to Skt. *-tā* forming an abstract noun look as if they have been written with *-sa* and so have been transliterated as such. See under *s-*.

d-. The diacritic vowel *-e* is normally attached to the top of the basic sign . In BC 11 there is a wider variety, ranging from top to bottom: .

bh-. Generally, the glyph for *bh* is written with two strokes, with the first consisting of a straight horizontal line which then proceeds down in a curve. The second stroke builds the stem (e.g., 11r39). In 11r32 it is written differently insofar as the first stroke is to the right and then down as the stem. After this, a semicircle is attached to the right (*bhu*).

y-. This character is written with two strokes. In most cases it is rather round at the top , but there are also a few instances where it displays an acute angle . In comparison to test letters from other manuscripts (Glass 2007: 106, table 15), it can be placed between the BL and the RS manuscripts, being nearer to the latter. The *terminus post quem* for this form is the beginning of the Kuṣāṇa era.

r-. The *ra* is written either flat on the top or slightly curved . It is possible to confuse the latter with *ḍa* if the context is not clear (e.g., in 11r25 *-saṣ̱araṇa-*, in 11r46 *-dharaṇa-*).

ś/ś̱/ś̱̄-. There are two forms, one with a straight or slightly left-bent right leg and one with a slightly right-bent right leg . In one instance (4r25), *ṇaś̱ae* is written with an additional horizontal stroke above it (cf. Lenz 2010: 55–56), leading to the complicated but consistent transliteration *ṇaś̱̄ae*. The distribution is as follows (words found with both forms in bold):

ś BC 4: *aṇuśaśa-*, ***aṇuśaśidava, (a)kuśala-***, *(a)śuha*, *deśidavo*, *śaki*, *śeṣ̱ae*, *śuña-*, *śoa*; future forms: *ataraṣ̱aïśati*, *upajiśati*, *cariśe*, *bhikṣiśe*, *vaïśadi*
BC 11: *aṇuśaśa*, *avaśi / avaśa*, ***akuśale,*** *(a)śuha-*, *ṇaśadi*, ***ṇaśida,*** *paśita*, ***mahaśie,*** *vidimiśa*, *śali*, *śiṭha*, *śida*, *śile*, *śuñagareṇa*; future form: *bhaviśadi*
BC 6: *aśalasaña*, *duśama*, *duśaṣ̱i*, *duśiadi*, *duśieadi*, *śaleṇa*, *śeṣ̱a*; future form: *dakṣiśati*

ś̱ BC 4: ***(a)kuś̱alaṇa***, *(a)śpriś̱aṇaṇa*, *iś̱emi*, *deś̱a-*, *deś̱amaṇa*, *ṇaś̱ae*, *ṇaś̱e*, *ṇaś̱ea*, *ṇaś̱ee*, *viś̱adi*, ***ś̱aṣ̱idava***
BC 11: *-aś̱ea-* or *-aśrea-*, ***kuś̱aleṇa***, *-deś̱a-*, *ṇaś̱iea*, ***ṇaś̱ida,*** *ṇaś̱e*, *ṇaś̱eati*, ***mahaś̱ie***
BC 6: *(a)kuś̱alasa*, *drudeś̱a*, *vovaś̱amo*

ś̱̄ BC 4: *ṇaś̱̄ae*

śp-. In BC 4 and BC 11 this sign is written where Sanskrit has *sp*, *sm*, or *sv* (cf. chapter 5 on phonology). It is written with a single stroke, resulting in a small loop at the bottom where the pen turns upwards again . In cases where a post-consonantal *r* is attached to it (*śpr*), it is written with two strokes, first the stem with the *r*-curve and then the curve to the right (*śpri*).

ṣ/ṣ̱-. There are two forms for this character, similar to *ś/ś̱* and *g/g̱*. The first is written with a straight or slightly left-bent stem , the second with a kind of foot mark where the tip of the stem is bent to the right . The distribution is as follows (words found with both forms in bold):

ṣ	BC 4:	***miṣo***, *ṣaṣadaeṇa*, *-ṣa-*
	BC 11:	*piṣita*, *ṣadimeṇa*, *ṣade/ṣado*, *ṣaṣadae*
	BC 6:	*phaṣadi*, *d(*u)ṣaṇa*
ṣ̱	BC 4:	*(a)sapuruṣ̱a-*, *-niṣ̱aṇa*, *-paribhaṣ̱idava-*, *paribhaṣ̱ehi*, ***miṣ̱o***, *ś̱aṣ̱idava*, *śeṣ̱ae*
	BC 11:	*apoṣ̱aṇa*, *amiṣ̱a*, *uaṇiṣ̱a*, *uṣ̱ata*, *eṣ̱a*, *edeṣ̱a*, *tuṣ̱e*, *teṣ̱a*, *doṣ̱a*, *bheṣ̱aje*, *viṣ̱a{ja}jita*, *ṣ̱ahi*
	BC 6:	*eṣ̱a*, *doṣ̱a*, *śeṣ̱a*

A theoretically reasonable rule "*ṣ* in the beginning, *ṣ̱* in intervocalic position" is proved wrong by the spellings *d(*u)ṣaṇa*, *miṣo*, *ṣaṣadae(ṇa)*, *piṣita*, *phaṣadi*, and *ṣ̱ahi*.

ṣ̄-. A superscript line is used to denote Skt. *ṣṇ* in *śidaüṣ̄a*- (11r46).

s/s̱/s̄-. Both types of *s* are used, the "normal" and the "corkscrew" . A third "underbarred" variety appears in BC 4 *as̱ivas̱idae* (for more details, see chapter 5 on phonology). Another unusual extension applied to *s̱a* (presumably for Skt. *-sya*) can be seen in 11v15 *-saparaïas̱a* . In one instance in BC 4 it is uncertain if *-sa* is a scribal mistake for *-ta* (Skt. *-tā*) and if it perhaps should be transliterated as *-ṯa* (4v11 *śpabhavasa*).[7] The same is seen four times in BC 6, where also *-sa* seems to be written for etymological *-tā*: 6v1 *abodhasa* , 6v2 *egagracitasa* , 6v2 *avikṣitacitasa* , 6v3 *(*e)grag̱acitasa* .

h-. It is sometimes difficult to distinguish between the glyphs for *hu* or *ho*. Originally, *hu* has a small circle or semicircle and *ho* a straight short line . Here, the shape of this line is sometimes in between, looking like a slightly bent stroke (11r25 *bahu*, 4v12 *sahoro*). Both *hu* and *ho* can be used for the same words, e.g., *śpaho/śpahu*, *amaho/amahu*, indicating that the two were also very similar in pronunciation.

3.4.3 Conjunct Characters

-ṃ (anusvāra). In the case of *sapati* it is sometimes difficult to tell with certainty if the scribe intended to write an anusvāra or not. An anusvāra could be possibly read in the following examples: 4r14 *sapati*, 4r17 *sapati*, and 4v12 *sahoro*. However, the *sa* in other words

7 For the irregular development *t* > *s*, cf. Glass 2007: 116 (though he does not exclude the possibility of scribal confusion, writing *jaṇasa* for Skt. *jānataḥ* and, similarly, *paśas̱a* for Skt. *paśyataḥ*). For *t* > *s* being a scribal mistake in the Senavarma and Indravarma inscription cf. Falk 2003a: 577 (*solite* = Skt. *tolitaḥ*, *-samughaso* = Skt. *-samudghāto*) and Falk 2014: 17.

where no nasal is to be expected is written similarly: 4v1 *sata*, 4r12 *sarva*, 4r13 *sarva*, 4v4 *sapuruṣaṇa*. A clearly written anusvāra can only be observed in 4r15 *asaṃkhedehi* , 4v4 *saṃsara* , 11r17 *sasaṃra* , and 4r23 *paṃca* (presumably also in 11r7 *paṃḍidaṇa* and 11r21 *paṃḍida*). When compared to these notations it thus does seem that no distinctive anusvāra was intended in the writing of *sapati*. In BC 6, four akṣaras stand for Skt. *saṃ-* and have been transliterated as such, even though other examples of *sa* look the same, and hence the anusvāra is not necessarily justified: 6v1 *saṃthidomaṇas̱a*, 6v5 *saṃthidae*, 6v5 *saṃthido*, 6v6 *saṃthidomaṇas̱a*.

*r*C- (pre-consonantal *r*-). In one instance, in 4r20 *rva* , the curve of the marker for pre-consonantal *-r-* is elongated, making it similar to *rvya* in other documents, but the circle is still open to the left and also the meaning is clear, so the reading *par⟨*i⟩ṇirvahido* is free of doubt with regard to the *rva*. In *karpa* it is used for double consonants, cf. P *kappa* = Skt. *kalpa* (4r15 *karpehi* , 11r35 *karpa* , 11r37 *karpa*).

C*r*- (post-consonantal *-r*). Regarding *tr* and *dr*, it is almost impossible to tell which one was intended only on paleographic grounds. Based on the context, words that go back to Skt. *daur-/ dur-* have been consistently transliterated as *dr-* (*droaca-*, *droatie*, *drogadi-*, *drugaṇa-*, *drujaṇa-*, *drudeś̱a-*), words that correspond to Skt. *tri-/-tra-/-tr̥̄-*, as *tr* (BC 4 *añatra*, *trae*, *triṇa*, *dharetrami*, *matra*, *sarvatra*; BC 11 *atra*, *amitra-*, *tatra*, *yatra*, *sarvatra-*; BC 6 *tatra*).

In BC 6, *mradua* for Skt. *mr̥duka*, the *mr* is written with the extension of the right upward stroke into a hook instead of being written with a pre-consonantal *r* as in *rmidu* (Anav[L], cf. Salomon 2008: 95) or *rmaḏo* (SĀ[S1], cf. Glass 2007: 102) = Skt. *mr̥du*.

C*v*- (post-consonantal *-v*). What is transliterated as *tva* goes back to either Skt. *ttva* or *tma*. In the latter it might also have been understood as *tma*, and should therefore perhaps be transliterated as such. However, there is no graphic distinction discernible to decide whether the Kharoṣṭhī sign refers to Skt. *ttva* or *tma* (see table 5).

Table 5. Writing of *tv* < *ttv* or *tm* in BC 4, BC 6, and BC 11.

ttv	4r17	4r21	4r22	4r22	11r19	11r21	11r24	11r47	6v2	
	-s̱atva	*satva-*	*satva*	*s̱atva*	*-s̱atva-*	*satva-*	*-s̱atvehi*	*-s̱atva-*	*tatva*	
tm	4r22	11r26	11r47	11v18	11v13	11v24	11v26	11v26	6r1	6r10
	atva	*atve*	*atva-*	*aṇatva-*	*ajatva-*	*ajatvia*	*ajatvia*	*ajatvia*	*atva*	*atva-*

3.5 Numerals

In BC 4 six numbers are written at the end of paragraphs. In BC 11 two numbers (1 and 4) are found (11v17, 11v30), probably also used to label paragraphs. BC 6 contains no numbers. In the following table, how these numbers have been written is compared to the survey of Andrew Glass (2000), which includes evidence from the Aśokan inscriptions, the British Library Collection, the Khotan *Dharmapada*, and the Niya documents. Where relevant, a short reference is made to the Senior Collection (based on personal communication with Mark Allon).

Table 6. Writing of numbers in BC 4.

<table>
<tr><th></th><th>#</th><th>Line</th><th>Remarks</th></tr>
<tr><td></td><td>1</td><td>4r12</td><td>–</td></tr>
<tr><td></td><td>2</td><td>4r14</td><td>The first stroke is very short but not distinctly connected to the second one. In Aśokan times and also, for example, in BL 2, the two strokes are parallel and equally long. In the Khotan Dharmapada the first stroke is already shortened. In the Niya documents, finally, the formerly separate strokes are connected; the same form is applied in the Senior Collection.
<table><tr><th>Aśokan</th><th>BL 2</th><th>KDhp</th><th>Niya</th><th>Schøyen</th></tr><tr><td></td><td></td><td></td><td></td><td></td></tr></table> (Glass 2000: 139)</td></tr>
<tr><td></td><td>3</td><td>4r17</td><td>Here, the strokes are almost connected to the final long stroke, indicating a slightly later date. Compared to the survey of Andrew Glass, the form lies between the Khotan Dharmapada and the Niya documents. The Senior Collection has again the same form as in the Niya documents, with the three strokes connected.
<table><tr><th>BL 2</th><th>KDhp</th><th>Niya</th><th>Schøyen</th></tr><tr><td></td><td></td><td></td><td></td></tr></table> (Glass 2000: 140)</td></tr>
<tr><td></td><td>4</td><td>4r19</td><td>Only in Aśokan inscriptions is the number four written with four vertical strokes. Later, as here, it is generally written as a cross rotated 45 degrees, like a saltire.</td></tr>
<tr><td></td><td>5</td><td>4r20</td><td>In Aśokan inscriptions the number five is written with five strokes. In all later documents it is indicated by a combination of a cross and a bar, 4 [+] 1 = 5. (Interestingly, the BL scribe 2 writes the combined number in the reverse; cf. Lenz 2010: 18.)</td></tr>
<tr><td></td><td>6</td><td>4r22</td><td>The number six is written as 4 [+] 2. In contrast to the notation of a single number 2, the two strokes here are connected, which brings us closer to the Niya documents.</td></tr>
</table>

With regard to the numerals, BC 4 is similar to the Khotan *Dharmapada* (1st or 2nd century) and the Senior Collection (ca. 140 CE), as well as the later Niya documents (3rd or 4th century). In the BL fragments published until now, the numbers 2 and 3 are written with separate and unconnected strokes (BL 1 and BL 2; cf. Lenz 2010: 18), making the first half of the first century a *terminus post quem* for BC 4, if we leave aside possible geographical factors, which could also have played a role in writing styles.

3.6 Punctuation

In BC 4 sometimes—very rarely—small dots are placed at the end of sentences. After each longer paragraph, circles of varying sizes are written, sometimes followed by a number. In BC 11 punctuation, consisting of dots and circles, is applied very irregularly. In cases where punctuation is found, it is almost always at the end of a sentence or paragraph, but sometimes it is found in places where it is unexpected. There is one example where a small circle (◦) indicates a break ("Sprechpause") within a sentence, making its application similar to today's use of a dash: 11v28 *pariña prahaṇakarmo ca · ruve* ◦ *a̱sa va · aruve*. Instead of writing a circle to mark the end of a paragraph, sometimes the rest of the line is left blank on purpose.

In addition to · and ◦, BC 6 contains two double circles ◎ (§ 1, § 2) as well as an ×-shape enclosed in a circle ⊗ (§ 4), all used to conclude paragraphs. In the other cases (§ 3, § 5), the end of the paragraph is missing.

Similar double circles are found in the *Ekottarikāgama*-like manuscript BL 12+14, though these look more like spirals or large circles (which is how they have been transliterated; cf. Allon 2001: 66) written twice. In BL 1, the *Anavataptagāthā* written by the same scribe as BL 12+14, a group of punctuation marks similar to those in BC 6 is used, ranging from small dots to bigger circles (see Salomon 2008: 95, 98). A large circle concludes the recitations of Śroṇa and Nandika, whereas another sign resembling a rectangular or oblong box, with an × inside, hence transliterated as ⊠, concludes the verses of Nanda and Bharadvāja.

Another very similar double concentric circle is found in a verse commentary held in the British Library (Nird^{L2} 9·59). In Baums 2009, it has been transliterated as ❁, thus interpreting the two concentric circles as the stylized lotus flower that is used at the end of all other paragraphs. Concentric circles are also used in this commentary as margin markers to indicate where sections end, these inserted at the same height as the corresponding punctuation marks within the text (see Baums 2009: 105–6). Although in this case (Nird^{L2} 9·59) it is quite likely that the concentric circles are an abstract version of a stylized lotus flower, in other manuscripts (like BC 6) two concentric circles simply mark the ends of sections, in the same way single circles do.

In BC 11, the text is structured by smaller and bigger circles, which subdivide it into units of thought. At the end of the text "○ × · –" is written. The diagonal cross (resembling a saltire) usually denotes the cipher 4, but on pot inscriptions this sign is also used to signify the end of an inscription.[8] Since it is found at the end of the written text of BC 11, it is possible that the cross has this meaning, despite there being no ambiguity that this is the end of the text. However, at another place in the text (11v17), a vertical line is inserted above a big circle, presumably

[8] Two inscriptions on water pots from Gandhāra (to be published by Ingo Strauch; cf. Strauch 2010b).

denoting the cipher 1, which suggests that the cross denotes the cipher 4. The ciphers 2 and 3 would then be missing due to parts of the birch bark being lost, in which case they could have been written at the beginning of 11v20 and 11v28. This, however, does not make much sense with regard to the content. On the other hand, there is no space for a cipher at places where marking the end of a paragraph would seem more appropriate. Only in the gloss might there have been a cipher. Another possibility is that the numbers refer to paragraphs 1 and 4 in BC 4 insofar as they deal with similar topics. Other scholastic texts of the Bajaur Collection also contain numbered paragraphs, ranging from 1 to 5, whereby sections with the same number contain identical or similar keywords.[9] Between BC 4 and BC 11, however, there is no strong indication that they are referring to one and the same subject. Thus the placement and meaning of the ciphers 1 and 4 remain unclear.

3.7 Paleographic Dating

All manuscripts of the Bajaur Collection are written in a late form of Kharoṣṭhī, i.e., not earlier than the Common Era. Based on their degree of cursivity—especially noticeable in the shape of the letter *k*—they have been divided into two groups by Ingo Strauch (2008: 108). Of these, BC 4, 6, and 11 clearly belong to the younger, cursive group B, even though occasional traces of older, archaic letter forms can be discerned (cf. *e* and *k*-). In general, the Bajaur Collection has been provisionally dated between the second half of the first and the first half of the second century CE, "with a tendency towards the later part of this period" (Strauch 2008: 111). Based on the shape of the letter *k* and especially due to the similarity of the hand to that of the scribe of the Senior Collection, this period seems very likely for BC 4, 6, and 11.[10]

9 BC 12, 14, 16, 18: § 1 *dukha*, § 2 *aïdaṇa/aṇica*, § 3 *(ṇir)atva*, § 4 *(ṇi)jiva*, § 5 *(ṇi)dhama*.

10 Regarding other test letters such as *c*-, *ch*-, *y*-, and *s*-, the differences are often not easily discernible. In general, the letters are similar to the graphemes presented by Allon (2001: 67) and Glass (2007: 106, table 15), which would mean assigning BC 4/6/11 to a still earlier period, i.e., the first half of the first century CE, like the BL manuscripts. However, the form of the letter *k* speaks against this.

Table 7. Kharoṣṭhī script as found in BC 4, BC 6, and BC 11.
If a sign occurs only in one manuscript, the respective manuscript number has been added.

	a	*i*	*u*	*e*	*o*
–					
k-					
kṣ-					
kh-		6	4		
k̲h̲-	6				
g-		11	11	4	
	rga *gra*	*gri* 6			*gro* 11
g̲-					
gh-					
	rgha				
c-					4
c̲/c̲̄-	*c̲̄a* 11, (4)	*c̲i* 6			
ch-					
j-					
		rji 4			
j̄-					

	a	*i*	*u*	*e*	*o*
jh-					
ñ-				4	
ṭ-					
ṭh-		4			
ṭh́-		6			
ḍ-				6	
ḍ̱-					
ḍ̱h-					
ṇ-					
t-					
	tra	*tri*		*tre*	*tro*
	tva	*tvi*		*tve*	
ṯ-		4			
th-					
	rtha			*rthe*	*rtho*
d-					
		dri	*dru*		*dro*
ḏ-	11				

	a	*i*	*u*	*e*	*o*
dh-					
n-					
p-					
	rpa *pra* *paṃ*	*pri*			*pro*
ph-	6				
b-		11			
bh-				11	11
m-			11		
	rma 11 *mra* 6			*rme* 11	*rmo* 11
y-					
	rya			*rye*	
r-					
l-		11		11	
v-					
	rva *rva*			*rve*	
vh-					
ś-					

	a	*i*	*u*	*e*	*o*
ś- (cont.)	*rśa*	*śri*			
ś̱/s̱̄-	*s̱a* *s̱̄a* 4				
śp-					
		śpri			
ṣ-					
s̱-		4			
ṣ̄-					
s-					
	saṃ *sva*				
ş-		4			
s̱-				6	
st-					
sp-					
h-					

Punctuation and numerals

	6 6 4
1–6	

Chapter 4

Orthography

While orthography includes matters of spelling, it also has to do with the correspondence between graphemes and phonemes. Since the orthographic system in Gāndhārī seems to have been rather fluid and flexible during the period under consideration (and might perhaps be more suitably characterized as an ensemble of idiolects), this chapter is mainly about different spellings as found in the texts edited here. The relationship between phonemes and graphemes will be discussed in the following chapter 5 on phonology. In both chapters, Orthography and Phonology, references to line numbers are mostly omitted to enhance readability (see the indices on page 290 and following if necessary). The Gāndhārī words are given as they appear in the text. In cases of several occurrences, the most complete reading is taken.

4.1 Anusvāra

Anusvāra is mostly left unwritten.[1] The few occurrences where it is applied are: BC 4 *asaṃkhedehi*, *-paṃca-*, *saṃsara-*; BC 11 *asakeṃa karpa* (in addition to *asakhea karpa*), *paṃḍidaṇa*, *sasaṃra* / *saṃsara*; BC 6 *saṃthida-*. In the case of *sasaṃra*, the scribe added the anusvāra in a second step, but in the wrong place. In the second occurrence of this word, it is uncertain where the anusvāra was intended, if at all, since the birch bark is broken off at this point. It has been transliterated as *saṃsara*, but in analogy to the preceding instance, *sasaṃra* might also be possible. Since *sa* is often written with a curved lower part, it is difficult to tell what was intended. Also in BC 6 it is hard to say if an anusvāra was written in the two occurrences of the word *saṃthida-* or not.

An anusvāra would have been expected etymologically in *aṇuśaśa* and *aṇuśaśidava*, although the development *ṃs* > *ś* may account for its omission; it is the same for *ś̱aṣ̱idava* (*ṃs* > *ṣ̱*) and *viś̱adi* (here the anusvāra may have been produced by the lengthening of the preceding vowel, as in P *vīsati*).[2] The remaining cases are all *sa-* for Skt. *saṃ-* preceding consonants: *sakṣiteṇa*, *sagha*, *saña*, *sadriṭhia*, *sapati*, and probably *sahoro*, where the anusvāra is replaced by

---

1 It is never written in the Senior Collection and only rarely in the British Library Collection, for example in Khvs[L] (cf. Salomon 2000: 76–77). Within the Bajaur Collection it is definitely written in several manuscripts (BC 1, 2, 3, 5, 7, 9), but at this preliminary stage nothing can be said about the systematic application of anusvāra in general. It is usually not written in the Khotan *Dharmapada* (Brough 1962: § 14) and inconsistently / irregularly in the Niya documents (cf. Burrow 1937: 17–18).

2 Also in other documents (Niya, Senavarma inscription, MS 28, and a "Copper Manuscript in Five Sheets"; cf. Falk 2010: 17–9) normally *viśati* is written, but cf. *viṃśati 20* (with a clear horizontal stroke above the *ś*, i.e., *ś̄*) in the "Shahi Kot Relic Slab" (cf. Falk 2003b: 71–4; also Baums 2012: 242).

a homorganic nasal before a stop, represented by the stop alone in the Kharoṣṭhī script. In those cases where the anusvāra is still written, it may have been retained due to the cluster *-ṃkhy- (asaṃkhedehi*, etc.), or because it is part of a special—numeric or technical—term (*paṃca, saṃsara, paṃḍida*). However, in BC 6, the last is clearly written *paḍide* without anusvāra.

4.2 Distribution of *n* / *ṇ*

As is common for many inscriptions of the first century CE, as well as for most of the Gāndhārī manuscripts examined so far, *n* is not distinguished from *ṇ*, with *ṇ-* written for every nasal.[3]

4.3 Distribution of *t* / *d*

It is sometimes difficult to differentiate between these two characters. Still there are some clear examples of etymologically unjustifiable writings of *-ti* for the 3rd sg. ending *-di* (*hakṣati* instead of *hakṣadi*), as well as some words written with *-t-* instead of the phonologically expected *-d-* (see chapter 5 on phonology under *d-*). Similar observations have been made by Andrew Glass with regard to SĀ[S1], in which essentially no distinction is made between *t* and *d*. He suggests "that the shapes of these letters were merging, perhaps under the influence of a phonetic merger" (Glass 2007: 107).

4.4 Distribution of *s* / *s̱*

In addition to *s*, the modified characters *s̱* and, in BC 4 in one instance, *s̮* are applied (the third with a subscript line; see chapter 3 on paleography, p. 57). The modified *s̱* is used where it represents an original intervocalic *-th-*/*-dh-* (compound boundaries are treated as the beginning of a new word, e.g., *loadhadu*). While it does not occur in gen. sg. endings (Skt. *-sya* / P *-ssa*), it quite often replaces normal *-s-* in the middle of words or at the beginning of compound elements (e.g., BC 4 *alas̱ia*, *cedas̱ia*; *as̱apuruṣa*, *bos̱is̱atva*). Sometimes *s* or *s̱* (for both Skt. *-s-* and *-th-*) are applied interchangeably. In BC 4: *ṇis̱amartha* as well as *ṇisamartha*; in BC 11: *sarva-s̱atva-* but *sarva-sapati-*, *ṇis̱amartha-* as well as *ṇisamartha-*, *as̱akeṃa* as well as *asakhea*, and *kas̱a* as well as *kasa*. In BC 11 *sayavisa* (for *sayas̱avi* = BHS *sayyathāpi*), *sa* is written where etymologically *s̱a* would be expected. Probably, BC 11 *driṭhadhami⟨*a⟩saparaïas̱a* contains a gen. sg. ending otherwise written with normal *-sa*. However, there is also an unusual extension at the bottom of the letter, so the scribe himself may have corrected the *s̱a* to *sa*.

4.5 Modified Consonants

The most common modification is a small rightward extension at the bottom of a character, in some editions called a foot mark. The scribe of the manuscripts under consideration preferred to write such extensions on intervocalic medial letters. The most prominent is *g*, also used in many other manuscripts. Similarly, a small hook to the right at the bottom of certain letters is prevalent for the scribe: *k̲h̲*, *c̱*, *ḍ̱*, *ḍ̱h*, *ś̱*, *ṣ̱*, *s̱*, but also "non-hooked" forms exist (cf. 4.8 "Scribal Inconsisten-

3 After the Aśokan period, the distinction between these two sounds was leveled (Konow 1929: civ, Salomon 1999a: 121, Salomon 2000: 75, Glass 2007: 107) and the use of the retroflex or dental sign consequently no longer indicated phonetic values. The use of one or the other became a scribal preference (e.g., Salomon 1999a: 121, 124).

cies" below). Other modified forms of certain consonants, like *ṯ* or *ḏ* with a rightward extension of the foot, are usually not used. There are only a few examples of a modified form of *t* or *d*, namely *hakṣaṯi* for Skt. *bhaviṣyanti* in BC 4 and *(a)paribhuḏa-*, next to *(a)paribhuta-*, for Skt. *(a)paribhukta-* in BC 11 (see chapter 3 on paleography, p. 56).

4.6 Diacritic Additions to Consonant Signs

Horizontal lines placed above certain consonants to indicate consonantal clusters or modified pronunciation can be found in BC 11: *ṣ̄* = Skt. *ṣṇ* / P *ṇh*, *j̄* = Skt. *dhy* / P *(j)jh*, and *c̄* = Skt. *śc* / P *cch*. The underlying rule in Gāndhārī seems to be that Middle Indo-Aryan aspiration of a consonant (cluster) is indicated by a superscript line above a single consonant. In BC 4 there is only one instance of such a line, but the letter underneath it is broken off (4r15). Similarly in 4r28 *pac̄a*, the birch bark above the sign is broken off, so we cannot be sure if the horizontal line was written (as in 11r27 *pac̄a*) or not (as in 6v8 *pac̱i*). Since the spelling is closer to BC 11 with respect to the closing vowel, it has been transliterated as *pac̄a*. In the case of *siha* (Skt. *sneha* / P *sineha*) there is definitely no superscript line, thus *si⟨*ne⟩ha* is probably to be reconstructed. G *maja* or *maje* (Skt. *madhya-* / P *majjha-*) is written without a line above the *-j-*. The only other occurrence for Skt. *-dhy-* is BC 11 *aj̄atvia* = Skt. *adhyātmika-*.

4.7 Notation of Geminate Consonants

Geminates are principally not written, but are represented by a singular consonant. An indirect notation is used when writing *karpa* for Skt. *kalpa* / P *kappa* (for this peculiarity among the BL scrolls in general, cf. Salomon 1999a: 122 and 2000: 77).

4.8 Scribal Inconsistencies

There are several inconsistent spellings in BC 4:

- vacillation between *-kh/h-* in: *dukha-* (11×) / *duha-* (2×)
- vacillation between *-g̱/ø-* in: *-log̱a(*dhadu)* (1×) / *-loadhadu* (3×)
- vacillation between *-k/g̱-* in: *akicaṇa* (1×) / *ag̱icaṇa* (1×)
- vacillation between *-ḍ/ḏ-* in: *praoḍidave* (1×) / *praoḏidave* (3×)
- vacillation between *-ś/ś̱-* in: *(a)kuśala-* (2×) / *(a)kuś̱ala-* (6×)
- vacillation between *-s/s̱-* in: *ṇisamartha-* (5×) / *ṇis̱amartha-* (7×), *aṣ̱ivasidae* (1×) / *aṣ̱ivas̱idae* (1×)
- vacillation between *-s̱/ṣ̱-* in: *as̱ivasidae* (1×) / *aṣ̱ivas̱idae* (1×)
- use of *-ti* instead of *-di* for 3rd sg. endings (e.g., *hakṣati*; see p. 83 under "*d*")
- confusion between consonants: *pracaparamido* for *prañaparamido* (if this interpretation is correct)
- vacillation between *ca* / *ya* for Skt. *ca*
- general inconsistent spelling of: *arida* / *aride* / *arede*; *kerea* / *keraa* / *karaï* / *karae* / *karao* / *ko*; *aharea* / *aharae*; *ṇaś̱e* / *ṇaś̱ee* / *ṇaś̱ae* / *ṇaś̱ea*
- *durgadi* as well as *drogadi* (Skt. *dur-*), also *drugaṇa* (Skt. *dur-*)
- *mos̱imaḍa-* for *bos̱imaḍa-* seems to be a scribal error

In BC 11 the inconsistencies are:

- vacillation between *-h/ø-* in: *-suhami* (3×) / *-suami* (1×)
- vacillation between *-kh/k-* in: *asakhea* (1×) / *as̱akeṃa* (1×)
- vacillation between *-ś/s̱-* in: *ṇaśida* (2×) / *ṇas̱ida* (1×)
- vacillation between *-s/s̱-* in: *ṇisamartha-* (7×) / *ṇis̱amartha-* (1×)
- confusion between consonants: *achatvia* (1×) for *aǰatvia* (4×); *gada* (1×) for *gaḍa-* (5×); *chata* (1×) for *chade* (3×); *sarpasapatie* (1×) for *sarvasapati-* (10×)[4]
- occasional omission of post- or pre-consonantal *-r-*: *pa-* for *pra-* (*pajahidava*); Skt. *prati-* written as *pradi-*, *padi-* or *paḍi-* (*pradig̱arasuhe*, *pradibhava*, *padilabhe*, *paḏitiṭ́ha*, *paḏiladha*); probably *kaye* for *karye*
- other inconsistent spellings: *sa{r}gharya* instead of the prevalent *sagharya-*; *gro* and *roa* (for Skt. *roga-*)
- inconsistencies regarding vowels (see 4.9 "Confusion of Vowels" below)
- incorrectly placed anusvāras (*sasaṃra*, *as̱akeṃa*; see 4.1 "Anusvāra" above)
- metathesis of consonants: *sayavisa* for *sayas̱avi* (similarly, in BC 2 there is one instance of this being written *sayas̱avis̱a*)

In BC 6 the inconsistencies are:

- vacillation between *-p/v-* (?): perhaps one instance of *aparimaṇa* in addition to *avarimaṇa*, although the context is missing (and thus this could be a case of just *parimaṇa*)
- metathesis of consonants: *(*e)grag̱acitasa* for *egagracitasa*, as otherwise found
- one inconsistency regarding vowels (see 4.9 "Confusion of Vowels" below)

4.9 Confusion of Vowels

Some vowel confusions might be explained by the vowel marker having been forgotten. These are: BC 4 *aṇag̱ada* → *aṇag̱ade*, *paraṇirvahido* presumably → *pariṇirvahido* (cf. annotations, p. 174), *paribhaṣidava* → *paribhaṣidave*, *bos̱imaḍa* → *bos̱imaḍe*, *maha* → *mahi*, *ṣaha* → *ṣahi*; BC 11 *abhae* → *ubhae*, *uhaa* → *uhae*, *kica* → *kici*, *ṇeva* → *ṇevi*, *paracaïta* (3×) → *paricaïta*, *paracea* → *paricea*, *sudiṇag̱araṇa* → *sudiṇag̱areṇa*.

In BC 11 *parubhuteṇa* < *pari∘* (next to *aparibhuteṇa*) and *bhio* < *bhuyaḥ*, the vacillation between *i/u* can be explained linguistically (cf. chapter 5 on phonology).

Other confusions are: BC 11 *meme* → *mame*, *avaramiṇa* (2×) → *avarimaṇa*, *yidi* → *yadi*, *paricaeta* (2×) → *paricaïta*; BC 6 *payela-* for *peyala-* (?).

---

4 This might be an example for the usual development of intervocalic *p* > *v* but not seen before in combination with pre-consonantal *r*, where the *v* is normally retained. It could however also be explained by influence of the following *pa* in *-sapatie*, in that the sound or written word is being anticipated; cf. *sa{r}gharya* instead of *sagharya* in the same text.

4.10 Inconsistencies Regarding Pre- and Post-Consonantial *r*

In BC 11, *a<u>s</u>akeṃa karpa* seems to have been written first with *kra* before being amended to *karpa* (in the subsequent passage, another correction of *va* to *a* suggests a temporary inattentiveness of the scribe; additionally, the anusvāra in *a<u>s</u>akeṃa* has been applied to the wrong letter). In a few instances, pre-consonantal *r* has been omitted, but these are uncertain or can be explained in other ways. In 11r1–2 *kaye* is written twice, presumably for *karye*, since *kaye* = Skt. *kāya* seems unlikely due to context. However, the scribe wrote *karye* elsewhere. Perhaps *karye* is the historic spelling (with respect to the scribe) and *kaye* indicates the scribe's own pronunciation. Likewise, the writing of *pajahidava* for *prajahidava* may be considered as indicative of Middle Indo-Aryan, since *pa-* for *pra-* is a common observation in other Gāndhārī manuscripts (cf. e.g., Salomon 2008a: 121).

4.11 Oral/Aural Features

Most of the given examples are best explained by orality/pronunciation and not as problems of the graphic letter forms. They indicate the scribe's tendency to represent the pronunciation familiar to him (close to his own vernacular), rather than using historic spellings. Other irregularities, such as the wrong placement of anusvāras, indicate that the writing was done rather carelessly, or that the scribe was uncertain about the correct historic spelling.

Thus, some orthographical features could point to the scribe listening to an oral presentation, or reflect the scribe simultaneously uttering the text (audibly or silently) while writing it down. To some extent, the following examples work against the idea of the scribe relying on a written template:

- Vacillation between consonants that are not similar graphically, but are similar in sound, as for example, *achatvia* instead of *ajatvia* and *gada* instead of *gaḍa*[5] (other examples given above).
- Deaspiration. The graphemes of aspirated or nonaspirated akṣaras are usually clearly different (e.g., *kh* vs. *k*), but this is not the case for their pronunciation, since in Gāndhārī, and Middle Indo-Aryan in general, there was an apparent levelling of the phonetic distinction between aspirate/nonaspirate consonants.
- Confusion between vowels (e.g., *avaramiṇa* for *avarimaṇa*). I presume that confusing (two subsequent) vowels rather happens when listening, not when following a written template, which is simply copied.[6] In the case of the metathesis of consonants (*sayavisa* for *saya<u>s</u>avi*), however, either (a written or an audible source) is imaginable.
- Occasional omissions of post- or pre-consonantal *-r-* suggest to the scribe's own pronunciation rather than a written template.

---

[5] The former is an example for a phonetic merger of *-c(h)/j-* (see Glass 2007: 108), the latter, a loss of retroflexion, both commonly observed processes in Gāndhārī (Blair Silverlock, personal communication).

[6] Due to strokes often being connected (between basic sign and vowel marker, and also between two distinct letters), I dismiss the possibility of a writing process in which the diacritics were added in a second step, during which they could have been forgotten or attached to the wrong basic sign.

- Misspellings in anticipation of the following letter are more likely to happen when writing something down for the first time (hearing it or thinking it), rather than copying it from somewhere else (e.g., *sarpasapatie* for *sarvasapatie*).[7]

4.12 Haplography (Omissions)

Omissions of letters in BC 4 are predominantly in the middle of words and may simply have been forgotten in the process of writing: 4r12 *sarvasi⟨*ṇe⟩ha*, 4r14 *gaga⟨*ṇadi⟩valiasa̱maloadhadu*, 4r23 *yo praṇide ⟨*ka⟩rae*, 4r23 *ya⟨*ṣa⟩bhudehi*, 4v1 *ahiva⟨*di⟩dava*, and perhaps twice the conjunction *⟨*ca⟩* in 4v9 and 4v11. This is different in SĀ[S1], where the omissions are at the end of words, which led Andrew Glass to the conclusion "that the scribe's attention had already moved on to the next term" (Glass 2007: 104). In BC 11 there are only a few omissions of single letters: 11r25 *u⟨*a⟩ṇiṣa{ṣa}suhe*, 11v1 *prajahaṇapri⟨*di⟩* and 11v15 *driṭhadhami⟨*a⟩ saparaïaṣa*, all near the end of the line. In addition, sometimes conjunction particles like *ca* or *va* have been forgotten: 11r21 *divacakṣu va paracitañaṇa ⟨*va⟩*; 11r25 *pradigarasuhe ⟨*ca⟩ u⟨*a⟩ṇiṣa{ṣa}suhe ca*; 11v1 *pariñapridi prajahaṇapri⟨*di ca⟩*; 11v9 *ṇisamartha ⟨*ca⟩ dukha ca aśuha ca*. In one instance, *bhio* is written as just *bhi*, probably simply an omission of *-o*, but it might also be considered a different spelling (or a weakening of the final ending). There are no obvious omissions in BC 6.

4.13 Dittography (Erroneous Repetitions)

BC 4: *saṃsara*(4v5)*{ra}badhaṇaṇa* (cf. annotations, p. 189).

BC 11: *u⟨*a⟩ṇiṣa*(11r26)*{ṣa}suhe*, *labhadi {di}*, *dukha sa{r}gharya*.

The first two are easily explained by the beginning of a new line. For *labhadi* there is no obvious reason other than erroneous duplication. In *sa{r}gharya* the scribe may already have moved on to the next akṣara (cf. Allon 2001: 98 for other examples of anticipatory *r*).

4.14 Interlinear Insertions

BC 4 has a number of interlinear additions, mostly *maje ṇisamarthe*, etc. At first sight, one might assume a systematic process in which certain remarks or categorizations have been made, resulting in two planes of text. But there are other insertions as well, which add forgotten words that can be found in other places in normal lines of text. It seems that the scribe himself went through the text in a second revision process. Where he had forgotten something, he added it to make the text complete or more comprehensible. The same can be observed with regard to the numbers, which are sometimes found within lines and other times are added above them. The same holds true for BC 11. There are no interlinear insertions or glosses in BC 6.

The insertions in BC 4 are:

- 4r5 《 *(*trae sapuruṣa)darśaṇa hakṣati budhapracea (*trae drugaṇa ṇa hakṣati ·) ? ? ? ? mapurvagama (*asapuruṣa)*》
- 4r13 《*ṇisamartha*》

[7] Although, of course, in the theoretical case of a copying process, the original could have already contained the misspelling and the copyist then simply transferred the mistake without correcting it.

- 4r13 *ta《ra》ṇ{u}ia*
- 4r20 《*5*》
- 4r23 《*ede uhae mis̱o*》
- 4r25 《*maje ṇis̱amarthe* ·》 and 《*budhaṇa*》
- 4r25 《*maj(*e)*》
- 4r28 《*maje ca ṇ(*i)s̱amarth(*e) purve dukhe pac̱a dukhe ma(*je ca ṇi)samarthe purve aśuha pa(*c̱a a)śuha maja ṇisamartha sarvatra ithu kaṭave*》
- 4v4 《*maj(*e) ca ṇis̱a(*marthe)*》
- 4v9 《*codidave varjidave*》
- 4v10 《*matra*》
- 4v10 《*ca*》

The phrase *maje* or *maje ṇis̱amarthe*, etc., appears only in interlinear insertions. It is probably some kind of comment upon what is "useless," since it is inserted in the vicinity of *sapurus̱aṇa ṇaś̱ae*, *as̱apurus̱aṇa a(*hara)e* (both 4r25) and *kamapramuhaas̱apurus̱aṇa* (4v4) as well as *gagaṇadivalias̱amaloga(*dhadu) taraṇia śaki uadiaṇa* (4r12–13). In one passage (4r28), it seems that an explanation is being given of what the passage means, namely to apply the following formula: "in the middle useless, before painful, afterwards painful, in the middle useless, before unpleasant, afterwards unpleasant" (cf. annotations, p. 185).

In BC 11, the interlinear insertions are:
- 11r32 《 *suverao* 》
- 11r48 《 *ṇis̱amarthavidimiśasuhe* 》
- 11v15 《 *loieṇa tava karaṇeṇa* 》
- 11v17 《 *ṣade* 》
- 11v17 《 *1* 》

4.15 Corrections

In BC 4 at the end of lines r14 and r15, some letters have been overwritten. The second layer of writing includes the same letters as well as corrected ones:
- (1) 4r14 *mokṣas̱apati* → *mokṣasapati*
- (2) 4r15 *paḏhamacitupade* → *paḏhamacitupade* (without rewriting the *i*-vowel)

Other corrections are:
- (3) 4r4 *trae kus̱a* → *trae ca kuś̱ ala*
- (4) 4r21 *dharmo* → *dharme*
- (5) 4r22 *hacadi ?* → *hakṣadi ◦ 4 2*

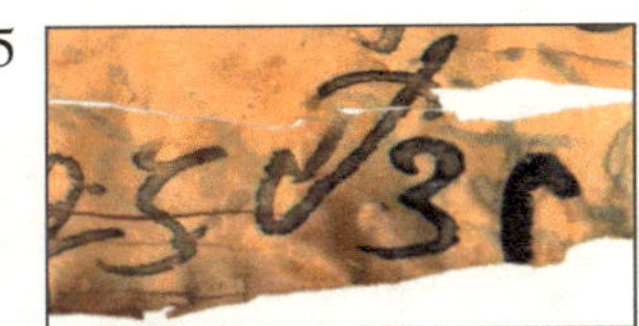

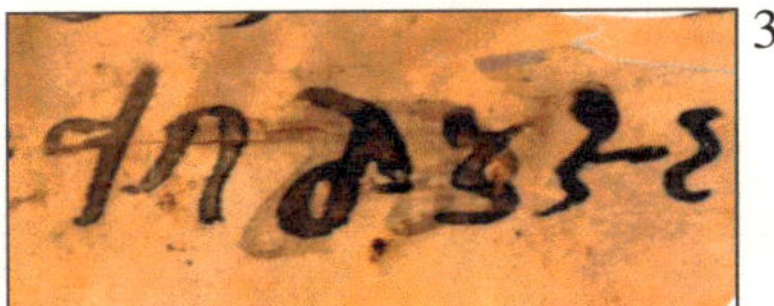

Fig. 29. Corrections in BC 4.

BC 11: In the sequence *sarva aśuhe aṇubhavi{da}ea sarve śuhe ṇa bhavi{da}ea sarva akuśale aṇubhaviea*, the first two occurrences of the same verb are very difficult to read (see figures below). Since in the following parallel phrase, the word *aṇubhaviea* is clearly written, it is assumed that the scribe first wrote *aṇubhaviea*, then corrected it (erroneously) to *aṇubhavidaea*, after which the *da* was deleted.

3

2

1

Fig. 30. Corrections in BC 11.

Other corrections in which a letter is not inserted but written over another one involve the addition of vowel marks (e.g., 11r17 *aadiea* > *uadiea*), the emendation of similar graphemes (11r35 *vacida* > *acida*) or simply the rewriting of a wrong letter (11r8 *yasade* > *yavade*). In 11v10 the scribe began to write *avarari* before amending it to *avaramiṇa* for *avarimaṇa*. In 11v8 *viṣ̄ajajita* the first *ja* is perhaps to be replaced by the following *ji*, although this remains uncertain, since the *ja* is clearly written and the *i*-vowel marker may have simply been applied to the already written consonant.

4.16 Nonphonetic Traces of Ink

BC 4 is relatively clean and void of dripped ink. BC 11, on the other hand, is full of stray and smudged drops of ink, especially on the recto. BC 6 is free of spilled ink except for one unintentional dot at the end of v3.

Chapter 5

Phonology

In the following, the phonetic features of all three texts are summarized. The texts belong to the middle Gāndhārī period and contain typical features observed also in other Gāndhārī manuscripts.[1] Due to their application of *s*/*s̱* they may be considered close to the Robert Senior collection. In their use of the reflex *śp* they are similar to the Niya documents and the British Library fragments.

5.1 Vowels

5.1.1 Alternations

-am > *-u*. This would seem to be the normal reflex *-o* for Skt. *-am*, but written with *-u*, this being phonetically similar to *-o* (see below, "u/o"). Attested forms are: BC 4, BC 6 *ithu* = Skt. *ittham*; BC 11 *ahu*, BC 6 *aho* (?) = Skt. *aham*; BC 11 *amahu*, *amaho*, *asvahu* = Skt. *asmabhyam*; BC 11 *śpahu*, *śpaho* = Skt. *svayam*.

-ā > *-i*. There are a few examples of adverbs ending in *-i*. Two cases have in common that they can be derived from the ending *-ā* in Vedic Sanskrit and Pali: BC 6 *aji* = Skt. *adya*, Vedic *adya* / *adyā*, P *ajja* / *ajjā*; BC 6 *paci̱* = Skt. *paścāt*, Vedic *paścā*, P *pacchā*. Another case, namely BC 11 *ṇevi* = Skt. *naiva*, might also be related to a long vowel at the end; cf. MW s.v. *eva*: "in the Saṃhitā also *evā*"). For *yavi*, which should correspond to Skt. *yāvat*, P *yāva*, no long vowel at the end is attested, but perhaps there was a general tendency to write adverbs ending in *-ă(t)* with an *i*-vowel at the end. (Alternation of final *a* and *i* is also attested in some of the BL manuscripts; cf. Allon 2001: 74, Lenz 2003: 167.) In both instances in BC 6 and BC 11, *yavi* is written after *sakṣiteṇa*, whereas elsewhere *yava* is written. Thus one might suspect a special meaning or use of *yavi* as opposed to *yava*. In other Gāndhārī manuscripts, however, this is not the case: In the BL avadānas, *yavi* is most often used at the beginning of sentences and means "then" (Lenz 2010: 64), with one exception, where it is used in an abbreviation formula in the sense of "up to" (Lenz 2010: 81). In the BL verse commentary (Nird[L2], Baums 2009) it is used in the sense of "until."

[1] In the early stage (best attested in Aśoka's major rock edicts at Shahbazgarhi and Mansehra), intervocalic consonants were mostly retained as in the original Old Indo-Aryan form. In the middle stage (inscriptions and manuscripts, first century BCE to the middle of the second century CE), intervocalic consonants are voiced, elided, or modified to fricatives. In the late stage (later second and early third centuries CE), phonological developments are masked by re-Sanskritization (cf. Salomon 2008b).

ā > o. A change from *ā* to *o* is possibly seen in BC 4 *sahoro* = Skt. *saṃ(b)hāra-*, but the equivalence is not completely certain. Nevertheless, the alternation is theoretically possible and documented elsewhere in cases of the nominal ending *-ā* = *-o* (Brough 1962: § 22, Salomon 2000: 80) but also in medial positions (von Hinüber 2001: § 121, e.g., Dhp^{K} 161 *-[mo]ṇa[so]* = Skt. *-mānaso* or Dhp^{K} 284 *samokadu* = Skt. *samāgata-*).

i > e. An example for this alternation might be BC 4 *siha* for *sneha* (in other manuscripts written *s̄eha*), but it is more likely that it should be reconstructed as *si⟨*ṇe⟩ha*. In BC 11, *paricaeta* instead of *paricaïta* seems to be written twice.

i > u and *u > i*. In *parubhuteṇa* (next to *aparibhuteṇa*) = Skt. *paribhukteṇa* the change *i > u* is the result of labialization (von Hinüber 2001: § 157); in *bhio* = Skt. *bhūyaḥ* / P *bhiyyo* the *u* is palatalized to *i* in the vicinity of palatal sounds (Oberlies 2001: § 7.11) and the *y* is dropped: *bhūyaḥ* > **bhiyaḥ* / P *bhiyyo* > *bhiyo* > *bhio*.

u/o. Generally in Gāndhārī texts, *u* and *o* alternate frequently (Allon 2001: 76, Salomon 2008a: 104–5). While in some cases this seems to be a distinctive habit of certain scribes (e.g., "hand 1 of the BL" writes *aṇo-* instead of *aṇu-*), most such variations seem to be "a more or less arbitrary graphic alternation" (Salomon 2008a: 105). In the Khotan *Dharmapada*, usually *-o* instead of *-u* is found after *h* and *pr*, e.g., *amaho* (Burrow 1937: § 4).[2] Burrow remarks that the signs for post-consonantic *-u*/*-o* are very similar, so probably *-u* is generally intended. Since the graphemes for both *h* and *pr* are open to the right and have a closed curve where the *u*-vowel marker is normally attached, the reason for this vowel change could indeed be merely graphic. In BC 4 there are two occurrences of an unambiguous *hu* (*hurahu*) and several instances of *ho* with a bent stroke to the left, which without comparison could also be transliterated as *hu*: *ohoro*, *(*o)horo*, *o(*ho)ro*. This term may be related to P *hura*, although the prefix *o-* remains problematic (cf. annotations, p. 189).

5.1.2 Developments of Old Indo-Aryan *ṛ*

Original OIA *ṛ* is represented as *(r)a* or *(r)i* and perhaps also as *(r)u*:

ṛ > a	BC 4: *śpadimo* = Skt. *smṛtimat*, P *satīmaṃ* (cf. Sn 212)
	BC 6: *phaṣadi* = Skt. *spṛśati*, P *phusati* / *phassati*
	BC 11: *uṣ̄ata* (word uncertain), *tati* = Skt. *tṛpti* / P *titti*
ṛ > ra	BC 6: *mradua-* = Skt. *mṛduka-*, P *muduka-*
	BC 11: *parigrahida* = Skt. *parigṛhīta-*, P *pariggahīta-*
ṛ > i	BC 4: *akicaṇa*, *agicaṇa*, *kicaṇa* = Skt. *(a)kṛtya-*, P *(a)kicca-*
	BC 6: *kica*, *kicakica* = Skt. *(a)kṛtya-*, P *(a)kicca-*

[2] Cf. also Brough 1962: § 21, who likewise gives several examples for *hu* written as *ho* in medial position (regularly *baho-*) and both *-hu*/*-ho* in word-final syllables. The Gāndhārī ending *-o* is explained by Baums (2009: 127) as a merger of MIA word-final *-u* and *-o*.

ṛ > ri BC 4: *aśpriṣaṇaṇa* = BHS *aspṛśana-*, P *aphusana-*
BC 4/6/11: *driṭha-* = Skt. *dṛṣṭa-*, P *diṭṭha-*
BC 6: *pragri(*de)* = Skt. *prakṛta-*, P *pakata-*

ṛ > ru BC 4: *vrude* = Skt. *vṛ(t)tam* (uncertain; cf. annotations, p. 168)
BC 11: *matupayeaṣi* = Skt. *mātṛ-* ? (unclear)

5.1.3 Reductions (Monophthongization)

No long vowels have been written. Among the diphthongs, *ai* and *au* are regularly reduced to *e* or *o*. Combinations with *-y-* are usually reduced to *e* or *i* ("palatalization"; cf. Brough 1962: § 37, Salomon 2000: 79, 86). For the elision of *-y-* in *bhio* = Skt. *bhūyaḥ* / P *bhiyyo*, see above "*i > u* and *u > i*." For other elisions of *-y-*, see 5.4 "Anaptyxis (Svarabhakti)" below.

The sequence *-aya-/-ayi-* in word medial position is reduced to *e* or *i*. Most frequently, this occurs in causative (or class X) verbal forms. In the case of BC 4 *codidavo* and *varjidavo*, it is uncertain whether they are based on the base verb or the causative.

The reduction *ava-* to *o-* is common also in other MIA dialects. Across compound boundaries (including prefixes and the negative particle) there is no reduction. Thus, BC 11 *avaśi* is stable because of Skt. *a-vaśvyam*, *aṇavaṭie* because of Skt. *an-ā-vartika-*.

In the following chart the occurrences documenting vowel changes are summarized.

Table 8. Gāndhārī reflexes of vowels.

Skt.	Gāndhārī	Examples
ay	*i*	BC 4: *io* BC 11: *citiadi*
	e	BC 4: *-pracea* BC 11: *avayea, aśrea, uayea-*
ya	*i*	BC 6: *-aïdaṇa* BC 11: *aïdaṇa, khaïti*
	e	BC 4: *asaṃkhedehi, kṣae* BC 6: *uadae*
yā	*a*	BC 4: *pialo* (including *e > i*) BC 11: *akhaïta, khaïti, pialo* (including *e > i*)
	e	BC 4: *asaṃkhedehi*
iy	*i* [or: *y* > Ø]	BC 4: *bhio* (including *ū > i*) BC 6: *pria-*
yi	*i* [or: *y* > Ø]	BC 4: *kaïa, saparaïa* BC 11: *akhaïta, dhaṇaïta*
ye	*e* [or: *y* > Ø]	BC 4: *vivaryaeṇa* BC 11: *aṣakeṃa, asakhea*
aya	*e*	BC 4: *varedi*
ayi	*i*	BC 4: *ahivadidava, upadidave, codidava* (?), *deśidavo, praoḏidave, varjidava-* (?) BC 6: *karitava* BC 11: *bhavidave*
	e	BC 4: *dharetrami*
av(a)	*o*	BC 4: *hoita* BC 6: *bhoti/bhodi, samoṣaṇeṇa* BC 11: *osagra, olaïa* (?) , *-samoṣaṇa-, hoidava*

5.2 Consonants

5.2.1 Deaspiration

Before Prakrit was imported into Central Asia, the majority of intervocalic aspirates had become *h* (Burrow 1937: § 27).[3] In BC 4, BC 6, and BC 11 this applies for *-kh-*, *-gh-* and *-bh-* (as well as *bh-*): e.g., *uhae*, *lahuṭ́haṇa*, *pramuha*, *śuha*, *suha*, *hakṣati* (see also detailed notes on "*bh*" on p. 83).

A further reduction is *duḥkha* > *dukkha* > *dukha* > *duha*. The writing of *dukha* is more prevalent, but *duha* is as well attested in other manuscripts, such as Dhp^{K}. BC 4 has both *dukha* and *duha*, side by side, although *dukha* is more frequent. BC 6 and BC 11 only use *dukha*. Again, in a next step, the *h* is elided, as for example in BC 6 and BC 11 in the variation *sua* for *sukha*, and in BC 4 *akṣati* for otherwise *hakṣati* = Skt. *bhaviṣyanti* (cf. Burrow 1937: § 28). Further deaspirations are: BC 6 *spura* = Skt. *sphura(t)*; BC 11 *as̱akeṃa* (along with *asakhea*) = Skt. *asaṃkhyeya-*, *hoḏe* = Skt. *hoḍha-*, *amuḏa* and *muḏeasa* = Skt. *(a)mūḍha-* (?). In BC 4 *uadi* is related to Skt. *upadhi*, but may be phonologically developed from P *upādi* rather than being an instance of deaspiration.

5.2.2 Single Consonants

In initial position, single consonants usually do not change. Parts of compounds are often treated as word-initials.[4] Word-initial exceptions to this rule are: *akṣati* / *hakṣati* / *hakṣadi* = Skt. *bhaviṣya(n)ti*; *vaṇa* = Skt. *punar* / P *paṇa*; *vi* = Skt./P *(a)pi*; *ṣada* = BHS *śāta* / P *śāta* (?); *ṣaṣada* = Skt. *śāśvata* / P *sassata*; *ho* = Skt. *khalu* / P *kho*[5]. Single consonants in medial position are generally voiced (e.g., *k* > *g*, *t* > *d*, *ṭ* > *ḍ*), and *p* becomes *v*.

The following chart summarizes the reflexes of single (mostly) intervocalic consonants as encountered in the manuscripts BC 4, BC 6, and BC 11. Consonants that do not change are not listed (such as *r*, *v*, or *l*). The expected changes do not occur in some 3rd pers. sg. endings (for examples, see notes under "*d*" on p. 83). The general convergence of *t* and *d* can also be seen in *chata* for otherwise *chada* = Skt. *chanda*, or *yati* for otherwise *yadi* = Skt. *yadi*.

Table 9. Gāndhārī reflexes of single consonants.

Skt.	Gāndhārī	Examples
k	*k*	BC 4: *akica(*ṇa)*
	g̱	BC 4: *agicaṇa*, *(*sarva)g̱areṇa*, *ahig̱akṣidave*, *log̱ado*, *l(*o)g̱a(*dhadu)* BC 6: *eg̱agracitasa*, *ṭ́hidig̱ica* BC 11: *-ag̱areṇa*, *viveg̱a-*, *pradig̱ara-*
	Ø	BC 4: *aloa-*, *kaïa-*, *kavalaeṇa*, *khaḍaeṇa*, *driṭhadhamia-*, *loadhadu*, *valia*, *śoa* BC 6: *amaṇas̱iara*, *taṇua*, *-dhamiasaparaïa-*, *pariapo*, *bhaṭarea-*, *mradua-* BC 11: *aj̄atvia*, *aṇavaṭie*, *avedea*, *(a)sagaṇia-*, *cedas̱ia*, *driṭhadhamia-*, *loutareṇa*, *sacea*

---

3 Cf. also Glass 2007: 108 ("deocclusion," Lenz 2010: 28).

4 E.g., BC 4 *praña-paramida*. Counterexample: BC 4 *agicaṇa* as well as *akicaṇa*. The general pattern in Gāndhārī is the non-voicing across a word boundary, but variations are not uncommon (cf. Salomon 2000: 82, referring to Konow 1929: xcviii and Brough 1962: 91, 106–7, that is §§ 38, 66).

5 The initial *kh* should be stable, but here it is treated as intervocalic in an enclitic word (Salomon 2008a: 109 and 150–51, as well as Brough 1962: §§ 48, 68).

Skt.	Gāndhārī	Examples
kh	*kh*	BC 11: *asakhea-*
	k	BC 11: *as̱akeṃa-*
	h	BC 4: *pramuha-*, *suha-* BC 6: *suha-* BC 11: *pramuha-*, *suha-*; word-initial: *ho*
	∅	BC 6: *sua* BC 11: *-suami*, *sue*
g	*g*	BC 4: *durgadi*, *drugaṇa*, *drogadi*, *-purvagama*, *sugadi* BC 6: *-akuhicagamaṇa* BC 11: *-akuhicagamaṇa*, *(*a)varimaṇaguṇavidimiśa*, *durgadi*, *sugada-*
	g̱	BC 4: *aṇag̱ada-*, *jag̱ariaṇa*, *-log̱a-*, *virag̱a* BC 6: *akuhicaag̱amaṇa-*, *arog̱a*, *rag̱a* BC 11: *akuhicaag̱amaṇa-*, *aṇag̱ada*, *atog̱ada*, *viveg̱agadasa*
	gr	BC 4: *viragraaṇuśaśe* BC 11: *viveg̱averagrasuha-*, *veragrasuha-*
	y	BC 11: *kamabhoyi*
	h	BC 4: *juhos̱idave*
	∅	BC 4: *apalios̱eṇa*, *-droaca-*, *palios̱e* BC 6: *droaca*, *droatie*, *palios̱eṇa* BC 11: *aroa*, *-droaca-*, *paricae*, *suverao*
gh	*kẖ*	BC 6: *akẖada-*
	h	BC 4: *lahuṭ́haṇa-*
c	*j*	BC 6: *ja* for *ca* (?)
	y	BC 4: *moyea*, *ya* for *ca* (in addition to *ca*) BC 11: *amoyaṇa* (?), *avayea-*, *uayea-*
j	*j*	BC 11: *-drujaṇa-*, *pajahidava*, *prajahaṇa-*, *prajahati*, *prajahita*, *bahujaṇasas̱araṇadukha*
	y	BC 11: *pariyaṇeo*, *parvayidehi*
	∅	BC 4: *paricaïta*, *pariceaṇa* BC 11: *paricaïta*, *paricaïdave*, *-bio/-bie*
ṭ	*ḍ̱*	BC 4: *trikoḍ̱i* BC 6: *kuḍ̱ae*, *kuḍ̱eami*
ḍh	*ḍ̱*	BC 11: *amuḍ̱a* (?), *muḍ̱easa* (?), *hoḍ̱e*
t	*t*	BC 4: *paḍ̱itiṭ́ha* BC 6: *karitava* (?) BC 11: *ete*
	d	BC 4: *adide*, *idara-*, *eda-*, *-cadura-*, *-cedas̱ia*, *jadi*, *durgadi*, *drogadi-*, *-dhadu-*, *prañaparamida-*, *pridi*, *viś̱adi*, *śpadimo*, *ṣaṣadaeṇa*, *satidehi*, *sugadi-*, *-hida* BC 6: *-aïdaṇa*, *jadi-* BC 11: *aïdaṇa*, *adida-*, *eda-*, *edes̱a*, *jado*, *-dhadu*, *padilabhe*, *paramida-*, *pradig̱ara-*, *pradibhave* (?), *pridi*, *vidimiśa*, *ṣaṣadae*, *sugada-*, *-hida-* generally: verbal endings in 3rd sg. (*-di*), gdv. (*-dava*), pp. (*-da*)
	ḍ̱	BC 4: *paḍ̱i-* (retroflex in combination with *pra-*) BC 6: *vipaḍ̱is̱ara* (retroflex in combination with *pra-*)
	s (?)	BC 4: *śpabhavasa* BC 6: *abodhasa*, *abhavasa*, *avikṣitacitasa*, *egagracitasa*
	∅	BC 4: *praïṭhavamaṇa* BC 11: *acitieṇa* (?), *citiae* (?), *vayaeṇa* (?)

Skt.	Gāndhārī	Examples
th	*s*	BC 11: *kasa*
	s̱	BC 4: *yas̱a-* BC 6: *kas̱a*, *tas̱e*, *yas̱a*, *yas̱ave* BC 11: *as̱a va*, *kas̱a*, (*sayavisa* misspelled for *sayas̱avi*)
	ḑh	BC 4: *paḑhama* (retroflex in combination with *pra-*)
d	*t*	BC 4: *kahati*, *hakṣati* BC 6: *kareati*, *upajati*, *bhoti*, *siati* BC 11: *khaveati*, *ṇaś̱eati*, *yati* (1×)
	d	BC 6: *yadi* BC 11: *yadi* (4×), *yidi* (for *yadi*, 1×) all other cases of Skt. *-d-*
dh	*dh*	BC 4: *driṭhadhamia-*, *b(*u)dhadharmasagho* BC 6: *driṭhadhamia-* BC 11: *aparihaṇadhama*, *driṭhadhamia-*, *śidaüṣadharaṇa-*
	s̱	BC 4: *ataras̱aïśati*, *apalios̱eṇa*, *as̱ivasidae*, *bos̱imaḍa-*, *bos̱is̱atva*, *bos̱a* BC 6: *palios̱eṇa-*, *samos̱aṇeṇa* BC 11: *aparas̱iṇa-*, *asas̱araṇe*, *-samos̱aṇa-*, *bahujaṇasas̱araṇa-*, *bos̱i*, *svaas̱iṇa-*
	ş	BC 4: *aşivas̱idae*
p	*p*	BC 4: *apalios̱eṇa*, *ekadutracadurepaṃcaṣaha*, *prañaparamida*, *suparibhaşidavo* BC 6: *aparimaṇa*, *paripuṇa* BC 11: *atvahisaparahisa-*, *aparas̱iṇa-*, *aparibhujitrea-*, *aparibhuta-*, *aparihaṇadhama*, *aprañati*, *amitrahoḑeapoşaṇam*, *ṇaṇaparigrahidia*, *dupadua*
	v	BC 4: *aṇuvadaṇa*, *avarimaṇa-*, *kavalaeṇa*, *paveṇa*, *vivaryaeṇa*; word-initial: *vaṇa*, *vi* BC 6: *avarimaṇa*, *karavidae*, *vovaś̱amo*; word-initial: *vaṇa*, *vi* BC 11: *ajavi*, *(a)ruva-*, *avaṇao*, *avayeasa*, *avarimaṇa*, *avi*, *uavati*, *ṭ́havaṇia*, *sayavisa* (for *sayas̱avi*); word-initial: *vaṇa*, *vi*
	d	BC 4: *sudiṇoamo* BC 6: *sudi(*ṇa)* BC 11: *sudiṇa-*
	∅	BC 4: *uadaṇa*, *uadi*, *uadiaṇa*, *uadiṇae*, *uekṣidae*, *sudiṇoamo* BC 6: *uadae* BC 11: *uayea-*, *uaṇişa*, *uavati*
b	*b*	BC 4: *tribos̱ae* BC 6: *abodhasa* BC 11: *aȷ̄atvabahira*, *dukhabio*
	v	BC 6: *savalo*
bh	*bh*	BC 4: *paribhaşidava-*, *paribhaşehi*, *paribhujidave*, *margabhavaṇe*, *śpabhavasa*; word-initial: *bhavid.* BC 6: word-initial: *bhava*, *bhaveadi*, *bhoti* BC 11: *aṇubhavaṇa*, *aṇubhavavida*, *aṇubhaviea*, *(*a)ṇubhavidave*, *(a)paribhuteṇa/-bhuḏasa*, *aparibhujitrea*, *abhae* (for *ubhaye*); word-initial: *bhaviea*, *bhavidave*, *bhaviśadi*, *bhave*, *bhavea*, *bhodu*
	vh	BC 4: *lavha*, *lavheti* BC 11: *avhiña-*
	h	BC 4: *ahigakṣidave*, *ahivadidava*, *aśuha-*, *uhae*, *śuha-*; word-initial: *hakṣati/hakṣadi*, *hoita* BC 11: *aśuha*, *uhae*, *śuha*; word-initial: *hoidava/hoidave*, *hodu*, *hode*, *hakṣati*
	∅	BC 4: *aïvadida*; word-initial: *akṣati*

Skt.	Gāndhārī	Examples
ś	*ś*	BC 4: *akuśala-* (1×), *kuśala-* (3×), *deśidavo* BC 11: *akuśale* (1×), *ṇaśida* (2×)
	ś̱	BC 4: *akuś̱ala-* (5×), *(a)śpriś̱aṇa-*, *kuś̱ala-* (3×), *ṇaś̱ae* (2×), *ṇaś̱e*, *ṇaś̱ea*, *ṇaś̱ee*, *deś̱a*; word-initial: *ś̱aṣ̱idava* BC 6: *(a)kuś̱ala-*, *drudeś̱a-*, *vovaś̱amo* BC 11: *kuś̱ala-* (4×), *ṇaś̱e*, *ṇaś̱iea*, *ṇaś̱ida* (1×), *ṇaś̱eati*, *deś̱a-*
	ś̳	BC 4: *ṇaś̳ae* (1×)
	ṣ	BC 4: word-initial: *ṣada*, *ṣaṣada-* BC 6: *phaṣadi* (in combination with preceding *ṛ* > *a*) BC 11: word-initial: *ṣade*/ *ṣado*, *ṣadimeṇa*, *ṣaṣada-*
ṣ	*ṣ*	BC 4: *paribhaṣidave* (1×); *-ṣa-* (treated as word-initial) BC 6: *d(*u)ṣaṇa* BC 11: *piṣita*
	ṣ̱	BC 4: *-ṇiṣ̱aṇa*, *-doṣ̱ehi*, *-paribhaṣ̱idava-* (4×), *paribhaṣ̱ehi*, *-puruṣ̱a-*, *śeṣ̱ae* BC 6: *doṣ̱a*, *śeṣ̱a* BC 11: *-apoṣ̱aṇa-*, *amiṣ̱a-*, *uaṇiṣ̱a-*, *edeṣ̱a*, *eṣ̱a*, *teṣ̱a*, *tuṣ̱e*, *doṣ̱a-*, *bheṣ̱aje*, *ṣ̱ahi*
s	*s*	BC 4: *as̱ivasidae*
	s̱	BC 4: *as̱atia-*, *as̱apuruṣ̱a-*, *as̱ivas̱idae*, *gagaṇadivalias̱ama*, *cedas̱ia*, *bos̱is̱atva*, *sarvas̱atva-* BC 6: *jaṇas̱i*, *duśas̱i*, *maṇas̱a*, *rajas̱i* BC 11: *as̱akeṃa*, *cedas̱ia-*, *sarvas̱atva-*
h	*ś̱*	BC 4: *iś̱emi* = Skt. *iha* (exception)
	s̱	BC 11: *pras̱aṇa-* = Skt. *prahāṇa-* (exception and confusion with Skt. *pradhāṇa-*)

Notes

k. Adjective endings in *-aka* are regularly rendered as *-ea* in Gāndhārī (*aka* > *aya* > *ea*). In the cardinal number *eka*, the *-k-* is usually retained.[6] There is only one exception in BC 6, where *egagra-* (Skt. *ekāgra-*) is found, although another word, namely *ekakalava*, is written with *-k-*. Maybe the long vowel in *ekāgra-* accounts for this.

g/*g̱*. When Gāndhārī manuscripts were initially being studied, *g* and *g̱* were not differentiated consistently by every editor because the two signs did not imply a difference in meaning. Since they do reflect a phonological difference, in this publication a distinction is maintained. Normal *g* is used at the beginning of words or compound parts, e.g., BC 4 *su-gadi*, BC 6 *a-gaḍa-saña*, BC 11 *-akuhica-gamaṇa*. The *g̱* with a rightward extension at the base of the stem is used in almost all other cases, that is, when found in an intervocalic position (e.g., BC 4/11 *aṇag̱ada*, BC 11 *ag̱amaṇa*). The few cases of an intervocalic position written with normal *g*, such as BC 4 *arogaṇa*, *gaga-* and *nagao*, go back to consonant clusters.

6 "The tendency to preserve *k* in *eka-* is widespread in MIA, including Gāndhārī, where it was presumably pronounced *ekka* (Konow 1929: xcviii; Burrow 1937: 6). The same alternation in the forms of the word for 'one' is also attested in the Central Asian Kharoṣṭhī documents (Stein 1935–37: 763; Norman 1992b: 200) and is reflected among modern Dardic and Nuristani languages (Berger 1992: 246)" (Salomon 2000: 82).

gh. There are two possible reflexes of singular *gh*. It is either written with *-h-* (BC 4 *lahuṭ́haṇa* = Skt. *laghūtthāna*), confirming a development observed in other manuscripts, as for example Anav[L] (Salomon 2008a: 110). Or it is written with a modified form of *-kh-*, as in BC 6 *(aṇ) ak̲h̲ada* = Skt./P *(an)āghāta*.

In BC 11 is found *sagharya*, which may be based on the underlying cluster *ṅgh* > *ṃh* (Skt. **saṅghārya* / **saṃhārya* in the sense of Skt. *saṃhāraṇa*, P *saṅgharaṇa* = *saṃharaṇa*). Alternatively, G *sagharya* might be connected to Skt. *saṃskārya* in the sense of Skt. *abhisaṃskāra* / P *abhisaṅkhāra*, this supported by the equivalent *saghara* = Skt. *saṃskāra* / P *saṅkhāra* in the Khotan *Dharmapada*.

c. In initial positions, *c* is retained. In a few instances of enclitic *ca*, the consonant is treated as intervocalic and rendered as *y*. Word-internally, in BC 4 the only example for *-c-* > *-y-* seems to be *moyea*, although it is unclear what it corresponds to exactly, namely Skt. *mocakaḥ* or *mocayet* (P *moceyya*) or *mocāya*. In BC 11, *amoyaṇa* may be equivalent to Skt. *amocana*, more certain are *avayea-* < Skt. *apacaya-* and *uayea-* < Skt. *upacaya-*. The remaining occurrences of intervocalic *c* are explainable by clusters: *vucadi* = Skt. *ucyate*; others go back to *-ty-*.

j. Intervocalic *-j-* is regularly represented by *-y-*, which can be dropped (or represented only by *-i-*). Examples for *-j-* > *-y-* are BC 11 *parvayidehi* = Skt. *pravrajita-* and *pariyaṇeo* = Skt. ~ *parijñeya-*. In BC 4 *puyamaṇa*, *-jy-* has first been assimilated to *jj*, then reduced to *j* and changed to *y*. Examples for *-j-* > ø are BC 4/11 *paricaïta* and similar derivatives of Skt. *parityaj*, or BC 11 *-bio*/*-bie* for Skt. *bīja-*. In BC 11 *pajahidava*, *prajahaṇa*, *prajahati*, and *prajahita*, it is likely that *-j-* is being treated as an initial after a prefix. Of uncertainty is the exact equivalence to *viṣ̄ajajita* in BC 11 (cf. annotations, p. 226).

t. Normally, *t* in medial position becomes voiced in Gāndhārī (*t* > *d*). The Old Indo-Aryan prefix *prati-* is regularly rendered as *paḍi-* (and one instance in BC 11, as *padi-*, in *padilabhe*). Once or twice it is rendered *pradi-* (BC 11 *pradigara*, *pradibhave* if this reading is correct), and once it is elided, resulting in *praï-* (BC 4 *praïṭ́havamaṇa*). Both forms, *paḍi-* and *pradi-*, occur also side by side in the BL *Ekottarikāgama*-type fragments (Allon 2001: 82), as well as in the Khotan *Dharmapada* and the Niya documents (*paḍi-* and *prati-*). The spelling *praï-* is also attested in the word *praïstaveti* in the Reliquary Inscription of Caṃdrabhi (found in Kalawan and dated 87/88 CE; last edited in Baums 2012: 236, no. 29).

Another case of elision of intervocalic *-t-* appears to be BC 11 *acitieṇa* = Skt. *acintitena*, and possibly also *citiae* = Skt. *cintitāya* (cf. annotations on 11r14 *citiae*, p. 202, for further remarks) and *vayaeṇa* for *vayieṇa* = Skt. *vyayitena* (?).

Original *t* is retained in clusters with *tr*, although it is sometimes difficult to tell if not indeed *dr* was written (cf. chapter 3 on paleography). Moreover, *t* is retained in the cluster *tm* and/or *tv* (cf. chapter 3 on paleography), in absolutive endings (Skt. *-itvā* / P *-itta*), which are written as *-ta*, as well as in other clusters in which only *t* is written in Kharoṣṭhī: *kt*, *tt*, *nt*, *pt*.

There are two cases in which *-t-* is possibly retained in a demonstrative pronoun. These are: 11r6 *ete* and 11r14 *eta*. In the first case both syllables are hardly legible and the following two syllables are also unclear, so there is no context and the translation remains uncertain. In the second case the separation of letters is open to question; they are currently transliterated as two words, one ending in *-e* followed by *ta* (11r14 *ciri me ta ṣado*).

d. Original single intervocalic *d* is usually stable in Gāndhārī. Examples for original *-d-* being irregularly written as *-t-* are: BC 11 *yati*, next to *yadi*, for Skt. *yadi* (cf. Burrow 1937: § 129) and *chata*, next to *chade*, for Skt. *chanda-*. Sometimes the irregular ending *-ti* (instead of *-di*) for 3rd sg. is used: BC 4 *kahati*, *hakṣati*; BC 6 *kareati*, *upajati*, *bhoti*, *siati*; BC 11 *khaveati*, *ṇaś̱eati*.

th. Original intervocalic *th* becomes *s̱*. In the cluster of semivowel *r* before *th* it is retained (e.g., *artha-*). In BC 4, Skt. *prathama* becomes *paḏhama*, similar to P *paṭhama*.

dh. Original intervocalic *dh* as a rule becomes *s̱*. There is apparently one exception: BC 11 *sudhu*. This may be an equivalent to G *sudha*, which is (according to Burrow 1937: § 91) an indeclinable with the meaning of "only." It is documented only in the Niya documents and its etymology is unclear (Burrow 1937: 131). It is possible that the *dh* is retained here because it is being treated as a word initial (*su-dhu*), or because it stems from P *suddha*.

p. Intervocalic *p* is most frequently represented by *v*. The rendering *svapna* > *sudiṇa* is explained by the further development *p* > *v* > *d* (cf. annotations, p. 166). Elision is common in the case of the OIA prefix *upa-*: BC 4 *uadaṇa* = Skt. *upādāna-*; *uadi* = P *upādi* (Skt. *upadhi*); *uadiaṇa* = Skt. *upādiyāna-*; *uadiṇae* = BHS *upādinna-*; *uekṣidae* = Skt. *upekṣita-*; *sudiṇoama* = Skt. *svapnopama*. If preceded by a negative prefix, *upa* is treated as medial: *aṇuvadaṇa* = Skt. *anupādāna-*. BC 11 documents *uaṇis̱a-* = BHS *upaniṣat-/upaniṣā-*; *uayeasa* = Skt. *upacaya-*; and *uavati* = Skt. *upapatti*. In BC 6 one finds *uadae* = Skt. *upādāya*.

In cases where *p* is written, it goes back to a cluster (*mp*, *tp*), or it is treated as word-initial at a compound break. After a negative prefix, both *p* and *v* are possible: BC 4 *apalios̱eṇa* but *avarimaṇa*; BC 6 *aparimaṇa* along with *avarimaṇa*. In BC 11 there is one instance in which the prefix *ava-* seems to be retained, but the reading and interpretation is not certain: *avakra ? + +*, perhaps a derivation of *ava√kram*.

bh. Intervocalic *bh* is retained mainly after prefixes or at the beginning of compound parts of words. In BC 11, *abhae* seems equivalent to *ubhaye*, which is otherwise written *uhae*.

Original *-bh-* becomes *-h-* in *uhae* and *(a)śuha-*. The development *-bh-* > *-h-* is familiar from nominal word endings in the instr. pl. (*-hi* < *-bhiḥ*). Also Skt. *ṣaḍbhiḥ* is reflected by BC 4 *ṣah⟨*i⟩* / BC 11 *s̱ahi* and thus is reduced twice (*ḍbh* > *bh* > *h*).

At the beginning of words, both reflexes, *bh-* and *h-*, occur in derivations of √*bhū*: BC 4 *bhavid.*, *hakṣati/hakṣadi*, *hoita*; BC 6 *bhava*, *bhaveadi*, *bhoti*; BC 11 *bhaviea*, *bhavidave*, *bhaviśadi*, *bhave*, *bhavea*, *bhodu*, but also *hoidava/hoidave*, *hodu*, *hode*, *hakṣati*. Moreover, *hakṣati* is apparently reduced once further to *akṣati* in BC 4.

Intervocalic *-bh-* is written as *-vh-* in BC 4 *lavheti* (= Skt. *labhate*, in contrast to *labhadi* = Skt. *labhyate*) and *lavha* (cf. von Hinüber 2001: § 191: *-bh-* > *-β-* > *-v/vh-*). The prefix *abhi-* is found as *ahi-* (5×), *aï-* (1×), or *avhi-* (1×, in *avhiña*). In BC 11 *labheṇa* and *padilabhe* the spelling *-bh-* can be explained by going back to *-mbh-*.

y. In combination with vowels, original *y* is reduced to *i* or is elided (see 5.1.3 "Reductions" above). In clusters with consonants, it is assimilated (see 5.2.3.3 "Clusters with Semivowel" below). Intervocalic *y* is retained in: BC 4 *bhuyo* (maybe due to double consonants in MIA), *svaya-* (perhaps from Skt. *svaka-* rather than *svaya-*); BC 11 *aya, kaya, (a)kṣaya-, śriya-*. It is also regularly retained in original clusters with *r*: BC 4 *vivaryaeṇa*; BC 11 *karye, sagharya*. In the reverse, *-y-* replaces original *-g-* / *-j-* / *-c-*: *y* < *g* (BC 11 *kamabhoyi*), *y* < *j* (BC 11 *parvayidehi, pariyaṇeo*), *y* < *c* (BC 11 *amoyaṇa*).

l. Normally *l* is stable. The only anomalies in BC 4 are *palaśpidava* and *palaśpada* if they derive from OIA *pari* √*smṛ*. These words, however, are currently understood as derivations from √*pāl*, although this is uncertain.

v. Original *v* is most commonly retained, both word initially and medially. Despite frequently being represented in Gāndhārī as *b* (see, e.g., Allon 2001: 78 or Salomon 2008a: 116), this is never the case here.

ś/*ś̱*/*ṣ*/*ṣ̱*. Intervocalic *ś* is usually written with a small rightward extension at the base, transliterated here as *ś̱*. In one instance, the same is found in word-initial position: *ś̱aṣ̱idava* (BC 4). After prefixes treated as an initial, it remains *ś*: BC 4/11 *aṇuśaśa*, *aśuha*, BC 6 *aśala-*. Nothing can be said about *ś* following *r* (BC 4 *darśaṇa*), because of the way that preconsonantal *r* is graphically combined with *ś*; for convenience it has been transliterated here as normal *ś*. In some cases intervocalic *ś* is retained, although alternative spellings with *ś̱* exist in the same manuscript: BC 4 *akuśala-*, *kuśala-*, *deśidavo*; BC 11 *akuśale*, *ṇaśida*.

In the case of *ṣada-*/*ṣadima-* (BC 4/11), *ṣ* seems to reflect Skt. *ś*. Usually initial *ṣ* goes back to *śr*, but there are counterexamples: *ṣaṣada-* = Skt. *śāśvatā* in BC 4 and BC 11; *ṣade* = Skt. *śāta* in the Niya documents (Burrow 1937: 126 referring to N.Pers. *šad*, etc.); *ṣiṣa-* = BHS *śīrṣa-* in Av^{L1} 146 (Lenz 2010: 27); and *aṣaga* = Skt. *aśokam* / P *asokaṃ* in Dhp^{K} 46.[7]

An anomalous shift *s* > *ś* (in one instance *ṣ̱*) is found in BC 4/11 *aṇuśaśa-* and BC 4 *aṇuśaśidava*, *ś̱aṣ̱idava*, but in all examples the etymological nasal + sibilant combination *ṃs* may account for this. A similar sporadic sound change is *śaśaṇa-* = Skt. *śāsana-* (Dhp^{K} 258, cf. Brough 1962: § 50; CKD 510; Anav^{L} 23, 57, 69, 77, cf. Salomon 2008a: 117); *viśpaśa* / *vaśpaśa* = Skt. *viśvāsa-* (Dhp^{K} 66, 162, 325, cf. Brough 1962: § 50); also *śaśaga-* = Skt. *saṃśaya-* (Nird^{L2} 9·143, 148, 155, 159); and *śaśea* = Skt. *śaṃset* (Nird^{L2} 18·7), for which palatal assimilation can be provided as the explanation (cf. Baums 2009: 187–88).

Similar to the distribution of *ś*/*ś̱* there are alternative spellings with either *ṣ* or *ṣ̱* in an intervocalic position. The variant with the rightward extension is more prevalent. The few cases where it is written without are: BC 4 *paribhaṣidav⟨*e⟩* (1×, along with 4× *paribhaṣ̱idave*); *-ṣa-* (treated as word-initial, but cf. BC 11 *ṣ̱ahi*); BC 6 *d(*u)ṣaṇa*; BC 11 *piṣita*.

---

7 Similar anomalous development of *ṣ* < *s* is attested in Dhp^{K} 46 *ṣaga* = Skt. *saṅgam* / P *saṅgaṃ* and Dhp^{K} 274 *aṣajamaṇa* = P *asajjamānaṃ*; cf. Brough 1962: §§ 50, 57.

s/s̮/s̱/h. The modified *s̱a* is not used for the gen. sg. ending (Skt. *-sya* / P *-ssa*), as is common in many Kharoṣṭhī manuscripts, but only for *-th-/-dh-* or for *-s-*, the latter usually at the beginning of a new compound part, but sometimes in the middle of a word (for examples, see 4.4 "Distribution of *s/s̱*" in chapter 4 on orthography). The text therefore seems to have been written during a transition stage of *s̱* shifting to *s*. The difference between *s* and *s̱* must have been very slight and/or not well known, and *s̱* notation seems to depend merely on the (presumed) voiced pronunciation (cf. Glass 2007: 107).

In a unique example of the word *as̮ivas̱idae* (4r20), a third kind of *s* can be seen, resembling a normal *s* with a rightward foot mark added as a more or less horizontal stroke at the bottom. For want of an established special character for this modified form (*s̱* being used for the "corkscrew"-*s*), I have transliterated this as *s̮* (*s* with breve, U+032E).[8] The easiest explanation for this sign would be the development of *s* to *s̱* as follows:

Fig. 31. Different writings of *as̮ivas̱idae* and *as̱ivasidae*.

normal *s* → underbent *s̮* for voiced sibilants corresponding to *-th-/-dh-* → corkscrew *s̱* for voiced sibilants corresponding to *-th-/-dh-* and *-sya/-ssa*, later also alternated with intervocalic *s*

Hitherto, transliterations have only distinguished between the first and last form. According to Glass (2000: 107) "[t]his form [i.e., *s̱*] first appears in the Bajaur casket inscription." However, the sign in Glass is closer to an underbent *s̮a* than a corkscrew *s̱a* (although used to indicate a gen. sg. ending, which is usually presented by *-s̱a* or *-sa*).[9] Here, I would like to differentiate systematically between *s̱a* and *s̮a*, first to see if they were used in different ways (since both appear side-by-side in the manuscripts of the Bajaur Collection), and secondly to prove (if possible) that *s̱a* did not develop graphically from a right-curving *sya*, as assumed by Senart (1914: 570–72) and Brough (1962: 68),[10] but from the addition of a *cauda* as in *g̱* and *ḏ*, as has been suggested by Glass (2000: 108).

The manuscripts that have survived until today may reflect a phase in which differentiation between the three signs and their usage had already become quite blurred, and thus it may not

---

8 This notation was agreed upon with Andrew Glass at the Gāndhārī Workshop in Munich, July 2013, against *şa*, proposed by Harry Falk (2011: 14), since combinable characters are now preferred.

9 B *Viyakamitras̱a apracaraj̱asa*, "Shinkot reliquary inscription," CKI 176. Cf. Falk 2005 and Baums 2012: 202–3 regarding the question of genuineness of the inscriptions. If genuine, inscription B would fall in the reign of Vijayamitra, 8/7 BCE (cf. Baums 2012: 202 n. 2, referring to Salomon 2005: 382) or 4/5 CE according to the "Index of dated objects and inscriptions" by Britta Schneider in Falk 2013.

10 "[… T]he regular inversion of the conjunct *-y* on the Wardak vase, and the appearance on the silver objects […] of *sa*, *sya*, and *sya* with inverted *-y*, seem to make it certain that the Dharmapada and Niya *s̱a* is a direct descendant of the inverted *sya* appearing on the two silver cups from Sirkap" (Brough 1962: 68).

be possible to determine their original application with certainty. Still, a comprehensive examination of the different graphemes will help us to consider the use of *s*/*s̱*/*ȿ* around the time these manuscripts were written. For a comprehensive study, of couse, inscriptions would have to be included as well.

To my knowledge, Harry Falk was the first to differentiate between three types of *sa* (in connection with a fragment from the Split Collection containing parts of the *Arthapada* / P *Aṭṭhakavagga*): "one of the corkscrew type, usually transcribed as *s̱a*, either corresponding to an initial *sa* or wherever it stands for Skt. gen. *-sya*. The third variety is again 'under-bent', transcribed here with a *ȿa* (Unicode U+023F). It occurs where Skt. would have a *dha*, as in *viȿasu* <≈ *vidhāsu*, *aȿivasaeha* <≈ *adhivāsayeyya*; *kuȿaya* <≈ *kudhayā*, *bahuȿa* <≈ *bahudhā*. Unfortunately, this application is not the only one; the under-bent *ȿa* also occurs where a *saṃ* is expected, as in *pratiȿajaneṇa* <≈ *paṭisaṃyujeyya*, and *aviȿabhunea* <≈ *abhisaṃbhaveyya*. There is no common logic apparent behind these two uses" (Falk 2011: 14). Nevertheless, it would indeed be encouraging to discern that a system once stood at the beginning of a development which ended in an apparently chaotic system of personal preferences of different scribes.[11]

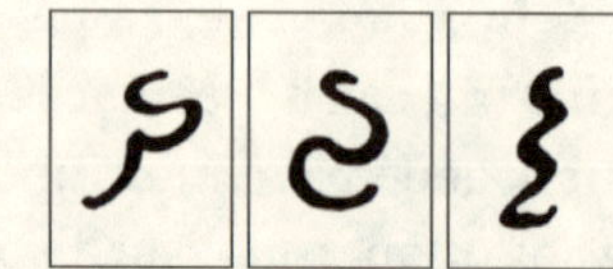

Fig. 32. Different writings of *sa*/*ȿa*/*s̱a* in the Split Collection.

There is one case in BC 11 where *s̱* seems to stand for original *h*: *pras̱aṇa*, found parallel to *prahaṇa*:

11r23 *eȿa pras̱aṇakarmo ruve · as̱a va aruve*
11v28 *pariña prahaṇakarmo ca · ruve ∘ as̱a va · aruve*

The first case (11r23 *pras̱aṇa*) suggests Skt. *pradhāna*, the second one (11v28 *prahaṇa*) Skt. *prahāṇa*. If one assumes that both occurrences mean the same, they either stand for Skt. *prahāṇa* (then: *pras̱aṇa* < Skt. *prahāṇa*) or they stand for Skt. *pradhāna* (then: *prahaṇa* < Skt. *pradhāṇa*). The development *s̱* < *h* is attested in SĀ[S1] (Glass 2007: 119)[12] and in the SaṅgCm[L] (Baums forthcoming); *h* < *dh* is, as far as I know, not yet attested elsewhere. There are, however,

---

[11] It seems that at the time the fragment from the Split Collection (SC 1, *Arthapada*) was written, two signs—(1) *saṃ*, in Aśokan inscriptions written as a half-moon placed in the middle of the base of a stem, and (2) *ȿa* later to become *s̱a*, written as a horizontal stroke attached to the base of the stem—were combined into one (*ȿa*). In a metal plate from Buner (Falk 2006: 395, dated to Azes 9 = 39/38 BCE) and also in a paleographically similar reliquary inscription from Buner (Falk 2012 [2007]: 139), the *saṃ* is still written with this half-moon, similar to the grapheme for *sma* (*saṃ* is written with a half-circle open to the left at least from 16/17 CE onward, e.g., on the Indravarma casket, Azes 63). In the Gomitra slab, which may be dated to the second or first century BCE (Salomon 2009, cf. Sadakata 2003), the grapheme corresponding to Skt. *-th-* is written with a clear horizontal stroke at the base of the *s* (i.e., *ȿ*).

[12] "Medial *h* has become *s̱* twice, *samepas̱aṇaṇa* = Skt. *samyakprahāṇānām* (34, 38). According to Mark Allon, this is likely due to confusion with Skt. *pradhāna-* / P *padhāna-*, which commonly occurs with it in the P compound *pahānapadhāna* (= G *prasaṇa-prasaṇo*; see Allon 2001: § 5.2.2.8, pp. 256–60; BHSD s.v. *pradhāna*; and text note on *samepas̱aṇaṇa*, ch. 11, l. 34)" (Glass 2007: 119).

examples of *h* < *s*,[13] which could have been a secondary development from *h* < *s*/*s̱* < *dh*. Thus, theoretically, both options are possible: *prahaṇa* < **prasaṇa* < Skt. *pradhāna*, or *prasaṇa* < **prahaṇa* < Skt. *prahāṇa*. Nonetheless, I consider Skt. *prahāṇa* to be intended in both cases, since this is supported by the general topic of the text.

Likewise, in the adverb *iś̱emi* = Skt. *iha*, the development *ś* < *h* seems to have taken place. The writing *iśa*/*iśe* is well attested in inscriptions (Fussman 1989: 472), the Niya documents (Burrow 1937: § 91) and also in other manuscripts (Lenz 2003: 168, Glass 2007: 119). It is sometimes written with a superscript line indicating an underlying cluster, which may be *hy*, since the development *ś* < *hy* is attested elsewhere (Dhp[L] 8 *vighaśa* = Skt. *vigāhya* or *vigṛhya*; cf. Lenz 2003: 44; *[a]r(*u)ś[a]* = Skt. *āruhya*, *daśamaṇa* = Skt. *dahyamānam*, *vigri[śo]* = Skt. *vigṛhyam*, *daśaṇ[o]* = Skt. **dayhanā*, Nird[L2;]; cf. Baums 2009: 171, 182). Cf. also *guhya* > *guza* in SĀ[S1] ("[a] derivation of *guza* from *guhya* assumes *hy* > *ś* (> *ź*) > *z*," Glass 2007: 161; cf. also Baums 2009: 149, 171, 182).[14] The explanation by Burrow (1937: § 17) is: *iha* > (Aś. Shah) *ia*, i.e., *iya* > *iyya* > *iśa*, *ija* (= **iźa*).

5.2.3 Consonant Clusters

Original geminates are written as the corresponding single consonant, e.g., *citta* > *cita*. Clusters of nonaspirates and aspirate are represented by the simple aspirate, e.g., *buddha* > *budha*. Anusvāra is written only sporadically (cf. chapter 4 on orthography); most often it is represented by a (non-written) nasal before homorganic stop (ṃC > NC > C). Where it is used, in some cases it is applied to the wrong consonant (*sasaṃra*, *as̱akeṃa*).

There are two words whose Sanskrit includes a visarga: Skt. *duḥkha* and *niḥsāmarthya*. In both cases, the visarga has been dropped, resulting in *dukha*/*duha* or *ṇisamartha*/*ṇis̱amartha*. Similarly, in BC 11: *ṇikhalida* = Skt. **niṣkālita*.

5.2.3.1 Stop + Stop

As in other MIA dialects, clusters of the type stop + stop undergo assimilation. The latter member predominates over the former, for example: *kt* > *tt* > *t*; *tk* > *kk* > *k*.

5.2.3.2 Clusters with Nasal

Anusvāra is written very irregularly and is not always certain (see 4.1 "Anusvāra" above). In rare cases, it is used to substitute a nasal: *paṃca* = Skt. *pañca* (BC 4), *paṃḍida-* = Skt. *paṇḍita-* (BC 11).

Clusters with nasal are mostly nasal + consonant, which are usually represented by the respective homorganic consonant alone. If the cluster is the opposite (consonant + nasal), it

---

13 Examples for *h* < *s* can be found in the Dhp[L] (*acahari* for P *accasārī*, *pracahari* for P *paccasārī*) According to Lenz (2003: 43) "[s]uch a phonetic development is found in Iranian languages, as well as in the P future tense (e.g., *padāhisi* for P *padassati*, *-ss-* > *-h-*; see Geiger and Norman 2000: § 150), but is generally marginal in IA dialects. The appearance of this development in the Dhp[L] is apparently part of a general tendency toward the weakening of *s* and *ś* to *h*."

14 A parallel development in the opposite direction (*ś* > *h*, sometimes also > Ø) is found in: *-yoṇiho* < *yoniśaḥ*, *baïhoda*/*baïhodu* < *vaśībhūtaḥ* and *baki[a]* < **vaṅkīśaḥ* (Anav[L], Salomon 2008a: 117) and *caduveharajada-* (Nird[L2], Baums 2009: 150).

changes: *jñ* > *ñ*; exception: *gn* > *g*. In combinations *n*/*ṇ* + *y* it is palatized to *ñ*; *ṣ* + *ṇ* is written as *ṣ̄*; *sm* is represented by *sv* or *śp* (with *sv* possibly used in word-medial position, and *śp* in word- or compound part-initial position).

The conjunct *tm* becomes *tv* in *atva-*, *aȷ̄atva-* and *aȷ̄atvia*. While the graphic sign transliterated as *tv* could also be taken as *tm*, there is no clear differentiation between *tv* used for *ttv* or *tm* (see chapter 3 on paleography, p. 58).

5.2.3.3 Clusters with Semivowel

Clusters with *y*. In clusters (including nasal) with *y* as a second member, the *y* is assimilated to the preceding consonant (geminated and then reduced). If the consonant is a dental—and not preceded by *r*—it is palatized.[15] The developments documented in BC 4, 6, and 11 are listed as follows. Assimilation: *khy* > *kh*; *gy* > *g*; *cy* > *c*; *jy* > *j* / *y*; *py* > *p*; *bhy* > *bh*; *rthy* > *rth*; *lp* > *p* (or: *rp*); *ly* > *l*; *vy* > *v*; *śy* > *ś*, *sy* > *s*. Assimilation + palatization: *ṇy* / *ny* > *ñ*; *ty* > *c*; *dy* > *j*; *dhy* > *j* / *ȷ̄* (one instance of *ch*[16]); *ṣy* > *ś*. Sometimes the consonant cluster is also resolved by the insertion of the glide *i*; see 5.4 "Anaptyxis (Svarabhakti)" below.

Clusters with *r*. Clusters with *r* as the latter member are usually preserved in Gāndhārī. In BC 11 they most frequently occur in the combination *pra*. In one instance, in *parvayidehi*, the prefix *pra-* is "metathized" to *par-*.[17] A regular exception to this rule is *prati-*, which becomes *paḏi-* in analogy to Pali *paṭi-* (BC 4 *paḏiladha*, *paḏitiṭha*; BC 6 *vipaḏiṣ̱ara*). In BC 11, there is one instance of this being further simplified to *padi-* (*padilabhe*; cf. *pajahidava* for *prajahidava*). The *pra* of OIA *prati-* is retained in BC 11 *pradigarasuha-* and perhaps in *pradibhave*, as well as in BC 4 *praïṭhavamaṇa* = *pratiṣṭhāpyamāna-*.[18] A special case seems to be BC 4 *picara* = Skt. *pratyarham* (cf. annotations, p. 187). Other clusters with *r* include *kr* (e.g., *avakra ? + +*), *gr* (e.g., *parigrahida*) and *tr* (e.g., *atra*, *añatra*, *matra*, *sarvatra*).

Regarding *śr* in BC 11, it is sometimes difficult to decide whether the post-consonantional *r* is retained or not, since here the Kharoṣṭhī sign for OIA *ś* is frequently written with a rightward foot mark (transliterated here as *ś̱*), usually standing for *ś* in intervocalic position. Especially in the word *mahaś̱ie* this would denote BHS *śrīyā*, but I do not think the foot mark can be interpreted here as post-consonantal *r*, because this is marked clearly and differently, with the foot rising high above the top of the *śi* in *śriyaṇa* (cf. chapter 3 on paleography). Glass (2007: 124) explains this as assimilation *śr* > *śś* > *ś* (which in our case would be mostly *ś̱*), but *śr* can also be rendered as *ś* (BC 11 *vidimiśa*) without any sign of foot mark or post-consonantal *r*. On the

---

15 For instance, *rthy* > *rth*, but *mithyā* > *micha* (Salomon 2008a: 259, 436) and **kvathya* > *kvachia* (Salomon 2008a: 119).

16 G *achatvia* for *aȷ̄atvia*, see chapter 4 on orthography.

17 In other Kharoṣṭhī manuscripts it is written with *pra-* (Av[L6] *pravayido*, Khvs[L] *prav(*ra)y(*i)da*, and likewise *pravajita-* in RE 12 at Shahbazgarhi and Mansehra), or it is also metathized as *par-* (Anav[L] *parvaïdu*, Dhp[K] *parvaïda-*).

18 The elision of original intervocalic dentals is "a characteristic feature of later stages of Gāndhārī (Fussman 1989: esp. 462–4), as of other MIA languages" (Salomon 2000: 81), that is "from approximately the second century A.D. onward" (Salomon 2000: 85, see Salomon 1999a: 126, 152). This phenomenon is however already attested in the Dhp[L] (Lenz 2003: 42).

other hand, in BC 4 *miśra* is written as *miṣo* / *miṣ̱o*, which is the usual development in Gāndhārī (but, according to Salomon 2008a: 125, *śr* can also be presented as *rś*, *sr*, or *śir*).

Clusters with *r* preceding the consonant are often subject to metathesis: *dur-*/ *daur-* > *dru-*/*dro-* in BC 4, 6, and 11 (e.g., *drugaṇa*, *drujaṇa*, *droaca*, *droatie*, *drogadi-*, but also *dur-gadi-*); BC 6 *pūrve* > *prove* (as well as *purve*); BC 11 *avasarga* > *osagra-*.

The cluster *r* + C is usually preserved: BC 4 *artho*,[19] *karma*, *ṇisamartha-*, *durgadi-*, *dharma-* (as well as two instances of *-dhamia-*); BC 6 *viarthae*, *ṇisamartha-*; BC 11 *karye* (as well as *kaye*?), *dharma-* as well as *dhama-*, *ṇirvaṇa* as well as *ṇivaṇu*, *ṇisamartha-*, *durgadi*, *purve*, *marga*, *varjamaṇa*, *varjita*, *sagharya*, *sarva*. Thus, the following clusters are usually stable: *rg* (with exceptions of metathesis), *rj*, *rth*, *rm*, *ry*, *rv*. Regarding *dharma* / *dhama*: Possibly these words were intentionally written differently, since almost always *dharma* is applied when "the Dharma" is meant, but *dhama* / *dhamia* in cases referring to "elements" or "phenomena," etc.[20] There is, however, one exception in 11r5 *(*kuṣ̱a)laṇa dharmaṇa*, where *dharma* (written with an *r*) seems to stand for "things" or "qualities" rather than "the Dharma." In BC 6 there are three examples where pre-consonantial *r* is not preserved: *dhama* (Skt. *dharma*, P *dhamma*, as "elements" or "phenomena"), *paripuṇa* (Skt. *paripūrṇa*, P *paripuṇṇa*), *sava* (Skt. *sarva*, P *sabba*).

The reflex *rt* > *ṭ* is documented in BC 4 / 11 *kaṭave*, BC 6 *kaṭava* = Skt. *kartavya-*, and BC 11 *aṇavaṭie* = Skt. *anāvartikam*. In other published Gāndhārī documents, Skt. *kartavya-* is usually written *kartav(y)a-* or rarely also *katava-* without the pre-consonantal *r* (Dhp^{K} 293 *kata[v]i*, Dhp^{Sp} 3 *katava*, 72 *katavo*). It is sometimes written with retroflex in the Niya documents and the rock inscriptions of Mansehra and Shahbazgarhi, as well as in other manuscripts from the Bajaur Collection (BC 3, BC 16).

Clusters with *l*. Skt. *kalpa* is written as *karpa* (BC 4 *asaṃkhedehi karpehi*, BC 11 *asakhea karpa* / *aṣ̱akeṃa karpa*), as elsewhere in the Bajaur Collection (e.g., BC 5, BC 18). In other Kharoṣṭhī manuscripts, it is either written as *kapa* (Anav^{L} and Dhp^{K}) or as *karpa* (~~*sakarpa*~~ in Av$^{\mathrm{L1}}$, Lenz 2010: 33), the pre-consonantal *r* thus functioning as a diacritic indicating a geminate: *lp* > *pp*, with *pp* represented by *rp* in Kharoṣṭhī. In BC 4 / 6 / 11 there are no other occurrences of pre-consonantal *r* for double consonants. In BC 6, Skt. *parikalpa* is spelled *pariapo*, thus without the pre-consonantal *r*. Possibly this is due to it being part of the stock phrase *pariapo uadae* = Skt. *parikalpam upādāya*.

In BC 4 *gelaña-* the cluster with *l* is dissolved by an epenthetic vowel as is done in Pali (Skt. *glāna*, BHS *glānya*, P *gelañña* or *gilāna*). Other Gāndhārī documents have *gilanago* = Skt. *glānakaḥ* (Av$^{\mathrm{L6}}$) or *[ghil](*a)ṇo* (Anav^{L}; cf. Salomon 2008a: 121 for more examples).

---

19 In other Gāndhārī documents (e.g., Anav^{L}) *rth* becomes *tth* > *th* ("In general, the retention or assimilation of predental *r* seems to be an area of inconsistency in Gāndhārī phonology and orthography," Salomon 2008a: 122).

20 The "Dharma": 4r21 *dharme*, 4r21 *b(*u)dhadharmasagho*, 11r51 *dharmadaṇe*. "Elements": 4r25 *driṭhadhamio*, 4v5 *driṭhadhamia*; 6r8 *dhama*; 11r3 *(*dha)mehi*, 11r10 *driṭhadhamiasa*, 11r52 *dhama*, 11v3 *aparihaṇadhama*, 11v15 *driṭhadhami⟨*a⟩*.

Clusters with *v*. Clusters with *v* as the latter member are retained in *sattva* > *satva* and *tattva* > *tatva*. Absolutives ending in *-(i)tvā* change to *(i)tta* > *(i)ta*. No absolutives ending in *-(i)tvāna* are found in these manuscripts. For *sv* > *śp* / *sp* / *sv*, see 5.2.3.4 "Cluster with Sibilants" below.

The cardinal number *dva* / *dvi* appears as *du* in its stem form (which conforms with Pali, where *du* is likewise possible within compounds) and as *due* or *dum(*e)* = *duve* in the nominative. The change of intervocalic *v* to *m* is well attested in the Dhp[K] and also in EĀ[L], here mostly within *ema* for *evam* (Allon 2001: 86). The change of semivowel to vowel (*dva* > *du*, *saṃprasāraṇa*) is similar to *svapna* > *sudiṇa*; cf. also *tuo* for Skt. *tvam* in BC 6.

5.2.3.4 Clusters with Sibilant

The clusters *kṣ* and *st* are retained as usual (e.g., BC 4 *mokṣa*, BC 11 *kṣaya*, *dakṣiṇe*; *asti*). The only exception is BC 11 *khaveati* corresponding to BHS *kṣepayati* / P *khepeti*. In the combination sibilant + labial (*v*, *p* or *m*) the reflex is mostly *śp*; for other developments see the list below. In the case of *sva-* or *svayam-* as a prefix, the *sva(ya)-* is retained, with the exception of *svabhāvatā* written as BC 4 *śpabhavasa* and *svayam* written as BC 11 *śpahu* / *śpaho*. In one instance in BC 6 *svayam-* as a prefix seems to be further reduced to *saï-*, but the term and its translation are uncertain (*saïthida* = Skt. *svayaṃsthita* (?); cf. annotations on 6v4–5 *saïthida*, p. 257).

sp > *śp*	BC 4	*(a)śpriṣ̄aṇa-*
sp > *ph*	BC 6	*phaṣadi*
sph > *sp*	BC 6	*spura-*
sm > *śp*	BC 4	*palaśpada* (?), *palaśpidava-* (?), *śpadimo*
sm > *sv*	BC 4, 6	*tasva*
sv > *śp*	BC 4, 11	*śpabhavasa*, *śpahu* / *śpaho*
sv > *sp*	BC 6	*aspamia*
sv > *sv*	BC 4	*sva-doṣ̄ehi*, *sva-droacehi*, *sva-sapatihi*, *svaya-aṇuśaśehi*

If all published Gāndhārī manuscripts are compared, the development of sibilant + labial is inconsistent. The reflexes of sibilant + *m*/*v* in strong position are summarized in Baums 2009: 175, which has served as a basis for the following observations.

For *sp* > *śp* there are no other attestations.[21] Otherwise the development is *sp(h)* > *ph* (word-initial, Dhp[K], Khvs[L], EĀ[L], Anav[L]; cf. Salomon 2000: 90, Allon 2001: 77, and Salomon 2008a: 125) or *sp* > *p* (word-initial, EĀ[L]; cf. Allon 2001: 90 and 95 for √*spr̥ś*). But compare *pph* > *śp* in SĀ[S1] (Glass 2007: 158). Thus, *sp* in derivations from √*spr̥ś* is "irregularly" rendered as *ph* in Dhp[K], Khvs[L], and EĀ[L], similar to MIA, whereby the scribe in BC 4 seems to be more consistent and closer to OIA.

The development *sm* > *śp* only occurs in BL fragments (Anav[L], Av[L6], Dhp[L], EĀ[L], BL 4), otherwise it becomes *s*, *sv*, *sm*, or *sp*.

The development *sv* > *śp* is attested in Niya, BL and RS manuscripts (Anav[L], Av[L6], Dhp[L], EĀ[L], BL 4; Anav[S], SĀ[S1]); *sv* > *sp* is attested in Dhp[K] and Nird[L2]; *sv* > *sv* is found in Bbs, Dhp[K],

21 But cf. *ps* > *śp* in Anav[L] *juho[śpi](*da)* / *joho[śp](*ida)*, "apparently by way of metathesis," according to Salomon 2008a: 124.

Niya. The mixed rendering *sv* > *śp* / *sv* is only common to the Niya documents. But there *sm* is stable, while being rendered as *śp* or *sv* in BC 4. For a comparison, in the following chart I have collected all occurrences of G *śp* in so far published editions.

Table 10. Gāndhārī reflex *śp* and its Sanskrit equivalents.

śp =	G	Skt.	Reference
śp	*aśpavarmano*	*aśvavarmaṇā* (Old Iranian *ašpa-*)	Lenz 2010: 40
	[a]śpavarmo / āśpava[r]ma	*aśvavarmā*	Lenz 2010: 32
śv	*aśpamutreṇa*	*aśvamūtreṇa*	Salomon 2008a: 124, 138
	iśpare	*īśvaraḥ*	Salomon 2008a: 124, 136
	Dhp[K] generally		Allon 2001: 96
**ṣv / sv*	*dhriśpa*	*dṛṣṭvā*	Salomon 2008a: 125, 159
	[dh]r[iśpa]ṇa	*dṛṣṭvā*, P *disvāna*	Allon 2001: 77, 117
	dhriśpaṇa	*dṛṣṭvā* (**dṛṣṭvāna*)	Salomon 2008a: 106, 125, 159–60, 432
sv	*śpaśariru*	*svaśarīre*	Salomon 2008a: 125, 139
	śpai / śpae / śpaya	*svayam*	Salomon 2008a: 102, 125, 151
	śpagam	*svakam*	Lenz 2003: 128, 140
	śpagho	*svakam*	Salomon 2008a: 108, 125, 137
	śpara	*svara* (impv.)	Salomon 2008a: 152
	*prabh(*a)[śp](*a)ra*	BHS *prabhāsvarāṇi*	Allon 2001: 96
	viśparo	*visvaram*	Salomon 2008a: 125
	*[śp](*ay)i[ta]*	BHS *svādayitvā* (*āsvādya*)	Allon 2001: 83 n. 4, 91, 96
	śpeḏa	*svedaḥ*	Glass 2007: 127; 123
	pariśpeiḏaṇa	*parisvedāni*	Glass 2007: 128, 134; 123
	śpa⟨⟨ṇa⟩⟩vaṇo	*svarṇavarṇaḥ*	Salomon 2008a: 122, 134
	Niya documents generally		Burrow 1937: § 49
śm	*śpaśaṇasaña*	*śmaśānasaṃjñā*	Salomon 2008a: 124, 141
ṣm / sm	*aśpado*	*āyuṣmataḥ*, P *āyasmato*	Lenz 2003: 127
	aśpataṇa	P *āyasmantāṇaṃ*	Lenz 2003: 127 (referring to RS 12)
sm	*śpi*	*asmi*	Allon 2001: 116; Salomon 2008a: 124, 151
	-śpi (loc. or abl. sg.)	*-asmin, -asmāt*	Allon 2001; Salomon 2008a: 133
	taśpa, taśpi	*tasmāt*	Salomon 2008a: 124, 147
	taśpi (abl. sg.)	*tasmin*	Allon 2001: 190 n. 108 (cf. Salomon 2008a: 147 n. 15)
	imaśpi	*asmin*	Salomon 2008a: 124, 147, 424
	ugha[daśpi]	**udgatasmin (udgate)*	Salomon 2008a: 112, 124, 139
	kayaśpi	**kāyasmin*	Salomon 2008a: 124, 139
	[lo]gha[śpi]	*lokasmin*	Allon 2001: 95

śp =	G	Skt.	Reference
sm (cont.)	*samasiśpi*	**samādhismin*	Salomon 2008a: 124, 139
	thuvaśpi	**stūpasmin*	Salomon 2008a: 124, 139
	śpadi	*smṛti*	Allon 2001: 77
	śpave[dr]. /// (?)	*smṛtīndriyaḥ*	Lenz 2010: 35
	spaḏoṭhaṇaṇa	*smṛtyupasthānānām*	Glass 2007: 112
	śpara	*smara*	Salomon 2008a: 124
	[śpa]rami	*smarāmi*	Salomon 2008a: 124
ṣp	*puśpu*	*puṣpam*	Salomon 2008a: 124, 137
pph	*pa[śpru]s̱a*	*phupphusa*, P *papphāsaṃ*	Glass 2007: 158
ps	*juho[śpi](*da)/ joho[śpi](*da)*	*jugupsitam*	Salomon 2008a: 124

All other clusters involving sibilants as the first member show assimilation and can be found in table 11 summarizing the consonant clusters (below). The exception *ṣṭh* > *ṭh* (instead of *ṭh*) in *pratitiṣṭhā* > *paḏitiṭha* seems to be based on √*sthā* (see chapter 3 on paleography). For the combination with post-consonantal *r* and *y*, see 5.2.2.3 "Clusters with Semivowel." In BC 4, apparently Skt. *-ps-* / P *-cch-* is reflected as *s̱* (Skt. **jugupsitavya-* / P **jigucchitabba-* > *juhos̱idave*), but the orthography of this word seems also to have varied in Pali (cf. annotations on 4r24 *juhos̱idave*, p. 181).

Table 11. Gāndhārī reflexes of consonant clusters.

Skt.	Gāndhārī	Examples
ṃ/ṅkṣ	*kṣ*	BC 4: *ahigakṣidave, sakṣiteṇa* BC 6: *sakṣiteṇa* BC 11: *sakṣiteṇa*
ṃ/ṅkhy	*k, ṃkh, kh*	BC 4: *asaṃkhedehi* BC 11: *as̱akeṃa, asakhea, sakhadaasakhadasa*
ṃ/ṅg	*g*	BC 4: *gaga* BC 11: *(a)sagaṇia-, jugida, jugidea*
ṃ/ṅgh	*gh*	BC 4: *sagha*
ṃ/ñc	*ṃc, c*	BC 4: *-paṃca-* BC 11: *mucami* (or *cy* > *c* ?)
ṃ/ñj	*j*	BC 4: *paribhujidave* BC 6: *rajaṇa* BC 11: *aparibhujitrea* (?)
ṃjñ	*ñ*	BC 6: *saña-*
ṃ/ṇḍ	*ṃḍ, ḍ*	BC 4: *khaḍaeṇa, bos̱imaḍa-/mos̱imaḍa-* BC 6: *(a)gaḍa-, paḍide* BC 11: *gaḍa-, paṃḍida*
ṃ/nt	*t, t̠*	BC 4: *citaṇe, citidasa, hakṣat̠i* BC 6: *matreadi* BC 11: *acitieṇa, atogada, kṣati* generally: verbal endings in 3rd pl. (*-ti*)

Skt.	Gāndhārī	Examples
ṃ/nd	*d, t*	BC 4: *sadriṭhia* BC 6: *evadukhami* BC 11: *chata* (1×), *chade* (3×), *chidita* (?)
ṃ/ndh	*dh*	BC 4: *-badhaṇa-* BC 6: *kadha-*
ṃn	*ṇ*	BC 6: *evaṇisamarthami*
ṃ/mp	*p*	BC 4: *sapati, saparaïa* BC 11: *sapati-, -sapara(*ia)*
ṃ/m(b)h	*h*	BC 4: *-sahoro* (?)
ṃś	*ś̱*	BC 4: *viś̱adi*
ṃs	*ṃ, ṃs*	BC 4: *saṃsara-* BC 6: *saṃthido-* BC 11: *sasaṃra / saṃsara* (or twice *sasaṃra*)
	ś, ṣ̱	BC 4: *aṇuśaśa, aṇuśaśidava, ś̱aṣ̱idava*
ḥkh	*kh*	BC 4: *dukha-* BC 6: *dukha-* BC 11: *dukha-*
	h	BC 4: *duhe* (in addition to usually *dukha-*)
ḥs	*s, s̱*	BC 4: *ṇisamartha-* (6×), *ṇis̱amartha-* (6×) BC 6: *ṇisamartha-* (4×) BC 11: *ṇisamartha-* (7×), *ṇis̱amartha-* (1×)
kt	*t, ḏ*	BC 4: *vatave, viratasa* BC 11: *aparibhuteṇa, parubhuteṇa* (read *paribhuteṇa*), *(a)paribhuḏasa*
kṣ	*kṣ*	BC 4: *uekṣidae, puñakṣae, bhikṣiśe, mokṣa-* BC 6: *avikṣitacita-, dakṣiśati* (?) BC 11: *akṣaye, kṣati, divacakṣu, mokṣa-, sakṣi*
	kh	BC 11: word-initial: *khaveati*
khy	*kh*	BC 11: *akhaïta*
gn	*g*	BC 4: *ṇagao*
gy	*g*	BC 4: *arogaṇa*
gl	*gel*	BC 4: *gelañaṇa*
cch	*ch*	BC 6: *ichiadi, ichidava* BC 11: *ichiea, gachiea*
cy	*c*	BC 4: *vucadi* BC 6: *vucadi* BC 11: *mucami* (or *ñc* > *c* ?), *vucadi*
jj	*j*	BC 11: *viṣ̱a{ja}jita* (?)
jñ	*ñ*	BC 4: *ñaṇa-, pariña(*e), praña-* BC 6: *ñaṇa-* BC 11: *aprañati, aviñati, avhiña, ñaṇa-, pariña*
jy	*j*	BC 4: *varjamaṇa* BC 6: *rajama, rajas̱i, rajiadi, rajieadi* BC 11: *bheṣ̱aje*
	y	BC 4: *puyamaṇa*
ḍbh	*h*	BC 4: *ṣah⟨*i⟩* BC 11: *ṣ̱ahi*

Skt.	Gāndhārī	Examples
ṇy	*ñ*	BC 4: *puña-* BC 11: *puña*
tt	*t*	BC 4: *cita-*, *-sapati-* BC 6: *-cita-*, *patade* BC 11: *-uavati-*, *-cita-*, *loutareṇa*, *-sapati-*
	tr	BC 6: *vitrae*, *vitrasua*
tth	*th*	BC 4: *ithu*, *ithumi* BC 6: *ithu*
	ṭ́h	BC 4: *lahuṭ́haṇaṇa*
ttv	*tv*	BC 4: *satva-* / *-s̱atva-* BC 6: *tatva* BC 11: *satva-* / *-s̱atva-*
tp	*p*	BC 4: *as̱apuruṣ̱a-*, *upajiśati*, *upadidave*, *citupade*, *sapuruṣ̱a-* BC 6: *upajati*, *upajadi*, *upajeadi* BC 11: *upajea*, *upaṇa*
tm	*tv*	BC 4: *atva-* BC 6: *atva-* BC 11: *aȷ̄atvia*, *(aṇ)atva-*
ty	*c*	BC 4: *kica-*, *paricaïta*, *pariceaṇa*, *picara*, *-pracea* BC 6: *ṭ́hidigica*, *ṇica-*, *droaca*, *paricae*, *parimaṇasacea* BC 11: *(a)ṇica-*, *kice*, *droaca-*, *paricaade*, *paricaïta*, *paricaïdave*, *paricaea*, *saca*, *sacea*
tr	*tr*	BC 4: *añatra-*, *ekadutracadurepaṃcaṣahayavasata-*, *trae*, *trikoḏi*, *triṇa*, *tribos̱ae*, *tr(*e)dhaduade*, *matra-*, *matreadi*, *sarvatra* BC 6: *tatra* BC 11: *atra*, *amitra-*, *tatra*, *yatra*, *sarvatra-*
	h	BC 6: *akuhicaagamaṇaakuhicagamaṇa* (cf. P *kuhiñci*) BC 11: *akuhicaagamaṇaakuhicagamaṇaagareṇa*
tv	*t*	absolutives (*-tvā* > *-ta*)
	tu	BC 6: *tuo*
dy	*j*	BC 6: *aji*, *upajati*, *upajadi*, *upajeadi* BC 11: *ajavi*, *upajea*, *vijadi*
dv	*du*	BC 4: *-du-*, *dum(*e)* BC 11: *due*, *duehi*
ddh	*dh*	BC 4: *budha-*, *midha-* BC 11: *budhehi*, *sudhu* (?)
dhy	*j*	BC 4: *maja*, *maje* BC 11: *maja*, *maje*
	ȷ̄	BC 11: *aȷ̄atva-*, *aȷ̄atvia*
	ch	BC 11: *achatvia* (scribal error)
ny	*ñ*	BC 4: *aña*, *añatra*, *gelaña*, *śuña-* BC 6: *aña* BC 11: *śuña*, *vihañadi*
pt	*t*	BC 4: *as̱atia* (?), *sata* BC 6: *avikṣitacita-*, *sakṣiteṇa* BC 11: *tati* (?), *viñati*, *sakṣiteṇa*

Skt.	Gāndhārī	Examples
pr	*pr*	BC 4: *praïṭhavamaṇa, praoḏidave, pracupaṇe, -pracea, prajahati, prañа-, praṇide, -pramuha-, praladhe, pridi* BC 6: *pragri(*de), pria-* BC 11: *aprañati, -pracupaṇehi, prajahaṇa-, prajahita, pradig̱ara-, pradibhave* (?), *-pramuhe, pras̱aṇa-, -prahaṇa-, prahadava, -pridi*
	p…r	BC 11: *parvayidehi*
	p	BC 4: *paḏitiṭ́ha, paḏiladha, paḏhamacitupade, picara* BC 6: *vipaḏis̱ara* BC 11: *padilabhe, pajahidava, picu* (?)
py	*p*	BC 11: *arupadhadu*
ps	*s̱*	BC 4: *juhos̱idave*
bdh	*dh*	BC 4: *paḏiladha, praladhe, ladhe, suladha*
bhy	*bh*	BC 4: *labhati*
mbh	*bh*	BC 11: *(a)labha-, padilabhe*
rg	*gr*	BC 11: *osagra-*
	rg	BC 4: *durgadi-* BC 11: *durgadi-*
	r…g	BC 4: *drugaṇa-, drogadi-*
	r…	BC 4: *-droaca-* BC 6: *droaca-* BC 11: *-droaca-*
rṇ	*ṇ*	BC 6: *paripuṇa*
rt	*ṭ*	BC 4: *kaṭave* BC 6: *kaṭava* BC 11: *aṇavaṭie, kaṭave*
rthy	*rth*	BC 4: *ṇisamartha-* / *ṇis̱amartha-* BC 6: *ṇisamartha-* BC 11: *ṇisamartha-* / *ṇis̱amartha-*
rm	*rm*	BC 4: *(a)karmaṇa, dharme, b(*u)dhadharmasagho* BC 11: *-karmo, dharmaṇa, dharmadaṇe*
	m	BC 4: *driṭhadhamia-* BC 6: *driṭhadhamia-, dhama* BC 11: *aparihaṇadhama, driṭhadhamia-, dhama, (*dha)mehi*
ry	*ry*	BC 11: *karye, sagharya*
	ri	BC 4: *jagaria*
	r	BC 4: *karamaṇa*
	y (?)	BC 11: *kaye* (?)
rh	*h*	BC 6: *tahi, yahi*
lp	*rp*	BC 4: *karpehi* BC 11: *asakheakarpa*
	p	BC 6: *pariapo*
ly	*l*	BC 6: *śala-*

Skt.	Gāndhārī	Examples
vy	*v*	BC 6: *vovaś̱amo* BC 11: *avayedeṇa* (?), *divacakṣu*, *paricaïdave* generally: gdv. (*-dava*)
	vi	BC 6: *viarthae*
śc	*c̱̄*, *c̱*	BC 4: *pac̱̄a* or *pac̱a* BC 6: *pac̱i* BC 11: *pac̱̄a*
śy	*ś*, *ś̱*	BC 4: *deś̱amaṇa* BC 11: *avaśi / avaśa*, *ṇaśadi*, *paśita*
śr	*śr*	BC 11: *-aśrea-*, *-śriya-*
	ś, *ś̱*	BC 11: *mahaś̱ie*, *-vidimiśa*
	ṣ, *ṣ̱*	BC 4: *miṣo / miṣ̱o*
śv	*ṣ*	BC 4: *ṣaṣada-* BC 11: *ṣaṣada-*
ṣk	*kh*	BC 11: *ṇikhalida*
ṣṭ	*ṭh*	BC 4: *driṭhadhamio*, *paribhaṭha*, *sadriṭhia* BC 11: *driṭha-*, *śiṭha*
ṣṭh	*ṭh*, *ṭ́h*	BC 4: *paḏitiṭ́ha*, *praïṭhavamaṇa* BC 6: *suṭhu* BC 11: *suṭhu*
ṣṇ	*ṣ̄*	BC 11: *uṣ̄a*
ṣy	*ś*	BC 4: *cariśe*, *bhikṣiśe*, *vaïśadi* BC 6: *dakṣiśati* (?), *duśama*, *duśas̱i*, *duśiadi*, *duśieadi* BC 11: *bhaviśadi*
sk	*k*	BC 6: word-initial: *kadha-*
sth	*ṭ́h*	BC 4: *lahuṭ́haṇa* BC 6: *aṭ́ha*; word-initial: *ṭ́hidigica* BC 11: *aṭ́haṇo*; word-initial: *ṭ́haṇa-*, *ṭ́havaṇia*
	th	BC 6: *saïthida*, *saṃthida-*
sn	*siṇ* (?)	BC 4: *sarvasi⟨*ṇe⟩ha*
sp	*śp*	BC 4: *(a)śpriś̱aṇaṇa*
	ph	BC 6: word-initial: *phaṣadi*
sph	*sp*	BC 6: *spura*, *spuramaṇas̱a*
sm	*śp*	BC 4: *palaśpada* (?), *palaśpidava* (?), *śpadimo* (?)
	sv	BC 4: *tasva* BC 6: *tasva*
sy	*s*	generally: gen. sg. endings
	si, *s̱i*	BC 4: *alas̱ia-* BC 6: word-initial: *siati / siadi* BC 11: word-initial: *siadi*
sv	*śp*	BC 4: *śpabhavasa* BC 11: *śpahu / śpaho*
	sp	BC 6: *aspamia*

Skt.	Gāndhārī	Examples
sv (cont.)	*sv*	BC 4: *svadoṣehi, svadroacehi, svayaaṇuśaśehi, svasapatihi* BC 11: *svaaṣiṇasuhe*
	s	BC 4: *sudiṇoamo* BC 6: *saïthida* (?), *sudi(*ṇa)* BC 11: *sudiṇa-*

5.3 Metathesis

The so-called dardic metathesis with the liquid *r* shifting to an adjoining segment is a common feature of the northwestern Indo-Aryan languages (Morgenstierne 1947, according to Salomon 2000: 92; cf. also "Clusters with *r*" under 5.2.3.3). In addition to this, *gro* seems to correspond to *roga* (BC 11). Also in *viragra-*, *veragra-* (BC 11) the *r* has spread to the adjoining *g*, indicating the pronunciation *gr* in the vicinity of *r*. Permutations occur in BC 11 *sasaṃra* (in addition to *saṃsara*) = Skt. *saṃsāra-*, although this might be an example of the anusvāra applied at the wrong consonant, similar to *aṣakeṃa* instead of *aṣaṃkhea*. Clear permutations of two consonants are BC 11 *sayavisa* instead of *sayaṣavi* (BHS *sayyathāpi* / P *seyyathāpi*), BC 6 *(*e)graġacita* instead of the previously correctly written *egagracita* = Skt. *ekāgracitta*, and probably BC 6 *payeladukheṇa* for *peyaladukhena* = Skt. *paryāyaduḥkha* / P *paryāyadukkha*.

5.4 Anaptyxis (Svarabhakti)

The resolution of consonant clusters through the insertion of an epenthetic vowel can be seen in BC 4 *alaṣia* = Skt. *ālasya* / P *ālassa*, *gelaña* = Skt. *glāna* / BHS *glānya* / P *gelañña*, *jagaria* = Skt. *jāgaryā* / P *jāgariyā*, *si⟨*ne⟩ha* = Skt. *sneha* / P *sineha* (if the reconstruction is correct); BC 6 *viartha(e)* = Skt. *vyartha(ka)*, *siati* / *siadi* = Skt. *syāt* / P *siyā*; BC 11 *siadi*.

5.5 Sandhi

Generally "Gāndhārī […] tends to elide the prior vowel, while Pali tends to elide the latter vowel" (Allon 2001: 201, Salomon 2008a: 127). The examples in BC 4/6/11, however, agree with the tendency in Pali: BC 4 *citupada* = BHS *cittotpāda* / P *cittuppāda*; BC 11 *loutara* = Skt. *lokottara* / P *lokuttara*. In BC 11 *aṇicagareṇa*, *aṇatvagareṇa*, *śuñagareṇa*, *ruvaruva*, as well as in BC 6 *egagracitasa* and *kicakica*, the sandhi *a* + *a* = *ā* is implied. BC 4 *sudiṇoamo* attests the sandhi *a* + *u* = *o*.

Regarding *vucadi* (Skt. *ucyate* / P *vuccati*) it has been stated that "[t]he initial *v* […] may represent a fossilized sandhi form (Geiger 1994: § 66.1) [i.e., *-v-ucadi*, author's note]. However, others take P *vuccati* to be derived from the guṇa grade of the root (see Norman's n. 5 to Geiger 1994: § 66.1; and von Hinüber 1986: § 270)" (Allon 2001: 101; cf. also Baums 2009: 191). I prefer to understand it as a *saṃprasāraṇa* phenomenon *vu*/*u* in derivations of √*vac*, in accordance with Norman.

Original final *m*, which is normally weakened or dropped, is retained when preceding a word that begins with a vowel: BC 4 *ekamekasa*, *edam io*; BC 6 *yam ida*; BC 11 *-apoṣaṇam iva*, *evam eva*, *kim asuhe*.

Chapter 6

Morphology

Some of the phonological and morphographic features of BC 4, BC 6, and BC 11 give the impression of a form of "Niya-ism," in that they encompass features which until now have only been seen in documents stemming from Niya. This is seen, for example, in a special type of compound future tense (e.g., BC 4 *a̱sivasidae hakṣadi*, BC 6 *karavidae siadi*) comparable to the compound past tense known from Niya (cf. Burrow 1937: § 114), as well as certain spellings common to Niya documents: BC 11 *amahu / amaho* (Skt. *asmabhyam*),[1] BC 4 / BC 6 *ithu* (Niya *iṃthu*),[2] BC 4 *i̱semi* (Skt. *iha*; otherwise G *iśa* or *iśe*), BC 11 *ṇevi* (Skt. *naiva*; cf. CKD 335), BC 4 *picara* (Skt. *pratyarha*), BC 4 *yati* (Skt. *yadi*), BC 6 / BC 11 *yahi* (cf. Burrow 1937: § 131), BC 4 / BC 11 *hakṣati*[3] (otherwise G *bhaviśadi* and the like). Of course, for most of these examples it may be pure coincidence that no parallels in other Gāndhārī manuscripts have as yet been found; these words may simply not have occurred in those texts. Still, BC 4, BC 6, and BC 11 do share some peculiarities with the Niya documents, as well as with certain fragments from the Senior Collection and a few avadānas in the British Library Collection. Instead of designating such features as "Niya-isms," which might ultimately be misleading, it should be noted that the language or dialect reflected in BC 4, BC 6, and BC 11 contains some features common to other manuscripts thought to have been written directly in Gāndhārī and not translated from a Buddhist Middle Indic source text (cf. Salomon 1999a: 139–40).

6.1 Nominal Forms

In Gāndhārī, the distinction between masculine and neuter gender has weakened, or the two have merged into a single Gāndhārī declension (see Baums 2009: 211 ff.). In the manuscripts under consideration, neuter or feminine nouns are sometimes found with masculine endings. For example, 6r1 *ime kadhadhaduaïdaṇa* points to the noun being taken as masculine, although in other Buddhist texts this compound is usually inflected as neuter (Skt. *skandhadhātvāyatanāni*).

---

[1] Another example may be BC 4 *mahi* (Skt. *mahyam* / P *mahyam*). While found frequently in the Niya documents, it is also documented in Anav^{S} (*mahia*, Salomon 2008a: 375), the Senavarma inscription (*mahia*, von Hinüber 2003: 14 and Baums 2012: 227), and the two Wardak vase inscriptions (*mahiya*, Baums 2012: 244 and 245).

[2] Also in RS 22 (*ithu ami*), BC 7 (*ithu ami*) and BC 18 (*ithumi*); cf. annotations on 4r28 *maja ṇisamartha sarvatra ithu kaṭave*, p. 185.

[3] This spelling is also attested in the Senavarma inscription (*hakṣati*) and the Shahbazgarhi Rock Edict 13 (*akṣati*). The only other Gāndhārī manuscripts are avadānas (Av^{L1} *hakṣadi*, cf. Lenz 2010: 48; Av^{L6} *hakṣe*, cf. Lenz 2003: 141).

Or, as another example, in 11r2 *ṣahi paramidehi* the feminine noun (Skt. *pāramitā*) has a masculine ending. Gender assignments are thus based on Sanskrit or Pali equivalents in this publication.[4] Additionally, according to Baums (2009: 211, 215), the nominative and accusative cases have combined into a new direct case. In the following table, I have listed these separately for historical reasons.

Table 12. Nominal endings
(arranged in order of frequency; Ⓜ masculine, Ⓝ neuter, Ⓕ feminine).

OIA stem		*-a/-an*		*-ā*	*-i*			*-in*	*-u*			*-ṛ*
Gender		Ⓜ	Ⓝ	Ⓕ	Ⓜ	Ⓝ	Ⓕ	Ⓜ	Ⓜ	Ⓝ	Ⓕ	Ⓕ
Singular	nom.	*o* *e*	*e* *a* *o*	*a* *e* *o* (?)	*i*		*i*	*i* *iṇa* (?)			*u* (?)	
	acc.	*a*	*o* *a*	*o* (?)			*i*					
	instr.	*eṇa*		*ae* (?)								
	dat.	*ae*										
	abl.	*ade* *ado*										
	gen.	*asa*					*ie*					
	loc.	*e* *ami*					*i* (?)				*u* (?)	*ami*
Plural	nom.	*a*	*a*				*i*				*u* (?)	
	acc.	*a*	*a*								*u* (?)	
	instr.	*ehi*		*ehi*			*ihi*					
	dat.											
	abl.											
	gen.	*aṇa*		*aṇa*			*iṇa*					
	loc.										*u* (?)	

In the case of *idara/idaro* (nom. sg., 4r28, 4v3) and *idara* (nom. or acc. sg., 4v11), it is unclear which gender is being followed. Also the forms *same/samo* (4r17–18) are uncertain and not taken into consideration in the above table; probably it is *same* = m. nom. pl. and *samo* = n. nom. sg. The ending *-o* usually occurs in adjectives or nouns being used adverbially (n. acc. sg.), e.g., *miṣo*, *pialo*, and *sadakalo* (BC 4). In general, the nom. sg. endings *-e* and *-o* are used interchangeably. A clear example of this is the same phrase written in two different forms found in BC 11: *ṇa ida ṭhaṇe vijadi* and *ṇa ida ṭhaṇo vijadi*.

---

4 For gender shifts in Gāndhārī, especially the distinction between masculine and neuter, cf. Salomon 2000: 93; von Hinüber 2001: § 291–93; Allon 2001: 106 and 115; Lenz 2003: 46; Salomon 2008a: 134 and 138; Baums 2009: 238; Lenz 2010: 43.

According to Brough 1962: § 76, the nom. sg. in *-e* is characteristic of (Ardha-) Māgadhī in the later period of Middle Indian (which is why such occurrences in Pali have been labeled "Māgadhisms"). The Aśokan inscriptions, with the exception of those in Girnar and Shahbazgarhi, regularly have *-e* forms. Post-Aśokan inscriptions have nominatives in both *-e* and *-o*, so that "it seems likely that [e.g.] the Mansehra *-e* is a real Gāndhārī form rather than a Māgadhism." Later inscriptions attest *-e* to the west of the Indus and *-o* to the east, with only sporadic exceptions (Konow 1929: cxii). Konow (1929: cxiii) states that the *-e* forms cannot "be considered as Māgadhisms, but rather as links connecting the northwestern Prākrit with Iranian forms such as we find in Sakish *ā*, *i*, and comparable with the pronominal *e*-forms in modern Dardic." Another possible explanation for the different endings of nominals is, according to Fussman (1989: 460, confirmed by further examples in Salomon 1999a: 130), that "the final vowels were no doubt pronounced very weakly, to the point that they were no longer differentiated." Around the beginning of the Common Era, the distinction between *e* and *o* was probably no longer audible (Fussman 1989: 480).

The nom. pl. of words ending in *-i* is *-i* instead of the expected *-ie* (cf. Baums 2009: 220); see for instance 4r3 *viṣ̄adi pridi* and *trae durgadi*.

6.2 Pronouns

The following table summarizes all personal, demonstrative, and relative pronouns found in the manuscripts. As the case with nouns, a leveling of the distinction between masculine and neuter forms can be observed. Thus, for example, the n. nom. sg. of the pronoun *idam* appears as *ida* (and also perhaps, in one instance, as *(i)de*), *imo*, *io*, and *aya*. The only expected historical form is G *ida*, but in Pali one finds *imaṃ* as well, and the extension of *ayam* to other genders is parallel in Ardhamāgadhī (n./f.; cf. Pischel 1900: § 429) and Pali (m./f.; cf. von Hinüber 2001: § 382 and Salomon 2008a: 148), likewise the attribution of *sa* as neuter (cf. Pischel 1900: § 423 and von Hinüber 2001: § 375). For the use of G *maha*/*mahi* = Skt. *mahyam* / P *mayham*, cf. annotations, p. 167.

Among the relative pronouns, *yo* in 4r23 could be either m. or n.; since the context is still unclear, this remains ambiguous. In BC 11, *yo*/*ya* relate to G *vela* = Skt. *velā*, which is originally feminine, but in the phrase *yaṃ velaṃ* … *taṃ velaṃ* the ending is usually shortened and treated as m. acc. sg. (cf. annotations, p. 208). This case is not included in the following table.

Table 13. Pronoun forms
(small superscript numbers 4, 6 or 11 = BC 4, BC 6 or BC 11).

		personal pronouns					demonstrative pronouns				relative pronouns		
		1st *ma*	2nd *tua*	3rd *ta*			3rd *eda*		3rd *ida*		3rd *ya*		
		Ⓜ Ⓝ Ⓕ	Ⓜ Ⓝ Ⓕ	Ⓜ	Ⓝ	Ⓕ	Ⓜ	Ⓝ	Ⓜ	Ⓝ	Ⓜ	Ⓝ	Ⓕ
Singular	nom.	*ahu*[11] *aho* (?)[6]	*tuo*[6]	*so*[4?, 6, 11] *se*[4?, 11]	*ta*[4, 6, 11] *sa*[4] *so* (?)[4]	*sa* (?)[11] *se* (?)[4]	*es̱a*[11]	*edam*[4] *es̱a*[6, 11]		*ida*[6, 11] *(i)de*[6] *imo*[4] *io*[4] *aya*[11]	*ya*[6, 11] *yo* (?)[4] *ye*	*ya*[4, 6, 11?] *yo*[4?, 11] *yam*[6]	*ya*[11]
	acc.					*ta* (?)[11]		*es̱a*[11]				*yo*[4]	
	instr.			*teṇa*[11]			*edeṇa*[4]		*imeṇa*[6]		*yeṇa*[11]		
	dat.												
	abl.			*tasva*[4, 6, 11]									
	gen.	*mama*[4, 11] *mame*[11] *meme*[11] *me*[4] *mahi*[4]		*tasa*[6]			*edes̱a*[11]						
	loc.												
Plural	nom.	*mio* (?)[11]					*ede*[4, 6]		*ime*[4, 11]	*ime*[6]			
	acc.												
	instr.						*edehi*[11]		*imehi*[11]				
	dat.												
	abl.												
	gen.	*asvahu*[11] *amahu*[11] *amaho*[11]		*tes̱a*[11]									
	loc.												

The table above does not contain interrogative or indefinite pronouns. These are: *ko* (m. nom. sg., BC 4, BC 6), *ki* or *kim* (n. nom. sg., BC 4, BC 11), and *keṇa* (n. sg. instr., BC 11). In combination with the enclitic particle *-ci* (Skt. *-cid*), the indefinite pronouns are *ṇa kici* or *ṇa kica* (to be read as *kici*), "nothing" (n. nom. sg., BC 11). In BC 11, *ku ṇa* is uncertain, but *ku* may denote Skt. *kū* (= *kva*) / P *ku*, "how? where? when? whither? whence?"

The pronominal adjectives and adverbs are: *aña* (m. nom. pl., BC 4, BC 6), *uhae* (m./n. nom. sg./pl., BC 4, BC 11; also written *uhaa* = *uhae* or *abhae* = *ubhae*), *śpahu*/*śpaho* = Skt. *svayam*/P *svayaṃ* (BC 11; written *svaya-* or *saï-* in compound, BC 4 and BC 6).

In all of the manuscripts, *sarva* is sometimes taken as an adjective and sometimes as the first part of a compound. Since the endings in Gāndhārī are often ambiguous, the compounds may also have dissolved into adjective + noun. As there are clear cases of compounds (e.g., *sarvasapatie* or *sarvadroacade*), also ambiguous cases have been written together in the transliteration.

6.3 Numbers

6.3.1 Cardinal Numbers

The cardinal numbers show no difference in gender, as for example, *trae* = mfn. nom. pl. (opposed to Skt. *trayaḥ / tisraḥ / trīṇi* or P *tayo / tisso / tīṇi* mfn.) and likewise *triṇa* = mfn. gen. pl. (opposed to Skt. *trayāṇām* mn. / *tisṛṇām* f. or P *tiṇṇannaṃ* mn. / *tissannaṃ* f.); cf. Salomon 2008a: 149.[5]

The numeral "four" with the G base form *cadura* or *cadure* is used in BC 4 in *ekadutra-cadurepaṃcaṣaha-yava-satahi aloehi* and *ekadutracadurapaṃcaṣa-yava-sata aloa*, as well as in BC 11 in /// ? *duehi caduraguḏiehi* (cf. Baums 2009: 227 for *cadure* as gender-neutral).

With respect to the incomplete *duehi* in BC 11, it is uncertain if this is really an instr. pl. of *du*, "two."

Table 14. Cardinal numbers
(small superscript numbers 4, 6 or 11 = BC 4, BC 6 or BC 11).

	1	2	3	4	5	6	7	20
stem	*eka* [4, 6] *ega* [6]	*du* [4]	*tra* [4] *tri* [4]	*cadura* [4, 11] *cadure* [4]	*paṃca* [4]	*ṣa* [4]	*sata* [4]	
nom.		*due* [11] *dume* [4]	*trae* [4]					*viśadi* [4]
instr.		*duehi* (?) [11]				*ṣaha* [4] *ṣahi* [11]	*satahi* [4]	
gen.			*triṇa* [4]					

6.3.2 Ordinal Numbers

The only ordinal number in these manuscripts appears in BC 4 as *paḏhama-*, "first."

6.4 Case Usage

Instr. pl. for loc. pl. BC 4 *añatradeṣehi* and BC 11 *sarvatradeṣehi, adidaaṇagadapracupaṇehi*. Cf. BHSG § 7.30: "In BHS, historic instr. forms are extensively used in loc. function [...] This is especially true of plural forms, particularly of *a*-stems." See also von Hinüber 2001: § 321.

Instr. pl. *yaṣabhudehi* ... The instrumental usually designates the means by which something is done. It can furthermore denote the reason "on account of" or "due to" which something happens (cf. Durioselle 1977: § 599).

Instr. + gen. + *karya*. In BC 11 *karya* (as well as *kica*) is combined with a genitive of persons and an instrumental of things, presumably expressing the special meaning that "something is of use for someone" (cf. annotations on 11r1–3 *kaye / karye / kice*, p. 196).

Loc. sg. In BC 11 a few words must be translated as "with regard to ..., related to ..." These mostly end in *-e*, which could be interpreted as accusative or locative. For the use of accusative

5 "The form *trae* (instead of expected *trayo*) will be due to analogy with *due*" (Baums 2009: 227).

instead of the expected locative, cf. BHSD § 7.23, although this specific case is not listed. In BC 6 a similar case is clearly in the loc. sg. (*evadukhami* and *evaṇisamarthami*, "with regard to such painful [and] useless [dharmas]"). Thus, also the cases ending in *-e* have been understood as locatives rather than accusatives.

6.5 Verbal Forms

In general, the 3rd sg. and pl. endings *-di* and *-ti* are not easy to differentiate paleographically, but there are also clear examples of the spelling *-ti* where only singular is possible.

6.5.1 Present

The verbal forms in the present tense occurring in all three manuscripts are:

- BC 4: 3rd sg. *prajahati*, *lavheti* (caus.?), *varedi* (caus.)
- BC 6: 2nd sg. *duśas̱i*, *jaṇas̱i*, *rajas̱i*; 3rd sg. *phaṣadi*, *bh(*odi)/bhoti*;
  1st pl. *duśama*, *rajama*
- BC 11: 3rd sg. *asti*, *citiadi* (or pass.?), *vacadi* (or pass. *vucadi*?); 3rd pl. *jaṇati*

In some verbs the suffix *-ia-* is indicative of the MIA passive form (cf. Nird[L2] *phaṣiadi*, Baums 2009: 231, referring to von Hinüber 2001: § 458). These are: 6v3 *rajiadi … duśiadi* (as opposed to the spellings *rajama*, *rajas̱i*, *duśama*, and *duśas̱i*, or also, for example, *duśadi* in Nird[L2]) as well as 6v8 *ichiadi*. The passive forms are:

- BC 4: 3rd sg. *labhadi*, *vucadi*
- BC 6: 3rd sg. *ichiadi*, *duśiadi*, *rajiadi*, *vucadi*
- BC 11: 1st sg. *mucami* (or active?); 3rd sg. *khaïti*, *labhadi*, *vijadi*, *vihañadi*, *vucadi*

6.5.2 Optative

In BC 4, *ṇas̱ea* seems to be a regular optative form, but several different spellings (*ṇas̱ae*, *ṇas̱e*, *ṇas̱ee*) make this uncertain. Similarly, the form *aharea* used in addition to *aharae* gives rise to the question of whether both cases intended a noun in the dat. sg., or an adjective with the suffix *-aka* (see annotations on 4r25 *ṇas̱e/aharae*, p. 183). In BC 11, *aharae* and *ṇas̱e* are consistent, pointing to a noun/adjective.

In BC 6, *upajeadi* could also be a causative, but an identical form in the Gāndhārī *Prajñāpāramitā* is clearly a simple optative: AsP[Sp] 5-54 *avaro bosisatvo upajeati* ~ AsP *athāparaḥ kauśika bodhisattvo mahāsattva utpadyeta* (Falk and Karashima 2013: 160/162). Thus, the verbal endings *-eadi/-eati* seem to be synonymous with *-ea*, the choice of one or the other depending on the scribe's preference or habit (cf. also Caillat 1992b: 113–15 [§ 3.4]).

The endings *-iea* have been understood as passive forms in the optative: 11r15–17 *gachiea … aṇubhavi{da}ea* (later written *aṇubhaviea*) … *bhavi{da}ea … uadiea … ṇas̱iea* and 11v3, 11v6 *ichiea*. Likewise the ending *-ieadi* (6v3 *rajieadi … duśieadi*).

The optative forms occurring in the three manuscripts are (3rd sg. if not stated otherwise):

- BC 4: no clear examples
- BC 6: *adahea*, *upajeadi*, *kareadi/kareati*, *duśieadi*, *paricae* (read *paricea* ?), *bhaveadi/bhaveati*, *matreadi*, *siadi/siati* (sg. and pl.), *rajieadi*

- BC 11: *aṇubhaviea, ichiea, uadiea, upajea, gachiea, jugidea, ṇaś̱iea, ṇikhalidea, par⟨*i⟩cea, bhave* (1×), *bhaviea* (1×), *bhavea* (4×), *siadi*; uncertain if sg. or pl.: *khaveati, ṇaś̱eati*

6.5.3 Imperative

BC 4: only *paḏitiṭha* as 2nd sg.; BC 11: *bhodu* 3rd sg. with an optative sense, expressing a wish ("may be, let be"). For *bhodu* = Skt. *bhavatu*, cf. Burrow 1937: § 98, Konow 1929: cxv.

6.5.4 Future

- BC 4: 1st sg. *bhikṣiśe, cariśe*; 3rd sg. *vaïśadi, hakṣadi*, probably also *kahati* (cf. annotations on 4r24, p. 183); 3rd pl. *hakṣati* (in one instance probably *akṣati*[6]), *ataraṣ̱aïśati, upajiśati*
- BC 6: 3rd sg. *dakṣiśati* (perhaps future of **dakṣadi* = Skt. **drakṣyati* / P *dakkhati*, or maybe another future form based on a different root)
- BC 11: 3rd sg. *bhaviśadi*; 3rd pl. *hakṣati, hakṣadi*

The unique instance of *bhaviśadi* in 11v24 (... *ṇica bhaviśadi aṭhaṇo*) could be due to its being part of an idiomatic expression, or being "cited" as part of an argumentation, since it is written as *hakṣadi / hakṣati* in all other cases. On the other hand, *hakṣadi* could also be understood as an optative (as observed by Burrow regarding the Niya documents)[7] and thus *bhaviśadi* rather as a "real" future form. This would correspond well with the abundant use of optatives in BC 4.

Until now, the future form *hakṣad/ti* = Skt. *bhaviṣya(n)ti* is only known from the Senavarma inscription (*hakṣati*), the Shahbazgarhi Rock Edict 13 (*akṣati*), the Niya documents, and the Gāndhārī pūrvayoga and avadāna texts (Av^{L6} *hakṣe*, Lenz 2003; Av^{L1} *hakṣadi*, Lenz 2010). According to Lenz (2003: 141), it can be assumed that the future form *hakṣe* "is a colloquial form and that *bhaviṣe* was borrowed from the source dialect of the text from which it was ultimately derived." His conclusion is based on the fact that *hakṣe* appears in a text written in a "colloquial form of Gāndhārī" (Av^{L6}) but *bhaviṣe* is found in a text that seems to be a "translation or transposition of a text originally written in a MIA dialect other than Gāndhārī" (EĀ^{L}, Allon 2001).[8] The Central Asian documents have the same future form and they, too, were originally composed in Gāndhārī, although in a provincial spoken form that is "overlain with stereotyped legal and bureaucratic jargon" (Salomon 1999a: 139–40).

---

6 For *ākṣeti* as an origin for P *acchati* "to be," cf. Turner 1936. On p. 802 he refers to *akṣaṃti* in Shahbazgarhi (Hultzsch 1925: *vrakṣaṃti*).

7 Burrow 1937: §§ 99–100 and 127 ("used for both *siyati* and *bhaviṣyati*. The optative sense is the more usual," Burrow 1937: 133).

8 Salomon (1999: 138–40) classifies the stylistic varieties of Gāndhārī into two main forms: (A) colloquial Gāndhārī, and (B) translated Gāndhārī. The latter is subdivided into (B1) scholastic/commentarial style, and (B2) narrative/poetic style. According to him, avadāna-type texts are generally written in this more informal Gāndhārī "in its original form" (Salomon 1999a: 114), supposedly as "Gandhāran lore" (Salomon 1999a: 139).

Therefore, we might assume that our manuscripts (BC 4, BC 6, and BC 11) were written directly in Gāndhārī and not translated from some other source. This might also help explain why no other parallel in any Indian language has yet been found.

6.5.5 Preterite

BC 4/6/11: The only finite preterite verb form (perfect tense) is *aha* = Skt. *āha*,[9] which however could also be translated in a present tense-meaning. In the Niya documents, *āha* receives present-tense terminations: G *ahati*, "says"; cf. also Baums 2009: 230 for *aha* as 3rd sg./pl. in a present-tense meaning in the Nird^{L2}.

6.5.6 Absolutives (Gerunds)

While a wide range of absolutive endings are evident in Sanskrit and Pali,[10] in BC 4, BC 6, and BC 11 the majority have the ending *-ita* = Skt. *-itvā*. It is not always evident whether a simple or causative form is intended, but most are probably not causatives. G *hoita*, for instance, could be interpreted as an absolutive of the causative of √*bhū*, i.e., Skt. *bhāvayitvā* / P *bhāvetvā*,[11] but in analogy to P *bhavitvā* (Sn 56, next to *hutvā* in Sn 43 and *hutvāna* in Sn 281; cf. PTSD s.v. *bhavati*), G *hoita* may as well be an absolutive of the base verb (Skt. *bhūtvā* / P *bhavitvā*).

Some of the forms ending in *-ta* can represent an absolutive or a past participle, since on rare occasions *-t-* is written where etymologically *-d-* is expected (see chapter 5 on phonology, p. 83). Examples of this are: 11r6–7 *akhaïta*, *khaïta*, *varjita*, as well as 11r34 *chidita*, *uṣ̄ata*, *piṣita*. Even though it might be possible to understand those forms as adjectives / past participles, they have been usually been translated as absolutives.

Absolutives in *-ita* (Skt. *-itvā*):

- BC 4: *paricaïta*, *hoita*
- BC 6: *jaṇita*
- BC 11: *akhaïta*/*khaïta* (?), *uṣ̄ata* (?), *chidita* (?), *citita*, *dhaṇaïta*, *paśita*, *paricaïta*, *piṣita* (?), *prajahita*, *varjita* (?), *viṣ̄a{ja}jita* (?)

Absolutives in *-ya*:

- BC 6: *uadae* (within a stock phrase)
- BC 11: *upaje*

9 Salomon 2008a: 158: "Other than the frozen forms *aha* and *ahu* = Skt. *āha*, *āhuḥ* in the Dhp^{K}, there seem not to be any other clear cases of old perfects surviving in Gāndhārī."

10 That is: *-(i)tvā*, *-ya*, *-tvāna*, *-tu* / P *-tvā*. For the last two, cf. Allon 2001: 117.

11 Cf. Baums (2009: 116): "The problematic form *parihoita* appears to be an absolutive of a causative with regular analogical replacement of the OIA termination *-ayitvā* (§ 5.1.4.8; but see also the text note on line 9·228). The root vowel *o* is unexpected since labialization before [*v*] otherwise only applies to short [*a*], making it likely that the root has been analogically reshaped under the influence of the presence stem, as previously observed in the past participle *hoda-* (§ 4.2.2.1.1). Alternatively and less likely, it could be a direct development from OIA *paribhāvayitvā*, with rare contraction of *āva* > *o* (von Hinüber 2001: § 145)."

6.5.7 Participles

6.5.7.1 Present Participles

The following rare occurrences have been explained as corresponding to the OIA present participle ātmanepada ending *-āna*: *pariceaṇa* and *uadiaṇa*. In all other cases the suffix *-maṇa* for Skt. *-māna* has been used: BC 4 *deṣ̱amaṇa*, *puyamaṇa*, *praïṭhavamaṇa*, *varjamaṇa*, *karamaṇa*; BC 11 *varjamaṇa*. In general, present participles seem not to have been declined—or the nom. sg. may have ended in *-a* (cf. Salomon 2000: 94).

6.5.7.2 Past Participles

The past participles ending in *-(i)da* (Skt. *-(i)ta*) are:

- BC 4: *aïvadida*, *codida*, *paḏiladha*, *paricata*, *pariñad.* (uncertain since incomplete), *par⟨*i⟩ṇirvahido*, *paribhaṭha*, *palaśpada*, *praṇide*, *praladhe*, *ladhe*, *varjida*, *virata-*, *vrude* (uncertain meaning), *suladha*
- BC 6: *likhida-* (also *likhidae*)
- BC 11 *acida*, *aṇubhavavida*, *aparibhuta-*, *jugida*, *ṇaśida*, *ṇikhalida-*, *dukhavida*, *parigrahida* (also *ṇaṇaparigrahidia*), *paribhuta-*, *vuto*, *hode*

Past participles ending in *-ṇa* (Skt. *-na*):

- BC 4: *-ṇiṣ̱aṇa*
- BC 6: *paripuṇa*
- BC 11: *upaṇa*

Some past participles have been nominalized and translated as nouns: *aṇagade*, *adidaaṇagada-pracupaṇa-*, *adide*, *parvayida-*, *pracupaṇe*, *budha-*, *vivegagada-*.

In 4r20 certain past participle forms (*uadiṇae*, *aṣ̱ivaṣ̱idae*/*aṣ̱ivasidae*, *uekṣidae*, and *paricatae*) are used in combination with *hakṣadi*, probably forming some kind of "compound future tense" comparable to the "compound past tense" labeled by Burrow 1937: § 114 with regard to the Niya documents for the construction *-dae* in combination with an auxiliary verb like G *siyati* (cf. annotations, p. 174). Also in BC 6 such a construction is used, here combined with *siadi*: 6v4–5 *karavidae*, *vitrae*, *saṃthidae* (cf. annotations, p. 256).

6.5.7.3 Future Passive Participles (Gerundives)

In all three manuscripts the gerundive suffix *-dava* (Skt. *-tavya*) is quite prevalent; in a few instances *-aṇia*/*-aṇea* (Skt. *-anīya*) as well as *-ya* (Skt. *-ya*) also occur. The endings of *-dava* are quite regular: m. nom. sg. *-o*, nom. pl. *-a*; n. nom. sg. *-e*, n. pl. *-a*; only *vatave* related to *dume uhae* seems to be pl. despite appearing singular (probably parallel to the flexibility of *uhae* being sg. or pl.). From the mere Gāndhārī form it is often not discernible if a gerundive is based on the causative or the base verb (cf. Baums 2009: 236).

Gerundives ending in *-(i)dava* (Skt. *-(i)tavya*):

- BC 4: *aṇuśaśidava*, *abhi(*ṇadi)dave* (reconstruction uncertain), *ahigakṣidave*, *ahivadidava*, *upadidave*, *kaṭave*, *codidava*, *juhoṣ̱idave*, *deśidavo*, *paribhaṣ̱idave*, *paribhujidave*, *palaśpidava*, *praoḏidave*, *vatave*, *varjidava*, *ṣ̱aṣ̱idava*, *suparibhaṣ̱idavo*

- BC 6: *ichidava*, *kaṭava*, *karitava* (? uncertain due to context, but also because of *-t-* instead of *-d-*)
- BC 11: *(*a)ṇubhavidave*, *ecakhaïdave* (*eca-* uncertain), *upajidave*, *kaṭave*, *citidave*, *pajahidava*, *paricaïdave*, *prahadava*, *bhavidave*, *hoidava*

Gerundives ending in *-aṇia/-aṇea* (Skt. *-anīya*):
- BC 4: *taraṇia* / *ta《ra》ṇ{u}ia* (uncertain)
- BC 11: *ṭ́havaṇia*, *pariyaṇeo*, *pidivaṇeo* (uncertain meaning)

Gerundives ending in *-ya* (Skt. *-ya*):
- BC 4: *(*vitre)a* / *vitrea* (uncertain)
- BC 11: *karye* (possibly also twice written *kaye*), *kice*

Chapter 7

Text Edition

For all three manuscripts, first the text is presented as it appears in the reconstructed scrolls. Next, the reconstructed text and a translation are provided on facing pages. Missing passages have been added to the text and it is structured into paragraphs, indicated by §. This structure is not visible in the original manuscripts, but it is implicit, at least in BC 4, through numbers written at the end of some of the paragraphs. Interlinear additions are marked in the reconstructed text as well as in the translation, since most of them are glosses rather than omitted words.

Grey shading in the reconstruction indicates unclear and therefore untranslated passages. Passages in square brackets [ ] within the translation are additions by the editor for a better understanding of the text. Sometimes Sanskrit words in their stem form are added in round brackets ( ) to clarify which term is being referred to in the English translation. Translations of very uncertain reconstructions given only in the footnotes are marked with "(*?)," as opposed to translations of quite certain reconstructions marked by "(*)" and presented in the general reconstruction. The sign "(?)" after a word or sentence indicates that the translation itself is uncertain.

The sequence of manuscripts is first BC 4, second BC 11, and third BC 6, since BC 6 refers to passages in both BC 4 and BC 11.

7.1 Transliteration

7.1.1 BC 4

4r1 ? ? ? + ? ? ? ? ? ? ? + + + + + ? +

4r2 ṇa hakṣati · se apalios̱eṇa margabhavaṇe hakṣadi [d]u[kho] + ? ? ? +

4r3 [ś]. citaṇe hakṣadi citidasa vis̱adi pridi hakṣati vis̱adi śoa ṇa hakṣati trae [ca] + + [di ṇa hakṣa]ti trae ca su[gadi] + + [ti] trae ca saparaïa mokṣa [hakṣati] trae [sadriṭhi]a

4r4 ? ? trae sadriṭhia suha hakṣati [kaï]ac[e]das̱ia trae ca duha ṇa hakṣati trae ca śu[ha] + + ti trae aśuha ṇa hakṣati trae ca[1] kus̱ala hakṣati trae akus̱ala ṇa hakṣati

4r5 ⟪ /// [da]rśaṇa hakṣati budhapracea + + + + + + + + + + + ? ? ? ? [ma]p[u]rvagama /// ⟫ + + + + + + [ha]kṣati sarvasapati + + + + + + + + + + + + + + + + + + + [kṣa]ti · vado ṇidaṇa ca akus̱ala paveṇa ka[ra] + + + raṇe kuśale puñakṣae ṇa ha[kṣadi]

4r6 + [karaṇa] vaïśadi [bhavid]. [d]. + + + + + + + + + + + + + + +

4r7 + ○ k[i hakṣadi] ? +

4r8 + [i]śadi kus̱ala ca karaṇa vaïśadi [to do c]. .[u h]. ? r.. [pa]lios̱e · ṇa hakṣati [apalios̱]. [ṇa] + r[gabha]

4r9 + tr. dhaduade viratasa viragraaṇuśaśe citaṇe hakṣadi citidasa vis̱adi pridi

4r10 hakṣati vis̱adi śoa ṇa hakṣati trae ca durgadi ṇa hakṣati tra[e ca] .u + + + + + + e [ca] + + + ? ti [sadr]iṭhia ca [trae s]. [ha hakṣati] trae dukha ṇa hakṣati [kaïa]ce

4r11 das̱ia trae ca śuha hakṣati trae aśuha ṇa hakṣati trae kuśala hakṣati tra[e] + + s̱ala ṇa hakṣati trae sapurus̱adarśaṇa [ha]kṣati budhaprac. a trae drugaṇa + hakṣati

4r12 ya mama ta sakṣiteṇa sarvadroaca ◈ ṇa hakṣati sarvasapati hakṣati mokṣasuha ca ha + [di] ime aṇuśaśa hakṣaṯi sarvasiha paricaïta ◦ 1 gagaṇadivalias̱amaloga

4r13 + + [ta]raṇia ⟪ṇisamartha⟫ śaki uadiaṇa gagaṇadivalias̱amaloadhadu .u + + + [a śaki] + [a]diaṇa ko varedi p[a] ? [pe] gagaṇa[diva]lias̱amalo◈adhadu ta⟪[ra]⟫ṇuia śaki

4r14 [pariceaṇa gagavalias̱ama]loadhadusuha vitrea śaki paricea[ṇa] g̱a ko [va]redi ta a [ro] pa[ri]cata ṇa uadi ṇa uadaṇa [te sa]rve duhe aṇuvadaṇa te sarva sapati mokṣasa[2]pati ca · 2

4r15 + + + + + + + ? + ? t[r]ibos̱ae ta asaṃkhe[dehi ka]rpehi [praña] + + + + + + + ?[3] ? ṇisamartho ya dukho ya sudiṇoamo ca prajahati ca se maha is̱emi jadi paḏhamacitupa[de]

4r16 ca [vr]ud[e] prañaparamida ca paḏiladha ṇis̱amartho ca dukho ca sudiṇoamo [ca pari]ña[d]. + ? hi [mo] + ? [pra]l[adhe] ? + + ? [ti] ṇi pa do ṇa praoḏidave ? ? ? ? [ca] + ? + ? ?

---

1 Corrected from *ku*. Also the next letter is overwritten, perhaps correcting a *s̱a*.

2 Apparently corrected from *s̱a*.

3 Character with a horizontal stroke above it.

4r17 varjidavo ca deśidavo ca ◦ 3 yo aña bos̱is̱atva bos̱imaḍami lavheti sa mahi i + [mi dha]retrami ladhe ñaṇe ta ṇa suladha me lavha ṇa ca praoḏidave aha ta ki samo bos̱imaḍami

4r18 labha[di sa]mo añatradeṣ̱ehi ta vucadi samo mos̱imaḍaṇiṣ̱aṇa so so ya bos̱imaḍe śuñe [i] .[e ca] + ña ca deṣ̱a śuña · samo bos̱imaḍa dukhe ca ṇisamarthe ca same ime ca añe ca deṣ̱a tasva same

4r19 ya ti ṇa praoḏidave ◦ 4 khaḍaeṇa kavalaeṇa bhikṣiśe ṇagao ca hoita ṇa vaṇa imo + ṇo [praoḏidave] + .[oñaṇo ca] + [s̱ama]rthañaṇo ca pracaparamido ca pari ? ? pra ? ? + +

4r20 ta ki hakṣati · ⟪5⟫ edeṇa dukhañaṇaṇisamarthañaṇeṇa sarve dukha u[adiṇae a]ṣ̱ivas̱idae ha[kṣadi] uekṣidae hakṣadi sarve suhe paricatae as̱ivasidae hakṣadi ta paraṇirvahi[do]

4r21 [lo]gado cariśe aku[śa]lo varja◈maṇa kuśalo [karamaṇa] + + [g̱a]re[ṇa b]. [dhadha]rma sagho puyamaṇa satvaṇa ca a[r]tho [karama]ṇa dharme[4] ca edam=io ṇis̱ama .tha dukhañaṇo deṣ̱amaṇa

4r22 satva ya bo◈ṣ̱a praïṭhavama[ṇa]◈ṇa ciri [ve] + r[va]sapati ca me [ha] + [di] sarvadroaca ca ṇa hakṣadi atvahida ca parahida ca sarvas̱atvahida ca hakṣadi[5] ◦ 6

4r23 ekadutracadurepaṃcaṣahayavasatahi aloehi yo ari[da] karae as̱atiade ca + loṇeade ca yo praṇide rae ⟪ede uhae miṣ̱o⟫ suparibhaṣ̱idavo ca yabhudehi paribhaṣ̱ehi codidav[a ca]

4r24 [yas̱abhude]hi svadoṣ̱ehi svadroacehi varjidava ca s[u]duro adide vi juhos̱idave pracu[pa]ṇae ṇa [a] + + didave aṇagada ṇa [a] .i + + dave trikoḏi kahati paribhaṣ̱idave codidave ca vatave [dum]. [uha]e

4r25 tava triṇa sugadiṇa ṇaṣ̱e triṇa dro[ga]diṇa ahara[e] triṇa ⟪maje ṇis̱amarthe ·⟫ sapuruṣ̱aṇa ⟪budhaṇa⟫ ṇa[ṣ̱a]e triṇa as̱apuruṣ̱aṇa ⟪ma[j].⟫ [a] + + e triṇa mokṣaṇa ṇaṣ̱ae triṇa badhaṇaṇa aharae driṭhadhamio triṇa suhaṇa ṇas̱̄ae triṇa [d]. [khaṇa]

4r26 aharae triṇa śuhaṇa ṇaṣ̱e triṇa aśu[haṇa a] + + + + + + + [laṇa ṇa]ṣ̱ee triṇa akuṣ̱alaṇa aharae triṇa + + + + + + + a triṇa mi + + + [ha]rea triṇa [lah]. [ṭ̄haṇa] + + .e[a]

4r27 triṇa alas̱iaṇa aharea triṇa kicaṇa ṇaṣ̱ea triṇa aki[caṇa] + [har]. [a] triṇa [ka]rmaṇa + .e + .iṇa akarmaṇa aharea triṇa śpriṣ̱aṇaṇa ṇaṣ̱ea + + + [śpr]. [ṣ̱aṇa]ṇa aharea .[r]. [ṇa arogaṇa]

4r28 ṇaṣ̱ea triṇa gelañaṇa aharea ⟪maje ca ṇ. s̱amarth. purv[e] dukhe pa[c̱]a dukhe [ma] + + + [sama]rthe purve aśuha pa + + śu[ha] maja ṇisamartha sarvatra ithu kaṭave⟫ śeṣ̱ae patade hi vivaryaeṇa matra ca idara ca ahi + [d]. dava ca yas̱abhudaaṇuśaśeṇa ca aṇuśaśidava palaśpidava ca

4v1 [e]kadutracadurapa[ṃca]ṣayavasata aloa aṇaride kerea · as̱atia ca a[loṇe] + ca aṇari[de ke]rao ede tava uhae miṣo ahivadidava yas̱abhuda picara ahivada[va]

4v2 codidava ca ṣ̱aṣ̱idava ca yas̱abhudehi svayaaṇuśaśehi svasapatihi palaśpidava + + ? + + + + + + + + + + + ḏa cite upadidave pracupaṇe ca ṣaṣadaeṇa matro ca

4v3 idaro ca paribhujidave aṇagade ca śpadimo [ahi]ga[kṣidave] ? ? + + [ka ra ṣ]. [d]. [ṣ]. [m]. + + + + + + + + + + + + + + + + + + ? [ca] kahati ahivadidave ka[hati] codidave

---

[4] Initially written as *dharmo*.

[5] Some of the letters (*kṣadi* ◦) are written over something else.

4v4 vatave dume uhae · triṇa drogadiṇa ṇaś̱ea moyea triṇa sugadiṇa aharea triṇa 《maj. ca ṇi[s̱a]》 [kama]pra[mu]haas̱apuru[ṣ̱aṇa] ṇaś̱ea triṇa budhapramuhasapuruṣ̱aṇa aharea triṇa sa[ṃ]sa[ra]

4v5 rabadhaṇaṇa ṇaś̱ea triṇa mokṣaṇa [aharea · driṭhadhamia] triṇa du + [ṇa ṇa]ś̱ea triṇa suhaṇa a + [re]a · triṇa aś. + + ṇaś̱ea triṇa śuhaṇa aharea triṇa akuś̱alaṇa ṇaś̱ea

4v6 [tri]ṇa kuś̱alaṇa aharea triṇa midhaṇa ṇaś̱ea triṇa jag̱ariaṇa aharea triṇa ala[s̱i] + ṇa ṇaś̱e[a] ◈ triṇa lahuṭ́haṇaṇa aharea triṇa ag̱icaṇa ṇaś̱ea

4v7 triṇa kicaṇa aharea triṇa akarmaṇa ṇaś̱ea triṇa karmaṇa aharea triṇa aśpriś̱a + [ṇa] ṇaś̱ea triṇa ◈ śpriś̱aṇaṇa aharea triṇa gelañaṇa ṇaś̱ea triṇa

4v8 arogaṇa aharea sakṣiteṇa sadriṭhia saparaïa avarimaṇaṇa triṇa triṇa do + + + ś̱ea triṇa triṇa sapatiṇa aha[rea] ? ? ? ? ? + ? [ithumi] ohoro satahi

4v9 arede [k]erea paribhaṣidava ◈ h[o]r[o] as̱atia al[o]ṇe[a] + [aride ka]raï paribhaṣ̱idave 《[codidave va]r[jidave]》 [○] ithumi ohoro sata matra aṇaride keraa

4v10 as̱atia aloṇ[e]o ca [o] + ro aṇaride [ko] paribhaṣ̱idave codidave palaśpidave ki aṇuśaśe hakṣadi te satahi 《matra》 arida keraa aloṇea as̱atiade 《ca》 idarade arida [kere] +

4v11 paribhaṭha ya codida ca varjida ca akṣati te śpabhavasa ataras̱aïśati ṇa ca bhuyo upajiśa[ti ○] te sata matra alo[a aṇari] + .[e]rea aloṇea as̱atia idara aṇarid[e] k[e]rea aïvadida ca

4v12 codida ca palaśpada ca sadakalo paḏi[ti]ṭ́ha sati[dehi] ṣadasa aṇag̱ade ca tomi u[j]u ca ṇe [a] p. [ci] + [va] ? pialo i[th]umi hurahu ekamekasa kaṭave [ma]tra[sa]horo · idarasahoro

7.1.2 BC 11

Part 1r

11r1 + + + + + ? khaï[ti] baho ca śpaho ca ta vucadi ṇevi edes̱a kuś̱aleṇa kaye ṇevi kuś̱a

11r2 + + + + + + + + + + + [ṇa] karye ṇa marga[suhe]ṇa ṇevi edes̱a s̱ahi paramidehi kaye ṇeva suheṇa

11r3 + + + + + + + + + + + + mehi kice ṇevi suheṇa ◦ ṇevi jaṇati ya es̱a śpahu ca [ba] + + + ? ?

11r4 + + + + + + + + + + + edehi khaïti e[de]hi ecakhaïdave [a]svahu [va]ṇa avi kice kuś̱alehi

11r5 + + + + + + + + + + + + ? ? + ? + + + l[aṇa] dharm[a]ṇa [tati] a[sva]hu suverao paricaïdave yas̱a ṇa [aña]

Part 2r

11r6 + + + + + + + + + + vi khaïta dukha kayadukhe avi varjamaṇa dukhe ci[ta]dukhe [ete] ? ? ◊

11r7 due dukha paṃḍidaṇa ho vaṇa avi akhaïta kayasuhe avi varjita citasuhe aṇubhavaṇa tasva suṭhu

11r8 ñaṇami abhae kaṭave pariñaprahaṇa ñaṇami yava[6]de uhae suha hakṣati uhaa ca dukha ṇa hakṣati

11r9 + + + + + + + [ha]rae sarvasapatie ca ṇaś̱e [ma]je ca ṇisamarthe ◊[7]

11r10 + + + + + + + + + + ricaae sarvadroacasa aharae sarvasapatie ca ṇaś̱e driṭhadhamiasa

11r11 + + + + + + + + + asa cedas̱iasa ○ uayeasa avayeasa ○ sakhadaasakhadasa droacasa aharae

11r12 + + + + + + [ś̱]. ? + ? ṇa sarvadroacasa ahara[e sa] .[va] + patie ca ṇaś̱e śpahu ca bahu ca keṇa

11r13 ṣaṣadae paricaea parameṇa ṣadimeṇa paricaïdave · ṇa vaṇa citiadi tati mama ṇa parica

11r14 [i] + .[e] sudhu vaṇa citiae ta parameṇa ṣadimeṇa paracea ṇa vacadi ahu mio sakṣi ? ciri me ta ṣado

Part 3r

11r15 + ? ? ? ca sarva durgadi gachiea

11r16 + + + + + + + + + + + + + .o sarva aśuhe aṇubhavidaea sarve śuhe [ṇa bhavida]ea sarva akuśale aṇubhaviea

11r17 ? ? ? ? ? [e e] piala yava sasaṃra u[8]adiea ṇivaṇ[u] ca bos̱i ca ṇaś̱iea ○ · osagrasuhe ṇame as̱a di di maha[ś̱]. +

11r18 pariñasuhe ca mahaś̱ie · aparas̱iṇasuhe ◈ svaas̱iṇasuhe [a]viñatis. he ? kṣi ṇe [a] g̱[a] ? [ṇ]. ? suhe ? .u ?

11r19 s. he sa .va [s̱atva] .i [ya] ṇ. s. h. sarvas̱atva ṇa ma sa ṇi va suhe sudeś̱asuhe su[gada] dhamos̱aṇasuhe ya vela chata yatra chade suhe

---

6 Overwritten and corrected from *sa*.

7 Rest of the line left blank, perhaps due to the surface of the birch bark.

8 Corrected from *a* to *u* by an additional circle at the lower end.

11r20 + + + + + + + + + + + [to]g̱adasuhe śuhe atog̱adasuhe mokṣasuhe avhiñaaśreasuhe vivег̱asuhe asagaṇia[suh].

11r21 + + + + + + + + + + ? [ṇa] suhe paṃḍidaśriyaṇa suhe divacakṣu va paracitañaṇa śriyaṇa suhe satvahidasuhe

11r22 + + + + + + + + + + + sakṣiteṇa avarimaṇados̱a avakra ?[9] + + + [va]rimaṇagu[ṇa]vi[di] miśa aharea suhe

11r23 + + + + + + + + + + ? [s]uhe mahaś̱ie ○ aha ki es̱a pras̱aṇaka[rmo] ruve · as̱a va aruve ◊

Part 4r

11r24 ? ? ? + ? ? ? ? ? ? [ita] ṭ́havaṇia ya ṇa sarvas̱atve[hi] parigrahida ṇa se[10] kamabhoyi

11r25 asti ye ṇaṇaparigrahidia eva bahujaṇasas̱araṇadukha ◦ es̱a vi pradig̱arasuhe uṇis̱a

11r26 s̱asuhe ca ṇa ṇi[ca] ṇa atve ṇa ka suhiṇa bhave es̱a vi pradig̱ara[s]. [he ca ua]ṇi[s̱a]suhe ca ◊

11r27 + + + + + + + + + [maja ṇisa]martha purve aśuhe pac̱a aśuhe maja ṇisamartha ṇa karye ◊

11r28 + + + + + + + + + + [r]ita osagrasa ca aṇuśaśa paśita citita .u ? [da ṇa] ? avarimaṇa ◊

11r29 + + + + + + + + + + + muḏeasa yati pridi ṇa upajea śiṭha ? ? ? ? upaṇa ◊

11r30 + + + + + + + + + + + pajea pridi ṇikhalidea ta upaje jugidea sa upajea jugida sa upa[je]

11r31 + + + + + + + + + + + [je]a ◦ parvayidehi ṇikhalida sa upaje pridi budhehisa upajea aprañati

11r32 [upaj]. a pridi paribhu[ḏ]asa upajea aparibhu[ḏ]asa 《suverao》 upajea sakṣiteṇa sarvatradeś̱ehi sarvatradea

11r33 ṇicakalo ṇa jado yaṇa upajea sagaṇia upajea viveg̱ag̱adasa upajea ○ ◊

11r34 ? ? + ? ? + + + + [a jibha] pramuha chidita tulie us̱ata [ya] atra piṣita kim=asuhe teṇa ṇa karye

11r35 ? ? ? + + + + + + + ? duehi caduraguḏiehi as̱akeṃa karpa a[11]cida ca dukhavida ca

11r36 suhade ca ṇaś̱ida sarvadroaca aṇubhavavida s[arvasapati] ṇaś̱ida sakṣiteṇa yavi mokṣade ṇaśida

11r37 ajavi asakhea karpa droace khaveati sapati ṇaś̱eati mokṣo ṇaś̱eati ta imehi ṇa karye sudhu

11r38 sarvadroacade mucami sarvasapati labhadi mokṣa ca ◦ ṇa bhio amaho labheṇa ṣade hoidave adidaaṇa

11r39 g̱ad[a]p.ac. paṇehi alabheṇa ṣade hoidave · ṇa bhi amahu parubhuteṇa ṣade hoidava aparibhuteṇa ṣa

11r40 d. hoidava adidaaṇag̱adapracupaṇehi amitrahoḏeapos̱aṇam=iva ṇa bhiu vayaeṇa

11r41 ṣade ho◈idave ava[yede]ṇa ṣade hoidave

---

9 Probably *m.* or *t.*

10 Corrected from *[a]*.

11 Corrected from *va*.

Part 5r

11r42 + + + + + + + + + + suhe viñatidukhavidimiśasuhe yo vela cha[d]. [ta v]ela ṇa labhadi dukhavidimiśa[s]u +

11r43 + + + + + + + + .o vidimiśasuhe yatra des̱e chade tatra ṇa labhadi di dukhavidimiśasuhe aśuha ◊

11r44 [vidimiśas]uhe [ka]yadukhacitadukhavidimiśasuhe sarvakayadukhavidimiśasuhe citadukhavidimi

11r45 śasuhe cedas̱iadukhavidimiśasuhe d[u]rgadidukhavidimiśasuhe saṃsaraüavatiṇirvaṇa

11r46 [ṇa]s̱a[dukhavidi]miśasuhe śidaüs̱adharaṇadukhavidimiśasuhe civarakṣayakayakṣaya

11r47 amoya[ṇakṣaya]dukhavidimiśasuhe atvahisaparahisasarvas̱atvahisavidimiśasuhe ◊

11r48 «ṇis̱amarthavidimiśasuhe» [eda]pramuhe avarimaṇa[dukha]vidimiśasuhe kamasuhehi ṇa ka[r]ya avaramiṇaguṇavidimiśa viveg̱averagra

11r49 suhe ṇa karye atra ca viveg̱asuhami veragrasuhami ca aya kamasuhe atog̱ado avaśi ṇa siadi

11r50 ? ? ? ? ṇa ida ṭ́haṇe vijadi avaśi vi + g̱asuami veragrasuhami kamasuhe atog̱ade keṇa karaṇeṇa

11r51 ◈ ta vucadi śile atog̱ade kṣati atog̱ade daṇe atog̱ade daṇe atog̱ade avi amis̱adaṇe avi dharmadaṇe

11r52 atog̱ade te yatra ime dhama atog̱ada ta kamasuhe ṇa atog̱ade bhavea ṇa ida ṭ́haṇo vijadi

11r53 sayavisa śali sarvarthae śali vuto avi palale atog̱ade yavasa tus̱e atog̱ade

Part 5v

11v1 ma tu pa ye a s̱i ola[ia] es̱a pridi[suhe] upajadi ṇi li ṇi .o .e pa[r]iñapridi prajahaṇap[r]i

11v2 hoidave pridi hoidave pridi avaśi hoidave pridisuha acala pridi asas̱araṇe

11v3 pridi aṇavaṭie pridi aparihaṇadhama pridi akṣaye pridi yadi va ṇa ichiea ◊

11v4 ta avaśa hode pridi ṇisamartha ca dukho ca aśuho ca paricaïta kas̱a pridi ṇa upajea ◊

11v5 es̱a ca ṇisamarthe ca dukhe ca aśuhe ca paricaïta [a]varimaṇaṇa dos̱aṇa avarimaṇaṇa droacaṇa ṇas̱e

11v6 avarimaṇaṇa sapatiṇa aharae paricaeta [ka]sa paricaïta ṇa pridi upajea yidi va ichiea

11v7 mame pri[dis]uhe upajea ta avaśi upaṇa pridi yahi amuḏa khaïta mame kayesuho bhodu

11v8 ta avaśi suhe ṇa bhavidave vis̱a[jaji]ta mame suho bhodu meme dukhaavaṇao bhodu avaśi hode

11v9 + + + [avaśi ho]de sue va ṇisamartha ◈[12] dukha ca aśuha ca paracaïta mame pridi

11v10 + + + + + + + + ? vado ca paricaade avarami[13]ṇados̱aprahaṇa avarimaṇaṇa sapatiṇa aharae

11v11 + + + + + + + + + + pridisuhe ṇa ida ṭ́haṇe vijadi avaśi upajidave sudhu citidave

---

[12] There is space for about four akṣaras after *ṇisamartha*, but no writing is discernible except perhaps the upper half of a middle dot before the following *dukha*.

[13] The scribe started to write *ri*, then corrected it to *ma*.

Part 4v

11v12 ola[i]a jaṇe vihañadi + digarasuhasa arthae jaṇe vihañadi uaṇiṣ̱asuhasa ca artha[e]

11v13 jaṇe vihañadi [ya]hi due gaḍa dupadua aj̄atvabahira teṣ̱a ca bheṣ̱ajesuhe ṇaśadi gro

11v14 upajea iva eṣ̱a so ya ṇisamartho aroa gaḍaṇa bheṣ̱aje yadi va kamadhadu yadi va ruvadhadu

11v15 yadi va arupadhadu ○ 《loi[e]ṇa tava karaṇeṇa》 c[a cha] paricaïta sarvadroacade mokṣe sarva[sa]patie ca driṭhadhamisaparaïa[s̱]a[14]

11v16 pradibh[ave ku ṇa] ? ? + ? ṣado paricae aloieṇa tava karaṇeṇa picu ṇa puña dhaṇaïta sarvasa

11v17 + + + + + + + + + + [ṇ]. 《ṣade》 paricae ○ 《1》 loutareṇa bhudañaṇeṇa ṇa kica paricaïta aṇicag̱a

11v18 reṇa aṇatvag̱ar[e]ṇa śuñag̱areṇa aparibhujitreaag̱areṇa avedeaag̱areṇa sudiṇag̱araṇa

11v19 akuhicaag̱amaṇaakuhicag̱amaṇaag̱areṇa parimaṇasaceaag̱areṇa ṇa kici paricaïta

11v20 + + + + + + + + ? ? [sarva]droacasa ṇaṣ̱e sarpasapatie ca padilabhe ku ṇa acitieṇa

11v21 + + + + + + + + + + + + ? [d]ukho paricaïta dukhabio pari[caïta] ◇

11v22 + + + + + + + + + + + + dukhabie paracaïta dukhasargharya gaḍa[sagha]rya roasagharya

11v23 + + + + + + + + + [gha]rya paracaïta keṇa karaṇeṇa dukhasagha .ye [ta v]. [ca] di ? [ya] tra [yeṇa]

11v24 + + + + + + + + + + + ta ? j̄a e ṇica bhaviśadi aṭ́haṇo evam=eva āj̄atvia aïdaṇa dukha bahi

11v25 ra aïdaṇa dukha te[ṣ̱a] sagharyade suho bhavea suho upajea ṇa ida ṭ́haṇo vijadi achatvia gada

11v26 + hira gaḍa teṣ̱a [sa] + + + + ho bhavea ṇa ida ṭ́haṇo iva pialo āj̄atvia aśuha bahira aśuha āj̄atvia

11v27 + + + + + + + + + + + + + + + ? l. a[jatvia gaḍa b]. [h]. [r]. [g]. [ḍ]. .[e] + [s]. gh. [y]. [s]. [ho] bhavea ṇa ida ṭ́haṇo

Gloss [teṇa karaṇe] + [du]kho [pa]ri + + + [sa]gh[arya] + + + + + + + + + + + + +
line1 /// ? + ? di bhavea ///
line2 /// + ricaïta ///

Part 3v

11v28 + + + + + + + + + + ? pariña prahaṇakarmo ca · ruve ◦ as̱a va · aruve ta vucadi avi ruve avi aruve ruvaruva

11v29 + + + + + + + + + + + + riyaṇeo pariyaṇeo prahadava pidivaṇe [pidi]vaṇeo pajahidava prajahita prajaha

11v30 + + + + + + + + + + + ṇubhavidave avaśa upaṇa pridi tae teṇa karaṇeṇa avi ruve avi aruve ○ 4 · –

---

14 The last three characters are written above the line due to lack of space.

7.1.3 BC 6

6r1 karitava pariapo uadae ime kadhadhaduaïdaṇa ṇi[c]e [dakṣiśati atva] ? ? + + + + + + + + apar[i]maṇa ? ? [ce a] ? droatie ? ? ? ? ? [a] ? kuhicaag̱amaṇa

6r2 + [h]. + + + + [ca bhaveadi] ? ? [ca] bhaveadi [bhava ca bha]veati ◦ [ta e d]. ? + ? ? ? + ? ? ? ? ? [yam=ida r]. [g̱e] +

6r3 yam=ida gaḏeṇa yam=ida [śaleṇa] ◈ yam=ida ak̲h̲adeṇa yam=ida payeladukh[e]ṇa [yam=ida] ? + + yam=ida jadidukhayava[maraṇa]dukheṇa priaviṇabha[vaa]gradukheṇa yam=ida drude[s̱a] +

6r4 drujaṇasamos̱aṇeṇa yam=ida sakṣiteṇa [yavi dukheṇa samosa]ṇeṇa [t]. ? ? ? [yeṇa] ? ? ? ? + ? + + + + ? ? ṇ. ? ? ? [ṇeṇa] yam=ida [dri]ṭha[dha]mi[a]sapara[ia] avarimaṇeṇa dukheṇa [ṇa] ichidava

6r5 kadhadhaduaïdaṇi siati ◎ ya [ṇi p]u .u [t]. [a] ? ? .u ? ? ? .u + ? ? ? + [śa]la c[a aṇa]k̲h̲ada ca siati ṇa ca avarimaṇa

6r6 dukha siati yas̱a aji hi [de] likhid[a |[15]] droaca ṇa siati · ta ṇi ? ? ? ? ? ? ṇ. [i] + + + + ? + + + .u ? ? ? ṇ. ? ? ◈ ? ? ? ? ? ? ? ? ? ? ? [ca] aspami[a ca]

6r7 eka[kalava ca] parimaṇasacea ca akuhicaag̱amaṇaakuhicag̱amaṇa ca su[di] + ? ? ? ? ? ? ? abhava ca ta imeṇa ṇisamartheṇa ṇa [ichidava] siati kadhadhaduaïdaṇa ◎

6r8 aha ta yadi [a]d[a]h[ea] ed[e] dhama dukha ca ṇisamartha ca eṣ̱a bhude eṣ̱a [pragri] + + ṣ̱a yas̱a[ve] eṣ̱a tas̱e [ta kas̱a] ra[ga ca doṣa ca upajadi e]vadukhami [eva]ṇisamarthami ◊

6r9 t[uo] ca ya ithu jaṇas̱i ◦ kas̱a rajas̱i ca duśas̱i [ca] ta vucadi ta ṇa ka a bo ? ? + ? ? ? ? ? ? + + + + + + + + + + [agaḏasaña] ca aroga[sa] + + ◊

6r10 aśalasaña ca aṇak̲h̲adasaña ca ◦ ṇicasaña ca a[tva]saña ca jivasaña ca bha[va] +

6r11 śeṣ̱a patade likhidae ◊

6v1 aha ta kas̱a abodhasa upajati kas̱a baleṇa ta vucadi saval[o] ? ? ? ca s[ua] vi[bo] + + [ṇa saṃ]thidomaṇas̱a bhoti yadi va maṇa[s̱a bh]. + + + + + ? ? [g]. [b]. [ṇ]. paripuṇa ◊

6v2 ṇa tatva ṇa [e]g̱a[gracitasa] ṇa avikṣitacita[sa] mraduamaṇas̱a bhoti ṇa + + th. do bahumaṇa bhoti aña kuś̱a[la]s[a] viarthae aña [ba]la[va ma ra] amaṇas̱iara akuś̱alasa vi

6v3 arthae ṇa spuramaṇas̱a bhoti ta rajiadi c[a] duśiadi ca ya vaṇa spura upajea[di] + + [gra] g̱acitasa aṭ̱ha ⊗ ya ra[ji]eadi [ca] duśi[e]adi [ca ◊ ya]hi [ñaṇo] ṇa kuḏae suṭhu

6v4 [phaṣa]di ta [ta]raṇae ca siadi tatra ca purve bahu taṇua saña karavi[da] + + + + ? ? [vitra]e ca siadi tatra ca purve suh[e vi]trasu[a] ṇa karavidae siadi saïthida ca ◊

6v5 pura [vi saṃ]thidae siadi · so ca sa[ṃ]thido matreadi taṇua [e a] ? + + + + + + + + + ? + + s. ṇ. abh[a]v[asa] k[ar]eadi kicakica hi [ṭ̱hi]dig̱ica kar[e]adi prove ya dukha jaṇita tasa dukhasa

6v6 vovaś̱amo kareati t[e] tatra tasa bhaṭareasa suha[saña upaj]. [adi] ◊ [t]. [ṇa a e] + + + + + + [+ + vovaś̱am]o ṇa sa[ṃ]thidomaṇas̱a siadi yadi va maṇas̱a siadi taṇu sp. r[a] ṇa cita eg̱a[g]. + + +

---

15 A little vertical stroke above the line, similar to an apostrophe, a small daṇḍa, or the number 1.

6v7 ṇa bahumaṇeṇa yahi aji tahi s[a]va ◈ pada kaṭava ◇ yava aña kica paliosẹṇa ṇa spuramaṇaṣa [bh]. + [+ + +] ta[tra] kuḏ[e]ami rajiadi ca a[ṇ]. + ? + + + + + + + + + + + + + + + + ? ? ? ? + ? ?

6v8 + + ? ? ? [ṇi likh]ide [ith]u ra[jama ja d]u[ś]ama ca ◇ tasva spurami ? ? ? + + + + + + + + [ñ]. [ṇ]. ? ? ? k. ? + [ya] ichiadi ṇa rajaṇa ṇ[a] d. ṣaṇa ma pac̱i vipaḏis̱ara [aho]

6v9 ? [vi] ca ko paḏide ṇisamartha ca dukha ca ṇa par[ica]e [a]h[o] ṇa ya [v]. + + + + + + + + + + + + ? ? [ṇ]. p. [r]. ◈ [diadi] ? ◈

7.2 Reconstruction and Translation

7.2.1 BC 4

§ 1A1

[4r1] ? ? ? + ? ? ? ? ? ? ? + + + + + ? + **[4r2]** ṇa hakṣati · se apalioṣ̱eṇa margabhavaṇe hakṣadi ⟨*·⟩ dukho + ? ? ? + (*tredhaduade viratasa viragra-aṇuśa)**[4r3]** ś(*e)[1] citaṇe hakṣadi ⟨*∘⟩

§ 1A2

citidasa viś̱adi pridi hakṣati viś̱adi śoa ṇa hakṣati ⟨*·⟩ trae ca (*durga)di ṇa hakṣati trae ca sugadi (*hakṣa)ti trae ca saparaïa mokṣa hakṣati ⟨*·⟩ {trae sadriṭhia} **[4r4]** {? ?} trae sadriṭhia suha hakṣati kaïacedaṣ̱ia trae ca duha ṇa hakṣati ⟨*·⟩ trae ca śuha (*hakṣa)ti trae aśuha ṇa hakṣati ⟨*·⟩ trae ca kuś̱ala hakṣati trae akuś̱ala ṇa hakṣati ⟨*·⟩ **[4r5]** ⟪(*trae sapuruṣ̱a)darśaṇa hakṣati budha-pracea (*trae drugaṇa ṇa hakṣati ·) ? ? ? ? mapurvagama (*aṣ̱apuruṣ̱a)⟨*∘⟩ ⟫

§ 1A3

(*sarvadroaca ṇa) hakṣati sarvasapati (*hakṣati) + + + + + + + + + + + + + +[2] (*ha)kṣati · vado ṇidaṇa ca ⟨*·⟩ akuś̱ala paveṇa kara(*ṇeṇa) ⟨*·⟩ (*ka)raṇe kuśale puñakṣae ṇa hakṣadi ⟨*·⟩ **[4r6]** + karaṇa vaïśadi ⟨*·⟩ bhavid. d. + + + + + + + + + + + + + + + **[4r7]** + ○

---

1 For the reconstructions in § 1A, cf. § 1B.

2 Uncertain what to reconstruct. Based on 4r12 (§ 1B3), *mokṣasuha ca hakṣati ime aṇuśaśa* would be possible, however without the concluding *sarvasi⟨*ṇe⟩ha paricaïta*.

§ 1A1

[4r1] … **[4r2]** there will be no … Thus, by being free from desire, developing of the path will 6v7
exist. Suffering … (*For one who is dispassionate with regard to the triple world) **[4r3]** there 11r23
will be contemplation on (*the benefit of dispassion).

§ 1A2

For the one who has contemplated, twenty joys will exist, twenty sorrows will not exist. Three 11r28
bad destinations will not exist, three good destinations will exist, three liberations relating to future life will exist. **[4r4]** Three happy [states] relating to present life will exist, relating to body and mind, three painful [states] will not exist. Three pleasant [states] will exist, three unpleasant [states] will not exist. Three wholesome [states] will exist, three unwholesome [states] will not exist. **[4r5]** ⟪(*Three) meetings (*with worthy men) will exist, [i.e., those] based on [trust in] the Buddha(s),[1] (*three bad companies will not exist, [i.e., with] unworthy men) preceded by …[2]⟫.

§ 1A3

There will (*not) be (*any misery), [but] every fortune (*will exist) … will exist. The state- 6r6
ment and [underlying] theme is: [There will be] an unwholesome [state] on account of a bad [deed]; in the case of a wholesome [deed], there will be no decay of merit **[4r6]** … will speak of … [as a] cause (?) … developed (?) … **[4r7]** …

---

1 In 4r24 (§ 7A2) is found *sapuruṣ̱aṇa* ⟪*budhaṇa*⟫, thus perhaps "Buddhas" in general.

2 Perhaps Kāma (?) as in § 7B2a *kamapramuhaas̱apuruṣ̱aṇa*, but cf. annotations on p. 159.

§ 1B1

ki[3] hakṣadi ? + **[4r8]** +[4] (*va)iśadi kus̱ala ca karaṇa vaïśadi ⟨*·⟩ to do c. .u h. ? r..[5] palios̱e {·} ṇa hakṣati ⟨*·⟩ apalios̱(*e)ṇa (*ma)rgabha**[4r9]**(*vaṇe hakṣadi) ⟨*·⟩ (*dukho)[6] + tr(*e)dhaduade viratasa viragraaṇuśaśe citaṇe hakṣadi ⟨*◦⟩

§ 1B2

citidasa vis̱adi pridi **[4r10]** hakṣati vis̱adi śoa ṇa hakṣati ⟨*·⟩ trae ca durgadi ṇa hakṣati trae ca (*s)u(*gadi hakṣati tra)e ca + + + ? ti ⟨*·⟩ sadriṭhia ca trae s(*u)ha hakṣati trae dukha ṇa hakṣati kaïace**[4r11]**das̱ia ⟨*·⟩ trae ca śuha hakṣati trae aśuha ṇa hakṣati ⟨*·⟩ trae kuśala hakṣati trae (*aku)s̱ala ṇa hakṣati ⟨*·⟩ trae sapurus̱adarśaṇa hakṣati budhaprac(*e)a trae drugaṇa (*ṇa) hakṣati ⟨*◦⟩

§ 1B3

[4r12] ya mama ta sakṣiteṇa ⟨*·⟩ sarvadroaca ṇa hakṣati sarvasapati hakṣati mokṣasuha ca ha(*kṣa)di ⟨*·⟩ ime aṇuśaśa hakṣat̠i sarvasi⟨*ṇe⟩ha paricaïta ◦ 1

§ 2

gagaṇadivalias̱amaloga**[4r13]**(*dhadu) taraṇia ⟪ṇisamartha⟫ śaki uadiaṇa ⟨*·⟩ gagaṇadivalias̱amaloadhadu(*d)u(*ha[7] vitre)a śaki (*u)adiaṇa ⟨*·⟩ ko varedi pa ? pe ⟨*◦⟩

gagaṇadivalias̱amaloadhadu ta⟪ra⟫ṇ{u}ia śaki **[4r14]** pariceaṇa ⟨*·⟩ gaga⟨*ṇadi⟩valias̱amaloadhadusuha vitrea śaki pariceaṇa {ga} ⟨*·⟩ ko varedi ta a ro ⟨*◦⟩

paricata ṇa uadi ṇa uadaṇa ⟨*·⟩ te sarve duhe aṇuvadaṇa ⟨*·⟩ te sarva sapati mokṣasapati ca · 2

---

[3] Cf. 4r20 (§ 5) *ta ki hakṣati* and 4v10 (§ 7C2) *ki aṇuśaśe hakṣadi*. Alternative reading: *ko*, but less likely.

[4] Reconstruct as *(*akus̱ala karaṇa)*? Or possibly negated: *(*akus̱ala karaṇa ṇa)*.

[5] *suhavarga*? *duhavarga*?

[6] Cf. 4r2 (§ 1A1).

[7] Possibly also *(*s)u(*ha)*, but in section § 6, *duha* is connected to *upa-ā√dā* and *suha* to *pari√tyaj*.

§ 1B1

What will happen? … **[4r8]** … will speak of …[3] and will speak of wholesome [deeds as a] cause.
… there will be no desire [for] … By being free from desire, developing of the path **[4r9]** (*will 6v7
exist. Suffering) … For one who is dispassionate with regard to the triple world, there will be 11r23
contemplation on the benefit of dispassion.

§ 1B2

For the one who has contemplated, twenty joys **[4r10]** will exist, twenty sorrows will not exist. 11r28
Three bad destinations will not exist, three good (*destinations will exist, three) … Relating to present life, three happy [states] will exist, three painful [states] will not exist, relating to body and mind. **[4r11]** Three pleasant [states] will exist, three unpleasant [states] will not exist. Three wholesome [states] will exist, three unwholesome [states] will not exist. Three meetings with worthy men will exist, [i. e., those] based on [trust in] the Buddha(s), three bad companies will (*not) exist.

§ 1B3

[4r12] As for what [will be] mine, that in brief is: There will not be any misery, [but] every 6r6
fortune will exist, and the bliss of liberation will exist. These benefits will exist, having let go 11r13–14
of every affection. [End of section] 1.

§ 2

One could cross world **[4r13]** (*systems) as [numerous as] the sands of the river Gaṅgā while
clinging 《useless》; one could (*go through (?)) [all kinds of] (*suffering) in [these] world 11r34–37
systems as [numerous as] the sands of the river Gaṅgā while clinging. Who chooses (?) … ?

One could cross world systems as [numerous as] the sands of the river Gaṅgā **[4r14]** while letting go; one could go through (?) [all kinds of] happiness in [these] world systems as [numerous as] the sands of the river Gaṅgā while letting go. Who chooses (?) … ?

[When everything is] let go, [there will be] no [more] attachment [to worldly possessions and] no [more] clinging [to existence]. Thus, every suffering [will be] without clinging [to it]. Thus, [there will be] every fortune and [especially] the fortune of liberation. [End of section] 2.

---

3 Probably: "will speak of unwholesome [deeds as a] cause." This could point to § 7A. The wholesome deeds then would point to § 7B.

§ 3

[4r15] + + + + + + + ? + ? tribos̱ae ⟨*·⟩ ta asaṃkhedehi karpehi praña(*paramida) + + + ?[8] ? ṇisamartho ya dukho ya sudiṇoamo ca prajahati ca[9] ⟨*◦⟩

se mah⟨*i⟩ is̱emi jadi paḏhamacitupade **[4r16]** ca vrude prañaparamida ca paḏiladha ⟨*·⟩ ṇis̱amartho ca dukho ca sudiṇoamo ca pariñad. + ? hi mo + ? praladhe ? + + ? ti ṇi pa do ṇa praoḏidave ? ? ? ?[10] ca + ? + ? ? **[4r17]** varjidavo ca deśidavo ca ◦ 3

§ 4

yo aña bos̱is̱atva bos̱imaḍami lavheti sa mahi i(*s̱e)mi dharetrami ladhe ñaṇe ⟨*·⟩ ta ṇa suladha me lavha ṇa ca praoḏidave ⟨*◦⟩

aha ta ⟨*·⟩ ki samo bos̱imaḍami **[4r18]** labhadi samo añatrades̱ehi ⟨*·⟩ ta vucadi ⟨*·⟩ samo mos̱imaḍaṇis̱aṇa[11] ⟨*·⟩ so so ya bos̱imaḍe śuñe i(*m)e ca (*a)ña ca des̱a śuña · samo bos̱imaḍ⟨*e⟩ dukhe ca ṇisamarthe ca same ime ca añe ca des̱a ⟨*·⟩ tasva same **[4r19]** ya ti ṇa praoḏidave ◦ 4

§ 5

khaḍaeṇa kavalaeṇa bhikṣiśe ṇagao ca hoita ṇa vaṇa imo (*ña)ṇo praoḏidave ⟨*·⟩ (*dukh)oñaṇo ca (*ṇi)s̱amarthañaṇo ca pracaparamido[12] ca pari ? ?[13] pra ? ? + + ⟨*·⟩ **[4r20]** ta ki hakṣati[14] · ⟪5⟫

§ 6

edeṇa dukhañaṇaṇisamarthañaṇeṇa sarve dukha uadiṇae as̱ivas̱idae hakṣadi uekṣidae hakṣadi ⟨*·⟩ sarve suhe paricatae as̱ivasidae hakṣadi ⟨*·⟩ ta par⟨*i⟩ṇirvahido **[4r21]** log̱ado cariśe ⟨*·⟩ akuśalo varjamaṇa ⟨*·⟩ kuśalo karamaṇa ⟨*·⟩ (*sarva)g̱areṇa[15] b(*u)dhadharmasagho puyamaṇa ⟨*·⟩ satvaṇa ca artho karamaṇa ⟨*·⟩ dharme ca edam io ṇis̱ama(*r)thadukhañaṇo des̱amaṇa ⟨*·⟩ **[4r22]** satva ya bos̱a praïṭhavamaṇa ⟨*·⟩ ṇa ciri ve (*sa)rvasapati ca me ha(*kṣa)di sarvadroaca ca ṇa hakṣadi ⟨*·⟩ atvahida ca parahida ca sarvas̱atvahida ca hakṣadi ◦ 6

---

8 Character with a horizontal stroke above it.

9 The position of this *ca* is syntactically obscure. It might, however, be possible to understand it as connecting two sentences, of which the verb of the first is now lost to us but would have followed *praña(*paramida)*.

10 Maybe *codidave*.

11 Read *bos̱imaḍa◦*.

12 Read *prañaparamido*.

13 Perhaps reconstruct as *pariñado*. The following could be *praoḏidave*, but there is no space for a negation.

14 Cf. 4v10 (§ 7C2.1) *ki aṇuśaśe hakṣadi.*

15 Uncertain reconstruction.

§ 3

[4r15] … for the sake of the three [kinds of] awakening (?). Thus, for innumerable eons […]
(*the perfection of) insight …,[4] and [one] abandons [what is] useless and painful and like a 6r8, 6v9,
dream. 11v4, 11v9

Thus, here in this lifetime, by me the first resolve [to strive for perfect awakening] **[4r16]** is performed (?) and the perfection of insight is obtained. It is thoroughly understood [what is] useless and painful and like a dream … is seized, …[5] should not be thrown away, …, … **[4r17]** should be avoided and should be shown. [End of section] 3.

§ 4

The knowledge other bodhisattvas obtain on the seat of awakening, that was obtained by me here on this [spot on the] ground. It was not easily obtained, it is for my gain, and it should not be thrown away.

[Someone] says: [Is it] the same [that] **[4r18]** is obtained on the seat of awakening, [and is it] the same [that is obtained] in other places? It is said: [It is] the same [as] "sitting on the seat of awakening." This and that [, i.e., every] seat of awakening is empty, and these and other places are empty. The same seat of awakening is painful and useless, [and it is] the same [in the case of] these and other places. Therefore **[4r19]** [that], which I say is the same (?), should not be thrown away. [End of section] 4.

§ 5

[Even if] I will [have to] beg with a broken bowl and having become a naked [mendicant], this knowledge should not be thrown away. The knowledge of [what is] painful and the knowledge of [what is] useless as well as the perfection of insight are thoroughly (*? understood) … **[4r20]** Then, what will happen? 《[End of section] 5.》

§ 6

By this knowledge of [what is] painful and this knowledge of [what is] useless, every suffering 6r8, 6v9,
[that will be] taken up will be accepted [and] looked at with an even mind. Every happiness 11v4, 11v9
[that will be] given up will be accepted. In this way, having reached complete extinction, **[4r21]**
I will leave this world. Avoiding [what is] unwholesome, doing [what is] wholesome, honoring
Buddha, Dharma, and Sangha in (*every) respect, acting for the profit of [all] living beings,
teaching this Dharma, which is the knowledge of [what is] useless and painful, **[4r22]** and
establishing [all] beings in awakening, [then] certainly before long every fortune will exist for
me and every misery will not exist; [there] will be welfare for myself, welfare for others, and 11r1 ?
welfare for every living being. [End of section] 6. 11r21

---

[4] Perhaps: "[one] obtains the perfection of insight, and [one] abandons [what is] useless and painful and like a dream."

[5] In § 4 and § 5 it is knowledge which should not be thrown away, but here the remaining traces of ink on the manuscript do not suggest such a reading (i.e., *ñaṇo*).

§ 7A1

[4r23] ekadutracadurepaṃcaṣaha-yava-satahi aloehi yo arida karae ⟨*·⟩ as̱atiade ca (*a)loṇeade ca yo praṇide ⟨*ka⟩rae ⟨*·⟩ ⟪ede uhae miṣ̱o⟫ suparibhaṣ̱idavo ca ⟨*·⟩ ya⟨*s̱a⟩bhudehi[16] paribhaṣ̱ehi codidava ca ⟨*·⟩ **[4r24]** yas̱abhudehi svadoṣ̱ehi svadroacehi varjidava ca ⟨*·⟩ suduro adide vi juhos̱idave ⟨*·⟩ pracupaṇae[17] ṇa a(*hiva)didave ⟨*·⟩ aṇagad⟨*e⟩[18] ṇa a .i + + dave[19] ⟨*·⟩ trikoḏi kahati paribhaṣ̱idave codidave ca ⟨*·⟩ vatave dum(*e)[20] uhae **[4r25]** tava ⟨*·⟩

§ 7A2a

triṇa sugadiṇa ṇaś̱e triṇa drogadiṇa aharae ⟨*·⟩ triṇa ⟪maje ṇis̱amarthe ·⟫ sapuruṣ̱aṇa ⟪budhaṇa⟫[21] ṇaś̱ae triṇa as̱apuruṣ̱aṇa ⟪maj(*e)⟫ a(*hara)e ⟨*·⟩ triṇa mokṣaṇa ṇaś̱ae triṇa badhaṇaṇa aharae ⟨*·⟩ driṭhadhamio triṇa suhaṇa ṇaś̱ae triṇa d(*u)khaṇa **[4r26]** aharae ⟨*·⟩ triṇa śuhaṇa ṇaś̱e triṇa aśuhaṇa a(*harae) ⟨*·⟩ (*triṇa kuś̱a)laṇa ṇaś̱ee triṇa akuś̱alaṇa aharae ⟨*·⟩

§ 7A2b

triṇa (*jagariaṇa[22] ṇaś̱e)a triṇa mi(*dhaṇa a)harea ⟨*·⟩ triṇa lah(*u)ṭhaṇa(*ṇa ṇaś̱)ea **[4r27]** triṇa alas̱iaṇa aharea ⟨*·⟩ triṇa kicaṇa ṇaś̱ea triṇa akicaṇa (*a)har(*e)a ⟨*·⟩ triṇa karmaṇa (*ṇaś̱)e(*a tr)iṇa akarmaṇa aharea ⟨*·⟩ triṇa śpriś̱aṇaṇa ṇaś̱ea (*triṇa a)śpr(*i)ś̱aṇaṇa aharea ⟨*·⟩ (*t)r(*i)ṇa arogaṇa **[4r28]** ṇaś̱ea triṇa gelañaṇa aharea ⟨*◦⟩

§ 7A3

⟪maje ca ṇ(*i)s̱amarth(*e) purve dukhe pac̱a[23] dukhe ⟨*·⟩ ma(*je ca ṇi)samarthe purve aśuha pa(*c̱a a)śuha ⟨*·⟩ maja ṇisamartha sarvatra ithu kaṭave⟫

śeṣ̱ae patade hi vivaryaeṇa matra ca idara ca ahi(*va)d(*i)dava ca yas̱abhudaaṇuśaśeṇa ca aṇuśaśidava palaśpidava ca ⟨*◦⟩

---

16 For the reconstruction, cf. 4r24 as well as 4v1 and 4v2.

17 Read *pracupaṇe* (cf. 4v2).

18 Cf. 4v3.

19 Reconstruct as *abhiṇadidave*? Cf. annotations, p. 182.

20 Cf. 4v4.

21 The first interlinear addition starts shortly after *tri* (of *triṇa*), and thus refers to this word. The second insertion starts above the last *ṇa* of *sapuruṣ̱aṇa*, presumably because the first insertion already took the space up to *sapuru*; hence the dot after the first insertion indicates its end here.

22 For the reconstructions in this passage, cf. 4v6–7 (§ 7B2b).

23 Or *paca*. Likewise in the following reconstruction.

§ 7A1

[4r23] Who/which *arida karae* by one, two, three, four, five, six—up to—seven *aloa*, and who/which *praṇide karae* from [the group] up to seven and from the *aloṇea*; 《these, both indiscriminately,》 should be thoroughly admonished; and with truthful admonitions [they] should be exhorted; **[4r24]** and due to [their] true inherent faults [and] inherent miseries, [they] should be avoided. Even with regard to the distant past, [they] should be abhorred; with regard to the present, [they] should not be saluted; with regard to the future, [they] should not be (*? rejoiced at). With regard to the three points of time [one] should do [what] is to be admonished and exhorted. **[4r25]** Now, both these two should be spoken.

§ 7A2a

[It would be for] destroying the three good destinations, procuring the three bad destinations; 11r9, 11r15
destroying the three worthy men 《[such as] the Buddhas》, 《in the middle useless,》 procuring the three unworthy men, 《in the middle [useless]》;[6] destroying the three liberations, procuring the three fetters; relating to present life, [it would be for] destroying the three happy [states], **[4r26]** procuring the three painful [states]; destroying the three pleasant [states], procuring the three unpleasant [states]; destroying the (*three) wholesome [states], procuring the three unwholesome [states].

§ 7A2b

[It would be for] destroying the three (*wakefulnesses), procuring the three sleepinesses; destroying the three physical alertnesses, **[4r27]** procuring the three idlenesses; destroying the three things to be done, procuring the three things not to be done; destroying the three [good] activities, procuring the three bad activities; destroying the three comforts, procuring the (*three) discomforts; **[4r28]** destroying the three healths, procuring the three sicknesses.

§ 7A3

《In the middle useless, before painful, afterwards painful; in the middle useless, before un- 11r9, 11r27
pleasant, afterwards unpleasant. "[In the] middle useless"—[when this is written,] in every case it should be done thus.》

For the remainder, on the reverse [side of the scroll], inversely the full measure [of seven] as well as the other [group] should be saluted, and on account of [their] true benefit [they] should be praised and maintained (?).

---

6 The first insertion seems to refer to the destruction of worthy men and the second seems to refer to unworthy men. In the repetition of the list (§ 7B2a), the inserted gloss is placed above the *triṇa* preceding the *aṣapuruṣaṇa* compound, thus clearly referring to unworthy men.

§ 7B1

[4v1] ekadutracadurapaṃcaṣa-yava-sata aloa aṇaride kerea · as̱atia ca aloṇe(*a) ca aṇaride kerao ⟨*·⟩ ede tava uhae miṣo ahivadidava ⟨*·⟩ yas̱abhuda picara ahiva⟨*di⟩dava **[4v2]** codidava ca ś̱aṣ̱idava ca ⟨*·⟩ yas̱abhudehi svayaaṇuśaśehi svasapatihi palaśpidava ⟨*·⟩ + + ? + + + + + + + + + + + ḏa cite upadidave ⟨*·⟩ pracupaṇe ca ṣaṣadaeṇa matro ca **[4v3]** idaro ca paribhujidave ⟨*·⟩ aṇag̱ade ca śpadimo ahig̱akṣidave ⟨*·⟩ ? ? + + ka ra ṣ. d. ṣ. m. + + + + + + + + + + + + + + + + + ? ca kahati ahivadidave ⟨*·⟩ kahati codidave ⟨*·⟩ **[4v4]** vatave dume uhae ·

§ 7B2a

triṇa drogadiṇa ṇaś̱ea moyea triṇa sugadiṇa aharea ⟨*·⟩ triṇa ⟪maj(*e) ca ṇis̱a(*marthe)⟫[24] kamapramuhaas̱apuruṣ̱aṇa ṇaś̱ea triṇa budhapramuhasapuruṣ̱aṇa aharea ⟨*·⟩ triṇa saṃsara-**[4v5]**{ra}badhaṇaṇa ṇaś̱ea triṇa mokṣaṇa aharea · driṭhadhamia triṇa du(*kha)ṇa ṇaś̱ea triṇa suhaṇa a(*ha)rea · triṇa aś(*uhaṇa) ṇaś̱ea triṇa śuhaṇa aharea ⟨*·⟩ triṇa akuś̱alaṇa ṇaś̱ea **[4v6]** triṇa kuś̱alaṇa aharea ⟨*·⟩

§ 7B2b

triṇa midhaṇa ṇaś̱ea triṇa jag̱ariaṇa aharea ⟨*·⟩ triṇa alas̱i(*a) ṇa ṇaś̱ea triṇa lahuṭhaṇaṇa aharea ⟨*·⟩ triṇa ag̱icaṇa ṇaś̱ea **[4v7]** triṇa kicaṇa aharea ⟨*·⟩ triṇa akarmaṇa ṇaś̱ea triṇa karmaṇa aharea ⟨*·⟩ triṇa aśpriś̱a(*ṇa)ṇa ṇaś̱ea triṇa śpriś̱aṇaṇa aharea ⟨*·⟩ triṇa gelañaṇa ṇaś̱ea triṇa **[4v8]** arogaṇa aharea ⟨*◦⟩

§ 7B3

sakṣiteṇa sadriṭhia saparaïa avarimaṇaṇa triṇa triṇa do(*ṣ̱aṇa ṇa)ś̱ea triṇa triṇa sapatiṇa aharea ⟨*◦⟩

---

24 The insertion is placed above and before *triṇa*.

§ 7B1

[4v1] [Who/which] *aṇaride kerea* the one, two, three, four, five, six—up to—seven *aloa*, and [who/which] *aṇaride kerao* [the group] up to seven and the *aloṇea*; now, these, both indiscriminately, should be saluted; truthfully [and] according to [their] merit [they] should be saluted **[4v2]** and exhorted and commended; [and] due to [their] true inherent benefits [and] inherent fortunes, [they] should be maintained (?). (*With regard to the past,) … one should produce the thought …, with regard to the present, constantly the full measure [of seven] **[4v3]** as well as the other [group] should be enjoyed (?), with regard to the future, [they] should be desired mindfully. … [One] should do [what] is to be saluted, [one] should do [what] is to be exhorted. **[4v4]** Both of these two should be spoken.

§ 7B2a

[It would be for] destroying the three bad destinations [and] liberating [oneself], procuring the three good destinations; destroying the three 《in the middle useless》 unworthy men headed by Kāma (?), procuring the three worthy men headed by the Buddha(s); destroying the three **[4v5]** fetters to the cycle of existence, procuring the three liberations; relating to present life, [it would be for] destroying the three painful [states], procuring the three happy [states]; destroying the three unpleasant [states], procuring the three pleasant [states]; destroying the three unwholesome [states], **[4v6]** procuring the three wholesome [states].

§ 7B2b

[It would be for] destroying the three sleepinesses, procuring the three wakefulnesses; destroying the three idlenesses, procuring the three physical alertnesses; destroying the three things not to be done, **[4v7]** procuring the three things to be done; destroying the three bad activities, procuring the three [good] activities; destroying the three discomforts, procuring the three comforts; destroying the three sicknesses, **[4v8]** procuring the three healths.

§ 7B3

In brief, [it would be for] destroying each of the immeasurable three[fold] faults [and] procuring each of the [immeasurable] three[fold] fortunes, relating to this life and the next. 6r4

§ 7C1.1
? ? ? ? ? + ? ithumi ohoro satahi **[4v9]** arede kerea paribhaṣidav⟨*e⟩ ⟨*·⟩ (*o)horo aṣ̱atia aloṇea(*de) ⟨*ca⟩[25] aride karaï paribhaṣ̱idave ⟪codidave varjidave⟫ ○

§ 7C1.2
ithumi ohoro sata matra aṇaride keraa ⟨*·⟩ **[4v10]** aṣ̱atia aloṇeo ca o(*ho)ro aṇaride ko paribhaṣ̱idave[26] codidave palaśpidave ⟨*◦⟩

§ 7C2.1
ki aṇuśaśe hakṣadi ⟨*·⟩ te satahi ⟪matra⟫ arida keraa ⟨*·⟩ aloṇea aṣ̱atiade ⟪ca⟫ idarade arida kere(*a) **[4v11]** paribhaṭha ya codida ca varjida ca akṣati ⟨*·⟩ te śpabhavasa ataraṣ̱aïśati ṇa ca bhuyo upajiśati ○

§ 7C2.2
te sata matra aloa aṇari(*de k)erea ⟨*·⟩ aloṇea aṣ̱atia ⟨*ca⟩[27] idara aṇaride kerea aïvadida ca **[4v12]** codida ca palaśpada ca ⟨*◦⟩

§ 7C3
sadakalo paḏitiṭha satidehi ⟨*·⟩ ṣadasa aṇag̱ade ca tomi uju ca ṇe a p. ci + va ? pialo ⟨*·⟩ ithumi hurahu[28] ekamekasa kaṭave matrasahoro · idarasahoro ⟨*○⟩

---

25 Cf. 4v10 (§ 7C2.1). The birch bark is broken here due to the folding of the manuscript. Most probably only the ending of *aloṇea(*de)* was written, since there does not seem to be enough space for two letters.

26 Apparently wrong for *ahivadidave*, cf. 4v11 (§ 7C2.2).

27 Cf. 4v10 (§ 7C1.2).

28 Reconstruct as *hurahu⟨*ro⟩*?

§ 7C1.1
… in this life [and] the next (?) **[4v9]** *arede kerea* by the seven should be admonished; in the next life (?) *aride karaï* (*from) [the group] up to (?) seven and the *aloṇea* should be admonished, ⟪exhorted, avoided⟫.

§ 7C1.2
In this life [and] the next (?) *aṇaride keraa* the full measure [of] seven, **[4v10]** [and] in the next life (?) *aṇaride ko* [the group] up to (?) seven and the *aloṇea* should be admonished [= saluted], exhorted, maintained (?).

§ 7C2.1
Which benefit will there be? Thus, *arida keraa* by the ⟪full measure [of]⟫ seven, [and] *arida kerea* from the other [group] up to (?) seven ⟪and⟫ the *aloṇea* **[4v11]** will be admonished and exhorted and avoided. Thus, the states of intrinsic nature will disappear and not rise anew.

§ 7C2.2
Thus, *aṇarida kerea* the full measure [of] seven *aloa* [and] *aṇarida kerea* the other [group] up to (?) seven and the *aloṇea* are saluted **[4v12]** and exhorted and maintained (?).

§ 7C3
Always establish [yourself] by the sevenness (?). Of the one who is content (?) the future …, etc., in short: In this life [and] from existence to existence (?), for each one, the collection of the full measure [of seven as well as] the collection of the other [group] should be done.

7.2.2 BC 11

Part 1r

[11r1] + + + + + ?[1] khaïti baho ca śpaho ca ⟨*·⟩ ta vucadi ⟨*·⟩ ṇevi edes̱a kus̱aleṇa kaye ṇevi kus̱a**[11r2]**(*l).[2] + + + + + + + + + ṇa karye ṇa[3] margasuheṇa ⟨*·⟩ ṇevi edes̱a s̱ahi paramidehi kaye ṇev⟨*i⟩ suheṇa ⟨*·⟩ **[11r3]** + + + + + + + + + + (*dha)mehi kice ṇevi suhena ∘

ṇevi jaṇati ya es̱a śpahu ca ba(*hu ca)[4] ⟨*·⟩ + ? ? **[11r4]** + + + + + + + + + + ⟨*·⟩ edehi khaïti ⟨*·⟩ edehi ecakhaïdave ⟨*·⟩ asvahu vaṇa avi kice kus̱alehi **[11r5]** + + + + + + + + + + ? ? + ? + (*kus̱a)laṇa dharmaṇa tati ⟨*·⟩ asvahu suverao ⟨*·⟩ paricaïdave yas̱a ṇa aña[5]

Part 2r

[11r6] + + + + + + + + (*a)vi khaïta dukha kayadukhe ⟨*·⟩ avi varjamaṇa dukhe citadukhe ⟨*·⟩ ete ? ?[6] **[11r7]** due dukha ⟨*·⟩ paṃḍidaṇa ho vaṇa avi akhaïta kayasuhe ⟨*·⟩ avi varjita citasuhe aṇubhavaṇa ⟨*·⟩ tasva suṭhu**[11r8]**ñaṇami abhae[7] kaṭave pariñaprahaṇa ⟨*·⟩ ñaṇami yavade uhae suha hakṣadi uhaa[8] ca dukha ṇa hakṣati ⟨*∘⟩

[11r9] (*sarvadroacasa a)harae sarvasapatie ca ṇas̱e ⟨*·⟩ maje ca ṇisamarthe **[11r10]** + + + + + + + + + (*pa)ricaae ⟨*·⟩ sarvadroacasa aharae sarvasapatie ca ṇas̱e ⟨*·⟩ driṭhadhamiasa **[11r11]** (*saparaïasa ○ kaï)asa cedas̱iasa ○ uayeasa avayeasa ○ sakhadaasakhadasa droacasa aharae **[11r12]** (*sapatie ca ṇa)ś̱(e) ⟨*·⟩ ? + ? ṇa[9] sarvadroacasa aharae sa(*r)va(*sa)patie ca ṇas̱e ⟨*·⟩ śpahu ca bahu ca ⟨*∘⟩

keṇa **[11r13]** ṣaṣadae paricaea parameṇa ṣadimeṇa paricaïdave · ṇa vaṇa citiadi tati mama ṇa parica**[11r14]**ï(*dav)e ⟨*·⟩ sudhu vaṇa citiae ta parameṇa ṣadimeṇa par⟨*i⟩cea ⟨*·⟩ ṇa vacadi ahu mio sakṣi ? ⟨*·⟩ ciri me ta ṣado ⟨*∘⟩

---

1 The letter *a* is excluded as a possibility; perhaps a *ña*.

2 Either *kus̱aleṇa* or a compound beginning with *kus̱ala-*.

3 To be reconstructed as *ṇ(*e)⟨*vi⟩* or taken together with *karyeṇa*, and thus as an adjective modifying *margasuheṇa*.

4 Cf. 11r12 as well as 11r1.

5 It is uncertain whether one line is missing or the text continued directly in 11r6.

6 Uncertain, perhaps *d. m.*; the rest of the line seems to have been left blank.

7 Read *ubhae*.

8 Read *uhae*.

9 Probably *sa(*kṣi)t(*e)ṇa*.

Part 1r

[11r1] … is declared[1] for many and for oneself? It is said: For them, there is no use (? *kārya*) for 4r22 ?
a wholesome [deed], nor for wholesome **[11r2]** … no use (? *kārya*) for …, nor (?) for the happiness of the path. For them, there is no use (? *kārya*) for the six perfections, nor for happiness **[11r3]**…, there is (*no) use (? *kṛtya*) for […] dharmas (?), nor for happiness.

Neither do they know what that [is], for many and for oneself,[2] … **[11r4]** … By these it is declared, by these it should be explained/neglected (?). For us, on the other hand, there is use (? *kṛtya*) for wholesome **[11r5]** … satisfaction with wholesome (?) dharmas. For us, there is complete dispassion. [One] should let go, like no other […]

Part 2r

[11r6] […][3] even though [it] has been declared, there is suffering, suffering of the body; even though [it] is being avoided, there is suffering, suffering of the mind. These … **[11r7]** [are] the two kinds of suffering. But for the wise, even though [it] has (not?) been declared, there is happiness of the body; even though [it] has been avoided, there is happiness of the mind, [the]
experience [of it]. Therefore, in proper (?) **[11r8]** knowledge both must be done: the thorough 6v3
understanding [of suffering] and the abandoning [of its origin]. As long as [one is abiding] in [this] knowledge, both kinds of happiness will exist and both kinds of suffering will not exist.

[11r9] [It would be for] procuring (*every misery) and destroying every fortune; in the middle 4r25–28
useless **[11r10]** … for the relinquishment [of …]; procuring every misery and destroying every fortune [means:] procuring [any] misery (*and destroying [any] fortune) relating to this life **[11r11]** (*or the next), relating to body or mind, increasing or decreasing, enumerated or non-enumerated; **[11r12]** in brief (?): procuring every misery and destroying every fortune, for oneself and for many.

How, **[11r13]** for the sake of permanent relinquishment, should one who is highly content let go? 4r12
[One] does not think, "My satisfaction is not to be given up." **[11r14]** Only by thinking, "This [is done] being highly content," should [one] let go. [One] does not say, "I, we (?) …[4]" [Then] for a long time [there will be] this contentment for me (?).

---

1 In 11r6–7 suffering (*dukha*) or happiness (*suha*) are declared / made known, but the character preceding "is declared" is neither *kha* nor *ha*.

2 Possibly in the sense that both "many" and "oneself" are empty words?

3 Perhaps the paragraph started with *avi* ("even"). It is also possible that *edeṣa* was written at the beginning ("For them") in apposition to *paṃḍidaṇa* in 11r7. The beginning of the physical line most probably belongs to the preceding paragraph.

4 G *sakṣi* or *sakṣito* or even *sakṣi⟨*ka⟩tvo* with different translations, cf. annotations on p. 203.

Part 3r

[11r15] + ? ? ? ca ⟨*·⟩ sarva durgadi gachiea ⟨*·⟩ **[11r16]** + + + + + + + + + + + + + .o[10] ⟨*·⟩ sarva aśuhe aṇubhavi{da}ea ⟨*·⟩ sarve śuhe ṇa bhavi{da}ea[11] ⟨*·⟩ sarva akuśale aṇubhaviea ⟨*·⟩ **[11r17]** ? ? ? ? ?[12] e e ⟨*·⟩ piala yava sasaṃra uadiea ṇivaṇu ca bos̱i ca ṇaś̱iea ○ ·

osagrasuhe ṇame as̱a di {di} mahaś̱(*ie) ⟨*·⟩ **[11r18]** pariñasuhe ca mahaś̱ie · aparas̱iṇasuhe sva-as̱iṇasuhe aviñatis(*u)he ? kṣi ṇe a g̱a ? ṇ. ? suhe ? .u ? **[11r19]** s(*u)he sa(*r)vas̱atva .i ya ṇ. s(*u)h(*e) sarvas̱atvaṇamasaṇivasuhe sudeś̱asuhe sugadasamos̱aṇasuhe ⟨*◦⟩

ya vela chata yatra chade suhe **[11r20]** + + + + + + + + + + (*a)tog̱adasuhe śuhe ⟨*·⟩ atog̱ada-suhe mokṣasuhe avhiñaaśreasuhe viveg̱asuhe asagaṇiasuh(*e) **[11r21]** + + + + + + + + + + ? ṇa suhe paṃḍidaśriyaṇa suhe ⟨*·⟩ divacakṣu va paracitañaṇa ⟨*va⟩ śriyaṇa suhe ⟨*·⟩ satvahidasuhe **[11r22]** + + + + + + + + + + + ⟨*·⟩ sakṣiteṇa avarimaṇados̱a avakra ? + + (*a)varimaṇaguṇa-vidimiśa aharea suhe[13] **[11r23]** + + + + + + + + + ?[14] suhe mahaś̱ie ○

aha ⟨*·⟩ ki es̱a pras̱aṇakarmo[15] ruve · as̱a va aruve ⟨*◦⟩

---

10 Maybe reconstruct as *sarvasugadi ṇa gachiea (iva) pialo*, although usually *piala yava* is found if used as an abbreviation. In BC 4 (§ 7A2a), the sequence is *durgadi / sugadi*, *as̱apuruṣ̱a / sapuruṣ̱a*, *badhaṇa / mokṣa*, *dukha / suha*, *aśuha / śuha*, *akuś̱ala / kuś̱ala*.

11 Perhaps read *⟨*aṇu⟩bhavi{da}ea*.

12 Analogously, one would expect *sarve kuśale ṇa bhaviea*, but this does not seem to be written here.

13 The meaning of these two words is unclear in this context.

14 Possibly reconstruct as *(*osa)gra*, as at the beginning of the preceding paragraph.

15 Cf. 11v28 *pariña prahaṇakarmo ca · ruve ◦ as̱a va · aruve*.

Part 3r

[11r15] … [one] would go to every bad destination, **[11r16]** (*? every good destination one would 4r25–26
not go to—etc., up to—) [one] would experience every unpleasant [state], every pleasant [state, one] would not experience, [one] would experience every unwholesome [state], **[11r17]** (*? every wholesome [state, one] would not experience)—etc., up to—[one] would hold on to the cycle of existence and [one] would destroy extinction as well as awakening.

The happiness of release is now indeed (?) a great fortune, **[11r18]** and also the happiness of thorough understanding [is] a great fortune. [They are] the happiness that is not dependent on anything else, the happiness that is [only] dependent on oneself, the happiness due to non-cognition, the happiness …, **[11r19]** the happiness …, the happiness … of all beings, the happiness … of all beings, the happiness due to a good place, the happiness due to meeting the "Sugata."

When there is the wish, wherever there is the wish, **[11r20]** [this kind of] happiness (*is obtained / will come into existence)[5] … the inner happiness is pleasant, the inner happiness, [that is,] the happiness of liberation, the happiness whose basis is the supernatural knowledges, the happiness of detachment/seclusion (*viveka*), the happiness of being without company, **[11r21]** …, the happiness of …, the happiness of the fortunes of the wise, the happiness of the fortunes
[such as] the divine eye or the knowledge of others' thoughts, the happiness of the welfare for 4r22
[all] beings **[11r22]** … In brief: immeasurable faults … mixed with immeasurable qualities [of the objects of sensual pleasure][6] … **[11r23]** …, the happiness (*? of release) [is] a great fortune.

[Someone] says: Is this act of abandoning related to form or to the formless?

4r2, 4r9 (4r12, 4r14, 4r15)

---

5 Cf. 11r42 for "obtained" and 11v4 ff. for "arise / come into existence."

6 Cf. 11r48 *avaramiṇaguṇavidimiśa*.

Part 4r

[11r24] ? ? ? + ? ? ? ? ? ? ita[16] ṭhavaṇia ⟨*·⟩ ya ṇa sarvasa̱tvehi parigrahida ṇa se kamabhoyi **[11r25]** asti ⟨*·⟩ ye ṇaṇaparigrahidia eva bahujaṇasasa̱raṇadukha ◦

eṣa̱ vi pradiga̱rasuhe ⟨*ca⟩ u⟨*a⟩ṇiṣa̱**[11r26]**{ṣa̱}suhe ca ṇa ṇica ṇa atve ṇa ka suhiṇa bhave ⟨*·⟩ eṣa̱ vi pradiga̱ras(*u)he ca uaṇiṣa̱suhe ca **[11r27]** + + + + + + + +[17] ⟨*·⟩ maja ṇisamartha purve aśuhe paca̱ aśuhe ⟨*·⟩ maja ṇisamartha ṇa karye **[11r28]** + + + + + + + + + rita ⟨*·⟩ osagrasa ca aṇuśaśa paśita citita .u ? da ṇa[18] ? avarimaṇa[19] **[11r29]** + + + + + + + + + + muḏeasa ⟨*◦⟩

yati pridi ṇa upajea śiṭha ? ? ? ?[20] upaṇa **[11r30]** + + + + + + + + + (*u)pajea pridi ṇikhalidea ⟨*·⟩ ta upaje jugidea ⟨*·⟩ sa upajea jugida ⟨*·⟩ sa upaje **[11r31]** + + + + + + + + (*upa)jea ◦

parvayidehi ṇikhalida sa upaje pridi budhesa[21] upajea aprañati **[11r32]** upaj(*e)a ⟨*·⟩ pridi paribhuḏasa upajea ⟨*·⟩ aparibhuḏasa ⟪suverao⟫ upajea ⟨*·⟩ sakṣiteṇa sarvatradeṣ̱ehi sarvatradea **[11r33]** ṇicakalo ṇa jado yaṇa upajea sagaṇia upajea vivega̱gadasa upajea ○

[11r34] ? ? + ? ? + + + + a jibha pramuha chidita ⟨*·⟩ tulie uṣa̱ta ya ⟨*·⟩ atra piṣita ⟨*·⟩ kim asuhe ⟨*·⟩ teṇa ṇa karye ⟨*·⟩ **[11r35]** ? ? ? + + + + + + + ? duehi caduraguḏiehi asa̱keṃa[22] karpa acida ca ⟨*·⟩ dukhavida ca ⟨*·⟩ **[11r36]** suhade ca ṇaśi̱da ⟨*·⟩ sarvadroaca aṇubhavavida ⟨*·⟩ sarvasapati[23] ṇaśi̱da ⟨*·⟩ sakṣiteṇa yavi mokṣade ṇaśida ⟨*·⟩ **[11r37]** ajavi asakhea karpa droace khaveati sapati ṇaśe̱ati mokṣo ṇaśe̱ati ⟨*·⟩ ta imehi ṇa karye ⟨*·⟩ sudhu **[11r38]** sarvadroacade mucami sarvasapati labhadi mokṣa ca ◦

ṇa bhio amaho labheṇa ṣade hoidave ⟨*·⟩ adidaaṇa**[11r39]**gadap(*r)ac(*u)paṇehi alabheṇa ṣade hoidave · ṇa bhi⟨*o⟩ amahu parubhuteṇa[24] ṣade hoidava ⟨*·⟩ aparibhuteṇa ṣa**[11r40]**d(*e) hoidava ⟨*·⟩ adidaaṇaga̱dapracupaṇehi amitrahoḏeapoṣa̱ṇam iva ⟨*·⟩ ṇa bhiu vayaeṇa[25] **[11r41]** ṣade hoidave ⟨*·⟩ avayedeṇa[26] ṣade hoidave ⟨*◦⟩

---

16 Maybe reconstruct as *ṭhavaïta*.

17 Perhaps reconstruct as (⟪*maje ṇisa̱marthe*⟫) *purve dukhe paca̱ dukhe*; cf. 4r28 *maje ca ṇ(*i)-sa̱marth(*e) purve dukhe paca̱ dukhe ⟨*·⟩ ma(*je ca ṇi)samarthe purve aśuha pa(*ca̱ a)śuha*. Or possibly the sequence was different here, with *maja ṇisamartha* at the end.

18 Perhaps read *uadaṇa*.

19 Usually *avarimaṇa* is followed by *doṣa̱/droaca* and then (*avarimaṇa-*) *sapati/guṇa* …; cf. 11r22, 11v5, 11v10, and 4v8.

20 In Schlosser 2016, this was reconstructed as *avaśa* (cf. 11v3, 11v6, 11v30), but there seem to be four rather than three akṣaras. An alternative reading of *uajaya* for *upajea* is too uncertain to reconstruct.

21 Read *budhasa*. First written *budhehi*, but the *hi* seems to have been deleted by the scribe adding *sa*, however, without deleting the now superfluous *e*-vowel mark above the *dha*.

22 Read *asa̱ṃkea* for *asa̱ṃkhea*.

23 Probably reconstruct as *sarvasapati⟨*e⟩* in anology to *suhade/mokṣade ṇaśida*.

24 Read *paribhuteṇa*.

25 Read *vayieṇa*?

26 Read *avayideṇa* or even *avayieṇa*?

Part 4r

[11r24] … to be established. Who[soever] is not surrounded (?) by all kinds of beings, he is not someone who enjoys sensual pleasures; **[11r25]** but who is surrounded (?) by different kinds [of beings, he partakes of the] suffering common to many people.

Moreover, happiness due to a remedy, as well as **[11r26]** happiness due to a cause, is not permanent, has no self, is not at all a continuous state of possessing happiness. Moreover, happiness
due to a remedy, as well as happiness due to a cause **[11r27]** …; [in the] middle useless, before 4r28
unpleasant, afterwards unpleasant; [in the] middle useless, [there is] no use (?) **[11r28]** … And
having seen the benefit of release, having thought about it, … immeasurable **[11r29]** … 4r3, 4r9

[Even] if joy should not arise, the rest … arisen **[11r30]** […; if] … should arise, [one] should remove joy; if it has arisen, [one] should exclude it; it should arise [again after being] excluded; it should arise / having arisen[7] **[11r31]** … should arise.

[While] it has been removed by mendicants [but] having arisen [again], joy would arise for an
awakened one, [but along with it also] non-designation **[11r32]** would arise. Joy would arise out 6v6
of something that is enjoyed, 《complete dispassion》 would arise out of something that is not enjoyed. In brief: nowhere, in no way, **[11r33]** never, [and] not at all would a vehicle (? *yāna*) arise, would company arise, would [this] arise for someone who has gone into solitude (*viveka-gata*).

[11r34] … having the tongue cut out first (?), having been lifted up onto a pole (?), having the 4r13
intestines crushed. Why [this] unhappiness? There is no use for it (?) **[11r35]** … filled with four [hot iron] balls (?) for innumerable eons, pained, **[11r36]** deprived of happiness, caused to experience every misery, deprived of every fortune, in brief up to: deprived of liberation; **[11r37]** from now on, for innumerable eons [one] would spend time in misery, would destroy [any] fortune [and] would destroy liberation. Thus, there is no use for them (?). Only **[11r38]** [by thinking,][8] "I am released[9] from every misery," every fortune and liberation is obtained.

No further should we become content by obtaining [something], in past, **[11r39]** future, present we should become content by not obtaining [something]. No further should we become content by [something] enjoyed, **[11r40]** we should become content by [something] not enjoyed, just like in past, future, present not nourishing [ourselves] on what is stolen from enemies. No further **[11r41]** should we become content by [something] spent, we should become content by [something] not spent.

---

7 G *upaje* or *upajea*?

8 Cf. 11r14.

9 Possibly also meant in a more active sense: "I liberate [myself]."

Part 5r

[11r42] + + + + + + + + + + suhe viñatidukhavidimiśasuhe ⟨*·⟩ yo vela chad(*e) ta vela ṇa labhadi ⟨*·⟩ dukhavidimiśasu(*he) **[11r43]** + + + + + + + + .ovidimiśasuhe ⟨*·⟩ yatra deṣe chade tatra ṇa labhadi ⟨*·⟩ di dukhavidimiśasuhe aśuha ⟨*◦⟩

[11r44] vidimiśasuhe ⟨*·⟩ kayadukhacitadukhavidimiśasuhe sarvakayadukhavidimiśasuhe citadukhavidimi **[11r45]** śasuhe cedaṣiadukhavidimiśasuhe durgadidukhavidimiśasuhe saṃsara-uavatiṇirvaṇa **[11r46]** ṇaṣadukhavidimiśasuhe śidaüṣadharaṇadukhavidimiśasuhe civarakṣaya-kayakṣaya **[11r47]** amoyaṇakṣayadukhavidimiśasuhe atvahisaparahisasarvaṣatvahisavidimiśa-suhe ⟨*·⟩ **[11r48]** ⟪ṇiṣamarthavidimiśasuhe⟫ edapramuhe avarimaṇadukhavidimiśasuhe ⟨*◦⟩

kamasuhehi ṇa karya ⟨*·⟩ avaramiṇa[27]guṇavidimiśa vivegaveragra **[11r49]** suhe⟨*ṇa⟩[28] ṇa karye ⟨*·⟩ atra ca vivegasuhami veragrasuhami ca aya kamasuhe atogado avaśi ṇa siadi ⟨*·⟩ **[11r50]** ? ? ? ? ⟨*·⟩ ṇa ida ṭhaṇe vijadi ⟨*·⟩ avaśi vi(*ve)gasuami veragrasuhami kamasuhe atogade ⟨*·⟩ keṇa karaṇeṇa ⟨*·⟩ **[11r51]** ta vucadi ⟨*·⟩ śile atogade kṣati atogade daṇe atogade ⟨*·⟩ daṇe atogade avi amiṣadaṇe avi dharmadaṇe **[11r52]** atogade ⟨*·⟩ te yatra ime dhama atogada ta kamasuhe ṇa atogade bhavea ⟨*·⟩ ṇa ida ṭhaṇo vijadi ⟨*·⟩ **[11r53]** sayavisa[29] śali sarvarthae śali vuto ⟨*·⟩ avi palale atogade yavasa tuṣe atogade ⟨*◦⟩

---

[27] Read *avarimaṇa*.

[28] For the reconstruction of ⟨*ṇa⟩, cf. 11r34 *teṇa ṇa karye*, 11r37 *ta imehi ṇa karye*, and 11r1 *ṇevi edeṣa kuṣaleṇa kaye*; possibly also ⟨*hi⟩ (plural), as in the preceding *kamasuhehi*.

[29] Read *sayaṣavi*.

Part 5r

[11r42] … happiness …, happiness mixed with suffering due to cognition; when there is the wish, it is not obtained. Happiness mixed with suffering, **[11r43]** happiness mixed with …; wherever there is the wish, it is not obtained. Hence, happiness mixed with suffering is unpleasant.

[11r44] Mixed happiness [is]: happiness mixed with suffering of the body and suffering of the mind; happiness mixed with suffering of the whole body; **[11r45]** happiness mixed with suffering of the mind; happiness mixed with suffering due to mind factors; happiness mixed with suffering due to bad destinations; **[11r46]** happiness mixed with suffering due to rebirth in the cycle of existence and the destruction of extinction (*nirvāṇa*); happiness mixed with suffering due to enduring cold and hot; **[11r47]** happiness mixed with suffering due to loss of the robe, loss of the body, or loss of putting on [the robe]; happiness mixed with suffering due to harm to oneself, harm to others, or harm to all beings. **[11r48]** Headed by this《happiness mixed with the useless》[is] the happiness mixed with immeasurable [kinds of] suffering.

Happiness of sensual pleasures is of no use. Mixed with immeasurable qualities [of the objects of sensual pleasure], **[11r49]** happiness of detachment and dispassion is of no use. Here, in the happiness of detachment and the happiness of dispassion, the happiness of sensual pleasures should certainly not be included **[11r50]** … This is not possible. Certainly, in the happiness of detachment [and] the happiness of dispassion, the happiness of sensual pleasures is included. For what reason? **[11r51]** It is said: Morality is included, endurance is included, giving is included, [whereas] "giving is included" [means that] the giving of material sources as well as the giving of the Dharma **[11r52]** is included. Thus, where these things are included, the happiness of sensual pleasures should not be included? This is not possible. **[11r53]** Just as grain is called grain in all matters, even if the straw is included [or] the husk of corn is included.

Part 5v

[11v1] matupayeasi olaïa eṣa pridisuhe upajadi ⟨*·⟩ ṇiliṇi.o.e pariñapridi prajahaṇapri⟨*di ca⟩ **[11v2]** hoidave ⟨*·⟩ pridi hoidave ⟨*·⟩ pridi avaśi hoidave ⟨*·⟩ pridisuha acala ⟨*·⟩ pridi asaṣaraṇe ⟨*·⟩ **[11v3]** pridi aṇavaṭie ⟨*·⟩ pridi aparihaṇadhama ⟨*·⟩ pridi akṣaye ⟨*◦⟩

pridi yadi va ṇa ichiea **[11v4]** ta avaśa hode pridi ⟨*·⟩ ṇisamartha ca dukho ca aśuho ca paricaïta kaṣa pridi ṇa upajea ⟨*·⟩ **[11v5]** eṣa ca ṇisamarthe ca dukhe ca aśuhe ca paricaïta ⟨*·⟩ avarimaṇaṇa doṣaṇa avarimaṇaṇa droacaṇa ṇaṣ̱e **[11v6]** avarimaṇaṇa sapatiṇa aharae paricaeta[30] ⟨*·⟩ kasa paricaïta ṇa pridi upajea ⟨*◦⟩

yidi[31] va ichiea **[11v7]** mame pridisuhe upajea ta avaśi upaṇa pridi ⟨*·⟩ yahi amuḏa khaïta mame kayesuho[32] bhodu **[11v8]** ta avaśi suhe ṇa bhavidave ⟨*·⟩ viṣa{ja}jita mame suho bhodu meme[33] dukhaavaṇao bhodu avaśi hode **[11v9]** (*pridi va)[34] avaśi hode sue va ⟨*·⟩ ṇisamartha ⟨*ca⟩ dukha ca aśuha ca par⟨*i⟩caïta mame pridi **[11v10]** + +[35] + + + + + + ? vado ca paricaade avaramiṇa[36]doṣaprahaṇa avarimaṇaṇa sapatiṇa aharae **[11v11]** + + + + + + + + + +[37] pridisuhe ⟨*·⟩ ṇa ida ṭ́haṇe vijadi ⟨*·⟩ avaśi upajidave ⟨*·⟩ sudhu citidave ⟨*◦⟩

---

30 Read *paricaïta*.

31 Read *yadi*.

32 Read *kayasuho*. Or separate into *kaye suho*.

33 Read *mame*.

34 There is space for five akṣaras before *avaśi*, so *pridisuhe va* might be a possibility as well. However, *sue* is named separately afterwards, and thus, based on context, the current reconstruction makes the most sense.

35 Add *(*bhodu)*?

36 Read *avarimaṇa*.

37 Based on 11v6, perhaps reconstruct as *paricaïta kasa ṇa upaṇa* (cf. 11v7, 11v30) / *hode* (cf. 11v8–9).

Part 5v

[11v1] Attached to (?) …, the happiness of joy arises. … the joy of thoroughly understanding [suffering] and the joy of abandoning [its origin] **[11v2]** should come into existence. Joy should come into existence. Joy should certainly come into existence. The happiness of joy is immovable, joy is extraordinary, **[11v3]** joy is not leading to rebirth, joy is not subject to decline, joy is not decaying.

[Even] if joy is not wished for, **[11v4]** certainly there is joy. Having let go of [what is] useless 4r15
and painful and unpleasant, how should joy not arise? **[11v5]** And having let go of [what is] useless and painful and unpleasant, having let go, [for] destroying immeasurable faults [and] immeasurable miseries **[11v6]** [and for] procuring immeasurable fortunes; having let go, how should joy not arise?

If it is wished, **[11v7]** "may happiness of joy arise for me," then certainly joy is arisen. If non-perplexed (?) having declared, "may there be happiness of the body for me," **[11v8]** then certainly happiness should not come into existence. Having adhered to (?): "may happiness be for me, may the removal of suffering be for me," [then] certainly there is **[11v9]** (*joy), or certainly there is happiness. Having let go of [what is] useless and painful and unpleasant, [thinking:] "(*? may there be) joy for me" **[11v10]** … from the relinquishment[10] […] [for] abandoning immeasurable faults, [for] procuring immeasurable fortunes; **[11v11]** …[11] happiness of joy. This is not possible. Certainly it must arise, it only must be thought of.

---

[10] In the sense of "due to that relinquishment"?

[11] Probably: "having let go, how should there be no happiness of joy?"

Part 4v

[11v12] olaïa jaṇe vihañadi ⟨*·⟩ (*pra)digara[38]suhasa arthae jaṇe vihañadi ⟨*·⟩ uaṇiṣ̱asuhasa ca arthae **[11v13]** jaṇe vihañadi ⟨*·⟩ yahi due gaḍa dupadua aj̄atvabahira teṣ̱a ca bheṣ̱ajesuhe ṇaśadi gro **[11v14]** upajea ⟨*·⟩ iva eṣ̱a so ya ṇisamartho aroa gaḍaṇa bheṣ̱aje ⟨*·⟩ yadi va kamadhadu yadi va ruvadhadu **[11v15]** yadi va arupadhadu ○

⟪loieṇa tava karaṇeṇa⟫ ca cha paricaïta sarvadroacade mokṣe sarvasapatie ca driṭhadhami⟨*a⟩-saparaïaṣ̱a **[11v16]** pradibhave ⟨*·⟩ ku ṇa ? ? + ?[39] ṣado paricae ⟨*○⟩

aloieṇa tava karaṇeṇa picu ṇa puña dhaṇaïta sarvasa**[11v17]**(*pati) + + + + + + + + ṇ. ⟪ṣade⟫ paricae ○ ⟪1⟫

loutareṇa bhudañaṇeṇa ṇa kic⟨*i⟩ paricaïta aṇicag̱a**[11v18]**reṇa aṇatvag̱areṇa śuñag̱areṇa aparibhujitreaag̱areṇa avedeaag̱areṇa sudiṇag̱ar⟨*e⟩ṇa **[11v19]** akuhicaag̱amaṇaakuhicagamaṇa-ag̱areṇa parimaṇasaceaag̱areṇa ṇa kici paricaïta **[11v20]** + + + + + + + + ? ? sarvadroacasa ṇaś̱e sarpa[40]sapatie ca padilabhe ⟨*·⟩ ku ṇa acitieṇa **[11v21]** + + + + + + ⟨*◦⟩

+ + + + + ? dukho paricaïta dukhabio paricaïta ⟨*·⟩ **[11v22]** + + + + + + + + + + + + dukha-bie par⟨*i⟩caïta dukhasa{r}gharya gaḍasagharya roasagharya **[11v23]** (*śalasagharya akẖada-sa)gharya[41] par⟨*i⟩caïta ⟨*◦⟩

keṇa karaṇeṇa dukhasagha(*r)ye ⟨*·⟩ ta v(*u)cadi ⟨*·⟩ ?[42] yatra yeṇa **[11v24]** + + + + + + + + + + + ta ? j̄ae ṇica bhaviśadi ⟨*·⟩ aṭhaṇo ⟨*·⟩ evam eva aj̄atvia aïdaṇa dukha bahi**[11v25]**ra aïdaṇa dukha ⟨*·⟩ teṣ̱a sagharyade suho bhavea suho upajea ⟨*·⟩ ṇa ida ṭ́haṇo vijadi ⟨*·⟩ achatvia gada **[11v26]** (*ba)hira gaḍa ⟨*·⟩ teṣ̱a sa(*gharyade su)ho bhavea ⟨*·⟩ ṇa ida ṭ́haṇo ⟨*·⟩ eva pialo aj̄atvia aśuha bahira aśuha ⟨*·⟩ aj̄atvia **[11v27]** (*ṇisamartha bahira ṇisamartha)[43] ⟨*·⟩ (*eva pi)al(*o) ajatvia gaḍa bah(*i)ra gaḍa ⟨*·⟩ te(*ṣ̱a) sagha(*r)ya⟨*de⟩ s(*u)ho bhavea ⟨*·⟩ ṇa ida ṭ́haṇo ⟨*◦⟩

---

38 Cf. 11r25.

39 Three, four or even five akṣaras. The last one could be a *ṇa*, as is found in the paragraph after next.

40 Read *sarva◦*.

41 The reconstruction is based on 6r9; cf. also 6r3.

42 Possibly *sa*.

43 Usually, the sequence is *ṇisamartha*, *dukha*, *aśuha*; here the only missing term is *ṇisamartha*. The given reconstruction matches the number of presumably missing akṣaras perfectly.

Part 4v

[11v12] Attached to [anything] (?), mankind suffers. For the sake of happiness due to a remedy, mankind suffers. For the sake of happiness due to a cause, **[11v13]** mankind suffers. If [there were] two boils, consisting of two parts, inner and outer, and the happiness due to the medicine [against them] perishes, the disease **[11v14]** would arise [again]. Equally useless as this freedom from the disease is a medicine against boils. [This applies for] the desire realm, the form realm, **[11v15]** and also the formless realm.

《Now, for reasons relating to this world (*laukika*)》, having let go of ..., [there is] liberation from every misery and **[11v16]** ... of every fortune of the present life and the next. Why then let go of contentment ...?

Now, for reasons not relating to this world (*alaukika*), not having desired merit after death, [there is] every (*fortune.) **[11v17]** (*Why then) let go of contentment ...? 《[End of section] 1.》

By means of superworldly (*lokottara*) true knowledge not having given up anything; **[11v18]**
under the aspect of [being] impermanent, under the aspect of [having] no self, under the aspect
of [being] empty, under the aspect of "there is no one who enjoys," under the aspect of "there
is no one who experiences," under the aspect of [being like a] dream, **[11v19]** under the aspect 6r7
of "not coming from anywhere, not going anywhere," under the aspect of truth being the [only]
measure not having given up anything, **[11v20]** ... [for] destroying every misery and [for] obtaining every fortune. Why then **[11v21]** ... by way of not thinking (?)?

... having let go of suffering, having let go of the seed of suffering, **[11v22]** ... having let go
of the seed of suffering, having let go of the accumulation of suffering, the accumulation of 6r3, 6r5,
boils, the accumulation of diseases, **[11v23]** (*the accumulation of thorns,) the accumulation of 6r9
(*blows).

For what reason [is there] accumulation of suffering? It is said: ... where, by **[11v24]** ..., (*there) 6r1
... will be permanent. [This is] not possible. In the exact same manner, the inner sense bases are painful, the outer **[11v25]** sense bases are painful. From their accumulation happiness should develop, happiness should arise? This is not possible. The inner are [like] boils, **[11v26]** the outer are [like] boils. From their (*accumulation) happiness should develop? This is not possible. And so on in this way: the inner are unpleasant, the outer are unpleasant; the inner **[11v27]** (*are useless, the outer are useless.) And so on (*in this way): the inner are [like] boils, (*the outer are [like] boils. From their accumulation) happiness should develop? This is not possible.

Gloss[44]

teṇa karaṇe(*ṇa) dukho pari(*caïta) sagharya + + + + +[45] + + + + + + + + + **[line 1]** ? + ? di[46] bhavea /// **[line 2]** /// (*pa)ricaïta ///[47]

Part 3v

[11v28] + + + + + + + + + + ? pariña prahaṇakarmo ca · ruve ◦ as̱a va · aruve ⟨*·⟩ ta vucadi ⟨*·⟩ avi ruve avi aruve ruvaruva ⟨*·⟩ **[11v29]** + + + + + + + + + + + (*pa)riyaṇeo pariyaṇeo prahadava pidivaṇe pidivaṇeo pajahidava prajahita prajaha[48] **[11v30]** + + + + + + + + + + + (*a)ṇubhavidave ⟨*·⟩ avaśa upaṇa pridi ⟨*·⟩ tae teṇa karaṇeṇa avi ruve avi aruve ○ 4 · –

44 The gloss in the margin presumably starts at line 11v13, but seems to refer to the last paragraph of part 4v as a kind of summary, or as a continuation of it.

45 Probably add (*paricaïta).

46 G *di*, or perhaps *kho*; since in the previous paragraph *suho bhavea* is repeatedly written, reconstructing *sukho bhavea* might be reasonable here as well. However, Skt. *sukha* is always written *suha* in this manuscript.

47 It is uncertain if line 1 or line 2 was written first. The letters of line 1 are bigger and thus more likely to have been written first. It is also uncertain how much text preceded or followed *bhavea* and *(*pa)ricaïta*.

48 Reconstruct either as *prajaha(*di)* or *prajaha(*dava)* for *prajahi(*dava)*.

Gloss

For that reason, having let go of suffering, (*? having let go of) [its] accumulation, … **[line 1]** … there should be … **[line 2]** … having let go …

Part 3v

[11v28] … is thorough understanding and the act of abandoning related to form or to the formless? It is said: [It is related to] form as well as [to the] formless, form and formless. **[11v29]** … [one] should thoroughly understand, [one] should thoroughly understand; [one] should abandon, …, …, [one] should abandon; having abandoned, [one] abandons[12] **[11v30]** …, [one] should experience …[13] Certainly joy is arisen. Thus (?), for that reason: form as well as formless. [End of section] 4.

---

12 Skt. *prajahāti*, or "should abandon" (Skt. *prajahitavya*).

13 Most probably "[one] should experience joy"; cf. 11v1–7.

7.2.3 BC 6

§ 1

[6r1] karitava ⟨*·⟩ pariapo uadae ime kadhadhaduaïdaṇa ṇice dakṣiśati atva ? ? + + + + + + + + +[1] aparimaṇa ? ? ce[2] a ? droatie ? ?[3] ? ? ?[4] a ?[5] kuhicaagamaṇa**[6r2]**(*ku)h(*icagamaṇa) ca bhaveadi ? ?[6] ca bhaveadi bhava ca bhaveati ∘

ta e d. ? + ? ? ? + ? ? ? ? ? ?[7] ⟨*·⟩ yam ida r(*o)ge(*ṇa)[8] ⟨*·⟩ **[6r3]** yam ida gaḍeṇa ⟨*·⟩ yam ida śaleṇa ⟨*·⟩ yam ida akhadeṇa ⟨*·⟩ yam ida payeladukheṇa[9] ⟨*·⟩ yam ida ? + + ⟨*·⟩ yam ida jadidukha-yava-maraṇadukheṇa priaviṇabhava-agradukheṇa ⟨*·⟩ yam ida drudeṣa(*ja)**[6r4]**drujaṇasamoṣaṇeṇa[10] ⟨*·⟩ yam ida sakṣiteṇa yavi dukheṇa samoṣaṇeṇa t. ? ? ? yeṇa ? ? ? ? + ? + + + + + ? ? ṇ. ? ? ? ṇeṇa ⟨*·⟩ yam ida driṭhadhamiasaparaïa[11] avarimaṇeṇa dukheṇa ṇa ichidava **[6r5]** kadhadhaduaïdaṇi[12] siati ◎

§ 2

ya ṇi pu .u t. a ? ? .u ? ? ? .u + ? ? ?[13] (*a)śala ca aṇakhada ca siati ⟨*·⟩ ṇa ca avarimaṇa **[6r6]** dukha siati ⟨*·⟩ yaṣa aji hi de likhida |[14] droaca ṇa siati ·

ta ṇi ? ? ? ? ? ? ṇ. i + + + + ? + + + .u ? ? ? ṇ. ? ? ? ? ? ? ? ? ? ? ? ? ? ca aspamia ca **[6r7]** ekakalava ca parimaṇasacea ca akuhicaagamaṇaakuhicagamaṇa ca sudi(*ṇa)[15] ? ? ? ? ? ? ?[16] abhava ca ⟨*·⟩ ta imeṇa ṇisamartheṇa ṇa ichidava siati kadhadhaduaïdaṇa ◎

---

1 The exact horizontal placement of the following fragment (*aparimaṇa ? ? ce a*) is uncertain.

2 Perhaps read *droace*, but hardly legible.

3 This could be *bha*, perhaps the beginning of *bhaviśadi*.

4 Only faintly visible. Maybe either two letters resembling *di* or the sign for the number 4 twice, i.e., 4+4 = 8. Or a combination: *di 4*.

5 Perhaps *ha* for *aha*.

6 Perhaps *atva* or *jadi* (as a synonym for *bhava*). Or maybe three akṣaras, and then perhaps *ṇicada*.

7 Looks like the upper parts of *aśaleṇa*, but the meaning in this position is unclear.

8 Only the upper parts of the akṣaras are preserved, so the reconstruction is uncertain and mainly based on parallels; cf. 6r9–10 as well as the annotations on p. 239.

9 Probably read *peyala*∘.

10 Reconstruction of (*ja) uncertain; probably as part of a compound with the following word, since there is no space for another *yam ida* in between, and the lower part of a letter can still be seen.

11 Cf. 11v15 *driṭhadhami⟨*a⟩saparaïa*.

12 Correct to ∘*aïdaṇa* as in all other cases (6r1, 6r7).

13 Could be *agaḍa* (cf. sequence in 6r3, which matches the usual sequence in other Buddhist texts), or *(*a)r(*o)ga ca* (cf. sequence in 6r9).

14 A little vertical stroke above the line, similar to an apostrophe, a small daṇḍa, or the number 1.

15 Cf. the sequence *aṇica, aṇatva, śuña, aparibhujitvea, avedea, sudiṇa, akuhicaagamaṇakuhicagamaṇa, parimaṇasacea* in 11v17–19.

16 The letters are only very faintly visible.

§ 1

[6r1] The subject matter [is] (?)[1]: Assuming the hypothetical case that [someone] will consider (?)
these aggregates, elements, and sense bases as permanent, [having] a self (?)[2] … immeasurable … 11v24
of bad destination (?) …, [this] would be coming from anywhere, **[6r2]** (*going anywhere), [this] 11v19
would be …, [this] would be existence.

… such as a disease (?), **[6r3]** a boil, a thorn, a blow, indirect (?) suffering, …, suffering due
to birth—up to—suffering due to death, suffering due to being separated from loved ones and
so on (?)[3], **[6r4]** meeting bad people (*? coming from)[4] bad places; in brief, encountering [any
kind of] suffering, …, …, [because of all these] immeasurable [kinds of] suffering, related to 4v8
the present life or the next, [one] should not wish that **[6r5]** aggregates, elements, and sense
bases would exist.

§ 2

… would be […,] without thorns, without blows.[5] And immeasurable **[6r6]** [kinds of] suffering 11v23
would not exist, as it has just been written. [Any kind of] misery would not exist. 4r5, 4r12

…, not belonging to anyone, **[6r7]** existing at the same time (?), having truth as the [only] mea- 11v18–19
sure, not coming from anywhere, not going anywhere, [being like] a dream, …, non-existence.
Thus, because it is useless, [one] should not wish that aggregates, elements, and sense bases
would exist.

---

1 The exact meaning of G *karitava*, tentatively understood as Skt. *kārayitavya*, is unclear; cf. annotations on p. 238.

2 Cf. § 3 "A notion of [being] permanent, a notion of [having] a self, …"

3 "and so on" translates *agra*; cf. annotations on p. 247.

4 Or perhaps "bad persons (*in) bad places."

5 Cf. § 3 "… a notion [of being] without boils, a notion [of being] without disease, a notion [of being] without thorns, a notion [of being] without blows."

§ 3

[6r8] aha ta ⟨*·⟩ yadi adahea ede dhama dukha ca ṇisamartha ca ⟨*·⟩ es̱a bhude es̱a pragri(*de e)s̱a yas̱ave es̱a tas̱e ⟨*·⟩ ta kas̱a rag̱a ca dos̱a ca upajadi evadukhami evaṇisamarthami ⟨*·⟩ **[6r9]** tuo[17] ca ya ithu jaṇas̱i ◦ kas̱a rajas̱i ca duśas̱i ca ⟨*·⟩ ta vucadi ⟨*·⟩ ta ṇa ka a bo ? ?[18] + ? ? ? ? ? ? + + + + + + + + + + agaḍasaña ca arogasa(*ña ca)[19] **[6r10]** aśalasaña ca aṇak̲h̲adasaña ca ◦ ṇicasaña ca atvasaña ca jivasaña ca bhava(*saña ca)[20] +[21]

[6r11] śes̱a patade likhidae[22]

§ 4

[6v1] aha ta ⟨*·⟩ kas̱a abodhasa upajati ⟨*·⟩ kas̱a baleṇa ⟨*·⟩ ta vucadi ⟨*·⟩ savalo ? ? ?[23] ca sua vibo + + ṇa saṃthidomaṇas̱a bhoti ⟨*·⟩ yadi va maṇas̱a bh(*oti) + + + + ? ? g̱. b. ṇ. paripuṇa **[6v2]** ṇa tatva ṇa eg̱agracitasa ṇa avikṣitacitasa ⟨*·⟩ mraduamaṇas̱a bhoti ṇa + + th(*i)do bahumaṇa bhoti ⟨*·⟩ aña kus̱alasa viarthae ⟨*·⟩ aña balava ma ra amaṇas̱iara akus̱alasa vi**[6v3]**arthae ⟨*·⟩ ṇa spuramaṇas̱a bhoti ⟨*·⟩ ta rajiadi ca[24] duśiadi ca ⟨*·⟩ ya vaṇa spura upajeadi (*ta e)grag̱acitasa[25] aṭ́ha ⊗

---

17 The *o* seems to have been corrected from *a* by two strokes having been added, one vertical to elongate the base letter *a* and one diagonal for the vowel-marker.

18 Perhaps *abodhasa* as in the following paragraph, but the ink is faded and the letter incomplete.

19 No letters are visible here.

20 In BC 2 the sequence is *atva*, *satva*, *bhava*, *jiva*, *pugala* (Skt. *ātman*, *sattva*, *bhāva*, *jīva*, *pudgala*).

21 It is uncertain how much of the line was inscribed, since as in the line above, it does not seem to have been written out in full.

22 This sentence was perhaps written later, after the birch bark was cut to size, since there is only a little space left at the bottom margin. Also, the script looks a little different.

23 The letters are almost complete, but it is uncertain what they represent. The first could be *reṃ* or *ce*, the second might be an *a*, but it is unusually long, and the third could be *cha* or even *cho*.

24 Looks as if written as *ci*; maybe a scribal error.

25 The letters *gra* and *g̱a* have been reversed.

§ 3

[6r8] [Someone] says: If [one] accepts [that] these dharmas are painful and useless, [that] this is 4r15–16,
true, this is natural, this is as it is, this is real; then how do passion and hatred arise with regard 4r20–21,
to such painful [and] useless [dharmas]? **[6r9]** If you too understand it thus, how do you be- 11v4, 11v9
come passionate and hateful? It is said: … a notion [of being] without boils, a notion [of being] without disease, **[6r10]** a notion [of being] without thorns, a notion [of being] without blows. A notion of [being] permanent, a notion of [having] a self, a notion of [having] a life force, (*a notion) of [being of] existence, …[6]

[6r11] The remainder has been written on the reverse [side of the scroll].

§ 4

[6v1] [Someone] says: How does the state of not being awakened[7] arise? How by forceful exertion? It is said: With forceful exertion and … [one] awakens to (?)[8] happiness, [but one] does not have a composed mind. Or if [one's] mind is […] full of …, **[6v2]** [there is] no true state, no state of a concentrated mind, no state of an undistracted mind. [One] has a pliant mind, [but] … no/not …[9] [held in] high esteem. Some [are of the opinion]: unprofitable for [anything] wholesome. Others [are of the opinion]: Possessed of forceful exertion (?) … not mentally engaged, 11r31
[thus at least] unprofitable for [anything] unwholesome. **[6v3]** [One] does not have an agitated mind. Then, [one] becomes passionate or hateful. But if agitation arises [again], the state of a concentrated mind is unstable (?).

6 First positive types of notions are listed, and then, after the punctuation mark, the negative types. Thus, presumably every kind of notion is listed and should be given up. In all cases, the notion should refer to dharmas (that is, a notion of dharmas being without boils, etc., and a notion of dharmas being permanent, etc.).

7 G *abodhasa* = P *abuddhatā*. The suffix *-sa* for Skt. *-tā* is unusual, but makes most sense here, as well as in four other cases in the text (6v2, 6v2, 6v3, 6v5); cf. annotations on p. 254.

8 G *vibo* + +, tentatively reconstructed as *viboǰadi* = Skt. *vibudhyate*. Cf. Anav[L] 37 *vioǰita* = absolutive of Skt. *vibudhyate*, P *vibujjhati* (Skt. **vibhuyitvā* for *vibudhya*). In BC 6, the letter after *vibo* could be *ǰ*, but too little is preserved to reconstruct it with certainty.

9 According to the context, "[but] one is neither composed [nor held in] high esteem" would make sense, so perhaps reconstruct as *ṇa saṃthido bahumaṇa bhoti*. The exact syntactic structure is uncertain, since a second negation before *bahumaṇa* seems to be missing.

§ 5

ya rajieadi ca duśieadi ca ⟨*·⟩ yahi ñaṇo[26] ṇa kuḏae suṭhu **[6v4]** phaṣadi[27] ⟨*·⟩ ta taraṇae ca siadi ⟨*·⟩ tatra ca purve bahu taṇua saña karavida(*e)[28] + + + ? ? vitrae ca siadi ⟨*·⟩ tatra ca purve suhe vitrasua ṇa karavidae siadi ⟨*·⟩ saïthida ca **[6v5]** pura vi saṃthidae siadi · so ca saṃthido matreadi taṇua e a ? + + + + + + + + + ? + + s. ṇ. abhavasa kareadi ⟨*·⟩

kicakica hi ṭ́hidigica kareadi prove ya dukha jaṇita tasa dukhasa **[6v6]** vovaś̱amo kareati ⟨*·⟩ te tatra tasa bhaṭareasa suhasaña upaj(*e)adi ⟨*·⟩

t. ṇa a e + + + + + + [+ +][29] vovaś̱amo[30] ṇa saṃthidomaṇas̱a siadi ⟨*·⟩ yadi va maṇas̱a siadi taṇu sp(*u)ra ṇa cita egag(*ra siadi) **[6v7]** ṇa bahumaṇeṇa ⟨*·⟩ yahi aji tahi sava pada kaṭava ⟨*·⟩ yava aña kica palios̱eṇa ṇa spuramaṇas̱a bh(*odi)[31] ⟨*·⟩ [+ + +][32]

tatra kuḏeami rajiadi ca aṇ. + ? + + + + + + + + + + + + + + + + + ? ? ? ? + ? ? **[6v8]** + + ? ? ? ṇi likhide ithu ⟨*·⟩ rajama ja[33] duśama ca ⟨*·⟩ tasva spurami ?[34] ? ? + + + + + + + + ñ. ṇ. ? ? ? k. ? + ya ichiadi ṇa rajaṇa ṇa d(*u)ṣaṇa ⟨*·⟩ ma paci vipaḏis̱ara ⟨*·⟩ aho[35] **[6v9]** ? vi ca ⟨*·⟩ ko paḏide ṇisamartha ca dukha ca ṇa paricae[36] ⟨*·⟩ aho ṇa ya v. + + + + + + + + + + + + ? ? ṇ. p. r. diadi ?[37]

---

[26] Uncertain, since the letters are only partially preserved with the upper part being lost. It can be either two or three akṣaras, with the first two being connected.

[27] There is a small dot between *di* and the following *ta*, possibly indicating the word break.

[28] Perhaps also add (**siadi*).

[29] Perhaps nothing was written here due to defects on the surface of the birch bark.

[30] Uncertain reading, mainly based on context.

[31] Uncertain reconstruction.

[32] Perhaps nothing was written here due to defects on the surface of the birch bark.

[33] Probably *ja* = *ca*, which is rare but not unattested. Alternatively, the letter could be an *a* with the same meaning, which is even rarer but still possible (see, for example, Khvs^{L} 6b). In 4r15 and 4v11 *ya* and *ca* are found for Skt. *ca*.

[34] Either *cu* or *du*?

[35] Uncertain, possibly also *atra* or *vahe*. Perhaps there were two more akṣaras.

[36] Uncertain, looks like *parecae*. Translated as if *paricea*, cf. 11v16–17.

[37] This is the last clearly visible akṣara before a large knot. It is uncertain if or how many letters were written afterwards. Some darker areas are discernible, but they could also be due to shadows or variations in the surface of the birch bark.

§ 5
If [one] becomes passionate or hateful—when [one] touches not the deceitful [but] the proper 11r7–8
knowledge, **[6v4]** then this would indeed be for the overcoming [of passion and hatred]. And
thereby the notion, which was plentiful before, (*would have been) reduced … and […] would
have been acquired (?)[10]. And thereby happiness due to acquired possessions (?)[11], which was 11r38–41
[known as] happiness before, would not have been caused. And also [what was] scattered (?)
[6v5] before would have been made composed. And being composed, one would say:
"Reduced …," … [one] would cause the state of non-existence.

Because [one] would bring to a halt what is to be done and what is not to be done, **[6v6]** [one]
would bring to rest what was earlier known as suffering. Thus, thereby, the master's notion of 11r31–32
happiness would arise.

… bringing to rest (?) […][12], [one] would not have a composed mind. Or if [one's] mental
action would be reduced [but still] agitated, the mind (*would) not (*be) concentrated, **[6v7]**
[and one would] not [be held] in high esteem. Now every word should be done [as above]—up
to—Some [are of the opinion]: [If] what is to be done [is done][13] with desire (*paligodha*), [one] 4r2, 4r8
does not have an agitated mind. […]

Thereby in deceitful [knowledge (?) one] would become passionate and …[14] **[6v8]** … thus it is written: We become passionate, we become hateful. Therefore, in agitation … What should be wished for [is] neither the act of becoming passionate nor the act of becoming hateful. Do not have cause to regret it later. I (?) **[6v9]** … What wise [person] would not let go of [what is] useless and painful? I (?) …

---

10 G *vitra* = Skt. *vitta* (?); cf. the following *vitrasua*.

11 G *vitrasua* = Skt. *vittasukha* (?); cf. Dhp^{Sp} 6 *vitralabha* for Skt./P *vittalābha*.

12 Possibly "bringing to rest actions but still having desire (BHS *paligodha*)."

13 Theoretically also "if anything is done with desire," with *kica* emended to *kic⟨*i⟩*.

14 Based on the context, "one would become passionate but (*not hateful)" would make sense.

Chapter 8

Annotations

8.1 BC 4

4r2 *se apaliosena margabhavaṇe hakṣadi*. In 4r8–9 the corresponding reading is *apalios̱(*e)ṇa (*ma)rgabha(*vaṇe hakṣadi)*, hence 4r2 *se* is likely a separate word. It is uncertain if *se* is a personal pronoun referring to *margabhavaṇe*, then f. sg., or if it should be interpreted as Skt. *tad*, ind., "thus." A similar case can be found in 4r15, where *se* is found at the beginning of a sentence, either referring to *paḏhamacitupadae*, m. sg., four words later, or as an indeclinable to be translated as "thus." In both instances if it is a pronoun standing at the beginning of the sentence, it would be at a distance from the word it refers to. Another *se* in 11r24 is quite certainly a personal pronoun, m. sg., referring to the immediately following *kamabhoyi*. Examples for *se* = Skt. *tad* / P *taṃ* at the beginning of a sentence can be found in the rock edicts from Mansehra, while the edicts at Shahbazgarhi have *so*, translated as "but," "therefore," or "now" in Hultzsch 1925: RE 1 (G) Sh *so*, Ma *se*, "but …"; 4 (B) Sh *so*, Ma *se*, "but …"; 4 (I) Sh *so*, Ma *se*, "therefore, …"; 5 (D) Sh *so*, Ma *taṃ*, "now, …"; 5 (H) Sh *sa*, Ma *se*, "now, …"; 5 (I) Sh *so*, Ma *se*, "but …"; 6 (M) Sh –, Ma *se*, "now, …"; 9 (D) Sh *so*, Ma *se*, "now …"; 9 (H) Sh *so*, Ma *se*, "therefore …"; 12 (I) Sh *so*, Ma *se*, "therefore …"; 14 (E) Sh *so*, Ma *se*, "but …" (cf. also Caillat 1992b: 111 [§ 2.2]). Other Gāndhārī manuscripts published so far have exclusively the spelling *ta*. I have interpreted *se* in 4r2 and 4r15 as Skt. *tad*, "thus," introducing a sentence (although "now" as a clause-connecting particle would work as well).

The presumed Gāndhārī word *apalios̱a* occurs as *apalig[o]dha-* in the fifth Aśokan rock edict at Shahbazgarhi and as *apar[i]godha-* at Girnar, while other inscriptions (Mansehra, Kalsi, Dhauli) contain just *apalibodha-*, with nearly the same meaning.[1] Hultzsch (1925: 57 n. 1) explains *paligodha* as a Māgadhan form of *parigodha* with the development *pari* √*gṛdh* → *parigṛddha* > *paliguddha* → BHS *paligodha* along with *parigṛddha* > *paligiddha* → P *paligedha*.[2] Regarding the usage of *apalibodha* (Man, Kal, Dhau) instead of *apali-/aparigodha* (Shah, Gir),

---

1 RE 5 (K): Shahbazgarhi (Hultzsch 1925: 55) *apalig[o]dha* (Bühler, Thomas: *apalib[odhe]*, Hultzsch: read °*godhaye*, Senart: *aparigadha[ya]*, later: *apalibodhaṃ* according to Thomas 1915: 100), Girnar (Hultzsch 1925: 9) *apar[i]godhāya*; Mansehra (Hultzsch 1925: 75) *apalibodhaye*; Kalsi (Hultzsch 1925: 32) *apalibodhāye*; Dhauli (Hultzsch 1925: 87) *a[pa]libodhāye*; all meaning "freeing (them) from desire / the fetters (for/of worldly life)." (L): Shahbazgarhi *apalibodhaye*; Girnar –; Mansehra *apalibodhaye*; Kalsi *apalibodhāye;* Dhauli *apalib[o]dhāye*; all meaning "causing (their) fetters to be taken off."

2 Cf. Thomas 1915: 102, as well as BHSD s.v. *paligodha*, *paliguddha*, BHSG § 3.68. For the sound change *r* / *l*, cf., for example, G *palikhaïda* in Nird[L2] or *palikṣea* and *palikṣiṇa* in BC 2.

it should be noted that the two words were originally differentiated in Pali texts, with *apalibodha* meaning "without fetters, obstacles" and *apaligedha* meaning "without desire/greed."[3] They had been confused quite early (see Thomas 1915: 105).

According to BHSD, *paligodha* usually refers to worldly and thus unworthy objects. But this is not exclusively the case: in the *Śikṣāsamuccaya* (Bendall 1902: 50.15), for example, *vaiyāpr̥tyapaligodhe* (ms.) means "attachment/devotion to duties." Likewise at 100.3–4 *buddhadharmābhiyuktena bhavitavyaṃ rātriṃ divaṃ dharmapaliguddhamānasena* ("day and night he must have a longing desire for service to the Law," Bendall and Rouse 1922: 102). Nonetheless, the negative sense is more prevalent. Also in Pali texts, this term is used when referring to the "adherence to lust for sensual pleasures/views, bondage [to it], fixation [on it], obsession [by it], holding firmly [to it]" (Bodhi 2012: 158), which is to be overcome: *kāma-* and *diṭṭhi-rāgavinivesavinibandhapaligedhapariyuṭṭhānajjhosānaṃ* (AN I 66–67).

While in BC 4 it is clearly said that one should be free from longing desire (*apaligodha*), in BC 6 one statement of "others" is that if something is done with desire, one will not have an agitated mind (6v7). Thus it seems there to have a somewhat positive connotation, just as in some of the examples above. However, this appears only to be the opinion of others; the author of the text itself emphasizes that "what should be wished for is neither the act of becoming passionate nor the act of becoming hateful" (6v8). As I understand it, *apaligodha* is subsumed here under passion in general and should be avoided, in contrast to others who might allow it as an exception.

4r2 *margabhavaṇe*. The path (*mārga*) is traditionally the eightfold path leading to awakening, known as the last of the four noble truths. There are, however, also other explanations (see Buswell and Gimello 1992: 7–9 and *passim*). Additionally, in Mahāyāna texts a distinction is sometimes made between a worldly (*laukika*) and a supramundane (*lokottara*) path.[4] It is not clear which definition the author of BC 4 had in mind. The only thing that can be said is that here the focus is on being free of desire for worldly objects (*apaligodha*).

With respect to a later passage in the text (§ 1A3), a definition given by Asaṅga in his *Abhidharmasamuccaya* might be interesting (Gokhale 1947: 33 / Pradhan 1950: 70–71, tr. Boin-Webb 2001: 155–57). There, *mārgabhāvanā* is explained as being cultivation aimed at acquisition (*pratilambha*), practice (*niṣevaṇa*), purification (*nirdhāvana*), and counteracting (*pratipakṣa*). This means procuring favorable qualities (*kuśala*), keeping them stable and expanding them, as well as destroying unfavorable qualities (*akuśala*) and preventing them from arising anew. In § 1A3 it said that bad actions (*pāpa*) lead to unwholesome conditions, but in case of wholesome deeds (*kuśala*) there will be no decay of merit. This basic statement might be similar to the above definition. In another passage in BC 11, reference is made to *laukika*, *alaukika*, and *lokottara*, suggesting that there were also other definitions for *mārgabhāvanā*.

---

3 Similarly P *paligiddha* / BHS *paligr̥ddha* = "desirous" (cf. Thomas 1915 for examples, also Weller 1965: 127–28 n. 19). Khvs[L] (Salomon 2000: 227) has *agridha[ṃ]* = Skt. *agr̥ddham* / P *agedhaṃ*, "not greedy."

4 E.g., *Prasannapadā* 8.5 (de La Vallée Poussin 1903–13: 184).

4r2 ***(*tredhaduade viratasa viragraaṇuśa)ś(*e).*** The reconstruction is based on the parallel passage in the next section (§ 1B, 4r9), which is an only slightly varied repetition of the first. What is being pointed out is the benefit of being without passion or lust for the three realms of existence: *kāma*, *rūpa*, and *ārūpya*.

In general, an *anuśaṃsa* (G *aṇuśaśa*, BHS *ānuśaṃsa*, P *ānisaṃsa*) is the benefit derived from virtuous actions.[5] According to Conze (1978: 98), the *anuśaṃsa*s are especially "[t]he advantages gained from perfect wisdom. A passage similar to the one in BC 4 can be found in the *Aṣṭasāhasrikā* as well as in the *Larger Prajñāpāramitā* from Gilgit:

> *punar aparaṃ subhūte bodhisattvo mahāsattvaḥ svapnāntaragato 'pi śrāvakabhūmau vā pratyekabuddhabhūmau vā traidhātukāya ca spr̥hām anuśaṃsācittaṃ notpādayati | idam api subhūte 'vinivartanīyasya bodhisattvasya mahāsattvasyāvinivartanīyalakṣaṇaṃ veditavyam ||* (AsP, Mitra 1888: 380)
>
> It is another mark [of irreversibility] if, even in his dreams, neither the level of Disciple or Pratyekabuddha, nor anything that belongs to the triple world, becomes an object of his longing, or appears advantageous to him. (Conze 1973b: 227)
>
> *sacet punaḥ subhūte bodhisattvo mahāsattvaḥ svapnāntaragato 'pi śrāvakabhūmaye vā pratyekabuddhabhūmaye vā traidhātukāya vā na spr̥hayate, na anuśaṃsācittam utpādayati, svapnopamān eva sarvadharmān vyavalokayati, pratiśrutkopamān yāvan nirmitopamān eva sarvadharmān vyavalokayati* (LPG, fol. 215, Conze 1962: 3)
>
> Moreover, Subhūti, for the Bodhisattva, the great being, even in his dreams the level of a Disciple or Pratyekabuddha, or anything that belongs to the triple world, does not become an object of his longing, or appears advantageous to him. He beholds all dharmas as like a dream, like an echo, etc. to : like a magical creation. (Conze 1975: 431)

Here, as in BC 4, one does not long for anything that belongs to the triple world, because one understands that its elements are void and unreal, and thus holding on to them does not appear advantageous.

4r3 ***citaṇe*** is phonologically equated with *cintana*, n. = *cintā*, f., which generally has a rather negative connotation in the sense of "anxious thought." Here it is applied in the neutral meaning "thinking upon, consideration, contemplation," as it is used in manuscripts from Central Asia (translated as "Überdenken" in SWTF s.v.).

4r3 ***citidasa.*** This could correspond to Skt. *cintitasya*. The following passage lists what comes into existence for one who is dispassionate towards the world. Logically, G *citidasa* would be

---

5 BHSD s.v. *anuśaṃsa*. PTSD lists five: great wealth, good report, self-confidence, an untroubled death, a happy state after death. There are, however, also other lists with four, seven, eight, or eleven items (cf. PTSD s.v. *ānisaṃsa*).

a gen. sg. of a person: "for one who has contemplated [on the benefit], twenty joys, etc., will exist." Grammatically, however, it is a past participle, perhaps being used as abstract noun (n., "thought, reflection") and referring to *citaṇe* in the previous sentence. If this is the case, it should be translated as "based on [this] reflection, twenty joys will exist, twenty sorrows will not exist."

Alternatively, if not referring to *citaṇe* in particular, the statement may mean that there will be twenty joys of thinking, which would work well with the following opposite *śoa*, Skt. *śoka*, "sorrow." This would also come close to "twenty joyful minds" (see the annotations on 4r3 *viṣ̱adi pridi* …, below). Then the whole sentence as well as the subsequent passage would be illustrating contemplation on the benefits of dispassion. However, this would be only the case if there were such a construction in § 1A1 (as well as § 1B1). For this reason, *citidasa* is understood as being a link to the previous passage.

4r3 *viṣ̱adi pridi … viṣ̱adi śoa*. I have found no parallel for these terms in Pali or Sanskrit Buddhist texts. The only text mentioning twenty kinds of joy seems to be a Chinese translation called "The Sūtra of the Garland of a Bodhisattva's Primary Karmas" (T 24 no. 1485, 菩薩瓔珞本業經 *Púsà yīngluò běnyè jíng*). The corresponding passage in chapter 3 about the training of sages is translated by Rulu (2013: 52) as follows:

> First, on the Joyful Ground, he abides in the highest truth in the Middle Way, cultivates twenty joyful minds [二十歡喜心], and makes ten endless vows. He manifests a hundred bodies to teach sentient beings in Buddha Lands in the ten directions, displays the five transcendental powers, enters the Illusion Samādhi, manifests as a Buddha, and accumulates immeasurable merit.

Apparently, the twenty joyful minds to be cultivated are not explained here either.[6] Nevertheless they belong to the practice of a bodhisattva at the beginning of his career, together with making vows and accumulating merit.

Since in BC 4 the twenty joys (*prīti*) are opposed to twenty sorrows (*śoka*), they might also be tantamount to *viṃśatir guṇāḥ* and *viṃśatiḥ kalaṅkāḥ*. These terms are found in several *śāstra*s or commentaries on *prajñāpāramitā* texts[7] in descriptions of the ten *bhūmi*s that a bodhisattva must attain. In the *Abhisamayālaṃkāra* (1.59–65, Stcherbatsky and Obermiller 1929), twenty flaws (*kalaṅka*) are to be relinquished in order to attain the seventh *bhūmi* (the

---

6 There are two commentaries, both by unknown authors: "Of the first commentary, only the first fascicle is extant, which is collected into the Chinese Canon, the Taishō Tripiṭaka, as text 2798 (T85n2798). With some missing words, it explains chapters 1–3 of text 1485. Of the second commentary, only the second fascicle is extant, which is collected into the Extension of the Chinese Canon, the Shinsan Zokuzōkyō, as text 705 (X39n0705). It explains chapters 4–8 and part of chapter 3 of text 1485" (Rulu 2013: 33). T 85 no. 2798 gives no explanation either (according to Hiromi Habata, personal communication); I have not checked the other commentary.

7 *Abhisamayālaṃkāra* attributed to Maitreyanātha (ca. 4th century); *Abhisamayālaṃkāravṛtti Sphuṭārthā* of Haribhadra (ca. 8th century); *Sāratamā* of Ratnākaraśānti (ca. 11th century).

sixth *bhūmi* being characterized by practising the six *pāramitās*).[8] Examples are: being attached to a self (*ātman*), a living being (*sattva*), a life force (*jīva*), a person (*pudgala*), to destruction (*uccheda*) or eternity (*śāśvata*), or to the three realms (*traidhātuka*). Those who have removed these attachments proceed to the seventh level, which is characterized by *śūnyatā* and non-attachment. There they will partake of positive dharmas (*guṇa*), such as the three doors to deliverance (*trivimokṣa*, i.e., *śūnyatā*, *animitta*, *apraṇihita*), compassion (*karuṇā*), the knowledge of the non-origination of dharmas, calmness of mind, an unobstructed knowledge, and so on. In the commentary of Ratnākaraśānti (Jaini 1979: 8), the *kalaṅka*s are explained as *doṣa* but unfortunately not explicitly as *śoka*. Even though the six *pāramitās* are mentioned in BC 4, the ten *bhūmi*s are not, and thus it is unlikely that the twenty joys and twenty sorrows mentioned here refer in any way to these *guṇa*s and *kalaṅka*s of the *prajñāpāramitā* commentaries.

The *Larger Prajñāpāramitā* from Gilgit (fol. 213–14, tr. Conze 1975: 162) lists twenty advantages (the numbering is provided by Conze) that a bodhisattva achieves after having heard the "seal of the entrances into the letters A, etc." (that is, the *arapacana* syllabary). But even though the *arapacana* syllabary suggests a close connection to the Kharoṣṭhī script and Gandhāra, twenty *śoka*s are not mentioned in this passage.

4r3 (and *passim*) *trae*. This is a numeral in the nom. congruent with the following noun, as is clear in 4r25 *triṇa sugadiṇa* (etc.). It is not defined what exactly is meant by "three." In the text itself two triads are mentioned. The first is *maje*, *purve*, *paca̱* (§ 7A3, 4r28). The other is *adide*, *pracupaṇa*, *aṇagada* (§ 7A1, 4r24; § 7B1, 4v2). Although the words are different, both seem to refer to the same, just as it is common in the Pali canon to use *pubbe*, *majjhe*, *pacchā* for pointing to the past, present, and future.[9] Such groups of three are also used to express the universal aspect of something, abbreviated as P *tividha* in Sn 509, which is explained by Buddhaghosa as "before, during, and after" and thus complete. Also the triads found in *prajñāpāramitā* texts (analyzed in Conze 1973a) often refer to "three periods of time" (*tryadhva*), i.e., past, present, future (cf. also *trikālam*, "always"). Thus, *trae* should be understood as threefold, relating to the three times: in the beginning, in the middle, in the end, i.e., in the past, present, and future, or in other words "completely, always."[10] I have translated this only as "three" to remain close to the Gāndhārī and to keep the repetitive parts as short as possible. There is one exception in § 7B3, where *triṇa triṇa* is combined with *avarimaṇaṇa*, referring to *doṣ̱aṇa* as well as to *sapatiṇa*.

---

8 Cf. Sparham 2006: 120–21 for a translation. For other translations, see Brunnhölzl 2010: 323–24 and Conze 1954: 25–27. See also the explanatory passage in the *Sāratamā* (Jaini 1979: 8).

9 PTSD s.v. *majjha*. In the *Dīrghāgama* manuscript from Gilgit, the terms *ādau*, *madhye*, *paryavasāne* are used (Melzer 2010: 140). Likewise in BC 2 *ṇa aṣ̱i* [...] *ṇa maje* [...] *ṇa p(*r)ayoṣ̱aṇo*.

10 Cf. Baums (2009: 398) in his commentary on Nird[L2] 9·106–7: *ṇa yaho ṇa ya bheśadi · ṇa ca ederahi vijadi · trae ? ? y. s. · ya ta paḍipakṣiasa ya kileśasa samosaṇo* (It neither was nor will it be, nor does it exist now: [...]): "The akṣaras *trae* seem to represent the numeral 'three' and may refer to the three times past, present and future, but the expected word for 'time' (*adhva*-) does not seem to follow, so it cannot be ruled out that the reference of the numeral is the Three Sources or something else entirely. If it is the three times, then the statement of our commentary would seem to be quite simply that pādas c–d of the root verse refer to the three times and to the concurrence or simultaneity (*samosaṇa*-) of these with the defilements (*kileśa*-, i.e., the Three Sources)."

Here it has been translated as "each of the immeasurable three[fold] faults [and] … each of the [immeasurable] three[fold] fortunes."

4r3 *saparaïa mokṣa*. It is assumed that these are two words, adjective and noun, even though a compound G *saparaïamokṣa* would be equally possible, and likewise with the following G *sadriṭhia*. The expression itself (Skt. *sāmparāyika* / P *samparāyika* in combination with Skt. *mokṣa* / P *mokkha*) could not be found in either Buddhist Sanskrit texts or the Pali canon, although it gives the impression of being a common wording.

4r3–4 *trae ca saparaïa mokṣa hakṣati {trae sadriṭhia ? ?}* / 4r10 *(*tra)e [ca] + + + ? ti*. At the end of the sentence in 4r3–4 we would expect *ṇa hakṣati*. The last two letters, that is, the first two of 4r4, are not complete enough to assure the reading *kṣati*, but it is not impossible. The negation *ṇa* and *ha*° would have to be added editorially, since no trace of ink is discernible and based on the preceding and following lines, no akṣaras seem to be missing. However, *sadriṭhia* does not make sense here, since it is repeated immediately afterwards in 4r4 referring to *suha / duha* as in all other internal parallels (4r10; in 4r25 and 4v5 this corresponds to *driṭhadhamia/o*). The usual counterpart of (*saparaïa*) *mokṣa* is (*saṃsara*)*badhaṇa* (4r25, 4v4–5), but the remnants at the end of line 4r3 do not allow the reconstruction of *badhaṇa* much less *saṃsarabadhaṇa*, instead of the present reading *sadriṭhia*. In the repetition of the list (§ 1B2, 4r10), this part of the passage is missing entirely.

§ 1A2	4r3–4	*trae ca* ***saparaïa mokṣa*** *hakṣati {trae sadriṭhia ? ?}*
§ 1B2	4r10	*(*tra)e ca + + + ? ti*
§ 7A2a	4r25	*triṇa* ***mokṣaṇa*** *ṇaśae triṇa* ***badhaṇaṇa*** *aharae*
§ 7B2a	4v4–5	*triṇa* ***saṃsarabadhaṇaṇa*** *ṇaśea triṇa* ***mokṣaṇa*** *ahare*

Thus, *trae sadriṭhia ? ?* in 4r3–4 seems to me a scribal error, anticipating the following *trae sadriṭhia suha*, etc. It is also assumed that in § 1A2 and § 1B2 *trae ca* (*saparaïa*) *mokṣa hakṣati* is to be read as part of the sequence *trae ca durgadi* and *trae ca sugadi*, similar to the triad *droaca*, *sapati*, and *mokṣasuha* in 4r12 and *duhe*, *sapati*, and *mokṣa* in 4r14. No reconstruction for 4r10 has been offered, because the remnants of the letters before *ti* do not convincingly look like they could belong to a *kṣa*, thus allowing the reconstruction *hakṣati*.

4r4 / 4r10–11 *kaïacedas̱ia*. The syntactical position of this compound is unusual because it stands in apposition to *duḥkha*, once at the beginning and once at the end of the *ṇa hakṣati*-string. It seems to be synonymous with *sadriṭhia* or *driṭhadhamia*, which is placed in a similar apposition in section 7 (§§ 7A2a and 7B2a).

4r4	*trae sadriṭhia suha hakṣati*
	kaïacedas̱ia *trae ca duha ṇa hakṣati*
4r10–11	*sadriṭhia ca trae s(*u)ha hakṣati*
	trae dukha ṇa hakṣati ***kaïacedas̱ia***

4r5 ⟪ (*trae sapuruṣa)darśaṇa hakṣati budhapracea (*trae drugaṇa ṇa hakṣati ·) ? ? ? ? mapurvagama (*asapuruṣa) ⟫. The whole sentence seems to have been inserted between the lines as if originally forgotten. The repetition in § 1B2 reads *trae sapuruṣadarśaṇa hakṣati budhaprac(*e)a trae drugaṇa (*ṇa) hakṣati*. For *? ? ? ? mapurvagama (*asapuruṣa)* as a possible gloss on *drugaṇa*, see § 7, where the *asapuruṣa* are expressed by *kamapramuha*:

§ 7A2a	4r25–26	*triṇa ⟪ maje ṇiṣamarthe · ⟫ sapuruṣaṇa ⟪ budhaṇa ⟫ ṇaśae* *triṇa asapuruṣaṇa ⟪ maj(*e) ⟫ a(*hara)e*
§ 7B2a	4v4–5	*triṇa ⟪ maj(*e) ca ṇiṣa(*marthe) ⟫ kamapramuhaasapuruṣaṇa ṇaśea* *triṇa budhapramuhasapuruṣaṇa aharea*

However, in 4r5 the remaining traces of ink preceding *mapurvagama* do not look like *ka* but rather two distinct letters. There are no other occurrences of this phrase in the manuscript, thus the reading *kama* is uncertain, which is why it has not been reconstructed here. The other uncertain akṣaras preceding *mapurvagama* could be *maje* as an abbreviation for *maje (ca) ṇiṣamarthe*.

Based on the parallel constructions in the manuscript, the words *-pracea*, *-pramuha*, and *-purvagama* are synonymous (Skt. *-pratyaya*, *-pramukha*, *-pūrvagama*). They express that the *satpuruṣa*s are preceded or headed by the Buddha—or by Buddhas in general, as the plural is used in § 7A2. The *asatpuruṣa*s (*durgana*) are those who are headed or preceded by Kama (?).

While *-pramukha* and *-pūrvagama* are commonly used in compounds and in this context, *-pratyaya* is not. Aside from its most common translation as "having … as a cause" or "caused by, because of," if used as an adverb (i.e., BHS *pratyayā* / P *paccayā*), it can be translated as "resting on, being founded in" or also "believing in, having trust in" (cf. MW s.v. *sapratyaya*, PW s.v. *pratyaya*, CDIAL s.v. *pratyaya*, PTSD s.v. *paccaya*); hence the combined translation "based on trust in." A rather free translation that would also match the other two terms *-pramukha* ("headed by") and *-pūrvagama* ("preceded by") might be "being followers of the Buddha(s)."

In Pali texts, *-pamukha* frequently occurs in the phrase *buddhapamukhaṃ bhikkhusaṅghaṃ*, which indicates that the *satpuruṣa*s (P *sappurisa*) are ordained disciples of the Buddha. As stated in BHSD, the *satpuruṣa*s are a lay category, mentioned immediately after a list of bodhisattvas. They are supposed to live the life of *gṛhapati*s, but the term *satpuruṣa* may include monks as well. Lenz (2010: 88–89), too, suggests a "worthy man" to be a "layman who supports the Buddhist saṅgha" when referring to Mvu III 148.8–15, where *satpuruṣa*s give [alms] to beggars and thereby go to a heavenly abode. Another reference is the *Samādhirājasūtra*, which is more explicit:

> *tatra kataraḥ*[11] *satpuruṣāśrayaḥ | yad idaṃ buddhāvirahitatā | tatra katarat satpuruṣasamavadhānam | yad idaṃ buddhabodhisattvapratyekabuddhaśrāvakasevanatā | tatra katarāsatpuruṣavarjanatā | yad idaṃ upālambhikānāṃ kusīdānāṃ ca vivarjanatā |* (Dutt 1954: 636)

---

11 In Dutt's edition this part is abbreviated with *ta∘* for *tatra kataraḥ / katarā / katamā / katarat.* Likewise, *yad idaṃ* is abbreviated by *ya∘* in each case (cf. Dutt 1954: 628 n. 8 and 9). In the facsimile edition of

> *tatra katarā satpuruṣasaṃsevanā| yad idaṃ buddhābhiniṣevitā|*
> *tatra katarāsatpuruṣavivarjanatā| yad idaṃ tīrthikānām upālambhadr̥ṣṭikānāṃ vivarjanatā|*
> (Dutt 1954: 641)
>
> What is support of a good person? Not being deprived of a Buddha.
> What is meeting with a good person? Serving Buddhas, bodhisattvas, pratyekabuddhas, [and] disciples.
> What is avoiding a bad person? Avoiding those holding faulty views and indolent ones.
>
> What is associating with a good person? Attending the Buddha.
> What is avoiding a bad person? Avoiding *tīrthika*s holding faulty views.

This passage states that *satpuruṣa*s are Buddhas, bodhisattvas, pratyekabuddhas, and śrāvakas, and that *asatpuruṣa*s are those holding other, that is, faulty views. These *asatpuruṣa*s should be shunned; associating with them is, in other words, "bad company" (*durgaṇa*). The use of the term *gaṇa* may be an allusion to the Jainas, or simply a reference to people with differing spiritual views and goals.

The statement that the *asatpuruṣa*s are headed by Kāma (as seems to be found in BC 4) has not been found anywhere else. There is, however, a particularly interesting paragraph in a Gāndhārī manuscript from the British Library Collection (BL 10) that contrasts "worthy" and "unworthy persons" (Cox 2014: 41).[12] Among other things, the unworthy person is characterized as having sensual and cruel thoughts (*kāmavitarka*, *vyāpādavitarka*).[13] Hence, also in BC 4 the expression may allude to persons being dependent on sensuality or sensual perception in general. Good persons, on the other hand, are described in BL 10, for example, as those endowed with the "good law" (*saddharmasamanvāgata*) and undertaking "virtuous courses of action" (*kuśalakarmapatha*), thus followers of the doctrine of the Buddha, just as in BC 4.

4r5 / 4r12 *sarvadroaca … sarvasapati*. The term *daurgatya* ("adversity, distress, misery, woe") is opposed to *sampatti* ("prosperity, welfare, good fortune," rather than "attainment, accomplishment"), the first used to describe states or conditions that are bad, the second those that are good. The paramount "good state" is the happiness of liberation (*mokṣasukha*, 4r12).[14] In Pali (according to PTSD s.v.) *sampatti* ("fortune") is normally opposed to *vipatti* ("misfortune"), but an analogous pairing of terms is not evident in the Gāndhārī text. In Anav^{L} 21 and 36, *sapati (parami)* is used to designate the (highest) fortune that occurs in the last rebirth as a human being before the final attainment of awakening (in verse 21 the Gilgit parallel has *saṃpadā*).

---

the Gilgit manuscripts published by Kudo et al. 2018 this passage is not contained, but in the section previous to this one the sentences start with *tatra katara* (and not *katama*).

12 There are also several other Gāndhārī references to *sapuruṣa*/*asapuruṣa*, but none with further definitions of the term.

13 Cf. PTSD s.v. *vitakka*: "*kāma*°, *vihiṃsā*°, *vyāpāda*° (sensual, malign, cruel thought)."

14 The happiness of liberation is also called *vimuttisukha* in Pali, which designates the state of bliss experienced after awakening.

Soon thereafter, one becomes free of passion (verse 22; cf. *viadaraghale* in verses 34 and 44), this succeeded by the attainment of permanent bliss (*ayalu suho*, verse 22; see also verse 12) and the state of calming (*ṇibudi*), which is *nirvāṇa* (verses 16, 48, 87).

4r5 *vado nidaṇa ca akuśala paveṇa kara(*ṇeṇa ka)raṇe kuśale puñakṣae ṇa hakṣadi.* G *karaṇa* could be equivalent to either *karaṇa*, "doing, acting," or *kāraṇa*, "reason, cause." The latter is preferred, because in BC 11 the meaning clearly corresponds to *kāraṇa* "reason." The general position of this sentence, as well as of the whole text, is quite clear: Bad or evil actions cause unwholesome conditions, good actions cause wholesome conditions and the growth—or at least not the decline—of merit. The term *kuśala* designates any good deed that is conducive to progress on the spiritual path. It is applied in a moral sense and thus is synonymous with *puṇya*, whereas *akuśala* is "practically equivalent to *pāpa*" (PTSD s.v. *kusala*). Elsewhere, for example in the *Abhidharmasamuccaya* and the *Visuddhimagga*, the decay of merit (G *puñakṣae*, Skt. *puṇyakṣaya*, P *puññakkhaya*) is explained as a premature death.[15]

4r6 *vaïśadi* / 4r8 *(*va)ïśadi* / *vaïśadi*. Most likely this should be taken as a future form of √*vac* (Skt. *vakṣyati*, P *vakkhati*) expressing that someone will speak of, describe, or explain something, namely, the reasons (*kāraṇa*) for wholesome/unwholesome effects of wholesome/unwholesome deeds.

4r6 *bhavid.d.* The first part must be a form of *bhavida* (Skt. *bhāvita*, P *bhāvita*, "developed"). Since the following akṣara does not look like *ve*, *bhavidava* (Skt. *bhāvayitavya*, P *bhāvetabba*) is excluded.

4r10 *(*tra)e ? + + + ? ti*. Cf. annotations on 4r3 *trae*, p. 157.

4r12 *si⟨*ṇe⟩ha* = Skt. *sneha* / P *sineha*. In other Gāndhārī documents, this is written as *ṣeha* or *siṇeha*. The question is whether we are dealing with the (relatively common) vowel change

---

15 *Abhidharmasamuccaya* (Pradhan 1950: 39): *puṇyakṣayaḥ katamaḥ* | *akāle maraṇam apuṇyamaraṇam* | *yena sattvā āsvādasamāpattyāṃ rajyante* | *puṇyakṣayāc ca hetoḥ te jīvitāc cyavante*, "What is the expiration of merit? It is premature death (*akālamaraṇa*), death due to a lack of merit, because beings are attached to a delicious attainment. They therefore die due to the expiration of merit" (Boin-Webb 2001: 88). Vism 229 / Vism[W] 189: *tattha kālamaraṇaṃ puññakkhayena vā āyukkhayena vā ubhayakkhayena vā hoti. akālamaraṇaṃ kammupacchedakakammavasena. tattha yaṃ vijjamānāya pi āyusantānakapaccayasampattiyā kevalaṃ paṭisandhijanakassa kammassa vipakkavipākattā maraṇaṃ hoti, idaṃ puññakkhayena maraṇaṃ nāma*, "As intended here it is of two kinds, that is to say, timely death and untimely death. Herein, timely death comes about with the exhaustion of merit or with the exhaustion of a life span or with both. Untimely death comes about through *kamma* that interrupts [other, life-producing] *kamma*. Herein, death through exhaustion of merit is a term for the kind of death that comes about owing to the result of [former] rebirth-producing *kamma*'s having finished ripening although favourable conditions for prolonging the continuity of a life span may be still present" (Ñāṇamoli 2011: 225).

of *e* to *i* combined with the loss of the diacritic superscript stroke above the *s*, or simply with the omission of *ṇe*. Both versions are attested:

ṣ̄eha:

*ṣ̄eha(*ṃ)vayaṃ*, Khvs[L] 2 = Skt. *snehānvaya* (Salomon 2000)
ṣ̄ehaprahaṇa, Nird[L2] 13·84 / *ṣ̄ehaprahaṇo*, Nird[L2] 9·123 = Skt. *snehaprahāṇam* (Baums 2009)

siha / siṇeha:

*[si]⟨*ne⟩ho aviprahino*, Shahbazgarhi Rock Edict 13 (H)
si[ne]he avipahin[e], Mansehra Rock Edict 13 (H)
uchina siṇeha atvaṇo, Dhp[K] 299

Since there is no superscript stroke visible in BC 4, the second explanation of the *ṇe* having been forgotten, as in the Shahbazgarhi rock edict, seems more likely.

4r12 *gagaṇadivaliasama*. In Buddhist Sanskrit Mahāyāna texts, two forms of the last member of this compound are found, either *-sama* or *-upama*, whereby combinations with *upama* are more frequent, especially in *pāramitā* texts. Moreover, they vary between *vālikā* and *vālukā*. Both forms occur, but *vālukā* is more common; manuscripts often vary between °*ikā* and °*ukā* (BHSD). In Gāndhārī texts (SC 5[16], BC 2[17]), one always finds G *valias/ṣama*; and thus it might be asked whether *vālikāsama* was an earlier form.

In addition to *lokadhātu*s, other nouns often described as being countless "like the sands of the river Gaṅgā" are places like *buddhakṣetra*s, etc., beings like *buddha*s, *tathāgata*s, *bodhisattva*s, etc., and time periods like *(mahā)kalpa*, objects like *stūpa*, *puṣpapuṭa*, etc. Frequently, discussions refer to filling countless *lokadhātu*s with valuable objects in order to accumulate merit. Unfortunately, in BC 4 the words specifying what is happening in or with the *lokadhātu*s are hardly legible; the only parallel as yet known, T 24 no. 1485, merely contains the Chinese word for *gaṅgānadīvālikā* without a reference to *lokadhātu*s. Thus, it is only possible to speculate on the context here. Most probably the G *lo(g)adhadu* refers either to world systems to be crossed (cf. annotations on 4r13 *taraṇia / ta⟪ra⟫ṇ{u}ia*, below), or is used in reference to *sukha / duḥkha* as experienced in innumerable *lokadhātu*s.

4r13 *taraṇia / ta⟪ra⟫ṇ{u}ia*. The construction of the first two sentences in § 2 is nearly parallel, hence their words should be identical; the uncertain reading of *ta* in the first occurrence is based on the second occurrence. G *taraṇia* could be *taraṇīya* in Sanskrit ("to be crossed," i.e., "lived through, passed, traversed," similar to *atikrānta* / P *atikkanta* = *abhikkanta*). Parallel

---

16 AsP[Sp] 5-30 *gaganati*[sic]*valiasa* (5-31:) + + + + + + (Falk and Karashima 2013: 122). Later in the manuscript, the last part of the compound is extant, but the first missing: 5-47 + + + + *sameṣu logadhaduṣu* (Falk and Karashima 2013: 154). For the former, the Sanskrit parallel is *gaṅgānadīvālukopameṣu*, but "[c]f. the Brāhmī ms (Sander 2000b: 9, 38) *-vālikāsāmāṃ /-vālikāsamāṃ kalpaṃ tiṣṭatā / tiṣṭaṃto*" (Falk and Karashima 2013: 122 n. 27).

17 In BC 2 ∘*valiasama* is used in reference to innumerous *lokadhātu*s.

to that, G *vitrea* might be corresponding to **vitārya*, "to be gone through." Since all of these occurrences are followed by G *śaki*, they could also be infinitives, though this is phonologically doubtful; see below.

4r13 *śaki* (4×). G *śaki* can correspond to BHS *śakyā* (Vedic *śakyāt*) / P *sakkā* (cf. Pischel 1900: § 465), "it is possible, one can/could (with inf.)," or *śakya* / P *sakka*, "able, possible, capable of."[18] In the Niya documents, *śaki* is regularly combined with an infinitive ending in *-tum* (e.g., *na śakya kartu* in documents no. 91 and no. 399), though the infinitive more frequently used is *-ănāya* (cf. Burrow 1937: § 103). This infinitive is apparently also attested in Shahbazgarhi RE 13 (L) *śako kṣamanaye*, parallel to Girnar *sakaṃ chamitave* and Erragudi *khamitave* (cf. also Caillat 1992b: 113 [§ 3.2]), but it could also be the dative of an active noun used as a substitute for the expected infinitive. Although these examples suggest that the corresponding infinitive usually follows *śaki*, it can also precede it. Thus, in BC 4 it is understood as "being capable of crossing / going through" (G *taraṇia*, *vitrea*) rather than "being capable of clinging / letting go" (G *uadiaṇa*, *pariceaṇa*). Among the several possible infinitive endings in Middle Indo-Aryan, such as *-(i)tum*, *-(i)tave*, *-(tuṃ)je/ye*, *-ăye/āyă*, or *-ănāya* (cf. von Hinüber 2001: § 497), the Gāndhārī words could also correspond to **tar-aṇāya* and **vitar-āya* instead of being gerundives, although in this case one would expect the spellings *taraṇae* and *vitarae*. Thus, the combination gerundive + *śaki* seems more likely with *śaki* being used as an adjective (Skt. *śakya* / P *sakka*).

4r13 *uadiaṇa* / 4r14 *pariceaṇa*. Although both words could be taken as nouns in the gen. pl. (*uadiaṇa* = Skt. *upādikānām* for *upadhikānām*, "having a substrate of being, showing attachment leading to rebirth," and *pariceaṇa* = Skt. *parityāgānām*, "giving up, letting go"), a more likely etymological reconstruction is *uadiaṇa* < Skt. *upādiyāna* as a pres. part. ātmanepada ending in *-āna*, meaning "grasping/clinging [to the world/to rebirth]."[19] Based on this, *pariceaṇa* would correspond to Skt. *parityajāna* ("letting go/abandoning"). It is unclear if the two words are nom. sg. m. or acc. sg. n. used adverbially. The single akṣara after the second occurrence of *pariceaṇa* transliterated as *ga* (it could also be an *e*) is obscure.

4r13 *ko varedi pa ? pe* / 4r14 *ko varedi ta a ro*. In the first occurrence, it might be possible to reconstruct *ko varedi paṇa*, but the following character is unclear. It resembles *pe*. Since the subsequent repetition of *ko varedi* … is not identical, it is of no help here.

Concerning *varedi*, it can have two different meanings: (1) √*vṛ*, "cover, restrain, prevent," caus. *vārayati*, or (2) √*vṛ*, "choose," caus. *varayati* ("ep. also *vārayati*" MW). Edgerton (BHSD) lists *vārayati* with *vareti*, *varayati* as vv.ll. (My 11.442.2, prose) and translates "shares, hands out in turn (as gifts), distributes," although with some uncertainty. In other Buddhist texts it is most

[18] For the phonological development of *śaki* < *śakyă*, cf. G *śakimuṇi* as well as G *śakamuni* < *śākyamuni* and analogously G *avaśi* < *avaśyam* in BC 11.

[19] Cf. Geiger and Norman 2000: § 192 and Pischel 1900: § 562. PTSD s.v. *upādiyati* lists *upādiyamāna*, SN III 73 and Sn-a 409, and *upādiyāna* (°*ādiyāno*), Sn 470 and Dhp 20. The latter corresponds to G *aṇuvad[i]aṇu* in Dhp[K] 191 (*anupādiyāno* in Dhp 20).

often *vārayati*, thus probably rather "who restrains"; also in the Niya documents it is used in this meaning, e.g., CKD 399 "prevent." In BC 4, however, "choose" in the sense of "who would choose clinging / who would choose something other than letting go?" would make sense.

4r14 *paricata*. Since an absolutive is used more often than a past participle, especially in BC 11 (see, for example, 11v6), *paricata* should perhaps be reconstructed as *parica⟨*i⟩ta* (BHS *parityajitvā*, "having let go"), instead of being understood as Skt. *parityaktam*, "is let go."

4r14 *uadi / uadaṇa / aṇuvadaṇa*. Several words in this section, namely *uadiaṇa* (Skt. *upādiyāna*), *uadi* (Skt. *upādi*), *uadana* (Skt. *upādāna*), *anuvadaṇa* (Skt. *anupādāna*), go back to the root *upa-ā √dā* "to grasp at, to cling to." In Pali, *upādi* is normally only used in compounds for *upādāna* or synonymously with *upadhi*, especially in the compound *sa-/an-upādisesa* = Skt. *sa-/an-upadhiśeṣa*, "with(out) fuel remaining" (cf. G *aṇuadiśeṣa*, Nird^{L2}, Baums 2009).[20] P *upadhi* is thus rather the "substrate or foundation [for rebirth]," but also translated as a synonym of *upādāna* as "attachment, clinging [to rebirth]."[21] The basis (*upadhi*) of clinging to existence (*upādāna*) is usually explained as the group of five aggregates (Skt. *skandha* / P *khandha*), but also as defilements, sensual pleasures, or volitional formations.[22] All of these are origins of suffering. In BC 4, suffering "without clinging [to it]" (*anupādāna*) will thus create no foundation for new suffering. In summary, this paragraph states that if one were to let go of clinging to the elements of the *lokadhātu*, there would be no fuel left, no foundation for rebirth, and nothing by which one would experience a next birth. Stated more precisely, this would be the case if one were to let go of the desire (*tṛṣṇā*) for these elements, this desire being the cause for grasping existence, which in turn causes new births. By letting go of this desire, every misery or distress is without cause for the next, and liberation will be attained.

4r15 *tribosae ta asaṃkhedehi karpehi praña(*paramida) + + + ? ?*. The usage of *bodha* instead of *bodhi* is frequently attested in Buddhist texts, and especially in the dat. sg. In Gāndhārī texts, *bosa* seems to be as common as *bosi*. For example, the Gāndhārī *Prajñāpāramitā* has *bosa* as well as *bosi* (e.g., in AsP^{Sp} 5-54, Falk and Karashima 2013: 162), and in BC 2 *bosae / bosae* is mentioned in addition to *bosie*. In BC 4, the akṣara before *bosae* looks like *tri*. The term *tri-bodhi* is also mentioned in other Buddhist texts, where it is however not explicitly explained.

---

20 BHSD s.v. *upadhi*: "Acc. to Childers *upādi* means the *khandhas* alone, while *upadhi* includes also *kilesa* (with which PTSD makes it 'almost synonymous'), *kāma*, and *kamma*; [... b]ut it seems that even in Pali, *upadhi* and *upādi* are not always clearly distinguished."

21 But cf. SWTF s.v. *upadhi*, where it is differentiated from *upādāna* in the compound *upadhyupādāna* "Besitz-Beanspruchen und Ergreifen" (elsewhere *upadhi* is translated as "Daseinssubstrat / Grundlage irdischer Existenz" in addition to "Hängen an Besitz," obviously following Schmithausen, e.g., 1969, "Grundlagen [irdischer Existenz]"; in 1987: 270 n. 130 he translates *nirupadhiśeṣa* / P *anupādisesa* as "where no possessions [i.e., *skandhas*] remain"). In my translation I am following DP s.v. *upadhi*: "BHS worldly possessions or belongings [...]; attachment to such possessions (forming a basis for rebirth)."

22 According to CPD s.v., *upadhi* is equated with "*taṇhā*, *ādāna*, *upādāna*, *āsava*, *kamma*, in later systematization particularly with *kāmā*, *khandhā*, *kilesā*, *abhisaṅkhārā*."

One rare and maybe the earliest piece of written evidence is a fragment from Šorčuq on the northern Silk Road containing a Buddhist stotra:

> *prajñāvimuktās traividyāḥ, ṣaḍabhijñā maharddhikāḥ |*
> *tribodhiprasthitāś cāryā, iha saṃghe vasanti te ||*[23]
>
> The noble ones who are released by insight, possessing the three knowledges,
> possessing the six higher knowledges, set forth for the three kinds of awakening,
> they live here in the community.

In his edition, Schlingloff (1955: 94) interpreted *tribodhi* as the three things the Buddha realized at his awakening, equivalent to the Buddhist interpretation of *traividya*.[24] Schlingloff states that the term *tribodhi* does not seem to occur in Pali, but he refers to the Chinese translation of the *Mahāparinirvāṇasūtra* by Fǎxiǎn 法顯, where arhats are described as possessing the three kinds of awakening and the six insights (Waldschmidt 1944: 32).

Instead of referring to three knowledges, as assumed by Schlingloff, the term *tribodhi* might be interpreted as relating to the three different ways to (or levels of) awakening, namely that of a śrāvaka, pratyekabuddha, and samyaksaṃbuddha. In Sanskrit (Śrāvakayāna and Mahāyāna) texts, the term *tribodhi* is usually not mentioned but rather the three terms separately. For example, Vasubandhu explains in his *Abhidharmakośabhāṣya* (Pradhan 1975: 383): *pudgalabhedena tisro bodhaya utpadyante | śrāvakabodhiḥ pratyekabodhir anuttarā samyaksaṃbodhir iti*.[25] In Gāndhārī texts the term *tribodhi* has not as yet been attested elsewhere. However, the three ways to awakening are mentioned in BC 2 as *ṣ̄avaga-/praceabudha-/samasabudhayaṇa*, i.e., the paths of a śrāvaka, pratyekabuddha, and samyaksaṃbuddha. Thus, the context of *tribodhi* in BC 4 could very well be that on all three paths to awakening, the *prajnāpāramitā* should be practiced for innumerable eons—if the reconstruction *praña(*paramida)* is accepted.

Regarding the long period of practice, cf., for example, a passage in the "Treatise on *pāramī*s" from the commentary on the *Cariyāpitaka*: "(xiv) How much time is required to accomplish them [the *pāramī*s]? As a minimum, four incalculables (*asaṅkheyya*) and a hundred thousand great aeons (*mahākappa*); as a middle figure, eight incalculables and a hundred thousand great aeons; and as a maximum, sixteen incalculables and a hundred thousand great

---

23 SHT 434/1+2, line 3. The reading by Schlingloff (1955: 94) is to be corrected with regard to *cānya*, which is actually *cārya* in the manuscript, written for *cāryā* (cf. the reading *cārya* in ms. Or.15009/502 of the British Library collection, and *cāryāḥ* in ms. 3510, 26 of the Pelliot collection according to Pauly 1957: 296).

24 His footnote to *traividyāḥ*: "Das dreifache Wissen der Buddhisten, Wissen um frühere Daseinsformen, um die Schicksale der Wesen, um die Erlösung, wird in Aṅg. Nik. I, 163–166 (P.T.S.) bewußt dem dreifachen Wissen der Brahmanen, den drei Veden, entgegengesetzt."

25 In the *Saddharmapuṇḍarīkasūtropadeśa* the three kinds of / paths to awakening are called *śrāvakayāna*, *pratyekabuddhayāna*, and *bodhisattvayāna*—in addition to *mahāyāna* and *buddhayāna*, and next to the general *ekayāna*. Cf. also the *Abhidharmadīpa* with its commentary *Vibhāṣāprabhāvṛtti* (Jaini 1959: 357–58): *sā punar eṣā bodhiḥ kṣayānutpādajñānarūpāsatī pudgalabhedena tridhā bhidyate | tisro bodhayaḥ | buddhapratyekabuddhaśrāvakabodhayaḥ |*.

aeons" (Bodhi 1996: 54). For the connection between the attainment of the *prajnāpāramitā* and the three forms of awakening, cf., for example, the *Pañcaviṃśatisāhasrikā* and the *Prasannapadā* with reference to the *Aṣṭasāhasrikā*.[26] In every case the *prajñāpāramitā* must be understood and practiced in order to arrive at the three kinds of *bodhi*.

It is unclear what Gāndhārī word followed *(*paramida)* in the manuscript. The last akṣara of + + + *? ?* could be read as *ti*, especially under the assumption that a finite verb is missing, parallel to *prajahati ca* at the end of the next sentence. The second-to-last akṣara was a letter with a horizontal superscript stroke (still preserved on the birch bark). Such strokes have been applied in other places in this manuscript to represent *dhy*, *śc*, or *ṣṇ*, and thus one of these would be a likely candidate. Based on the vague parallels mentioned above, a possible reconstruction and translation might be: "Therefore, for innumerable eons (*[one] accomplishes / learns / practices the perfection of) insight and [one] abandons [what is] useless, etc." Especially with regard to *prajñāpāramitā* texts, the root *śikṣ* seems most suitable. Hence the reconstruction *praña(*paramidae śikṣ̄ati)*, "one trains / practices oneself in the *prajñāpāramitā*," is reasonable. Normally one would expect this to be written *śikṣati*, without a horizontal stroke above, as in the Gāndhārī *Prajñāpāramitā* at AsP^{Sp} 1-17 in relation to *prañaparamida* (Falk and Karashima 2012: 34), but CKD 510 has *śikṣ̄atu* for *śikṣatu* (in the Niya documents, *kṣ* is generally written with a superscript stroke).

Another problem with this fragmentary sentence is that the subject (agent) is missing. Most likely, it is the ideal practitioner of the proposed path to awakening, as was the case in the preceding paragraphs. Alternatively, it could refer to "other bodhisattvas" as mentioned later in § 4 to the effect that they must train a very long time before they finally obtain the *prajnāpāramitā* (i.e., the *anuttarajñāna* = *bodhi*). In contrast to this, the practitioner of the way proposed in this manuscript would reap the fruits of his efforts much more quickly, needing just one lifetime from the first intention to strive for awakening until its attainment.

4r15 *sudiṇoamo* = Skt. *svapnopama-*. The equivalence of *sudiṇo* to Skt. *svapna* is confirmed by a passage in BC 2, where parallels support the translation. There, *puruṣo sudiṇataragada* corresponds to "a person in a dream" (*puruṣaḥ svapnāntaragataḥ*). For the phonological development of Skt. *svapna-* / P *supina-* > *sudiṇo* (*p* > **v* > *d*) compare Skt. *vihaṃgama-* / P *vihaṅgama-* >

[26] *Pañcaviṃśatisāhasrikā* (Kimura 1986, II–III: 97–98): *ye 'pi te daśadiśi loke 'saṃkhyeyeṣu lokadhātuṣu śrāvakā, ye ca pratyekabuddhās tiṣṭhanti dhriyante yāpayanti te 'pīmām eva prajñāpāramitām āgamya śrāvakabodhipratyekabodhiprāptās. tat kasya hetos? tathā hy atra prajñāpāramitāyāṃ trīṇi yānāni vistareṇopadiṣṭāni, tāni punar animittayogenānutpādānirodhayogenāsaṃkleśāvyavadānayogenānābhisaṃskārayogenānāyūhāniryūhayogenānutkṣepāprakṣepayogenānudgrahānutsargayogena.* Cf. also the *Larger Prajñāpāramitā* from Gilgit (fol. 12v1–2, Zacchetti 2005: 185–86 and 304 n. 465): *punar aparaṃ śāradvatīputra yāvanto daśadigloke sarvalokadhātuṣu satvās tān sarvāṃ śrāvakapratyekabuddhayānena ca parinirvāpayitukāmena bodhisatvena mahāsatvena prajñāpāramitāyāṃ śikṣitavyam.* The passage in the *Prasannapadā* (de La Vallée Poussin 1903–13: 353) is: *ata evoktaṃ bhagavatā āryāṣṭasāhasrikāyāṃ bhagavatyām | śrāvakabodhim abhisaṃboddhukāmena subhūte 'syām eva prajñāpāramitāyāṃ śikṣitavyaṃ | pratyekabodhim abhisaṃboddhukāmena subhūte 'syām eva prajñāpāramitāyāṃ śikṣitavyaṃ | anuttarāṃ samyaksaṃbodhim abhisaṃboddhukāmena subhūte bodhisattvena mahāsattvenāsyām eva prajñāpāramitāyāṃ śikṣitavyam ity ādi.*

dihaghama- with the similar development *v* > *d* (Allon 2001: 78, 330), or Skt. *chavi* / P *chavi* > *chaḏi* (Glass 2007: 118, 155–56). The form *supina* occurs for example in the Gilgit manuscript of the *Vajracchedikā* (Schopen 1989: 107, but cf. also BSHD s.v.). In Prakrit (Ardhamāgadhī, Jaina-Māhārāṣṭrī) *sumiṇa* is attested along with *suviṇa* and even *siviṇa* (Pischel 1900: §§ 133, 177, 248).[27]

Regarding the content, *svapna* is common in Buddhist texts dealing with *śūnyatā* and is used to express the dreamlike character of all phenomena. To understand reality as it really is, i.e., empty, is to wake up. Interestingly, there is a distinction between *soppa* and *supina* in Pali (both *svapna* in Sanskrit). Whilst *soppa* denotes a dream while sleeping, *supina* is used for a dreamlike, oneiric vision (Pinault 2009: 243, cf. also Hanneder 2009: 66–67).

4r15 *se*. This could either be a nom. sg. m. referring to *citupade* (Skt. *cittutpāda*) three words later, or it is an adverb (Skt. *tad* / P *taṃ*). A similar case is seen in 4r2, where *se* stands at the beginning of the sentence, either corresponding to Skt. *tad* used adverbially, or referring to the noun after the next word (4r2 *se apalioṣ̱eṇa margabhavaṇe*), in which case it would be nom. sg. f. The only other attestation of *se* as Skt. *tad* / P *taṃ*, "thus, then," is found in the Mansehra rock edicts (see annotations on 4r2 *se* ..., p. 153).

4r15 *mah⟨*i⟩*, cf. 4r17 *mahi i(*ṣ̱e)mi*. In the Niya documents, *mahi* is equivalent to *mahyam* and used as dat. or gen. sg. of the first person (cf. Burrow 1937: § 78). As a genitive it can be used as the agent of a sentence (Burrow 1937: § 119, cf. also Jamison 2000: 74 n. 36 and 77 n. 47). Note also the use of *mama kr̥tam* for *mayā kr̥tam* in the Aśokan edicts (Caillat 1992a: 489 = Caillat 2011: 211).

4r15 *iṣ̱emi* ("here," adv.) is so far only known from the Niya documents, where it is frequently used (Burrow 1937: §§ 91 and 133, as well as Caillat 1990: 16). Other edited Gāndhārī manuscripts use *iha* or *iśe*.

4r15 *jadi*. Maybe loc. sg. (= Skt. *jātyām* / P *jātiyā*, *-yaṃ*), congruent with *iṣ̱emi*, although in other Gāndhārī documents this is usually rendered *-ie* (e.g., *śavastie*, Allon 2001: 111; cf. also Baums 2009: 219–20 for examples ending in *-ie* as well as *-ia*). Alternatively, it could be taken as acc. sg. (= Skt. *jātim* / P *jātiṃ*) whether used for loc. (cf., e.g., Duroiselle 1997: § 598 or BHSG § 7.23), or to express a duration of time ("during this lifetime").

4r15 *paḏhamacitupade ca vrude prañaparamida ca paḏiladha*. The *prathamacittotpāda* is the "first arising of the thought/aspiration/intention [to attain awakening]" or the "initial resolve/resolution [to strive for perfect awakening]."[28] Cf. BC 2 *aṇutarae samasabosae · cito upadema*;

[27] In Niya document no. 157, *sumiṃna* is written (*ahu sumiṃna triṭhemi*, "I saw a dream," and *puna arikungeya sumiṃna triṭha*, "Again the *ari* Kungeya saw a dream ...," Burrow 1940: 29). Cf. Brough 1962: § 36 (also Allon 2001: 85) for the alternation of *m*/*v* (*m* for original *v* seems to be preferred in the Dhp^{K}, which might apply here as well).

[28] For different kinds of *cittotpāda*, cf. Wangchuk 2007: 149 ff.

cito upadido; AsP[Sp] *aṇutarae samasaṃbosae cito upadeaṃsu* (Falk and Karashima 2013: 152ff.). This resolve marks the beginning of the bodhisattva career, whose end is achieved with awakening for the sake of other beings, usually expressed by "the attainment of the *prajñāpāramitā*" or "sitting on the seat of awakening." In Sanskrit *prajñāpāramitā* texts, the duration of progressing on the bodhisattva path is often paraphrased as *prathamacittotpādam upādāya yāvad bodhimaṇḍaniṣaṇṇa-* ("from the arising of the first resolution until sitting on the seat of awakening").[29] The attainment of the *prajñāpāramitā* (or synonymously *anuttarasamyaksaṃbodhi*, *sarvākārajñatā*, *anuttarajñāna*) on the seat of awakening is often expressed with the verb *prati* √*labh*.[30] After the first resolve to attain perfect awakening, a bodhisattva practices the six *pāramitās*[31] and develops other qualities.[32] Regarding *ca vrude* in BC 4, the link between the "first thought

---

29 For example, LPG, fol. 239a (Conze 1962: 96), fol. 240a (Conze 1962: 98, 99), fol. 249b (Conze 1962: 135). Similarly: *prathamacittotpādam upādāya yāvad bodhimaṇḍaniṣadanāt* (PvsP, Kimura 1992, V: 97, and LPG, fol. 274a, Conze 1974: 27). Also *Kāśyapaparivarta* (SI P/2, fol. 21r3–4; Vorobyova-Desyatovskaya 2002): *prathamacittotpādiko bodhisatvo yāvad bodhimaṇḍaniṣadanā tāvat sarvasatvopajīvyo nirvikāro (ni)ṣpratikāro bhavati.* For reaching buddhahood on the seat of awakening, cf. LPG, fol. 239b, Conze 1962: 97–98 ("[the Bodhisattva] does not realise that Dharmahood until he is seated on the terrace of enlightenment, and there wins the knowledge of all modes, immediately thereafter to turn the wheel of Dharma," Conze 1975: 496).

30 E.g., LPG, fol. 17r (Zacchetti 2005: 387): *kecit puna(ḥ) śāradvatīputra bodhisatvā mahāsatvā gambhīrā prajñāpāramitāpratilabdhā*; *Gaṇḍavyūha* (Suzuki and Idzumi 1949: 288): *duṣprajñānāṃ sattvānāṃ prajñāpāramitāpratilābhāya dharmaṃ deśayāmi*; *Karuṇāpuṇḍarīkasūtra* (Yamada 1968: 400): *evaṃrūpaṃ tasya tathāgatasya pūrvaṃ prathamacittotpāditānuttarajñānapratilābhāya praṇidhānaṃ babhūva*. Cf. also LPG, fol. 296b (Conze 1974: 100–101): *tat kasya hetoḥ ? tathā hi mayā prathamacittotpādam upādāya nānyaṃ cittaṃ pratilabdham anyatra-anuttarasyā samyaksaṃbodheḥ.* Likewise, PvsP (Kimura 2006, VI–VIII: 122): *tat kasya hetoḥ ? tathā hi tena bodhisattvena mahāsattvena prathamacittotpādam upādāya nānyatra cittaṃ pratilabdham anyatrānuttarāyāḥ samyaksaṃbodheḥ.*

31 Cf. LPG, fol. 260b–261a (Conze 1962: 183): *bodhisattvo mahāsattvo prathamacittotpādam upādāya ṣaṭsu pāramitāsu carann aṣṭau bhūmīñ jñānena ca darśanena ca atikrāmati* … ("the Bodhisattva […] beginning with the first thought of enlightenment, coursing in the six perfections, transcends the eight stages [of the Disciples and Pratyekabuddhas] with his cognition and vision," Conze 1975: 541). Cf. also LPG, fol. 293b (Conze 1962: 91): *katamo bhagavan bodhisattvasya mahāsattvasya bodhimārga yatra bodhisattvena mahāsattvena caratā sattvāḥ paripācayitavyā buddhakṣetraṃ ca pariśodhayitavyaṃ? bhagavān āha: iha subhūte bodhisattvo mahāsattva prathamacittotpādam upādāya dānapāramitāyāṃ caraṃc chīlapāramitāyāṃ kṣāntipāramitāyāṃ vīryapāramitāyāṃ dhyānapāramitāyāṃ prajñāpāramitāyāṃ caran yāvad aṣṭādaśasv āveṇikeṣu buddhadharmeṣu caraṃ sattvāṃś ca paripācayati buddhakṣetraṃ ca pariśodhayati*, "What is the enlightenment-path of a Bodhisattva, coursing in which he should mature beings and purify the Buddha-field? The Lord: Here the Bodhisattva, from the first thought of enlightenment onwards, courses in the six perfections, etc. *to* : in the eighteen special Buddhadharmas, and both matures beings and purifies the Buddha-field" (Conze 1975: 610). For "practising the six *pāramitā*s from the time of his initial production of the thought [of awakening] until he seats [sic] at Bodhi-tree," cf. Zacchetti 2005: 336 § 3.17.

32 For the things the bodhisattva has to learn on his way regarding the teaching of the Buddhas, i.e., *sūtra*, *geya*, *vyākaraṇa*, and so on, cf. LPG, fol. 258a (Conze 1962: 171–72, tr. Conze 1975: 532).

of awakening" and the "attainment of the *prajñāpāramitā*" is not entirely clear. It was certainly not *upādāya*, which however would be expected based on the aforementioned phrase. The obscure word could refer to the verbal uttering of a *praṇidhāna*[33] in the sense of it having already happened (G *vrude* = **vr̥tam* for *vr̥ttam*). Since the last grapheme does not look like a *t.*, a correspondence to *ukta-* is unlikely. Also the presumed reading *vru* points to G *vrude* = Skt. *vr̥t(t)a-*. This seems indeed possible, since similar derivations of √*vr̥t* are combined with *cittotpāda* in other texts, as for example: *cittotpādā divasam anuvarteran* (AsP 234), *cittotpāde vartamāna* (*Gaṇḍavyūha*, Suzuki and Idzumi 1949: 522.13), *cittotpādaparivartaiḥ* (Larger *Sukhāvativyūha* § 8.19, Fujita 2011: 18.8). Moreover, the *triskandhaka(dharmaparyāya)* is combined with *pravr̥t* in the *Śikṣāsamuccaya* (Bendall 1902: 171 *triskandhakadharmaparyāyapravartanena* [tr. Bendall "engaging in the recitation…"], Bendall 1902: 290 *triskandhakapravartanam*). Thus, if G *vrude* = Skt. *vr̥t(t)aḥ*, this might involve some sort of oral performance.

4r16 *pariñad*. What has been written after *ña* cannot be safely identified. A little chip is lying on top of this spot of the manuscript fragment, making it impossible to reconstruct anything with the help of any remaining traces of ink. Based on the preceding and following past participles, we would expect a Gāndhārī form *pariñada* corresponding to Skt. *parijñāta* / P *pariññāta*.

4r16 *praladhe*. Most of the birch bark is broken off here. However, the context and especially the following passage make the reading quite likely: In 4r17 (§ 4), it is knowledge (G *ñaṇa*) which is obtained and should not be thrown away. This does not seem to have been written here, because one or two letters before *praladhe*, the remnants of a letter look like *mo*. This could point to *mokṣa*, "liberation." However, no such parallel has been found in other Buddhist texts, though there are expressions with *(bodhisattva-vi)mokṣa* and verbal forms of *pratilabh* in Sanskrit Mahāyāna texts, as well as *vimokkha* + *paṭilabh* in Pali texts.

4r17 *boṣimaḍa-*. In 4r18, *boṣimaḍa* is written as *moṣimaḍa* (*ta vucadi samo moṣimaḍaniṣaṇa*). Most probably this is merely a scribal error, with *mo* written twice instead of proceeding with *bo*. Another possibility is that this indeed represents a different pronunciation or orthography. Since it is not explained or referred to any further, and the emphasis seems to be on the difference between *boṣimaḍami labhadi* and *moṣimaḍaniṣaṇa*, I prefer to attribute the unfamiliar spelling to the inattention of the scribe. Nevertheless, in the *Lalitavistara* the seat of awakening is once called *mahīmaṇḍa* (verses 21.82–83, Lefmann 1902–08, I: 316).[34] The same term occurs in the

33 In the *Bodhisattvabhūmi*, the *cittotpāda* is the first of five *praṇidhāna*s: *tatra katamad bodhisattvasya bodhisattvapraṇidhānam | tat samāsataḥ pañcavidhaṃ draṣṭavyam | cittotpādapraṇidhānaṃ upapattipraṇidhānaṃ gocarapraṇidhānaṃ samyakpraṇidhānaṃ mahāpraṇidhānañ ca | tatra prathamacittotpādo bodhisattvasyānuttarāyāṃ samyaksaṃbodhau cittotpādapraṇidhānam ity ucyate* (Dutt 1966: 186). The idea of a verbal uttering was first suggested to me by Vincent Tournier.

34 First noted by Ingo Strauch. The passage reads: *yatha merucakravāḍāś candrāsūryaś ca śakrabrahmāṇaḥ | vr̥kṣāś ca parvatavarāḥ praṇate sarve mahīmaṇḍaṃ || niḥsaṃśayu puṇyabalī prajñābalavāṃś ca jñānabalavāṃś ca | kṣāntibala(vāṃś ca) vīryabalavān abalaṃkartā namucipakṣāṃ*, "As mount Meru and the surrounding ranges, the moon and the sun, Śakra and Brahma, the trees and the best of mountains all bow down to the seat of awakening (*mahīmaṇḍa*), certainly someone with

Mahāvastu (Mvu I 161 *mahīmaṇḍagato* or Mvu II 401 *mahīmaṇḍaṃ*), where it has been translated as "high ideal" (Mvu I 161)[35] or "best place" (Mvu I 161),[36] or as "bodhi throne" (Mvu II 401).[37]

In the examples above, the word *bodhimaṇḍa / mahīmaṇḍa* represents the time and space where one attains awakening and thereby becomes a Buddha. Although it was indeed a certain spot on the ground where Siddhārtha Gautama realized the ultimate truth, this came more and more to denote an intellectual, abstract state of mind. In this sense, the *Vimalakīrtinirdeśa* gives a detailed explanation of what is meant by *bodhimaṇḍa* (§§ 3.54–60). Among other things, it is the seat of generosity, morality, tolerance, meditation, and insight, in other words, it is the seat of the six *pāramitās*. As in the *Vimalakīrtinirdeśa*, so also in other Buddhist works, especially of course those concerning the *prajñāpāramitā*, the *bodhimaṇḍa* is explicitly connected with the *pāramitā*s, because they are to be practiced as long as is needed to attain perfect awakening.[38] In short phrases, this moment of awakening is often expressed as "sitting on the seat of awakening" (*bodhimaṇḍa* + *niṣad-/niṣanna-*). However, I have not found it in close combination with a form of √*labh*, as is the case in this Bajaur manuscript (*yo aña bosiṣatva bosimaḍami lavheti sa mahi i(*ṣ̄e)mi dharetrami ladhe ñaṇe … samo bosimaḍami labhadi*). A partial parallel is found in the *Suvikrāntavikrāmiparipṛcchā*, where the bodhisattva quickly approaches the seat of awakening and quickly obtains the knowlege of the omniscient (*bodhisattvaḥ … kṣipraṃ ca bodhimaṇḍam upasaṃkrāmati, kṣipraṃ ca sarvajñajñānaṃ pratilabhate*, Hikata 1958: 116).

4r17 ***lavheti***. Judging from context, this should be a third person plural present tense active form of √*labh*, "obtain" (*labhanti/te*). In BC 4, the Kharoṣṭhī sign transliterated as *-vh-* stands for Skt. *-bh-* (as in *lavha* = Skt. *lābha-*), while *-bh-* reflects Skt. *-bhy-* (as in *labhadi* = Skt. *labhyate*).

---

the power of merit (*puṇya*), of insight (*prajñā*) and of knowledge (*jñāna*), of endurance (*kṣānti*) and vigor (*vīrya*) will render the wings of Māra powerless."

35 Mvu I 161 […] *tato priyaṃ budhyati jñānam uttamaṃ | svayaṃ mahīmaṇḍagato tathāgato*, "That is why the Tathāgata, reaching his high ideal, awakens to that unsurpassed knowledge which is dear to him" (Jones 1949–56, I: 128).

36 Mvu I 161 "infolge davon erwacht er zum erwünschten höchsten Wissen, (er) der selbst zum besten Ort auf der Erde gelangte Tathāgata" (Leumann and Shiraishi in Shiraishi 1988: 244–45). The *bodhimaṇḍa* is rendered as *byang chub snying po* in Tibetan ("supreme / essence of enlightenment," cf. BHSD s.v. *bodhimaṇḍa*), taking *maṇḍa* as a synonym for *sāra*, which is further justified by the commentary *bodher maṇḍaḥ sāro 'treti bhūpradeśaḥ paryaṅkākrānto bodhimaṇḍaḥ* (*Abhisamayālaṃkārālokā*, Wogihara 1932–35: 206, cf. Lamotte 1962: 198–200 n. 105 for further references). Cf. also PTSD s.v. *maṇḍa*.

37 Mvu II 401 […] *yathā tṛṇāni gṛhṇāsi yathā yācasi svastikaṃ | yathopesi mahīmaṇḍaṃ adya buddho bhaviṣyasi*, [Kāla, the nāga king, speaks to the Buddha sitting at the river Nairañjanā before his final defeat of Māra, i.e., his awakening:] "From the way thou holdest the grass, from the way thou dost ask Svastika for it, from the way thou dost approach the bodhi throne, today thou wilt become Buddha" (Jones 1949–56, II: 357; no translation by Leumann and Shiraishi).

38 *Abhidharmasamuccayabhāṣya* (Tatia 1976: 107): *yad bodhisattvas tāṃ śīlapāramitābhāvanāparaṃparāṃ yāvat prajñāpāramitābhāvanāparaṃparamā* (ms. *°paraṃparāmā*) *bodhimaṇḍaniṣadanān na bhraṃśayati na vicchinattīti*; cf. *Adhyardhaśatikā Prajñāpāramitā* (Tomabechi 2009: 5 and 8); *Larger Prajñāpāramitā* from Gilgit, fol. 222b (Conze 1962: 29–30, tr. Conze 1975: 448) and fol. 237a (Conze 1962: 86–87, tr. Conze 1975: 490–91).

The *e*-vowel in the Gāndhārī form, however, suggests a causative (*-aya-*), but this does not fit the context (cf. von Hinüber 2001: § 447 for MIA *-e-* verbs without a causative sense).

4r17 *dharetrami*. In concordance with *boṣimaḍami*, this is taken as a loc. sg. of *dhārayitṝ* (also *dharitrī*), f., "earth," in the meaning of "on this very spot on the ground." Also in the *Suvarṇabhāsottama* a connection is made between the place where the sūtra is expounded and the earth-goddess Dṛḍhā (see Emmerick 2001: 54–55).

4r17 *ta ṇa suladha me lavha ṇa ca praoḍidave*. The phrase recalls the common *labdhā me sulabdhā lābhā*, *sulabdhā me lābhā*, and other variants (*Aṣṭasāhasrikā Prajñāpāramitā*, *Larger Prajñāpāramitā* from Gilgit, *Pañcaviṃśatisāhasrikā Prajñāpāramitā*, *Mahāvastu*, *Gaṇḍavyūha*). In Pali texts it is *lābhā … suladdhaṃ* or *lābhā … suladdhalābhā*, most often in the phrase *lābhā vata me suladdhaṃ vata me*.[39] The form P *lābhā* is explained as dat. sg. in PTSD (s.v. *lābha*: "dat. sg. *lābhā* [for *lābhāya*] is used adverbially with foll. genitive in meaning of 'for my [our] gain,' 'it is profitable,' 'good for me that' "). The Gāndhārī form *lavha* could be either nom. sg. m. or a short adverbial dat. sg. form, as in the Pali tradition.

Here, the *ta* at the beginning is taken as a demonstrative pronoun, n. nom. sg. ("it, this"), but it could also have been used in an adverbial sense ("thus"), meaning "because I have not easily obtained this, it should not be thrown away."

4r17 *praoḍidave*. Cf. Burrow 1937: 81: *oḍeti* = "let go, send away, allow." According to Burrow the etymology is not clear: "It may be connected with Pali *oḍḍeti* 'throw away, reject' (Pv. A. 256 *oḍḍayāmi* = *chaḍḍayāmi*) and *oḍḍeti* 'to set or lay a snare' (*pāsa*)." Based on the meaning in the Niya documents, it is understood here as "to be thrown away, rejected, relinquished" and synonymous with BHS **prachorayitavya* / **prachoḍ(ḍ)ayitavya* / **prachaḍḍayitavya* / P **pachaḍḍetabba*.[40]

4r17 *samo* / 4r18 *same*. G *samo* / *same* should correlate to Skt./P *sama* ("the same"), but phonologically, Skt. *samyak* / P *sammā* ("properly") is also possible.[41] However, *samyak* is not known

---

39 E.g., in the *Visuddhimagga* (Vism 223 / Vism[W] 184): *lābhā vata me suladdhaṃ vata me* […] *lābhā vata me ti mayhaṃ vata lābhā* […] *suladdhaṃ vata me ti yaṃ mayā idaṃ sāsanaṃ manussattaṃ vā laddhaṃ, taṃ suladdhaṃ vata me*, "It is gain for me, it is great gain for me, that […] Herein, 'it is gain for me': it is my gain, advantage. […] 'It is great gain for me': it is great gain for me that this Dispensation, or the human state, has been gained by me" (Ñāṇamoli 2011: 220). Or, e.g., Mil 17 *lābhā no tāta, suladdhaṃ no tāta*, "It is a gain for me, my dear, it is well gotten by me, my dear, …" (Horner 1963: 23).

40 PTSD s.v. *chaḍḍeti*: "Vedic *chardayati* & *chṛṇatti* to vomit; […] to throw away; abandon, leave, reject; […] grd. *chaḍḍetabba* […]." BHSD s.v. *chaḍḍeti*: "(= Pali id.) abandons: °*ti* Mv ii.170.18; iii.291.14; mss. corrupt in both, but context makes Senart's em. seem certain; in iii.291.14 the only ms. *choḍḍeti* (lacuna in other ms.)." Cf. also PTSD s.v. *pachaḍḍana*: "vomiting, throwing out Sdhp 137." On a related note, Nird[L1] (Baums forthcoming) documents *chorida* from *chorayati* (rarely *choḍayati*, cf. BHSD s.v. *chorayati*) in the meaning "let go, release, abandon, remove," etc.).

41 In the Senavarma inscription, Oskar von Hinüber (2003: 15) translates *same* as "vollständig," interpreting it as *samyak*. Also Stefan Baums (2009: 315) translates *same* in Nird[L2] 13·67 with "right."

in direct connection with *bodhimaṇḍa*. Although the syntactical construction in BC 4 is not entirely clear, I think we can exclude *samyak* due to context and translate *sama*.[42] What is meant by "the same" is that the "traditional" awakening (*bodhi*) is identical with the "new" knowledge (*jñāna*), which is further explained as the realization that everything, i.e., all *dharma*s—and this also includes the *bodhimaṇḍa*—are devoid of inherent existence (*śūnya*) and are therefore causing suffering (*duḥkha*) and useless (*niḥsāmarthya*) with regard to liberation. This is the core statement of the *prajñāpāramitā*, and this seems to be meant by "the knowledge of [what is] painful and the knowledge of [what is] useless" (G *dukhañaṇaṇisamarthañaṇa*) in the following sections § 5 and § 6 in BC 4.

With reference to *prajñāpāramitā* texts, two passages may be mentioned here. One is a statement in the *Vajracchedikā* from Gilgit which says that every place (*pṛthivīpradeśa*) where the *prajñāpāramitā* is proclaimed becomes a place to be worshipped, similar to a *bodhimaṇḍa*. Usually, however, the term *caitya* is used instead of *bodhimaṇḍa* (cf. Schopen 1975). In the *Saddharmapuṇḍarīka*, both *caitya* and *bodhimaṇḍa* are named: *yasmiṃś ca kulaputrāḥ pṛthivīpradeśe 'yaṃ dharmaparyāyo vācyeta* [...] *tasmin pṛthivīpradeśe tathāgatam uddiśya caityaṃ kartavyam | tat kasya hetoḥ | sarvatathāgatānāṃ hi sa pṛthivīpradeśo bodhimaṇḍo veditavyas* [...] (Kern and Nanjio 1912: 391). Further, in the *Aṣṭasāhasrikā Prajñāpāramitā* it is emphasized that "all dharmas have neither place nor locality," and that this is how a bodhisattva should approach the *prajñāpāramitā* (AsP 235 *sarvadharmādeśāpradeśataḥ prajñāpāramitā anugantavyā*; cf. also AsP 196 and 476).

4r18–19 ***tasva same ya ti ṇa praoḍidave***. Within *ya ti ṇa*, the second akṣara is broken off at the top, but the remaining strokes resemble *ti* rather than *di*. For *ya ti* there are several options. First, G *yati* corresponding to (1) Skt. *yadi*, "if," is not an uncommon variant, although it is restricted to the Niya documents and apparently to BC 2 and BC 11 (both of these documents also have the alternative spelling *yadi*). Another reason for this may be that the editors of other manuscripts or inscriptions, when in doubt, preferred to transliterate *yadi* since it is etymologically expected. Other solutions are (2) *ca iti*, (3) *yad iti*, or (4) *yati* ("an ascetic, one who has restrained his passions and abandoned the world," MW; cf. PTSD). Among these options, (3) is the most likely considering the overall context, which is emphasizing that the knowledge one has obtained should not be thrown away (cf. section § 5).

4r19 ***khaḍaeṇa kavalaeṇa ... ṇagao***. Phonetically, the first word should correspond to Skt. *khaṇḍaka-*, meaning either "fragment, piece" or "evil, false" (cf. BHSD s.v. *khaṇḍaka*). The second word, *kavalaeṇa*, most likely correlates to Skt. *kapālaka-*, i.e., a bowl made from a skull.

There is an interesting wordplay on *samyak* and *sama* in the Gilgit *Vajracchedikā* (fol. 10): "However, Subhūti, that dharma is the same as any other (*sama*), and there is nothing at all different (*viṣama*) about it. That is why it is called 'supreme and perfect (*samyak*) awakening.' By virtue of being devoid of a soul, being devoid of a living being and being devoid of a person, that supreme and perfect awakening [*samyaksaṃbodhi*] is fully awakened to as being the same [*sama*] as all wholesome dharmas" (Harrison in Harrison and Watanabe 2006: 155).

42 In the translation, *sama* is taken as an adjective referring to "knowledge" in the preceding passage, but it could also be translated as an adverb: "in the same way."

The second meaning of Skt. *khaṇḍaka* would lead to the translation "even if I will beg with a false bowl and having become a naked mendicant" with G *ṇagao* = Skt. *nagnaka-* referring to non-Buddhist ascetics (*khaṇḍakāpālika* is attested in the *Kathāsaritsāgara* as a name for an inferior Kāpālika ascetic; see MW s.v.). The first meaning as "fragmentary" or "broken" is supported by *khaṇḍena pātreṇa* as a term for a broken begging bowl in the *Bhikṣuṇīvinaya*.[43] A *nagnaka* is simply a monk who has lost all his clothes. The entire passage would thus express that a monk would give up or throw away everything he owns (food, or a proper means to get food, as well as his clothes), but not the very precious knowledge by which he attains liberation.

4r19 *imo (*ña)ṇo praoḏidave*. G *imo* is nom. sg. n. corresponding to *idaṃ (jñānam)*, as also in Pali *imaṃ* as well as *idaṃ* as nom./acc. sg. n. is known (cf., e.g., Duroiselle 1997: § 307 or Pischel 1900: § 429). See also chapter 6 on morphology ("Pronouns").

4r19 *pracaparamido*. This is tentatively read as equivalent to G *prañaparamido* = Skt. *prajñā-pāramitā*, even though it is clearly written *praca*°. This could be a scribal error. But it could also indicate an oral transmission if one assumes that *prajñā* was pronounced similarly to *praca*.[44] Identifying *pracaparamido* with *prañaparamido* is furthermore supported by the triad 4r15 *ṇisamartho ya dukho ya sudiṇoamo ca*, which seems to correspond directly to 4r19 *(*dukh)o-ñaṇo ca (*ṇi)ṣamarthañaṇo ca pracaparamido ca*, since "being like a dream" (G *sudiṇoamo* = Skt. *svapnopama*) is a very common way to describe emptiness.

The following akṣaras *pari ? ? pra ? ?* + + are for the most part hidden by a small fragment (folded back from the recto), so it can only be guessed that the first was *pariñado* and the second most probably *praoḏidave*.

4r20 *dukhañaṇaṇisamarthañaṇeṇa*. The knowledge of what causes suffering and of what is useless most likely corresponds to the knowledge that one obtains on the seat of awakening, referring to the realization of emptiness, the core element of the *prajñāpāramitā* doctrine. G *dukhañaṇa* seems to refer to the knowlege of suffering as the first of the four noble truths in a general sense.[45]

I have not found *duḥkhajñāna* or P *dukkhañāṇa* in juxtaposition with *niḥsāmarthyajñāna* / P **niratthañāṇa*, or even the latter alone. According to PTSD s.v. *nirattha*, "useless" is applied in the *Sīlakkhandhavaggaṭīkā* to useless prattle by which happiness and welfare are destroyed. In the *Aṣṭasāhasrikā Prajñāpāramitā* the term occurs in the compound *niḥsāmarthyakriyā* (AsP 552), translated as "ineffectual action" by Conze. The context is the Bodhisattva Sadāprarudita

43 Niḥsargika-Pācattika-Dharma 12, § 174a (Roth 1970: 169): *sthūlanandān nāma bhikṣūṇī omalina-malinehi cīvarehi pāṭitavipāṭitehi khaṇḍena pātrena chidravichidreṇa piṇḍapātam aṇvati*.

44 See Pischel 1900: § 276 for the reflex *jñ* > *jj* (among others Hc. 2, 83 *pajjā* < *prajñā*). In the dialect of the Senior Collection, *j* and *c* have merged and are effectively interchangeable; see Glass 2007: 115 (§ 5.2.1.2) and Silverlock 2015: 222 (§ 6.3.1).

45 This suffering is equally mental and physical, as stated in BC 4 and also in BC 11. In other Buddhist texts, *duḥkha* is sometimes characterized as belonging in particular to the body (*kāyika*), as opposed to mental pain / distress, which is expressed as *daurmanasya* (e.g., Nett 12 *duvidhaṃ dukkhaṃ: kāyikaṃ ca cetasikaṃ ca. yaṃ kāyikaṃ idaṃ dukkhaṃ, yaṃ cetasikaṃ idaṃ domanassaṃ*).

offering his own body to the Bodhisattva Dharmodgata. The breaking up of his body is for the sake of "gaining the good law" and for the accumulation of wholesome roots (*kuśalamūla*) in opposition to "ineffectual actions" done during many previous lifetimes, which were for the sake of sense pleasures (*kāma*). Analogously, in the *Suvarṇavarṇāvadāna* the term *sāmarthya* is linked to *puṇya* [= *kuśala*]: *puṇyānāṃ sāmarthya* (Roy 1971: 344), "efficacy of meritorious actions" (Rajapatirana 1974). Thus, in BC 4 *niḥsāmarthyajñāna* might best be understood in the sense of knowing what is unwholesome (*akuśala*) and hence "ineffectual" or "useless" with regard to liberation, since it is insufficient to produce the desired result.

4r20 *uadiṇae aṣ̄ivaṣ̄idae ... uekṣidae ... paricatae aṣ̄ivasidae*. These forms could be seen as dat. sg. from past participles (Skt./BHS *upādinnāya*, *adhivāsitāya*, *upekṣitāya*, *parityaktāya*). The passage might then be translated as "every suffering will come into existence to be taken up, to be accepted/endured, and to be looked at with an even mind; every happiness will come into existence to be given up and to be accepted/endured." The current translation is, however, based on the periphrastic past tense common in the Niya documents. It is formed by the ending *-taka*/*-taga* or *-tae*/*-dae*, usually in combination with an auxiliary verb like *siyati*, although this is occasionally omitted (Burrow 1937: § 114). If we accept *hakṣati* in place of *siyati* within some kind of periphrastic future (cf. Burrow ibid.), then we can translate the phrase as "every suffering [that will be] taken up will be accepted/endured [and] looked at with an even mind; every happiness [that will be] given up will be accepted/endured."

4r20 *par⟨*i⟩ṇirvahido*. The last two akṣaras cannot be read with certainty due to the broken-off birch bark. An alternative reading would be *◦hedi*. The current reconstruction is supported by *sarvasatva pariṇivaïto* in the Indravarma reliquary inscription (CKI 241), translated as "all beings are caused to attain *nirvāṇa*" by Salomon (1996: 428–29). Salomon (1996: 429 n. 23) points to *sarvasatva [para]ṇivaïti* in the "Aśoraya" inscription (on the halo of a standing Buddha, CKI 256), translated as "all beings are brought to *nirvāṇa*" (Skt. *parinirvāpita*) by Bailey (1982: 149–50). In addition to these inscriptions, BC 2 contains the verb *paraṇivaïśati* = Skt. *parinirvāsyanti*, "they will attain final extinction." Interestingly, the spelling *para-* is more common than *pari-* (occurring only in the Indravarma vessel inscription and once in BC 2). If we do not assume a scribal error from our current point of view (*para-* instead of *pari-*), the reading in BC 4 could as well be *para ṇirvahedi* = Skt. *parān nirvāhayati*, "he leads out other (beings)," i.e., he helps others to reach *nirvāṇa*.[46] However, the continuation of the sentence in the first person singular (*logado cariśe*, "I will go from this world") makes this unlikely.

The *-h-* in G *-ṇirvahido* suggests Skt. *-nirvāhita*, but I have not found anything corresponding to this (Skt. *parinirvāhita* / P *parinibbāhita*) or to Skt. *parinirvāhayati* / P *parinibbāheti*.[47]

---

46 Cf. Book of Zambasta, verses 13.131–32: "... 'He is "*paranärväta-*"', so it is said in the *sūtra*. There is another meaning of this expression. 'Another' being is said to be '*para-*'. A '*närvr̥ta-*' is one who extinguishes *kleśa*s. 'He extinguishes the *kleśa*s of others'—this is the meaning of that expression" (Emmerick 1968). For a similar case, cf. SWTF s.v. *paranirmita* (v.l. *parinirmita*).

47 Only a *Mahāparinirvāṇasūtra* manuscript from Central Asia (Waldschmidt 1950–51: 210, Vorgang 16.10) has *parinirvāhi* corresponding to P *parinibbātu* ("may [the Venerable One] attain complete

Only as a partial parallel, a commentary on the *Mokṣopāya* (2,17.43, Slaje 1993: 135) explains *nirvāhita* as "led (*nīta*) to cessation (*avasāna*)." The *-h-* can thus be better interpreted as a glide that has been inserted after a consonant or semivowel has been dropped (see Allon 2007: 247–48 for examples and references). Usually, this glide *-h-* replaces *-y-*, which then leads to Skt. *parinirvāyita* / P *parinibbāyita*.

Instead of *parinirvāhita* or *parinirvāyita* the form *parinirvāpita* is frequently met in *prajñāpāramitā* texts (*Aṣṭasāhasrikā*, *Pañcaviṃśatisāhasrikā*, *Vajracchedikā*) and the *Sukhāvatīvyūha*. BHSD translates *parinirvāti* as "enters complete enlightenment," the causative *parinirvāpayati* as "brings to …" (see also BHSG § 2.47). But the causative can also be used with a non-causative meaning, as, for example, in the *Divyāvadāna* (Cowell and Neil 1886: 90): *yathāyaṃ bhagavān … parinirvāsyati, evam aham api … parinirvāpayeyam*, "… so may I also enter complete *nirvāṇa*" (BHSD s.v. *parinirvāti*). Likewise in BC 4, *pariṇirvahido* = Skt. *parinirvāyita* does not refer to other beings having been brought to *nirvāṇa*, but to the bodhisattva having reached complete extinction by the aforementioned practice and knowledge of what is painful and useless. The extinction referred to here (Skt. *parinirvāṇa* / P *parinibbāna*) is the complete release or emancipation from all cravings and worldly desires.[48]

4r21 ***logado cariśe***. The ending *-do* instead of *-de* for the abl. sg. is unusual in this manuscript. It is however not unusual in Middle Indo-Aryan dialects in general (cf. von Hinüber 2001: § 300) or Kharoṣṭhī manuscripts in particular (cf. Lenz 2010: 40 and Baums 2009: 208).

As regards the meaning, it is unclear to me if the speaker ("I") is referring to the distant future in which he finally leaves the world, i.e., when he dies and does not come back, having led all beings to the state of *nirvāṇa*, or if his leaving the world should be taken metaphorically in the sense that he has relinquished all desires and thereby cut off the fetters of existence and the causes for rebirth, thus being "in this world, but not of this world." With regard to the latter possibility, cf. AN II 37–39, where Doṇa asks the Buddha if he is a god, a *gandharva*, a *yakṣa*, or human. The Buddha rejects the very premises, saying that he has abandoned all defilements that could identify him as any of them: "Just as a blue, red, or white lotus flower, though born in the water and grown up in the water, rises above the water and stands unsoiled by the water, even so, though born in the world and grown up in the world, I have overcome the world and dwell unsoiled by the world. Remember me, brahmin, as a Buddha" (Bodhi 2012: 426). This story is also preserved in a Gāndhārī manuscript (EĀ[L]; see Allon 2001: 124–25).

---

extinction"). There are few other parallels with *nirvāhayati* withouth a prefix, but they have nothing in common with BC 4. The Pali form *parinibbāhisi* is a future form, where *-h-* replaces *-ss-* (see Geiger and Norman 2000: § 150).

48 For the etymology of *nibbāna*, see Norman 1994. Regarding *parinibbāna* he states (1994: 217): "I prefer to follow the view of Thomas, who more than once reminded us that the difference between *nibbāna* and *parinibbāna* is a grammatical one. […] He states, '*Nirvāṇa* is the state of release; *parinirvāṇa* is the attaining of that state. The monk *parinirvāti* "attains *nirvāṇa*" at the time of enlightenment as well as at death. […] He *parinibbāyati*, attains the state, and then *nibbāyati*, is in the state expressed by *nibbāna*'" (cf. Norman for references and footnotes). On page 222 Norman concludes that *nibbāna*, "extinction," was only an explanation to *nibbuti* (Skt. *nirvṛti*) meaning "happiness, bliss, rest, ceasing," which is the original meaning.

4r21 ***dharme ca edam io ṇiṣ̱ama(*r)thadukhañaṇo***. The scribe seems to have first written *dharmo* and then emended it to *dharme*, which points to *dharma* being understood as a neuter instead of the more common masculine (although neuter is documented occasionally in Sanskrit and Pali texts). The first pronoun *edam* (Skt. *etad* / P *etaṃ*) is similar to Skt. *idam* / P *idaṃ* in the same meaning ("this"), but it is quite safely equated with *etad*, the more so since *etad* generally refers to what precedes, especially when connected with *idam*, the latter then referring to what follows (MW s.v. *etad*).

4r22 ***satva ya boṣ̱a praïṭhavamaṇa***. Instead of *boṣ̱a* we would expect a loc. sg. *boṣ̱e*, cf. AsP^{Sp} 5-22 *jaṃbudive satva te sarve sadavatiphale p(r)adiṭhavea* = AsP *jambūdvīpe sattvāḥ tān sarvān … srotaāpattiphale pratiṣṭhāpayet* (Falk and Karashima 2013: 118).

At the end of *praïṭhavamaṇa* the last *ṇa* is faded. What follows is a hole in the manuscript with the length of about eight akṣaras, most probably due to the condition of the birch bark. Because there are no traces of ink on the remaining parts, and because the text does not call for any wanting words, I assume that nothing was written here.

4r22 ***ṇa ciri ve***. This corresponds to Skt. *na cirād vai*, "certainly after a short time, very soon," although the ending *-i* would be better explained by a sandhi *cirā(d) + iva* or *eva*, comparable to P *na cirass' eva*, "after a short time, shortly."

4r23 ***satahi aloehi yo arida karae***, etc. The equivalents of both G *aloa* and *aloṇea* are uncertain, as is the meaning of *aride / praṇide kerea* and *aṇaride kerea*. These words are central to the last section (§ 7) and occur several times. The general structure of this section is as follows:

- § 7A1: [Who / which] *arida karae* by the one to seven *aloa*, or [who / which] *praṇide karae* from the *aṣ̱atia*[49] and the *aloṇea*, they both should be admonished / exhorted / avoided. With respect to all three times, both should be spoken.
- § 7A2: The result would be negative (Skt./BHS *durgati*, *asatpuruṣa*, *bandhana*, *duḥkha*, *aśubha*, *akuśala*; *middha*, *ālasya*, *akṛtya*, *akarman*, *aspṛśana*, *glānya*), which is why it / they should be avoided.
- § 7B1: *aṇaride kerea* the one to seven *aloa*, or *aṇaride kerao* the *aṣ̱atia* and the *aloṇea*, they both should be saluted / exhorted / commended / maintained. Both should be spoken.
- § 7B2: The result would be positive (Skt. *sugati*, etc.).

The following overview shows the parallel structure of § 7A1 and § 7B1. Words with negative connotations are marked with red, those with positive connotations, with green, and neutral ones, with yellow. Uncertain words are marked with grey.

---

49 G *aṣ̱atia* probably means "up to seven" (Skt. **āsaptika*), because *sata* is the last member of the enumeration "one, two, three, four, five, six, seven." Alternatively, G *aṣ̱atia* could mean "not seven" (Skt. *asaptika*), if *aloṇea* is the opposite of *aloa* and not a derivative of it.

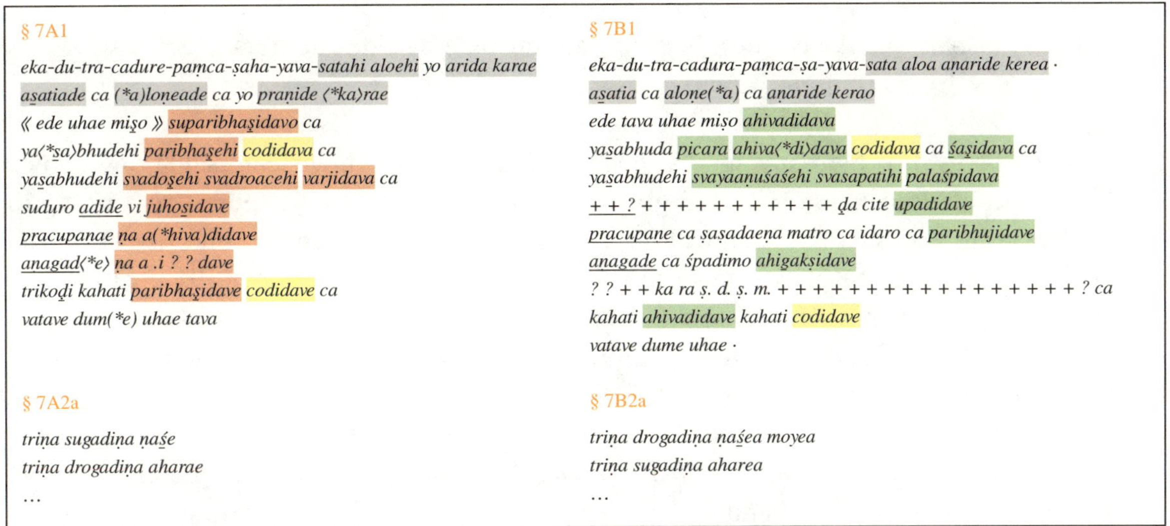

§ 7A1

eka-du-tra-cadure-paṃca-ṣaha-yava-satahi aloehi yo arida karae
*as̱atiade ca (*a)loṇeade ca yo praṇide ⟨*ka⟩rae*
⟪ ede uhae miṣo ⟫ suparibhaṣidavo ca
*ya⟨*ṣa⟩bhudehi paribhaṣehi codidava ca*
yas̱abhudehi svadoṣehi svadroacehi varjidava ca
suduro adide vi juhoṣidave
*pracupanae ṇa a(*hiva)didave*
*anagad⟨*e⟩ ṇa a .i ? ? dave*
trikoḍi kahati paribhaṣidave codidave ca
*vatave dum(*e) uhae tava*

§ 7A2a

triṇa sugadiṇa ṇaṣe
triṇa drogadiṇa aharae
…

§ 7B1

eka-du-tra-cadura-paṃca-ṣa-yava-sata aloa aṇaride kerea ·
*as̱atia ca aloṇe(*a) ca aṇaride kerao*
ede tava uhae miṣo ahivadidava
*yas̱abhuda picara ahiva⟨*di⟩dava codidava ca śaṣidava ca*
yas̱abhudehi svayaaṇuśaśehi svasapatihi palaśpidava
+ + ? + + + + + + + + + + + ḍa cite upadidave
pracupaṇe ca ṣaṣadaeṇa matro ca idaro ca paribhujidave
anagade ca śpadimo ahigakṣidave
? ? + + ka ra ṣ. d. ṣ. m. + + + + + + + + + + + + + + + + + ? ca
kahati ahivadidave kahati codidave
vatave dume uhae ·

§ 7B2a

triṇa drogadiṇa ṇaṣea moyea
triṇa sugadiṇa aharea
…

In the last paragraph, § 7C, these statements are repeated with addition of *ithumi* and *ohoro*, as well as *matra* and *idara*. The statements made in the last section can be illustrated as follows:

ithumi ohoro	through	*sata (matra)*	*arede kerea* *arida keraa*	to be admonished … avoided *paribhaṣidave … varjidave*	**benefit**: state of inherent existence (*śpabhavasa*) will disappear
ohoro	from	*as̱atia aloṇea (idara)*	*aride karaï* *arida kere(*a)*		
ithumi ohoro		*sata aloa (matra)*	*aṇaride keraa* *aṇari(*de) kerea*	to be saluted … maintained (?) *aïvadidave … palaśpidave*	
ohoro		*as̱atia aloṇea (idara)*	*aṇaride ko* *aṇaride kerea*		

What can be concluded from this, is:

- *satahi aloehi* as well as *as̱atia* (and) *aloṇeade aride kerea* is bad and to be avoided, *sata aloa* as well as *as̱atia* (and) *aloṇea aṇaride kerea* is good and to be maintained.
- The result is that the state of inherent existence (Skt. *svabhāvatā*) will disappear.
- *as̱atia aloṇea* are equal appositions according to § 7A–B, since they are conjoined by … *ca* … *ca*.[50]
- *as̱atia* and *aloṇea* seem to be derivations from *sata* and *aloa* with the addition of the suffix *-aka/-ika*.
- The difference is between *aride* (bad) and *aṇaride* (good) *kerea*.[51]

---

50 In two of the other four occurrences in § 7C, the *ca* is, however, only written once at the end and could thus be interpreted as a conjunction between the two parts of the sentence. Then, *as̱atia-aloṇeo* (§ 7C1.2) and *aloṇea-as̱atiade* (§ 7C2.1) might be understood as compounds. In the other two occurrences, no *ca* is written by the scribe.

51 G *-kerea* seems to be functioning as an adjective-marker corresponding to Pkt./BHS *-keraka* = Skt. *kāryaka*, cf. Pischel 1900: § 176; cf. also BHSD s.v. *parakeraka*, "belonging to another."

- *sata aloa* is likely to be positive (§ 7C3: "established [yourself] by the sevenness"), probably also *asatia aloṇea* (in § 7C3 they are put side by side and treated equally: *matrasahoro* [= *aloa*] · *idarasahoro* [= *aloṇea*]).

For all uncertain words there are several possibilities, none of which seem satisfying, which is why no definite translation has been given. Nothing in the text itself points to a group of seven. According to usual phonological developments, *aloa* could correspond to Skt. *ăloka*, *ăloga*, *ălopa*, *ălavaka*.[52] Of these, *āloka* in the meaning of "[inner] light," "illumination," or "insight" seems the most probable. In the Nikāyas of the Theravāda canon, *ālokasañña* ("perception of light") is a meditation technique to avoid drowsiness (P *thīnamiddha*).[53] It is intriguing that in BC 4, in §§ 7A2b and 7B2b, the terms *jāgaryā* and *middha* point to beneficial conditions during meditation practice. In the *Śrāvakabhūmi* there are four kinds of *ālokasaṃjñā* mentioned: *dharmāloka*, *arthāloka*, *śamathāloka*, *vipaśyanāloka*.[54] In the *Lalitavistara* (Lefmann 1902–08, I: 31), one hundred and eight *dharmālokamukha*s ("gateways to the light of the Dharma") are listed, beginning with *śraddhā*, *prasāda*, *prāmodya*, *prīti*, *kāyasaṃvara*, *vāksaṃvara*, *manaḥsaṃvara*.[55] In the *Daśabhūmikasūtra* (Rahder 1926: 37–38), ten *dharmālokapraveśa*s ("entries into the light of the Dharma") are mentioned and said to provide entry to the fourth "blazing" stage for one who has "purified vision" (*supariśuddhāloka*). They are explained as contemplations on the realms of *sattva*, *loka*, *dharma*, *ākāśa*, *vijñāna*, *kāma*, *rūpa*, *ārūpya*, *udārāśayādhimukti*, and *māhātmyāśayādhimukti*. Although none of these listings agree with the Bajaur text in comprising seven items, and none of the first-listed items is mentioned in the Bajaur text (except *prīti*), *āloka* may still point to the same context of contemplation and consideration (*āloka*; *ālocana(ka)*, *ālokanīya*, *ālocanīya*). However, I have not found any

---

52 If one includes the possibility of the sound change *r*/*l*, then a derivation of *ā√ruc*, "to announce, declare," might fit the context. In the Niya documents this occurs as *arocemti* ("approve"), in the rock edicts of Shahbazgarhi and Mansehra the same base is attested in Sh RE 4 *loceṣu* / Man RE 4 *alocayisu*, and Sh RE 14 *aloceti*. Thus, a spelling *l* for *r* would not be impossible.

53 It is mentioned in descriptions of the third *jhāna* and/or regarding the development of concentration that leads to the attainment of knowledge and vision (P *ñāṇadassanapaṭilābha*); e.g., DN III 223 (tr. Walshe 1987: 488) or AN II 44 (tr. Bodhi 2012: 431, cf. Ṭhānissaro 2010: 207). Likewise, the *Visuddhimagga* uses *āloka* relating to concentration techniques (among others, *ālokakasiṇa*) similar to the *ālokasaññā*. A more detailed passage occurs in the *Arthaviniścaya*, where *āloka* is compared to the "daylight at high noon" (Samtani 2002: 142). The commentary gives the explanation " 'perception of daylight', meaning 'perception of illumination': 'evenly luminous' [mind]" (Samtani 2002: 143). Samtani (2002: 143 n. 132) adds: "The idea of evenly luminous mind is close to the idea of very bright, resplendent (*pabhassaracitta*) mind in the early Pali Tradition, AN I, p. 10. Compare the later Teachings of the Mahāyāna Yogācāra school, based on the theory of 'mind only' (*cittamātratā*)." The *āloka* may first have been a means in meditation to stay awake and/or reach a clearer state of mind, later becoming a synonym for the understanding gained after having reached that clear state of mind. The *Nettippakaraṇa*, for example, names *āloka* as a synonym of understanding (§ 294, Ñāṇamoli 1962: 81, with reference to § 440, Ñāṇamoli 1962: 106). Cf. also Dhs 292, Peṭ 15, 494, 503, 541.

54 Śrāvakabhūmi Study Group edition 2007: 140.

55 The last three are, for example, also included in a long list of *samādhi*s in the *Samādhirājasūtra* (Dutt 1941: 15, GMNAI II.3: 4 folio (6), verso, line 3); they are, however, not called *āloka*.

Buddhist text preserved in an Indic language in which a particular set of seven "lights" (Skt. *sapta āloka*, P *satta āloka*) is mentioned.

When looking for groups of seven, what immediately comes to mind are the *satta bojjhaṅga*s, the seven factors of awakening,[56] but there are no references to these anywhere else in our manuscript. The sets of seven found in T 24 no. 1485 and related texts (cf. p. 20) also have no clear connection to the content of BC 4.[57] In addition to referring to seven items of a group, the number could also refer to some kind of seven-limbed poem or prayer to be uttered in a ritual, similar to the seven-limbed prayer of Śāntideva in the *Bodhicaryāvātara*, which lists seven verses about rejoicing in the awakening mind and finally dedicates the accumulated virtue to the complete removal of the pain of every living creature.

Theoretically, G *aloa* = Skt. *ălavaka* in the meaning "(not) cutting off" and G *aloṇea* = Skt. *ălavanīya*, "(not) to be cut off," or Skt. *ălūnaka*, "(not) cut off," are possibilities, but they do not seem to match the context. Something that would fit is Skt. *ālayanaka* as a derivation from *ālaya* in the meaning "attachment, clinging,"[58] but the phonological development *aya* > *o* is not attested elsewhere. Also, it seems more likely that *aloa*/*aloṇea* is positive in meaning.

Both terms, G *sata aloa* and *aṣatia aloṇea*, are combined with the equally uncertain words G *aride kerea* and *aṇaride kerea*, in variant spellings:

arida karae (1×) = *praṇide ⟨*ka⟩rae* (1×)	*aṇ-aride kerea* (3×)
arede kerea (1×)	*aṇ-aride kerao* (1×)
aride keraï (1×)	*aṇ-aride keraa* (1×)
arida keraa (1×)	*aṇ-aride ko* (1×)
*arida kere(*a)* (1×)	

Syntactically, *arida* takes an instr. or abl. and *aṇarida* a nom. or acc. Furthermore, in combination with *sata aloa*, *arida* apparently has a negative connotation and *aṇarida* a positive one. Once, in 4r23, *aride karae* is replaced by *praṇide ⟨*ka⟩rae* according to the analogously constructed passage. G *praṇide* may be the same as G *praṇito* in the Senavarma inscription (12a, see von Hinüber 2003: 37), where it corresponds to Skt. *praṇīta* / P *paṇīta*, "advanced, excellent, superior" or "noble" (see CPD s.v. *atipaṇīta*). Thus, the more frequently used G *arida* could then be equated to Skt. *āryatas*, "honorable, excellent," Skt. *āryatā*, "state of being honorable,"[59] or Skt. *ārita*, "praised." However, these words have positive connotations, which seems

---

56 Mindfulness (*sati*), investigation of the Dhamma (*dhammavicaya*), energy (*viriya*), joy (*pīti*), tranquility (*passaddhi*), concentration (*samādhi*), equanimity (*upekkha*), as, e.g., in SN V 71.

57 The groups of seven mentioned in T 24 no. 1485 and akin texts are: seven features of purity (see Rulu 2013: 85, 101–2 and 108 n. 12), seven *bodhi* factors (Rulu 2013: 49, 162, 275), seven stages of the bodhisattva way (Rulu 2013: 276), seven grounds (Rulu 2013: 26), seven noble treasures (Rulu 2013: 74), seven guiding instructions from all Buddhas (Rulu 2013: 199–200).

58 For *ālaya* as "abode," cf. T 24 no. 1485 (Rulu 2013: 51). Here there are seven levels of abiding, whereby during the first six, a bodhisattva practices the *pāramitā*s. At the sixth level he practices the *prajñāpāramitā*, realizes emptiness, and enters the seventh level, whence he never regresses.

59 Skt. *ārya* is usually written *aria* in Gāndhārī. Nevertheless, in the Niya documents, *ari* is sometimes used as a title before personal names, most probably denoting *ārya* (Burrow 1937: 76).

unlikely in this context (see above). Quite the opposite would be G *arida* = Skt. *aritā*, "emnity," and G *aṇaride* = Skt. *anaritā*, "without emnity." G *praṇide*, however, then remains unexplained.

Unfortunately, none of the several proposed options seems convincing. A similar term to G *aloa*/*aloṇea* used in a possibly similar context is Pkt. *āloyaṇā* or *ālocanā* (cf. Amg. *āloei*, Jaina Skt. *ālocayati*). It stands for a Jaina confession practice, where in Buddhist contexts P *paṭideseti* / BHS *pratideśāyati* would be used (cf. Caillat 1975: 116 ff.). There are seven moments in this process, which leads the sinner from confession to the expiation of his faults. The confession is to be executed three times (*āloyāventi te u tikkhutto*, Caillat 1975: 123). Though this sounds promising and similar to BC 4, the details are different. For example, only step one of the seven moments entails a confession or declaration of faults (cf. Caillat 1975: 117). Also, only the word G *aloa* would be explained as corresponding to Skt. *āloca*[*nā*], maybe with G *aloṇea* being a derivative thereof, something like **ālocanaka*. The other two terms *arida karae* / *aṇaride kerea* are still unexplained. Nevertheless, with this background the whole section § 7 of BC 4 could be seen as a description of a confession ritual. In § 7A the sins would be reported with regret, whereas in § 7B one would rejoice at the good things. Similar acts are also performed in the *triskandhaka* ritual (see p. 7). Also in the *Survarṇabhāsa* there is a chapter on confession, according to which one should regret (with regard to the past, present, and future), do good things, and avoid evil deeds (Emmerick 2001: 8–18). This is basically the same as in BC 4, possibly summarizing what is to be done by a bodhisattva on his way to become a Buddha.

4r23 *suparibhaṣidavo ... paribhaṣehi*. Although the verb *paribhāṣ* can have a neutral meaning ("to address; to declare") it is more often, especially in Buddhist texts, used in a negative sense.[60] In the *Pañcaviṃśatisāhasrikā Prajñāpāramitā* (and other *prajñāpāramitā* texts; cf. Conze 1973a) *paribhāṣ* means "to revile" and is a synonym of *vivad* ("dispute") and *ākruś* ("accost").[61] Also in the *Saddharmapuṇḍarīka* (8.40, Kern and Nanjio 1912: 213) *paribhāṣ* has been translated, for example, as "reprimand" (Kern 1884), "rebuke" (Watson 1993) and "reproach" (Kubo and Yuyama 2007). In the Niya documents it occurs as *parihaṣa* = Skt. *paribhāṣā* ("claim," Burrow 1937: § 27) and *paribhaṣati* = Skt. *paribhāṣate* ("revile, abuse," Burrow 1937: 104 with the note: "The meaning is obviously something like 'complains' "). I decided to translate it as "admonish" as long as the context (G *aloa*, *aloṇea*, etc.) is not clear, since "revile" would rather point to a person, which however is also the case with its antonym G *ahivadidave*.

4r23 *codidava*, "to be exhorted." For other translations, cf. Conze 1973a: *codayati*, "exhort, warn against," and *saṃcodita*, "impelled." The Niya documents record *codeyati* (CKD 592, 654, 715) / *coteyati* (CKD 71, 572, 579, 580, 581, 586, 587, 590, 591) / *coteyāti*, "to bring up" (CKD 571, 572, 587), "dispute" (CKD 592, 579, 580, 586, 591), "disagree" (CKD 582, 590), "fault with" (CKD 564, 715); *cotaṃna* (CKD 345, 572, 582) = *codaṃna* (cf. § 13) / *cotaṃti* (CKD 592),

60 In Sanskrit both meanings are known, in Pali and BHS only the negative one. Cf. also Bhattacharya and Sarkar 2004: 1035.

61 Cf., e.g., PvsP (Kimura 1992, V: 26): *yāvad vivaded vā ākrośed vā paribhāṣed vā kalahayitvā vā bhaṇḍayitvā vā vigrahayitvā vā vivādayitvā vā ākrośayitvā vā paribhāṣayitvā vā.*

"bringing up" (Burrow 1940). In BC 4 it is applied in a neutral sense, since it is used in a negative and positive context alike:

negative:

4r23–24	*suparibhaṣ̄idavo ca … codidava ca … varjidava ca*
4v9	*paribhaṣ̄idave ⟪codidave varjidave⟫*
4v11	*paribhaṭha ya codida ca varjida ca*

positive:

4v1–2	*ahiva⟨*di⟩dava codidava ca ṣ̄aṣ̄idava ca*
4v10	*paribhaṣ̄idave* [= *ahivadidave*] *codidave palaśpidave*
4v11–12	*aïvadida ca codida ca palaśpada ca*

4r23 *svadoṣ̄ehi*. In §§ 7A1 and 7B1, G *doṣ̄a* is used as an antonym of *aṇuśaśa* ("benefit, advantage"), next to *droaca / sapati*:

§ 7A1	*ya⟨*ṣ̄a⟩bhudehi paribhaṣ̄ehi codidava ca*
	yaṣ̄abhudehi ***svadoṣ̄ehi*** *svadroacehi varjidava ca*
§ 7B1	*yaṣ̄abhuda picara ahiva⟨*di⟩dava codidava ca ṣ̄aṣ̄idava ca*
	yaṣ̄abhudehi ***svayaaṇuśaśehi*** *svasapatihi palaśpidava*

4r24 *suduro*. The top of the first akṣara looks like a *tra* at first sight, but the lower half is only blurred, as is the following letter *du*. While the last akṣara could be *ro* or *ṭha*, the sign for *ṭha* is normally curved at the top (like a *va* with an additional stroke to the left). Therefore the transliteration as *ro* may be justified, although it is unusually large and sprawling. For a similar form of *ra / ro*, see, for example, 4r27 *aharea* and 4v8 *ohoro*.

4r24 *juhoṣ̄idave*. This is equivalent to Skt. **jugupsitavyam* ("to be abhorred / disgusted"), supported by evidence from other Gāndhārī manuscripts such as BL 1 (AnavL 33, Salomon 2008: 177):

sarvo aya roaghado	All this which consists of
yasa su kuṇavu tasa ◦	physical form is like that
atepudi ayokṣa ca	corpse, putrid within and
*sarvam edu juhośpi(*da ◦)*	filthy; all of this is repulsive.

G *juhośpi(*da)* is also written *johośp(*ida)* in Anav^{L} 30,[62] both going back to Skt. *jugupsita*, "repulsive" (as proven by the parallel in the Gilgit manuscript of the *Mūlasarvāstivādavinaya*; cf. Salomon 2008a: 234). The readings in Anav^{L} are, however, uncertain (discussed by Salomon 2008a: 229 and also 124). In the first instance, *śpi* is only retained on a separated chip whose original position was not necessarily here. In the second occurrence it is hardly legible, since half of the akṣara is broken off. Still, what remains does not resemble a *ṣ̄i* as in BC 4, but indeed

62 The glyph looks like a combination of *ju* and *jo*, having both a circle at the bottom and a diagonal stroke to the left.

rather a *śp*. The same word, apparently, also occurs in BC 2, where it is written as *juhosvia* or *juhosviaṇi*, both related to *kāma*. Thus, we would have the following developments: Skt. *ps* > G *śp* (Anav[L]) / *sv* (BC 2) / *s̱* (BC 4) in addition to P *cch* and a non-historical hyper-Sanskritized form BHS *st* (cf. BHSG § 2.19 as well as BHSD s.v. *jugupsana* and PTSD s.v. *jigucchati*). For the spelling in BC 4, the development would be: G *juhos̱idave* = BHS **jugupsitavya-* for Skt. *jugupsanīya-* / P *jigucchitabba-* (P *jugucchitabba-* is not documented, but cf. Śaurasenī *juguch°* according to von Hinüber 2001: § 238).

4r24 *a(*hiva)didave* / 4v3 *ahivadidave*. G *vadidave* can be derived from √*vad* ("say") or √*vand* ("salute, venerate"), both of which result in the same meaning "to salute respectfully," especially with the prefix *abhi-* (cf. PTSD s.v. *vandati*).[63] According to CPD s.v. *abhivadati*, the meaning "to salute (respectfully)" is more frequently related to causatives. Other meanings are "maintain, assert; approve of, assent to." A neutral translation of *abhivad* would be "to declare, speak of," but in BC 4 *ahivadidave* is used analogously to *paribhas̱idave*; thus "welcome, salute" as opposed to "admonish" seems more appropriate (4r24 *kahati paribhas̱idave codidave ca* vs. 4v3 *kahati ahivadidave kahati codidave*). Moreover, in Pali texts *abhivadati* in the sense of "salute, greet, welcome" is often used in combination with *abhinandati*, which may have been found in the following passage with respect to *aṇagad⟨*e⟩*.

4r24 *aṇagad⟨*e⟩ ṇa a .i + + dave* = *aṇagad⟨*e⟩ ṇa abhi(*ṇadi)dave* (?). Due to distortions of various parts of the manuscript, fragment 4.1r L could not be repositioned perfectly in the general reconstruction so that both sides are linked to adjacent fragments. In the figure below the fragment is located a little further to the left to demonstrate how the remaining traces of ink on the surrounding fragments have been rearranged relative to each other. The gap and letter remnants do not make it easy to tell what verb is meant. Based on context, G *abhiṇadidave* = Skt. *abhinanditavya-* (PTSD "to be rejoiced at, be delighted with [acc.], welcome, praise, applaud, approve," CPD "to greet with joy or welcome") could be reconstructed (cf. Nird[L2] "look forward to" and EĀ[L] "rejoice"), although the expected form of *ṇa* does not match the remaining traces perfectly. Furthermore, G *ahi-* would be expected, as in other spellings of Skt. *abhi-* throughout BC 4, but *hi* is definitely excluded on the basis of the still visible parts of the akṣara. The parallel sentence on the verso (4v3, see figure below) is not very well preserved either, but can quite safely be transliterated as *aṇagade ca śpadimo ahigakṣidave*. It clearly uses another verb, although with a similar meaning (Skt. *abhikāṅkṣati* / P *abhikankhati*, "to long for, desire after, wish for"). On this equivalence, see Baums 2009: 28. Cf. also the annotations on 4v3 *ahigakṣidave*, p. 188.

Fig. 33. Comparison of 4r24 *aṇagad⟨*e⟩ ṇa a .i + + dave* (left) and 4v3 … *ahigakṣidave* (right).

---

63 Dhp[K] 321 *ahivadaṇa* = Dhp 108 *abhivādana* ("respectful salutation"). Likewise Dhp[K] 172 = Dhp 109.

4r24 *trikoḍi*. In BHSD s.v. *trikoṭi*, this term is defined as "three alternatives" or more generally as "three points." According to the PTSD, *koṭi* also means "division of time, with reference either to the past or the future." Although this seems limited to two points/ends of time, i.e., the past and the future, it may not be too farfetched to translate *trikoṭi* here as "three points of time," referring to the aforementioned past, present, and future[64]—or probably also as "three times a day/at night" (cf. the Introduction, p. 8).

4r24 *kahati*. This most likely corresponds to BHS *kāhiti*, a 3rd sg. future of √*kṛ*. Cf. BHSG § 31.18; Geiger and Norman 2000: § 153 (*kāhiti*/*kāhati*); Pischel 1900: §§ 520, 533; von Hinüber 2001: §§ 469–70; Oberlies 2001: § 49 (*kāhiti*/*kāhati*).[65] The future form is translated here as an instruction to the reader or practitioner meaning "one should do (G *kahati*) what is to be admonished/exhorted/saluted" (cf., e.g., Speyer 1886: 266 § 344). Thus it would be used similarly to G *kaṭave* in 4r28, in the sense of "apply the formula with regard to '*paribhaṣidave*/*codidave*/*ahivadidave*.' "

4r25 *ṇaṣ̄e*/*aharae*, etc. The spellings of *ṇaṣ̄a-* and *ahara-* are inconsistent. At the beginning of the list (§ 7A2a) it is: *ṇaṣ̄e*, *ṇaṣ̄ae*, *ṇaṣ̄ae*, *naṣ̄ae*, *ṇaṣ̄e*, *ṇaṣ̄ee* and *aharae*, *a(*hara)e*, *aharae*, *aharae*, *(*aharae)*, *aharae*. Subsequently (§ 7A2b, § 7B1–2), the ending is *-ea*, indicating a 3rd sg. optative (P *-eyya*).[66] The syntactical construction in combining this with a noun in the genitive is, however, puzzling.[67] In this respect, the endings in § 7A2a would be better understandable as substantives in the dat. sg. (*-āya*) meaning "for (the sake of)," but then the frequent ending *-ea* is unusual, though not totally excluded.[68] Another, and perhaps the most likely solution is to understand the different spellings *-ea* and *-ae* (as well as *-e* or *-ee*) going back to the suffix *-aka*. In BC 11 the two words are consistently written as *aharae* and *ṇaṣ̄e* in combination with a genitive. In one instance (11v10), *ṇaṣ̄e* is replaced by *prahaṇa* ("abandoning") and in another (11v20), *aharae* is replaced by *padilabhe* ("obtaining"), supporting the understanding of *ṇaṣ̄(a)e* and *aharae* as nouns rather than verbs and corresponding to Skt. *nāśaka* and *āhāraka*. The meaning of these antonyms should be "destroying, annihilating" (perhaps also "losing"), on the one hand, and "procuring, bringing near," on the other (cf. MW and PW s.v. *nāśaka*, with gen. or comp., as well as MW s.v. *āhāraka*). All forms seem to be in the nom. or acc. sg., probably in the sense of "this would be for destroying/procuring" or "by this one would destroy/procure" (with "this" referring to *arida karae* / *praṇide karae* in § 7A1 and *aṇaride kerea* / *aṇaride kerao* in § 7B1).

---

64 Cf. *Ratnāvalī* verse 1.70, where the Chinese translation of Paramārtha renders *ādimadhyāvasānāni* as 三際, lit. meaning "three ends." But the characters can also be translated as "three time periods," "before, between, and after," or "past, present, and future" according to DDB s.v.; cf. Okada 2006: 61.

65 Cf. also Caillat (1977–78: 103 = 2011: 127) for a discussion of *kariṣyati*.

66 Although G *-ea* can also be 1st sg. opt. (P *-eyyaṃ*), predominantly *-ea* is 3rd sg. opt, and *-ae* 1st sg. opt.; cf., e.g., Salomon 2008a: 151–52.

67 For the unexpected use of genitives with various verbs, cf. BHSG § 7.65 and also Salomon 2008a: 282 with reference to Mvu I 376. However, none of the given examples is applicable.

68 Cf. Lenz 2003: 74 for the unusual *bhave[a]* = Skt. *bhavāya* (as confirmed by parallels). There are no attestations in other Gāndhārī manuscripts edited so far.

4r26 *(*jagariaṇa)* / 4v6 *jagariaṇa*. According to PTSD, *jāgariyā* ("wakefulness") is especially used in the sense of being cautious of the dangers that are likely to befall one who strives for perfection.

4r26 *mi(*dhaṇa)* / 4v6 *midhaṇa*. This is part of one of the five hindrances (*nīvaraṇa*) in the Pali Nikāyas that should be abandoned in order to enter *samādhi* and reach the *jhānas*: *kāmarāga, byāpāda, thīna-middha, uddhacca-kukkucca, vicikicchā* ("sense-desire, aversion, sloth and torpor, restlessness-regret, doubt"; cf., e.g., Giustarini 2005: 157). In the *Śūraṃgamasamādhisūtra* the hindrances to meditation are: *abhidhyā, vyāpāda, styāna-middha, auddhatya-kaukr̥tya, vicikitsā* ("covetousness, aversion, sloth and torpor, restlessness-regret, doubt"; cf. Lamotte and Boin Webb 2003: 13). Moreover, the *Abhidharmahr̥daya* states that "[s]leepiness [*middha*] exists only in a desirous mind,"[69] indicating a special relation to the problem of desire and passion, which is also at the heart of the Gāndhārī texts BC 4, BC 6, and BC 11.

4r26 *lah(*uṭhaṇaṇa)* / 4v6 *lahuṭhaṇaṇa*. In Pali texts this term only occurs in phrases like *appābādhaṃ appātaṅkaṃ lahuṭṭhānaṃ balaṃ phāsuvihāraṃ*, not in combination with P *ālassa* / *ālasiya* (Skt. *ālasya*). The five terms are part of a polite phrase used when approaching the Blessed One: *bhagavato pāde sirasā vandati, appābādhaṃ appātaṅkaṃ lahuṭṭhānaṃ balaṃ phāsuvihāraṃ pucchati* (e.g., DN II 73). In Sanskrit texts the formulation is, for example, as follows:[70] *bhagavataḥ pādau śirasā vanditvālpābādhatāṃ pr̥cchanty alpātaṅkatāṃ ca laghūtthānatāṃ ca yātrāṃ ca balañ ca sukhañ cānavadyatāṃ ca sparśavihāratāṃ ca* ("… they bow down to the feet of the Blessed One and ask about him having little affliction, little sickness, lightness, livelihood, strength, happiness, faultlessness, and a comfortable life"). Another example from the *Visuddhimagga* is:

> *ayaṃ pana ānisaṃso appābādhatā appātaṅkatā lahuṭṭhānaṃ balaṃ phāsuvihāro* (Vism 69 / Vism[W] 56)
>
> The benefits are these. He has little affliction and little sickness; he has lightness, strength, and a happy life. (Ñāṇamoli 2011: 65)

The commentary *Paramatthamañjūsā* (B[e] I 96) annotates *lahuṭṭhāna* as being especially the lightness and flexibility of the body: *appābādhatā ti arogatā. appātaṅkatā ti akicchajīvitā sarīradukkhābhāvo. lahuṭṭhānan ti kāyassa lahuparivattitā. balan ti sarīrabalaṁ. phāsuvihāro ti sukhavihāro*. Cf. also de La Vallée Poussin 1909: 345, where he briefly discusses the term *laghūtthāna* (with reference to the *Saddharmapuṇḍarīka*, the *Divyāvadāna*, and the *Mahāvyutpatti*). In the commentary on the *Bodhicaryāvatāra* it is explained as being physically alert

---

69 Willemen 2006: 106–7: "because a sleepy mind is closed, sleepiness exists only in the realm of desire in the mental stage. It is associated with all afflictions of the realm of desire. All afflictions proceed at the moment of sleepiness" (n. 162 on "closed": "*abhisaṃkṣipta*? This would be a view held by the masters in Gandhāra. Kośa VII 18").

70 Cited from the *Avadānaśataka* (Speyer 1906–09, I: 326).

so that one is able to get up quickly, even during the night (*laghūtthānaḥ śīghram evottiṣṭhet*, de La Vallée Poussin 1901–14: 151, referring to verse 5.96).

4r27 *kicaṇa* … *akicaṇa* / 4v6–7 *kicaṇa* … *agicaṇa*. Very basically, this encompasses everything that is "to be done" and "not to be done." In the commentary on the *Suttanipāta* (Sn 715), *kiccākicca* is glossed as *kusalākusala* (cf. Nyanaponika 1955: 301). Here both *kicca* and *akicca* are to be given up in order to abandon every craving.[71] A similar statement is found in 6v5–6.

In a Mahāyāna context, *kṛtya* denotes the actions that are to be performed for the benefit of all beings. Through the knowledge of performing what is to be done (*kṛtyānuṣṭhānajñāna*), a Tathāgata knows how to benefit all beings in order to help them on their way to awakening.[72] In BC 4, however, the terms *kica* and *akica* seem to be used in a general sense, as is the case in BC 6.

4r27 *karmaṇa* / 4v7 *karmaṇa*. On the one hand, *karman* is the execution of an action (activity). On the other hand, it is the result or consequence of this action. In a sequence with G *kica* it might denote actual activities done with one's body, voice, or mind. The *karman* as an action of a bodhisattva reminds one of the title of T 24 no. 1485, "The Sūtra of the Garland of a Bodhisattva's Primary Karmas," which deals exclusively with the bodhisattva-*śīla* (cf. p. 20 and 156).

4r27 *śpriṣ̄aṇaṇa* / 4v7 *śpriṣ̄aṇaṇa*. This is equivalent to Skt. *sparśana-* / BHS *spṛśana-* / P *phusana-*, "touch, contact." In other Gāndhārī documents, initial *spṛ-* appears as *ph-*: *phuṣita* = Skt. *spṛṣṭvā* / BHS *spṛśitvā* / P *phusitvā* (EĀ[L] 54, Allon 2001: 94) and *phaṣea* = Skt. **sparśeyam* (Anav[L] 16, Salomon 2008a: 123 and 125).[73] The Gāndhārī reflex *śpr* is attested once in SĀ[S1] 3 *pa[śpru]ṣ̄a*, although in medial position, corresponding to Skt. *phupphusa* / BHS *phuṣphasa* / P *papphāsa*, "lungs" (cf. Glass 2007: 158 for variant forms).[74]

In BC 4, the emphasis should be laid on "touch" as a "pleasant or unpleasant feeling" or "comfort or discomfort," similar to "health or sickness," which are the next items in the list.[75]

4r28 *maja ṇisamartha sarvatra ithu kaṭave*. This signifies an exegetical instruction to the reader: in every case it must be done "thus" (G *ithu*). What exactly "every case" (*sarvatra*)

71 Sn 715 *yassa ca visatā n' atthi chinnasotassa bhikkhuno, kiccākiccappahīnassa pariḷāho na vijjati*, "In whom there is no craving, in the bhikkhu who has cut across the stream, (and) has given up what is to be done and what is not to be done, no fever is found" (Norman 1992: 81).

72 The *kṛtyānuṣṭhānajñāna* is one of the five knowledges of a Tathāgata, cf. *Dharmasaṃgraha* 94 (Müller and Wenzel 1885: 22), *Sāratamā* (Jaini 1979: 175), or Mvy 110–14. In *Mahāyānasūtrālaṃkāra* 9.67 and 9.74 (Lévi 1907: 46, 47), only four are listed.

73 Cf. also Anav[L] 27 *phaṭiṣ[u]* = Skt. **asphaṭṭīt*.

74 BHSD s.v. *phuṣphasa* gives the spellings: *phaphasa, phuṣphuṣa, phusphuṣa* (Skt. and Pkt. *phupphusa*).

75 Cf. MW s.v. *sparśa*. Also BSHD s.v. *sparśavihāratā*: "state of comfort, agreeable condition," and s.v. *asparśavihāra*: "discomfort" with reference to AsP 253 *na cāsyā asparśavihāra amana āpaḥ kaye utpadyeta*. Especially in combination with *-vihāra* it means the state of "comfort" or "ease" (according to PTSD s.v. *phāsu*), synonymous with *sukha (-vihāra)*, e.g., *yathāsukhaṃ yathāphāsu* (cf. BHSD s.v. *phāsu*).

refers to is open to discussion. (1) It could mean to repeat the previous sentences—*maje ca ṇ(*i)ṣamarth(*e) purve dukhe paca̱ dukhe ma(*je ca ṇi)samarthe purve aśuha pa(*ca̱ a)śuha*—replacing *dukhe* or *aśuha* with every other negative term of the list in § 7A2 (4r25–4r28). This would result, for example, in *maja ṇisamartha purve akuśala paca̱ akuśala*. Or (2), it could be explaining that the abbreviation *maje ca ṇiṣamarthe* within the text, which occurs in lines 4r13, 4r25 [2×], and 4v4 (as well as in 11r9 and 11r27 [2×]), should be extended in this manner, i.e.: "each time you come across this, read: *maje ca ṇiṣamarthe purve dukhe paca̱ dukhe*, *maje ca ṇiṣamarthe purve aśuha paca̱ aśuha*." The second option is more likely, since the list of § 7A2 does not start with *dukha* and also contains items that are not adjectives. The abbreviation *maje ca ṇiṣamarthe*, or sometimes only *maje* or only *ṇiṣamarthe*, is found exclusively as an interlinear gloss in BC 4, making it even more plausible that the sentence *maja ṇisamartha sarvatra ithu kaṭave* in 4r28 was intended to explain this.

G *ithu* here is an indeclinable (Vedic *itthā* / Skt. *ittham* / P *itthaṃ*) in the meaning "thus," while G *ithumi* later on seems to refer to "here, in this world" (BHS *itthaṃ*; see NWS s.v. *ittham* and BHSD s.v. *etthaṃ*, and cf. P *itthatta* or *itthabhāva*, possibly from **ittha* = *ettha*, "here"). The confusion between P *ittha-* as either "here" or "thus" (see PTSD and CPD s.v. *itthatta*) seems to be avoided in our text by the different endings. Schwarzschild 1956: 268 assumes an artificial differentiation in Prakrit between *itthaṃ*, "thus," and *ittha* = *ettha*, "here." G *ithu* in the sense of "thus" also appears in other (not yet published) Gāndhārī manuscripts. In BC 7 (*Karmavācanā* formulae, Strauch forthcoming) it is written *ithu ami*, corresponding to Skt. *ittham api* / P *itthaṃ pi*, "in this way," or *ithuṇamo* = P *itthaṃnāma*, "N. N." With the same meaning it is attested in RS 22: *ithu ami veḏaṇa saña sakhara*, "so also feeling, perception, and volitional formations," the text giving form (*ruo*) and consciousness (*viñaṇa*) in full (Mark Allon, personal communication). In BC 18 it is written *ithumi* as in BC 4, but the context is not yet clear. In the Niya documents, *iṃthu ami* is attested in addition to *iṃthu* (in Burrow 1937: § 91 written together as *iṃthuami* and explained as *iṃthu* with the suffix *-mi*, *-emi*, both translated as "so").

4r28 *śeṣae patade hi*. The ending of the first word (*-ae*) could indicate a dative or locative singular of *śeṣa* = Skt. *śeṣa* / P *sesa* (m./n., "remainder"). In the case of a locative, we would expect the Gāndhārī form *śeṣe*, but the loc. sg. ending *-ae* for words ending in *a* is prevalent, at least in epigraphic sources. Alternatively, one could think of Skt. *śeṣaka* in the loc. sg. but with the same meaning as *śeṣa* (cf. PTSD s.v. *sesa*).

The following *patade* seems to go back to **patta* ("back, behind, after"), which is peculiar to the northwest of India (cf. CDIAL s.v. ²*patta*). In Niya, similarly, *patama* is used (adv., "back," Burrow 1937: § 91).[76]

The same combination with *śeṣa* is documented in 6r11 *śeṣa patade likhidae*. While in BC 6 nothing is written in addition, BC 4 also includes an injunction about what is to be done on the other side: 4r28 *śeṣae patade hi vivaryaeṇa matra ca idara ca ahi(*va)d(*i)dava* … ("For

[76] While less likely, it may also be derived from *prānta* ("edge, border," *prāntatas* "along the border"), but the post-consonantial *r* should then be retained.

the remainder, on the reverse [side of the scroll] inversely the full measure [of seven] as well as the other [group] should be saluted …").

4r28 *vivaryaeṇa*. Literally, this means "by the opposite," akin to Skt. *viparyāye*, *-ena* and *-āt* (ind.), "in the opposite case, otherwise, to the contrary." In combination with a gerundive it is often used in Pali commentaries to express that the opposite of the situations/conditions just expressed should be known. Often the "white half," i.e., the good alternative, is implied here, e.g.: Vism 427 / Vism^{W} 361 *vuttavipariyāyena sukkapakkho veditabbo*. In combination with P *sesa*, the formulation is for example: *sesaṃ vuttavipariyāyena veditabbaṃ*.

4r28 *matra ca idara ca*. This is repeated several times, with *matra* referring to *sata aloa*, and *idara* to *asatia* and *aloṇea*. With *matra* = Skt. *mātra* in the meaning of "consisting of, measuring, numbering …" or "the full or simple measure of anything" (MW) it is understood as "the full measure [of seven *aloa*] and the other [group, i.e, the *asatia aloṇea*]."

4r28 *palaśpidava*. The Kharoṣṭhī sign transliterated as *śp* is written for Skt. *śp*, *śm*, *śv*, *ṣp*, *ṣm*, *sm*, *sv*, or *ps* in different Gāndhārī manuscripts. In BC 4/6/11 *sv(a)*, *sp(r̥)* and *sm(r̥)* occur (cf. chapter 5 on phonology, p. 90). G *pala-* should correspond to *pălă-*, since *r* and *l* usually remain unchanged (Salomon 2000: 86, Allon 2001: 86).[77] Nevertheless, G *pali-* for *pari-* is attested in some Gāndhārī textual sources, so that *palaśpidava* could be Skt. *pari-*, if we further accept that the scribe forgot to write the vowel sign.[78] But since it is always written *pala-* (*palaśpidava* [2 ×], *palaśpidave*, *palaśpada*), this is unlikely. Also, no case of G *pala-* = Skt./P *pără-* has yet been found in any text. Thus, most probably this is an unclear derivation from Skt. √*pāl* in the sense of "to be guarded, protected, maintained," since it is opposed to G *varjidava*, "to be avoided," in 4r24/4v2. Unfortunately, there is no evidence of G *śp* = *y*, and also the letter as such cannot be mistaken for *y*, which makes G *palaśpidava* = Skt. *pālayitavya-* unjustified.

4v1 *picara*. Until now, this Gāndhārī word was only known from the Niya documents, either standing on its own: CKD 288 *tehi picara syati*, "will be worthy of you" (Burrow 1940), or as part of a compound: CKD 107 *picaradivyavarṣaśatayupramaṃna-* and CKD 247 *piṃcaradivyavarṣaśatāyupramāna-*, "having a life span of a hundred divine years worthy of him/them." In other Niya documents, *picara-* is replaced with *yogya-*, "proper, fit or qualified for, suitable": CKD 140 and 307 *yogyadivyavarṣaśataayupramana-*, CKD 161 *yogyadivyavarṣaśatāyupramana-*, Skt. *yogyadivyavarṣaśatāyupramāṇa*, and CKD 399 *yogyadivyavarṣaśatayuka-*, Skt. *yogyadivyavarṣaśatāyuṣka*, "having a life (span) of a hundred divine years suited to him/them."

Regarding the loss of *r* in *picara* = BHS *pratyarham*, Thomas (1934: 66 n. 9) refers to *picavidavo* = Skt. *pratyarpitavya* and suggests a dissimulative influence of the following *r*

77 One exception is the eastern loan word G *saleloa* = Skt./P *saroruha* (Dhp^{L} 8, Lenz 2003: 42).

78 The examples are: Nird^{L2} 9·113 *palikhaïda* = Skt. *parīkṣita-* / P *parikkhita-*, Hirayama fragment 8 *palikṣiviśati* (*palikṣivitva*) = fut. of Skt. *parikṣipati* / P *parikkhipa*, Mathura Lion Capital *palichina* = Skt. *paricchinna* / P *paricchinna*.

(Thomas 1936: 792–93). There is, however, no suggestion for the change of the vowel in the first syllable from *a* to *i* (see also Burrow 1937: 105).

Thomas furthermore points to Mvu I 143 *kā ca pratyarahasaukhyā*, translating this as "qui a un bonheur proportionné à son mérite" (Thomas 1934: 66 n. 9) or "happiness according to desert" (Thomas 1936: 792; cf. Jones 1949–56, I: 113: "Who has merit to win such honor?"). In other Buddhist texts, *pratyarha* is often combined with *yathā-* as *yathāpratyarha*, "according to deserts/merit," or it occurs as *yathārha*, "according to merit" (MW s.v. *yathārha* and *yathāpratyarham*, BHSD s.v. *yathāpratyarha*). In BC 4, *picara* = BHS *pratyarham* has the meaning of "according to merit," not only "worthy." This agrees with the equivalence of *picara-* and *yogya-* in the Niya documents, where both have the meaning of "according to [his/their] merit."

4v2 *ṣaṣadaeṇa*. This should correspond to Skt. *śāśvata* / P *sassata*, or rather Skt. *śāśvatika*, "eternal, permanent," but involving the unusual development *ś-* > *ṣ-*. In other published Gāndhārī manuscripts, *śāśvata* is written as *śaśvada* (Dhp[K]) or *saspada-* (Nird[L2]). In the two Wardak vases, *śaśvetiga*/*śaśvatiga* stands for Skt. *saṃsvedika* / P *saṃsedika*, "sweat-born," but, according to Falk (2008: 73), *śaśvatiga* must have been a misconception deriving *saṃsedika* from *śaśvat* as *śāśvatika* ("eternal creature"). In BC 2 *ṣa[ṣa]to* occurs, most likely for Skt. *śāśvatam*, even though the passage is very fragmentary. Nevertheless, I assume that *ṣaṣadaeṇa* in 4v2 has been written for Skt. *śāśvatikena*, and, correspondingly, *ṣaṣadae* in 11r13 for Skt. *śāśvatāya* / P *sassatāya* (dat. sg.), both in the meaning "forever, incessant(ly), eternal(ly), constant(ly)." In view of this parallel, we might also have to separate *ṣaṣadae ṇa* in BC 4, resulting in *ṣaṣadae ṇa matro ca idaro ca*, "for evermore not only the full measure [of seven] but also the other [group] should be enjoyed" or even "for evermore neither the full measure [of seven] nor the other [group] should be enjoyed," even though we would expect a different syntax then (for example, *ṇevi … ṇevi …*). But cf. also 4r28–29 *śeṣae patade hi vivaryaeṇa matra ca idara ca ahi(*va)d(*i)dava ca*, where the *ṇa* before *matra* more likely belongs to the preceding word.

4v3 *ahigakṣidave*. This should correspond to Skt. *abhikāṅkṣitavya-* / P *abhikankhitabba-* from *abhi* √*kāṅkṣ*, "to long for, desire," or in a more neutral translation, "to hope for, expect, await." In the parallel section in § 7A1 the corresponding word seems to be *abhiṇadidave*, which, for example, in Th 196 and 606, etc., can have the same meaning "to long for" (Norman 1969: 24, 60 etc.); cf. annotations on 4r24 *aṇagad⟨*e⟩ ṇa a .i + + dave*, p. 182. So far, *abhighakṣada-* (Anav[L]) or similarly *paḏigakṣidava-* (BC 2) are attested in other Gāndhārī documents. Despite the satisfying reconstruction in BC 4, it should be noted that the first letter looks slightly like an initial *u*, the second could as well be an *a*, and *kṣi* could also be *ji*, resulting in the possible alternative reading *uagajidave*.

4v4 *moyea*. In analogy to the interpretation of *ṇaśea* and *aharea* as Skt. *nāśaka* and *āhāraka* (see p. 183), *moyea* should correspond to Skt. *mocaka*, "liberating, emancipating."

4v4 *kamapramuhaasapuruṣaṇa*. The reconstruction of G *kama* is uncertain, but highly likely. It stands in contrast to *budhapramuhasapuruṣaṇa*. If we assume a person opposed to the Buddha, we would think of Māra, for whom an epithet like P *kaṇha* would be suitable. Usually P *kaṇha* corresponds to G *kriṣ̱a* (= Skt. *kr̥ṣṇa*), which cannot be reconstructed here. Since Māra is more or less a personification of desire, passion, and longing (*kāma*), which is one of the central topics in this text, the reading as *kama* may be justified.[79]

4v4–5 *saṃsara{ra}badhaṇaṇa*. The last akṣara in 4v4 has to be *ra*. However, the first akṣara in 4v5 also looks like a *ra*. Hence, the writer appears to have repeated the same letter erroneously (dittography). If we dissolve the compound (*saṃsarabadhaṇa*) as a genitive *tatpuruṣa* one would expect *saṃsarasa badhaṇa*. Since the upper half of the letters *sa* and *ra* can look very similar, this is not impossible, but on balance the letter in question is more likely to be a *ra*, as the upper stroke is rather horizontal, and therefore it is transliterated here as such.

4v8 *do(*ṣ̱aṇa)*. This stands in opposition to G *sapati*. Normally (in this text) we would expect *droaca* as the counterpart to *sapati*; in one instance (4r14) it is *duhe*. The first letter here, however, is clearly *do*, and what is left of the next akṣara resembles more a *ṣ̱a* than an *a*. Further arguments supporting this interpretation are the closeness of the two words in the following phrases: 4r24 *svadoṣ̱ehi svadroacehi*, 11v5 *avarimaṇaṇa doṣ̱aṇa avarimaṇaṇa droacaṇa ṇaś̱e*. Therefore *doṣ̱aṇa* is more probable than the assumption of a scribal mistake, even though the expected counterpart would be *aṇuśaśe* and not *sapati*, since the pairs are *doṣ̱a* and *aṇuśaśa* as well as *droaca* and *sapati*.

4v8–9 *ithumi ohoro … (*o)horo* / 4v9–10 *ithumi ohoro* … *o(*ho)ro* / 4v12 *ithumi hurahu*. The meaning of *ithumi* in combination with *ohoro* is uncertain. Usually, *ithu* means "thus" (see annotations on 4r28 *maja ṇisamartha sarvatra ithu kaṭave*, p. 185) corresponding to Skt. *ittham*, P *itthaṃ*. There is, however, a second meaning to BHS / P *ittha-* denoting "here, in this world, in this existence," cf. BHS *itthatva*; P *itthatta* /*-bhāva*[80] → Skt. *iha*(*loka*) / P *idha*(*loka*), more often written *idha* in Pali or Buddhist Sanskrit texts in the phrase *idha vā huraṃ vā*, "here or there; in this world or the next." As such it is documented in Dhp^{K} 191 *idha va horo va* = Dhp 20 *idha va horo va*, "in this world and the next" (Norman 1997). Similarly, Dhp^{K} 91 *(*hora)[h]oru* stands for Dhp 334 *hurāhuraṃ*, "hither and thither" (Norman 1997), in the sense of "from existence to existence" (or "from life to life" as translated by Müller 1881).[81]

---

79 Cf. *Buddhacarita* 13.2: *yaṃ kāmadevaṃ pravadanti loke, citrāyudhaṃ puṣpaśaraṃ tathaiva, kāmapracārādhipatiṃ tam eva, mokṣadviṣaṃ māram udāharanti* (Johnston 1935: 145), "Him who in the world they call the god of Love, him of the bright weapon and also the flower-arrowed, that same one, as the monarch of the activities of the passions and as the enemy of liberation, they style Māra," Johnston 1936: 188).

80 In the Turfan fragments we find the scribal error *iṃthābh(āva)* for *itthaṃbhāva* ("das Sosein; Existenz in dieser Form," the opposite of *anyathībhāva*); cf. SWTF s.v. *iṃthābh(āva)*.

81 According to PTSD s.v., the adverb *huraṃ* is of uncertain origin. For an attempt at an explanation, see Norman 1969: 42 and 189, where he discusses *hurāhuraṃ* in Th 399 = Dhp 334. One commentary, Dhp-a IV 44, gives *bhave bhave* for *hurāhuraṃ*; a commentary on Ud 37, Ud-a 237, circumscribes it with *aparāparaṃ* or *idhalokaparalokato*. The commentary on Th 10 *idha vā huraṃ vā* explains: *idhā ti, imasmiṃ loke attabhāve vā. huran ti, parasmiṃ anāgate attabhāve vā. idhā ti vā ajjhattikesu āyatanesu. huran ti, bāhiresu* (cf. Norman 1969: 121). Thus *hura* principally means

In BC 4, *ithumi* occurs twice side by side with *ohoro*, and once together with *hurahu*. It seems therefore likely that it is to be understood as "here (in this life)," while *ohoro* stands for "there, in the next life" and *hurahu* for "from existence to existence" (thus probably *-ro* is to be added: *hurahu⟨*ro⟩*). The precise phonological development, however, is difficult to explain; perhaps *ohoro* stands for Skt./P *vā huraṃ (vā)*. If a prefix, *o-* must remain unexplained.[82] It might also be asked whether G *ohoro* corresponds to *hurāhuraṃ*, not only *huraṃ*, even though it is written *ohoro* four times and only once *hurahu* (and even then we would have to reconstruct the last akṣara). A possible explanation then could be a development *hurahu* > **oroho* (equivalence of *u*/*o* and the occasional writing of *-o-* for Skt. *-ā-*, together with the elision/dropping of initial *h* [cf. *atha khalu* > *asa ho* > *asa o* in SĀ[S1]]) > *ohoro* (metathesis). While the first step might be accepted, a combination with the second seems implausible. However, a similar kind of metathesis can be observed in BC 11 in the spelling *sayavisa* instead of *sayaṣavi*. Moreover, especially the type of metathesis involving a liquid *r* and an adjacent syllable is a widely attested phenomenon in MIA languages (cf. Geiger and Norman 2000: § 47.2). Examples in Gāndhārī are: *maduru* = Skt. *mārutaḥ* (Dhp[K] 69), *aparado* = Skt. *alpataram* (Dhp[K] 145); *uraḍa-* = Skt. *udāra-* / P *uḷāra-* (Khvs[L] 24, 32), *koviraḍo* = Skt. *kovidāraḥ* / P *koviḷāro* (Khvs[L] 19); *palaḍiputr(*e)* = Skt. *pāṭaliputre* (Av[L6] 16). If we choose to accept that *hurahu* and *ohoro* mean the same ("from existence to existence," BHS / P *hurāhuraṃ*), we would again have to consider translating *ithumi* as "in this manner" instead of "in this life."

As regards the context, the phrases *idha vā huraṃ vā* (e.g., SN I 12, Sn 224, 468, 470, 496, 801, Th 10, Dhp 20) and *hurāhuraṃ* (e.g., Dhp 334 = Th 399 or Vism 107 / Vism[W] 87) usually occur in verses about letting go or non-grasping either "here" or "there," being without desire for treasures "here or there," "in this world or the next."[83] These are quite similar to the overall subject in BC 4.

With respect to the occurrence of these phrases in the last paragraph of BC 4, where it is described what things are to be done, it is also tempting to think of *ahorātra* "day and night" in relation to the *triskandhaka* ritual (cf. p. 7), which must be performed three times during the day and three times during the night. Unfortunately, G *ohoro* = Skt. *ahorātram* / P *ahorattaṃ* is even less likely, since it is written *ahoratra* in Dhp[K] 50. Also, immediately preceeding the last section with *ohoro* and *hurahu*, reference is made to "this life and the next" (4v8 *sadriṭhia saparaïa*), which also speaks in favor of the given translation.

4v10 *ki aṇuśaśe hakṣadi*. The syntactic function of *ki* is uncertain. It is currently translated as being an interrogative pronoun referring to *aṇuśaśe*, although this word should be masculine or feminine, not neuter, based on the genders of BHS *ānuśaṃsa* (m., or *anuśaṃsā*, f.), and P

anything "over there (outside)," i.e., "not here (inside)," which can be translated as "there" or "in the next life" depending on the context. In this respect, Th 399 is a nice play on words, describing a monkey jumping "here and there / hither and yon" from limb to limb searching for tasty fruits, just like a human jumping from existence to existence searching in vain for satisfaction.

82 Several other suggestions for *ohoro*, like *avahāra* / *ohāra* or *vohāra* for *vyavahāra* appear improbable in terms of the content.

83 Sn 224 "here or elsewhere"; Sn 468 and Sn 801 "here or in the next world" (alternative translation for Sn 468 "here or hereafter"); Sn 496 "in this world or the next" (Norman 1992a).

ānisaṃsa (m.). As another possible spelling, the BHSD lists *ānr̥śaṃsa*, n., for which MW gives the slightly different meaning "absence of cruelty or harm, mildness, kindness, benevolence." This spelling occurs in manuscripts, for example in the *Buddhacarita* 6.12 (Johnston emended to *anuśaṃsa*) and in the title of the *Saddharmapuṇḍarīka*, chapter 18 (according to Kern 1884: 226 n. 1, but the edition has °*nu*°; both citations are based on BHSD s.v. *anuśaṃsa*). Moreover, de La Vallée Poussin assumes *ānr̥śaṃsa* to be the original form (in *Bodhicaryāvatārapañjikā* 22 n. 3, cited from BHSD s.v. *anuśaṃsa*). Thus it might be possible that in Gāndhārī, *aṇuśaśa* was considered a neuter corresponding to BHS *ānr̥śaṃsa* or Skt. *anr̥śaṃsa*. The pronoun in 4r12 *ime aṇuśaśe*, however, seems to point to masculine (nom. pl.). Then again, in 6r1 *ime kadhadhaduaïdaṇa* the pronoun is referring to a noun in the neuter (albeit spelled or even understood as a masculine).[84] In any case, the use of *ime* is not conclusive evidence for a noun being considered masculine.

In other places in all three manuscripts, *ki* is either used as an interrogative pronoun, for which similar examples are 4r7 *ki hakṣadi*, 4r20 *ki hakṣadi* (other instances use different cases, namely *ko* or *keṇa*), or *ki* is used as an indeclinable simply to introduce a question. Examples for this are 4r17–18 *aha ta ki samo bos̱imaḍami labhadi samo añatrades̱ehi* as well as 11r23 *aha ki eṣa pras̱aṇakarmo ruve · as̱a va aruve*. A third possiblity, not attested in these manuscripts but found in other Kharoṣṭhī documents, is to understand *ki* as "why, how."

Thus, as an alternative to the current translation ("Which benefit will there be?") implying the understanding of either *ki* as masculine or *aṇuśaśe* as neuter, two possibilities would be to take *ki* as introducing a question ("Will there be a benefit?") or interpeting *ki* as indeclinable ("How will there be a benefit?"). The first of these two options seems unlikely; the second might be a valid alternative in view of the following sentences.

4v10–11 ***te*** is used thrice at the beginning of sentence. The form alone can correspond either to Skt. *te* or *tā* as a nominative plural, or to Skt. *tad* / P *taṃ* used as an adverb in the sense of "thus, then." The latter is more likely here, because *te* is only used at the beginning. If it were a pronoun it should also be found before 4v10 *aloṇea* and 4v11 *aloṇea* (as is the case in 4r23, where similarly *yo* is written once before *arida karae* and repeated before *praṇide ⟨*ka⟩rae*.

4v11 ***śpabhavasa*** = Skt. *svabhāvatā*, "state of intrinsic nature / inherent existence" (for the spelling *-sa* for Skt. *-tā*, see chapter 3 on paleography under *s*/*s̱*/*ṣ*-).[85] This intrinsic nature of things is rejected in the *prajñāpāramitā* literature as well as by Mahāyāna adherents in general, and above all by Nāgārjuna in his Madhyamaka doctrine, which extends "selflessness" not only to human beings (as in the Śrāvakayāna literature) but to all phenomena (*dharmanairātmya*). According to this doctrine, everything is devoid or empty (*śūnya*) of any kind of *svabhāva*.[86]

---

84 The nom. pl. form is written twice as *kadhadhaduaïdaṇa*, but also once as *kadhadhaduaïdaṇi*, possibly indicating some uncertainty.

85 Cf. Ronkin 2013 with reference to (especially) Gethin 2004: 533 and Cox 2004.

86 Cf. Keown 2004 s.v. *svabhāva*, as well as Williams 2009 (p. 52 for *svabhāva* in *prajñāpāramitā* texts and especially n. 18 on p. 285 regarding *svabhāva* in the context of letting go of everything, p. 63, pp. 67–68 for Madhyamaka, p. 93 for Yogācāra, p. 108 for its relationship to the *tathāgatagarbha*).

"This is seen through *prajñā*, analytic understanding" (Williams 2009: 70). For the Mādhyamikas, "*śūnyatā* is an exact equivalent of *niḥsvabhāvatā*, absence of *svabhāva*" (Williams 2009: 70 n. 31).

Interestingly, Edgerton (BHSD s.v. *svabhāva*) mentions that *svabhāva* is used in the *Laṅkāvatārasūtra* in a peculiar way, namely, it is specified as being sevenfold: "there are seven kinds of self-nature: collection (*samudaya*), being (*bhava*), characteristic marks (*lakṣaṇa*), elements (*mahābhūta*), causality (*hetu*), conditionality (*pratyaya*), and perfection (*niṣpatti*)" (Suzuki 1932: 35).[87] These are not explained here or elsewhere, and Suzuki has no explanation either.[88] So, unfortunately, this also does not help us understand the group of seven in BC 4.

Seven *svabhāvas* are given in the *Abhisamayālaṃkāravṛtti Sphuṭārthā* as the "seven trainings in the knowledge of all aspects" (*sarvākārajñātāyāḥ sapta svabhāvāḥ*, commenting on *Abhisamayālaṃkāra* 4.31, tr. Brunnhölzl 2011: 56–57). Together with the four trainings in the all-knowledge and the five trainings in the knowledge of the path, they constitute the sixteen *svabhāvas*, the "facets of the subject that is the wisdom devoid of reference points" (Brunnhölzl 2011: 57). In this list they are the last seven points that , which refer to "suchness" (*tathatā*) as the nature of this training of a bodhisattva.[89] This nature of the training is again the last part of a fourfold group of defining characteristics of the training, according to the *Abhisamayālaṃkāra* (4.13, namely 1. knowledge, 2. distinction, 3. activities, 4. nature; cf. Brunnhölzl 2011: 48–49; see also Brunnhölzl 2011: 18–19 and 308 for an overview of the complete training in all aspects). In this system, it is a path of accumulation.[90] Although the context is similar to BC 4, that is, defining the training of a bodhisattva with special emphasis on *śūnyatā* as the essential teaching of the *prajñāpāramitā*, this does not seem to be a direct parallel that would help clarify the meaning of the seven G *aloa* / *aloṇea*, which are nonetheless somehow connected with the realization of the non-existence of a state of intrinsic nature (*svabhāva*).

4v12 *paḏitiṭha*. Skt. *pratitiṣṭha*. This direct address in the second singular imperative is suprising but not unique. Also in BC 6 the reader or listener is addressed directly, once in 6r9 (*tuo ca ya ithu jaṇaṣi* ◦ *kaṣa rajaṣi ca duśaṣi ca*, "If you too understand it thus, how do you become passionate and hateful?") and once in 6v8 (*ma paci vipaḏiṣara*, "Do not have cause to regret it later."), where it is likewise written near the end of the text.

A similar instruction is given in the *Pratyutpannabuddhasaṃmukhāvasthitasamādhisūtra*, now known to have existed in Gāndhārī (see p. 17), where it is said, "establish yourself properly

87 *Laṅkāvatārasūtra* (Nanjio 1923: 39): *saptavidho bhāvasvabhāvo bhavati yad uta samudayasvabhāvo bhavasvabhāvo lakṣaṇasvabhāvo mahābhūtasvabhāvo hetusvabhāvaḥ pratyayasvabhāvo niṣpattisvabhāvaś ca saptamaḥ.*

88 Suzuki (1932: 35 n. 1): "What is exactly meant by these concepts regarded as self-nature (*svabhāva*) is difficult to define as far as the *Laṅkāvatāra* is concerned."

89 One point (15) in the commentary of the Eighth Karmapa on the *Abhisamayālaṃkāra* is given as "devoid of arising—coming into existence newly" (Brunnhölzl 2011: 57 n. 78 on p. 570), which is similar to the statement *te śpabhavasa ataraṣaïśati ṇa ca bhuyo upajiśati*, "the states of inherent existence will disappear and not rise anew" in BC 4.

90 "The first temporary result of such training is the mahāyāna path of accumulation, which is called 'the factors conducive to liberation' (IV 32–34)." The next path is the path of preparation, followed by the culmination training, etc. (cf. Brunnhölzl 2011: 19 ff.).

in the four stoppings of thoughts" (Harrison 1998: 66). Likewise, in another passage it is said that the bodhisattvas "set themselves to study this meditation" (Harrison 1998: 74).

4v12 *satidehi*. If we assume that this word corresponds to an instrumental plural of Skt. **saptitā* for *saptatā* (f.), it should be written *satidahi*, though the general shift to masculine forms in the case of cardinal numbers may have also affected derivations of them (cf. 11r2 *ṣahi paramidehi*).

4v12 *ṣadasa*. In the Niya documents, the adjective *ṣada* is used to express "being pleased" (e.g., CKD 157 *ahu suṭha ṣada hudemi*, "I am very pleased"; CKD 305 *ṣada bhavidavo*, "you will be pleased"; CKD 247 *ṣadosmi*, "I am pleased"; CKD 399 *ṣadama*, "we are pleased"; CKD 399 *ṣada bhavitavya*, "you should be pleased"). The etymology is uncertain. In addition to the possibility of an Iranian influence,[91] it could be derived from *śānta* ("appeased, pacified") or *śrānta* ("calmed, tranquil"), the second at least a lexicographically documented variant of *śānta* (cf. MW s.v. *śrānta*), although in its usual sense this word has negative connotations ("wearied").[92] Nevertheless, *śr-* would explain the retroflex *ṣ-* in Gāndhārī (Burrow 1937: § 38). Then again, *-nt-* should be written *-t-* in Kharoṣṭhī, which is not the case in any of the occurrences known. This is why I consider BHS *śāta* / P *sāta* ("pleasant, agreeable; n. pleasantness, pleasure") to be the most likely possibility.

While in BC 4 only *ṣadasa* is used, in BC 11 the term is written as *ṣade*/*ṣado* nine times and twice as *ṣadimeṇa*, being the instrumental singular of *ṣadima* = Skt. **śāntimant*/**śrāntimant* or **śātimant*. Among these choices, Skt. *śānti* is of course the most common term, denoting tranquility, peace or calmness of mind.

Although the etymology is not yet entirely clear, the context in BC 4/11 is much in line with the translation "pleased" in the Niya documents, and I therefore suggest understanding *ṣada* as "pleased," or better, "content" in the sense of "satisfied, appeased, tranquil" in the absence of passion and desire. Thus, *ṣada* or *ṣadima* describe a state of mind abiding in a neutral, contented, wishless state of peaceful happiness. Cf. also BC 5, verse 10, *ṣado logo krido sadevamaṇuyo ya prata boṣi śiv(*a)*, "The world with [its] gods and men was made content, because blissful awakening was attained" (Gudrun Melzer, personal communication).

While in BC 4, BC 5, and in the Niya documents *ṣada* is used as an adjective, in BC 11 it seems more often to be a noun ("contentment"). Possibly this is the reason for the different form of *ṣadima* introduced in BC 11, which can thus be translated as "possessing contentment" or simply "being content."

---

91 Burrow 1937: 126: "*ṣada*: See *B.S.O.S.* VII, 514. There are two alternatives: (1) that it = N.Pers. *šād*, etc. 'pleased'. If so it is interesting, because the Khotanese Saka is excluded as the dialect from which it was borrowed. They have *tsāta-*; (2) that it is Indian Pali *sāta* 'pleasant', *assāta-* 'unpleasant', out of *śrāta-*, 'cooked', hence 'sweet'. In view of the prevalence of Iranian influence in the language, the first alternative is probably to be preferred, as being less complicated." Although phonologically *śṛta* or *śrāta* ("boiled") would be the expected Sanskrit equivalent for G *ṣada*, this is excluded by the context.

92 Similarly, P *samaṇa* (BHS *śramaṇa*) is derived from √*śram* ("to be weary, exhausted"), but was often etymologically connected with √*śam* ("to be quiet, calm, satisfied, contented"); cf. PTSD s.v. *samaṇa*.

4v12 *tomi*. In the Niya documents *tomi* occurs as a genitive singular, usually in the use of an instrumental (agent). The form has been explained as *to* [= *tava*] + *mi*, which is frequently appended to pronominal forms (Burrow 1937: 96; cf. also Burrow 1937: § 91, with the examples *tasyemi*, *teṣemi*).

4v12 *uju*. This could correspond to Skt. *ṛju* / P *uju* (cf. Dhp 33 *ujuṃ karoti*, Dhp[P] 342 *ujjuṃ karoti*, "makes straight"; only the initial *u* is preserved in Dhp[K] 136). In BC 4 the meaning might be "straight, right, honest" or, as an adverb, "in the right manner, correctly."

4v12 *ṇe a p. ci + va*. The reading of these only partly preserved akṣaras is uncertain, and it is also uncertain if after the supposed *va* and the following *pialo* there was something written or not. One suggestion is to read *pacidava* = Skt. *pracitavya*, "should be collected/accumulated." If *uju* means "right" (Skt. *ṛju* / P *uju*), *ṇea* could correspond to Skt. *naya*, "behavior," leading to the translation "your future correct behavior should increase." But this does not fit syntactically with the rest of the preceding words. Based on the two *ca*s, *ṣadasa aṇagade* and *tomi uju* should be parallel, both being the object or subject of *ṇe a p. ci + va*. (Reading *ṣadasa aṇagade ca tomi pracupaṇe* is tempting but impossible, most of all because of the *ca* where a *pa* should be.)

The last *va* could also belong to the following *pialo*, then to be reconstructed as *eva pialo* as in 11v26 and 11v27, which would leave *ṇe a p. ci*. Both are unlikely, that is, *eva pialo* with a gap of one akṣara between *eva* and *pialo* and a verb or verbal noun *ṇe a p. ci*. All in all, this part of the last paragraph remains unclear.

4v12 *pialo*. BHS *peyālam* / P *peyyālaṃ*, an indicator for the omission of a repetition, commonly used adverbially in the meaning of "etc.," literally "here (follows) the formula (*pariyāya*)" (PTSD s.v. *peyyāla*). It can be used "where the passage has not occurred before in the text in question, but where presumably its sense is regarded as well known or obvious" (BHSD s.v. *peyāla*). In the *Saddharmapuṇḍarīka* (Kern and Nanjio 1912: 424) it has the connotation "in short, in a word." In the *Lalitavistara* (Lefmann 1902–08, I: 295) it opens a series of stanzas: *peyālam eṣa*, "in brief, …" (cf. BSHD s.v. *peyāla*).

In 4v12 *pialo* appears to be used as a summarizing conclusion in the meaning of "etc., in short," but perhaps also in the sense of "so once more." In 11v26 and 11v27 *eva pialo* introduces a repetition. First, this repetition replaces one word by another only syntactically: 11v26–27 *eva pialo ajatvia* ***aśuha*** *bahira* ***aśuha*** *⟨*.⟩ ajatvia (*****ṇisamartha*** *bahira* ***ṇisamartha****)* is taking up the previous 11v24–25 *ajatvia aïdaṇa* ***dukha*** *bahira aïdaṇa* ***dukha***. Second, the repetition is exactly the same as before: 11v27 *(*eva pi)al(*o) ajatvia gaḍa bah(*i)ra gaḍa ⟨*.⟩ te(*ṣa) sagha(*r)ya⟨*de⟩ s(*u)ho bhavea ⟨*.⟩ ṇa ida ṭhaṇo ⟨*◦⟩* is repeating the previous 11v25–26 *achatvia gada (*ba)hira gaḍa ⟨*.⟩ teṣa sa(*gharyade su)ho bhavea ⟨*.⟩ ṇa ida ṭhaṇo*. Both are translated as "and so on in this way," but in the second instance "so once more" is possible as well.

Table 15. Abbreviations used in BC 4, BC 6, and BC 11.

sakṣiteṇa	"in short, to sum up"	summarizing a preceding passage	4r12, 4v8, 6r4, 11r20, 11r30, 11r34
yava	"up to"	abbreviating an obvious sequence	6r3
yava, yavi	"up to"	abbreviating an obvious sequence, but with nothing missing	4r23, 4v1, 11r36
piala yava	"etc., up to"	abbreviating an apparently known sequence	11r17
pialo	"etc., in short"	summarizing/concluding	4v12
eva pialo	"and so on in this way"; "so once more"	repeating something	11v26, 11v27

4v12 *hurahu*. Cf. annotations on 4v8–9 *ithumi ohoro*, p. 189.

4v12 *sahoro*. Tentatively translated as "collection" based on Skt./P *saṃhāra*, "collection, abridgment, compendium, manual." Skt. *saṃhāra* is also often interchanged with *sambhāra* in the same meaning, with the additional meanings "completeness; multitude, number, quantity" (MW). In Buddhist contexts, Skt. *saṃhāra*/*saṃbhāra* denotes the requisites or equipment for (those destined for) awakening.[93] It has to be admitted, however, that the development *-ā-* > *-o-* is uncommon, although still occasionally attested in the Khotan *Dharmapada* and the Niya documents.

93 For example, the title *Bodhisaṃbhāraśāstra* is translated as "provisions for enlightenment" by Dharmamitra (2009). The commentary explains "provisions" as "that which preserves, that which raises and nurtures, that which forms the causal basis for *bodhi* and that which represents the complete adequacy of the essential component parts of *bodhi*" (Dharmamitra 2009: 76).

8.2 BC 11

11r1 *śpaho* / 11r3 *śpahu* / 11r12 *śpahu* = Skt. *svakam* or *svayam* / P *sakam*. Other spellings in Gāndhārī manuscripts are: *śpaya*, *śpagho*, *śpae*, *śpaï* in Anav[L] 24, 82, 83, 89 (cf. Salomon 2008a: 175ff.), but the most expected development occurs in Av[L6] 21 *śpagam* < *svakam* (Lenz 2003: 132). Word-final G *-hu* for *-kam* is attested in SĀ[S1] *tuspahu* = Skt. *yuṣmākam* / P *tumhākaṃ* (cf. Glass 2007: 179).

11r1 *kuṣaleṇa*. Skt. *kuśala* / P *kusala* can mean both "wholesome [deed]" or the result of it, i.e., "merit." If the following G *kaye* is Skt. *kāryam*, "wholesome [deed]" is more likely.

11r1–3 *kaye* / *karye* / *kice*. In the translation, *kaye* has been tentatively understood as *karye* = Skt. *kāryam*, despite the fact that the scribe clearly writes *karye* in other places (11r27, 11r34, 11r37, 11r49). Still, *kaye* for Skt. *kāyam* ("body") seems inappropriate here. Also, in a few syntactically parallel sentences the word *kice* (Skt. *kr̥tyam*) is used, which supports a translation in the sense of Skt. *kāryam*, since *kāryam* and *kr̥tyam* can be used interchangeably.

In line 11r2 it is uncertain if *karye ṇa* should be emended to *karye ṇ(*e)⟨*vi⟩* as in the other instances of *kaye ṇevi* corresponding to Skt. *kāryaṃ naiva*, or if it should be read as one word *karyeṇa* referring to the following *margasuheṇa* ("the happiness of the path which is to be practised").

Both words, *ka(r)ye* and *kice*, are used together with a genitive of persons and an instrumental of things. As such, *kārya* is known from other texts in the meaning of "something is of use to, someone cares about" (MacDonell 1929, s.v. *kārya*); "there is need of, someone has business with" (MW s.v. *kārya*, example: *tr̥ṇena kāryam*, "there is need of a straw"; *na bhūmyā kāryam asmākam*, "we have no business with the earth"; cf. Capeller 1891 s.v. *kārya*, *na kāryam asmākam*, "we have no business with or need of [instr.]," and Apte 1957–59 s.v. *kārya*: "want, need, occasion, business [with instr.]"). Likewise, the combination with *kr̥tya* can be translated as "anybody (gen.) is concerned about (instr.)" (MW s.v. *kr̥tyam*). PW gives for both *kārya* and *kr̥tya* the possible meaning "es ist Jmd zu thun um" (PW s.v. *kārya* and *kr̥tya*), or also "es kann Jmd Gebrauch machen von" (only s.v. *kārya*). NWS gives the meaning "Wirkung, Zweck" for both *kārya* and *kr̥tya*.

Thus, in BC 11 the translation alternatives range between: "Neither do they care about wholesome […], nor …"; "Neither are they concerned about wholesome […], nor …"; "Neither do they need wholesome […], nor …"; "Neither do they have business with wholesome […], nor …"; "Neither can they make use of wholesome […], nor …"; "Neither is there for them a use of wholesome […], nor … ."

In other places in the same manuscript, a similar syntactical construction is used, namely in 11r34 *teṇa ṇa karye* and in 11r37 *imehi ṇa karye*, even though here only with the instrumental, which then should refer to things, not persons. Both sentences follow a description of suffering and unhappiness, and the statement seems to be "There is no use for this" / "This is of no use" or "This serves no purpose" / "This is to no purpose," probably saying that suffering does not help achieve liberation.

All in all, the translation "there is (for them/us, gen.) no use for … (instr.)" or "… (instr.) is of no use (for them/us, gen.)" seems to fit well.

11r2 *margasuheṇa*. There are three kinds of happiness or bliss known in commentaries on the Pali canon: *jhāna-*, *magga-* and *phala-sukha*.[94] Superior to all is *nibbāna(sukha)*, the highest bliss.[95] According to commentaries on the *Aṅguttaranikāya*,[96] the mind leads to bliss in the following sequence: *māṇusaka-*, *dibba-*, *jhāna-*, *vipassanā-*, *magga-*, *phala-*, *nibbāna-sukha*. Having accomplished the *maggasukha*, one reaches the *phala-* and *nibbānasukha*.[97]

11r2 *ṣahi paramidehi* = Skt. *ṣaḍbhiḥ pāramitābhiḥ*. In the *Ugraparipṛcchā* (chapter 7, § 22A) the practice of the six *pāramitā*s is presented as the essential characteristic of Mahāyāna practice: "[…] the practice of giving, morality, endurance, exertion, concentration, and insight—in other words, the practice of the Mahāyāna."[98] Also in other Gāndhārī manuscripts, the set of *pāramitā*s consists of six items.[99] They are not explicitly enumerated, but applied as if commonly known.

Based on the list of six, different *pāramitā*s are stressed in different texts. Thus, in the *prajñāpāramitā* text of the Split Collection (AsP^{Sp}) naturally the *prajñāpāramitā* is emphasized, as in BC 4. In contrast, in the *Ugraparipṛcchā* the *dānapāramitā* is stressed. But at the same time, in BC 2, there is no mention of any *pāramitā* at all (cf. Strauch 2010a: 27). According to Strauch (referring to Vetter 1994), the introduction of the *prajñāpāramitā* literature was a later, or at least not original process within the Mahāyāna movement, which developed simultaneously with a "de-arhatization" and the establishment of "easy" devotional practices. Rather than being explained chronologically, this inclusion or non-inclusion could also be due to geographical or ideological reasons. In any case, BC 2 indicates that even without an emphasis on *prajñāpāramitā*, there were conceptions of bodhisattvas and buddhafields like Abhi-

---

94 E.g., DN-a, *Tividhaokāsādhigamavaṇṇanā*: II 643 *sukhassādhigamāyāti jhānasukhassa maggasukhassa phalasukhassa ca adhigamāya* or II 269 *'sukhassā' ti idaṃ tiṇṇam pi sukhānaṃ sādhāraṇavacanan ti āha 'jhānasukhassa maggasukhassa phalasukhassā' ti*.

95 E.g., MN-a, *Māgaṇḍiyasuttavaṇṇanā*: III 218 *yaṃ kiñci jhānasukhaṃ vā maggasukhaṃ vā phalasukhaṃ vā atthi, nibbānaṃ tattha paramaṃ, natthi tato uttaritaraṃ sukhan ti nibbānaṃ paramaṃ sukhaṃ*.

96 AN-a, e.g., *Akammaniyavaggavaṇṇanā*, *Anubuddhasuttavaṇṇanā*, or *Papatitasuttavaṇṇanā*.

97 KN-a, *Vakkalittheragāthāvaṇṇanā*: II 149 *viharissāmīti yathāvutte bodhipakkhiyadhamme bhāvento maggasukhena tadadhigamasiddhena phalasukhena nibbānasukhena ca viharissāmi*. In the *Bhaddajisutta* (AN V 170), Ānanda asks Bhaddaji what the highest bliss is (*kiṃ sukhānaṃ aggaṃ*); Bhaddaji answers that it is the happiness of gods (*te santaṃ yeva tusitā sukhaṃ paṭivedenti, idaṃ sukhānaṃ aggaṃ*). Ānanda on the contrary says that when pleasantness is without an interval, desires get destroyed; that is the foremost pleasantness (*yathā sukhitassa anantarā āsavānaṃ khayo hoti, idaṃ sukhānaṃ aggaṃ*). In the commentary (AN-a, *Bhaddajisuttavaṇṇanā*) the "*yathā sukhitassa*" is glossed as "*yena maggasukhena sukhitassa*."

98 This passage only occurs in the earliest versions of Ān Xuán 安玄 and Yán Fótiào 嚴佛調 (180–90 CE, T 12 no. 322), as well as that of Dharmarakṣa (3rd or 4th century CE, T 12 no. 323); cf. Nattier 2003: 280 n. 472. For an explanation of each *pāramitā*, see chapter 8, § 25L of the *Ugraparipṛcchā* (Nattier 2003: 304 ff.).

99 (1) Fragments of the Schøyen Collection containing the *Bhadrakalpikasūtra*, roughly dated to the 3rd/4th century CE: *paramida ṣo* (Baums, Glass, and Matsuda 2016: 203 and elsewhere). (2) *Prajñāpāramitā* from the Split Collection: *ṣah[i p]. ///* ~ AsP *ṣaṭpāramitāsu śikṣante* (Falk and Karashima 2013: 168–69).

rati or Sukhāvatī, where Buddhas such as Akṣobhya or Amitābha resided. Williams (2009: 47 ff.) takes these phenomena as two separate yet equally important strands: one philosophical (*prajñāpāramitā*) and the other religious (*buddhakṣetra*). These strands later mixed.

It is not known when the *pāramitās* in general were introduced into Buddhism, or the set of six, but one passage in the *Vibhāṣā* (Kātyāyanīputra, first century BCE, translated by Xuánzàng 玄奘 in the 7th century, T 27 no. 1545 p. 892a24) claims that the quantity of six *pāramitās* was distinctive of Gandhāra. In this passage, a bodhisattva practices the four *pāramitās* for an immeasurable length of time, gaining the four perfections of *dāna*, *śīla*, *vīrya*, and *prajñā*. But the *Vibhāṣā* also mentions that there are other traditions, namely the "Foreign Masters," who claim that there are six *pāramitās*, adding *kṣānti* and *dhyāna*. All Śāstra masters in Kashmir would say that these two are already included in the four (T 27 no. 1545 p. 892b23, according to Qing 2001: 23). Those "Foreign Masters" are also called "Western Masters," this referring to Abhidharma teachers from Gandhāra to the west of Kashmir (Qing 2001: 23 n. 72).

As indicated, there are other sets consisting of four or—in Pali literature—ten perfections.[100] However, the most prevalent set in Mahāyāna literature is that of six,[101] and in most texts the traditional sequence is: *dāna*, *śīla*, *kṣānti*, *vīrya*, *dhyāna*, *prajñā* (generosity, virtue, patience, energy, concentration, insight). The sequence in 11r51, which lists only three, is *śīla*, *kṣānti*, and *dāna* (G *śile*, *kṣati*, *daṇe*). Instead of the usual order, *dāna* is probably put at the end because it is needed as a topic of argumentation, being referred to in more detail in the following passage. There is, to my knowledge, no other text that has the sequence *śīla*, *kṣānti*, and *dāna*.

11r4 *ecakhaïdave*. Because of the parallel construction *edehi khaïti edehi ecakhaïdave*, *eca-* is tentatively understood as a prefix to *khaïdave* (*ati* + *ā* + √*khyā*). The same prefix *eca-* occurs in Dhp^{K} 86, where *ecasari* corresponds to P *accasārī*, and likewise *precasari* to P *paccasārī*

---

100 In Pali texts these are: *dāna*, *sīla*, *nekkhamma*, *paññā*, *viriya*, *khanti*, *sacca*, *adhiṭṭhāna*, *mettā*/*metti*, *upekkhā* (generosity, virtue, renunciation, insight, energy, patience, truthfulness, resolution, loving-kindness, equanimity). This group is not found in texts of the older Pali literature, but only in two apocryphal texts, the *Buddhavaṃsa* and the *Cariyāpiṭaka* of the *Khuddakanikāya* (cf. Nyanatiloka 1952), as well as in later jātakas or avadānas. In the *Visuddhimagga* (IX) it is said that by developing the four *brahmavihāras*, the ten *pāramitās* are obtained (Nyanatiloka, ibid.). See Skilling 2004: 151–52 for more details about the ten perfections. In some texts the list of six and ten are combined, or at least attempts are made to do so, for example in the "Treatise on the Pāramīs," originally composed by Dhammapāla and extant in at least two places in the Pali exegetical literature, once in a complete version in the *Cariyāpiṭakaṭṭhakathā* and once in an abridged version in the subcommentary (*ṭīkā*) on the *Brahmajālasutta*. In this text, ten *pāramitās* are listed, although it is mentioned immediately afterwards that "some say there are six" (see Bodhi 1996 for more details).

101 But cf. Bodhi 1996: "Later Mahāyāna texts add four more—resolution, skillful means, power, and knowledge—in order to co-ordinate on a one-to-one basis the list of perfections with the account of the ten stages of the bodhisattva's ascent to Buddhahood. The Pāli works, including those composed before the rise of Mahāyāna, give a different though partly overlapping list of ten [...]. Unlike the Mahāyāna, the Theravāda never developed a theory of stages, though such may be implicit in the grading of the *pāramīs* into three degrees as basic, intermediate, and ultimate [...] The set of ten *pāramīs* itself comes from the Buddhavaṃsa, as does the discussion of the great aspiration (*abhinīhāra*) with its eight qualifications."

(Brough 1962: § 22a), being a 3rd sg. pret. of P *atisarati* and *paṭisarati* (Skt. *atisarati* and *pratisarati*). The *e*-vowel is explained by palatalization in the neighborhood of a palatal consonant.

The only attestation for *atyākhyā* is found in BHSD s.v. *atyākhyāya*, where the reading *'tyākhyāya tāṃ te gatiṃ gamiṣyanti* is cited from Lefmann's edition of the *Lalitavistara* (1902–08, I: 88), but it is written as *vyākhyā°* ("to explain") in almost all manuscripts (cf. Lefmann 1902–08, II: 39). Hence, this is not valid evidence and the reading *'tyākhyāya* is probably wrong.

Skt. *ati√khyā* is given in MW and PW as "to overlook" or "to neglect," but only in Vedic texts. Since the context in BC 11 is lost, it is unclear which meaning is more likely, "to explain" or "to neglect."

11r5 *yaṣ̱a ṇa aña.* It is impossible to tell if this is the end of the sentence or not. If the sentence is complete, it might mean "just so, not otherwise" (Skt. *yathā nānyad*) in the sense that only letting go of things helps achieve satisfaction or the bliss of liberation. Theoretically, one should also let go "like no other" (Skt. *yathā nānyaḥ*). If the sentence is not complete but continues, *yaṣ̱a ṇa aña* could mean "so that no other ..."

11r6–7 *avi khaïta / avi akhaïta.* The syntax and meaning of the first few sentences in 11r6–7 are unclear. First of all, it is uncertain if the *a-* in *akhaïta* is a negation (*a-*) or a prefix (*ā-*). Then, it is unclear if 11r5 *khaïta*, 11r7 *akhaïta*, and 11r7 *varjita* are past participles or absolutives, since sometimes, though rarely, *t* is written for *d* (see chapter 5 on phonology, p. 83). In general, *ta*-endings have been translated as absolutives.

Moreover, the appositional *aṇubhavaṇa* at the end of the third sentence is syntactically unusual. It has been understood as referring to the preceding *citasuhe* and most likely also to the previous *kayasuhe*. Perhaps then both nouns are in the loc. sg. instead of the nom. sg. ("[experience] with regard to happiness of the body" and "experience with regard to happiness of the mind"), but *kayadukhe* and *citadukhe* in the first sentence, with the same ending and syntactically being used in a similar way, are in the nom. sg.

As regards *dukhe / dukha* in the first sentence, it is open to discussion if they stand on their own or if they should be understood as objects of the preceding *khaïta / varjamaṇa*. Then the translation would be: "[...] even though suffering has been declared / is known, there is suffering of the body; even though [this] suffering is being avoided, there is suffering of the mind" (instead of "even though [it] has been declared, there is suffering, suffering of the body; even though [it] is being avoided, there is suffering, suffering of the mind").

Despite these uncertainties the statement of the passage is that for some group of persons (this part of the sentence is lost at the beginning of 11r6) there is suffering of body and mind, but for the wise there is the experience of happiness of the body and the mind due to the right kind of knowledge.

11r6–7 *kayadukhe* ... *citadukhe* ... *kayasuhe* ... *citasuhe*. Both Skt. *kāya-/citta-duḥkha* and *-sukha* are feelings situated in the body and the mind. "The corporeal feeling is that which arises on the support of five senses, and the mental is that which arises on the support of the sixth sense" (*Satyasiddhiśāstra*, chapter 82 on *duḥkhasatyaskandha*, tr. Sastri 1978: 169).[102] Cf., for example, also a passage in the *Dukanipāta* of the *Aṅguttaranikāya*, where both are named, but the mental happiness is said to be the better:

> *dve 'māni bhikkhave sukhāni. katamāni dve? kāyikañ ca sukhaṃ cetasikañ ca sukhaṃ. imāni kho bhikkhave dve sukhāni. etad aggaṃ bhikkhave imesaṃ dvinnaṃ sukhānaṃ yadidaṃ cetasikaṃ sukhan ti.* (AN I 81)
>
> Bhikkhus, there are these two kinds of happiness. What two? Bodily happiness and mental happiness. These are the two kinds of happiness. Of these two kinds of happiness, mental happiness is foremost. (Bodhi 2012: 171)

11r7 *suṭhu* = Skt. *suṣṭhu* / P *suṭṭhu*. This can either be an adverb following Burrow (1937: 40 § 91), who translates *sutha* = Skt. *suṣṭhu* < **suṣṭham* as "well" (CKD 399; in his index he also gives the translation "very," Burrow 1937: 131), or, alternatively, *suṭhu* can be an adjective with the meaning "excellent" in Buddhist Hybrid Sanskrit as well as in Ardhamāgadhī (BHSD s.v. *suṣṭhu*). In the *Mahāvyutpatti* (Mvy 2531) it is also listed among "synonyms of *anuttara*" (BHSD s.v. *suṣṭhu*). It is translated as "[it was] excellent" in the *avadāna*s preserved on BL 1 (Lenz 2010: 79). The same is the case with BL 4, where *aha suṭhu* means "He said, 'Excellent.'" (Lenz 2010: 79).

In 11r7 theoretically either is possible, *suṭhu* as an adverb or adjective, but both are rather unconvincing. If read as an adverb, it would stand apart from the verb to which it belongs when translated "therefore, both have to be done well [as long as one abides] in knowledge" (11r7 *tasva suṭhu ñaṇami abhae kaṭave*). If it is an adjective, this would form the compound *suṭhuñaṇa* (BHS **suṣṭhujñāna*), but this is not known as a valid alternative to *anuttarajñāna*, which makes it doubtful. However, in BC 6 *suṭhu* seems to be used as an adjective in contrast to *kuḏae* (Skt. *kūṭaka*), both related to *ñaṇa*: 6v3 *yahi ñaṇo ṇa kuḏae suṭhu phaṣadi*. Both *kuḏae* and *suṭhu* could also be translated as adverbs here ("when [one] touches knowledge not deceitfully [but] properly"), but later in 6v7 *kuḏeami* is an adjective in the locative singular, possibly used in the same way as it was in 11r7 *suṭhuñaṇami* (if written together and understood as a compound). In the case of 6v7 *kuḏeami* the reference to *ñaṇa* would have to be supplied on the basis of 11r7 as well as of 6v3.

Although there is no other evidence, in both manuscripts BC 6 and BC 11 *suṭhu* seems to refer to a "proper" kind of knowledge as opposed to a deceitful one.

11r8 *pariñaprahaṇa*. The expression "understanding and abandoning" means the thorough understanding of suffering (*duḥkhasya parijñāna*) and the abandoning of its origin (*samudayasya prahāṇa*).[103] Thus, one should understand and eliminate those factors that cause suffering and rebirth. In the Gāndhārī *Ṇatuspahusūtra* (SĀ[S1] 19–21, Glass 2007: 183), these causes are the

---

102 For other interpretations in the Pali canon, cf. Giustarini 2005: 173–76.

103 Cf., e.g., *Prasannapadā* (de La Vallée Poussin 1903–13: 477) *duḥkhasatyaparijñānaṃ duḥkhasamudayasya ca prahāṇaṃ*, or *Sphuṭārthā Abhidharmakośavyākhyā* (Wogihara 1932–36: 37) *parijñā*

skandhas: One should give up what does not belong to a self (G *ya ṇa tuspahu ta pacahaṣa*), i.e., G *ruo*, *vedaṇa*, *saña*, *ṣakhara*, *viñaṇa* ("form, feelings, conception, conditioned forces, perceptual consciousness"). By fully understanding (G *pariyaṇo*) form, etc., one is released (G *parimucadi*) from birth, aging, sickness, and death, grief, lamentations, suffering, despair, and frustration (G *jaḏijaraviaṣimar(*a)ṇ(*a)s(*pa) śoḵaparidev(*adukhadomaṇasta) uayaṣa*, SĀ[S1] 25–27, Glass 2007: 190). Cf. also Nird[L2] 9·4–5 (Baums 2009: 329–30): *tiṇo · kileśado · aya samudeaprahaṇo · muto dukhado · aya dukhapariña*, "crossed over from defilements; this is abandoning of the origin. Liberated from pain; this is diagnosis of pain," and Nird[L2] 9·31–32 (Baums 2009: 345): *avare vahita pavaga (*dhama dukha)pariña ca · samudagaprahaṇa ca*, "Others: Warding off evil (*dharmas): both the diagnosis (*of pain) and abandoning of the origin."

11r8 *ñaṇami yavade*. I translate this as "as long as [one is abiding] in [this] knowledge." It possibly means "only if [one is abiding] in [this] knowledge." A perhaps similar use of *yāvatā* can be seen in Dhp[K] 114 *na tavada dhamadharo yavada baho bhaṣadi* ~ Dhp 259 *na tāvatā dhammadharo yāvatā bahu bhāsati* ("A man is not an expert in the doctrine simply because he talks much," Norman 1997) or Dhp[K] 67 *na bhikhu tavada bhodi yavada bhikṣadi para | veśma dharma samadaïbhikhu bhodi na tavada* ~ Dhp 266 *na tena bhikkhū hoti yāvatā bhikkhate pare | vissaṃ dhammaṃ samādāya bhikkhu hoti na tāvatā* ("One is not a bhikkhu simply because one begs others for alms: having adopted the domestic way of life, thereby one is not a bhikkhu," Norman 1997).

11r9 *(*sarvadroacasa a)harae sarvasapatie ca ṇaṣ́e*. The connection of this sentence with the previous paragraph is not apparent. In the preceding sentence it is said that both kinds of happiness will exist. This sentence, in contrast, states that something not further specified will destroy every fortune. Thus, the two sentences cannot refer to each other. One possibility is to insert an "otherwise, …" in the translation. Another possibility, and probably the more likely one, is to understand the beginning of the sentence *(*sarvadroacasa a)harae sarvasapatie ca ṇaṣ́e* […] as a citation, for which an explanation is given in the following text. For a discussion of *(*a)harae* and *ṇaṣ́e*, cf. annotations on 4r25 *ṇaṣ́e/aharae*, p. 183.

11r11 *uayeasa* and ***avayeasa*** are understood as characterizing the items of list 1 in BC 4 (see p. 5), thus referring to the increase (Skt. *upacaya*) or decrease (Skt. *apacaya*), respectively, of good or bad things, as for example, the increase of wholesome (*kuśala*) or pleasant (*śubha*) states. Theoretically, the combination of these terms could also be applied to the fate of people in the meaning "prosperity and decay" or "rise and fall" (cf. MW s.v. *upacayāpacaya*). In contrast to all other terms in the list, *uayea* and *avayea* seem to be nouns rather than adjectives.

11r11 *sakhadaasakhadasa*. Probably a first genitive singular ending *-sa* should be reconstructed in analogy to the preceding pairs: *sakhada⟨*sa⟩ asakhadasa*. There are two possible

---

duḥkhasya prahāṇaṃ samudayasya, or (Wogihara 1932–36: 542) *tadyathā duḥkhasya parijñānaṃ samudayasya prahāṇaṃ*.

equivalents for *sakhada*: (1) Skt. *saṃskṛta* / P *saṅkhata*, "constructed, conditioned"; or (2) Skt. *saṃkhyāta* / P *saṅkhāta*, "named, considered, enumerated." Since the preceding pairs are about the characterization of the items in list 1 of BC 4, and because there is no "non-constructed" item mentioned in that list (which would be *nirvāṇa*), the second option, "enumerated or not-enumerated," seems more likely here. This would complete the list by saying that everything that was "mentioned" is included, but also everything else that has "not been mentioned."

11r13 *ṣaṣadae*. Cf. the annotations on 4v2 *ṣaṣadaeṇa*, p. 188.

11r13 *parameṇa ṣadimeṇa*. Although similar, I rule out G *ṣadima* as corresponding to Skt. *smṛtimant* / P *satimant* (cf., e.g., P *paramena satinepakkena samannāgato*, "possessing supreme mindfulness and alertness," Bodhi 2012: 999), most of all because Skt. *smṛtimant-* is spelled *svad(*ima)* (Khvs[L]), *spadivata* (Nird[L2]), *svadimada* (Dhp[K]), *spaḏima* (RS 12), or *śpadimo* (BC 4) in Gāndhārī, and the references to *ṣade* in BC 11 and *ṣadasa* in BC 4 have been equated to Skt. *śāta* / P *sāta*, "pleased, content" (cf. annotations on 4v12 *ṣadasa*, p. 193).

11r13 *citiadi* may correspond to Skt. *cintayati* (pres. active) or, more likely, to Skt. *cintyate* (pres. passive). G *vacadi* in the following sentence could be analogous to Skt. **vacati* (active, for *vakti* / P *vatti*, similar to *vadati*) or a misspelling for *vucadi* = Skt. *ucyate* / P *vuccati* (passive).

11r14 *citiae* is understood as instr. sg. as in Mil 92 *ekacintitāya*, "by thinking of one thing (only)" (Horner 1963, I: 128). The gender seems to be feminine (Skt./P *cintitā*, Skt. instr. sg. *cintitayā*, P instr. sg. *cintitāya*), even though *cintita* is usually neuter. Alternatively, it may come from *cintaka*, mfn., "thinking," but then the *-e* in the Gāndhārī form would be superfluous.

A similar form *acitieṇa* is seen in 11v20, which may correspond to Skt. *acintya* / BHS *acintiya* / P *acintiya*, but the sentence is too incomplete to ensure this meaning. From what is left, translating this as "by way of not thinking" would make the most sense. Thus, perhaps both occurrences are to be understood as Skt./P *(a)cintita*, "(not) thinking," as in the *Milindapañha*, even though the phonetic development would be rather exceptional. Other elisions of intervocalic *-t-* in these manuscripts are 4r22 *praïṭhavamaṇa* and perhaps 11r40 *vayaeṇa* for *vayieṇa* = Skt. *vyayitena*.

Other examples for elision of original intervocalic *-t-* are found in inscriptions as early as the beginning of the first century CE, one example being *maülena* = Skt. *mātulena* (Salomon 1999: 126), another *caüṭha* = Skt. *caturtha-*, which is also known from manuscripts. Both of these are elisions preceding *u*, as in another example from the Gāndhārī *Anavataptagāthā*, where *piu* (corrected to *pi[d]u* or vice versa) stands for Skt. *pitur* (Salomon 2008: 114). Other examples, not involving *u*, are: *upaïdo* = P *uppatitaṃ* (Dhp[L] 5, Lenz 2003: 41) and *añeare* = Skt. *anyataraḥ* (SĀ[S1] 31, Glass 2007: 116). Furthermore, *[a]bhiñae* in EĀ[L] 19 seems to be misunderstood as an absolutive (Skt. *abhijñāya*), where the parallels preserve the past participle Skt. *abhijñātam* / P *abhiññātaṃ*, which also fits better in the general structure of the verse (cf. Allon 2001: 83). Thus, a few examples in Kharoṣṭhī documents attest the possible elision of original intervocalic *-t-*, which is why the same can be assumed here, namely, *(a)citia* corresponding to Skt. *(a)cintita* instead of Skt. *(a)cintya*.

11r14 *sudhu*, "only, solely." Cf. Burrow 1937: § 91 *sudha* = "only" referring to Niya document no. 272, but the etymology is not clear (Burrow 1937: 131). It may be connected to P *suddha*, "clean, pure," but also "simple, mere, nothing but …" (PTSD s.v. *suddha*).

11r14 *mio*. Next to *ahu* (Skt. *aham* / P *aho*), *mio* should be first person plural, equivalent to P *mayaṃ*, which occurs alongside P *vayaṃ* = Skt. *vayam*. Cf. 4r21 *io* = Skt. *ayam*.

11r14 *sakṣi*. What is written after *sakṣi* cannot be transliterated with certainty. It looks like *tro*, but the word *sakṣitro* is unknown. If it is *sakṣito*, it might correspond to Skt. *saṃkṣiptam*, but the texts normally uses *sakṣiteṇa* for Skt. *saṃkṣiptam*, "in brief," which makes this possibility rather unlikely.

Perhaps *sakṣi* and the next letter are two separate words, with *sakṣi* corresponding to Skt. *sākṣin*, "seeing with the eyes, observing; witness," or in a more philosophical sense "ego" or "subject." If this is the case, then it possibly means that one should not think of oneself as having an ego, or at least one should not identify oneself with that ego or subject. Or, in a more basic sense, one should not think of oneself as being a witness to the experience of contentment.

Another interpretation of *sakṣi* could point to Skt. *sākṣātkr̥tvā*, "having realized," even though one letter would have to be added: *sakṣi⟨*ki⟩ta*. The translation would then be: "One does not say, 'I, we have realized,'" which could mean that one should not think of oneself as having attained arhatship. Similar phrases are known from the Pali canon in descriptions of becoming an arhat, e.g.:

> … *tad anuttaraṃ brahmacariyapariyosānaṃ diṭṭheva dhamme sayaṃ abhiññā sacchikatvā upasampajja vihāsi. "khīṇā jāti. vusitaṃ brahmacariyaṃ. kataṃ karaṇīyaṃ. nāparaṃ itthattāyā"ti abbhaññāsi.* (DN I 177)

> … that unexcelled culmination of the holy life, having realised it here and now by his own super-knowledge and dwelt therein knowing: 'Birth is destroyed, the holy life has been lived, what had to be done has been done, there is nothing further here.' (Walshe 1987: 157)

In Vasubandhu's *Abhidharmakośabhāṣya*, the word is found in another context, here referring to the realization of joy with the body (cf. also *Sphuṭārthā Abhidharmakośavyākhyā*, Wogihara 1932–36: 674):

> *"yasmin samaye āryaśrāvakaḥ pravivekajāṃ prītiṃ kāyena sākṣātkr̥tvopasaṃpadya viharatī"ty* (Pradhan 1975: 439)

> "At which time the *āryaśrāvaka*, having realized joy born from seclusion with his body, entered it and dwelled in it."

Similary, in some Buddhist texts it is used to refer to the realization of the third *vimokṣa*. One example from the *Pañcaviṃśatisāhasrikā* is:

> *śubhaṃ vimokṣaṃ kāyena sākṣātkr̥tvopasaṃpadya viharaty ayaṃ tr̥tīyo vimokṣaḥ.* (Kimura 2006, VI–VIII: 57)

> Having realized the pleasant *vimokṣa* with his body, he enters it and dwells in it. This is the third *vimokṣa*.

In the *Visuddhimagga* the term *kāyasakkhi* stands for the realization of extinction through the body rather than through a vision:

> *phuṭṭhantaṃ sacchikato ti kāyasakkhī.* [...] *jhānaphassaṃ paṭhamaṃ phusati pacchā nirodhaṃ nibbānaṃ sacchikarotī ti kāyasakkhī.* (Vism 660 / Vism[W] 566)

> ... he has realized [nibbāna] by experiencing, thus he is a body witness [...] he first experiences the experience of jhāna and afterwards realizes cessation, nibbāna, thus he is a body witness. (Ñāṇamoli 2011: 689)

Thus, perhaps also in BC 11 the term *sakṣi* points to a bodily, "eyewitnessed" realization and experience, here related to contentment or satisfaction. That is, one should not become conceptionally aware of one's own experience of contentment, because this would cause attachment to it. Or, one should not become aware of one's separation from the experience itself through a dualistic reality being called to mind in which there is a distinction between subject and object.

A last possibility would be to read *sakṣito* for Skt. *sākṣiptam*, "with absence of mind, thoughtlessly" (MW s.v.). Then the sentence would be: "One does not say, 'I [am], we [are] thoughtless/absent-minded'" used in the same way as the previous statement: "One does not think, 'I shall not let go of satisfaction.'" While then both satisfaction and thoughtlessness would be positive conditions, one should not think about them, since attachment would arise. Cf. 11v20 *ku ṇa acitieṇa*.

11r14 *ciri me ta*. The separation of words is uncertain, and perhaps it is *cirim eta* ("for a long time [there will be] this contentment"). The sequence has been split up into three words, because *ta* for Skt. *tad* is more common than *eta* for Skt. *etad*, which should be written *eda*, although both are possible. G *ciri* should correspond to Skt. *cirāt* ("after long") rather than *ciraṃ* ("for long"), but the context here suggests it being used in the sense of *ciraṃ* ("for a long time"); cf. SĀ[S1] 6 *ṇa jira jiviśami*, "I will not live long" (Glass 2007: 138–39), or Anav[L] 53/74 *ṇiraghehi kṣeviṣu ciru/ciro*, "I spent a long time in hells" (Salomon 2008a: 181, 184). Skt. *cirāt* would make sense if it were combined with *na*, but here the uncertain letter preceding *ciri* cannot be read as a *ṇa*.

11r15 ff. *gachiea* ... *aṇubhaviea* ... *uadiea* ... *ṇaṣ̄iea*. Possibly, the Gāndhārī ending *-ea* does not correspond to P *-eyya* (3rd sg. opt.) but to P *-eyyaṃ* (1st sg. opt.).

11r17 *osagrasuhe*. Since *osagrasukha* is juxtaposed with *pariñasukha*, G *osagra* (Skt. *avasarga* / P *vossagga*, "letting loose, relinquishing, abandonment") is here synonymous with *prahaṇa* (Skt. *prahāṇa* / P *pahāna*). Cf. 11r8 *pariñaprahaṇa*, p. 200.

11r17 *ṇame aṣa di {di}*. The correct separation of these letters and their Sanskrit correspondents are uncertain. They could either be separated as *ṇameaṣa di*, corresponding to Skt. *nāmadheyam (i)ti*, "thus the name," which, however, should be spelled *ṇamaṣeo di* in Gāndhārī, or *ṇamadheo* as in AsP[Sp] 1-29 *ṇamadh(*e)o*. The sentence *osagrasuhe ṇameaṣa* (read *ṇamaṣeo*) *di {di} mahaś(*ie)* would then be translated as "what is called 'happiness of release' is a great fortune." Or, they could be separated as *ṇame aṣa di* for Skt. *nāma atha (i)ti*, with *nāma* as either "called" or "indeed." Then, the sentence *osagrasuhe ṇame aṣa di {di} mahaś(*ie)* would be translated as either "now (*atha*), thus (*iti*), what is called (*nāma*) 'happiness of release' is a great fortune" or "now, thus, the happiness of release is indeed (*nāma*) a great fortune." The subsequent addition *pariñasuhe ca mahaśie*, without the *ṇame aṣa di*, makes *nāma* as "indeed" a bit more likely. Otherwise one might expect *nāma* in the sense of "called" or "named" to be repeated. In all cases the second *di* seems superflous.

11r18 *aparaṣiṇasuhe*. The only textual evidence for *(a)parādhīnasukha* I could find is a passage in a commentary on the *Nimijātaka* (Jā VI 99):

ye ve adutiyā na ramanti ekikā
vivekajaṃ ye na labhanti pītiṃ
kiñcāpi te indasamānabhogā
te ve parādhīnasukhā varākā ti.

Those who do not rejoice themselves alone,
those who do not obtain the joy born from detachment,
those have [only] the same enjoyments as Indra,
those have [only] the impure pleasures that depend on something else.

11r18 *aviñatis(*u)he*. The term Skt. *avijñapti* / P *aviññatti* means basically "non-information" or anything "unmanifest."[104] Contrary to *vijñapti*, which is the act of "making known," of cognizing and perceiving an object by its external or material appearance,[105] *avijñapti* is free from limited or exoteric knowledge. In *prajñāpāramitā* contexts a translation as "non-perception" or "non-cognition" (based on Schmithausen 1987, Index) seems to be the most appropriate.

---

104 According to the *Abhidharmakośabhāṣya* (de La Vallée Poussin and Pruden 1988–90, I: 35), *avijñapti* belongs to the *dharmāyatana* in contrast to *rūpāyatana*. Vasubandhu gives several other opinions (de La Vallée Poussin and Pruden 1988–90, I: 47): "Dharmaśrī [...] Action of the *manas* is solely *avijñapti* [...] because this action is not visible"; "Upaśānta [...] Mental action is called *avijñapti* because it does not inform others"; "Dharmatrāta [...] replaces the terms *vijñapti* and *avijñapti* with 'doing' and 'not doing'." Cf. also de La Vallée Poussin and Pruden 1988–90, I: 73–74: "*vedanāskandha*, *saṃjñāskandha*, *saṃskāraskandha*, plus *avijñapti* and the three unconditioned things, are seven things which are called *dharmāyatanas* or *dharmadhātu*." According to the *Abhidharmahṛdaya* and also the **Satyasiddhiśāstra*, *avijñapti* is mainly characterized by being unmanifest or invisible. Cf. Willemen 2006: 60; Sastri 1978: 191–92 (*avijñapti* = unmanifest action; *vijñapti* = manifest action), Sastri 1978: 245 ("The action done by the body and speech is *vijñapti*").

105 Cf. Schmithausen 1987: 85, 97, 203.

11r18–23 ***-suhe***. Several of the kinds of happiness listed here cannot be identified at this point in time, or maybe never, since the preservation status of the birch bark is very poor, in addition to the somewhat careless style of the scribe. A passage in the *Kathāvatthu* lists several kinds of bliss akin to the passage in BC 11, but apparently none of the so far illegible ones is included. The discussion is between the Gokulikas, who claim that everything is ill ("all is on fire"), and the Theravādins, who try to convince them of the opposite:

> *sabbe saṃkhārā anodhikatvā kukkuḷā ti? āmantā.*
>
> *nanu atthi sukhā vedanā, kāyikaṃ sukhaṃ, cetasikaṃ sukhaṃ, dibbaṃ sukhaṃ, mānusakaṃ sukhaṃ, lābhasukhaṃ, sakkārasukhaṃ, yānasukhaṃ, sayanasukhaṃ, issariyasukhaṃ, adhipaccasukhaṃ, gihīsukhaṃ, sāmaññasukhaṃ, sāsavaṃ sukhaṃ, anāsavaṃ sukhaṃ, upadhisukhaṃ, nirupadhisukhaṃ, sāmisaṃ sukhaṃ, nirāmisaṃ sukhaṃ, sappītikaṃ sukhaṃ, nippītikaṃ sukhaṃ, jhānasukhaṃ, vimuttisukhaṃ, kāmasukhaṃ, nekkhammasukhaṃ, pavivekasukhaṃ, upasamasukhaṃ, sambodhisukhan ti?* (Kv 208–9)
>
> Controverted Point. – That all conditioned things are absolutely [*anodhikatvā*, "without distinction"] cinderheaps.
>
> Th. – You affirm this; but is there not such a thing as pleasurable feeling, bodily pleasure, mental pleasure, celestial happiness, human happiness, the pleasures of gain, of being honoured, of riding-and-driving [*yānasukha*, lit. vehicle-pleasure], of resting, the pleasures of ruling, of administrating, of domestic-and-secular life, of the religious life, pleasures involved in the intoxicants [*āsava*] and pleasures that are not, the happiness [of *nibbāna*], both while stuff of life remains and when none remains [*upadhisukha* and *nirupadhisukha*], worldly and spiritual pleasures, happiness with zest and without zest, *jhāna*-happiness, the bliss of liberty, pleasures of sense-desires, and the happiness of renunciation, the bliss of solitude, of peace, of enlightenment? (Aung and Davids 1915: 127–28; their footnotes are given in abbreviated form within the brackets)

In the following debate several statements attributed to the Buddha are cited, with the Gokulikas referring to the sorrowfulness of everything connected with the field of senses and mind, and the Theravādins countering with similar passages giving evidence that there are still some pleasing things. In reply to the Gokulikas' reference to the impermanence of everything conditioned, which inevitably involves suffering, the Theravādins bring forward giving and virtue as examples of something that causes the opposite of sorrow and that is not undesired, unpleasant or disagreeable (note that also in 11r53 *dāna* is brought forward as an argument for the existence of *kāmasukha*). The Theravādins finish with the following citation (Udāna II.1),[106] which remains without reply; hence they win the debate:

---

[106] Translation by Aung and Davids 1915: 129, see there for further parallels.

sukho viveko tuṭṭhassa	Happy is solitude who, glad at heart,
sutadhammassa passato,	Hath learnt the norm and doth the vision see!
abyāpajjaṃ sukhaṃ loke	Happy is that benignity towards
pāṇabhūtesu saṃyamo.	the world which on no creature worketh harm.
sukhā virāgatā loke	Happy the freedom from all lust, th' ascent
kāmānaṃ samatikkamo,	Past and beyond the needs of sense-desires.
asmimānassa yo vinayo	He who doth crush the great 'I am'-conceit:
etaṃ ve paramaṃ sukhaṃ	This, even this, is happiness supreme.
taṃ sukhena sukhaṃ pattaṃ	This happiness by happiness is won,
accantasukham eva taṃ,	Unending happiness is this alone.
tisso vijjā anuppattā	The Threefold Wisdom hath he made his own.
etaṃ ve paramaṃ sukhan ti	This, even this, is happiness supreme.

Also here, *viveka-* and *vairāga-sukha* are considered the foremost happinesses, although the *paramaṃ sukhaṃ* might also refer to *nirvāṇa* itself, which is declared to be supreme bliss in the *Atthasālini* (and elsewhere). But, in the words of Nārada (1987: 172): "This does not mean that there is a pleasurable feeling in Nibbāna although the term *sukha* is used. Nibbāna is a bliss of relief. The release from suffering is itself Nibbānic bliss."

11r19 *sarvaṣatvaṇamasaṇivasuhe*. Either this is one compound, or it should be separated as *sarvaṣatvaṇa ma°* or *sarvaṣatvaṇam a°*. Thus we are left with three possibilities for the second word: *ṇamasaṇivasuhe*, *masaṇivasuhe*, or *asaṇivasuhe* "of all beings." The reading of *sa* is uncertain and it could also be transliterated as *su* or *taṃ* (however, anusvāra is rarely used by this scribe). The reading *va*—as opposed to *ma*—is based on how the letter is written, namely, beginning at the top right (instead of on the left). Since the top is slightly angular, it should be *va* rather than *a*, although the latter cannot be excluded. Based on the following *sudeṣasuhe* (Skt. *sudeśasukha*) and *sugadasamoṣaṇasuhe* (Skt. *sugatasamavadhānasukha*), maybe *ma⟨*ha⟩ saṇiva⟨*ta⟩* = Skt. *mahāsaṃnipātasukha*, "the happiness due to a great assembly of all beings" could be meant, although two akṣaras would have to be reconstructed. Based on the overall content and the other kinds of happiness, *asaṇiasuhe* = Skt. **āsannikasukha*, "the happiness of being near [a Tathāgata or awakening]," may be taken into consideration as well.

11r19 *sudeṣasuhe*. G *sudeṣasuhe* can be explained as Skt. *sudeśasukha* ("happiness due to a good place") or as Skt. *sūddeśasukha* ("happiness due to a good instruction"). It is difficult to judge from the context which one is more likely, since the previous four types of happiness are unclear. The following *sugadasamoṣaṇasuhe* = Skt. *sugatasamavadhānasukha* ("happiness due to meeting the 'Sugata'") matches both possibilities: either G *sudeṣa* is a good place in the sense of offering favorable conditions for meeting the Sugata, or it is understood as listening to a good instruction given by the Sugata. In Kharoṣṭhī spelling one would expect *sūddeśasukha* to be rendered as *suudeṣasuhe*, as in BC 3 *suu[ta](*ma)* = Skt. *sūttama* (cf. Strauch 2014: 75) or Nird[L2] 13·38 *suuaṭhidacito* = Skt. *sūpasthitacitta* (cf. Baums 2009: 504). Although the *u* of

°*udeṣa* could have been forgotten, or the *su°* could imply a sandhi (Skt. *su-uddeśa*), this possibility is less likely and *sudeṣasuhe* = Skt. *sudeśasukha* preferred. The occurrence of *drudeṣa-* in 6r3 as something that is to be avoided might support this as well.

11r19 *sugadasamoṣaṇasuhe*. First read as *sugadadha(*r)moṣaṇasuhe* (Skt. *sugatadharmāvadhāna-sukha*, "happiness due to the concentration on the Dharma of the Sugata;" Schlosser 2016: 194–95), this word should better be understood as Skt. *sugatasamavadhānasukha* (thanks to Richard Salomon for this new reading). A similar compound *buddhasamavadhāna* is found in the *Śikṣā-samuccaya* citing the *Bṛhatsāgaranāgarājaparipṛcchā* and the *Śraddhābalādhānāvatāramudrā-sūtra* (Bendall 1902: 309–11). Meeting the Buddha is not only seeing him in reality (*svarūpeṇa*), but also seeing him in a painting or in a manuscript (*citrakarmalikhitaṃ vā pustakakarmakṛtaṃ vā buddhaṃ paśyed*; Bendall 1902: 311; tr. Bendall 1922: 278).

11r19 *ya vela*. Cf. 11r42 *yo vela … ta vela*. Skt./P *velā*, "(point of) time," is used in adverbial phrases attested in the *Mahāvastu* with shortening of the ending to *-aṃ*: *yaṃ velaṃ … taṃ velaṃ*, "when … then" (BHSD s.v. *velā* and also BHSG § 7.18). In the Niya documents the phrase is *vela velaya*, "from time to time" (CKD 358 and CKD 371), or *yaṃ vela veya atra agachiṣyama taṃ vela …*, "When we come there, at that time, …" (CKD 231, tr. Burrow 1940: 44).

11r20 *atogada-*. Although later in the text, G *atogada* must be translated as "included," here "turned inwards" in relation to the mind being withdrawn from the senses makes more sense (cf. Mvu I 237 *antogatehi indriyehi avahirgatamānasena*, "with his faculties turned inwards, with a mind not turned to external things," Jones 1949–56, I: 193, or Mvu I 301 *antargatehi indrayehi abahirgatena mānasena*, "his faculties were turned inwards; his mind was not turned outwards," Jones 1949–56, I: 250).

11r20 *avhiña-* = Skt. *abhijñā* / P *abhiññā*. Only someone who has gained the fifth *jhāna* can develop the higher supernormal or supernatural knowledges.[107] They are the final attainments

---

[107] Cf., for example, *Abhidhammatthasaṅgaha*, chapter 9, § 21: *abhiññāvasena pavattamānam pana rūpāvacarapañcamajjhānam abhiññāpādaka pañcamajjhāna vutthahitvā adhittheyyādikam āvajjitvā parikammam karontassa rūpādisu ālambanesu yathāraham appeti. abhiññā ca nāma: iddhividham dibbasotam paracittavijānanā. pubbenivāsānussati dibbacakkhū'ti pañcadhā*, "Having emerged from the fifth jhāna as a basis for direct knowledge, having adverted to the resolution, etc., when one does the preliminary work, one enters the fifth fine-material-sphere jhāna occurring by way of direct knowledge with respect to such objects as visible forms, etc. The direct knowledges are fivefold: the supernormal powers, the divine ear, knowledge of others' minds, recollection of past lives, and the divine eye" (Bodhi 2007: 343). These supernormal or direct knowledges are said to be mundane. Sometimes a sixth supramundane knowledge is mentioned, which is the knowledge of the destruction of the taints (P *āsavakkhaya*) arisen through insight (cf. Bodhi 2007: 344). The Sanskrit terms are, e.g., according to *Dharmasaṃgraha* 20 (Müller and Wenzel 1885: 4): *divyacakṣus, divyaśrotra, paracittajñāna, pūrvanivāsānusmṛti, ṛddhi*. Cf. also the terms in the *Dīrghāgama* manuscript from Gilgit (Melzer 2010: 18–19): *ṛddhiviṣaya, divyaśrotrajñāna, cetaḥ-paryāyajñāna, pūrvanivāsānusmṛtijñāna, cyutyupapādajñāna, āsravakṣayajñāna* (for *cyutyupapāda-*

within the method of meditation for developing calm (P *samatha*).[108] BC 11 (r21) names only two of them, namely *divacakṣu* (Skt. *divyacakṣus* / P *dibbacakkhu*) and *paracitañaṇa* (Skt. *paracittajñāna* / P *paracittavijānana*) by way of example.

11r20 ***avhiñaaśreasuhe***. Presumably, this is the "happiness whose basis (*āśraya*) is the supernatural knowledges." Alternatively, *aśrea* might be understood as Skt. *aśreya* in the sense of *niḥśreya(sa)*, "having no superior; n. ultimate bliss" or also "final emancipation, liberation." For the last meaning, cf. *naiḥśreyasa* in *Ratnāvalī* verse 1.3, 1.4, and 1.75 (Hahn 1982: 2, 30), which is translated as "Erlösung" (= liberation) by Okada (2006: 36–37), reflecting Paramārtha's translation of *naiḥśreyasa* as 解脱 = Skt. *mokṣa*. Then it could be translated as "happiness of final emancipation/liberation [coming along with] supernatural powers," especially in sequence of 11r20 *mokṣasuhe*.

In the following line, two *abhijñā*s are apparently enumerated as examples for *śriyā* (= *śrī*, "fortune, wealth"): 11r21 *paṃḍidaśriyaṇa suhe divacakṣu va paracitañaṇa ⟨*va⟩ śriyaṇa suhe*.

11r22 ***avakra ? + +***. The letter after *kra* could be *ma* or *ta*, leading to *avakrata* or *avakram.*, which could go back to Skt. *ava√kram*, "to enter," also in the meaning of entering a condition or state (cf. SWTF s.v. ³*avakram* and *avakrānta*). It could, however, also be related to *apakram*, "to go away," in the sense of overcoming immeasurable faults.

11r23 ***praṣaṇakarmo***. In accordance with the usual phonetic development, *praṣaṇa* should go back to Skt. *pradhāna*. Since in 11v28 it is written *pariñaprahaṇakarmo* in a syntactically parallel construction, this is doubtful and I take both as Skt. *prahāṇa*, "abandoning" (cf. chapter 5 on phonology, p. 86).[109] Nevertheless, in BHS both *pradhāna* and (more often) *prahāṇa* are used for *pradhāna*, "effort, endeavor." The regular development *praṣaṇa* < Skt. *pradhāna* ("effort") is attested in SĀ[S1]; in EĀ[L] it is written with normal *s*: *prasaṇa* < Skt. *pradhāna.*[110] G *praṣ/saṇa* = Skt. *prahāṇa* ("abandoning") is apparently attested only once in SaṅgCm[L] as a unique exception in addition to the otherwise used *prahaṇa*.[111] Probably the best example for the confusion between the two meanings and spellings is *[pra]saṇaprasaṇ[o]* = BHS *prahāṇaprahāṇaṃ* / P *pahānappadhānaṃ*, "effort of abandoning," in EĀ[L] 39–40 (cf. Allon 2001: 258–59). Another piece of evidence for the confusion of the two senses can be seen in

jñāna = *divyacakṣusjñāna*, cf. Bodhi 2007: 344 stating that "the knowledge of the passing away and rebirth of beings" is included in the "divine eye").

108 For more detailed explanations, see Bodhi 2007: 344.

109 Alternatively, MW lists Skt. *pradhānakarman* / P *padhānakamma* as "chief or principal action." Since the general topic of BC 4/6/11 is abandonment, I do not think this applies here.

110 SĀ[S1] 34 *samepaṣaṇaṇa* = Skt. *samyakprahāṇa* [sic], "right striving" (cf. Glass 2007: 203). EĀ[L] 39–40 *catvarime bhikṣave prasaṇa ◦ satu savijamaṇa loghaśpi ◦ (*kadara / kadama catvari / catvaro ◦) sabaraprasaṇe aṇorakṣaṇaprasaṇe bhavaṇaprasaṇo ◦ prasaṇaprasaṇo*, "Monks, these four efforts are found existing in the world. (*What four?) The effort of restraint, the effort of protecting, the effort of development, the effort of abandoning" (Allon 2001: 255).

111 In the commentary on the *catvāry āryavaṃśāḥ*, G *paṣaṇaramo* is written once, in addition to, otherwise, *[p]r[aha]ṇaramo* = Skt. *prahānarāma-* (Stefan Baums, personal communication).

the inconsistent Chinese translations for *pradhāna* (cf. BHSD s.v. *pradhāna*). According to Jan Nattier (see Allon 2001: 259), translators before Kumārajīva used "abandon/cut-off," those contemporary with Kumārajīva used "exertion," and those contemporary with Xuánzàng used "cutting off" again.

As regards the following *ruve · aṣa va aruve* (cf. also 11v28 *pariña prahaṇakarmo ca · ruve ◦ aṣa va · aruve*), *ruve* and *aruve* have been interpreted as locative, so that *prahaṇakarmo*, "the act of abandoning," is "[related to] form or formless" rather than being "form or formless" itself. This decision is supported by the statement 11v14–15 *yadi va kamadhadu yadi va ruvadhadu yadi va arupadhadu*, "[This applies for] the desire realm, the form realm, and also the formless realm," which refers to the inner and outer sense bases (being compared to boils) causing suffering in either of the three realms. Since the first one, the *kamadhadu*, is addressed throughout the manuscript, it is reasonable that the question refers only to the other two realms, the form and the formless.

11r24–25 *ya ṇa sarvaṣatvehi parigrahida ṇa se kamabhoyi asti ye ṇaṇaparigrahidia eva bahujaṇasaṣaraṇadukha*. There are several possible interpretations of 11r24 *ya ṇa* (1. *yad/yo na*, 2. *yāna*, 3. *yena*) and 11r25 *ye ṇaṇa* (1. *yena na*, 2. *ye/yo/yaṃ/yad nānā-*), as well as different meanings of *parigr̥hīta*. I have chosen the adopted translation (reflecting Skt. *yo na* …, *yo nānā-* …), because it agrees with other statements in the texts, where detachment and solitude are recommended. For the combination *parigrahida* with *ṣatvehi*, cf., for example, *sattvaparigr̥hīta* in the *Abhidharmasamuccaya*, translated as "surrounded by beings," where these beings are those who reject the Mahāyāna (Fujita 2009: 104 n. 11).[112]

In BC 4, this sentence could stress the necessity for a bodhisattva to follow the instructions of the text to live alone in solitude, not surrounded by others, since the company of others is not conducive to the abandonment of pleasures and desires, which is one of the main issues throughout the manuscripts, because pleasures (*kāma*) are the origin of suffering.

In the Pali canon, a *kāmabhogin* is a householder (*gihin*, in contrast to those having left home, *pabbajita*), who, as a layperson, may enjoy sensual pleasures (cf., e.g., AN II 69 or also SN I 78). Opposed to that, someone who has gone forth into homelessness should not pursue happiness through sensual pleasures (see SN IV 330 ff. and cf. AN V 176 ff.). Thus, BC 4 seems to speak in favor of those having left their homes, focusing here on the aspect of not being surrounded by other people.

As for the position of *asti*, it can either stand at the end of a sentence or at its beginning (then: "[But] there is the one who is surrounded (?) by different kinds [of beings, and that one partakes of the] suffering common to many people."). G *eva* can either emphasize the preceding *ṇaṇaparigrahidia*, like Skt. *eva*, or refer to the following *dukha*, like Skt. *evam* ("and thus he partakes of the suffering …"). Moreover, *-saṣaraṇa-* in the last compound might be understood as Skt. *saṃsaraṇa*, "passing through the cycle of existences," instead of Skt. *sādhāraṇa*.

---

[112] It may be noted that *pari* √*grah* can also have the meaning "to help [others]" (cf. MW s.v. *parigraha* and *parigrahītr̥*) or "to understand, comprehend." Moreover, *aparigr̥hīta* is a common term in *prajñāpāramitā* literature for the "non-grasping" to form, etc. (*aparigr̥hītasamādhi*), so maybe there is also a wordplay involved here.

11r25–26 *pradigarasuhe*. For the happiness resulting from a remedy (Skt. *pratīkārasukha*), cf. a passage in the *Saundarananda* of Aśvaghoṣa (11.28):

> *ākāṅkṣec ca yathā rogaṃ pratīkārasukhepsayā* |
> *duḥkham anvicchati bhavāṃs tathā viṣayatr̥ṣṇayā* || (Johnston 1928: 78)
>
> As a man might wish for disease in order to secure the pleasure to be derived from remedies, so you seek suffering out of longing for the objects of the senses. (Johnston 1932: 63)

This happiness is only temporary, as explained in 11v12. Similarly, in a passage of the **Satyasiddhiśāstra* it is stated that there is no pleasant feeling in the absolute sense if the happiness is caused by an antidote (chapter 78 on *vedanā*; for a Sanskrit translation of the Chinese, see Sastri 1975: 187):

> When there is a factor for stopping the suffering, on that occasion the happiness is felt. When a man, e.g., is oppressed by a severe cold, a touch of the fire causes pleasure to him. Q[uestion]. The pleasant feeling is not existent; for, the hot touch being intensive, causes suffering. A[nswer]. It exists in the empirical sense but not in the absolute sense. The hot touch causes pleasure to one who is desirous of it. That is when the touch serves as remedy of one's previous suffering, it causes pleasure. When the suffering has already been removed, the hot touch causes no more pleasure. Therefore there is no pleasant feeling in the absolute sense. (Sastri 1978: 157)

In the following text of the **Satyasiddhiśāstra* it is discussed whether happiness exists in a nominal sense, in other words, if there is "even in the realm of desire a pleasant feeling." In the end this is rejected with the statement "when the misery is less intensive the people wrongly conceive of it as happiness." On this, cf. also *Ratnāvalī* verses 4.48 and 4.62 (Hahn 1982: 110, 116).

11r25–26 *u⟨*a⟩ṇiṣasuhe* / 11r26 *uaṇiṣasuhe*. The equivalent of G *uaṇiṣa* is BHS *upaniṣad* or *upaniṣā* / P *upanisā* in the meaning of "cause, basis" as a synonym for *hetu*, *pratyaya*, *nidāna*, *kāraṇa*, *nimitta*, *liṅga*. Cf. Wogihara (1908: 20) regarding *upaniṣad*:

> [...] in ZDMG 58 p. 454 hat Professor Leumann drei Verwendungen dieses Wortes unterschieden. Zur zweiten stellt sich folgender Zusammenhang (Abhidharmak.-vy. Calc.-MS fol. 48b): *duḥkhôpaniṣac chraddhā*, *duḥkham upaniṣad asyāḥ*, *sêyaṃ śraddhā duḥkhôpaniṣat*, *duḥkha-hetukêty arthaḥ*. Hiuenthsang übersetzt hier *upaniṣad* mit 'Stütze, Anhaltspunkt', was ich erwähne, weil Prof. Leumann (wie in ZDMG. 62 p. 101(2) kurz angedeutet ist) jetzt ein altbuddhistisches Wort **upaniśrā* (im Dialekt **upanissā*) mit den Bedeutungen 'Grundlage, Stütze, Nähe' voraussetzt, welches man bei Vereinfachung des *ss* von *upanissā* für das brahmanische Wort *upaniṣad* gehalten und dementsprechend umgestaltet habe. [...] Das Substantiv finde sich außer in der bei Childer verzeichneten Dhammapada-Stelle in

> Saṃyutta-nikāya II p. 30–32, wo *-upanisa* in einer dem Pratītyasamutpāda ähnlichen Reihe genau so wie sonst *-paccaya* gebraucht sei.

I could not find a direct parallel to *upaniṣa(t)-/upaniṣā-/upanisā-sukha*, but probably *hetusukha* denotes the same. This is named in the *Bodhisattvabhūmi* (chapter 1.3) as one of five kinds of bliss: *hetusukhaṃ veditasukhaṃ duḥkhaprātipakṣikaṃ sukhaṃ veditopacchedasukham avyābādhyañ ca pañcaṃ sukham* (Dutt 1966: 17).[113] The *hetusukha* ("caused bliss") is said to have two components: the senses and their objects. The cause for the feeling of bliss is touch (*sparśa*) that leads to a result (*phala*) in this life or the next.[114] The third type of *sukha*, the *duḥkhaprātipakṣikasukha* ("bliss antithetical to pain") could be a synonym of *pratikārasukha*. It is explained as the notion of bliss that comes into existence when suffering is appeased. Suffering can be due to different reasons, such as enduring cold or heat, hunger or thirst, etc., and bliss is felt due to the respective remedy.[115] The last kind of *sukha*, the *avyābādhyasukha* ("indestructible pleasure"), may be comparable to the *avasargasukha* (G *osagrasuhe*) mentioned in 11r17, as well as other types of happiness listed in the following passage (11r20–21). In the *Bodhisattvabhūmi*, the *avyābādhyasukha* is described as fourfold: (1) *naiṣkramyasukha* ("bliss of renunciation"), (2) *pravivekasukha* ("bliss of seclusion," equivalent to *prītisukha* experienced in the first *dhyāna* due to the cessation of *kāma-*, *pāpaka-* and *akuśaladharma*), (3) *upaśamasukha* ("bliss due to calmness" achieved through the cessation of *vitarka* and *vicāra* in the second *dhyāna*), (4) *saṃbodhisukha* ("bliss of perfect awakening" due to the total liberation from worldly fetters and the perfect comprehension of reality as it really is).[116]

11r26 *ṇa ṇica ṇa atve ṇa ka suhiṇa bhave*. This phrase is reminiscent of the three marks of conditioned phenomena (Skt. *trilakṣaṇa* / P *tilakkhana*): they are impermanent (Skt. *anitya* / P *anicca*), without a self (Skt. *anātman* / P *anattā*), and painful (Skt. *duḥkha* / P *dukkha*). G *ṇa ka suhiṇa bhave* should correspond to Skt. *na kaṃ sukhinaḥ* (= *sukhitasya*) *bhāvaḥ*, "not at all [is it / is there] a continuous state of possessing happiness / being happy." For G *suhiṇa* = Skt. *sukhitasya*, cf. SaṅgCm^{L} *suhiṇa cite samaṣiaḏi* corresponding to Skt. *sukhitasya cittaṃ samādhīyate* (Stache-Rosen 1968: 149) / P *sukhino cittaṃ samādhiyati* (DN III 241).

---

113 Cf. Bendall and de La Vallée Poussin 1906: 215–16.

114 *tatra sukhapakṣyadvayam indriyaṃ viṣayaś ca | taddhetukaś ca yaḥ sparśaḥ sukhavedanīyaḥ yac ca kiñcid iṣṭaphalaṃ karma dr̥ṣṭe dharme abhisaṃparāye vā tat sarvam aikadhyam abhisaṃkṣipya hetusukham ity ucyate* (Dutt 1966: 17).

115 *śītoṣṇakṣutpipāsādikānām anekavidhānāṃ duḥkhānāṃ bahunānāprakārāṇām utpannotpannānāṃ śītoṣṇakṣutpipāsādiduḥkhapratikāreṇa praśamāt tasminn eva duḥkhopaśamamātrake yā sukhabuddhir utpadyate idam ucyate duḥkhaprātipakṣikaṃ sukham* (Dutt 1966: 17–18).

116 *avyābādhyasukhaṃ punaḥ samāsataś caturākāraṃ veditavyam | naiṣkramyasukhaṃ pravivekasukham upaśamasukhaṃ saṃbodhisukhañ ca | samyag eva śraddhayā agārād anāgārikāṃ pravrajitasya āgārikavicitravyāsaṅgaduḥkhanirmokṣān naiṣkramyasukham ity ucyate | kāmapāpakākuśaladharmaprahāṇavivekāt prathame dhyāne vivekajaṃ prītisukhaṃ pravivekasukham ity ucyate | dvitīyādiṣu dhyāneṣu vitarkavicāropaśamād upaśamasukham ity ucyate | sarvakleśātyantavisaṃyogāj jñeyavastuyathābhūtābhisaṃbodhāc ca yat sukham idam ucyate saṃbodhisukham* (Dutt 1966: 18).

11r28 *paśita* = Skt. *paśyitvā*, "having seen." Cf. Silk (2013: 183), where the verses of the *Kāśyapaparivarta* are examined: "Looking more directly at morphology, we find the non-Sanskritic gerunds *paśyitva*" (other occurrences of this form can be found in the *Daśabhūmika-sūtra*, *Ratnaguṇasaṃcayagāthā*, *Saddharmapuṇḍarīkasūtra*, and *Mahāvastu*). Cf. also Av^{L6} 48 *paśi[do]* = Skt. *dr̥ṣṭaḥ* / P *diṭṭho*, "seen," pp. of √*dr̥ś* / *paś* (Lenz 2003: 188). Likewise, Av^{L1} 169 and Av^{L2} 1 *paśido* (Lenz 2010: 79 and 97).

11r29 *muḏeasa*. Probably related to Skt. *mūḍha*, "stupefied, bewildered, perplexed, confused." Cf. 11v7 *amuḏa khaïta* = "non-perplexed (?) having declared."

11r30 *ṇikhalidea* / 11r31 *ṇikhalida*, pp. from *niṣ* √*kal*, "to remove, expel, take out, send back." Cf. *nikhalita* CKD 331 "he took (her) up (from the ground)"; *nikhalitaṃti* CKD 63 "they took out"; *nikhalidavo* CKD 64 "are to be sent back" (Burrow 1937: § 92), CKD 272 "to be taken," CKD 714 "to be removed"; *nikaliṣyati* [sic] CKD 188 "to remove" (Burrow 1937: § 24).

11r30 *jugidea* ... *jugida*. Both words may be derivations from √**juṅg* / **yuṅg*, "to exclude, desert, relinquish, abandon," attested only in the *Dhātupāṭha* (v. 50 *yuṅgati*, v. 51 *juṅgati*, see MW ss.vv.). The adjective *juṅgita* ("deserted, abandoned") is attested in the *Vasiṣṭhadharmasūtra* (21.10), translated as "degraded man" in Olivelle 2000: 437.

11r31 *parvayidehi*, instr. pl. of *parvayida* = Skt. *pravrajita* / P *pabbajita*, "mendicant." The *pravrajita* appears to be placed in opposition to a Buddha a few words later; one might ask whether *pravrajita* is here a synonym of *śrāvaka*.

11r31 *aprañati*. The Sanskrit term *aprajñapti* stands for "non-designation," which means the state of being without any verbal or conceptual notion of things, without cognizing things by way of designation. In combination with the emergence of joy (Skt. *prīti*), it refers to a state in meditation during which one experiences joy but is without any kind of conceptual thinking, similar to (or identical with) the second *dhyāna*, which is without *vitarka* and *vicāra*, that is, noticing and investigating an object roughly and in more detail.

11r32 *paribhuḏa* is understood as Skt. *paribhukta* / P *paribhutta*, "enjoyed, possessed, consumed," pp. of *pari* √*bhuj*, since also in other passages of BC 11 this meaning is more appropriate than, for example, Skt. *paribhūta*, "despised." Cf. also the spelling *parubhuteṇa* (read *paribhuteṇa*) and *aparibhuteṇa* in 11r39. The derivation from √*bhuj* is further justified by 11v18 *aparibhujitrea* and 4v3 *paribhujidava*.

11r32 *sarvatradea*. Cf. BHSD s.v. *sarvatratāye*: "adv. (app. instr. of **sarvatra-tā*; = Pali *sabbattatāya* or *sabbatthatāya*), altogether, in every way." If correct, the Gāndhārī form should be *sarvatradae*, but this is not reason enough to dismiss the equivalence. Instead it would be another argument for interpreting the ending *-ea* in BC 4 as dative singular *-āya*. Cf. annotations on 4r25 *ṇaś̱e* / *aharae*, p. 183.

11r33 *yaṇa*. The way *yaṇa* is used here, without any specification or emphasis, makes it slightly uncertain if indeed Skt./P *yāna*, "path, vehicle," is meant. In relation to the other words in this context, namely *sagaṇia* (Skt. *saṃgaṇikā*) and *vivegag̱ada* (Skt. *vivekagata*), an understanding of *yāna* in the sense of a community of shared values and common interests seems plausible.

11r33 *vivegag̱adasa* is translated as Skt. *vivekagatasya* (gen. sg.). The last repeated *upajea* seems superfluous, but the alternative *vivekagatatā* (nom. sg.), "state of having gone into seclusion," causes difficulties, as it is contrary to *saṃgaṇikā*. These problems could be solved by adding a "but" to the translation ("... [but] the state of having gone into seclusion would arise"). This solitude can refer to physical or mental isolation, and although elsewhere in this text mental detachment is generally meant, in this context—in juxtaposition with *yāna* and *saṃganikā*—physical seclusion might be intended. The same is the case in 11r20 *vivegasuhe asagaṇiasuh(*e)*, "the happiness of detachment / seclusion (*viveka*), the happiness of being without company (*asaṃgaṇikā*)." Cf. on this topic a passage in the *Aṣṭasāhasrikā*:

> *punar aparaṃ subhūte māraḥ pāpīyān vivekaguṇena bodhisattvaṃ mahāsattvam upasaṃkramya codayiṣyati smārayiṣyati* || *kathaṃ ca subhūte māraḥ pāpīyān vivekaguṇena bodhisattvaṃ mahāsattvam upasaṃkramya codayiṣyati smārayiṣyati* | *iha subhūte māraḥ pāpīyān bodhisattvaṃ mahāsattvam upasaṃkramiṣyati upasaṃkramyaivaṃ vakṣyati* | *vivekasya tathāgato varṇavādī araṇyavanaprasthagiriguhāśmaśānapalālapuñjādiṣu viharttavyam iti* | *na cāhaṃ subhūte bodhisattvasya mahāsattvasya evaṃvidhaṃ vivekaṃ vadāmi, yad utāraṇyakāni prāntāni śayanāsanāni vijanapadāni viviktāni vividhāni vanaprasthagiriguhāśmaśānapalālapuñjādīni* || *subhūtir āha* | *katamaḥ punaḥ sa bhagavan bodhisattvasya mahāsattvasyānyo viveko yadi vā 'raṇyakāni prāntāni śayanāsanāni vijanapadāni viviktāni vividhāni vanaprasthagiriguhāśmaśānapalālapuñjādīni yadi tāni nādhyāvasati kiyad rūpaḥ punar bhagavan bodhisattvasya mahāsattvasyānyo vivekaḥ* || *evam ukte bhagavān āyuṣmantaṃ subhūtim etad avocat* | *sa cet subhūte bodhisattvo mahāsattvo vivikto bhavati śrāvakapratisaṃyuktair manasikārair vivikto bhavati pratyekabuddhapratisaṃyuktair manasikārair evaṃ sa bodhisattvo mahāsattvo vivikto viharati* | (Mitra 1888: 391)
>
> Furthermore, Mara the Evil One may come to the Bodhisattva and exhort and inform him in connection with the quality of detachment that the Tathagata has praised detachment, and that that means that one should dwell in a remote forest, in a jungle, in mountain clefts, burial grounds, or on heaps of straw, etc. But that is not what I teach as the detachment of a Bodhisattva, that he should live in a forest, remote, lonely and isolated, or in a jungle, mountain clefts, burial grounds, on heaps of straw, etc. Subhuti: If that is not the detachment of the Bodhisattva, what then is it? The Lord: A Bodhisattva dwells detached when he becomes detached from the mental activities associated with the Disciples and Pratyekabuddhas. (Conze 1975: 233)

11r31–33 *-sa* or *sa*. In the entire paragraph the interpretation of *sa* either as a gen. sg. ending or as a personal pronoun is a matter of uncertainty. Tentatively, (almost) all occurrences have been interpreted as a gen. sg. ending, whether in the meaning of "for" (11r31 *pridi budhesa*

[= *budhasa*] *upajea*, "joy would arise for an awakened one [i.e., in the mind of a Buddha]," or 11r33 *vivegagadasa upajea*, "would arise for someone who has gone into solitude"), or in the meaning of "if / in case," perhaps as a kind of genitive absolute, although without an antecedent (11r32 *pridi paribhutasa upajea*, "joy would arise out of something that is enjoyed" in the sense of "in case something is enjoyed," etc.). In my understanding, the message is that this joy, which is removed in the meditation practice of *pravrajita*s (as a synonym of *śrāvaka*s?), arises for a fully awakened one who realizes emptiness and is free from conceptual thinking (*aprajñapti*). In such a state of mind the experience of joy can arise, since it is not the same joy as for an ordinary being and there is no attachment to it.

11r34 *jibha pramuha chidita*. G *pramuha* has been translated as "first" (adv., Skt. *pramukham*). In view of the presumed hell-description context, however, it could also mean that the tongue has been removed from the mouth (Skt. *pramukhāt*), as is described in the commentary on the *Saṃkiccajātaka* (see below 11r35 *caduragu̱diehi*). This, however, seems unlikely, since we would expect the spelling *pramuhado* or ◦*de*.

As for *chidita* as well as the following *u̱sata* and *piṣita*, it is not clear if the forms are past participles (irregularly with the ending -*ta* and not -*da*), or if they are absolutives. I have translated them as absolutives and in a passive sense based on the context.

11r34 *tulie u̱sata ya*. The *ya* is written in two separate parts, thus it could also be two letters (*a* and *ṇa*/*da*) written very small. In the case of *ya* = *ca*, the syntactical position would be odd, but I have no other explanation. G *tulie* (loc. sg.?) should correspond to Skt. *tulā*, "balance," or more basically a "beam" or "pole" for lifting something (cf. PTSD). G *u̱sata* then could mean "hanging from a beam" (*ava*√*śr̥̄*, cf. CDIAL s.v. *avaśrayati*) or "being fixed on a pole" (cf. MV s.v. √*śri*). Or it could refer to something being "raised" (*ud* √*śr̥̄*, BHS rarely *utsr̥ta*, next to *ucchr̥ta*, for Skt. *ucchrita*) onto a balance in order to be weighed, as is often seen in hell depictions, or it means being "lifted up onto" or "impaled on" a stake, as in the description of criminals who are tortured in the *Ambasakkarapetavatthu* of the *Petavatthu* (Pv 45–57, *sūle āropeti*).[117] While the Pali term is *sūle*, in BC 11 it is clearly written with a *t* at the beginning, i.e., *tulie*, but it nevertheless might mean the same. In general, this is reminiscent of hell tortures as described, for example, in the *Kokālikasutta* of the *Suttanipāta*:

> *ayosaṃkusamāhataṭṭhānaṃ, tiṇhadhāraṃ ayasūlam upeti*
> *atha tattaayoguḷasannibhaṃ, bhojanam atthi tathā patirūpaṃ* (Sn 667)
>
> He goes to the place of impaling upon iron spikes, to the iron stake with its sharp blade. Then there is food like a ball of heated iron, thus appropriate. (Norman 1992a: 77)

Even though the exact wording is not entirely certain, this short passage refers to descriptions of hell, in which one has to spend as much time as is needed in order that all "evil action has exhausted its result." This is stated for example in the *Devadūtasutta* (MN III 178–87) and in

117 See also *sūle uttāseti*, "impale on a spike" (AN I 48; Jā I 326; Jā II 443; Jā IV 29).

the *Suhṛllekha* attributed to Nāgārjuna (verses 77–82), in which various painful situations in hell are described, demonstrating that one is reborn as a consequence of one's own ill-conduct and evil deeds.

11r35 *caduraguḏiehi*. The exact meaning of this word is open to discussion. At first sight, it could be an instrumental plural of *caturaṅgulika*, "four fingers long/broad" (i.e., four inches). Cf. Anav^{L} 21 *caduraghulu* = Skt. *caturaṅgulam*, "four fingers long" (Salomon 2008a: 429), referring to soft hair on the soles of the feet. The immediate context in BC 11 is not clear, but also in the *Suvikrāntavikrāmiparipṛcchā* a similar term is mentioned apparently quite out of context: "Just as in space no one has ever seen the full reality of (an object) five fingers broad, just so no one has ever seen the own-being of the full reality of the perfection of wisdom" (Conze 1973b: 46).[118] Thus the word might simply refer to any object that can be measured in such dimensions (that is, what is graspable with the hand). The length/width of four fingers could also refer to the cloth with which the sexual organ of a naked monk should be covered, while he is "repeatedly [sustaining] these and other various painful feelings" as described in the *Ācārāṅgasūtra* of the Jainas, a scripture describing "the progress of the faithful towards the highest perfection" (Jacobi 1884: xlviii).[119] Although the context does indeed fit the word, the plural of *caturaṅgulika* presents a problem; it is still open to question which noun it classifies.

Perhaps, *caturaṅgulika* also stands in relation to the immeasurably long time during which one experiences suffering. A similar formulation to express the same notion is for example used in the *Saṃyuttanikāya* (SN II 178). Here, a man cuts down all the trees, branches, etc. in Jambudvīpa, piles them, works them into four-inch square pieces (*caturaṅgulaṃ ghaṭikaṃ*) and counts them (cf. Lamotte 1944–80, IV: 2099–100).

As yet another possibility, especially in relation to the descriptions of hell previously mentioned, the term might be equivalent to Skt. *caturguḍaka*, "four [hot iron] balls." Related spellings for *guḏie* = Skt. *guḍaka* are P *guḷa* ("ball," cf. P *ayoguḷa* / Skt. *ayoguḍa*, "[hot] iron ball"), P *guḷikā* ("little ball"), and Skt. *guṭikā* ("small ball, pill"). The phonetic development would present no problems at all. However, there is normally no direct statement of it being four balls in particular. But since the preceding word, which probably also stands in connection with *caduraguḏie*, is incomplete, nothing definite can be said.

---

118 Hikata (1958: 46): *tadyathāpi nāma Śāradvatīputrākāśe na jātu kenacit pañcāṅguliparinịṣpattir dṛṣṭapūrvā, evam eva Śāradvatīputra na jātu kenacit prajñāpāramitāparinịṣpattisvabhāvo dṛṣṭapūrvaḥ.*

119 Cf. Jacobi 1884: 73 (footnotes given in square brackets and according to current transliteration conventions): "(5) Seventh Lesson: To a naked [n.: *acela*] monk the thought occurs: I can bear the pricking of grass, the influence of cold and heat, the stinging of flies and mosquitos; these and other various painful feelings I can sustain, but I cannot leave off the covering of the privities. Then he may cover his privities with a piece of cloth [n.: This is the *kaṭibandhana* or *colapaṭṭaka*; it should be four fingers broad and one *hasta* long]. A naked monk who perseveres in this conduct, sustains repeatedly these and other various painful feelings: the grass pricks him, heat and cold attack him, flies and mosquitos sting him. A naked monk (should be) aspiring to freedom from bonds. Penance suits him. Knowing what the Revered One has declared, one should thoroughly and in all respects conform to it."

Hot iron balls often occur in hell descriptions.[120] One is found in the *Saṃkiccajātaka*:

> *tattaṃ pakaṭṭhitaṃ* [B^e^ *pakkuthitam*] *ayoguḷañ ca*
> *dīghe ca phāle cirarattatāpite*
> *vikkhambham ādāya vibhajja rajjuhi* [B^e^ *rajjubhi*]
> *vatte* [B^e^ *vivaṭe*] *mukhe saṃsavayanti* [B^e^ *sampavisanti*] *rakkhasā.* (Jā V 268)

> The red-hot iron ball being cooked,
> when an iron-rod has been heated for a long time,
> taking the prop and binding it with a rope [to prop open the mouth],
> the Rakkhasas drop the [the ball] into the open mouth. (Marino 2017: 78)

The function of the iron ball is explained further in the commentary:

> *tattaṃ pakkaṭṭhitam* [B^e^ *pakkuthitam*] *ayoguḷañ cā 'ti puna pakkaṭṭhitagūthakalalañ* [B^e^ *pakkuthitaṃ gūthakalalañ*] *c'eva jalitaayoguḷañ ca khādāpenti, so pana taṃ āhariyamānaṃ disvā mukhaṃ pidheti, ath'assa dīghe ciratāpite jalamāne phāle ādāya mukhaṃ vikkhambhetvā vivaritvā rajjubaddhaṃ ayabalisaṃ khipitvā jivhaṃ nīharitvā tasmiṃ vatte vivaṭṭe* [B^e^ *vivaṭe*] *mukhe taṃ ayoguḷaṃ saṃsavayanti* [B^e^ *sampavisanti*] *pakkhipanti, rakkhasā ti nirayapālā.* (Jā V 273–274)

> "Heated, boiled iron ball": Now [the demons] make [the person] eat boiled excrement and a hot iron ball. The person, seeing [the demon] bringing [the heated items], shuts tight his mouth. Then, taking up an iron ploughshare that had been heated for a long time, [the demons] prop open [the person's] mouth, drop in an iron fishhook attached to a rope, pull out the tongue, and shove the iron ball into the open mouth. "Rakkhasā-s" [refers to] guardians of hell. (Marino 2017: 78)

Also in BC 11 *caduraguḏiehi … acida* could refer to being filled with hot iron balls, especially since near the beginning of the paragraph (11r34) *jibha pramuha chidita* might describe the tongue being pulled out and—in a second and more drastic step—even being cut off, after which one would be impaled on a stake (G *tulie uṣ̄ata*) while the intestines are crushed (G *atra piṣita*). A similar description serves as the background for a passage in the *Anguttaranikāya*:

> *taṃ kiṃ maññatha bhikkhave, katamaṃ nu kho varaṃ: yaṃ balavā puriso tattena ayosaṅkunā ādittena sampajjalitena sajotibhūtena mukhaṃ vivaritvā tattaṃ lohagulaṃ ādittaṃ sampajjalitaṃ sajotibhūtaṃ mukhe pakkhipeyya, taṃ tassa oṭṭham pi daheyya mukham pi daheyya jivham pi daheyya kaṇṭham pi daheyya udaram pi daheyya antam pi antaguṇam pi ādāya adhobhāgā nikkhameyya, yaṃ vā khattiyamahāsālānaṃ vā brāhmaṇamahāsālānaṃ vā gahapatimahāsālānaṃ vā saddhādeyyaṃ piṇḍapātaṃ paribhuñjeyyā ti?* (AN IV 131–32)

[120] For the simile of a red-hot iron ball in hell descriptions, cf. Marino 2017: 75–82. See there for different readings of the following citations, as well as for more references to other descriptions.

> What do you think, Bhikkhus? Which is better, for a strong man to force open one's mouth with a hot iron spike—burning, blazing, and glowing—and insert a hot copper ball—burning, blazing, and glowing—which burns one's lips, mouth, tongue, throat, and stomach, and comes out from below taking along one's entrails, or for one to consume almsfood given out of faith by affluent khattiyas, brahmins, or householders? (Bodhi 2012: 1092)

11r35 *acida*. Apparently first written *va*, the initial letter was corrected to *a* resulting in *acida*, which most probably corresponds to Skt./P *ācita* (pp. of *ā* √*ci*), "accumulated," with instr. "loaded, covered, filled with." Since the beginning of the sentence is missing, the syntax is not clear, and thus it could either describe a state of "being covered or filled with something that is four fingers long" or "being filled with four [hot iron] balls" (see previous annotations on 11r35 *caduragu̱diehi*) or "having accumulated [something] for innumerable eons."

11r37 *khaveati* is most probably derived from √*kṣip* (BHS *kṣepayati*, P *khepeti*; cf. Baums 2009: 237) in the meaning "to spend time" → "would spend innumerable *kalpa*s in misery (*daurgatya*)." In this, it would be very close to a statement in Anav[L] 53 *ṇiraghehi kṣeviṣu ciru* / 74 *ṇiraghehi kṣeviṣu ciro*, "I spent a long time in hells" (Salomon 2008a: 181, 184, annotations 264). This is paralleled in the *Divyāvadāna* (Cowell and Neil 1886: 367): *narakavedanīyāni karmāṇi kṣepayitvā*, "having spent (exhausted) their deeds that had to be suffered-for in hells" (BHSD s.v. *kṣepayati*). Similarly, in BC 11 *khaveati* (possibly to be emended to *kh⟨*e⟩veati*) would indicate that one spends a long time under miserable conditions due to bad karma.

11r38 *ṇa bhio* / 11r39 *ṇa bhi⟨*o⟩* / 11r40 *ṇa bhiu* = Skt. *na bhūyaḥ* / P *na bhiyyo*, "not at all, no more." In BC 4 this is written *bhuyo*. In the Niya documents it occurs as *bhuya*, *bhui*, *buo* (Burrow 1937: § 91). Since as so far known, nowhere else is this written only as *bhi*, it has been reconstructed to *bhi⟨*o⟩* in 11r39.

11r38 *amaho* / 11r39 *amahu*. The form suggests a dative (Skt. *asmabhyam*), but it is used as genitive plural; also in Pali both the dative and genitive plural are *amhākaṃ* / *asmākaṃ* / *amhaṃ*. The Gāndhārī form *amaho* / *amahu* occurs only in the Niya documents, *amahu* being more frequent; cf. Burrow 1937: § 78, where it is likewise applied as genitive plural.

11r38–39 *ṣade*. Cf. annotations on 4v12 *ṣadasa*, p. 193.

11r40 *amitrahoḏeapoṣ̱aṇam iva*. The current translation "like the not nourishing on what is stolen from enemies" is based on the following considerations: *apoṣ̱aṇa* might be synonymous with *aparibhuta* = Skt. *aparibhukta*, thus *apoṣ̱aṇa* as the negation of Skt. *poṣaṇa* / P *posana*, "nourishing, feeding, support," is reasonable.

G *hoḏe* corresponds to Skt. *hoḍha*, "stolen [goods]." Cf. also MW s.v. *hoḍṛ*: "(?) m. a robber, highway-robber," MW s.v. *ūḍha*, "stolen," and PTSD s.v. *oḍḍha*: "[better spelling *oḍha*, pp. of *ā* + *vah*] carried away, appropriated," apparently only in the compound *sahoḍha*: Vism 180 / Vism[W] 147 *sahoḍḍhaṃ coraṃ*, "thief with the goods" (Vism[W] with the note "C *sabhaṇḍaṃ*; Sanskrit *sahoḍhaṃ*"); cf. MW *sahoḍha*, "one who has the stolen property with him."

G *amitra* is Skt. *amitra*, probably as a synonym of *ari*, which again is a synonym of *kleśa*. Thus, in a metaphorical sense, this phrase expresses that just as one should not support/feed oneself by something stolen from enemies, so also one does not produce joy or pleasure by *kleśa*s (that is, various kinds of passion or lust causing clinging to existence), since they do not belong to oneself, are impermanent, and ultimately cause suffering.

11r40–41 *vayaeṇa* … *avayedeṇa*. Based on the preceding contrastive pairs *labheṇa – alabheṇa* and *par⟨*i⟩bhuteṇa – aparibhuteṇa*, these two words should be antonyms. Most probably they refer to Skt. *vyayaka*, "making payments, spending,"[121] or Skt. *vyayita*, "spent" (then to be read as G *vay⟨*i⟩eṇa*) and Skt. *avyayita*, "not spent." This fits well with the aforementioned terms *lambha*, "obtaining," and *paribhukta*, "enjoyed, used, employed."

If *avayedeṇa* = Skt. *avyayitena* is correct, it might be better transliterated as *avayideṇa*, that is, with *yi* instead of *ye*. On the scan of the manuscript a little chip covers the letter, making it hard to tell if the vowel marker crossed the consonant sign or not. In any case it seems that the scribe did not write the left arm of the *y*-. Also in the next letter transliterated as *de*, it seems to be corrected either from *e* or perhaps also the other way around, from *de* to *e*, which would make it the same spelling as in the preceding term *vayaeṇa* or *vay⟨*i⟩eṇa*.

11r42 *vidimiśa* = Skt. *vyatimiśra* / P *vītimissa*, "mixed with, intermingled with, tainted by"; cf. a passage in the *Dharmasamuccaya* (5.171–72, Lin 1946: 248–499):

> *duḥkhamiśraṃ sukham idaṃ pracchannam eva vidyate* |
> *padmamālāparicchinno viṣapūrṇo yathoragaḥ* ||
> *odanaṃ viṣasaṃmiśraṃ maraṇāntāya tad yathā* |
> *tathā saukhyam idaṃ sarvaṃ narakāntaṃ bhaviṣyati* ||
>
> This happiness is mixed with suffering, well hidden,
> like a serpent full of poison wrapped in a lotus garland.
> Just like rice mixed with poison ends in death,
> so all this comfort will end in hell.

In BC 4, the two main categories are mental happiness, indicated by *viñatidukhavidimiśasuhe*, and physical happiness, indicated by *dukhavidimiśasu(*he)*. Both are unpleasant and ineffectual.

11r47 -*amoyaṇakṣaya*-. G *amoyaṇa* can correspond to Skt. *amocana*, "not losing or letting go," or to Skt. *āmocana*, "undressing, letting go," or, quite contrary, "putting on [a garment or ornament]." In the sequence with *cīvara* ("robe") and *kāya* ("body"), "undressing" or "putting on" makes sense, combining the previous two terms. Since "putting on" is the more common meaning of *āmocana*, this has been chosen.

---

121 Cf. P *vyaya* [*vi+aya*] or *vaya* [*vi+i*], "expense, loss," or also *veyyāyika*, "(nt.) [fr. *vyaya*] money to defray expenses, means" (PTSD).

11r47 ***atvahisaparahisasarvasatvahisa-*** with *hisa* = Skt. *hiṃsā* / P *hiṃsā*, "violence, harm." I have not found this triad in combination with *hiṃsā*, but *parahiṃsā* or *sattvahiṃsā* occur for instance in hell descriptions, thus they fit the preceding *śidaüṣadharaṇadukha* (Skt. *śītoṣṇa-dhāraṇaduḥkha*), which may refer to the suffering experienced specifically in cold and hot hells. In its syntactical composition, the phrase is parallel, but in a contrasting sense, to 4r22 *atvahida ca parahida ca sarvasatvahida*.

11r48 ***kamasuha***. The letters in *kamasuhehi ṇa karya* could also be separated as *kamasuhe hi ṇa karya*, then agreeing with the following *vivegaveragrasuhe ṇa karye*. Both words have been transliterated or reconstructed as instrumentals because of other occurrences of the phrase *ṇa karye* that are combined with an instrumental sg. or pl. (see p. 196).[122]

Skt./P *kāmasukha* is the happiness of sensual pleasures. In contrast to the supreme bliss gained through meditation, it is impure and mediocre.[123] Happiness of sensual pleasures is also called worldly or material happiness (P *āmisasukha*), as opposed to mental or spiritual happiness that is free from sensual desires (P *nirāmisasukha*; see Kalupahana 1992: 95).

The *guṇa* in the following 11r48 *avaramiṇaguṇavidimiśa* may refer to the qualities or attributes of anything created (see MW s.v. *guṇa*). Through these qualities, such as shape or sound, objects are perceived by means of the five senses. It is based on this that desire can develop. In Buddhist texts, *guṇa* is regularly found in the compound *(pañca)kāmaguṇā*, "the (five) strands of sensual pleasure" or "the (five) objects of sensual pleasure," namely form, sound, smell, taste, and touch (see, for example, CPD s.v. *kāmaguṇa*).[124] The *kāmaguṇā* are the "pretty things in the world" (P *citrāni loke*), with *kāma* being the desire for them by way of intention (P *saṅkapparāgo*; both AN III 411). In BC 11, the qualities are referred to as immeasurable, so it is uncertain if exactly the five strands of sensual pleasures are meant, or more generally the various qualities of the objects of sensual pleasure. The statement is the same, in that the happiness of detachment and dispassion is of no use when mixed with sense perception (11r48–49 *avaramiṇaguṇavidimiśa vivegaveragrasuhe⟨*ṇa⟩ ṇa karye*).

11r48–49 ***vivegasuha***. Detachment or seclusion (Skt. *viveka*) can be related to the body (*kāya-viveka*) as well as to the mind (*cittaviveka*). Bodily seclusion means that the monk or practitioner is alone in a forest, on a mountain, in a cave, etc. Mental seclusion is developed by meditation. In 11r48–49, *vivegasuha* (Skt. *vivekasukha*) is juxtaposed with *veragrasuha* (BHS *virāgasukha*). Thus, *viveka* could refer to bodily seclusion and *virāga* to mental seclusion. In 11r20, *vivegasuha* is followed by *asagaṇiasuha* ("happiness of being without company"), and thus possibly also here, what is meant is not mental but bodily seclusion. Generally, however,

---

122 In Schlosser 2016, *kamasuhe* was part of the last sentence of the preceding paragraph, and *-hi ṇa karya* was read as *hiṇakaya-*, "of the wretched body." The current reconstruction seems more likely, since the letters in question resemble *karya* rather than *kaya* and the first two sentences of the paragraph now have a parallel syntactical construction, with both ending in *ṇa karya* / *ṇa karye*.

123 See, for example, MPPŚ IV 1966–67; or also MPPŚ I 443 and II 711, 1021, 1044.

124 SWTF s.v. *kāmaguṇa*: "(fünf) Eigenschaft(en der Dinge), auf welche sich die Begierde richtet; (fünf) Gegenstände sinnlicher Freuden; (fünf) Sinnesobjekt(e)."

in BC 11 mental seclusion is being referred to, although this may imply physical seclusion for meditation (cf. annotations on 11r33 *vivegagadasa*, p. 214).

11r48–49 *veragrasuha*. BHS *virāga*[125] / P *virāga*, "absence of (worldly) desire or passion, renouncement of desire" (Skorupski 2002), "without attachment" (Dessein 2009: 50). In the *Buddhacarita* (12.48) this absence of desire (*vairāgya*, also *virāga*) is praised as the highest happiness (*paraṃ śivaṃ*). It is a synonym of *nirāmiṣaṃ sukhaṃ*, "detached/disinterested happiness, free from sense-pleasures, as opposite to physical pleasure" (Anderson 2001: 38 referring to the *Pañcattayasutta*, MN II 228–38).

11r51–52 *daṇe atogade avi amiṣadaṇe avi dharmadaṇe atogade*. The *amiṣadaṇa* (Skt. *āmiṣa-* / P *āmisadāna*) comprises material resources, the *dharmadaṇa* (Skt. *dharma-* / P *dhammadāna*) religious and spiritual teachings, of which the *dharmadaṇa* is superior.[126] Cf., for example, a passage in the *Aṅguttaranikāya*:

> *dvemāni, bhikkhave, dānāni. katamāni dve? āmisadānañ ca dhammadānañ ca. imāni kho, bhikkhave, dve dānāni. etadaggaṃ, bhikkhave, imesaṃ dvinnaṃ dānānaṃ yad idaṃ dhammadānan ti.* (AN I 91)
>
> Bhikkhus, there are these two kinds of gifts. What two? The gift of material goods and the gift of the Dhamma. These are the two kinds of gifts. Of these two kinds of gifts, the gift of the Dhamma is foremost. (Bodhi 2012: 182)

According to Findly (2003: 195),[127] P *dhammadāna* is an action of "renunciants," P *āmisadāna* an action of "non-renunciants." The *āmisadāna* is in general the giving of food or clothes from lay followers to monks. In contrast, the *dhammadāna* is the giving of teachings by monks to lay followers. Ideally, the lay follower gives out of pure generosity and the monk teaches out of pure compassion (*anukampā*). In reality, obtaining merit (*puṇya*) by giving was certainly an issue, since teachings would have also taken place in return for material support.

A passage in the *Larger Prajñāpāramitā* from Gilgit (fol. 278b, Conze 1974: 42 ff., tr. Conze 1974: 170–71) lists *dāna* as one of "four means of conversion" by which a bodhisattva helps

---

125 In Sanskrit, also *vairāga* or *vairāgya* is possible, but *vairāgya* should be written as *veraga* in Gāndhārī, with a non-modified *g* open to the left (cf. BC 4 *aroga* = Skt. *ārogya*). Other spellings in BC 4 and BC 11 are: 4r9 *viragraaṇuśaśe*, 11r48–49 *vivegaveragrasuhe*, 11r49 and 11r50 *veragrasuhami*, 11r5 and 11r32 *suverao*. Especially the last shows that the *e*-vowel is combined with a single *g* (in this case not written). Even though it is more often written with *ve-* (Skt. *vai-*) instead of *vi-*, I have decided to understand all occurrences as Skt. *virāga* as based on the spelling in Pali.

126 An early commentary partially preserved in MS 2373/1/1 of the Schøyen Collection (palm leaf, Sanskrit, Kuṣāṇa Brāhmī, ca. second century CE) also deals with the concepts of "material gift" (*āmiṣadāna*) and "gift of doctrine" (*dharmadāna*); see Schmithausen 2002: 249–52.

127 For *āmisadāna*, see Findly 2013: 195–96 and 259; for *dhammadāna*, see Findly 2013: 59, 113, 142, 184–85 (referring to AN IV 364), 195, 361, 389.

other beings.[128] The category of *dāna* is again divided into *āmiṣa-* and *dharma-*. The *āmiṣadāna* is the giving of material things like gold, silver, or elephants; the *dharmadāna* is subdivided into *laukika-* (worldly Dharma) and *lokottara-* (supramundane Dharma).[129]

A threefold division is given for example in the *Cariyāpiṭakaṭṭhakathā* in a section about the instruction on the practice of the *pāramī*s:

> *dānapāramiyā tāva sukhūpakaraṇasarīrajīvitapariccāgena bhayāpanudanena dhammopadesena ca bahudhā sattānaṃ anuggahakaraṇaṃ paṭipatti. tattha āmisadānaṃ abhayadānaṃ dhammadānan ti dātabbavatthuvasena* [PTS: *dānabba°*] *tividhaṃ dānaṃ. tesu bodhisattassa dātabbavatthu ajjhattikaṃ bāhiran ti duvidhaṃ.* (Cp-a 303)
>
> The perfection of giving, firstly, is to be practiced by benefiting beings in many ways—by relinquishing one's own happiness, belongings, body, and life to others, by dispelling their fear, and by instructing them in the Dhamma. Herein, giving is threefold by way of the object to be given: the giving of material things (*āmisadāna*), the giving of fearlessness (*abhayadāna*), and the giving of the Dhamma (*dhammadāna*). Among these, the object to be given can be twofold: internal and external.[130] (Bodhi 1996: 26)

The same triad of *dāna* is documented in a commentary on the *Vajracchedikāsūtra* of Master Fu (497–569): *āmiṣa*, *dharma*, and *abhaya* ("wealth alms, dharma alms, fearless mind alms," Yakup 2010: 125). At the time of the writing of BC 11 apparently only the division into two categories was known.

The reason why *dāna* is subdivided into *āmiṣa-* and *dharmadāna* in the Gāndhārī text seems to be that the author is in need of an argument for *kāmasukha* to be included together with *viveka-* and *virāgasukha*, hence part of the practice recommended in this manuscript. Since this method is based on the *pāramitā*s, he lists three of them ending with *dāna*, which also pertains to the world of senses in the giving of material gifts. This thus gives rise to *kāmasukha.*

---

128 These are: gifts (*dāna*), kind words (*priyavadyatā*), actions for other's benefit (*arthacaryā*), concistency between words and deeds (*samānārthatā*).

129 (I) *kathaṃ ca subhūte bodhisattvo mahāsattva dānena sattvān saṃgṛhṇāti? iha subhūte bodhisattvo mahāsattvo dvābhyāṃ dānābhyāṃ sattvān saṃgṛhṇāti. katamābhyāṃ dvābhyāṃ? yad uta* (Ia) *āmiṣadānena ca* (Ib) *dharmadānena ca.* (Ia) *kathaṃ ca subhūte bodhisattvo mahāsattvaḥ āmiṣadānena sattvān saṃgṛhṇāti?* [. . .] (Ib) *kathaṃ ca subhūte bodhisattvo mahāsattvaḥ prajñāpāramitāyāṃ caran sattvān dharmadānena anugṛhṇāti? dve ime subhūte dharmadāne* (Iba) *laukikaṃ ca* (Ibb) *lokottaraṃ ca* [. . .], "And how does the Bodhisattva help beings with gifts? He helps them with two kinds of gifts, i.e., material gifts and the gift of Dharma. And how does he help beings with material gifts? [. . .] And how does the Bodhisattva who courses in perfect wisdom help beings with the gift of Dharma? There are two kinds of the gift of Dharma—the worldly and the supramundane. [. . .]." Cf. Conze 1975: 198–99. Regarding *dāna* as part of the perfections, cf. Findly 2003: 185 or Amore 1971: 94. Regarding *dharmadāna*, cf. Skorupski 2002: 8 (and *passim*).

130 For more details on the method of practicing the perfection of giving, see Bodhi 1996 or 1978.

11r53 ***sayavisa śali sarvarthae śali vuto avi palale atogade yavasa tuṣ̄e atogade*.** This simile is given to illustrate that *kāmasukha* is inevitably included in all kinds of *sukha*, as long as one abides on earth in human form. In it, *śāli* may denote every kind of happiness, while the kernel or essence of a grain may point to *viveka-* and *virāgasukha* and the husk, on the other hand, to *kāmasukha*.[131] In order to reach the kernel of the grain, we have to remove the husk. Likewise, in order to reach inner bliss, we have to remove the pleasure acquired by senses. Thus, sensual pleasure might be considered a necessary evil, for, just as one cannot hold water without a vessel, so too the Buddha's doctrine relies on a form. That is, to transport the message of the Buddha in this life, one has to deal with the medium of a human sensory body and mind.

Another fascinating aspects of this simile is the fact that by removing the husk, the corn is no longer able to sprout. Thus, if you separate yourself from the husk of *kāmasukha*, it will no longer spring forth and there will be no more rebirth. Cf. Frauwallner 1973: 332–33:[132]

> As long as these taints (*kleśāḥ*) are present, the actions (*karmāṇi*) are able to bring about fruit. Their relation is like that of a rice-corn which, as long as it carries husks, is able to put forth sprouts, but no longer when the husks are removed.

This simile is given and explained in Vyāsa's commentary on Patañjali's *Yogasūtra* 2.13 (see Bryant 2009: 198–202). In general, the commentary on this and the following verses of the *Yogasūtra* refers largely to the same issue being discussed in BC 11, namely, that the happiness based on sense-experience is only temporary and ultimately causes suffering (see Bryant 2009: 202–12). The same statement is made in the *Abhidharmakośabhāṣya* (Abhidh-k-bh III 36–37), where it "is explained that defilement is like a seed, a Nāga, a root, a tree, a husk of grain [...] Grain, even though intact, does not germinate when it is stripped of its husk. [...] Action is like grain with its husk" (Pruden 1988–1990, II: 437–38). Also in a Central Asian manuscript, a husk (*tuṣa*) is equated with defilements (*kleśa*), while *karma* is equated with a corn of rice (*taṇḍula*): SHT VIII 1840 *tuṣasthānīyaḥ kleśaḥ taṇḍulasthānīyaṃ karma*. A similar comparison can be found in the *Aṅguttaranikāya* (AN I 242), where a monk abandons all taints and thus attains or is established in the core (i.e., the core of *sīla*, or of *sīla*, *samādhi*, and *paññā*, according to the commentary of Buddhaghosa), just like a farmer, who, having cut his [rice] plants (*sāli*), removes the straw (*palāla*) and chaff (*bhusika*) and winnows it. Then he pounds it and removes the husk (*thusa*), thus reaching the pure core (*sāra*).

In BC 11, *yavasa* could perhaps also be transliterated as *yavaṣ̄a* or even *yavaṯa*, since a small part of the Kharoṣṭhī sign is broken off, leaving several options. One would be that it corresponds to BHS/P *yāvatā*, "up to, as far as," but normally this develops into G *yavada* or *yavaḏe*. In 11r8 it is written *yavade*, which makes a different spelling rather unlikely.

For a further discussion of this simile, see Schlosser 2018.

11v1 ***matupayeaṣ̄i*.** Although the characters are quite clear and legible, leaving not many choices, it is not clear what is meant. The most obvious translation of *matu* as Skt. *mātṛ*, "mother,"

[131] For the association of the husk being impure, cf., e.g., Vism 346 / Vism[W] 289–90, or DN III 199.

[132] Thanks to Elisabeth Steinbrückner for pointing this passage out to me.

makes no sense to me here. Another possibility might be to understand *matu* = Skt. *mātṛ* as "a knower, one who has true knowledge" (MW s.v. ¹*mātṛ*), but this use is rather rare. Since relying or even being attached to *matu*, the happiness of joy (Skt. *prītisukha*) would arise, the whole compound could refer to some kind of *samādhi* or exposition—if the following translation of G *olaïa* as "attached" is correct at all.

11v1 *olaïa* / 11v12 *olaïa*. Most probably this is a derivation from Skt. *avalagati* / P *olaggati* as a past participle (Skt. **avalagita* for *avalagna* / P *olagga*), "fastened/attached to (something)." CDIAL lists the Prakrit forms *olagga*, "attached to" (s.v. *avalagna*), as well as *olaïa*, "touching" (s.v. *avalagati*). For another similar Prakrit form, *olaggio* = P *olaggiya*, see Haribhadra's *Dhuttakkhāṇa*, verse 4.72.[133] Cf. also DP s.v. *olaggeti* for references where *olaggita* is apparently synonymous with *olambita* (or likewise *olaggetvā* = *olambitvā*), "attached, clinging to (something)" or also "depending upon." Thus, perhaps G *olaïa* might also be a synonym of P *olambaka* as a derivation from *olamba* + suffix *ka* (cf. CPD s.v. *olambaka*) or *olambika* as a derivation from *olambi(n)* + suffix *ka* (cf. DP s.v. *olambika*), "hanging down from, clinging to" or ultimately "depending on" something.

11v1 *pridisuhe*. Skt. *prītisukha* is the happiness or bliss of experiencing joy during the first and especially the second *dhyāna*.[134] It arises having left behind the sensual pleasures (*kāmasukha*) produced by the five sensual strands (*pañca kāmaguṇāḥ*) while entering the first stage (cf. Choong 2000: 123). In other words, *prīti* is a first indication of *sukha* born from meditation (*samādhija*) and gained through detachment/seclusion (*viveka*) and the perfection of concentration. The difference between *prīti* and *sukha* is that *prīti* is a mental state (P *cetasika*) belonging to the group of mental factors (P *saṅkhārakkhandha*), while *sukha* belongs to feelings (P *vedanākkhandha*). For the difference between *prīti* / P *pīti* and *sukha*, see, for example, the definition in the *Visuddhimagga*:[135]

> *sati pi ca nesaṃ (pītisukhānaṃ)*[136] *katthaci avippayoge, iṭṭhārammaṇapaṭilābhatuṭṭhi pīti, paṭiladdharasānubhavanaṃ*[137] *sukhaṃ. yattha pīti, tattha sukhaṃ. yattha sukhaṃ, tattha na niyamato pīti. saṅkhārakkhandhasaṅgahitā pīti, vedanākkhandhasaṅgahitaṃ sukhaṃ. kantārakhinnassa vanantodakadassanasavaṇesu viya pīti, vanacchāyappavesana-udakaparibhogesu viya sukhaṃ.* (Vism 145 / Vism^{W} 117)

---

133 Krümpelmann (2000: 162–63): *olaggio ya Garuḍo samamṃtao deva-saya-sahassehiṃ | pariveḍhio ya bhaṇio amay'āhārī hao si tti* with the note: "Zu *olaggiya* vgl. (im PED) Pāli: *olaggeti* – to make stick to, to put on, hold fast, restrain; vgl. auch Gujarātī: *vaḷagvuṃ* – to clasp, to embrace."

134 In Pali (here cited from MN III 4): *savitakkaṃ savicāraṃ vivekajaṃ pītisukhaṃ paṭhamajjhānaṃ* [...] *avitakkaṃ avicāraṃ samādhijaṃ pītisukhaṃ dutiyajjhānaṃ.*

135 See also: *Dhammasaṅgani* (tr. Müller 1885: 10–11 n. 3), *Atthasālinī* (tr. Maung Tin 1920–21: 153–56), and *Abhidhammatthasaṅgaha* (tr. Wijeratne and Gethin 2002: 34–35).

136 Only Vism 145 (with n. 3: "B^{hm} S^{b} *omit*").

137 Vism 145 (with n. 4: "B^{hm} *paṭiladdhassānu*∘"), Vism^{W} 117 *paṭiladdhassānubhavanaṃ*.

> And wherever the two are associated, happiness [*pīti*] is the contentedness at getting a desirable object, and bliss [*sukha*] is the actual experiencing of it when got. Where there is happiness there is bliss (pleasure); but where there is bliss there is not necessarily happiness. Happiness is included in the formations aggregate [*saṅkhāra*]; bliss is included in the feeling aggregate [*vedanā*]. If a man, exhausted in a desert, saw or heard about a pond on the edge of a wood, he would have happiness; if he went into the wood's shade and used the water, he would have bliss. (Ñāṇamoli 2011: 139, terms in square brackets added by me)

Thus, *prīti* / P *pīti* is the joy in the expectation of the fulfillment of a wish; *sukha* is the pleasure after the wish is fulfilled and a desirable object of the senses is experienced.

In some Mahāyāna texts *prītisukha* seems to be used in reference to a peculiar kind of meditation concentrating on joy and happiness. Cf. for example the *Book of Zambasta*, verse 3.103: "All the *kleśa*s of beings are completely calmed for them. Their minds are calmed. They sit in *prītisukha*-meditation alone" (*puṣṣo ni näṣo'nda satvānu klaiśa biśśä, uī' ni näṣaunde prītti-sukhu ā're samu*, Emmerick 1968: 68–69).

For 11v1 *pridisuha acala*, cf. P *acalaṃ sukhaṃ* in verse 350 of the *Therīgāthā*:

> *vantā mahesinā kāmā ye dibbā ye ca mānusā*
> *khemaṭṭhāne vimuttā te pattā te acalaṃ sukhaṃ* (Thī 157)

> Sensual pleasures, those which are divine and those which are human,
> have been rejected by the great seers.
> They (the seers) are completely released in the place of security;
> they have arrived at unshakable happiness. (Norman 1971: 36)

11v1 *ṇiliṇi.o.e*. What is preserved of the letters cannot be safely reconstructed. Most probably it is *ṇiliṇiohe*, but the meaning is unclear.

11v3 *aṇavaṭie*. Phonetically, this should correspond to Skt. *anāvartika*, attested in BHSD within the compound *anāvartikadharma* (~ P *anāvattidhamma*, "characterized by no more returning [to rebirth]"), but also written BHS *anivartika* / P *anivattika*, BHS *anivartiya* / P *anivattiya*, "not liable to turning back." In the *Peṭakopadesa* (Peṭ 193) *anāvattika* occurs in the statement *sukhaṃ āpannassa anāvattikan*, which is translated by Ñāṇamoli (1964: 262 [§ 788]) as "[t]he pleasure that one who has entered upon [the attainment of cessation of perception and feeling] has does not belong to the [actual] occasion." In this footnotes, Ñāṇamoli comments on *anāvatthika*, deriving it from *ava* √*sthā* (→ *anāvasthika*) and interpreting it as "either anticipatory or retrospective." Although the overall context is very similar to BC 11 in that it is about the experience of *sukha* in meditation without perception, P *anāvattika* should probably be understood as "not leading to rebirth," just as in BC 11, meaning that someone who no longer perceives or feels anything is not accumulating any *karma* that keeps one bound to the cycle of rebirths.

11v7 *yahi*. Cf. Burrow 1937: § 131: "*yahi* is used with the future in the sense of 'when, as.' The form is probably to be compared with the Avestan *yezi* [...] It sometimes means 'if,' being indistinguishable from *yadi* with the future." [138] An easier solution is that it corresponds to Skt. *yarhi*, "when"; cf. 6v7 *yahi* … *tahi* …, and also CDIAL s.v. *yarhi*.

11v8 *viṣa{ja}jita*. The reading of the first *j*- is quite certain, the second *j*- however could also be a *ḍ*-, this being perhaps even more likely (cf. 6v9). If the reading is *viṣajajita*, the meaning might be "having adhered to," being derived from *vi√ṣañj* → *viṣajati*, "to hang to"; *viṣajjate*, "to be attached or devoted to" (cf. MW s.v. *viṣañj*). In Pali the form is *visajjati*, "to cling to, adhere (fig.)" (PTSD s.v. *visajjati*). The Gāndhārī absolutive form in BC 11 should be *viṣajita*. The additional -*ja*- in *viṣajajita* might indicate an unusual frequentative. It could also possibly be a scribal error. This, however, is uncertain, since the *ja* is clearly written and the *i*-vowel marker may have simply been added to the already written consonant.

Another possibility is a derivation from *vi√sṛj* (caus. Skt. *visarjayati* / P *vissajjeti*) with the meaning "to reply, answer." This makes sense in the context of BC 11 in that first the wish for bodily happiness is declared (and rejected), and then in reply the wish for [mental] happiness is declared (which proves successful). Also in this case the apparently superfluous first -*ja*- would have to be elided or the entire word read as *viṣajita* for Skt. *visarjayitvā*. However, in all attestations of this root in other Kharoṣṭhī documents it is written with *s* and not with *ṣ*, having the meaning "to send." Both speak against this possibility.

If the reading is *viṣajaḍita*, it could be related to Skt. *jaḍa*, "stupid," or *ajaḍa*, "not stupid," especially in view of the preceding *amuḍa* (Skt. *amūḍha*), "unperplexed (?)," but the exact meaning in combination with *viṣa*, which might correspond to Skt. *viṣa*, "poison," is unclear. The theoretical possibility "having conquered what is born from poison" (Skt. *viṣajaṃ jitvā*) is doubtful because of the missing context, unless poison is a metaphor for the bodily happiness in the previous sentence.

11v12 *vihañadi* (Skt. *vihanyate* / P *vihaññati*), "to be frustrated or disappointed, to suffer," especially in the sense that one "exert[s] one's self in vain" (MW s.v. *vihan*).

11v13 *gaḍa* corresponds to Skt./P *gaṇḍa*, "boil," which, according to the PTSD, is frequently used in similes referring to *kāma* and *kāya*. With regard to the context, cf., for example, *Ratnāvalī* verse 2.69 (Hahn 1982: 65): "There is pleasure when a sore is scratched, but to be without sores is more pleasurable still; There are pleasures in worldly desires, but to be without desires is more pleasurable still" (Hopkins et al. 1975: 42).

11v13 *gro* is a very unusual spelling for Skt. *roga*, "disease," but confirmed by the following *aroa* for Skt. *aroga*, "freedom from disease" and the overall context of the simile.

11v15 *loieṇa* / 11v16 *aloieṇa* / 11v17 *loutareṇa*. The three categories (Skt. *laukika*, *alaukika*, *lokottara* / P *lokuttara*) correspond to the three realms of the triple world referred to in 11v14–15, i.e., *kāmadhātu*, *rūpadhātu*, *ārūpyadhātu*, and to *nirvāṇa*:

---

[138] The glyphs for *hi* and *di* could also be mixed up graphically (mirroring); cf. Falk 2012 (2007): 139, where *he* and *di* have been interchanged in an inscription on a reliquary from Buner (CKI 827).

laukika = ordinary / normal[139] = *kāma*
alaukika = extraordinary / supernormal = *rūpa*, *ārūpya*
lokottara = transcendental / supramundane (= *nirvāṇa*)

They are furthermore attributed to the different levels of consciousness gained through meditation[140] insofar as the four absorptions (*dhyāna*) are associated with the *rūpadhātu*, and the four immaterial or formless absorptions / attainments (*samāpatti*) are associated with the *ārūpyadhātu*. This meditation process produces supernormal knowledges (Skt. *abhijñā* / P *abhiñña*), of which two are named in BC 11 (cf. p. 208). All of this is implied in the mundane path (*laukikamārga*), which is co-existent with the supramundane path (*lokottaramārga*), distinguishable in that they are said to use the same methods but in different ways. According to Deleanu (2006: 20) referring to the *Śrāvakabhūmi* "[t]he yogi practising the mundane path attains a series of ever deeper and more refined states of tranquillity, but these altered states of consciousness, to use a modern term, as well as the rebirth realms which they entail are temporary and cannot lead to the final Liberation. It is only the supramundane path which is conducive to Nirvana." The difference is mainly that on the supramundane path the mind is accompanied by insight while experiencing *nirvāṇa*.[141] The practitioner concentrates likewise on the four noble truths, especially the truth of suffering in respect to all conditioned things, but under certain aspects, namely impermanence (*anityākāra*), suffering (*duḥkhākāra*), emptiness (*śūnyākāra*), and non-self (*anātmākāra*).[142] Cf. also Dessein 2009: 42 with reference to the *Samayabhedoparacanacakra* (T 49 nos. 2031, 2032, 2033) of the Bahuśrutīyas, which names three points regarding their doctrine: supramundane teachings, mundane teachings, and the five points of Mahādeva (on the status of an arhat). The supramundane teachings (*lokottaraśāsana*) lead to the "attainment of the path of emancipation," they are teachings on *anityatā*, *duḥkha*, *śūnyatā*, *anātmatā*, *śānta*, i.e., impermanence, suffering, emptiness, selflessness, peace [of *nirvāṇa*].

11v16 *pradibhave*. If this is read correctly, it could correspond to Skt. *pratibhavam*, "for this and all future births." However, the preceding words, especially *sarvasapatie*, seem to be in the gen. sg., which would indicate a parallel structure having *sarvadroacade mokṣe* on the one hand and *sarvasapatie ca driṭhadhami⟨*a⟩saparaïaṣa pradibhave* on the other, making the translation "[there is] liberation from every misery and [there is] every fortune of the present life and the next" (Schlosser 2016) unlikely. (Even though in other Gāndhārī texts the ending *-ie* can indicate a f. nom. pl., there are no such examples in the manuscripts under consideration here; cf. the chapter 6

139 The designations *laukika* and *alaukika* as ordinary and extraordinary perception are also known from the Nyāya-Vaiśeṣika epistemology (Roshan 2012). For *laukika* / *alaukika*, cf. also Bäumer and Vatsyayan 2003: 122 ff.

140 Sinha 1934: 356 with reference to the *Abhidhammatthasaṅgaha* (tr. Aung 1910: 10 and 12).

141 This is also the main difference of higher levels of absorption in Brahmanic and Buddhist meditation practice: In Buddhism the emphasis was laid on *prajñā* even after nothing is perceived; in Brahmanism the aim was to dissolve everything and be "without any mental activity at all, 'like a log of wood' " (Wynne 2007: 109 with reference to Bronkhorst 1985 and 1993 among others).

142 *Śrāvakabhūmi* (Shukla 1973: 470): *caturbhir ākārair duḥkhasatyasya lakṣaṇaṁ pratisaṁvedayate | tadyathā 'nityākāreṇa duḥkhākāreṇa śūnyākāreṇa anātmākāreṇa ca*. Cf. Deleanu 2006: 22 and 31.

on morphology, p. 100). It is unclear to me what *pradibhava* (Skt. *pratibhāva* as "counterpart"?) could mean in relation to *sarvasapati* in the genitive. Perhaps *pradi* should be reconstructed as *pr⟨*i⟩di*, thus reading *pr⟨*i⟩dibhave* ("there is the existence of joy due to every fortune").

11v16 *ku ṇa*. This as well as the following is hardly legible, but *ku ṇa* occurs again at the end of 11v20 *ku ṇa acitieṇa ///*. It could correspond to Skt. *kū* (= *kva*) / P *ku*, "how? where? when? whither? whence?," in combination with *na*, "why then … ?" As regards *ṣado paricae*, this could either be a compound *ṣadoparicae* = Skt. *śātaparityāga*, or it could be a combination of an accusative object and a verb in the optative: *ṣado paricea* = Skt. *śātaṃ parityajet*. In 11v17 it is written *ṣade* (added between the lines) *paricae*, speaking in favor of object + verb (written wrongly as *paricae* instead of *paricea*). The sentence seems to be repeated three times at the end of three consecutive paragraphs:

11v16	*ku ṇa ? ? + ?* ṣado paricae*	(*three, four or five akṣaras)
11v17	+ + + + + + *ṇ. ⟪ṣade⟫ paricae* ○	
11v20	*ku ṇa acitieṇa* + + + + + +	(more missing akṣaras following)

Possibly the sentence is an identical refrain in all cases: *ku ṇa acitieṇa ṣado paricae*. But perhaps there were also minor spelling differences, but with identical syntax. Because of this uncertainty, in all three instances I have refrained from reconstructing the phrase in its entirety.

11v16 *picu*. Presumably, this corresponds to Skt. *pretya* / P *pecca*, "after having passed on," i.e., "having died, after death," based on AMg. *pĕccā*, *piccā* = **pretyā* = *pretya* along with *pītvā* (Pischel 1900: § 587). The less-expected reflex *p-* for original *pr-* is also observed in G *picara* (Skt. *pratyarha* / P **paccaraha*), while *-u* for *-ā* in word-final position is attested in BL 1 (Anav^{L}), especially in adverbs (*kṣip[u]* = Skt. *kṣipā*, *divasu* = Skt. *divasā*, *sadu* = Skt. *sadā*, but also *abhighakṣadu* = Skt. *abhikāṅkṣatā*; cf. Salomon 2008a: 103–4). The *pretyabhāva* is the state after death, "hereafter," as opposed to this world, the *ihaloka* (cf. MW s.v. *pretya* and *pretyabhāva* and also Pischel 1900: § 361 *pĕccabhave ihabhave ya*).

11v17 *loutareṇa bhudañaṇeṇa*. In *Mahāyānasūtrālāṃkāra* verse 19.48, the *bhūtajñāna* is said to be fourfold: *sarvasyānupalambhāc ca bhūtajñānaṃ caturvidhaṃ | sarvārthasiddhyai dhīrāṇāṃ sarvabhūmiṣu jāyate* (Lévi 1907: 168), "because of the non-apprehension of everything, true knowledge is fourfold; it arises for the wise on all stages, for the achievement of all aims." The commentary explains the "fourfold thorough knowledge of true reality" (*yathābhutaparijñāna*; thus interpreting *bhūtajñāna* as *yathābhūtaparijñāna*) of dharmas as being related to the investigation of their name (*nāma*), substance (*vastu*), ascriptive designations (*svabhāvaprajñapti*), and descriptive designations (*viśeṣaprajñapti*). All four are known through non-apprehension (*anupalambha*). Without going into detail regarding the definition as fourfold, what matters here is that G *bhudañana* = Skt. *bhūtajñāna* may safely be understood as Skt. *yathābhūtajñāna*. Moreover, this kind of knowledge is based on non-apprehension, that is, it is a direct knowledge of all phenomena without objectifying them, without having an idea of them, and without developing any conceptions.

In the commentary section on *Mahāyānasūtrālāṃkāra* verse 11.42, *lokottarā prajñā* ("superworldly insight") is part of the definition of *āloka* ("light"): *ālokaḥ sadasatvenārthadarśanaṃ lokottarā prajñā tathā sac ca sato yathābhūtaṃ paśyaty asaccāsataḥ* (Lévi 1907: 65), "light [is] the vision of objects as existent or non-existent, [it is] superworldly insight; thus it sees the existence of the existing and the non-existence of the non-existing as it really is."

The combination of both definitions suggests that 11v17 *loutareṇa bhudañaṇeṇa* can be understood as the knowledge or vision of things as they really are by way of non-apprehension. In BC 11, the following list of aspects, such as having no self, being empty, or being like a dream, describes the essencelessness of all phenomena, which is why they should or cannot be apprehended. This knowledge then leads to liberation, as is, for example, stated in *Ratnāvalī* verse 1.57 (Hahn 1982: 24):

> *nāstiko durgatiṃ yāti sugatiṃ yāti cāstikaḥ* |
> *yathābhūtaparijñānān mokṣam advayaniśritaḥ* ||
>
> Who believes in non-existence goes to a bad destination,
> who believes in existence goes to a good destination.
> Who, by thoroughly understanding [truth] as it really is,
> is based on non-duality goes to liberation.

11v17 *ṇa kica paricaïta.* Regarding this phrase, cf. a passage in the *Pañcaviṃśatisāhasrikā Prajñāpāramitā* about the difference between mundane and supramundane *prajñāpāramitā*:

> *śāriputra āha: katamāyuṣman subhūte prajñāpāramitā laukikī, katamā lokottarā? subhūtir āha: laukikī āyuṣman śāriputra prajñāpāramitā, iha bodhisattvo mahāsattvo dānaṃ dadāti upalambhaniśrito mātsaryacittaṃ mayā nigrahītavyam iti, tac cātmasattvadānasaṃjñāniśritaḥ sarvasvaṃ parityajati bāhyaṃ vā adhyātmikaṃ vā vastu upāttaṃ vā anupāttaṃ vā nāsti kiṃcid yaṃ na parityajati, …* (Kimura 2009, I-2: 169)
>
> Śāriputra: What is the worldly, and what the supramundane perfection of wisdom? Subhūti: This is the worldly perfection of wisdom: Here a Bodhisattva gives a gift, leaning on a basis, i.e., he thinks that "I should suppress all niggardly thought in myself." Leaning on the notions of self, being, and gift, he renounces all that he has, all inner and outer things, appropriated and unappropriated, and there is nothing that he does not renounce. (Conze 1975: 199–200)

Even though the message is contrary to the one in BC 11, the wording is similar.[143]

---

143 Cf. also MPPŚ IV 1950–51 (chapitre XLVI): "Enfin le Bodhisattva ne donne rien que ce soit (*na kiṃcit tyajati*), mais il met en œuvre les moyens salvifiques (*upāya*) pour que le êtres obtiennent vêtement, nourriture et autres avantages."

11v18–19 ***-agareṇa*** = Skt. *-ākāreṇa*, "under the aspect of ..." (for *ākāra*, see Skorupski 2002: XVIII ff.). In *prajñāpāramitā* texts this refers to the contemplation of the limbs of trances under several aspects, which forms an essential part of the path of a bodhisattva and/or the practice of the six *pāramitās*. For example, in the *Pañcaviṃśatisāhasrikā* the aspects *anitya*, *duḥkha*, *anātma*, *śānta*, *śūnya*, *animitta*, *apraṇihita* are named:

> *yadā bodhisattvo mahāsattvaḥ sarvākārajñatāpratisaṃyuktair manasikārais tā dhyānāpramāṇārūpyasamāpattīḥ samāpadyate ca vyuttiṣṭhate ca tāś cānityākāreṇa duḥkhākāreṇa anātmākāreṇa śāntākāreṇa śūnyākāreṇa animittākāreṇa apraṇihitākāreṇa pratyavekṣate na ca śrāvakanyāmaṃ vā pratyekabuddhanyāmaṃ vābhikrāmati iyaṃ bodhisattvasya mahāsattvasyāpramāṇeṣu carataḥ prajñāpāramitā. idam āyuṣman Śāriputra bodhisattvasya mahāsattvasya mahāyānam* (Kimura 2009, I-2: 42)
>
> If, with his attentions centred on the knowledge of all modes, he enters into the trances, Unlimited and formless attainments and emerges from them, and contemplates them under the aspects of impermanence, ill, not-self, of quietude, emptiness, signlessness and wishlessness, but does not go forward to the way of salvation of the Disciples and Pratyekabuddhas—then this is the perfection of wisdom of a Bodhisattva who courses in the Unlimited. This is the great vehicle of the Bodhisattva, the great being. (Conze 1975: 134)

The *Śikṣāsamuccaya* names "eighty ways [*ākāra*] of entering into hearing the word," citing the *Akṣayamatisūtra* as an example for a description of the learning in the *bodhisattvavinaya* (Bendall 1902: 190, tr. Bendall and Rouse 1922: 185). Among them, *anitya*, *duḥkha*, *anātma*, *śānta*, *śūnyatā*, *animitta*, and *apraṇihita* match the aspects given in *prajñāpāramitā* literature. In the *Suvikrāntavikrāmiparipṛcchā* (Hikata 1958: 94) the aspects are only *śūnya*, *śānta*, and *anātma*.

According to the MPPŚ (II 640–41) the term "aspect" (*ākāra*) denotes the gateways leading to insight (*prajñāmukha*). Among the Buddha's disciples there are eight kinds of consideration. For them, everything is impermanent (*anitya*), painful (*duḥkha*), empty (*śūnya*), without self (*anātmaka*), similar to an illness (*roga*), a boil (*gaṇḍa*), an arrow (*śalya*) stuck in the body, and a torment (*agha*). The terms *roga* and *gaṇḍa* also occur in BC 11 in the next passage (11v22–27), and the other two terms *śalya* and *agha* (though spelled as G *a<u>kh</u>ada*, corresponding to Skt. *āghāta*) are repeatedly named in BC 6, although they are not included in the list of aspects (11v17–19). Here the sequence is: G *aṇica*, *aṇatva*, *śuña*, *aparibhujitrea*, *avedea*, *sudiṇa*, *akuhicaagamaṇaakuhicagamaṇa*, *parimaṇasacea*. While the first three (Skt. *anitya*, *anātma*, *śūnya*) are rather general characterizations also occurring in other lists of aspects,[144] the latter refer to the *śūnyatā*-doctrine presented in *prajñāpāramitā* texts. But as shown above, those lists are not identical with the one in BC 11, for which I have found no parallel. Also in the

---

144 E.g., *Dharmasaṃgraha* 97 (Müller and Wenzel 1885: 23) *tatra duḥkhasatye catvāra ākārāḥ | tadyathā || anityato duḥkhataḥ śūnyato 'nātmataś ceti*; *Abhidharmahṛdaya* 100–101 (Willemen 2006: 121; the four aspects relating to the *duḥkhasatya* are Chinese terms equivalent to Skt. *anitya*, *duḥkha*, *śūnya*, and *anātmaka*); *Sphuṭārthā Abhidharmakośavyākhyā* (Wogihara 1932–36: 535): *anityākāreṇa vā duḥkhākāreṇa vā śūnyākāreṇa vā anātmākāreṇa*.

Śrāvakabhūmi the supramundane path is characterized by investigating the truth of suffering under several aspects, and along with the well-known set of four aspects, it adds another group of ten aspects, but none of them coincide with the additional ones in BC 11.[145]

11v18 *aparibhujitrea.* The exact spelling of this word is uncertain as there is no direct parallel for it. If the correct reading is *aparibhujitvea*, it might be derived from Skt. **aparibhuñjiyātmaka*, "having a self that is not be enjoyed" or "consisting of something that is not to be enjoyed" (matching the preceding aspects of selflessness and emptiness), or from **aparibhuñjātmaka*, "having the nature of not enjoying" (matching the following aspect of "there is no one who experiences").

If the reading is *aparibhujitrea* (which is more likely compared to other letter forms representing *tv-* or *tr-*), it could correspond to Skt. **aparibhuñjitr̥ka* or **aparibhuñjitrīka* in analogy to BHS *vedayitr̥ka*, "one who causes to feel or experience." In the *Larger Prajñāpāramitā* from Gilgit (fol. 237a, Conze 1962: 87) the passage *na vedakato na vedayitrīkato* is parallel to the spelling *na vedakato, na vedāpakato* in the later Nepalese *Pañcaviṃśatisāhasrikā Prajñāpāramitā* (Kimura 1992, V: 80).

If the last letter is *da* rather than *a*, the whole word would be *aparibhujitveda* or *aparibhujitreda*, for which, however, I have no suggestion.

Thus, the most likely is *aparibhujitrea* = Skt. **aparibhuñjitr̥ka.* Though the compound is somewhat strange, it fits the overall message that there is nobody who enjoys or consumes something (synonymous with Skt. *bhoktr̥*; see next paragraph).

11v18 *avedea* = Skt. *avedaka*, probably in the sense of "restoring to consciousness" and thus not perceiving consciously. Cf. BHSD s.v. *vedaka*: "one who experiences, feels" with reference to Mvy 421, 4679 and Lal 419.11 (vs) *na ca kārako 'sti tatha naiva ca vedako 'sti*, "there is no actor, and no experiencer either (= normal Skt. *bhoktar*, contrasting with *kartar*)." In BC 11 we have the combination **aparibhuñjitrīka* and *avedaka*, the term *kāraka* is not included.

Skt. *(a)vedaka* is commonly used in *prajñāpāramitā* texts in descriptions of how to not perceive a dharma, which is essentially the practice of the *prajñāpāramitā.* The term occurs in two passages in the *Aṣṭasāhasrikā*, for which Conze gives different translations. The first is "unfindable" (or "cannot be known"; cf. Conze 1973a: 87), referring to *dharma* as a passive object, the second is "[not a] feeler" (or "[not] one who experiences"; cf. Conze 1973a: 370), referring to *dharma* as an active subject (*vedaka* next to *kāraka*).

---

145 Cf. Deleanu 2006: 31–32. The group of ten aspects (*daśākāraḥ*), which is peculiar to the *Śrāvakabhūmi*, is "distributed over the four aspects in the following way. All conditioned things (*sarvasaṁskārāḥ*) are impermanent (*anitya*) because they are subject to change-and-decay (*vipariṇāma*), annihilation (*vināśa*), and separation (*viyoga*); these three aspects are imminent (*sannihita*), and this is the nature (*dharmatā*) of things. The conditioned things are characterised by suffering (*duḥkha*) because they are unpleasant (*aniṣṭa*), represent fetters and bondage (*samyojanabandhana*), and are not [conducive to] security (*ayogakṣema*). They are empty (*śūnya*) because no substantial self can be observed (*anupalambha*) as being the subject of the cognitive processes or the agent of rebirth. Finally, they are non-self (*anātman*) because they are not autonomous (*asvatantra*), i.e., they depend upon conditions."

> [...] *sarvadharmā hi ānandājānakā apaśyakā na kāryasamarthāḥ* || *tat kasya hetoḥ* | *nirīhakā hy ānanda sarvadharmā agrāhyā ākāśanirīhakatayā* | *acintyā hy ānanda sarvadharmā māyāpuruṣopamāḥ* | *avedakā hy ānanda sarvadharmā asadbhāvatām upādāya* || *evañ caranta ānanda bodhisattvā mahāsattvāś caranti prajñāpāramitāyaṃ na kañcid dharmam abhiniviśante* | *evaṃ śikṣamāṇā ānanda bodhisattvā mahāsattvāḥ śikṣante prajñāpāramitāyāṃ.* (Mitra 1888: 465–66)

> [...] all dharmas are of such a nature that they can be neither known nor seen, and they are incapable of doing anything. For all dharmas are inactive, they cannot be grasped, because they are as inactive as space. All dharmas are unthinkable, similar to illusory men. All dharmas are unfindable [*avedaka*], because they are in a state of non-existence. When he courses thus a Bodhisattva courses in perfect wisdom and he does not settle down in any dharma. When he trains thus, a Bodhisattva trains in perfect wisdom. (Conze 1973b: 270)

> *evaṃ khalu punaḥ subhūte bodhisattvo mahāsattvaḥ pratītyasamutpādaṃ vyavalokayan na kañcid dharmam ahetukam utpadyamānaṃ samanupaśyati na kañcid dharmaṃ nityaṃ vā dhruvaṃ vā śāśvataṃ vā 'vipariṇāmadharmakaṃ vā samanupaśyati na kañcid dharmaṃ kārakaṃ vā vedakaṃ vā samanupaśyati* | *iyaṃ subhūte bodhisattvasya mahāsattvasyemāṃ prajñāpāramitām akṣayābhinirhāreṇābhinirharato 'syāṃ prajñāpāramitāyāñ carataḥ pratītyasamutpādavyavalokanā.* (Mitra 1888: 470)

> A Bodhisattva who thus surveys conditioned coproduction does certainly not review any dharma that is being produced without a cause nor does he review any dharmas as permanent, stable, eternal, not liable to reversal, nor does he review any dharmas as a doer or a feeler [*vedaka*]. This is the surveying of conditioned coproduction on the part of a Bodhisattva who consummates this perfection of wisdom through the consummation of non-extinction, and who courses in this perfection of wisdom. (Conze 1973b: 272)

In BC 11, for *avedaka* both "unknowable" and "not experiencing" are possible translations—also depending on the understanding of *aparibhujitvea* / *aparibhujitrea* as either "not to be enjoyed" or as "not enjoying." Comparing the two citations from the *Aṣṭasāhasrikā*, the BC 11 passage is closer to the second one, thus rather "someone who does not experience." Cf. also the explanation in the *Sāratamā*, where *avedaka* is explained by the absence of someone who seizes (*gr̥hītuś cābhāvāt*):

> *na ca kiñcid dharmam iti skandhaiḥ saṃgr̥hītam* | *kutaḥ? pratītyotpādadarśanāt* | *nityam ity anādinidhanam* | *dhruvam iti sthiram* | *śāśvatam ity anidhanam* | *kārakaṃ vedakaṃ veti* | *īhatur gr̥hītuś cābhāvāt* | (Jaini 1979: 150)

> No dharma is grasped through the aggregates. Why? Because of realizing dependent origination. Permanent means having neither beginning nor end. Stable means steady. Eternal means having no end. Doer or feeler is said because of the absence of someone who endeavors [to obtain something] or of someone who seizes [sense objects].

The *Larger Prajñāpāramitā* from Gilgit gives another explanation: *avedakā … sarvadharmāś cittavigatatvāt*, which Conze translates as "because they elude all thought." This is reasonable in sequence with the other terms *ajānaka*, *apaśyaka*, *nirīhaka*, *agrāhya*, *acintya*, and *asāraka*. The entire passage reads:

> *na dharmo dharmasya ābhāsam āgacchati. na dharmo dharmaṃ paśyati. na dharmo dharmaṃ jānāti. sarvadharmā hy ānanda ajānakāḥ apaśyakāḥ akriyāsamarthāḥ. tat kasya hetoḥ? nirīhakā agrāhyā hy ānanda sarvadharmā ākāśanirīhakatayā, acintyā hy ānanda sarvadharmāḥ māyāpuruṣopamāḥ, avedakā hy ānanda sarvadharmāś cittavigatatvāt viṭhapanapratyupasthānalakṣaṇatvād asārakatāṃ copādāya. evaṃ caran bodhisattvo mahāsattvaś carati prajñāpāramitāyāṃ na ca kiṃcid dharmam abhiniviśate. evaṃ śikṣamāṇa ānanda bodhisattvo mahāsattvaḥ śikṣate prajñāpāramitāyāṃ.* (fol. 235b, Conze 1962: 81–82)
>
> [. . .] a dharma does not come within the range of a dharma, does not see a dharma, does not cognize a dharma. For all dharmas are unknowable, unseeable, incapable of doing anything. And why? All dharmas are unoccupied, unseizable, on account of the fact that they are unoccupied, like space; all dharmas are unthinkable like an illusory man; all dharmas cannot be known [*avedaka*], because they elude all thought, have the mark of being set up as mere fabrications, and on account of their insubstantiality. When he courses thus, the Bodhisattva, the great being, courses in the perfection of wisdom, but settles down in no dharma whatever. When he trains thus he courses in the perfection of wisdom. (Conze 1975: 487)

In a passage a little later on it is said:

> *evaṃ khalu subhūte bodhisattvo mahāsattvaḥ pratītyasamutpādaṃ vyavalokayan na kaṃcid dharmaṃ paśyaty ahetukam utpadyamānam na kaṃcid dharmaṃ nityaṃ samanupaśyati na nirudhyamānaṃ. na kaṃcid dharmam ātmataḥ samanupaśyati. na sattvato na jīvato na jaṃtuto na manujato na mānavato na poṣato na pudgalato na kārakato na kārāpakato na utthāpakato na samutthāpakato na vedakato na vedayitrīkato na jānakato na paśyakataḥ, na nityataḥ samanupaśyati na anityato na sukhato na duḥkhato na ātmato na anātmato na śāntato na aśāntataḥ. evaṃ khalu subhūte bodhisattvena mahāsattvena pratītyasamutpādo vyavalokayitavyaḥ prajñāpāramitāyāṃ caratā.* (fol. 237a, Conze 1962: 87)
>
> When he thus surveys conditioned coproduction, a Bodhisattva certainly does not see any dharma that is being produced without a cause, nor does he review a dharma that is permanent and never stopped. He reviews no dharma as a self, a being, a soul, a creature, a man, a youth, a person, a personality, a doer, one who feels [*vedaka*, *vedayitrīka*], one who knows, one who sees; nor does he review a dharma as permanent or impermanent, as ease or ill, as self or not-self, as appeased or not appeased. It is certainly thus that a Bodhisattva, a great being who courses in perfect wisdom, should survey conditioned coproduction. (Conze 1975: 491)

Finally, in a last example from the *Pañcaviṃśatisāhasrikā*, *vedaka* is part of a longer enumeration also including *ātman*, which is also part of the sequence in 11v18.

> *ātmānaṃ śāriputra nopalabhate, evaṃ sattvaṃ jīvaṃ poṣaṃ puruṣaṃ pudgalaṃ manujaṃ mānavaṃ kārakaṃ vedakaṃ jānakaṃ paśyakaṃ nopalabhate. tat kasya hetoḥ? atyantatayā hy ātmā na vidyate nopalabhate.* (Kimura 2007, I-1: 192)
>
> One does not find a self, and likewise one does not find a being, a life force, a personality, a man, a person, a human being, a human, a doer, an experiencer [*vedaka*], a knower, a seer. Why is that? Because a self does absolutely not exist, one does not find [it].

In most of these passages, *avedaka* is understood as actively "not experiencing" or "not feeling" in the sense of not having the ability to perceive or seize an object, to feel or cause to feel something. Thus, I have decided for the translation "not experiencing" / "there is no one who experiences." Accordingly, *aparibhujitrea* should be active as well, in the sense of "not enjoying" / "there is no one who enjoys," likewise related to objects of the senses.

11v18 *sudiṇagaraṇa*. For *sudiṇa* = Skt. *svapna*, cf. annotations on 4r15 *sudiṇoamo*, p. 166.

11v19 *akuhicaagamaṇaakuhicagamaṇa*. The expression "not coming from anywhere, not going anywhere" has a parallel in *Larger Prajñāpāramitā* from Gilgit:

> *subhūtir āha: yathā kathaṃ punar bhagavaṃ bodhisattvo mahāsattvaḥ prajñāpāramitāyāṃ caran pañcasu upādānaskandheṣu śikṣate?*
>
> *bhagavān āha: iha subhūte bodhisattvo mahāsattvaḥ prajñāpāramitāyāṃ caran rūpaṃ prajānāti. yathā ca rūpam utpadyate. yathā rūpaṃ nirudhyate. yathā rūpasya tathatā. kathaṃ rūpaṃ prajānāti iti? atyantacchidrataś ca atyantasuṣirataś ca. tadyathāpi nāma phenapiṇḍa asārakaḥ evaṃ rūpaṃ prajānāti. kathaṃ ca rūpasya utpādaṃ prajānāti? na rūpaṃ kutaścid āgacchati nāpi rūpaṃ kvacid gacchati ity akutaścid āgamanataś ca akvacid gamanataś ca rūpasya utpādaṃ prajānāti. yan na kutaścid āgataṃ na kvacid gataṃ, evaṃ hi subhūte bodhisattvo mahāsattva rūpasya utpādavyayaṃ prajānāti. kathaṃ ca rūpasya tathatāṃ prajānāti? na tathatā utpadyate vā nirudhyate vā na āgacchati na gacchati. na saṃkliṣyate na vyavadāyate. ni hīyate na vardhate. evaṃ tathatāṃ prajānāti.* (fol. 285a–b, Conze 1974: 65)
>
> Subhuti: And how does the Bodhisattva, coursing in perfect wisdom, train himself with regard to the five grasping skandhas?
>
> The Lord: Here the Bodhisattva, who courses in perfect wisdom, wisely knows form, and how form is produced and stopped, and also what is the Suchness of form. How does he wisely know form? Since it is altogether full of cracks and holes, he wisely knows form to be as unsubstantial as a mass of foam. And how does he wisely know the production of form? Since it is said that 'form does not come from anywhere nor does it go to anywhere',

> he wisely knows the production of form from the fact that 'form has not come from anywhere nor gone to anywhere'. It is thus that the Bodhisattva wisely knows the production and passing away of form. And how does he wisely know the Suchness of form? Suchness is not produced, or stopped, does not come or go, is not defiled or purified, does not grow or diminish—thus he wisely knows Suchness. (Conze 1975: 594)

In this passage, "not coming from anywhere, not going anywhere" is related to the perception of form as well as of the other *skandhas*. They should be known as being like foam (*phenapiṇḍa*) and without essence (*asāraka*). As regards the arising and disappearing of form (*rūpasya utpādavyaya*), one should consider it as "not coming from anywhere and not going anywhere" (*na rūpaṃ kutaścid āgacchati nāpi rūpaṃ kvacid gacchati*). It is the same with regard to the true reality of form (*rūpasya tathatā*), which does not arise or cease, does not come or go: *na tathatā utpadyate vā nirudhyate vā na āgacchati na gacchati*, where *ā √gam* is synonymous with *ut √pad* and *√gam* to *ni √rudh*.

In the *Ratnāvalī* verse 2.9–14 (Hahn 1982: 42–44) it is said that the world is like an illusion, like a magically created elephant that comes from nowhere, goes to nowhere, and stays nowhere (2.12). Also in Rāhulabhadra's *Prajñāpāramitāstotra* (Hahn 1988: 68) a similar phrase is found: *nāgacchasi kutaś cit tvaṃ na ca kva cana gacchasi | sthāneṣv api ca sarveṣu vidvadbhir nopalabhyase* || 13 ||.

11v19 *parimaṇasacea*. No parallel has been found for this compound. The same spelling is found in 6r7 so the reading is certain.

11v20 *acitieṇa* is an instrumental singular either of Skt. *acintaka*, "one who does not think or reflect upon," or of *acintita* (n.), "without thought or reflection." Since ignoring the *i*-vowel appears more problematic than assuming an elision of invervocalic *-t-*, which is rare but attested, especially from the second century CE onwards,[146] *acintitena*, "without reflection," is preferred. Cf. 11r14 *citiae*.

11v22 *sagharya*. Although the meaning of this word is quite clear, its equivalent in Sanskrit or Pali is not. It is either Skt. **saṅghārya* for *saṃhārya* in the sense of *saṃharaṇa*, "accumulation,"[147] as an abstract noun—in analogy to P *saṅgharaṇa* = *saṃharaṇa*, "accumulation" (PTSD)—or it might be connected to P *(abhi)saṅkhāra* in the same meaning and especially the accumulation of merit or demerit (PTSD s.v. *abhisaṅkhāra*; see also BHSD s.v. *abhisaṃskāra*). Since P *saṅkhāra* is derived from *saṃ√kṛ*, the direct equivalent to G *sagharya* would be *saṃskārya* with a parallel development G *saghara* < Skt. *saṃskāra* / P *saṅkhāra* in Dhp^{K} 10, 70, 106, 107, 163, and 181.

11v24 *jae*. Since *j* represents Skt. *dhy* / P *j(j)h*, there are not many possible equivalents. One is Skt. *dhyāyin* / P *jhāyin*, "self-concentrated, engaged in *jhāna*-practice," as also attested in

146 Salomon 1999a: 126, 152, Allon 2001: 82–83, Lenz 2003: 42, Glass 2007: 116, Salomon 2008a: 113.

147 Suggested by Ingo Strauch (personal communication).

Dhp[K] 50 *jaï* = Dhp 387 *jhāyī*. G *jae* could correspond to *dhyāyam*, "meditating on (acc.)," *dhyāyant*, "meditating" (MW), or *dhyāyin*, "in meditation" (BHSD). Unfortunately, unless the missing piece of birch bark preceding this part is found, nothing more can be said, since the akṣaras here might be the end of a word or compound.

11v24–25 *ajatvia aïdaṇa ... bahira aïdaṇa*. The inner and outer sense bases (*āyatana*) are the six sense organs and their respective objects.[148] The inner (Skt. *ādhyātmika-* / P *ajjhattika-*) are: *cakṣus*, *srotra*, *ghrāṇa*, *jihvā*, *kāya*, *manas*; the outer (Skt. *bāhira-* or *bāhya-* / P *bāhira-*) are their respective objects: *rūpa*, *śabda*, *gandha*, *rasa*, *spraṣṭavya*, *dharma*. Sometimes the inner and outer *āyatana*s are not related to sense organs and sense objects, but to faculties of oneself in contrast to others (Ronkin 2005: 37 and 44, referring to the *Vibhaṅga*[149] but also to the *Sutta-piṭaka* in the context of meditation).[150]

11v26 *eva pialo*. G *pialo* is here, in combination with *eva*, translated as "and so on in this way." The text passage that follows is a partial repetition and thus it is indeed "signifying a phrase to be repeated over and over again" (PTSD s.v. *peyyāla*). In addition, it may also refer to the usual pattern G *ṇisamartha ca dukho ca aśuho ca* (e.g., 11v4), and thus be some kind of abbreviation with the meaning "repeat [what was previously / is usually said]."

11v29 *pariyaṇeo prahadava*, etc. Cf., a passage in the *Mahāvagga* of the *Saṃyuttanikāya*, where it is described what a monk should do in order to practice the eightfold path:

> *ye dhammā abhiññā pariññeyya te dhamme abhiññā parijānāti,*
> *ye dhammā abhiññā pahātabbā te dhamme abhiññā pajahati,*
> *ye dhammā abhiññā sacchikātabbā te dhamme abhiññā sacchikaroti,*
> *ye dhammā abhiññā bhāvetabbā te dhamme abhiññā bhāveti.* (SN V 52)
>
> [...] he fully understands by direct knowledge those things that are to be fully understood by direct knowledge; he abandons by direct knowledge those things that are to be abandoned by direct knowledge; he realizes by direct knowledge those things that are to be

---

148 Nattier (2003: 303 n. 645). In the *Ugraparipṛcchā* § 27D, "to conceive of the sense doors as an empty city" is one of the "four items of pure morality" (Nattier 2003: 311 n. 713: "Since the Sanskrit word also means 'house, dwelling place', the application of the idea of no-self yields the image of the *āyatana*s as empty houses [i.e., houses with no resident] and by extension as an empty city.").

149 For more information about *āyatana*s, see Ronkin 2005: 44–45 and 101–2. Also in a definition given in the *Niddesa* the inner and outer *āyatana*s are listed as one way to paraphrase *idhā* and *hurā*, which can refer to "oneself" and "others," as well as to "this world of humans" and "the other world of gods," etc. (Nidd I 109 *idhā ti sakattabhāva, hurā ti parattabhāvo; idhā ti sakarūpavedanāsaññā-saṃkhāraviññāṇaṃ, hurā ti parakarūpavedanāsaññāsaṃkhāraviññāṇaṃ; idhā ti cha ajjhattikāni āyatanāni, hurā ti cha bāhirāni āyatanāni; idhā ti manussaloko; hurā ti devaloke; idhā ti kāmadhātu, hurā ti rūpadhātu arūpadhātu; idhā ti kāmadhātu rūpadhātu, hurā ti arūpadhātu*).

150 Ronkin 2005: 102. In the commentaries, *ajjhattaṃ* is explained as *attano* and *bahiddhā* as *parassa* (cf. Ronkin 2005: 127 n. 82, referring to Hamilton 1996: xxvi and Gethin 1992a: 53–54).

> realized by direct knowledge; he develops by direct knowledge those things that are to be developed by direct knowledge. (Bodhi 2000: 1557)

According to the following text passage, the things to be thoroughly understood (*pariññeyyā*) are the five aggregates subject to clinging (*pañcupādānakkhanda*), the things to be abandoned (*pahātabbā*) are ignorance and thirst for existence (*avijjā* and *bhavataṇhā*), the things to be realized (*sacchikātabbā*) are true knowledge and liberation (*vijjā* and *vimutti*), and the things to be developed (*bhāvetabbā*) are serenity and insight (*samatho* and *vipassanā*). All of this is done by developing the right view (*sammādiṭṭhi*) and the right concentration (*sammāsamādhi*), which is based on seclusion (*vivekanissitaṃ*), dispassion (*virāganissitaṃ*) and destruction (*nirodhanissitaṃ*) maturing in release (*vossaggapariṇāmiṃ*).[151]

Unfortunately, in this passage the unclear Gāndhārī word *pidivaṇeo* (with the preceding *pidivaṇe*) is not included, but it should be synonym to P *sacchikātabba*, "to be realized." One suggestion is **piṇḍīpanna* (*piṇḍa* + *āpanna*), "having gained concentration, union," and analogously **piṇḍīpanīya*, "to be concentrated, united," i.e., "one should concentrate."

11v30 *tae*. The form as such looks like Skt. *tayā* / P *tāya*, instr. sg. f., literally "by that," perhaps with reference to G *pridi*. Cf. Allon 2001: 288 for a similar case in EĀ^L 63, where it is interpreted either as instr. f. (referring to a following noun) or as representing *taṃ ca* (then to be transliterated as *ta e*). In 6r2, *tae* seems also to be used at the beginning of a sentence, but the following text is lost. It is quite unlikely that it refers to a preceding feminine noun here, even though the entire passage is no longer preserved. While in the example of EĀ^L, *tae* as instr. sg. f. is reasonable, in the other two cases (BC 11, BC 6) this is not convincing. There, a translation "thus" makes the most sense, even though the precise corresponding word in Sanskrit or Pali is as yet unclear. Perhaps it is also related to Vedic *tāt*, Pkt. *tā*, "thus, in this way,"[152] even though the ending *-ae* is still not explained thereby. G *e* could of course correspond to Skt. *ca*, but it is not used in this sense in BC 4, BC 6, or BC 11 (only *ya* = *ca* occurs five times in BC 4).

---

151 Cf. Ronkin 2005: 37. Regarding the wording of the Gāndhārī text, cf. Nird^L2 9·33–34 *abhiñeo · abhiñado · bhavidava ca · bhavido*, "What should be recognized is recognized and what should be developed is developed" (Baums 2009: 345).

152 MW s.v. *tāt*: ind. (obs. abl. of 2. *ta*), "thus, in this way"; SWTF s.v. *ātta-śrāmaṇya*: "*tān na* für *tāt na* (*tāt* ind.), so, in dieser Weise," with reference to Wackernagel, AiG Bd. III § 244. Cf. von Hinüber 2001: § 374: "Vedisches *tāt* lebt in Pkt. *tā* weiter," with reference to Pischel 1900 §§ 167, 425.

8.3 BC 6

6r1 *karitava*. This seems to be the very first word of the text, although we cannot be entirely certain if there was not originally another fragment attached to the top of the preserved scroll (see the discussion of the physical reconstruction of BC 6, p. 32). If we agree to assume this was indeed the beginning of the text, G *karitava* = Skt. *kārayitavya* must have a special application. Perhaps it corresponds to *kāryam ca* at the beginning of letters, as documented in the *Lekhapaddhati* in the meaning of "Und nun die Angelegenheit" (cf., e.g., Strauch 2002: 220, Eng. "And now the subject matter"), as it is translated here, even though the *Lekhapaddhati* is considerably later and from a different region. In the *Lekhapaddhati* the introducing words can also be replaced by *vijñāpyam* / v.l. *vijñapanīyaṃ* ("die Mitteilung, das Mitzuteilende") or *boddhavyam* ("die Mitteilung, das zu Beachtende, das zur Kenntnis zu Nehmende"). Thus, G *karitava* = Skt. *kārayitavyam* could be used as the equivalent of *kāryam* in the sense of "subject matter, issue, concern," or "purpose."

The spelling *karitava*, with *-t-* instead of the phonologically expected *-d-*, could be explained either by it being a technical term, or by the general nearness of *t* and *d* in the scribe's pronunciation (as is indicated by the ending *-ti* for both sg. and pl., as well as other instances of *-t-* being written for etymological *-d-*).

6r1 *kadhadhaduaïdaṇa*. This compound (Skt. *skandha* + *dhātu* + *āyatana*) summarizes the requirements for the human experience that forms our reality. The *skandha*s are the five conglomerations that constitute a person or personality, viz. *rūpa*, *vedanā*, *saṃjñā*, *saṃskāra*, *vijñāna* ("form, sensation, notion, mental formation, consciousness"). The *dhātu*s are (in this compound and context) the physical elements or factors of sensory experience. The *āyatana*s are the sense bases or spheres on which sense perception is based, i.e., the inner bases or organs of the senses, viz. *cakṣus*, *śrotra*, *ghrāṇa*, *jihvā*, *kāya*, and *manas* ("eye, ear, nose, tongue, body, mind"), and the outer bases or objects of the senses, viz. *rūpa*, *śabda*, *gandha*, *rasa*, *spraṣṭavya*, and *dharma* ("sight, sound, smell, taste, tactile sensation, knowable phenomenon").

6r1 *dakṣiśati*. This verb form is uncertain but possibly based on the same present *dakhati* (Skt. **drakṣyati*, P *dakkhati*) as in Shahbazgarhi and Mansehra RE 1 (D) *ba[hu]ka [hi] doṣa sa[maya] spi Devaṇapriy[e] Priadraśi ray[a da]khati* and *bahu[ka] hi [doṣa samajasa Devanaṃpriye] Priyadraśi raja [da]kha[ti]*, "For king Devānāṃpriya Priyadarśin sees much evil in festival meetings" (Hultzsch 1925: 51). Alternatively, a future form of √*dakṣ* may te taken into consideration ("these aggregates, etc. will increase permanently"). Still another possibility, though less likely, is to read G *ca kṣiyati* in the sense of either "remain" (*kṣiyanti*) or "perish" (*kṣīyanti*).

6r2 *bhaveadi*. It is open to question whether this optative is from the base verb (Skt. *bhavet*, P *bhaveyya*/*bhaveyyāti*) or from the causative (Skt. *bhāvayet*, P *bhāveyya*/*bhāveyyāti*). Thus, the translation can be "[this] would be coming from anywhere, (*going anywhere), [this] would be …, [this] would be existence" or "[this] would cause coming from anywhere, (*going anywhere), [this] would cause …, [this] would cause existence." The sequence of terms is again used in 6r6–7, there without any verb. It is also used in 11v17, where each term is an aspect (Skt. *ākāra*). This again refers to certain perspectives according to which one should consider all dharmas or all conditioned things. With this background, I think one should understand the lists in BC 6 as referring to those aspects and thus in the sense of "this would be [to perceive all dharmas under the aspect of] coming from anywhere, etc."

6r2–3 *r(*o)ge(*ṇa) ... gaḍeṇa ... śaleṇa ... ak͟hadeṇa*. A little later, in 6r9–10, another only partially preserved passage reads *agaḍasaña ca arogasa(*ña ca) aśalesaña ca aṇak͟hadasaña ca*. Combining the two, we can see that the sequence *gaḍa ... roga ... śala ... ak͟hada* (or *roga ... gaḍa ... śala ... ak͟hada*) was known to the author of the Gāndhārī text. This reminds us of the sequence Skt. *roga gaṇḍa śalya agha* / P *roga gaṇḍa salla agha* attested in other Buddhist texts. References in the Pali canon are numerous. One occurs in the *Mahāmālunkyasutta* (MN I 435–36), where it used in a meditation context, more specifically within the description of how to abandon the five lower fetters by secluding oneself from objects of attachment. In the first stage of meditation this is done by perceiving the five *skandha*s as a boil or tumor, a disease, and so on:

> And what, Ānanda, is the path, the way to the abandoning of the five lower fetters? Here, with seclusion from objects of attachment, with the abandoning of unwholesome states, with the complete tranquillization of bodily inertia, quite secluded from sensual pleasures, secluded from unwholesome states, a bhikkhu enters upon and abides in the first jhāna, which is accompanied by applied and sustained thought, with rapture and pleasure born of seclusion.
>
> Whatever exists therein of material form, feeling, perception, formations, and consciousness, he sees those states as impermanent, as suffering [*aniccato dukkhato*], as a disease, as a tumour, as a barb, as a calamity [*rogato gaṇḍato sallato aghato*], as an affliction, as alien, as disintegrating, as void, as not self [*ābādhato parato palokato suññato anattato*].
>
> He turns his mind away from those states and directs it towards the deathless element thus: 'This is the peaceful, this is the sublime, that is, the stilling of all formations, the relinquishing of all attachments, the destruction of craving, dispassion, cessation, Nibbāna.' Standing upon that, he attains the destruction of the taints. But if he does not attain the destruction of the taints, then because of that desire for the Dhamma, that delight in the Dhamma, with the destruction of the five lower fetters he becomes one due to reappear spontaneously [in the Pure Abodes] and there attain final Nibbāna without ever returning from that world. This is the path, the way to the abandoning of the five lower fetters. (Ñāṇamoli and Bodhi 1995: 539–40)

According to the notes of Bhikkhu Bodhi (1995: 1266 n. 655)[153] the six terms suffering, disease, tumor, barb, calamity, and affliction show the characteristic of suffering (as against the characteristic of impermanence or not-self). The occurrence of these four terms in BC 6 fits the general focus on happiness and suffering.

---

153 As well as according to the *Paṭisambhidāmagga* (II 241).

A more elaborate enumeration can be found in the *Mahāniddesa* and the *Paṭisambhidāmagga*. There, the full sequence is:

> *aniccato dukkhato* ***rogato gaṇḍato sallato aghato*** *ābādhato parato palokato ītito upaddavato bhayato upasaggato calato pabhaṅguto addhuvato atāṇato aleṇato asaraṇato rittato tucchato suññato anattato ādīnavato vipariṇāmadhammato asārakato aghamūlato vadhakato vibhavato sāsavato saṃkhatato mārāmisato jātidhammato jarādhammato byādhidhammato maraṇadhammato sokaparidevadukkhadomanassupāyāsadhammato saṃkilesikadhammato samudayato atthaṅgamato assādato ādīnavato nissaraṇato.* (Nidd I 53)

> *aniccato dukkhato* ***rogato gaṇḍato sallato aghato*** *ābādhato parato palokato ītito upaddavato bhayato upasaggato calato pabhaṅgato adhuvato atāṇato aleṇato asaraṇato rittato tucchato suññato anattato ādīnavato vipariṇāmadhammato asārakato aghamūlato vadhakato vibhavato sāsavato saṅkhatato mārāmisato jātidhammato jarādhammato byādhidhammato maraṇadhammato sokadhammato paridevadhammato upāyāsadhammato saṅkilesikadhammato.* (Paṭis II 238)[154]

A similar though not identical sequence is used in the *Pañcaviṃśatisāhasrikā Prajñāpāramitā* where it is applied to a practice of mind called *anupalambhayoga*, thus again referring to detachment from the world of senses by non-perception of the *skandha*s:

> *tatra kauśika bodhisattvasya mahāsattvasya katamā prajñāpāramitā, iha bodhisattvo mahāsattvaḥ sarvajñatāpratisaṃyuktaiś cittotpādaiḥ rūpam anityato manasikaroti duḥkhato 'nātmataḥ śāntato* ***rogato gaṇḍataḥ śalyato 'ghataḥ*** *arataḥ pralopadharmataś calataḥ prabhaṅgurato bhayata upasargata upadravato manasikaroti tac cānupalambhayogena, vedanā saṃjñā saṃskārā vijñānam.* (Kimura 1986, II–III: 3)

Also, according to the *Nidānasaṃyukta* (9.X and 9.Z; Tripāṭhī 1962: 125–26) one should consider that which appears to be dear and pleasant as a disease, etc. (*roga*, *gaṇḍa*, *śalya*, *aga* [sic], *anitya*, *duḥkha*, *śūnya*, *anātman*) in order to become unattached to the desire that binds one to the circle of existence. Through this practice, attachment and hence suffering would cease. Other examples for Sanskrit texts are:

---

154 Translation by Ñāṇamoli (1997: 402): "[He sees] the five aggregates as impermanent, as painful, as a disease, a boil, a dart, a calamity, an affliction, as fickle, perishable, unenduring, as no protection, no shelter, no refuge, as empty, vain, void, not self, as a danger, as subject to change, as having no core, as the root of calamity, as murderous, as due to be annihilated, as subject to cankers, as formed, as Māra's bait, as connected with the idea of birth, connected with the idea of ageing, connected with the idea of illness, connected with the idea of death, connected with the idea of sorrow, connected with the idea of lamentation, connected with the idea of despair, connected with the idea of defilement."

Avadānaśataka:

> *pañcopādānaskandhā* ***rogato gaṇḍataḥ śalyato 'ghato*** *'nityato duḥkhataḥ śūnyato 'nātmataś ca deśitāḥ.* (Speyer 1906–09, II: 168)

Sāratamā, referring to the *śrāvakabodhi* and the second of the Four Noble Truths:

> ***rogato gaṇḍataḥ śalyato 'ghataś*** *ca duḥkhahetutvād duḥkhotkarṣahetutvād* (Jaini 1979: 24)

Abhisamayalāṃkāravṛttiḥ Sphuṭārtha, referring to the second Noble Truth as part of the *śrāvakamārga*:

> *samudayasatyasya hetu-samudaya-prabhava-pratyayarūpatvena* ***roga-gaṇḍa-śalya-aghākārāḥ*** (Tripathi 1977: 27)

Prasannapadā, citing the *Śālistambasūtra*:[155]

> *ya imaṃ pratītyasamutpādam evaṃ yathābhūtaṃ samyakprajñayā satatasamitam ajīvaṃ nirjīvaṃ yathāvad aviparītam ajātam abhūtam akṛtam asaṃskṛtam apratigham anāvaraṇaṃ śivam abhayam anāhāryam avyayam avyupaśamasvabhāvaṃ paśyati, asatas tucchata ṛktato 'sārato* ***rogato gaṇḍataḥ śalyato 'ghato*** *'nityato duḥkhataḥ śūnyato 'nātmataḥ, na sa pūrvāntaṃ pratisarati | kiṃ nv aham abhūvam atīte 'dhvani āhosvin nābhūvam atīte 'dhvani, ko nv aham abhūvam atīte 'dhvani, kathaṃ nv aham abhūvam atīte 'dhvani.* (de La Vallée Poussin 1903–13: 593)
>
> Who sees, by correct gnosis, this dependent arising as it is, always deprived of a life force, devoid of a life force, as it is, unmistaken, unborn, unarisen, uncreated, unconditioned, without resistance, without obstruction, peaceful, fearless, ungraspable, imperishable, unappeased by its very nature; who recognizes it as non-existent, vain, hollow, without essence, **as a disease, a boil, a thorn, as evil**, impermanent, painful, empty, without a self, this one does not resort to the past, [asking], "Have I existed in the past, or have I not existed in the past? Who was I in the past? How was I in the past?" [etc.]

In one of the commentaries on the *Śālistambasūtra* (Kamalaśīla's *ṭīkā*; cf. Schoening 1995: 331) disease (*roga*) is explained by "[beings] suffer by the suffering of change even though experiencing a slight happiness." Boil (*gaṇḍa*) is explained by "[it] harms by the very suffering of suffering, like a pustule (*'bras*)"; a thorn (*śalya*) by "inasmuch as in all times [it] is endowed with precisely the suffering of the conditioning factors, the Noble Ones do not desire [it]"; evil (*agha*) by "inasmuch as [it] is sinful (*sdig pa'*), [it] is to be renounced."

155 See also *Śālistambasūtra*, de La Vallée Poussin 1913: 88. Cf. also the citation in the *Śikṣāsamuccaya* (Bendall 1902: 123), although there, *rogato gaṇḍataḥ śalyato* is missing.

In all the examples above, the fourth term is written Skt./P *agha*, whereas in BC 6 it is written *ak͟hada* corresponding to Skt./P *āghāta*. In the *Suvikrāntavikrāmiparipṛcchā* we see the term *agha* accompanied by *āghāta* in a position that in Pali texts is taken by *ābādha* (see above: *aniccato dukkhato rogato gaṇḍato sallato aghato ābādhato parato* ...):

> *sa evaṃ nairvedhikyā prajñayā samanvāgato, yat kiṃcit paśyati śṛṇoti jighrati āsvādayati, spṛśati vijānīte vā, tat sarvaṃ nirvidhyati. kathaṃ nirvidhyati? anityato duḥkhato* ***gaṇḍato rogataḥ śalyataḥ*** *śūnyato 'ghata* ***āghātataḥ*** *parataḥ [pralopataḥ] pralopadharmataś calataḥ prabhaṅgurato 'nātmato 'nutpādato 'nirodhato 'lakṣaṇata iti, ayam ucyate Suvikrāntavikrāmin śītībhūto viśalya iti. tad yathā 'pi nāma Suvikrāntavikrāmin viśalyā nāma bhaiṣajyajātiḥ sā yasmin sthāpyate tataḥ sarvaśalyān apanayati nirvidhyati, evam evaivaṃrūpair dharmaiḥ samanvāgato bhikṣur viśalyaḥ śītībhūto nairvedhikyā prajñayā samanvāgataḥ saṃsārātyantavihārī nairvedhikaprajño viraktaḥ sarvatraidhātukād atikrāntaḥ sarvamārapāśebhyaḥ.* (Hikata 1958: 9–10)

> One who is thus endowed with penetrating wisdom penetrates everything that he sees, hears, smells, tastes, touches, or discerns. How does he penetrate? [Seeing it as] impermanent, painful, **a boil, a disease, a thorn**, empty, evil, **a blow**, alien, a destruction, subject to destruction, unsteady, perishable, without a self, without arising, without cessation, without a characteristic mark. This, Suvikrāntavikrāmin, is called the "cooled freedom from thorns." Now, Suvikrāntavikrāmin, as for that kind of medicine called "freedom from thorns," if it is placed somewhere, it takes away and destroys all thorns. Likewise, a monk who is endowed with such dharmas is free from thorns, cooled, endowed with penetrating wisdom, dwelling beyond the border of *saṃsāra*, possessing penetrating wisdom, dispassionate regarding the entire triple world, having overcome all of Māra's traps. (translation based on Conze 1973b: 7)

I have found the term *āghāta* only in one other text within lists of these terms, namely, in the *Vibhāṣāprabhāvṛtti* on the *Abhidharmadīpa*, where reference is made to *rogagaṇḍaśalyāghātākārādibhir* (Jaini 1959: 330).

In general, Skt. *āghāta* denotes a "blow" (physically or metaphorically). In Buddhist Hybrid Sanskrit, however, it has the same meaning as in Pali, namely "anger, hatred, ill-will," or any malicious feeling (cf. BHSD and CPD). In the sequence *roga*, *gaṇḍa*, *śalya*, the term *āghāta* makes sense in its more literal meaning as a blow or the consequences thereof, such as a wound or a cut. All these terms have in common that they are specific things causing damage to the body and pain to the person experiencing it. In most Buddhist texts, however, the sequence contains the term *agha* ("evil, misery, adversity") and not *āghāta*, and the list continues with or contains other terms such as *anitya*, *duḥkha*, and *śūnya*, that is, more general abstract words. In this respect, *agha* fits well in its meaning of "evil" or "calamity."

It is hard to tell if the sequence in the Gāndhārī text originally contained more than the four preserved terms. In 11v14 only *aroa* and *gaḍa* are mentioned together. In 11v22–23 the terms *dukha*, *gaḍa*, and *roa* are written and editorially supplemented by *śala* and *ak͟hada* based on BC 6: *dukhabie par⟨*i⟩caïta dukhasa{r}gharya gaḍasagharya roasagharya* *(*śalasagharya akhadasa)gharya par⟨*i⟩caïta*. However, *dukha* has a special status in this sentence, which is why this passage is not an argument for including it in the full sequence. Since in other Buddhist texts *roga*, *gaṇḍa*, *śalya*, and *agha* (or *āghāta*) can stand alone, it is assumed that this was the entire phrase in BC 6 as well.

6r3 *payeladukheṇa*. This is tentatively understood as a misspelling of G *peyaladukheṇa* = P *pariyāyadukkha*. In the *Visuddhimagga* (apparently the only source for this term?), *pariyāyadukkha* denotes indirect suffering beginning with birth. Since this term also follows in the Gāndhārī text, this seems likely, even though another word has been written in between, but most of the letters are lost and it thus remains unclear. The explanation in the *Visuddhimagga* (Vism 499 / Vism[W] 424) is as follows:

> For there are many kinds of suffering, that is to say, intrinsic suffering (*dukkha-dukkha*), suffering in change (*vipariṇāma-dukkha*), and suffering due to formations (*saṅkhāra-dukkha*); and then concealed suffering (*paṭicchanna-dukkha*), exposed suffering (*appaṭicchanna-dukkha*), indirect suffering (*pariyāya-dukkha*), and direct suffering (*nippariyāya-dukkha*). (Ñāṇamoli 2011: 511, Pali terms partly supplied by me)

Buddhaghosa's subsequent explanation is:

> Except intrinsic suffering, all given in the exposition of the truth of suffering [in the Vibhaṅga] (Vibh 99) beginning with birth are also called *indirect suffering* because they are the basis for one kind of suffering or another. But intrinsic suffering is called *direct suffering*. (Ñāṇamoli 2011: 511–12)

The term *peyaladukha* then could introduce the following enumeration of *jadidukha* up to *maraṇadukha* as examples for indirect or implicit suffering (P *pariyāyadukkha*), because they are not painful in an apparent way and yet lead to suffering. The preceding enumeration of *gaḍa*, *śala*, and *akhada*, probably preceded by *roga*, might be examples for direct or explicit suffering (P *nippariyāyadukkha*), because it is apparent that they cause unpleasant feelings and suffering.

If P *pariyāyadukkha* corresponds to G *payeladukha*, then P *nippariyāyadukkha* should be written G *ṇipayeladukha* or, more correctly, *ṇipeyaladukha*. This is, however, difficult if not impossible to read in the manuscript, where only the upper parts of the letters are preserved. Before 6r3 *gaḍeṇa*, it is possible to read *rogeṇa* at the end of 6r2, preceded by another *yam ida*. Before that, theoretically, the summarizing term *ṇipayela-* / *ṇipeyala-dukheṇa* should have been written, but whatever the word is, it certainly does not end in *dukheṇa*. Instead, the three akṣaras rather look like *śaleṇa*, which does not make much sense here, since the term is included afterwards and would thus be given twice.

As another though less likely possibility of interpreting G *peyala*, it may also stand for BHS *peyāla* / P *peyyāla* as an abbreviation for a longer list of different kinds of suffering starting with *(roga,) gaṇḍa*, *śalya*, *āghāta* (see above). Other spellings for this term in Kharoṣṭhī documents published so far are *piyalo*, *peyalo*, *piala*, and *pialo*. In BC 4 and BC 11 *piala* / *pialo* is used in the sense of "etc." (11r17), or perhaps also "etc., in short …" (4v12), and "and so on in this way …" (*eva pialo*, 11v26, 11v27). In another text of the Bajaur Collection (BC 2), it is used once in the meaning of "and so forth … up until" (*pialo eva yava*) as an instruction to the reader to repeat the preceding formula with reference to *rūpa* in respect to the other aggregates, i.e., *vedanā*, *saṃjñā*, *saṃskāra*, *vijñāna*. Thus, also in BC 6 it could be an abbreviation for an otherwise longer, commonly known sequence of several kinds of sufferings. This possibility is less likely because of the consistent spelling as *piala/pialo* elsewhere in BC 4/6/11.

6r3 ***jadidukha-yava-[maraṇa]dukheṇa***. The abbreviation *yava* (Skt. *yāvat*) refers to *jarā* and *vyādhi*, which usually stand between *jāti* and *maraṇa*, as for example in the *Nidānasaṃyukta* (9.W–Z; Tripāṭhī 1962: 124–26): *jātijarāvyādhimaraṇaśokaparidevaduḥkhadaurmanasyopāyāsebhyaḥ*. For a more detailed parallel in Pali, an example from the *Sammādiṭṭhisutta* explaining the First Noble Truth of suffering is cited:

> *jāti pi dukkhā, jarā pi dukkhā, byādhi pi dukkho, maraṇam pi dukkhaṃ, sokaparidevadukkhadomanassupāyāsāpi dukkhā, yam p' icchaṃ na labhati tam pi dukkhaṃ, saṅkhittena pañc' upādānakkhandhā dukkhā. idaṃ vuccat' āvuso dukkhaṃ.* (MN I 48)
>
> Birth is suffering; ageing is suffering; sickness is suffering; death is suffering; sorrow, lamentation, pain, grief, and despair are suffering; not to obtain what one wants is suffering; in short, the five aggregates affected by clinging are suffering. This is called suffering. (Ñāṇamoli and Bodhi 1995: 134–35)

6r3 ***priaviṇabhavaagradukheṇa***. In the example given above, the description of the First Noble Truth only mentions the non-obtainment of things one longs for (P *yam picchaṃ na labhati tam pi dukkhaṃ*). In other descriptions the wording is somewhat different, using the phrase *apriyasaṃprayogo 'pi priyaviprayogo 'pi duḥkham*, as for example in the *Lalitavistara*:[156]

> *jātir api duḥkhaṃ jarāpi duḥkhaṃ vyādhir api duḥkhaṃ maraṇam api apriyasaṃprayogo 'pi priyaviprayogo 'pi duḥkham* | (Lefmann 1902–08, I: 417)

A combination of both formulations can be found in the *Arthaviniścaya* and the *Nidānasaṃyukta*:

> *jātir duḥkham* | *jarā duḥkham* | *vyādhir duḥkham* | *maraṇaṃ duḥkham* | *priyaviyogo duḥkham* | *apriyasaṃyogo duḥkham* | *yad apīcchan paryeṣyamāṇe na labhate tad api duḥkham* | *saṃkṣiptena pañcopādānaskandhā duḥkham* | *idam ucyate duḥkham āryasatyam* | (Samtani 1971: 14)

---

156 Similarly in the *Kāraṇḍavyūha* (cited from Mette 1997: 142, corresponding to the facsimile edition of Lokesh Chandra 1981: 124–25): *jātijalā[=jarā]vyādhimaraṇaduḥkhapriyaviprayogavihīnā bhaveyuḥ*, "[the bodhisattvas] would be without suffering due to birth, age, sickness, and death as well as separation from what is dear."

> *jātir (duḥ)kham* | *jarā duḥkham* | *vyādhir duḥkham* | *(mara)ṇaṃ duḥkham* | *priyaviprayogo duḥkham* | *apriyasa(ṃpra)yogo duḥ(kham)* | *yad apīcchate paryeṣamāṇo na labhate tad api du(ḥ)kha(m)* | *saṃkṣiptena pañcopādānaskandhā duḥkham* | *idaṃ duḥkha(m* | *evaṃ d)u(ḥ)khaṃ yathābhūtaṃ prajānāti* | (23.13b; Tripāṭhī 1962: 193)

The term *piyavippayoga* is rarely found in Pali texts; only in one verse of the Rhinoceros Sutta,[157] in the *Peṭakopadesa* (see below), in a few *jātakas*,[158] in the later *Visuddhimagga* (see below), and in other non-canonical texts.

The term *piyavinābhāva* as in the Bajaur text (G *priaviṇabhava*) is not used in the Pali canon. However, *vinābhāva* occurs in an explanation of *piyavippayoga* in the *Peṭakopadesa*. Moreover, *samodhāna* is given there for *sampayoga* in the following passage, just as in the Bajaur text:

> *amanāpasamodhānalakkhaṇo appiyasampayogo manāpavinābhāvalakkhaṇo piyavippayogo* (Peṭ 6)
>
> [A]ssociation with the loathed [has] the characteristic of meeting the disagreeable, dissociation from the loved the characteristic of losing the agreeable. (Ñāṇamoli 1964: 7)

Cf. also a passage in the *Visuddhimagga*:

> *piyavippayogo nāma manāpehi sattasankhārehi vinābhāvo* (Vism 505 / Vism^{W} 429)
>
> Separation from the loved is to be parted from agreeable beings and formations (inanimate things). (Ñāṇamoli 2011: 517)

The same phrasing *priyavinābhāva* as in BC 6 (G *priaviṇabhava*) can be found in the *Bodhisattvabhūmi*, the *Śrāvakabhūmi*, the *Rāṣṭrapālaparipṛcchā*, and the *Karuṇāpuṇḍarīkasūtra*, but the *Rāṣṭrapālaparipṛcchā* is closest in that it uses the term *samavadhāna* instead of *saṃyoga* in the other cases.

Bodhisattvabhūmi:

> *saptavidhaṃ duḥkham* | *jātir duḥkhaṃ jarā vyādhir maraṇam priyasaṃyogaḥ priyavinābhāvaḥ yad apīcchan paryeṣamāṇo na labhate tad api duḥkham* | (Dutt 1966: 167)

---

157 Sn 41 *khīḍḍā ratī hoti sahāyamajjhe puttesu ca vipulaṃ hoti pemaṃ, piyavippayogaṃ vijigucchamāno eko care khaggavisāṇakappo*. Commented upon in the *Cullaniddesa* and also mentioned in the *Apadāna*. For a Gāndhārī version, see Salomon 2000: 125, verse 7, but the term itself is missing in the Gāndhārī text. For references to the parallels, see Salomon 2000: 208 and 216.

158 *Matakabhattajātaka* (Jā I 168), generally circumscribing suffering as *jarāvyādhimaraṇāppiyasampayogapiyavippayogahatthapādacchedādi*. It is also used in the *Mahāummaggajātaka* (Jā VI 422, 430, 467), but in a different context.

Śrāvakabhūmi:

tatra duḥkhasatyaṃ katamat | tadyathā jātir duḥkhaṃ jarā duḥkhaṃ vyādhir maraṇam apriyasaṃprayogaḥ priyavinābhāva icchāvighātaś ca | saṃkṣepataḥ pañcopādānaskandhā duḥkham | (Śrāvakabhūmi Study Group edition 2007: 118; cf. 122)

Karuṇāpuṇḍarīkasūtra:

jarāvyādhimaraṇāpriyasaṃprayogapriyavinābhāvaduḥkhāṃ (Yamada 1968: 74)

Rāṣṭrapālaparipṛcchā, without the preceding *jarā*, etc.:[159]

apriyasamavadhānaṃ priyavinābhāvaṃ (Finot 1901: 39)

Saṃghāṭasūtra, with both *priyaviprayoga* and *priyād vinābhāva*:

dṛṣṭvā ca na jarā na vyādhir na śoko na paridevaḥ na priyaviprayogo nāpriyasaṃprayogaḥ na priyād vinābhāvaḥ na maraṇaṃ nākālamṛtyu (§ 226[160])

The term is also attested in one of the drama fragments from Central Asia,[161] though the context is lost (*/// (d)ukkho ⟨⟨ khu ⟩⟩*[162] *piyavinābhāvo* –), and also in the *Udānavarga*, where the compound is split into its components: *priyāṇāṃ ca vinābhāvād apriyāṇāṃ ca saṃgamāt* | *tīvra utpadyate śoko jīryante yena mānavāḥ* (verse 5.6 [127], Bernhard 1965–68: 140).

In summary, there seem to be only a few textual parallels for the terminology used in BC 6 (G *priaviṇabhava* = Skt. *priyavinābhāva*, P **piyavinābhāva*). The ones I have found are from the *Bodhisattvabhūmi*, the *Śrāvakabhūmi*, the *Rāṣṭrapālaparipṛcchā*, the *Saṃghāṭasūtra*, and the *Karuṇāpuṇḍarīkasūtra*, as well as two early sources from Central Asia, namely the drama fragments and the *Udānavarga*.[163] In Pali texts, the term is only indirectly used in explanations in the *Peṭakopadesa* and the *Visuddhimagga*. Nevertheless, the sequence as such is widely attested in all sorts of Buddhist texts.

---

159 However, in another passage it reads *jātījarāmaraṇaśokahataṃ priyaviprayogaparidevaśataiḥ* | *satatāturaṃ ca jagad īkṣya mune parimocayan vicarase kṛpayā* ‖ (Finot 1901: 52).

160 Unpublished edition by Oskar von Hinüber. One reading without the critical apparatus can be found on http://gretil.sub.uni-goettingen.de/gretil.htm or downloaded from www.sanghatasutra.net (accessed October 5, 2018). Cf. Canevascini 1993: 95: *dṛṣṭvā ca na jarāṃ, na vyādhiṃ, na śokaṃ, na paridevaṃ, na priyaviprayogaṃ, nāpriyasaṃprayogaṃ, na priyād vinābhāvaṃ, na maraṇaṃ, nākālamṛtyum*.

161 SHT 16 fragment 29 in Kuṣāṇa Brāhmī (Lüders 1911: 74).

162 Inserted below the line.

163 There is also a verse in the *Suvarṇavarṇāvadāna*, Roy (1971: 248, § 111): *adya me tat suvihitaṃ yat tvayoktaṃ mahātmane* | *sarvaiḥ priyair vinābhāvo bhavatīty unapatsthita iti*; Rajapatirana (1974: 45, verse 22): *adya me tat suvihitaṃ yat tvayoktaṃ mahātmanā* | *sarvaiḥ priyair vinābhāvo bhavatīty unapatsthita iti uttamaṃ vaca iti*.

As regards its meaning, *priyavinābhāva* can either be translated as "being separated from loved ones" (m.) or "from what is dear" (n.); cf. SWTF s.v. *priya* with reference to *Udānavarga* verse 5.6 (see above), and see also the commentary in the *Cullaniddesa*.[164]

Within the compound 6r3 *priaviṇabhavaagradukheṇa*, G *agra* is uncommon in this position and normally not used in the sense of "and so on." Possibly it is to be understood in a meaning similar to *ādi*, "beginning with, etc." (cf., e.g., SWTF *adyāgreṇa*, "from today/now on"; MW *agre* (s.v. *agra*), BHSD *agre*, PTSD *agge* [only in compounds], "from ..., beginning from ..."). Even though most of these examples refer to a point in time, interpreting *agra* as "beginning with" still seems likely because the preceding compound is also abbreviated in the middle by *yava* (Skt. *yāvat*). However, as can be seen in the examples given above, *priyavinābhāva*/*priyaviprayoga* is usually not the first item, but the last or second to last in a sequence beginning with *jātiduḥkha*, a term that is already mentioned in the Gāndhārī text. Since another *yam ida* is missing between them, they seem to belong to each other more closely (although the conjunction may simply have been forgotten). There are two possible solutions: (1) *priyavinābhāva* was, at the time of the composition of the text or in the mind of the author, the next item following *maraṇadukha* and thus *agra* is an abbreviation for all of the following items; (2) *agra* might have the function of referring to the "highest," i.e., "last" item in a list. Then one would have to assume that the full sequence ended with the *priaviṇabhava*. Yet another interpretation would be to combine *agra* with the following *dukha*, understanding it as the "highest," i.e., "worst" kind of suffering. This however is not entirely convincing in the context, as it is possible to think of something worse.

Another possibility is to read *vagra* instead of *agra*. G *vagra* then would stand for Skt. *varga*, and in combination with the preceding G *priaviṇabhava* would mean "the group of being separated from loved ones [etc.]," and would thus be another way of abbreviating a longer sequence. It is hard to tell if the letter in question is an *a* or a *va*, since the top is curled as if an *a*, but the bottom is straight as if a *va*.

6r3–4 *drudeṣa(*ja)drujaṇasamoṣaṇeṇa*. It cannot be determined what is missing between *drudeśa* and *drujaṇa*, except that it is not another *yam ida*, because there is only space for one letter at the end of line 6r3, of which only the lower part is preserved. Thus, it could very well be *ja*, resulting in the compound *drudeśajadrujaṇasamoṣaṇa* ("meeting bad people coming from bad places"). Such a compound is apparently not attested in any other Buddhist text (the only lexicographically attested form coming from the *Bhāvaprakāśa*; cf. PW), but I have also not found any other combination of Skt. *durdeśa* / P *duddesa* and Skt. *durjana* or *durgaṇa* / P *dujjana* or *duggaṇa*. Skt. *durjana* alone is mostly used in the Purāṇas. Other than that, it is attested in Āryaśūra's *Jātakamālā*, though in another context, in the *Rāṣṭrapālaparipṛcchā*, and

164 *Cullaniddesa* (B^e 247): ***piyavippayogaṃ vijigucchamāno****ti dve piyā – sattā vā saṅkhārā vā. katame sattā piyā? idha yassa te honti atthakāmā hitakāmā phāsukāmā yogakkhemakāmā mātā vā pitā vā bhātā vā bhaginī vā putto vā dhītā vā mittā vā amaccā vā ñātī vā sālohitā vā, ime sattā piyā. katame saṅkhārā piyā? manāpikā rūpā manāpikā saddā manāpikā gandhā manāpikā rasā manāpikā phoṭṭhabbā, ime saṅkhārā piyā.* ***piyavippayogaṃ vijigucchamāno****ti piyānaṃ vippayogaṃ vijigucchamāno aṭṭiyamāno harāyamānoti – piyavippayogaṃ vijigucchamāno, eko care khaggavisāṇakappo.*

in the *Kāśyapaparivarta*. In the *Rāṣṭrapālaparipṛcchā* the formulation is *durjanamadhyagata* (Finot 1901: 48), "being among bad or evil people," occuring in a list of things that are not conducive to a good rebirth, let alone supreme awakening. In the *Kāśyapaparivarta* it is used within a list describing the "immediate [result] of a bodhisattva's higher knowledge" (*kṣiprābhijñatā*, § 156, SI P/2, fol. 78v4–5; Vorobyova-Desyatovskaya 2002). All items in the list accord with the overall picture emerging from BC 4/6/11, focusing on solitude and serenity of mind (for example: *araṇyavāsaḥ kāyacittavivekatayā*, *jñānārtho 'tyantākopanārthatayā*, *vivekārtho atyantopa(śamā)rthatāyeti*). The ninth item is *asaṃsargo durja + na vivarjanatayā* ("By avoiding malignant persons [a bodhisattva] has no [undesirable] contact," Pāsādika 2015: 186, reconstructing *durjanāna* as gen. pl.). However, this does not help us find the missing link between *drudeṣa* and *drujaṇa* in BC 6. As another possibility, the sequence between *drudeṣa* and *drujaṇa* might also serve as an abbreviation marker such as *yava*, but the perserved lower part of the writing on the manuscript does not support this and rather looks like it belongs to only one akṣara.

6r4 *yavi dukheṇa*. Uncertain; especially, what is transliterated as *yavi* could also be *ava* or *yava*. One would expect *sarvadukheṇa*, but the first letter cannot be read as *sa*. Of all possibilities, *yavi* seems the most likely, as the wording *sakṣiteṇa yavi* would be the same as in 11r36 *sakṣiteṇa yavi*. In both cases it would be a summarizing conclusion:

6r4	*yam ida drudeṣa(*ja)drujaṇasamoṣaṇeṇa yam ida sakṣiteṇa yavi dukheṇa samoṣaṇeṇa*
11r36	*sarvadroaca aṇubhavavida sarvasapati ṇaṣida sakṣiteṇa yavi mokṣade ṇaśida*

Since in 11r36 nothing is left out or abbreviated, this is not expected in 6r4 either. The phrase *sakṣiteṇa yavi* would simply conclude the enumeration of different kinds of suffering. As such, G *yavi* is used in the sense of "in short, altogether, indeed" (cf. PTSD s.v. *yāva*), quasi-identical to G *sakṣiteṇa* and left untranslated here.

The combination of *samoṣaṇeṇa* (Skt. *samavadhāna*) with an instrumental (G *dukheṇa*) is different from the preceding use of *samoṣaṇeṇa* as a compound, but confirmed, for example, by a verse in Asaṅga's *Mahāyānasūtrālaṃkāra*:

> *buddhaiś ca samavadhānaṃ tebhyaḥ śravaṇaṃ tathāgrayānasya* |
> *adhimuktiṃ saha buddhyā dvayamukhatām āśu bodhiṃ ca* ‖ (Lévi 1907: 83)
>
> [...] encounters with the Buddhas, hearing the supreme vehicle from them,
> faith endowed with intelligence, the two doorways, and the swift enlightenment.
> (Thurman et al. 2004: 162)

6r6 *yaṣa aji hi de likhida*. Or perhaps *yaṣa aji hi de likhide*, but the ink is too faded to be certain. This statement ("as it has just been written") seems to function in the meaning of "see above." The Sanskrit equivalents for G *aji hi de* can be *adya* + *iha*/*hi* + *idam*/*tad*. Since in BC 15 a similar phrase is *yatha aji hi viśpaṭhe*, and in 6v7 it is written *yahi aji tahi* [...], the second word *hi* should correspond to Skt. *hi* rather than *iha*. As regards the third word *de*, there is so far no evidence for *de* = Skt. *tad* or *idam*. In BC 4/11, *ta* or *te* for Skt. *tad* are documented. Nonetheless, Skt. *te* can be written as G *de* (Anav[L] 82; Salomon 2008: 317) or *d̲e* (SĀ[S6] 19; Marino 2017: 220), Skt. *tena* as G *dena* (Niya documents 83, 164, 399), and Skt. *tasya* as G *d̲asa* (SĀ[S1]; Glass 2007: 116). Therefore understanding G *de* as Skt. *tad* should cause no problem, although G *hi de* can still involve a sandhi Skt. *hi* + *idam*. The corresponding Sanskrit *chāyā* of the whole formula is thus either *yathādya hi tal likhitam* or *yathādya hīdaṃ likhitam*, with the first being more likely.

6r6 *aspamia*. According to the usual phonological development rules, this most probably corresponds to Skt. *asvāmika*, "having no owner or master, not belonging to anyone." Two parallels are found in the *Śikṣāsamuccaya*, where the term is related to the body:

Śikṣāsamuccaya, citing the *Ratnarāśisūtra*:

> *yathaiṣāṃ bhāvanām* ***asvāmikānām*** *amamānām aparigrahāṇām* [...]
> *evam evāyaṃ kāyas tṛṇakāṣṭhakuḍyapratibhāsopamo* ***'svāmiko*** *'mamo 'parigraho* [...]
> (Bendall 1902: 201)
>
> Just as those external things **have no owner**, no "mine," no possessiveness, [...],
> in just the same way, this body [...] **has no owner**, no "mine," no possessiveness, [...]
> (Goodman 2016: 198)

Śikṣāsamuccaya, citing the *Dharmasaṃgītisūtra*:

> *ayaṃ kāyo* [...] *nādyantamadhye pratiṣṭhitamūlaḥ* | ***asvāmikaḥ*** | *amamaḥ* | *aparigrahaḥ* |
> (Bendall 1902: 229)
>
> This body [...] has neither beginning, nor middle, nor end, no established root, **no owner**, no "mine," and no possessiveness. (Goodman 2016: 222)

6r7 *ekakalava*. This term is unclear and not included in the parallel sequence in BC 11, just as the preceding term *aspamia* is not. While the following three terms agree with BC 11, the last term *abhava* (after some other illegible terms) is again peculiar to BC 6.

6r6–7	..., *aspamia*, *ekakalava*,
	parimaṇasacea, ***akuhicaagamaṇaakuhicagamaṇa***, ***sudi(*ṇa)***, ..., *abhava*.
11v17–19	*aṇica*, *aṇatva*, *śuña*, *aparibhujitvea*, *avedea*,
	sudiṇa, ***akuhicaagamaṇakuhicagamaṇa***, ***parimaṇasacea***.

The letters before *aspamia* in BC 6 are only partially preserved and cannot be read with certainty. Possibly, they were *aṇica ca aṇatva ca* ... *ca*, which would fit well with the sequence in BC 11. The last three-letter term is open to question, as it does not correspond to any of the terms in BC 11.

G *ekakalava* is unfamiliar as a technical term but corresponds most likely to Skt. *ekakāla-vat*, lit. "having the same time," which might be a description of the understanding that in true reality all dharmas are the same and thus exist at the same time.

6r8 *eṣa bhude eṣa pragri(*de e)ṣa yaṣave eṣa taṣe.* The four adjectives correspond to *bhūta*, *prakṛta*, *yathāvat* (v.l. in Pali: *yāthāvat*), and *tatha* (P) or *tathya* (Skt.). There is no parallel for the entire sequence, but the Pali canon attests the combination *abhūta* and *ataccha* as part of the longer sequence *yo ca panevarūpaṃ satthāraṃ codeti, sā codanā abhūtā atacchā adhammikā sāvajjā*, "and if anyone blames that teacher, his blame is improper, untrue, not in accordance with reality, and faulty" (e.g., DN I 234, tr. Walshe 1987: 185). Or also, in a shorter version: *atītañcepi kho cunda hoti abhūtaṃ atacchaṃ anatthasaṃhitaṃ, na taṃ tathāgato byākaroti*, "if 'the past' refers to what is not factual, to fables, to what is not of advantage, the Tathāgata makes no reply" (e.g., DN III 135, tr. Walshe 1987: 436). Cf. also this passage in the *Nidessa* (Nidd I 291): *etaṃ tucchaṃ, etaṃ musā, etaṃ abhūtaṃ, etaṃ alikaṃ, etaṃ ayāthāvan ti* (v.l. *ayāthāvaṃ etan*). The text comments upon *tucchaṃ* ("vain") and *musā* ("wrong") in the *Cūḷaviyūhasutta* and gives *abhūtaṃ* ("untrue"), *alikaṃ* ("false"), and *ayāthāvaṃ* ("not as it is") as synonyms.

Since the combination is usually *abhūta* and *ataccha* corresponding to Skt. *atathya*, the equivalent to G *taṣe* might be Skt. *tathya* / P *taccha*, but there is also the Pali adjective *tatha*, which seems to fit better to the general phonological development. At DN I 190 there is the combination *bhūta*, *taccha*, and *tatha* (*api ca samaṇo gotama bhūtaṃ tacchaṃ tathaṃ paṭipadaṃ paññāpeti dhammaṭṭhitaṃ dhammaniyāmakaṃ*), where the synonymous *tacchā* and *tatha* have been translated only once by Walshe 1987: "But the ascetic Gotama teaches a true and real way of practice which is consonant with Dhamma and grounded in Dhamma."

6r9 *rajaṣi ca duśaṣi ca.* Throughout the manuscript this contrastive pair is given in several variations: 6r9 *rajaṣi ca duśaṣi ca*, 6v3 *rajiadi ca duśiadi ca*, 6v3 *rajieadi ca duśieadi ca*, 6v8 *rajama ja duśama ca*, 6v8 *ṇa rajaṇa ṇa d(*u)ṣaṇa*. The forms with the suffix *-ia-* seem to indicate a passive construction, but are apparently used in the same meaning as the other forms, which already have a medio-passive sense.

In the Pali canon, the pair (P *rajjati* … *dussati*) is not as frequent as one might think (see below), and it is always continued with other terms such as *muhyati*, *kuppati*, *majjati*, *kilissati*.

> *yato kho bhikkhave bhikkhuno rajanīyesu dhammesu cittam* ***na rajjat****i vītarāgattā, dosanīyesu dhammesu cittaṃ* ***na dussati*** *vītadosattā, mohanīyesu dhammesu cittaṃ na muyhati vīta-mohattā, madanīyesu dhammesu cittaṃ na majjati vītamadattā so na chambhati na kampati na vedhati na santāsaṃ āpajjati na ca pana samaṇavacanahetu pi gacchatīti.* (AN II 120)
>
> *Bhikkhus*, when a *bhikkhu*'s mind **is not excited** by things that provoke lust because he has gotten rid of lust; when his mind **is not full of hate** toward things that provoke hatred because he has gotten rid of hatred; when his mind is not deluded by things that cause delusion because he has gotten rid of delusion; when his mind is not intoxicated by things that intoxicate because he has gotten rid of intoxication, then he does not cower, does not shake,

does not tremble or become terrified, nor is he swayed by the words of [other] ascetics. (Bodhi 2012: 500)

rajanīye ***rajjati****, dusanīye* ***dussati****, mohanīye muyhati, kopanīye kuppati, madanīye majjati. Imehi kho bhikkhave pañcahi dhammehi samannāgato thero bhikkhu sabrahmacārīnaṃ appiyo ca hoti amanāpo ca agaru ca abhāvanīyo ca.* (AN III 110)

(1) He **is filled with lust** toward that which provokes lust; (2) he **is filled with hatred** toward that which provokes hatred; (3) he is deluded by that which deludes; (4) he is agitated by that which agitates; (5) and he is intoxicated by that which intoxicates. Possessing these five qualities, an elder *bhikkhu* is displeasing and disagreeable to his fellow monks and is neither respected nor esteemed by them. (Bodhi 2012: 716)

rajanīye ***na rajjati****, dusanīye* ***na dussati****, mohanīye na muyhati, kopanīye na kuppati, madanīye na majjati. imehi kho bhikkhave pañcahi dhammehi samannāgato thero bhikkhu sabrahmacārīnaṃ piyo ca hoti manāpo ca garu ca bhāvanīyo cā ti.* (AN III 111)

(1) He **is not filled with lust** toward that which provokes lust; (2) he **is not filled with hatred** toward that which provokes hatred; (3) he is not deluded by that which deludes; (4) he is not agitated by that which agitates; (5) and he is not intoxicated by that which intoxicates. Possessing these five qualities, an elder *bhikkhu* is pleasing and agreeable to his fellow monks and is respected and esteemed by them. (Bodhi 2012: 716–17)

Interestingly, also here at the end of the paragraph it is mentioned that a monk who is not filled with lust or hatred, etc., would be respected and esteemed by others (P *garu ca bhāvanīyo ca*). This could point to *bahumaṇa bhoti* in BC 6 as being some kind of reward for taming one's mind. Other examples from Pali are:

cakkhunā rūpaṃ disvā rajanīye ***na rajjati****, dosanīye* ***na dussati****, mohanīye na muyhati, kopanīye na kuppati, kilesanīye na kilissati, madanīye na majjati.* (Nidd I 242)

Having seen form with the eye, he is **not filled with lust** toward that which provokes lust; he is **not filled with hatred** toward that which provokes hatred; he is not deluded by that which deludes; he is not agitated by that which agitates; he is not stained by that which stains; he is not intoxicated by that which intoxicates. (translation based on Bodhi 2012: 716–17)

cakkānuvattako thero mahāñāṇī samāhito
pathavāpaggi samāno ***na rajjati na dussati*** (Th 1014)

Keeping the wheel rolling, having great knowledge, concentrated,
being like earth, water, fire, the elder is **not attached, is not opposed.**
(Norman 1969: 93)

In Buddhist Sanskrit texts, the formula is *rajyati … duṣyati* (or *rajyeta … duṣyeta*), again accompanied by another term, namely, *muhyati* (or *muhyeta*). For examples see BHSD s.v. *duṣyati*. One occurrence is again from the *Kāśyapaparivarta*:

> *kataraṃ cittaṃ* ***rajyati*** *vā* ***duṣyati*** *vā muhyati vā | atītaṃ vā anāgataṃ vā pratyutpannaṃ vā | yadi tāvad atītaṃ cittaṃ tat kṣīṇaṃ | yād anāgataṃ cittaṃ tad asamprāptaḥ atha pratyutpannasya cittasya sthitir nāsti* | (§ 97, KP-SI P/2, fol. 49v; Vorobyova-Desyatovskaya 2002)[165]
>
> Which mind **is passionate**, **malicious** or confused? Is it one's past, one's future or present mind? In case of its being past, it no longer exists; one's future mind has not yet occurred, and one's present mind is evanescent. (Pāsādika 2015: 154)

A similar passage is found in the *Samādhirājasūtra* (VIII *Abhāvasamudgataparivarta*):

> 3) *sarvadharmāṇām abhāvasvabhāvajñānakuśalo hi kumara bodhisatvo mahāsatvaḥ sarvarūpaśabdagandharasaspraṣṭavyadharmebhyo* ***na rajyate na duṣyate*** *na muhyate. tat kasya hetoḥ? tathā hi sa taṃ dharmaṃ na samanupaśyati taṃ dharmaṃ nopalabhate.*
> 4) ***yo rajyeta****, yatra va rajyeta, yena vā rajyeta;* ***yo duṣyeta****, yatra vā duṣyeta, yena vā duṣyeta; yo muhyeta, yatra vā muhyeta, yena vā muhyeta, sa taṃ dharmaṃ na samanupaśyati, sa taṃ dharmaṃ nopalabhate taṃ dharmaṃ asamanupaśyann anupalabhamānaḥ sarvatraidhātukenānadhyavasito bhavati, kṣipram imaṃ samādhiṃ pratilabhate, kṣiprañ cānuttarāṃ samyaksaṃbodhim abhisaṃbudhyate.* (Régamey 1938: 30–31)
>
> 3) O Kumāra, the Bodhisattva-Mahāsattva who is an expert knower of the essence of the non-existence, **is neither attracted nor repulsed** nor infatuated by all the elements of sight, hearing, smell, taste and touch. For what reason? Because he does neither perceive nor apprehend this dharma.
> 4) He neither perceives nor apprehends the dharma **which is attracted**, neither the dharma which attracts, nor the dharma due to which the attraction is produced; neither the dharma **which is repulsed**, nor the dharma which repulses, nor the dharma due to which the repulsion is produced; neither the dharma which is infatuated, nor the dharma which infatuates, nor the dharma due to which the infatuation is produced. Neither perceiving nor apprehending this dharma, he does not cling to all the elements of the threefold world, soon reaches this *samādhi* and speedily attains the Supreme Enlightenment. (Régamey 1938: 65)

Based on paragraph 4 of this passage, where *rajyeta* is applied in reference to *dharma* as a subject, an object, or a reason, the *ya* in BC 6 § 5 might also refer to such a *dharma* (cf. 6v3–4 *ya rajieadi ca duśieadi ca ⟨*·⟩ yahi ñaṇo ṇa kuḏae suṭhu phaṣadi ⟨*·⟩ ta taraṇae ca siadi*, then to

[165] Cited in the *Śikṣāsamuccaya* (Bendall 1902: 233–34): *cittasmṛtyupasthānaṃ tu yathāryaratnakūṭe | sa evaṃ cittaṃ parigaveṣate | katarat tu cittaṃ | rajyati vā duṣyati vā muhyati vā | kim atītam anāgataṃ pratyutpannaṃ veti | tatra yad atītaṃ tat kṣīṇaṃ | yad anāgataṃ tad asaṃprāptaṃ | pratyutpannasya sthitir nāsti* | […].

be translated as "which [dharma] becomes attracted or hateful—if one touches the proper [...] knowledge, this would be for its [i.e., that dharma's] overcoming").

A little later, in the next chapter of the *Samādhirājasūtra* (IX *Gambhīradharmakṣāntiparivarta*), the pair is again used with respect to *dharmas* that are not perceived and hence cannot be desired or hated:[166]

> *sa gambhīrayā dharmakṣāntyā samanvāgato rañjanīyeṣu dharmeṣu* ***na rajyate*** *doṣaṇīyeṣu dharmeṣu* ***na duṣyate*** *mohanīyeṣu dharmeṣu na muhyate* |
> *tat kasya hetoḥ* | *tathā hi sa taṃ dharmaṃ na samanupaśyati taṃ dharmaṃ nopalabhate* | *yo rajyeta yatra vā rajyeta yena vā rajyeta* | *yo duṣyeta yatra vā duṣyeta yena vā duṣyeta* | *yo muhyeta yatra vā muhyeta yena vā muhyeta* | *sa taṃ dharmaṃ na samanupaśyati taṃ dharmaṃ nopalabhate* | *taṃ dharmam asamanupaśyann anupalabhamāno 'rakto 'duṣṭo 'mūḍho* ***'viparyastacittaḥ samāhita*** *ity ucyate* | (Dutt 1941: 95)[167]
>
> Endowed with [this] profound willingness to accept the dharmas [for what they are], he **does not desire** dharmas which may be objects of desire, **is not repelled** by dharmas which may be objects of repulsion, and is not deluded by dharmas which may be objects of delusion. And why is that so? Because he does not see any dharma, is not aware of any dharma which might desire or which he might desire or by means of which he might desire, nor [any dharma] which might feel repulsion or towards which he might feel repulsion or by means of which might feel repulsion, nor [any dharma] which might be deluded or with reference to which he might be deluded or by means of which he might be deluded. Such a dharma he does not see, such a dharma he is not aware of, and if [, in this way,] he neither sees nor is aware of such a dharma, is therefore free of desire, free of feelings of repulsion, free from delusion, and is one **whose mind has not been led astray**, then he is called '**concentrated.**' (Cüppers 1990: 7)

In this passage, the context is quite similar to that in BC 6 inasmuch as the mind is called concentrated (*samāhita*) when one does not become passionate or hateful. In BC 6 this state is called *saṃthido* or *egagra* (§ 5). What is called *aviparyastacitta* in the *Samādhirārajasūtra* corresponds to G *avikṣitacita* (§ 4). The only difference is that in BC 6, the method of non-perception is not explicitly mentioned, other than by saying the notions in the mind should be reduced and one should not become mentally engaged. It is, however, known from other texts of the Bajaur Collection, either described directly (BC 2 *ṇa samaṇupaśati*) or indicated through certain terms (BC 11 *aviñati*, *aprañati*).

---

166 Parts of this passage (from *yo rajyeta yatra vā rajyeta yena vā rajyeta* onwards) are also cited in the *Prasannapadā* at the end of chapter 6 and 23 (de La Vallée Poussin 1903–13: 143 and 472).

167 Cf. GMNAI II.3: 30–31, folio (32), verso, line 6 – folio (33), recto, line 3: */// yā kṣāntyā .amanvāgato raṃjanīyeṣu dharmeṣu na rajyate* | *doṣaṇīyeṣu na duṣyate* | *mohanīyeṣu dharmeṣu na /// .. nupaśya .i taṃ dharmaṃ nopalabhate* | *yo rajyeta* | *yatra vā rajyeta* | *yena vā rajyeta* | *yo duṣyeya* | *yatra vā duṣyeta* | *ye /// n. vā muhyeta* | *taṃ dharmaṃ na samanupaśyati* | *taṃ dharmaṃ nopalabhate* | *taṃ dharmaṃ na samanupaśyaty anupalabhamānaḥ araktaḥ a /// .. ta ity ucyate.*

6r9 *agaḍasaña* … *ṇicasaña* … Since the beginning of this sentence and the ending of the next sentence starting with *ṇicasaña* are not preserved, the meaning of these sequences is unclear. The first sequence starting with *agaḍasaña* should be the one which is desireable (to have a notion of dharmas being free from boils, etc.), while the following sequence obviously is the one which should not be practiced (to have a notion of dharmas being permanent, etc.). Possibly, this difference corresponds to *rajaṣi* and *duśaṣi*, respectively, meaning that the first notion is that which one desires and the second, that which one rejects. The general statement probably was that one should not have any notion at all.

6v1 *abodhasa*. Cf. PTSD *buddhatā* and similarly PTSD *buddhatta*, PW *buddhatva*, MW *abuddhatva*. The suffix *-sa* for Skt. *-tā* is unusual but makes most sense here, as well as in the four other cases in the text (6v2, 6v2, 6v3, 6v5). If one takes *-sa* as a genitive singular ending, another translation would be: "How does it arise for someone who is not awakened (*abuddha*)?" Then in the following, the translation "How for someone who is powerful (*balinā* [instr. for gen.])" might be reasonable. In both cases the last sentence could also be "How by a fool (*bāla*)?" but the following *savala* = Skt. *sabala* as well as later *balava* = Skt. *balavat* points to Skt. *bala* rather than *bāla*.

6v1 *baleṇa*, *savalo*, 6v2 *balava*. I have translated *bala* as "forceful exertion" based on my understanding that the author wants to express that if one tries to become awakened by forceful exertion or too much effort, then only an experience of happiness will arise but not the state of awakening, as one would not have a composed mind (G *ṇa saṃthidomaṇaṣa bhoti*). Since the sentences with *savalo* (Skt. *sabala-*) and *balava* (Skt. *balavat-*) are incomplete, this remains uncertain.

6v2 *avikṣitacitasa*. Skt. *avikṣiptacittatā* signifies a state of mind that is not confused or distracted (cf. SWTF s.v. *avikṣiptacitta*). Or, put the other way around, *vikṣipta* describes the state in which the mind processes a wide range of information without the ability to focus on one object. In a fragment from Central Asia, *avikṣiptacitta* is synonymous with *upasthitasmṛti* ("attentive or focused mindfulness"), and *avikṣipta* is glossed by *avikirat* ("not scattered").[168] In other texts *avikṣipta* is paraphrased with *samāhita*, *asaṅgapratibhāna*, *asaṃkliṣṭacitta*, etc.,[169] describing a state of mind destined to supreme awakening. An exact correspondence to G *avikṣitacitasa* occurs in the *Pañcaviṃśatisāhasrikā Prajñāpāramitā*:[170]

---

168 Hoernle, MR 1 *[saṃ]prajānena upasthitasmṛtinā avikṣiptacittena av[i]kiratā*.

169 *Pañcaviṃśatisāhasrikā Prajñāpāramitā* (Kimura 1986, II–III: 18): *yaṃ ca teṣāṃ buddhānāṃ bhagavatām antike dharmaṃ śroṣyanti sarvo 'sya dharmo na jātv antarā vicchetsyati yāvan nānuttarā samyaksaṃbodhir abhisaṃbuddheti sadā samāhitaś ca bhaviṣyati avikṣiptacittaḥ. samāhitayogena, asaṅgapratibhānaś ca bhaviṣyati, anācchedyapratibhānaḥ samāhitapratibhāno yuktapratibhānaḥ śliṣṭapratibhāno 'rthavatpratibhānaḥ sarvalokābhyudgataviśiṣṭapratibhānaś ca bhaviṣyati*; *Bodhisattvabhūmi* (Dutt 1966: 161): *nāpaviddham avikṣiptacittaḥ karoty asaṃkliṣṭacittaḥ*.

170 Cf. also LPG (fol. 241a; Conze 1962: 100): *dhyānapāramitāyāṃ sthita avikṣiptamanas*, where the description of "standing in the perfection of meditation" in relation to the perfection of morality is to not have any thought connected with greed, hate, delusion or harming (cf. tr. Conze 1975: 498).

> *santi śāriputra bodhisattvā mahāsattvāḥ prajñāpāramitāyāṃ caranto dhyānapāramitāyāṃ sthitvā sarvākārajñatāpanthānaṃ śodhayanti, atyantaśūnyatayā* ***avikṣiptacittatām*** *upādāya.* (Kimura 2007, I-1: 102)
>
> Śāriputra, *bodhisattva-mahāsattva*s coursing in the perfection of wisdom, having stood in the perfection of meditation, purify the roadway to the knowledge of all modes by means of absolute emptiness, having acquired the state of an undisturbed mind. (translation based on Conze 1975: 82–83)

As to the difference between *citta* and *manas*, both often translated as "mind" in English, *citta* is the basic "mind" and *manas*, "mental action" or "mentality." According to Bhikkhu Bodhi (commenting on SN II 94 *cittaṃ iti pi mano iti pi viññāṇaṃ iti pi*, also referring to DN I 21 *yaṃ … idaṃ vuccati cittan ti vā mano ti vā viññāṇan ti vā*), the three terms P *viññāṇa*, *mano*, and *citta* are generally used in distinct contexts: *viññāṇa* refers to the "particularizing awareness through a sense faculty" (eye-contact, etc.) as well as the "underlying stream of consciousness"; *mano* serves as an "action" (along with body and speech) and as the "sixth internal sense base" (along with the five physical sense bases) coordinating the data of the five senses and also cognizing mental phenomena (*dhammā*); *citta* signifies the mind as the "center of personal experience." "It is *citta* that needs to be understood, trained, and liberated" (Bodhi 2000: 769–70 n. 154).

6v2 *mraduamaṇaṣa*. G *mradua* = Skt. *mr̥duka* / P *muduka*. Cf. SĀ[S1] 11 *rmaḏo* = Skt. *mr̥du*, "pliant," for example in "[h]aving tamed and controlled his mind […] and having made it pliant and workable" (Glass 2007: 171) or also Anav[L] 21 *rmidu* = Skt. *mr̥du*, "soft [hair]."

6v2 *bahumaṇa bhoti* / 6v7 *bahumaṇeṇa*. Cf. annotations on 6r9 *rajaṣi ca duśaṣi ca*, p. 250, with reference to AN III 110, 111.

6v3 *spura*. There are several occurrences in BC 6 of G *spura*: 6v3 *spuramaṇaṣa bhoti*, 6v3 *spura upajeadi*, 6v7 *spuramaṇaṣa bh(*odi)*, 6v8 *spurami*. Most probably it corresponds to Skt. *sphura*, "quiver, throb," *sphurat* or *sphuramāṇa*, "trembling, quivering, shaking" (MW), in the sense of an unsteady or agitated mind. Cf. *sphuranmanasaḥ* in Āryaśūra's *Jātakamālā* (Kern 1891: 92, prose passage after verse 14.21; Hanisch 2005: 132), translated as "highly agitated" by J. S. Speyer (1895: 131).[171]

6v3 *aṭ́ha*. "Not stable, transient" is the most likely interpretation of G *aṭ́ha* based on the overall statements in this paragraph. Cf. also MW *asthāyin*, "not permanent, transient." Another possibility with the same meaning would be to consider it as an aorist form of √*sthā* (cf. CPD s.v. *aṭṭhā* = *aṭṭhāsi*, spelled as *[a]ṭ́haṣi* in RS 12; Silverlock 2015: 270), but then the syntax of the sentence would be unusual, since the lost negation would be positioned before the noun: *(*ṇa*

---

[171] In the combination *santrāsavaśagāḥ sphuranmanasaḥ* ("trembling with fear and highly agitated").

e)gragacitasa aṭ́ha instead of *egragacitasa ṇa aṭ́ha*. Another possibility is G *aṭ́ha* for Skt. *asthā* "at once," but this is not a common usage, and also rather unlikely in terms of the context.

Still another possibility is to understand G *aṭ́ha* as Skt. *artha*, but again this seems unlikely because of the preceding spelling *viartha*. One would thus expect it to be written *artha*. Moreover, this would imply the interpretation of *(*e)gragacitasa* as a gen. sg. m., as against nom. sg. f. in the preceding instances (6v2 *egagracitasa*, *avikṣitacitasa*).

6v3 *kuḍae* / 6v7 *kuḍeami*. The exact correspondence of G *kuḍea* is uncertain, but most probably it is derived from Skt. *kūṭa* + *ka*; cf. P *kūṭeyya* for *kūṭa*. Both G *kuḍae* and *suṭhu* could also be used adverbially in 6v3 ("when one touches knowledge, not deceitfully [but] properly"). They are translated as adjectives because *kuḍeami* in 6v8 seems to be an adjective rather than an adverb. Cf. also *suṭhuñaṇami* in 11r7–8, although here too it is uncertain if *suṭhu* is used as a separate adverb or as an adjective as the first part of a compound. For 6v3 *suṭhu*, cf. annotations on 11r7 *suṭhu*, p. 200.

If this interpretation is accepted, *kūṭaka* would refer to knowledge (*jñāna*). This deceitful knowledge again would refer to experiencing *sukha* at the time of being (deceitfully) awakened. It would thus be equivalent to the state of not being awakened (*abuddhatā*) mentioned at the beginning of § 4. Thus, the reasoning here seems to be that if you are experiencing *sukha* or if you are striving to experience *sukha* in the false assumption that it is a sign of awakening, then you are wrong. This argumentation possibly takes up the discussion of *sukha* in BC 11.

6v3–4 *ya … yahi … ta taraṇae ca siadi*. The whole sentence is: *ya rajieadi ca duśieadi ca* ⟨*.⟩ *yahi ñaṇo ṇa kuḍae suṭhu phaṣadi* ⟨*.⟩ *ta taraṇae ca siadi*. The general statement is that whatever the condition is for experiencing *rāga* or *dveṣa*, it is overcome when one reaches perfect knowledge and is awakened. Thus, possibly *ya* and *ta* could also be understood as relative pronouns (cf. the passage from the *Samādhirājasūtra* in the notes on 6r9 *rajaṣi*, p. 250).

In view of the verbal constructions in the following sentences, *taraṇae* might also be a past participle, then to be translated in the sense of "what[ever] could become passionate or hateful, that would have been overcome indeed, when one touches not the deceitful [but] the proper knowledge." However, there is no such form based on √*tṝ*, so one would have to interpret G *taraṇae* as a misspelling for *tirṇae* or the like (parallel to Skt. *tīrṇa* / P *tiṇṇa*). So far, the following spellings are attested in other Kharoṣṭhī manuscripts: (-)*tiṇo* (Skt. *tīrṇa*), *adirno* (Skt. *ātīrṇa*), *utrirno* or *utiṇo* (Skt. *uttīrna*), *vitiṇo* (Skt. *vitīrṇa*).

The position and meaning of *ca* is uncertain but tentatively interpreted here as a particle emphasizing the preceding word (cf. MW s.v. ²*ca*, "indeed"). Or perhaps it is *ca* for Skt. *cid* (MW "indeed").

6v4–5 … *karavida(*e)* … *vitrae ca siadi* … *karavidae siadi* … *saṃthidae siadi*. These verbal forms seem to be examples for the compound past tense known from the Niya documents; cf. Burrow 1937: § 114. G *-ae* corresponds to the ending of a past participle in *-ta* plus the suffix *-ka*, and it can be combined with auxiliary verbs in the third person singular, of which *siyati*, *huati*, and *hakṣati* are attested.

In the Niya documents, these verbal phrases are often applied in a sentence beginning with *yadi bhudartha* ("whether he has really…" or "if it is really so…," etc.):

karya kiṭae (siyati)	if … did [no] work … (*kr̥ta+ka*)
giḍaga hakṣati	has taken = should have taken (*gr̥hīta+ka*)
giḍaka hoati	has taken = should have taken (*gr̥hīta+ka*)
ditae siyati	should have given (**ditta + ka*)
ditae huati	has given (**ditta + ka*)
dharidae siyati	[whether] he has held (*dhārayita+ka*)
nidae siyati	has taken = should have taken/led/brought (*nīta+ka*)

In BC 6, *karavidae* and *saṃthidae* are clearly past participles. Based on that, *vitrae* also has to be a past participle, making Skt./P *vitta* the most likely candidate, especially since in the *Dharmapada* of the Split Collection, *vitralabha* is likewise found for Skt./P *vittalābha* (Dhp[Sp] 6).

6v4 *taṇua.* The term is once written *taṇua* (Skt. *tanuka*) and once *taṇu* (Skt. *tanu*): 6v4 *taṇua saña karavida(*e)*, 6v6 *yadi va maṇaṣa siadi taṇu.* Its meaning in the context of meditation is to reduce the objects of the mind, i.e., concepts, ideas, or ideations (*saṃjnā*), to a minimum so that they become small (*tanu*). In the *Milindapañha* the term is used to reduce *rāga*, *dosa*, and *moha* in order to make the mind "light" (*lahuka*) instead of "heavy" (*garuka*):

> *tatr' idaṃ tatiyaṃ cittaṃ vibhattim āpajjati. ye te mahārāja sakadāgāmino, yesaṃ rāgadosamohā tanubhūtā, tesaṃ taṃ cittaṃ pañcasu ṭhānesu lahukaṃ uppajjati lahukaṃ pavattati, uparibhūmisu garukaṃ uppajjati dandhaṃ pavattati.* (Mil 103)
>
> As to this, this third kind of mentality is distinguished [thus]: the mentality, sire, of those once-returners who have reduced attachment, aversion and confusion to the minimum [*tanubhūta*], arises buoyantly [*lahuka*], proceeds buoyantly in the five (lower) stages, but as regards the higher planes it arises with difficulty [*garuka*], proceeds sluggishly [*dandha*]. (Horner 1963: 144)

In the *Śrāvakabhūmi*, *pratanu√kr̥* is used in reference to reducing malice (*vyāpāda*) by means of benevolence (*maitrī*) in order to finally make the mind get rid of malice entirely:

> *tatra vyāpādacaritaḥ pudgalo maitrīṃ bhāvayan sattveṣu yo vyāpādas taṃ pratanūkaroti* | *vyāpādāc cittaṃ pariśodhayati* || (Śrāvakabhūmi Study Group 2007: 70)
>
> When a man with malicious behavior develops benevolence towards [all] beings, he reduces malice. He purifies the mind from malice.

6v4–5 *saïthida / saṃthidae.* The first term should correspond to Skt. *svayaṃsthita*, literally "standing by itself," synonymous with *svasthita* (MW "independent"). For the phonological development of the prefix, cf. Dhp[K] 171 *saïgada* for Skt. *svayamkṛta* / P *sayaṃkata*. This is an antonym of *saṃsthita*, literally "standing together" but more generally "standing firm, established, settled, composed." In the context of the mind, the terms might be translated as "scattered" or "scatterbrained" vs. "composed" (German "verzettelt, zerstreut" vs. "gesammelt, konzentriert"). Cf. annotations on 6v2 *avikṣitacitasa*, p. 254.

The term *svayaṃsthita* has only been found in Asaṅga's *Mahāyānasūtrālaṃkāra* (19.50, Lévi 1907: 169), where it is however used in another meaning. There, *svayaṃsthitaṃ* (or, more often, *sthitaṃ svayaṃ*), "self-established / standing on its own" (based on [true] nature), is opposed to *purataḥ sthāpitaṃ*, "established earlier" (imagined based on [sense] experience), both referring to *nimitta*. Cf. tr. Lévi 1911: 277 and Thurman et al. 2004: 307.

6v5 *prove ya dukha jaṇita tasa dukhasa vovaṣ̄amo kareati*. The current translation ("[one] would bring to rest what was earlier known as suffering") is based on the preceding sentence with the same syntax. It is also possible, however, to understand the sentence as "after having understood what suffering is, one would bring to rest this suffering."

6v6 *bhaṭareasa*. The use of the term *bhaṭarea* = Skt. *bhaṭṭāraka*, "master," is suprising here, as the word typically refers to a secular power. It can, however, also be used as a title for religious teachers, spiritual preceptors, or respected men in general (cf. MW, PW, and NWS s.v. *bhaṭṭāraka*). The term is not often attested in literary Buddhist Sanskrit texts (only in later ones), and never in Pali texts. In BC 6, I understand it as referring to the instructor of the teaching on the notion and development of happiness. This is particularly interesting, since it gives us a clue regarding the environment in which these manuscripts were produced.

6v7 *yahi aji tahi sava pada kaṭava yava*. Here, *yahi* … *tahi* should correspond to Skt. *yarhi* … *tarhi*, "when … then …" For G *tahi*, cf. AsP[Sp] 5-20 *dahi* = Skt. *tarhi* (Falk and Karashima 2013: 116). Another possibility would be to understand *tahi* as gen. sg. of *tvam*, as in the Niya documents, but with *yahi* = Skt. *yarhi* at the beginning, *tahi* = Skt. *tarhi* is more plausible.

The phrase *sava pada kaṭava* has not been found in any other Kharoṣṭhī document so far. Also, the combination *yahi aji tahi* … (Skt. *yarhi adya tarhi* …) is not familiar from any other Buddhist text (known to me). This might also lie, however, in the very nature of the texts being transmitted, as they are mostly standardized canonical texts drawing on the oral tradition and not later scholastic treatises composed in writing from the beginning. Similar abbreviations are known from the Gāndhārī avadāna and pūrvayoga texts. The closest formula to the one in BC 6 is *vistare sarvo karya*, "expansion; all should be done" (cf. Lenz 2003: 89 and Lenz 2010: 80), though not followed by *yava*. The particle *yāvat* is used in other common abbreviation formulae such as *pūrvavad yāvat*, "as previously, up to" (cf. Lenz 2003: 85).

As for *pada kaṭava*, there is a similar phrase in Patañjali's *Vyākaraṇamahābhāṣya* that could be a parallel: *yathālakṣaṇam padam kartavyam*, "words should be made according to grammar" (cf. Bronkhorst 2007: 340 n. 9).[172] The note *padam kartavyam* is apparently also used

[172] This phrase is used in several places: P 3,1.109 / KA II,84.15–85.5 / Ro III,206–7; P 6,1.207 / KA III,117.14–19 / Ro IV,530; P 8,2.16 / KA III,397.3–398.10 / Ro V,380–82. The whole sequence is

in other commentary texts, such as one by Śabara, where it is an instruction to replace a certain word with another: *jyotiṣṭome girā-padasya sthāne irā-padaṃ kartavyam iti*, "In the *jyotiṣṭoma* [sacrifice] instead of the word *girā* the word *irā* should be used."[173] Thus, the phrase *sava pada kaṭava yava* in BC 6 should mean "one should use every word up until (the following)." This then seems to point to an earlier text passage in BC 6, namely § 4, since several words are identical, hence the addition "as above" in the translation. The passage in § 5 (6v6–7) relates to the passage in § 4 (6v1–3) as follows:

§ 4	§ 5
ṇa saṃthidomaṇas̱a bhoti *yadi va maṇas̱a bh(*oti)* *+ + + + ? ? g̱. b. ṇ. paripuṇa* *ṇa tatva*	*ṇa saṃthidomaṇas̱a siadi* *yadi va maṇas̱a siadi* *taṇu* *sp(*u)ra*
ṇa eg̱agracitasa *ṇa avikṣitacitasa* *mraduamaṇas̱a bhoti*	*ṇa cita eg̱ag(*ra siadi)*
*ṇa + + th(*i)do bahumaṇa bhoti*	*ṇa bahumaṇeṇa*
aña kuś̱alasa viarthae *aña balava ma ra amaṇas̱iara akuś̱alasa viarthae* *ṇa spuramaṇas̱a bhoti*	***yahi aji tahi sava pada kaṭava yava*** *aña kica palios̱eṇa* *ṇa spuramaṇas̱a bh(*odi)*

It is not clear to me what the abbreviation refers to exactly, that is, if it points to the whole passage *aña kuś̱alasa viarthae aña balava ma ra amaṇas̱iara akuś̱alasa viarthae*, or only to parts of it. Logically it should abbreviate something, but in BC 11 *yavi* is used in a sequence where nothing is missing: 11r36 *sarvadroaca aṇubhavavida sarvasapati ṇaś̱ida sakṣiteṇa yavi mokṣade ṇaś̱ida* (the usual combination consists only of *droaca*, *sapati*, and *mokṣa*). Even clearer is the use of *yava* in 4r23/4v1 *ekadutracadurepaṃcaṣaha-yava-satahi*. Thus, perhaps also in 6v7 *yava* is only indicating the end of an enumeration, not necessarily something that has been omitted. In any case, § 5 *aña kica palios̱eṇa* should refer to either § 4 *aña kuś̱alasa viarthae* and/or *aña balava ma ra amaṇas̱iara akuś̱alasa viarthae*. This could mean that if one does a duty or something else with desire (G *palios̱eṇa*), some hold the opinion that this will not lead to anything wholesome, while others hold the opinion that at least it will not lead to anything unwholesome, as long as the mind is not agitated (G *ṇa spuramaṇas̱a bhoti*). These sentences suggest a special status for *paligodha* among certain people. In BC 4, however, *paligodha* is presented rather negatively, and also in BC 6 (v8) it is stated that both extremes, that is, any kind of aversion as well as any kind of longing, should be avoided.

---

na lakṣaṇena padakārā anuvartyāḥ | padakārair nāma lakṣaṇam anuvartyam | yathālakṣaṇam padam kartavyam.

173 Cited from Deshpande 1992: 237 n. 488. Śabara dates to an early century CE, perhaps the fourth.

6v8 *ṇa rajaṇa ṇa d(*u)ṣaṇa*. Skt. *rañjana* and *dūṣaṇa* are used as synonyms for *rāga* and *doṣa* (in the BHS sense for Skt. *dveṣa*) in the *Prasannapadā*, commenting on verse 23.7 of Nāgārjuna's *Madhyamakaśāstra*:

> *rāgasya dveṣasya mohasya | tatra rañjanaṃ rāgo raktir adhyavasānam | rajyate vā anena cittam iti rāgaḥ | dūṣaṇaṃ doṣaḥ, āghātaḥ sattvaviṣayo 'sattvaviṣayo vā dūṣyate vā anena cittam iti doṣaḥ* | (de La Vallée Poussin 1903–13: 457)
>
> Of passion, hatred, delusion: Among these, [passion is] the act of becoming passionate; passion, affection, clinging. Or when the mind becomes passionate by it, this is passion. [Hatred is] the act of becoming hateful; hatred, malicious feeling with regard to the sphere of beings or the sphere of non-beings. Or when the mind becomes hateful by it, this is hatred.[174]

6v8 *vipaḏiṣara*. The term Skt. *vipratisāra* / P *vippaṭisāra*, literally "thinking back [on the past]," is usually translated as "remorse, regret, guilt, repentance," or "atonement." In BC 6, the term is used within the phrase *ma paçi vipaḏiṣara*. In Sanskrit and Pali texts the phrasing is Skt. *mā paścād vipratisāriṇo bhaviṣyatha* (or *bhūta*) / P *mā pacchā vippaṭisārino ahuvattha*. The term occurs in the *Majjhima-*, *Saṃyutta-* and *Aṅguttaranikāya*s, always at the end of an instruction using the same stock phrase.[175] After stating what has been taught, the following statements are given, cited here from the most recent translation:

> Thus, *bhikkhu*, I have taught [...]. Whatever should be done; by a compassionate teacher out of compassion for his disciples, seeking their welfare, that I have done for you. These are the feet of trees, these are empty huts. Meditate, *bhikkhu*, do not be heedless. **Do not have cause to regret it later**. This is our instruction to you. (Bodhi 2012: 699)[176]

In Pali, the wording is as follows:

---

174 Cf. May (1959: 186): "De quoi? De la concupiscence, de la répulsion et de l'erreur. La concupiscence est «coloration» (*rañjana*); [elle est synonyme d']attraction, recherche délibérée (*adhyavasāna*); ou encore, elle se définit par la propriété de colorer la pensée (*rajyate vānena cittam iti*). L'aversion est perversion; hostilité ayant pour objet un être vivant ou une chose; elle se définit aussi par la propriété de pervertir la pensée. L'erreur est le fait des se tromper, la confusion [d'esprit], la connaissance imparfaite de la forme propre des choses (*padārthasvarūpa*); elle se définit aussi par le propriété de tromper la pensée."

175 It is also used in the *Dīghanikāya*, but not in the same stock phrase as in the other *nikāya*s. One example is: "It may be, monks, that some monk has doubts or uncertainty about the Buddha, the Dhamma, the Sangha, or about the path or the practice. Ask, monks! Do not afterwards feel remorse, thinking: 'The Teacher was there before us, and we failed to ask the Lord face to face!'" (DN III 145–155, tr. Walshe 1987: 270).

176 Other translations differ mainly in the last sentence: "Meditate, *bhikkhu*s, do not delay or else you will regret it later" (MN I 118, tr. Ñāṇamoli and Bodhi 1995: 210); "Meditate, *bhikkhus*, do not be negligent, lest you regret it later" (SN IV 133, tr. Bodhi 2000: 1212).

> *iti kho bhikkhu desito … yaṃ bhikkhu satthārā karaṇīyaṃ sāvakānaṃ hitesinā anukampakena anukampam upādāya kataṃ vo taṃ mayā. etāni bhikkhu rukkhamūlāni etāni suññāgārāni. jhāyatha bhikkhu mā pamādattha* ***mā pacchā vippaṭisārino ahuvattha****. ayaṃ vo amhākam anusāsanī ti.* (AN III 87)

In some Buddhist Sanskrit texts, the formula is similar, but with the addition of a few more places where to go for meditation purposes:

Divyāvadāna (24 *Nāgakumārāvadāna*),[177] citing the instruction itself (not at the end of text):

> *sa evaṃ śrāvakāṇāṃ dharmaṃ deśayati | etāni bhikṣavo 'raṇyāni śūnyāgārāṇi parvatakandaragiriguhāpalālapuñjābhyavakāśaśmaśānavanaprasthāni prāntāni śayanāsanāni dhyāyata bhikṣavo mā pramādata* ***mā paścād vipratisāriṇo bhūte****dam asmākam anuśāsanam |* (Cowell and Neil 1886: 344)
>
> He taught the dharma to his disciples as such: "You should meditate, monks, in forests, in empty chambers, in mountains, valley, hills, caves, heaps of straw, open spaces, cremation grounds, wooded plateaus, and in remote areas. Don't be careless, monks! **Otherwise, later on, you'll be filled with regret**. This is our teaching." (Rotman 2017, II: 157–58)

In other Sanskrit texts, the phrasing is a little shorter, comprising only the exhortation to meditate and not be heedless or careless so that one would not regret it in the future.

Arthaviniścaya, at the end of the sūtra:

> *dhyāyata bhikṣavo mā pramādyata | mā paścād vipratisāriṇo bhaviṣyatha | idam anuśāsanam ||* (Samtani 1971: 67)
>
> [The Blessed One has also said:] "[…] Meditate, monks; do not be indolent. Be not remorseful later." This is the instruction. (Samtani 2002: 43)

---

177 The *Nāgakumārāvadāna* is also cited in the *Pravrajyāvastu*; cf. Vogel and Wille 2002: 27, fol. 48v7–8: *sa evaṃ śrāvakāṇāṃ dharmaṃ deśayati etāni bhikṣavo 'raṇyāni vṛkṣamūlāni śūnyāgārāṇi parvatakandaragiriguhāpalālapuṃjābhyavakāśaśmaśānavanaprasthāni prāntāni śayanāsanāni dhyāyata bhikṣavo mā pramādyata* ***mā paścād vipratisāriṇo bhaviṣyatha*** *: asmākam iyam anuśāsanam iti*, "He taught the Law to his disciples *as follows*: 'These, monks, (are) lonely resting-places: forests, spots at the bases of trees, empty houses, mountain-valleys, mountain-caves, straw-stacks, spots in the open air, funeral places, and wooded tablelands. Meditate (there), monks, do not be inattentive, **do not become remorseful afterwards**! This (is) our instruction.'" (Vogel and Wille 2002: 39). The same text passage occurs also in the *Śayanāsanavastu* (Gnoli 1978: 35–36, A 326a–b): *uktaṃ bhagavatā: ekāny araṇyāni vṛkṣamūlāni śūnyāgārāṇi parvatakandaragiriguhapalālapuñjābhyavakāśaśmaśānavanaprasthāni prāntāni śayanāsanāni dhyāyata, bhikṣavaḥ, mā pramādyata,* ***mā paścād vipratisāriṇo bhūta*** *iti; āraṇyakatvasya ca bahudhā varṇo bhāṣitaḥ.*

Arthaviniścaya, commentary:

> *cittavivekaḥ punar akuśalavitarkavivarjanam | yat pratipādayann āha – dhyāyata bhikṣavo mā pramādyateti | upadeśaka evāham, pratipattyā tu yuṣmābhir eva niṣpādanīyam ity āha –* ***mā paścād vipratisāriṇa*** *iti vistaraḥ* | (Samtani 1971: 311)
>
> [...] mental detachment [in brief] is avoidance of unwholesome thoughts. To accomplish this, it is said, "Meditate, monks, do not be indolent. I am only the teacher: You must gain [the benefit] through your own practice." Hence it is stated, "**Be not remorseful later**." (Samtani 2002: 220)

In the *Rāṣṭrapālaparipṛcchā* the phrase is again used at the end of the text, but not with the exact same wording as in the examples given above:

> *ye yuktāś ca ihāpi harṣitā jinayāne śrutvā yukta sudurmanā bhavitāraḥ* |
> *tasmād vai janayeta śāsane adhimuktiṃ* ***mā paścād anutāpa bheṣyathā*** *vicaramāṇāḥ* ||
> (Finot 1901: 59)
>
> The disciplined are delighted in this vehicle of the Victors. When the undisciplined hear about it, they will become extremely dejected. Therefore, you should apply yourself earnestly in this teaching **lest you are haunted by regret in the future** when you go astray. (Boucher 2008: 169)

In the *Aṣṭasāhasrikā* and *Pañcaviṃśatisāhasrikā Prajñāpāramitā* the phrase is also used, but in another context:

> *sa ca dharmabhāṇakas tān kulaputrān evam abhivyāhariṣyati | amuṣmin kulaputrāḥ pradeśe durbhikṣabhayaṃ kaccit kulaputrā yūyam āgamiṣyatha* ***mā paścād vipratisāriṇo bhaviṣyatha*** *durbhikṣabhayaṃ praviṣṭāḥ | evaṃ te tena dharmabhāṇakena sūkṣmeṇopāyena pratikṣepsyate* | (Mitra 1888: 247)
>
> And that teacher will say to those sons of good family: "This place is short of food. Of course, sons of good family, you may come here if you wish. **But I am afraid that you will regret having come**." This is a subtle device by which he rejects them. (Conze 1973b: 169)[178]

---

178 The passage in the *Pañcaviṃśatisāhasrikā Prajñāpāramitā* is as follows: *punar aparaṃ subhūte dharmabhāṇakaś ca tena gamiṣyati, yena subhikṣaṃ sodakaṃ, dharmaśravaṇikāś cānubaddhā bhaviṣyanti, sa tān evaṃ vakṣyati, kiṃ yuṣmākaṃ kulaputrā āmiṣahetos tatra gantuṃ sucintitaṃ tāvat kuruta mā paścād vipratisāriṇo bhaviṣyatha piṇḍapātena labdhālabdhena, evaṃ tena dharmabhāṇakena sūkṣmeṇopāyena dharmapratyākhyānaṃ kṛtaṃ bhaviṣyati, te nirviṇṇarūpā evaṃ jñāsyanti pratyākhyānanimittāny etāni naitāni dātukāmatānimittāni, iyam api subhūte visāmagrī bhaviṣyati, iha gambhīrāyāṃ prajñāpāramitāyāṃ likhyamānāyām uddiśyamānāyāṃ svādhyāyamānāyāṃ vācyamānāyāṃ bhāvyamānāyām, idam api subhūte bodhisattvānāṃ mahāsattvānāṃ mārakarma veditavyam* (Kimura 1990, IV: 51). "Furthermore the teacher may want to go to a place which is short

Based on this last example, a possible alternative translation of the sentence in BC 6 could be: "Those who would neither wish for the act of becoming passionate nor the act of becoming hateful [will] not regret it afterwards." But the wording in BC 6 seems more closely related to its use in the Pali canon and the Sanskrit texts cited above, even more so, since the formula is placed near the end of the text, just as in the examples above at the end of an instruction. It does not exactly conclude it, but it nevertheless exhorts the reader/listener/addressee to neither become attracted nor repulsed, which is essentially the content of the instruction. Another difference is that an exhortation to meditate is missing. But assuming the stock phrase was well known, even though only a short piece of it is cited, this practice of becoming neither passionate nor hateful was to be developed by way of meditation and mental exercise, and one was not to become careless about it, lest one regret it later.

of food and water, but the pupil will not want to go there. Or the teacher may have gone to a place where there is plenty of food and water, and the pupils will follow him there. He, however, will say to them: 'You may think that it is a good thing for you to come here, because you think that your material needs will be supplied. But I am afraid that you will regret having come, when you see how little alms-food can be had here'. In this way the teacher refuses Dharma by means of a subtle device" (Conze 1975: 341–342).

Appendix

Kharoṣṭhī Bajaur Fragment 19

Mainly the left half of the manuscript is preserved. The longest strip is about 14 cm wide. The fold is still discernible about nine centimeters from the left margin. If we assume that the manuscript was folded in the middle, about nine akṣaras are missing at the beginning of the first line. At the top and bottom nothing seems to be missing, since both margins have been preserved. Based on these observations, the size of the original document was approximately 18 × 10 cm (width × height).

The fragment is stored in the same frame as BC 6 (and was previously labeled BC 6, part 3). Due to its poor state of preservation and the very faded script it is difficult to make much sense of what was once written. Apparently the recto and verso display a single text; punctuation marks are not visible. There is also no remark at the bottom of the recto to turn the page, as is found on BC 4 and BC 6. The text ends in the middle of the verso. All in all, there are twelve lines of writing: seven on the recto and five on the verso.

The size of the letters is rather big and there is more space between the lines than found on the other possibly related manuscripts (BC 4, BC 6, BC 11). Other than that, the ductus and handwriting is in general quite similar to the other three.

Regarding the content, I have abstained from offering a translation, since too many readings are uncertain and too many meanings are unclear. It is possible to say that the text is structured as a list of different opinions on some topic, this suggested by phrases such as *ta vucadi* "it is said" (19r4); *aña* "another [one]"; *aha* "[someone] says/aks"; *aña aha* "another [one] says"; and *tatra aha* "then [someone] says." What was written in between remains mostly in the dark. The only words that can be read with certainty are: 19r7 *bodhakṣetraṇa* ("of buddhafields") and 19r2 *matro* / 19v1 *matra* ("full measure"), which might indicate a connection to BC 4. Other sentences or parts thereof, such as 19v1 *ṇa bhi [atva]da uvagada* ("selfhood is not attained any more") and 19v3 *[suhovaṣaṇa]* ("basis for / causing happiness," Skt. *sukhopadhāna*), also suggest a similar context to that found in BC 4, BC 6, and BC 11.

[19r1] + + + + + + + + + ? [loge][1] dukhi[t]. ? ? ◊ sarvae[hi agap]iehi [vi]ṇa bhayaṇi ca sarva ? ? e[hi v]iṇa bha **[19r2]** + + + + + + + + + ya [ṇ]i ? i ? [e] ? ? [va] ta matro palaḏemaṇa[2] [ta] e mi [ṇa][3] labha **[19r3]** + + + + + + + + + ? ? ? ? ? ? ? ś. ? ? ? ṭa ma[tro] **[19r4]** + + + + + + + + + ? ? ? [hi] tayadi jaḍa ta ka [do he] śi [e] ta vucadi tayadi jaḍa ◊ **[19r5]** + + + + + + + + + ? ? [ṇ]. hi ? ? [vi] ve u s̱a vi [pra]di[4] bhava[d]i aña a ? [da va] **[19r6]** + + + + + + + + + ? [h]. + + + + + + ? p. d. [bha]veadi ta ya[b]a[5] uadae **[19r7]** + + + + + + + + + ? ? ? ? [+ +] .i śa [da va] ◊ bodhakṣetraṇa aña ṇa ◈ yi [v]i [de va][6]

[19v1] + + + + + + + + + ? ? ? ? ṇa bhi [atva]da uvag̱ada [va] ? ? [ya] matra a[ha] hu pa[ś]ami [aha] ki yeṇa mi ◊ apalaḏeṇeṇa **[19v2]** + + + + + + + + + ? jadi a + ? + ? ṇa vi ṇa ya ? ? + + + + + + + + + + [a] ? [aña aha a k]. ? ? ? ? kul[e]hi ua[va] ? + **[19v3]** + + + + + + + + + [suhovas̱aṇa] ? [ṇa] hu[m i]di vaceadi ◊ tatra aha **[19v4]** + + + + + + + + + ? ? karmaṇa khaḍia bhata ṇa bhi ? [mi ṇa hi] daṇi[e]ṇa [va hi] **[19v5]** + + + + + + + + + ? ◊ ṇa vea avarajati ◊

---

[1] Or *lohe*, but cf. the letter form in the following *[agap]iehi*.

References

Allon, Mark. 1997a. "The Oral Composition and Transmission of Early Buddhist Texts." In *Indian Insights: Buddhism, Brahmanism and Bhakti*, edited by Peter Connolly and Sue Hamilton, 39–61. London: Luzac Oriental.

———. 1997b. *Style and Function: A Study of the Dominant Stylistic Features of the Prose Portions of Pāli Canonical Sutta Texts and their Mnemonic Function*. Studia Philologica Buddhica Monograph Series 12. Tokyo: International Institute for Buddhist Studies.

———. 2001. *Three Gāndhārī Ekottarikāgama-Type Sūtras: British Library Kharoṣṭhī Fragments 12 and 14*. Gandhāran Buddhist Texts 2. Seattle: University of Washington Press.

———. 2007. "A Gāndhārī Version of the Simile of the Turtle and the Hole in the Yoke." *Journal of the Pali Text Society* 29: 229–62.

———. 2008. "Recent Discoveries of Buddhist Manuscripts from Afghanistan and Pakistan and Their Significance." In *Art, Architecture and Religion along the Silk Roads*, edited by Ken Parry, 153–78. Turnhout: Brepols.

Allon, Mark, and Richard Salomon. 2000. "Kharoṣṭhī Fragments of a Gāndhārī Version of the Mahāparinirvāṇasūtra." In Braarvig 2000: 243–73.

———. 2010. "New Evidence for Mahāyāna in Early Gandhāra." *The Eastern Buddhist* 41: 1–22.

Amore, Roy Clayton. 1971. "The Concept and Practice of Doing Merit in the Early Theravāda Buddhism." Ph.D. diss., Columbia University.

Andersen, Dines, and Helmer Smith. 1913. *Sutta-nipāta*. London: Henry Frowde.

Anderson, Carol S. 2001. *Pain and Its Ending: The Four Noble Truths in the Theravāda Buddhist Canon*. 1st Indian edition. Buddhist Tradition Series 45. Delhi: Motilal Banarsidass.

Apte, Vaman Shivaram. 1957–59. *Revised and Enlarged Edition of Prin. V. S. Apte's The Practical Sanskrit-English Dictionary*. 3 vols. Poona: Prasad Prakashan.

Aung, Shwe Zang, and C. A. F. Rhys Davids. 1910. *Compendium of Philosophy*. London: Henry Frowde.

———. 1915. *The Points of Controversy*. London: Humphrey Milford.

Bailey, H. W. 1982. "Two Kharoṣṭhī Inscriptions." *Journal of the Royal Asiatic Society of Great Britain & Ireland*, n.s., 114: 142–55.

Balogh, Josef. 1927. "Voces paginarum: Beiträge zur Geschichte des lauten Lesens und Schreibens." *Philologus* 82: 84–109, 202–40.

Barnes, Nancy J. 2012. "Rituals, Religious Communities, and Buddhist Sūtras in India and China." In *Buddhism Across Boundaries: The Interplay of Indian, Chinese and Central*

Asian Source Materials, edited by John R. McRae and Jan Nattier, 212–25. Sino-Platonic Papers, 222. Taipei: Fo Guang Shan Foundation for Buddhist and Culture Education / Sino-Platonic Papers.

Barua, Arabinda. 1982. *The Peṭakopadesa*. Revised edition. London: Routledge & Kegan Paul.

Barua, D. L., 1979. *Achariya Dhammapāla's Paramatthadīpanī: Being the Commentary on the Cariyā-piṭaka*. Second edition. London: Routledge & Kegan Paul.

Bäumer, Bettina, and Kapila Vatsyayan. 2003. *Kalātattvakośa: A Lexicon of Fundamental Concepts of the Indian Arts*. Revised edition. Delhi: Motilal Banarsidass.

Baums, Stefan. 2009. *A Gāndhārī Commentary on Early Buddhist Verses: British Library Kharoṣṭhī Fragments 7, 9, 13 and 18*. Ph.D. diss., University of Washington.

———. 2012. "Catalog and Revised Texts and Translations of Gandharan Reliquary Inscriptions." In *Gandharan Buddhist Reliquaries*, edited by David Jongeward, Elizabeth Errington, Richard Salomon, and Stefan Baums, 200–51. Seattle: Early Buddhist Manuscripts Project.

———. 2014. "Gandhāran Scrolls: Rediscovering an Ancient Manuscript Type." In *Manuscript Cultures: Mapping the Field*, edited by Jörg Quenzer, Dmitry Bondarev, and Jan-Ulrich Sobisch, 183–225. Berlin: De Gruyter.

Baums, Stefan, and Andrew Glass. 2002–a. *A Dictionary of Gāndhārī*. Accessed October 21, 2018. https://gandhari.org/dictionary.

———. 2002–b. *Catalog of Gāndhārī Texts*. Accessed October 21, 2018. https://gandhari.org/catalog.

Baums, Stefan, Andrew Glass, and Kazunobu Matsuda. 2016. "Fragments of a Gāndhārī Version of the Bhadrakalpikasūtra." In Braarvig 2016: 183–266.

Baums, Stefan, Jens Braarvig, Timothy J. Lenz, Fredrik Liland, Kazunobu Matsuda and Richard Salomon. 2016. "The Bodhisattvapiṭakasūtra in Gāndhārī." In Braarvig 2016: 267–82.

Beal, Samuel. 1884. *Si-yu-ki: Buddhist Records of the Western World; Translated from the Chinese of Hiuen Tsang (A.D. 629)*. London: Trübner and Co.

Bechert, Heinz. 1973. "Notes on the Formation of Buddhist Sects and the Origins of Mahāyāna." In *German Scholars on India*, vol. 1, 6–8. Varanasi: The Chowkhamba Sanskrit Series Office.

———. 1990. *Abkürzungsverzeichnis zur buddhistischen Literatur in Indien und Südostasien*. Sanskrit-Wörterbuch der buddhistischen Texte aus den Turfan-Funden, Beiheft 3. Göttingen: Vandenhoeck & Ruprecht.

Bechert, Heinz, Klaus Röhrborn, and Jens-Uwe Hartmann, eds. 1994–. *Sanskrit-Wörterbuch der buddhistischen Texte aus den Turfan-Funden und der kanonischen Literatur der Sarvāstivāda-Schule*. Göttingen: Vandenhoeck & Ruprecht.

Bendall, Cecil. 1902. *Çikshāsamuccaya: A Compendium of Buddhistic Teaching Compiled by Çāntideva Chiefly from Earlier Mahāyāna-sūtras*. Bibliotheca Buddhica 1. St. Petersburg: Académie impériale des sciences.

Bendall, Cecil, and W. H. D. Rouse. 1922. *Śikshā-samuccaya: A Compendium of Buddhist Doctrine Compiled by Śāntideva*. London: John Murray.

Bendall, Cecil, and Louis de La Vallée Poussin. 1906. "Bodhisattva-Bhūmi. A Text-book of the Yogācāra School. An English Summary with Notes and Illustrative Extracts from Other Buddhistic Works." *Le muséon. Revue d'études orientales*, n.s., 7: 213–30.

Berger, Hermann. 1992. "Modern Indo-Aryan." In *Indo-European Numerals*, edited by Jadranka Gvozdanović, 243–87. Trends in Linguistics, Studies and Monographs 57. Berlin: De Gruyter Mouton.

Bernhard, Franz. 1965–68. *Udānavarga*. Abhandlungen der Akademie der Wissenschaften in Göttingen, philologisch-historische Klasse, 3. Folge, Nr. 54. Göttingen: Vandenhoeck & Ruprecht.

Bhattacharya, J. N., and Nilanjana Sarkar. 2004. *Encyclopaedic Dictionary of Sanskrit Literature*. Delhi: Global Vision Publishing House.

Bhattacharya, Vidhushekhara. 1943. *The Āgamaśāstra of Gauḍapāda*. Calcutta: Calcutta University Press.

Bidyabinod, B. B. 1927. "Fragment of a Prajnaparamita Manuscript from Central Asia." *Memoirs of the Archaeological Survey of India* 32: 1–11.

Binz, Wolfgang. 1980. "Praṇidhāna und Vyākaraṇa. Untersuchungen zur Geschichte der Entwicklung des Bodhisatva-Ideals." Ph.D. diss., Ludwig-Maximilians-Universität München.

Bodhi (Bhikkhu). 1996. *A Treatise on the Pāramīs: From the Commentary to the Cariyāpiṭaka by Ācariya Dhammapāla; Translated from the Pāli by Bhikkhu Bodhi [Excerpted from 'The Discourse on the All-Embracing Net of Views: The Brahmajāla Sutta and Its Commentaries']*. Kandy, Sri Lanka: Buddhist Publication Society.

———. 2000. *The Connected Discourses of the Buddha: A New Translation of the Saṃyutta Nikāya*. 2 vols. Oxford: Pali Text Society.

———. 2007. *A Comprehensive Manual of Abhidhamma: The Abhidhammattha Saṅgaha of Ācariya Anuruddha*. Kandy, Sri Lanka: Buddhist Publication Society.

———. 2012. *The Numerical Discourses of the Buddha: A Translation of the Aṅguttara Nikāya*. Boston: Wisdom Publications.

Böhtlingk, Otto, and Rudolph Roth. 1855–75. *Sanskrit-Wörterbuch*. 7 vols. St. Petersburg: Kaiserliche Akademie der Wissenschaften.

Boin-Webb, Sara. 2001. *Abhidharmasamuccaya: The Compendium of the Higher Teaching (Philosophy) by Asaṅga; Originally Translated into French and Annotated by Walpola Rahula; English Version from the French by Sara Boin-Webb*. Fremont, California: Asian Humanities Press.

Bose, M. M. 1977. *Itivuttaka-aṭṭhakathā*. 2 vols. London: Humphrey Milford.

Boucher, Daniel. 1998. "Gāndhārī and the Early Chinese Buddhist Translations Reconsidered: The Case of the *Saddharmapuṇḍarīkasūtra*." *Journal of the American Oriental Society* 118: 471–506.

———. 2008. *Bodhisattvas of the Forest and the Formation of the Mahāyāna: A Study and Translation of the Rāṣṭrapālaparipṛcchā-sūtra*. Honolulu: University of Hawai'i Press.

Boyer, A. M., E. J. Rapson, E. Senart, and J. Noble. 1920–29. *Kharoṣṭhī Inscriptions Discovered by Sir Aurel Stein in Chinese Turkestan*. Oxford: Clarendon Press.

Braarvig, Jens, ed. 2000. *Buddhist Manuscripts in the Schøyen Collection*. Vol. 1. Manuscripts in the Schøyen Collection 1. Oslo: Hermes Publishing.

———. 2016. *Buddhist Manuscripts in the Schøyen Collection*. Vol. 4. Manuscripts in the Schøyen Collection. Oslo: Hermes Publishing.

Bronkhorst, Johannes. 1985. "Dhamma and Abhidhamma." *Bulletin of the School of Oriental and African Studies* 48: 305–20.

———. 1993. *The Two Sources of Indian Asceticism*. Bern/New York: P. Lang.

———. 2007. *Greater Magadha: Studies in the Culture of Early India*. Leiden: Brill.

———. 2011. *Buddhism in the Shadow of Brahmanism*. Leiden: Brill.

———. 2013. "Abhidharma in early Mahāyāna." Paper presented at 32nd Deutscher Orientalistentag, Münster, September 23–27, 2013.

Brough, John. 1962. *The Gāndhārī Dharmapada*. London: Oxford University Press.

———. 1965. "Comments on Third-century Shan-shan and the History of Buddhism." *Bulletin of the School of Oriental and African Studies* 28: 582–612.

Bryant, Edwin Francis. 2009. *The Yoga Sūtras of Patañjali: A New Edition, Translation, and Commentary with Insights from the Traditional Commentators*. New York: North Point Press.

Brunnhölzl, Karl. 2010. *Gone Beyond.* Vol. 1, *The Prajñāpāramitā sūtras, the Ornament of Clear Realization, and Its Commentaries in the Tibetan Kagyü Tradition*. Ithaca NY: Snow Lion Publications.

———. 2011. *Gone Beyond.* Vol. 2, *The Prajñāpāramitā sūtras, the Ornament of Clear Realization, and Its Commentaries in the Tibetan Kagyü Tradition*. Ithaca NY: Snow Lion Publications.

Bühler, Georg. 1896. *Indische Palaeographie von circa 350 a. Chr. – circa 1300 p. Chr.* Grundriss der indo-arischen Philologie und Altertumskunde 1,11. Strassburg: Trübner.

Burrow, Thomas. 1937. *The Language of the Kharoṣṭhi Documents from Chinese Turkestan*. Cambridge: Cambridge University Press.

———. 1940. *A Translation of the Kharoṣṭhi Documents from Chinese Turkestan*. London: The Royal Asiatic Society.

Buswell Jr., Robert E. 1990. "Introduction: Prolegomenon to the Study of Buddhist Apocryphal Scriptures." In *Chinese Buddhist Apocrypha*, edited by Robert E. Buswell Jr., 1–30. Honolulu: University of Hawai'i Press.

Buswell Jr., Robert E., and Robert M. Gimello. 1992. *Paths to Liberation: The Mārga and Its Transformations in Buddhist Thought*. Honolulu: University of Hawai'i Press.

Caillat, Colette. 1975. *Atonement in the Ancient Ritual of the Jaina Monks*. L. D. Series 49. Ahmedabad: L. D. Institute of Indology.

———. 1977–78. "Forms of the Future in the Gāndhārī Dharmapada." *Annals of the Bhandarkar Oriental Research Institute (Diamond Jubilee Volume)* 58/59: 101–6.

———. 1990. "Notes grammaticales sur les documents kharoṣṭhī de Niya." In *Documents et archives provenant de l'Asie centrale*, edited by Akira Haneda, 9–24. Kyoto: Association franco-japonaise des études orientales.

———. 1992a. "The constructions *mama kr̥tam* and *mayā kr̥tam* in Asoka's edicts." In *Proceedings of the XXXII. International Congress for Asian and North African Studies (Hamburg, 25th–30th August 1986)*, edited by Albrecht Wezler and Ernst Hammerschmidt, 489. Stuttgart: Franz Steiner Verlag.

———. 1992b. "Connections Between Asokan (Shahbazgarhi) and Niya Prakrit?" *Indo-Iranian Journal* 35: 109–19.

———. 2011. *Selected Papers*. Bristol: The Pali Text Society.

Canevascini, Giotto. 1993. *The Khotanese Saṅghāṭasūtra: A Critical Edition*. Beiträge zur Iranistik 14. Wiesbaden: Ludwig Reichert Verlag.

Capeller, Carl. 1891. *A Sanskrit-English Dictionary: Based upon the St. Petersburg Lexicons*. Strassburg: Trübner.

Ching, Keng. 2009. "Yogacara Buddhism Transmitted or Transformed? Paramartha (499–569 C.E.) and His Chinese Interpreters." Ph.D. diss., Harvard University.

Choong, Mun-keat (Wei-keat). 2000. *The Fundamental Teachings of Early Buddhism: A Comparative Study Based on the Sūtrāṅga Portion of the Pāli Saṃyutta-Nikāya and the Chinese Saṃyuktāgama*. Wiesbaden: Harrassowitz.

Cone, Margaret. 2001. *A Dictionary of Pāli*. Pt. 1, *a-kh*. Oxford: Pali Text Society.

Conze, Edward. 1954. *Abhisamayālaṅkāra*. Serie Orientale Roma 6. Rome: Istituto Italiano per il Medio ed Estremo Oriente.

———. 1962. *The Gilgit Manuscript of the Aṣṭādaśasāhasrikāprajñāpāramitā (I): Chapters 55 to 70 Corresponding to the 5th Abhisamaya*. Serie Orientale Roma 26. Rome: Istituto Italiano per il Medio ed Estremo Oriente.

———. 1973a. *Materials for a Dictionary of the Prajñāpāramitā Literature*. Tokyo: Suzuki Research Foundation.

———. 1973b. *The Perfection of Wisdom in Eight Thousand Lines and Its Verse Summary*. Bolinas: Four Seasons Foundation.

———. 1974. *The Gilgit Manuscript of the Aṣṭādaśasāhasrikāprajñāpāramitā (II): Chapters 70 to 82 Corresponding to the 6th, 7th and 8th Abhisamayas*. Serie Orientale Roma 46. Rome: Istituto Italiano per il Medio ed Estremo Oriente.

———. 1975. *The Large Sutra on Perfect Wisdom, with the Divisions of the Abhisamayālaṅkāra*. Berkeley: University of California Press.

———. 1978. *The Prajñāpāramitā Literature*. Bibliographia philologica Buddhica series maior 1. 2nd edition. Tokyo: Reiyukai.

Cousins, Lance S. 1983. "Pali Oral Literature." In *Buddhist Studies Ancient and Modern*, edited by P. Denwood and A. Piatigorsky, 1–11. London: Curzon Press.

Covill, Linda. 2007. *Handsome Nanda*. Clay Sanskrit Series. New York: New York University Press and the Clay Sanskrit Library.

Cowell, Edward B., and R. A. Neil. 1886. *The Divyāvadāna: A Collection of Early Buddhist Legends*. Cambridge: Cambridge University Press.

Cox, Collett. 2004. "From Category to Ontology: The Changing Role of Dharma in Sarvāstivāda Abhidharma." *Journal of Indian Philosophy* 32: 543–97.

———. 2014. "Gāndhārī Kharoṣṭhī Manuscripts: Exegetical Texts." In Harrison and Hartmann 2014: 35–49.

Cüppers, Christoph. 1990. *The IXth [Ninth] Chapter of the Samādhirājasūtra: A Text-Critical Contribution to the Study of Mahāyāna Sūtras*. Alt- und Neu-Indische Studien 41. Stuttgart: Steiner.

Deleanu, Florin. 2000. "A Preliminary Study of Meditation and the Beginnings of Mahāyāna Buddhism." *Annual Report of the International Research Institute for Advanced Buddhology at Soka University* 3: 65–113.

———. 2006. *The Chapter on the Mundane Path (Laukikamārga) in the Śrāvakabūmi: A Trilingual Edition (Sanskrit, Tibetan, Chinese); Annotated Translation, and Introductory Study*. 2 vols. Studia Philologica Buddhica Monograph Series XXa. Tokyo: International Institute for Buddhist Studies.

Deshpande, Madhav M. 1992. *The Meaning of Nouns: Semantic Theory in Classical and Medieval India*. Dordrecht: Springer-Science+Business Media.

Dessein, Bart. 2009. "The Mahāsāmghikas and the Origin of Mahayana Buddhism: Evidence Provided in the *Abhidharmamahāvibhāṣāśāstra." *The Eastern Buddhist* 40: 25–61.

Dharmamitra, Bhikshu. 2009. *Nāgārjuna's Guide to the Bodhisattva Path: Treatise on the Provisions of Enlightenment (Bodhisaṃbhāra Śāstra) with Selective Abridgment of Bhikshu Vaśitva's Early Indian Bodhisaṃbhāra Śāstra Commentary; Translation, Abridgement and Explanatory Notes by Bhikshu Dharmamitra*. Seattle: Kalavinka Press.

Drewes, David. 2010a. "Early Indian Mahāyāna Buddhism, I: Recent Scholarship." *Religion Compass* 4: 55–65.

———. 2010b. "Early Indian Mahāyāna Buddhism, II: New Perspectives." *Religion Compass* 4: 66–74.

———. 2011. "Dharmabhāṇakas in Early Mahāyāna." *Indo-Iranian Journal* 54: 331–72.

Dutt, Nalinaksha. 1934. *The Pañcaviṁśatisāhasrikā Prajñāpāramitā*. Calcutta Oriental Series 28. London: Luzac & Co.

———. 1941. *Gilgit Manuscripts*. Vol. 2, pt. 1. Calcutta: Calcutta Oriental Press.

———. 1954. *Gilgit Manuscripts*. Vol. 2, pt. 3. Calcutta: Calcutta Oriental Press.

———. 1966. *Bodhisattvabhumi*. Tibetan Sanskrit Works Series 7. Patna: Kashi Prasad Jayaswal Research Institute.

Edgerton, Franklin. 1953. *Buddhist Hybrid Sanskrit Grammar and Dictionary*. New Haven: Yale University Press.

Erdosy, George. 1990. "Taxila: Political History and Urban Structure." In *South Asian Archaeology 1987 – Proceedings of the Ninth International Conference of the Association of South Asian Archaeologists in Western Europe, Held in the Fondazione Giorgio Cini, Island of San Giorgio Maggiore, Venice*, edited by Maurizio Taddei and Pierfrancesco Callieri, 643–74. Rome: Istituto Italiano per il Medio ed Estremo Oriente.

Emmerick, Ronald E. 1968. *The Book of Zambasta: A Khotanese Poem on Buddhism*. London: Oxford University Press.

———. 2001. *The Sūtra of Golden Light: Being a Translation of the Suvarṇabhāsottamasūtra*. 3rd revised edition. Oxford: Pali Text Society.

Falk, Harry. 2003a. Review of Oskar von Hinüber, *Beiträge zur Erklärung der Senavarma-Inschrift*. *Orientalistische Literaturzeitung* 98: 573–77.

———. 2003b. "Five New Kharoṣṭhī Donation Records from Gandhāra." *Silk Road Art and Archaeology* 9: 71–86.

———. 2005. "The Introduction of Stūpa-Worship in Bajaur." In *Afghanistan, ancien carrefour entre l'Est et l'Ouest. Actes du colloque international organisé par Christian Landes & Osmund Bopearachchi au Musée archéologique Henri-Prades-Lattes du 5 au 7 mai 2003*, edited by Osmund Bopearachchi and Marie-Françoise Boussac, 347–58. Turnhout: Brepols.

———. 2006. "Three Inscribed Buddhist Monastic Utensils from Gandhāra." *Zeitschrift der Deutschen Morgenländischen Gesellschaft* 156: 393–412.

———. 2008. "Money Can Buy Me Heaven: Religious Donations in Late and Post-Kushan India." *Archäologische Mitteilungen aus Iran und Turan* 40: 137–48.

———. 2010. "Names and Titles from Kuṣāṇa Times to the Hūṇas: The Indian Material." In *Coins, Art and Chronology II: The First Millenium C.E. in the Indo-Iranian Borderlands*, edited by M. Alram, D. Klimburg-Salter, M. Inaba, and M. Pfister, 73–89. Vienna: Verlag der Österreichischen Akademie der Wissenschaften.

———. 2011. "The 'Split' Collection of Kharoṣṭhī Texts." *Annual Report of The International Research Institute for Advanced Buddhology at Soka University* 14: 13–23.

———. 2012 (2007). "Ancient Indian Eras: An Overview." *Bulletin of the Asia Institute*, n.s., 21: 131–45.

———. 2013. *Hariśyenalekhapañcāśikā: Fifty Selected Papers on Indian Epigraphy and Chronology.* Bremen: Hempen Verlag.

———. 2014. "The First-Century Copper-Plates of Helagupta from Gandhāra Hailing Maitreya." *Annual Report of The International Research Institute for Advanced Buddhology at Soka University* 17: 3–26.

———. 2015. "A New Gāndhārī Dharmapada (Texts from the Split Collection, 3)." *Annual Report of The International Research Institute for Advanced Buddhology at Soka University* 18: 23–62.

Falk, Harry, and Seishi Karashima. 2012. "A first-century Prajñāpāramitā Manuscript from Gandhāra – parivarta 1 (Texts from the Split Collection, 1)." *Annual Report of The International Research Institute for Advanced Buddhology at Soka University* 15: 19–61.

———. 2013. "A first-century Prajñāpāramitā Manuscript from Gandhāra – parivarta 5 (Texts from the Split Collection, 2)." *Annual Report of The International Research Institute for Advanced Buddhology at Soka University* 16: 97–169.

Falk, Harry, and Ingo Strauch. 2014. "The Bajaur and Split Collections of Kharoṣṭhī Manuscripts within the Context of Buddhist Gāndhārī Literature." In Harrison and Hartmann 2014: 51–78.

Fausbøll, Viggo. 1877–96. *The Jātaka Together with Its Commentary Being Tales of the Anterior Births of Gotama Buddha.* 6 vols. London: Kegan Paul Trench Trübner & Co.

Findly, Ellison Banks. 2003. *Dāna: Giving and Getting in Pali Buddhism*. Buddhist Tradition Series 52. Delhi: Motilal Banarsidass.

Finot, Louis. 1901. *Rāṣṭrapālaparipṛcchā: Sūtra du Mahāyāna*. St. Petersburg: Académie impériale des sciences.

Frauwallner, Erich. 1973. *History of Indian Philosophy*. Delhi: Motilal Banarsidass.

Fujita, Kotatsu. 2011. *The Larger and Smaller Sukhāvatīvyūha Sūtras*. Kyoto: Hozokan.

Fujita, Yoshimichi. 2009. "The Bodhisattva Thought of the Sarvāstivādins and Mahāyāna Buddhism." *Acta Asiatica. Bulletin of the Institute of Eastern Culture (Tōhō Gakkai)* 96: 99–120.

Funayama, Tōru. 2013. "Buddhist Theories of Bodhisattva Practice as Adopted by Daoists." *Cahiers d'Extrême-Asie* 20: 15–33.

Fussman, Gérard. 1989. "Gāndhārī écrite, gāndhārī parlée." In *Dialectes dans les littératures indo-aryennes*, edited by Colette Caillat, 433–501. Paris: Institut de civilisation indienne.

———. 2011. *Monuments bouddhiques de Termez, I: Catalogue des inscriptions sur poteries; Publications de l'Institut de civilisation indienne, fascicule 79*. Paris: Édition-diffusion de Boccard.

Geiger, Wilhelm. 1994. *Pāli Grammar*. Oxford: Pali Text Society.

Geiger, Wilhelm, and K. R. Norman. 2000. *A Pali Grammar*. Revised edition. Oxford: Pali Text Society.

Gethin, Rupert M. 1992a. *The Buddhist Path to Awakening: A Study of the Bodhi-Pakkhiyā Dhammā*. Brill's Indological Library 7. Leiden: Brill.

———. 1992b. "The Mātikās. Memorization, Mindfulness and the List." In *In The Mirror of Memory: Reflections on Mindfulness and Remembrance in Indian and Tibetan Buddhism*, edited by J. Gyatso, 149–72. Albany: State University of New York.

———. 2004. "He Who Sees Dhamma Sees Dhammas: Dhamma in Early Buddhism." *Journal of Indian Philosophy* 32: 513–42.

Glass, Andrew. 2000. "A Preliminary Study of Kharoṣṭhī Manuscript Paleography." M.A. thesis, University of Washington.

———. 2004. "Kharoṣṭhī Manuscripts: A Window on Gandhāran Buddhism." *Nagoya Studies in Indian Culture and Buddhism: Saṃbhāṣā* 24: 129–52.

———. 2006. *Connected Discourses in Gandhāra: A Study, Edition, and Translation of Four Saṃyuktāgama-Type Sūtras from the Senior Collection*. Ph.D. diss., University of Washington.

———. 2007. *Four Gāndhārī Saṃyuktāgama Sūtras: Senior Kharoṣṭhī Fragment 5*. Gandhāran Buddhist Texts 4. Seattle: University of Washington Press.

Gnoli. Raniero. 1978. *The Gilgit Manuscript of the Śayanāsanavastu and the Adhikaraṇavastu, Being the 15th and 16th Sections of the Vinaya of the Mūlasarvāstivādin*. Serie Orientale Roma 50. Rome: Istituto Italiano per il Medio ed Estremo Oriente.

Gokhale, V. V. 1947. "Fragments from the Abhidharmasamuccaya of Asaṃga." *Journal of the Bombay Branch of the Royal Asiatic Society*, n.s., 23: 13–38.

Gombrich, Richard. 1990. "How the Mahāyāna Began." In *The Buddhist Forum*, vol. 1, edited by Tadeusz Skorupski, 21–30. London: School of Oriental and African Studies.

Gómez, Luis O. 1976. "Proto-Mādhyamika in the Pāli Canon." *Philosophy East and West* 26: 137–65.

———. 1999. *Land of Bliss: The Paradise of the Buddha of Measureless Light; Sanskrit and Chinese Versions of the Sukhāvatīvyūha Sutras*. Honolulu: University of Hawai'i Press.

Goodman, Charles. 2016. *The Training Anthology of Śāntideva: A Translation of the Śikṣāsamuccaya*. New York: Oxford University Press.

Giustarini, Giuliano. 2005. "A Note on Saḷāyatanas in Pāli Nikāyas." *Annali dell' Università degli Studi di Napoli* 65: 153–78.

———. 2006. "Faith and Renunciation in Early Buddhism: Saddhā and Nekkhamma." *Rivista di Studi Sudasiatici* 1: 161–79.

Hahn, Michael. 1982. *Nāgārjuna's Ratnāvalī*. Vol. 1, *The Basic Texts (Sanskrit, Tibetan, Chinese)*. Indica et Tibetica 1. Bonn: Indica et Tibetica.

———. 1988. "Bemerkungen zu zwei Texten aus dem Phudrag-Kanjur." In *Indology and Indo-Tibetology: Thirty Years of Indian and Indo-Tibetan Studies in Bonn*, edited by Helmut Eimer, 53–80. Indica et Tibetica 13. Bonn: Indica et Tibetica.

Hakeda, Yoshito. 1967. *The Awakening of Faith*. New York and London: Columbia University Press.

Hamilton, Sue. 1996. *Identity and Experience: The Constitution of the Human Being According to Early Buddhism*. London: Luzac Oriental.

Hanisch, Albrecht. 2005. *Āryaśūras Jātakamālā*. Indica et Tibetica 43. Marburg: Indica et Tibetica Verlag.

Hanneder, Jürgen. 2009. "Dreams and Other States of Consciousness in the Mokṣopāya." In *The Indian Night: Sleep and Dreams in Indian Culture*, edited by Claudine Bautze-Picron, 64–99. New Delhi: Rupa & Co.

Hardy, E. 1902. *The Netti-pakaraṇa with Extracts from Dhammapāla's Commentary*. London: Henry Frowde.

Harrison, Paul. 1987. "Who Gets to Ride in the Great Vehicle? Self-Image and Identity Among the Followers of the Early Mahāyāna." *Journal of the International Association of Buddhist Studies* 10: 67–89.

———. 1993. "The Earliest Chinese Translations of Mahāyāna Sūtras: Some Notes on the Works of Lokakṣema." *Buddhist Studies Review* 10: 135–77.

———. 1995. "Searching of the Origins of the Mahāyāna: What Are We Looking For?" *Eastern Buddhist* 28: 48–69.

———. 1998. *The Pratyutpanna Samādhi Sutra*. Berkeley: Numata Center for Buddhist Translation and Research.

Harrison, Paul, and Jens-Uwe Hartmann, eds. 2014. *From Birch Bark to Digital Data: Recent Advances in Buddhist Manuscript Research; Papers Presented at the Conference 'Indic Buddhist Manuscripts: The State of the Field,' Stanford, June 15–19 2009*. Vienna: Verlag der Österreichischen Akademie der Wissenschaften.

Harrison, Paul, Timothy Lenz, and Richard Salomon. 2018. "Fragments of a Gāndhārī Manuscript of the *Pratyutpannabuddhasaṃmukhāvasthitasamādhisūtra* (Studies in Gāndhārī Manuscripts 1)." *Journal of the International Association of Buddhist Studies* 41: 117–43.

Harrison, Paul, Timothy Lenz, Qian Lin, and Richard Salomon. 2016. "A Gāndhārī Fragment of the *Sarvapuṇyasamuccayasamādhisūtra*." In Braarvig 2016: 311–19.

Hartmann, Jens-Uwe. 2011. "Sensationeller Fund eines Mahāyānasūtras aus dem 1. Jahrhundert." *Tibet und Buddhismus* 96: 30–34.

Hikata, Ryusho. 1958. *Suvikrāntavikrāmi-paripṛcchā Prajñāpāramitā-Sūtra*. Fukuoka: Kyushu University.

Hinnells, John R. 1995. *A New Dictionary of Religions*. Oxford, UK / Cambridge, MA: Blackwell.

Hinüber, Oskar von. 1986. *Studien zur Kasussyntax des Pāli, besonders des Vinaya-Piṭaka*. Munich: Kitzinger.

———. 1990. *Der Beginn der Schrift und frühe Schriftlichkeit in Indien*. Akademie der Wissenschaften und der Literatur, Mainz, Abhandlungen der geistes- und sozialwissenschaftlichen Klasse 1989, 11. Stuttgart: Franz Steiner Verlag.

———. 1994. *Untersuchungen zur Mündlichkeit früher mittelindischer Texte der Buddhisten*. Akademie der Wissenschaften und der Literatur, Mainz, Abhandlungen der geistes- und sozialwissenschaftlichen Klasse 1994, 5. Stuttgart: Franz Steiner Verlag.

———. 1996. *A Handbook of Pāli Literature*. Berlin: De Gruyter.

———. 2001. *Das ältere Mittelindisch im Überblick*. 2nd revised edition. Vienna: Verlag der Österreichischen Akademie der Wissenschaften.

———. 2003. *Beiträge zur Erklärung der Senavarma-Inschrift*. Akademie der Wissenschaften und der Literatur, Mainz, Abhandlungen der geistes- und sozialwissenschaftlichen Klasse 2003, 1. Stuttgart: Franz Steiner Verlag.

Hinüber, Oskar von, and K. R. Norman. 1995. *Dhammapada: Reprinted with Corrections*. Oxford: Pali Text Society.

Hirakawa, Akira. 1990. *A History of Indian Buddhism: From Śākyamuni to Early Mahāyāna*. Tr. Paul Groner. Asian Studies at Hawai'i 36. Honolulu: University of Hawai'i Press.

Hopkins, Jeffrey et al. 1975. *The Precious Garland of Advice for the King*. London: Allen & Unwin.

Horner, I. B. 1963. *Milinda's Questions*. 2 vols. London: Luzac & Company.

———. 1975. *The Minor Anthologies of the Pali Canon*. Vol. 3. London: Pali Text Society.

Hubbard, Jamie. 1994. "Original Purity and the Arising of Delusion." Accessed September 11, 2013. http://sophia.smith.edu/-jhubbard/publications/papers/OriginalPurity.pdf.

Hultzsch, Eugen. 1925. *Inscriptions of Asoka*. Corpus Inscriptionum Indicarum I. Oxford: Clarendon Press.

Insler, Stanley. 1987. "The Vedic Causative Type jāpáyati." In *Studies in Memory of Warren Cowgill (1929–1985): Papers from the Fourth East Coast Indo-European Conference, Cornell University, June 6–9, 1985*, edited by Calvert Watkins, 54–65. Berlin: De Gruyter.

Jacobi, Hermann Georg. 1884. *Gaina Sûtras*. Pt. 1, *The Âkârâṅga Sûtra. The Kalpa Sûtra*. Sacred books of the East 22. Oxford: Clarendon Press.

Jaini, Padmanabh S. 1959. *Abhidharmadīpa with Vibhāshāprabhāvṛtti*. Tibetan Sanskrit Work Series 4. Patna: Kashi Prasad Jayaswal Research Institute.

———. 1979. *Sāratamā: A Pañjikā on the Aṣṭasāhasrikā Prajñāpāramitā Sūtra by Ratnākaraśānti*. Tibetan Sanskrit Works Series 18. Patna: Kashi Prasad Jayaswal Research Institute.

Jamison, Stephanie W. 2000. "Lurching towards Ergativity: Expressions of Agency in the Niya Documents." *Bulletin of the School of Oriental and African Studies* 63: 64–80.

Johnston, E. H. 1928. *The Saundarananda of Aśvaghoṣa*. London: Oxford University Press.

———. 1932. *The Saundarananda or Nanda the Fair*. London: Oxford University Press.

———. 1935. *The Buddhacarita: Or Acts of the Buddha*. Vol. 1, *Sanskrit Text*. Panjab University Oriental Publications 31. Calcutta: Baptist Mission Press.

Johnston, E. H. 1936. *The Buddhacarita: Or Acts of the Buddha*. Vol. 2, *Cantos i to xiv Translated from the Original Sanskrit Supplemented by the Tibetan Version*. Panjab University Oriental Publications 32. Calcutta: Baptist Mission Press.

Johnston, E. H. 1971. *Formal Penmanship and Other Papers*. New York: Taplinger.

Jones, J. J. 1949–56. *The Mahāvastu*. 3 vols. Sacred books of the Buddhists 16, 18, 19. London: Lancaster.

Kalupahana, David J. 1992. *A History of Buddhist Philosophy: Continuities and Discontinuities*. Honolulu: University of Hawai'i Press.

Keown, Damien. 2004. "A Dictionary of Buddhism." Online version 2012. Accessed January 7, 2013. http://www.oxfordreference.com/view/10.1093/acref/9780198605607.001.0001/acref-9780198605607.

Kern, Hendrik. 1884. *The Saddharma-Pundarîka or the Lotus of the True Law*. Sacred books of the East 21. Oxford: Clarendon Press.

———. 1891. *The Jataka-Mala*. Harvard Oriental Series 1. Cambridge, MA: Harvard University Press.

Kern, Hendrik, and Bunyiu Nanjio. 1912. *Saddharmapuṇḍarīka*. Bibliotheca Buddhica 10. St. Petersburg: Académie impériale des sciences.

Kim, Jinah. 2013. *Receptacle of the Sacred: Illustrated Manuscripts and the Buddhist Book Cult in South Asia*. Berkeley: University of California Press.

Kimura, R. 1927. "Mahāyāna and Hīnayāna Works Known to Nāgārjuna." *Indian Historical Quarterly* 3: 412–17.

Kimura, Takayasu. 1986. *Pañcaviṃśatisāhasrikā Prajñāpāramitā II–III*. Tokyo: Sankibo Busshorin.

———. 1990. *Pañcaviṃśatisāhasrikā Prajñāpāramitā IV*. Tokyo: Sankibo Busshorin.

———. 1992. *Pañcaviṃśatisāhasrikā Prajñāpāramitā V*. Tokyo: Sankibo Busshorin.

———. 2006. *Pañcaviṃśatisāhasrikā Prajñāpāramitā VI–VIII*. Tokyo: Sankibo Busshorin.

———. 2007. *Pañcaviṃśatisāhasrikā Prajñāpāramitā I-1*. Tokyo: Sankibo Busshorin.

———. 2009. *Pañcaviṃśatisāhasrikā Prajñāpāramitā I-2*. Tokyo: Sankibo Busshorin.

Konow, Sten. 1929. *Kharoshṭhī Inscriptions with the Exception of Those of Aśoka*. Corpus Inscriptionum Indicarum 2.1. Calcutta: Government of India, Central Publication Branch.

———. 1942. *Central Asian Fragments of the Ashṭādaśasāhasrikā Prajñāpāramitā and of an Unidentified Text*. Memoirs of the Archaeological Survey of India 69. Calcutta: Government of India Press.

Krümpelmann, Kornelius. 2000. *Das Dhuttakkhāṇa: Eine jinistische Satire*. Frankfurt: Lang.

Kubo, Tsugunari, and Akira Yuyama. 2007. *The Lotus Sutra (Taishō Volume 9, Number 262): Translated from the Chinese of Kumārajiva*. BDK English Tripiṭaka Series. Berkeley: Numata Center for Buddhist Translation and Research.

Kudo, Noriyuki, Takanori Fukita, and Hironori Tanaka. 2018. *Gilgit Manuscripts in the National Archives of India: Facsimile Edition*, vol. 2.3, *Samādhirājasūtra*. Tokyo: The International Research Institute for Advanced Buddhology, Soka University / Delhi: The National Archives of India.

Kurumiya, Yenshu. 1978. *Ratnaketuparivarta: Sanskrit Text*. Kyoto: Heirakuji-Shoten.

La Vallée Poussin, Louis de. 1901–14. *Prajñākaramati's Commentary to the Bodhicaryāvatāra of Çāntideva*. Bibliotheca Indica 150. Calcutta: Asiatic Society.

———. 1903–13. *Mūlamadhyamakakārikās (Mādhyamikasūtras) de Nāgārjuna avec la Prasannapadā Commentaire de Candrakīrti*. St. Petersburg: Académie impériale des sciences.

———. 1909. "Notes sur le Grand Véhicule." *Revue de l'Histoire des Religions* 59: 338–48.

———. 1913. *Bouddhisme: Études et matériaux; Théorie des douze causes.* Gand: Librairie Scientifique E. van Goethem.

La Vallée Poussin, Louis de, and Leo M. Pruden. 1988–90. *Abhidharmakośabhāṣyam of Vasubandhu: Translated into English from the French Translation of Louis de La Vallée Poussin; English Translation by Leo M. Pruden.* 4 vols. Berkeley: Asian Humanities Press.

La Vallée Poussin, Louis de, and E. J. Thomas. 1916–17. *Niddesa I: Mahāniddesa.* London: Oxford University Press.

Lambert, H. M. 1953. *Introduction to the Devanagari Script for Students of Sanskrit, Hindi, Marathi, Gujarati, and Bengali.* London: Oxford University Press.

Lamotte, Étienne. 1944–80. *Le traité de la grande vertu de sagesse de Nāgārjuna (Mahāprajñāpāramitāśāstra).* 5 vols. Publications de l'Institut orientaliste de Louvain 2, 12, 24, 25, 26. Louvain-la-Neuve: Université de Louvain, Institut orientaliste.

———. 1954. "Sur la formation du Mahāyāna." In *Asiatica: Festschrift für Friedrich Weller zum 65. Geburtstag gewidmet*, edited by Johannes Schubert and Ulrich Schneider, 377–96. Leipzig: Harrassowitz.

———. 1962. *L'Enseignement de Vimalakīrti (Vimalakīrtinirdeśa).* Bibliothèque du Muséon 51. Louvain: Publications Universitaires.

Lamotte, Étienne, and Sara Boin-Webb. 2003. *Śūraṃgamasamādhisūtra: The Concentration of Heroic Progress; An Early Mahāyāna Buddhist Scripture.* First Indian edition. Delhi: Motilal Banarsidass.

Lee, Mei-huang. 2009. "A Study of the Gāndhārī Dārukkhandopamasutta ('Discourse of the Simile of the Log')." Ph.D. diss., University of Washington.

Lefmann, Salomon. 1902–08. *Lalitavistara.* 2 vols. Halle: Verlag der Buchhandlung des Waisenhauses.

Lenz, Timothy. 2003. *A New Version of the Gāndhārī Dharmapada and a Collection of Previous-Birth Stories: British Library Kharoṣṭhi fragments 16 + 25.* Gandhāran Buddhist Texts 3. Seattle: University of Washington Press.

———. 2010. *Gandhāran Avādanas: British Library Kharoṣṭhī Fragments 1–3 and 21 and Supplementary Fragments A–C.* Gandhāran Buddhist Texts 6. Seattle: University of Washington Press.

Lethcoe, Nancy R. 1977. "The Bodhisatva Ideal in the Aṣṭa. and Pañca. Prajñāpāramitā Sūtras." In *Prajñāpāramitā and Related Systems: Studies in Honour of Edward Conze*, edited by Lewis Lancaster, 263–80. Berkeley: University of California.

Lévi, Sylvain. 1907. *Mahāyāna-Sūtrālaṃkāra: Exposé de la Doctrine du Grand Véhicule; Tome I, Texte.* Paris: Librairie Honoré Champion.

———. 1911. *Mahāyāna-Sūtrālaṃkāra: Exposé de la Doctrine du Grand Véhicule; Tome II, Traduction—Introduction—Index.* Paris: Librairie Honoré Champion.

Limaye, Surekha Vijay. 1992. *Mahāyānasūtrālaṁkāra by Asaṅga: Sanskrit Text and Translated into English.* Delhi: Sri Satguru Publications.

Lin, Li-kouang. 1973. *Dharma-Samuccaya: Compendium de la Loi. 3e Partie (Chapitres XIII à XXXVI); Texte sanskrit édité avec la version tibétaine et les versions chinoises et traduit en français.* Annales du Musée Guimet, Bibliothèque d'Études 75. Paris: Adrien-Maisonneuve.

Lokesh Chandra. 1981. *Kāraṇḍavyūha and Other Texts: Sanskrit Manuscripts from Nepal, Reproduced from the Collection of Prof. Raghuvīra.* Śata piṭaka series 268. New Delhi: Sharada Rani.

Lüders, Heinrich. 1911. *Bruchstücke buddhistischer Dramen*. Kleinere Sanskrittexte 1. Berlin: Reimer.

Macdonell, Arthur Anthony. 1929. *A Practical Sanskrit Dictionary with Transliteration, Accentuation, and Etymological Analysis Throughout*. London: Oxford University Press.

Marino, Joseph. 2017. "Metaphor and Pedagogy in Early Buddhist Literature: An Edition and Study of Two Sūtras from the Senior Collection of Gāndhārī Manuscripts." Ph.D. diss., University of Washington.

Marshall, John. 1951. *Taxila: An Illustrated Account of Archaeological Excavations Carried out at Taxila under the Orders of the Government of India between the Years 1913 and 1934*. 3 vols. Cambridge: Cambridge University Press.

Martini, Guiliana. 2013. "Bodhisattva Texts, Ideologies and Rituals in Khotan in the Fifth and Sixth Centuries." In *Buddhism among the Iranian Peoples of Central Asia*, edited by Matteo de Chiara, Mauro Maggi, and Giuliana Martini, 13–69. Vienna: Verlag der Österreichischen Akademie der Wissenschaften.

Maung Tin, Pe. 1920–21. *The Expositor (Atthasālinī): Buddhaghosa's Commentary on the Dhammasaṅgaṇī, the First Book of the Abhidhamma Pitaka*. London: Milford.

May, Jacques. 1959. *Candrakīrti, Prasannapadā Madhyamakavṛtti*. Paris: Adrien-Maisonneuve.

Melzer, Gudrun. 2010. "Ein Abschnitt aus dem Dīrghāgama. Teil 1 [mit einigen Ergänzungen, 31.1.2010]." Ph.D. diss., Ludwig-Maximilians-Universität München.

Mette, Adelheid. 1997. *Die Gilgitfragmente des Kāraṇḍavyūha*. Monographien zu den Sprachen und Literaturen des indo-tibetischen Kulturraumes 29. Swisttal-Odendorf: Indica et Tibetica.

Mitra, Rājendralāla. 1888. *Ashṭasāhasrikā*. Calcutta: G. H. House.

Monier-Williams, Monier. 1899. *A Sanskrit-English Dictionary*. Oxford: Clarendon Press.

Morgenstierne, Georg. 1947. "Metathesis of liquids in Dardic." In *Festskrift til professor Olaf Broch på hans 80-årsdag fra venner og elever*, edited by Chr. S. Stang, Erik Krag, and Arne Gallis, 145–54. Oslo: Jacob Dybwad.

Müller, Edward. 1885. *The Dhammasaṅgaṇi*. Text Series 31. London: Oxford University Press.

Müller, F. Max. 1881. *The Dhammapada: A Collection of Verses; Being One of the Canonical Books of the Buddhists*. The Sacred Books of the East 10,1. Oxford: Clarendon Press.

Müller, F. Max, and H. Wenzel. 1885. *Dharmasaṃgraha*. Anecdota Oxoniensia, Aryan Series 1,5. Oxford: Clarendon Press.

Murakami, Shinkan. 2004. "Origin of the Mahāyāna-Buddhism." Paper presented at the International Congress for Asian and North African Studies (ICANAS) XXXVII, Moscow, August 16–21, 2004.

Ñāṇamoli (Bhikkhu). 1962. *The Guide (Netti-ppakaraṇaṃ) According to Kaccāna Thera*. London: Luzac & Company.

———. 1964. *The Piṭaka-Disclosure (Peṭakopadesa)*. London: Pali Text Society.

———. 1997. *The Path of Discrimination (Paṭisambhidāmagga)*. Revised edition. London: Pali Text Society.

———. 2011. *The Path of Purification (Visuddhimagga)*. 3rd revised online edition. Kandy: Buddhist Publication Society. Accessed October 29, 2019. https://www.accesstoinsight.org/lib/authors/nanamoli/PathofPurification2011.pdf

Ñāṇamoli (Bhikkhu) and Bodhi (Bhikkhu). 1995. *The Middle Length Discourses of the Buddha: A New Translation of the Majjhima Nikāya*. Boston: Wisdom Publications.

Nanjio, Bunyiu. 1923. *The Laṅkāvatāra-sūtra*. Kyoto: Otani University Press.

Nārada (Mahāthera). 1987. *A Manual of Abhidhamma: Being Abhidhammattha Saṅgaha of Anuruddhācariya; Edited in the Original Pali Text with English Translation and Explanatory Notes*. 5th edition. Kuala Lumpur: Buddhist Missionary Society.

Nasim Khan, M. 2008. *Kharoṣṭhī Manuscripts from Gandhāra*. Department of Archaeology, University of Peshawar.

Nattier, Jan. 1992. "The Heart Sutra: A Chinese Apocryphal Text?" *Journal of the International Association of Buddhist Studies* 15: 180–81.

———. 2003. *A Few Good Men. The Bodhisattva Path According to The Inquiry of Ugra (Ugraparipṛcchā)*. Honolulu: University of Hawai'i Press.

———. 2008. *A Guide to the Earliest Chinese Buddhist Translations: Texts from the Eastern Han and Three Kingdoms Periods*. Bibliotheca Philologica et Philosophica Buddhica 10. Tokyo: International Research Institute for Advanced Buddhology.

Neelis, Jason. 2011. *Early Buddhist Transmission and Trade Networks: Mobility and Exchange within and beyond the Northwestern Borderlands of South Asia*. Leiden: Brill.

Norman, H. C. 1906. *The Commentary on the Dhammapada*. 4 vols. London: Luzac & Company.

Norman, Kenneth R. 1969. *The Elders' Verses*. Vol. 1, *Theragāthā*. Pali Text Society Translation Series 38. London: Luzac & Company.

———. 1971. *The Elders' Verses*. Vol. 2, *Therīgāthā*. Pali Text Society Translation Series 40. London: Luzac & Company.

———. 1992a. *The Group of Discourses (Sutta-nipāta)*. Vol. 2, *Revised Translation with Introduction and Notes*. Pali Text Society Translation Series 45. Oxford: Pali Text Society.

———. 1992b. "Middle Indo-Aryan." In *Indo-European Numerals*, edited by Jadranka Gvozdanović, 199–241. Trends in Linguistics, Studies and Monographs 57. Berlin: De Gruyter Mouton.

———. 1994. "Mistaken Ideas about Nibbāna." In *The Buddhist Forum*, vol. 3, edited by Tadeusz Skorupski, 209–24. London: School of Oriental and African Studies.

———. 1997. *The Word of the Doctrine (Dhammapada)*. Pali Text Society Translation Series 46. Oxford: Pali Text Society.

Nyanaponika (Bhikkhu). 1955. *Sutta-Nipāta: Frühbuddhistische Lehr-Dichtungen aus dem Pali-Kanon*. Buddhistische Handbibliothek 6. Konstanz: Christiani.

———. 1952. *Buddhistisches Wörterbuch*. Konstanz: Verlag Christiani.

———. 1980. *Buddhist Dictionary: Manual of Buddhist Terms and Doctrines*. 4th revised edition. Kandy: Buddhist Publication Society.

Oberlies, Thomas. 2001. *Pāli. A Grammar of the Language of the Theravāda Tipiṭaka*. Berlin: De Gruyter.

Okada, Yukihiro. 2006. *Nāgārjuna's Ratnāvalī*. Vol. 3, *Die chinesische Übersetzung des Paramārtha*. Indica et Tibetica 48. Marburg: Indica et Tibetica Verlag.

Oldenberg, Hermann, and Richard Pischel. 1966. *The Thera- and Therī-Gāthā*. 2nd edition, with appendices by K. R. Norman and L. Alsdorf. London: Luzac & Company.

Olivelle, Patrick. 2000. *Dharmasūtras: The Law Codes of Āpastama, Gautama, Baudhāyana, and Vasiṣṭha*. Delhi: Motilal Banarsidass.

Pagel, Ulrich. 1995. *The Bodhisattvapiṭaka: Its Doctrines, Practices and their Position in Mahāyāna Literature*. Tring, U.K.: Institute of Buddhist Studies.

———. 2006. "About Ugra and his Friends: a Recent Contribution on Early Mahāyāna Buddhism. A Review Article." *Journal of the Royal Asiatic Society*, ser. 3, 16: 73–82.

Pāsādika (Bhikkhu). 2015. *The Kāśyapaparivarta*. New Delhi: Aditya Prakashan.

Pinault, Georges-Jean. 2009. "Sleep and Dream in the Lexicon of the Indo-European Languages." In *The Indian Night: Sleep and Dreams in Indian Culture*, edited by Claudine Bautze-Picron, 225–59. New Delhi: Rupa & Co.

Pischel, Richard. 1900. *Grammatik der Prakrit-Sprachen*. Strassburg: Karl J. Trübner.

———. 1981. *A Grammar of the Prākrit Languages*. 2nd revised edition. Delhi: Motilal Banarsidass.

Potter, Karl H. 1999. *Encyclopedia of Indian Philosophies*. Vol. 8, *Buddhist Philosophy from 100 to 350 A.D.* Delhi: Motilal Banarsidass.

Pradhan, Pralhad. 1950. *Abhidharma Samuccaya of Asanga*. Visva-Bharati Studies 12. Santiniketan: Visva-Bharati.

———. 1975. *Abhidharmakośabhāṣyam of Vasubandhu*. Tibetan Sanskrit Works Series 8. Patna: Kashi Prasad Jayaswal Research Institute.

Qing, Fa. 2001. "The Development of Prajñā in Buddhism From Early Buddhism to the Prajñāpāramitā System: With Special Reference to the Sarvāstivāda Tradition." Ph.D. diss., University of Calgary.

Rajapatirana, Tissa. 1974. "Suvarṇavarṇāvadāna, Translated and Edited Together with Its Tibetan Translation and the Lakṣacaityasamutpatti." Ph.D. diss., Australian National University, Canberra.

Rawlinson, Andrew. 1977. "The Position of the Aṣṭasāhasrikā Prajñāpāramitā in the Development of Early Mahāyāna." In *Prajñāpāramitā and Related Systems: Studies in Honor of Edward Conze*, edited by Lewis Lancaster, 3–34. Berkeley Buddhist Studies Series 1. Berkeley: University of California.

Régamey, Konstanty. 1938. *Philosophy in the Samādhirājasūtra: Three Chapters from the Samādhirājasūtra*. Warsaw: The Warsaw Society of Sciences of Letters.

Rhys Davids, C. A. F. 1920–21. *The Visuddhi-magga of Buddhaghosa*. 2 vols. London: Pali Text Society.

Rhys Davids, T. W., and William Stede. 1921–25. *The Pali Text Society's Pali-English Dictionary*. Chipstead: Probsthain.

Ronkin, Noa. 2005. *Early Buddhist Metaphysics: The Making of a Philosophical Tradition*. London/New York: RoutledgeCurzon.

———. 2013. "Abhidharma." In *Stanford Encyclopedia of Philosophy (Spring 2013 Edition)*, edited by Edward N. Zalta. Accessed February 7, 2016. http://plato.stanford.edu/archives/spr2013/entries/abhidharma.

Roshan, Baa. 2012. "Indian Philosophy." Accessed October 20, 2013. http://fikpani.wordpress.com/2012/11/23/mpy-001-indian-philosophy.

Rospatt, Alexander von. 1997. "Der Abhidharma." Paper presented within a series of lectures titled "Buddhismus in Geschichte und Gegenwart," January 8, 1997.

Roth, Gustav. 1970. *Bhikṣuṇī-vinaya: Including Bhikṣuṇī-Prakīrṇaka and a Summary of the Bhikṣu-Prakīrṇaka of the Ārya-Mahāsāṃghika-Lokottaravādin*. Patna: Kashi Prasad Jayaswal Research Institute.

Rotman, Andy. 2017. *Divine Stories: Divyāvadāna.* Vol. 2. Somerville: Wisdom Publications.

Roy, Sitaram. 1971. *Suvarṇavarṇāvadāna: Decipherment and Historical Study of a Palm-leaf Sanskrit Manuscript – an Unknown Mahāyāna (avadāna) Text from Tibet*. Patna: Kashi Prasad Jayaswal Research Institute.

Ruegg, David Seyfort. 2004. "Aspects of the Study of the (Earlier) Indian Mahāyāna." *Journal of the International Association of Buddhist Studies* 27: 3–62.

Rulu. 2013. *The Bodhisattva Way: Selected Mahāyāna Sūtras*. Bloomington: AuthorHouse.

Sadakata, Akira. 2003. "Pakisutan hōmen shutsudo no bukkyō moji shiryō パキスタン万面出土の仏教文字資料." *Chūgai nippō* 中外日報 2/15/2003: 6–7.

Saddhatissa, H. 1989. *The Abhidhammatthasaṅgaha of Bhadantācariya Anuruddha and the Abhidhammatthavibhāvinī-ṭīkā of Bhadantācariya Sumaṅgalasāmi*. Oxford: The Pali Text Society.

Sakaki, R. 1926. *Mahāvyutpatti*. 2 vols. Kyoto: Kyōto Bunka Daigaku.

Salomon, Richard. 1996. "An Inscribed Silver Buddhist Reliquary of the Time of King Kharaosta and Prince Indravarman." *Journal of the American Oriental Society* 116: 418–52.

———. 1999a. *Ancient Buddhist Scrolls from Gandhāra: The British Library Kharoṣṭhī Fragments*. Seattle/London: University of Washington Press / British Library.

———. 1999b. "A Stone Inscription in Central Asian Gāndhārī from Endere (Xinjiang)." *Bulletin of the Asia Institute* 13: 1–13.

———. 2000. *A Gāndhārī Version of the Rhinoceros Sūtra: British Library Kharoṣṭhī Fragment 5B*. Gandhāran Buddhist Texts 1. Seattle: University of Washington Press.

———. 2002. "A Fragment of a Collection of Buddhist Legends, with a Reference to King Huviṣka as a Follower of the Mahāyāna." In *Buddhist Manuscripts.* vol. 2, edited by Jens Braarvig, 254–67. Manuscripts in the Schøyen Collection 3. Oslo: Hermes Publishing.

———. 2005. "The Indo-Greek era of 186/5 B.C. in a Buddhist Reliquary Inscription." In *Afghanistan, ancien carrefour entre l'Est et l'Ouest: actes du colloque international au Musée archéologique Henri-Prades-Lattes du 5 au 7 mai 2003*, edited by Osmund Bopearachchi and Marie-Françoise Boussac, 359–401. Turnhout: Brepols.

———. 2006. "New Manuscript Sources for the Study of Gandhāran Buddhism." In *Gandhāran Buddhism: Archaeology, Art, Texts*, edited by Pia Brancaccio and Kurt Behrendt, 135–47. Vancouver: UBC Press.

———. 2008a. *Two Gāndhārī Manuscripts of the Songs of Lake Anavatapta (Anavatapta-gāthā): British Library Kharoṣṭhī Fragment 1 and Senior Scroll 14*. Gandhāran Buddhist Texts 5. Seattle: University of Washington Press.

———. 2008b. "Gāndhārī Language." Accessed October 28, 2012. http://www.iranicaonline.org/articles/gandhari-language.

———. 2009. "Why did the Gandhāran Buddhists Bury their Manuscripts?" In *Buddhist Manuscript Cultures: Knowledge, Ritual, and Art*, edited by Stephen C. Berkwitz, Juliane Schober, and Claudia Brown, 19–34. Abingdon: Routledge.

———. 2010. "Kharoṣṭhī Manuscripts in the Schøyen Collection." In *Traces of Gandhāran Buddhism: An Exhibition of Ancient Buddhist Manuscripts in the Schøyen Collection*, edited by Jens Braarvig and Fredrik Liland, xxxiii. Oslo: Hermes Publishing.

Samtani, Narayan Hemandas. 1971. "The Arthaviniścaya-sūtra & Its Commentary (Nibandhana) Written by Bhikṣu Vīryaśrīdatta of Śrī-Nālandāvihāra." Ph.D. diss., University of Delhi.

———. 2002. *Gathering the Meanings: The Compendium of Categories. The Arthaviniścaya Sūtra and Its Commentary Nibandhana*. Berkeley, California: Dharma Publishing.

Sander, Lore. 2000a. "Die 'Schøyen Collection' und einige Bemerkungen zu der ältesten Aṣṭasāhasrikā-Handschrift." *Wiener Zeitschrift für die Kunde Südasiens* 44: 87–100.

Sander, Lore. 2000b. "Fragments of an Aṣṭasāhasrikā Manuscript from the Kuṣāṇa Period." In Braarvig 2000: 1–51.

Sasaki, Shizuka. 2009. "A Basic Approach for Research on the Origin of Mahāyāna Buddhism." *Acta Asiatica* 96: 25–46.

Sastri, N. Aiyaswami. 1975. *Satyasiddhiśāstra of Harivarman*. Vol. 1, *Sanskrit Text*. Gaekwad's Oriental Series 159. Baroda: Oriental Institute.

———. 1978. *Satyasiddhiśāstra of Harivarman*. Vol. 2, *English Translation*. Gaekwad's Oriental Series 165. Baroda: Oriental Institute.

Schlingloff, Dieter. 1955. *Buddhistische Stotras*. Berlin: Akademie-Verlag.

———. 1964. *Ein buddhistisches Yogalehrbuch*. Berlin: Akademie-Verlag.

Schlosser, Andrea. 2016. "On the Bodhisattva Path in Gandhāra. Edition of Fragment 4 and 11 from the Bajaur Collection of Kharoṣṭhī Manuscripts." Ph.D. diss., Freie Universität Berlin. http://www.diss.fu-berlin.de/diss/receive/FUDISS_thesis_000000101376.

———. 2018. "Die Spreu vom Weizen trennen: Ein Gleichnis in buddhistischen Handschriften aus Gandhāra und Zentralasien." In *Saddharmāmṛtam: Festschrift für Jens-Uwe Hartmann zum 65. Geburtstag*, edited by Oliver von Criegern, Gudrun Melzer and Johannes Schneider, 369–81. Wiener Studien zur Tibetologie und Buddhismuskunde 93. Vienna: Arbeitskreis für tibetische und buddhistische Studien.

Schlosser, Andrea, and Ingo Strauch. 2016. "Abhidharmic Elements in Gandhāran Mahāyāna Buddhism. Groups of Four and the Abhedyaprasādas in the Bajaur Mahāyāna Sūtra." In *Text, History, and Philosophy: Abhidharma Across Buddhist Scholastic Traditions*, edited by Bart Dessein and Weijen Teng, 47–107. Leiden: Brill.

Schmithausen, Lambert. 1969. *Der Nirvāṇa-Abschnitt in der Viniścayasaṃgrahaṇī der Yogācārabhūmiḥ*. Vienna: Kommissionsverlag der Österreichischen Akademie der Wissenschaften.

———. 1987. *Ālayavijñāna*. Tokyo: The International Institute for Buddhist Studies.

———. 2002. "Fragments of an Early Commentary." In *Buddhist Manuscripts*, vol. 2, edited by Jens Braarvig, 249–54. Manuscripts in the Schøyen Collection 3. Oslo: Hermes Publishing.

Schoening, Jeffrey D. 1995. *The Śālistamba Sūtra and Its Indian Commentaries*. Vol. 1, *Translation with Annotation*. Wiener Studien zur Tibetologie und Buddhismuskunde 35,1. Vienna: Arbeitskreis für tibetische und buddhistische Studien.

Schopen, Gregory. 1975. "The Phrase '*sa pṛthivīpradeśaś caityabhūto bhavet*' in the *Vajracchedikā*: Notes on the Cult of the Book in Mahāyāna." *Indo-Iranian Journal* 17: 147–81.

———. 1987. "The Inscription on the Kuṣān Image of Amitābha and the Character of the Early Mahāyāna in India." *Journal of the International Association of Buddhist Studies* 10: 99–133.

———. 1989. "The Manuscript of the Vajracchedikā Found at Gilgit." In *Studies in the Literature of the Great Vehicle: Three Mahāyāna Buddhist Texts*, edited by Luis O. Gómez and Jonathan A. Silk, 89–139. Michigan Studies in Buddhist Literature 1. Ann Arbor: University of Michigan.

———. 2005. "The Mahāyāna and the Middle Period in Indian Buddhism: Through a Chinese Looking-Glass." In *Figments and Fragments of Mahāyāna Buddhism in India: More Collected Papers*, edited by Gregory Schopen, 3–24. Honolulu: University of Hawai'i Press.

Schwarzschild, L. A. 1956. "Quelques adverbes pronominaux du moyen indien." *Journal Asiatique* 244: 265–73.

Senart, Émile. 1882–97. *Le Mahâvastu: Texte sanscrit publié pour la première fois et accompagné d'introductions et d'un commentaire par É. Senart*. 3 vols. Paris: Imprimerie nationale.

———. 1914. "L'inscription du vase de Wardak." *Journal Asiatique* 4: 569–85.

Shimoda Masahiro. 2009. "The State of Research on Mahāyāna Buddhism: The Mahāyāna as Seen in Developments in the Study of Mahāyāna Sūtras." *Acta Asiatica* 96: 1–23.

Shiraishi Shindō. 1988. *Bukkyōgaku Ronbunshū* [The Collected Papers of Shiraishi Shindō], edited by Shiraishi Hisako. Sagamiharashi: Kyōbi Shuppansha.

Shukla, Karunesha. 1973. *Sravakabhumi of Acarya Asanga*. Tibetan Sanskrit Works Series 14, 28. Patna: Kashi Prasad Jayaswal Research Institute.

Shukla, N. S. 1979. *The Buddhist Hybrid Sanskrit Dharmapada*. Tibetan Sanskrit Works Series 19. Patna: Kashi Prasad Jayaswal Research Institute.

Silk, Jonathan A. 2002. "What, if Anything, is Mahāyāna Buddhism? Problems of Definitions and Classifications." *Numen* 49: 355–405.

———. 2013 (2009). "The Nature of the Verses of the Kāśyapaparivarta." In *Evo ṣuyadi: Essays in Honor of Richard Salomon's 65th Birthday.* Bulletin of the Asia Institute 23: 179–88.

Silverlock, Blair. 2015. "An Edition and Study of the Goṣiga-sutra, the Cow-Horn Discourse (Senior Collection Scroll No. 12): An Account of the Harmonious Aṇarudha Monks." Ph.D. diss., University of Sydney.

Sinha, Jadunath. 1934. *Indian Psychology: Perception*. London: Kegan Paul, Trench, Trübner & Co.

Skilling, Peter. 2004. "Mahāyāna and Bodhisattva: An Essay Towards Historical Understanding." In *Phothisatawa barami kap sangkhom thai nai sahatsawat mai [Bodhisattvaparami and Thai Society in the New Millennium]*, edited by Pakorn Limpanusorn and Chalermpon Iampakdee, 139–56. Proceedings of a seminar in celebration of the fourth birth cycle of Her Royal Highness Princess Maha Chakri Sirindhorn held at Thammasat University, 21 January 2546 (2003). Bangkok: Chinese Studies Centre, Institute of East Asia, Thammasat University.

———. 2014. "Birchbark, Bodhisatvas, and Bhāṇakas: Writing Materials in Buddhist North India." *Eurasian Studies* 12: 499–521.

———. 2018. "Namo Buddhāya Gurave (K. 888): Circulation of a Liturgical Formula across Asia." *Journal of the Siam Society* 106: 109–28.

Skorupski, Tadeusz. 2002. *The Six Perfections: An Abridged Version of E. Lamotte's French Translation of Nāgārjuna's Mahāprajñāpāramitāśāstra, Chapters XVI–XXX*. Buddhica Britannica, series continua 9. Tring, U.K.: Institute of Buddhist Studies.

Slaje, Walter. 1993. *Bhāskarakaṇṭhas Mokṣopāyaṭīkā. 2. Prakaraṇa (Mumukṣuvyavahāra)*. Graz: Leykam.

Smith, Helmer. 1916–18. *Sutta-Nipāta Commentary Being Paramatthajotika II*. 3 vols. London: Luzac & Company.

Sparham, Gareth. 2006. *Abhisamayālaṃkāra with Vṛtti and Ālokā: First Abhisamaya [Vṛtti by Ārya Vimuktisena, Ālokā by Haribhadra; English translation by Gareth Sparham]*. Fremont, California: Jain Publishing Company.

———. 2008. *Abhisamayālaṃkāra with Vṛtti and Ālokā: Second and Third Abhisamaya [Vṛtti by Ārya Vimuktisena, Ālokā by Haribhadra; English translation by Gareth Sparham]*. Fremont, California: Jain Publishing Company.

Speyer, J. S. 1886. *Sanskrit Syntax*. Leiden: Brill.

———. 1895. *Jātakamālā or Garland of Birth Stories*. London: Frowde.

———. 1906–09. *Avadānaçataka: A Century of Edifying Tales Belonging to the Hīnayāna*. 2 vols. Bibliotheca Buddhica 3. St. Petersburg: Académie impériale des sciences.

Śrāvakabhūmi Study Group. 1998. *Śrāvakabhūmi: The First Chapter; Revised Sanskrit Text and Japanese Translation*. Taishō University Sōgō Bukkyō Kenyūjo series 4. Tokyo: The Institute for Comprehensive Studies of Buddhism, Taisho University.

———. 2007. *Śrāvakabhūmi: The Second Chapter with Asamāhitā Bhūmiḥ, Śrutamayī Bhūmiḥ, Cintāmayī Bhūmiḥ; Revised Sanskrit Text and Japanese Translation*. Taishō University Sōgō Bukkyō Kenyūjo series 18. Tokyo: The Institute for Comprehensive Studies of Buddhism, Taisho University.

Stcherbatsky, Theodor, and Eugene Obermiller. 1929. *Abhisamayālankāra-Prajñāpāramitā-Upadeśa-Śāstra*. Bibliotheca Buddhica 23. Leningrad.

Stein, Marc Aurel. 1935–37. "The Numerals in the Niya Inscriptions." *Bulletin of the School of Oriental Studies* 8: 763–79.

Steinkellner, Ernst. 2012. "'Kanon' im Buddhismus und die Anfänge der schriftlichen Überlieferung." Accessed November 7, 2012. http://info-buddhismus.de/Kanon_im_Buddhismus_und_die_Anfaenge_der_schriftlichen_Ueberlieferung-Steinkellner.html.

Strauch, Ingo. 2002. *Die Lekhapaddhati-Lekhapañcāśikā: Briefe und Urkunden im mittelalterlichen Gujarat*. Berlin: Dietrich Reimer Verlag.

———. 2007/2008. The Bajaur Collection: A New Collection of Kharoṣṭhī Manuscripts – A Preliminary Catalogue and Survey – Online Version 1.1 (May 2008). Accessed February 7, 2016. http://resolver.sub.uni-goettingen.de/purl/?gr_elib-273.

———. 2008. "The Bajaur Collection of Kharoṣṭhī Manuscripts – A Preliminary Survey." *Studien zur Indologie und Iranistik* 25: 103–36.

———. 2010a. "More Missing Pieces of Early Pure Land Buddhism: New Evidence for Akṣobhya and Abhirati in an Early Mahayana Sutra from Gandhāra." *The Eastern Buddhist* 41: 23–66.

———. 2010b. "Mönche, Klöster und beschriebene Töpfe: neue Zeugnisse für die Geschichte und Geographie des buddhistischen Gandhāra." Paper presented at the 31. Deutscher Orientalistentag, Marburg, September 9, 2010.

———. 2014. "The Evolution of the Buddhist *rakṣā* Genre in the Light of New Evidence from Gandhāra: The **Manasvi-nāgarāja-sūtra* from the Bajaur Collection of Kharoṣṭhī Manuscripts." *Bulletin of the School of Oriental and African Studies* 77: 63–84.

Study Group on Buddhist Sanskrit Literature. 2006. *Vimalakīrtinirdeśa: A Sanskrit Edition Based upon the Manuscript Newly Found at the Potala Palace*. Tokyo: The Institute for Comprehensive Studies of Buddhism, Taisho University.

Suzuki, Daisetz Teitaro. 1932. *The Lankavatara Sutra: A Mahayana Text, Translated for the First Time from the Original Sanskrit*. London: Routledge & Kegan Paul.

Suzuki, Daisetz Teitaro, and Hokei Idzumi. 1949. *The Gandavyuha Sutra*. New revised edition. 4 vols. Kyoto: Society for the Publication of Sacred Books of the World.

Takakusu Junjirō (高楠順次郎), and Kaigyoku Watanabe (渡邊海旭). 1924–32. 大正新脩大藏經 *[Taishō shinshū daizōkyō]*. 東京 [Tōkyō]: 大正一切經刊行會 [Taishō issaikyō kankōkai].

Takeda, Kohgaku. 2000. "The Authorship of the Mahaprajnaparamitasastra (Summary)." *Journal of the International College for Advanced Buddhist Studies* 3: 211–44.

Tatia, N. 1976. *Abhidharmasamuccayabhāṣyam*. Tibetan Sanskrit Works Series 17. Patna: Kashi Prasad Jayaswal Research Institute.

Taylor, Arnold C. 1894–97. *Kathāvatthu*. 2 vols. London: Henry Frowde.

———. 1905–07. *Paṭisambhidāmagga*. 2 vols. London: Henry Frowde.

Ṭhānissaro (Bhikkhu). 1997. "The Dhammapada." Accessed September 11, 2018. https://www.dhammatalks.org/suttas/KN/Dhp/index_Dhp.html.

———. 2010. *The Wings to Awakening: An Anthology from the Pali Canon*. Revised 6th edition. Barre, Massachusetts: Dhamma Dana Publications.

Thomas, Frederick William. 1915. "Notes on the Edicts of Asoka." *The Journal of the Royal Asiatic Society of Great Britain and Ireland*: 97–112.

———. 1934. "Some Notes on the Kharoṣṭhī Documents from Chinese Turkestan." *Acta Orientalia* 12: 37–70.

———. 1936. "Some Words Found in the Central Asian Documents." *Bulletin of the School of Oriental Studies* 8: 789–94.

Thompson, John M. 2008. *Understanding Prajñā: Sengzhao's 'Wild Words' and the Search for Wisdom*. New York: Peter Lang.

Thurman, Robert A. F. et al. 2004. *The Universal Vehicle Discourse Literature (Mahāyānasūtrālaṁkāra) by Maitreyanātha/Āryāsanga Together with Its Commentary (Bhāṣya) by Vasubandhu*. New York: American Institute of Buddhist Studies.

Tomabechi, Tōru. 2009. *Adhyardhaśatikā Prajñāpāramitā: Sanskrit and Tibetan Texts*. Vienna/Beijing: Austrian Academy of Sciences Press / China Tibetology Publishing House.

Trenckner, Vilhelm. 1880. *The Milindapañho*. London: Williams and Norgate.

Trenckner, Vilhelm et al. 1924–. *A Critical Pāli Dictionary*. Copenhagen: Department of Asian Studies, University of Copenhagen.

Tripāṭhī, Chandrabhāl. 1962. *Fünfundzwanzig Sūtras des Nidānasaṃyukta*. Berlin: Akademie Verlag.

Tripathi, Ram Shankar. 1977. *Prajñāpāramitopadeśaśāstre Abhisamayālaṅkāravr̥ttiḥ Sphuṭārthā Ācāryaharibhadraviracitā*. Sarnath: Central Institute of Higher Tibetan Studies.

Tsai, Yao-ming. 2014. "On Justifying the Choice of Mahāyāna among Multiple Paths in Buddhist Teachings: Based on the *Prajñāpāramitā-sūtras*." In *Scripture:Canon::Text:Context. Essays Honoring Lewis Lancaster*, edited by Richard K. Payne, 257–78. Berkeley: Institute of Buddhist Studies and BDK America.

Tubb, Gary A., and Emery R. Boose. 2007. *Scholastic Sanskrit: A Handbook for Students.* New York: American Institute of Buddhist Studies.

Turner, R. L. 1936. "Sanskrit *ā́-kṣeti* and Pali *acchati* in Modern Indo-Aryan." *Bulletin of the School of Oriental and African Studies* 8: 795–812.

———. 1966–85. *A Comparative Dictionary of the Indo-Aryan Languages*. London: Oxford University Press / School of Oriental and African Studies.

Vetter, Tilmann. 1994. "On the Origin of Mahāyāna Buddhism and the Subsequent Introduction of Prajñāpāramitā." *Asiatische Studien. Zeitschrift der Schweizerischen Asiengesellschaft* 48: 1241–81.

———. 2001. "Once Again on the Origin of Mahāyāna Buddhism." *Wiener Zeitschrift für die Kunde Südasiens* 45: 59–89.

Vogel, Claus, and Klaus Wille. 2002. "The Final Leaves of the Pravrajyāvastu Portion of the Vinayavastu Manuscript Found Near Gilgit: Part 2, Nāgakumārāvadāna and Lévi Text." In *Sanskrit-Texte aus dem buddhistischen Kanon: Neuentdeckungen und Neueditionen* 4, edited by Jin-il Chung, Claus Vogel, and Klaus Wille, 11–76. Sanskrit-Wörterbuch der buddhistischen Texte aus den Turfan-Funden, Beiheft 9. Göttingen: Vandenhoeck & Ruprecht.

Vorobyova-Desyatovskaya, M. I. (in collaboration with Seishi Karashima and Noriyuki Kudo). 2002. *The Kāśyapaparivarta: Romanized Text and Facsimiles*. Bibliotheca Philologica et Philosophica Buddhica 5. Tokyo: International Research Institute for Advanced Buddhology, Soka University.

Waldschmidt, Ernst. 1944. *Die Überlieferung vom Lebensende des Buddha: Eine vergleichende Analyse des Mahāparinirvāṇasūtra und seiner Textentsprechungen. 1. Teil: Vorgangsgruppe I–IV.* Göttingen: Vandenhoeck & Ruprecht.

———. 1967. *Von Ceylon bis Turfan: Schriften zur Geschichte, Literatur, Religion und Kunst des indischen Kulturraumes; Festgabe zum 70. Geburtstag am 15, Juli 1967*. Göttingen: Vandenhoeck & Ruprecht.

Waldschmidt, Ernst et al., eds., 1965–. *Sanskrithandschriften aus den Turfanfunden*. Verzeichnis der orientalischen Handschriften in Deutschland 10. Wiesbaden/Stuttgart: Franz Steiner Verlag.

Waley, Arthur. 1952. *The Real Tripitaka and Other Pieces*. London: Allen & Unwin.

Walshe, Maurice. 1987. *The Long Discourses of the Buddha: A Translation of the Dīgha Nikāya*. Boston: Wisdom Publications.

Wangchuk, Dorji. 2007. *Resolve to Become a Buddha: A Study of the Bodhicitta Concept in Indo-Tibetan Buddhism*. Studia Philologica Buddhica, monograph series 23. Tokyo: The International Institute for Buddhist Studies of the International College for Postgraduate Buddhist Studies.

Warren, Henry Clarke, and Dharmananda Kosambi. 1950. *Visuddhimagga of Buddhaghosâcariya*. Harvard Oriental series 41. Cambridge: Harvard University Press.

Watson, Burton. 1993. *The Lotus Sutra*. New York: Columbia University Press.

Weller, Friedrich. 1965. *Zum Kāśyapaparivarta*. Heft 2, *Verdeutschung des sanskrit-tibetischen Textes*. Berlin: Akademie-Verlag.

Wijeratne, R. P., and Rupert Gethin. 2002. *The Summary of the Topics of Abhidhamma and Exposition of the Topics of Abhidhamma*. Oxford: Pali Text Society.

Willemen, Charles. 2006. *The Essence of Scholasticism: Abhidharmahṛdaya*. Delhi: Motilal Banarsidass.

Willemen, Charles, Bart Dessein, and Collett Cox. 1998. *Sarvastivada Buddhist Scholasticism.* Handbuch der Orientalistik 2.11. Leiden: Brill.

Williams, Paul. 2009. *Mahāyāna Buddhism: The Doctrinal Foundations*. 2nd revised edition. London: Routledge.

Windisch, Ernst. 1889. *Iti-vuttaka*. London: Henry Frowde.

Wogihara, Unrai. 1908. "Asanga's Bodhisattvabhūmi. Ein dogmatischer Text der Nordbuddhisten nach dem Unikum von Cambridge im Allgemeinen und lexikalisch untersucht." Ph.D. diss., Kaiser-Wilhelms-Universität zu Strassburg.

———. 1932–35. *Abhisamayālaṃkārālokā Prajñāpāramitā-vyākhyā: The Work of Haribhadra*. Tokyo: The Toyo Bunko.

———. 1932–36. *Sphuṭârthā Abhidharmakośavyākhyā by Yaśomitra*. 2 vols. Tokyo: Publishing Association of Abhidharmakośavyākhyā.

Woodward, F. L. 1926. *Paramattha-dīpanī Udānaṭṭhakathā (Udāna Commentary) of Dhammapālacariya*. London: Oxford University Press.

Wynne, Alexander. 2007. *The Origin of Buddhist Meditation*. Abingdon: Routledge.

Yakup, Abdurishid. 2010. *Prajñāpāramitā Literature in Old Uyghur*. Turnhout: Brepols.

Yamada, Isshi. 1968. *Karuṇāpuṇḍarīka: The White Lotus of Compassion; Edited with Introduction and Notes*. London: School of Oriental and African Studies.

Zacchetti, Stefano. 2005. *In Praise of the Light: A Critical Synoptic Edition with an Annotated Translation of Chapters 1–3 of Dharmarakṣa's Guang zan jing; Being the Earliest Chinese Translation of the Larger Prajñāpāramitā*. Bibliotheca Philologica et Philosophica Buddhica 8. Tokyo: International Research Institute for Advanced Buddhology.

Zürcher, Erik. 1959. *The Buddhist Conquest of China the Spread and Adaptation of Buddhism in Early Medieval China*. Leiden: Brill.

———. 1991. "A New Look at the Earliest Chinese Buddhist Texts." In *From Benares to Beijing: Essays on Buddhism and Chinese Religion in Honour of Prof. Jan Yün-hua*, edited by K. Shiara and G. Schopen, 277–304. Oakville: Mosaic Press.

Word Index

Each entry of the word index is given in the following format:

G *lemma*, grammatical category / gender (if noun), Skt. *equivalent*, P *equivalent*, "English translation." (Annotations to the lemma.)
Grammatical status, G *word* (as given in the reconstructed text), line number.
Cross-references.

The Gāndhārī lemmata (headwords) are presumptive, since they do not necessarily appear in the manuscript in this form. They are normalized but based on the evidence in BC 4, BC 6, and BC 11. For verbal forms, the present stem is used. Sanskrit and Pali equivalents, as well as English translations are given only once for each lemma. When the equivalent in Sanskrit or Pali does not phonetically correspond directly to the Gāndhārī form, this is indicated by the symbol ~ ("similar to"). All Sanskrit and Pali forms are reconstructed, since there are no parallels to the texts of the manuscripts in question. These equivalents are intended only as a help to the reader. Sometimes no Pali equivalent is given, for example, if a term is used only in Sanskrit and/or Mahāyāna literature.

The actual forms as they appear in the text editions are given in the subsequent listings. The sequence of the occurrences is based on their grammatical status, and within that, on their spelling. For the grammatical status, the sorting order is: m., mn., n., f., unclear cases. Within each gender category the sequence is nom.–loc. singular, nom.–loc. plural. Uncertainties are marked by "(?)." If the gender is completely unknown, the corresponding position in the grammatical status shows a question mark without brackets ("?").

For convenience, the index follows the more familiar *varṇamālā* sequence as it is known from other dictionaries of Indic languages; *s̱* is treated as *s*.

aïdaṇa n. Skt. *āyatana*, P *āyatana*, "sense base."
nom. pl. *aïdaṇa* 11v24, 11v25.

akarma n. Skt. *akarman*, P *akamma*, "bad activity."
gen. pl. *akarmaṇa* 4r27, 4v7.
Cf. ***karma***.

akica n. Skt. *akṛtya*, P *akicca*, "things not to be done."
gen. pl. *aki[caṇa]* 4r27, *ag̱icaṇa* 4v6.
Cf. ***kica***, ***kicakica***.

akuś̱ala adj. Skt. *akuśala*, P *akusala*, "unwholesome/bad [deed or state]."
n. nom. sg. *akuś̱ala* 4r5, *akuśale* 11r16, *aku[śa]lo* 4r21; gen. sg. *akuś̱alasa* 6v2; nom. pl. *akuś̱ala* 4r4, *(*aku)ś̱ala* 4r11; gen. pl. *akuś̱alaṇa* 4r26, 4v5.
Cf. ***kuś̱ala***.

akuhica see ***akuhicaag̱amaṇaakuhicag̱amaṇa-***, ***akuhicaag̱amaṇaakuhicag̱amaṇaag̱ara***.
Cf. ***kuhica***.

akuhicaag̱amaṇaakuhicag̱amaṇa n.
Skt. *akutracidāgamanākutracidgamana*, P *akuhiñcāgamanākuhiñcigamana*, "'not coming from anywhere, not going anywhere.'"
nom.(?) sg. *akuhicaag̱amaṇaakuhicag̱amaṇa* 6r7.
See also ***akuhicaag̱amaṇaakuhicag̱amaṇa-ag̱ara***. Cf. ***kuhicaag̱amaṇakuhicag̱amaṇa***.

akuhicaag̱amaṇaakuhicag̱amaṇaag̱ara m.
Skt. *akutracidāgamanākutracidgamanākāra*, P *akuhiñcāgamanākuhiñcigamanākāra*, "the aspect of 'not coming from anywhere, not going anywhere.'"
instr. sg. *akuhicaag̱amaṇaakuhicag̱amaṇa-ag̱areṇa* 11v19.

akṣati see ***bhodi***.

akṣaya adj. Skt. *akṣaya*, P *akkhaya*, "not decaying."
f. nom. sg. *akṣaye* 11v3.

akhaïta pp. Skt. ~ *ākhyāta*, BHS *ākhyāyita*, P *ākkhāyita*, or more probably abs. Skt. ~ *ākhyāya*, BHS *ākhyāyitvā*, P *ākkhāyitvā*, "(having been) declared." (Perhaps also negated as BHS *akhyāyita* or *akhyāyitvā*.)
n. nom. sg. *akhaïta* 11r7 (or abs.).
Cf. ***khaïta***, ***khaïti***.

ak̲h̲ada m. Skt. *āghāta*, P *āghāta*, "blow."
instr. sg. *ak̲h̲adeṇa* 6r3.
See also ***ak̲h̲adasagharya***.

ak̲h̲adasagharya n. Skt. *āghātasaṅghārya* (?) = ~ *āghātasaṃharaṇa*, P ~ *āghātasaṅgharaṇa*, "accumulation of blows."
acc. sg. *(*ak̲h̲adasa)[gha]rya* 11v23.

ag̱aḍa see ***ag̱aḍasaña***. Cf. ***g̱aḍa***.

ag̱aḍasaña f. Skt. *agaṇḍasaṃjñā*, P *agaṇḍasañña*, "notion [of being] without boils."
nom. sg. *[ag̱aḍasaña]* 6r9.

ag̱amaṇa see ***akuhicaag̱amaṇaakuhicag̱amaṇa-***, ***kuhicaag̱amaṇakuhicag̱amaṇa***.

ag̱ara see ***akuhicaag̱amaṇaakuhicag̱amaṇaag̱ara***, ***aṇatvag̱ara***, ***aṇicag̱ara***, ***avedeaag̱ara***, ***parimaṇasaceaag̱ara***, ***śuñag̱ara***, ***sarvag̱ara***, ***sudiṇag̱ara***.

ag̱ra see ***eg̱ag̱racitasa***, ***priaviṇabhavaag̱radukha***.

acala adj. Skt. *acala*, P *acala*, "immovable."
n. nom. sg. *acala* 11v2.

aciti(d)a n.(?) Skt. *acintita*, P *acintita*, "not thinking." (Uncertain; usually *acitia* corresponds to Skt. *acintya*, BHS/P *acintiya*, "inconceivable, unthinkable.")
instr. sg. *acitieṇa* 11v20.
Cf. ***citida***.

acida pp. Skt. *ācita*, P *ācita*, "filled with (?)."
m.(?) nom.(?) sg. *acida* 11r35 (or n. acc. sg. used adverbially?).

achatvia see ***aj̄atvia***.

aj̄atva see ***aj̄atvabahira***.

aj̄atvabahira adj. Skt. *adhyātmabāhira*, P *ajjhattabāhira*, "inner and outer."
m. nom. pl. *aj̄atvabahira* 11v13.

aj̄atvia adj. Skt. *ādhyātmika*, P *ajjhattika*, "inner."
n. nom. pl. *achatvia* 11v25, *aj̄atvia* 11v24, 11v26 [2×], *a[j̄atvia]* 11v27.

ajavi ind. Skt. *adyāpi*, P *ajjavi*, "from now on."
ajavi 11r37.

aji ind. Skt. *adya*, P *ajja/ajjā*, "just, now."
aji 6r6, 6v7.

aña adj. Skt. *anya*, P *añña*, "other."
m. nom. pl. *aña* 4r17, 6v2 [2×], 6v7, *(*a)ña* 4r18, *añe* 4r18; n.(?) nom. sg.(?) *[aña]* 11r5.

añatra see ***añatradeṣ̱a***.

añatradeṣ̱a m. Skt. *anyatradeśa*, P *aññatradesa*, "other places (pl.)."
instr. pl. *añatradeṣ̱ehi* 4r18.

aṭhaṇa n. Skt. *asthāna*, P *aṭṭhāna*, "impossibility; (here:) not possible."
nom. sg. *aṭhaṇo* 11v24.

***aṭha* (?)** adj. Skt. *astha*, "unstable, transient." (Uncertain; cf. annotations, p. 255.)
f.(?) nom. sg. *aṭha* 6v3.

aṇaḵẖada adj.(?) Skt. *anāghāta*, P *anāghāta*, "without blows." (noun or bv.)
n.(?) nom. sg. *[aṇa]ḵẖada* 6r5.
See also ***aḵẖada***, ***aṇaḵẖadasaña***.

aṇaḵẖadasaña f. Skt. *anāghātasaṃjñā*, P *anāghātasaññā*, "notion [of being] without blows."
nom. sg. *aṇaḵẖadasaña* 6r10.

aṇagada n. Skt. *anāgata*, P *anāgata*, "future."
loc. sg. *aṇagad⟨*e⟩* 4r24, *aṇagade* 4v3;
loc.(?) sg. *aṇagade* 4v12 (context unclear).
See also ***adidaaṇagadapracupaṇa***.

aṇatva see ***aṇatvagara***.

aṇatvagara m. Skt. *anātmākāra*, P *anattākāra*, "the aspect of [having] no self."
instr. sg. *aṇatvagar[e]ṇa* 11v18.

aṇarida (Uncertain; cf. annotations, p. 176.)
unclear: *aṇaride* 4v1, 4v9, 4v10, *aṇari[de]* 4v1, *[aṇari](*de)* 4v11, *aṇarid[e]* 4v11.
Cf. ***arida***.

aṇavaṭia adj. Skt. *anāvartika*, P *anāvattika*, "not leading to rebirth."
f. nom. sg. *aṇavaṭie* 11v3.

aṇica see ***aṇicagara***. Cf. ***ṇica***.

aṇicagara m. Skt. *anityākāra*, P *aniccākāra*, "the aspect of [being] impermanent."
instr. sg. *aṇicagareṇa* 11v17–11v18.
Cf. ***ṇica***.

aṇubhavaṇa n. Skt. *anubhavana*, P *anubhavana*, "experience."
nom. sg. *aṇubhavaṇa* 11r7.

aṇubhavavida pp. Skt. ~ *anubhāvita*, P *anubhāvāpita*, "caused to experience."
m.(?) nom.(?) sg. *aṇubhavavida* 11r36 (or n. acc. sg. used adverbially?).

aṇubhavidava gdv. Skt. *anubhavitavya*, P *anubhavitabba*, "to be experienced."
n. nom. sg. *(*a)ṇubhavidave* 11v30.

aṇubhodi v. Skt. *anubhavati*, P *anubhavati*, *anubhoti*, "experiences."
opt. 3rd sg. pass. *aṇubhaviea* 11r16, *aṇubhavi{da}ea* 11r16.

aṇuvadaṇa n. Skt. *anupādāna*, P *anupādāna*, "without clinging."
nom. sg. *aṇuvadaṇa* 4r14.

aṇuśaśa m. Skt. *anuśaṃsa*, BHS *ānuśaṃsa* (or f. *anuśaṃsā*), P *ānisaṃsa*, "benefit."
nom. sg. *aṇuśaśe* 4v10; acc. sg. *aṇuśaśa* 11r28; nom. pl. *aṇuśaśa* 4r12.
See also ***yaṣ̱abhudaaṇuśaśa***, ***viragraaṇuśaśa***, ***svayaaṇuśaśa***.

aṇuśaśidava gdv. Skt. *anuśaṃsitavya*, P *ānisaṃsitabba*, "to be praised (?)."
mn.(?) nom. pl. *aṇuśaśidava* 4r28.

atarasa̱edi v. Skt. *antardhatte/-dhīyate*, BHS *antaradhāyati*, P *antaradhāyati*, "disappear."
fut. 3rd pl. *atarasa̱ïśati* 4v11.

atog̱ada adj. Skt. *antargata*, BHS *antogata*, P *antogata*, "included."
m. nom. sg. *atog̱ade* 11r53; nom. pl. *atog̱ada* 11r52; mn. nom. sg. *atog̱ade* 11r53;
n. nom. sg. *atog̱ade* 11r50, 11r51 [3×], 11r52 [2×], *atog̱ado* 11r49; f. nom. sg. *atog̱ade* 11r51.
See also ***atog̱adasuha***.

atog̱adasuha n. Skt. *antargatasukha*, P *antogatasukha*, "inner happiness."
nom. sg. *(*a)[to]g̱adasuhe* 11r20, *atog̱adasuhe* 11r20.

[1]***atra*** ind. Skt. *atra*, P *atra*, "here."
atra 11r49.

[2]***atra*** n. Skt. *antra*, P *anta*, "intestines."
nom. sg. *atra* 11r34.

atva adj. Skt. *ātman*, P *atta*, "[having a] self." (bv.)
nom. sg. *atve* 11r26 (bv.); nom. pl. *[atva]* 6r1 (bv. or first part of a compound).
See also ***atvasaña***, ***atvahida***, ***atvahisaparahisasarvaṣ̱atvahisavidimiśasuha***.

atvasaña f. Skt. *ātmasaṃjñā*, P *attasaññā*, "notion of [having] a self."
nom. sg. *a[tva]saña* 6r10.

atvahida n. Skt. *ātmahita*, P *attahita*, "welfare for myself."
nom. sg. *atvahida* 4r22.

atvahisa see ***atvahisaparahisasarvas̱atvahisa-vidimiśasuha***.

atvahisaparahisasarvas̱atvahisavidimiśasuha n. Skt. *ātmahiṃsāparahiṃsāsarvasattvahiṃsā-vyatimiśrasukha*, P *attahiṃsāparahiṃsā-sabbasattahiṃsāvītimissasukha*, "happiness mixed with suffering due to harm to oneself, harm to others, or harm to all beings."
nom. sg. *atvahisaparahisasarvas̱atvahisa-vidimiśasuhe* 11r47.

adahadi v. Skt. *ādadhāti*, P *ādahati*, "accepts." (Uncertain but matching the context.)
opt. 3rd sg. *[a]d[a]h[ea]* 6r8.

adida n. Skt. *atīta*, P *atīta*, "past."
loc. sg. *adide* 4r24.
See also ***adidaaṇagadapracupaṇa***.

adidaaṇagadapracupaṇa n. Skt. *atītānāgata-pratyutpanna*, P *atītānāgatapaccuppanna*, "past, future, present."
instr. pl. *adidaaṇagad[a]p(*r)ac(*u)paṇehi* 11r38–11r39, *adidaaṇagadapracupaṇehi* 11r40.

aparas̱iṇa see ***aparas̱iṇasuha***.

aparas̱iṇasuha n. Skt. *aparādhīnasukha*, P *aparādhīnasukha*, "happiness that is not dependent on anything else."
nom. sg. *aparas̱iṇasuhe* 11r18.

aparibhujitreaagara m. Skt. *aparibhuñjitṛkākāra* (?), "the aspect 'there is no one who enjoys' (?)."
instr. sg. *aparibhujitreaagareṇa* 11v18.

aparibhuta pp. Skt. *aparibhukta*, P *aparibhutta*, "not enjoyed."
n. instr. sg. *aparibhuteṇa* 11r39; gen. sg. *aparibhu[ḏ]asa* 11r32.
Cf. ***aparibhujitreaagara***, ***paribhuta***.

aparihaṇa see ***aparihaṇadhama***.

aparihaṇadhama adj. Skt. *aparihāṇadharma*, P *aparihānadhamma*, "not subject to decline."
f. nom. sg. *aparihaṇadhama* 11v3.

apalios̱a m. BHS *apaligodha*, P *apaligedha*, "free from desire."
instr. sg. *apalios̱eṇa* 4r2, *[apalios̱](*e)[ṇa]* 4r8.
Cf. ***palios̱a***.

apos̱aṇa see ***amitrahoḏeapos̱aṇa***.

aprañati f. Skt. *aprajñapti*, P *appaññatti*, "non-designation."
nom. sg. *aprañati* 11r31.

abodhasa f. Skt. *abuddhatā*, P *abuddhatā*, "state of not being awakened." (Cf. annotations, p. 254.)
nom. sg. *abodhasa* 6v1.

abhava m. Skt. *abhāva*, P *abhāva*, "non-existence."
nom.(?) sg. *abhava* 6r7.

abhavasa f. Skt. *abhāvatā*, P *abhāvatā*, "state of non-existence."
acc. sg. *abh[a]v[asa]* 6v5.

amaṇas̱iara m. Skt. *amanasikāra*, P *amanasikāra*, "without mental engangement, not mentally engaged."
nom.(?) sg. *amaṇas̱iara* 6v2 (bv.?).

amahu / amaho see ***ma-***.

amitra see ***amitrahoḏeapos̱aṇa***.

amitrahoḏeapos̱aṇa n. Skt. *amitrahoḍhāpoṣaṇa*, "not nourishing on what is stolen from enemies."
nom. sg. *amitrahoḏeapos̱aṇam* 11r40.

amis̱a see ***amis̱adaṇa***.

amis̱adaṇa n. Skt. *āmiṣadāna*, P *āmisadāna*, "giving of material sources."
nom. sg. *amis̱adaṇe* 11r51.

***amuḏa* (?)** adj. Skt. *amūḍha*, P *amūḷha*, "non-perplexed (?)."
m.(?) nom.(?) sg. *amuḏa* 11v7 (or n. acc. sg. used adverbially).

amoyaṇa see ***civarakṣayakayakṣayaamoyaṇa-kṣayadukhavidimiśasuha***.

arida (Uncertain; cf. annotations, p. 176.)
unclear: *ari[da]* 4r23, *arida* 4v10 [2×], *[aride]* 4v9, *arede* 4v9.
Cf. ***aṇarida***.

arupa see ***arupadhadu***.

arupadhadu f. Skt. *ārūpyadhātu*, P *āruppadhātu*, "the formless realm."
loc. sg. *arupadhadu* 11v15.

aruva n. Skt. *arūpa*, P *arūpa*, "the formless."
loc. sg. *aruve* 11r23, 11v28 [2×], 11v30.
See also ***ruvaruva***.

aroa see ***aroga***.

aroga n. Skt. *ārogya*, P *ārogya*, "health."
gen. pl. *[aroganạ]* 4r27, *aroganạ* 4v8.

aroga m. Skt. *aroga*, P *aroga*, "freedom from disease."
nom. sg. *aroa* 11v14.
See also ***arogasaña***.

arogasaña f. Skt. *arogasaṃjñā*, P *arogasaññā*, "notion [of being] without disease."
nom.(?) sg. *aroga[sa](*ña)* 6r9.

artha n. Skt. *artha*, P *attha*, "profit; (dat. sg.:) for the sake of."
nom. sg. *a[r]tho* 4r21; dat. sg. *arthae* 11v12, *artha[e]* 11v12.

alabha m. Skt. *alambha* or *alābha*, P *alābha*, "not obtaining."
instr. sg. *alabhena̤* 11r39.

alas̱ia n. Skt. *ālasya*, P *ālassa*, "idleness."
gen. pl. *alas̱ianạ* 4r27, *ala[s̱i](*a)nạ* 4v6.

aloa (Uncertain; cf. annotations, p. 176.)
unclear: *aloa* 4v1, *alo[a]* 4v11, *aloehi* 4r23.

aloia adj. Skt. *alaukika*, P *alokika*, "not relating to this world."
n. instr. sg. *aloienạ* 11v16.
Cf. ***loia***.

aloṇea (Uncertain; cf. annotations, p. 176.)
unclear: *a[loṇe](*a)* 4v1, *aloṇea* 4v10, 4v11, *(*a)loṇeade* 4r23, *al[o]ṇe[a](*de)* 4v9, *aloṇ[e]o* 4v10.

avakra(madi) v. (a) Skt. *avakrāmati*, BHS also *avakramati*, P *avakkamati*, *okkamati*, "enters into [a state]"; (b) Skt. *apakramati*, P *apakkamati*, "goes away." (Uncertain.)
unclear: *avakra ?* + + 11r22.

***avayida* (?)** adj. Skt. *avyayita* (?), "not spent."
n. instr. sg. *ava[yede]ṇa* 11r41 (read *avayideṇa* or even *avayieṇa*?).
Cf. ***vayida* (?)**.

avayea m. Skt. *apacaya*, P *apacaya*, "decrease; (here:) decreasing."
gen. sg. *avayeasa* 11r11.
Cf. ***uayea***.

avarimaṇa adj. Skt. *aparimāṇa*, P *aparimāṇa*, "without measure, immeasurable."
m. gen. pl. *avarimaṇaṇa* 4v8 (referring to both m. and f.), *[a]varimaṇaṇa* 11v5; n. nom. sg. *avarimaṇa* 6r5; instr. sg. *avarimaṇeṇa* 6r4; gen. pl. *avarimaṇaṇa* 11v5; f. gen. pl. *avarimaṇaṇa* 11v6, 11v10; unclear: *apar[i]maṇa* 6r1 (context missing), *avarimaṇa* 11r28 (context missing).
See also ***avarimaṇaguṇavidimiśa***, ***avarimaṇadukhavidimiśasuha***, ***avarimaṇadoṣa***, ***avarimaṇadoṣaprahaṇa***.

avarimaṇaguṇavidimiśa adj. Skt. *aparimāṇaguṇavyatimiśra*, P *aparimāṇaguṇavītimissa*, "mixed with immeasurable qualities [of the objects of sensual pleasure]."
n.(?) acc.(?) sg. *avaramiṇaguṇavidimiśa* 11r48 (used adverbially?); unclear: *(*a)[va]rimaṇaguṇ[ṇa]vi[di]miśa* 11r22 (context missing).

avarimaṇadukhavidimiśasuha n. Skt. *aparimāṇaduḥkhavyatimiśrasukha*, P *aparimāṇadukkhavītimissasukha*, "happiness mixed with immeasurable [kinds of] suffering."
nom. sg. *avarimaṇa[dukha]vidimiśasuhe* 11r48.

avarimaṇadoṣa m. Skt. *aparimāṇadoṣa*, P *aparimāṇadosa*, "immeasurable faults."
acc.(?) pl. *avarimaṇadoṣa* 11r22.
See also ***avarimaṇadoṣaprahaṇa***.

avarimaṇadoṣaprahaṇa n. Skt. *aparimāṇadoṣaprahāṇa*, P *aparimānadosapahāṇa*, "abandoning immeasurable faults."
nom.(?) sg. *avaramiṇadoṣaprahaṇa* 11v10 (read *avarimaṇadoṣaprahaṇa*).

avaśa adv. Skt. *avaśyam*, P *avassaṃ*, "certainly."
avaśa 11v4, 11v30, *avaśi* 11r49, 11r50, 11v2, 11v7, 11v8 [2×], 11v11, *[avaśi]* 11v9.

avi ind. Skt. *api*, P *api*, "also, even though, moreover."
avi 11r4, 11r6, 11r7 [2×], 11r51 [2×], 11r53, 11v28 [2×], 11v30 [2×], *(*a)vi* 11r6, *vi* 11r25, 11r26.

avikṣita see ***avikṣitacitasa***.

avikṣitacitasa f. Skt. *avikṣiptacittatā*, P *avikkhittacittatā*, "state of an undistracted mind."
nom. sg. *avikṣitacita[sa]* 6v2.

aviñati see ***aviñatisuha***.

aviñatisuha n. Skt. *avijñaptisukha*, P *aviññatti-sukha*, "happiness due to non-cognition."
nom. sg. *[a]viñatis(*u)he* 11r18.
Cf. ***viñatidukhavidimiśasuha***.

avedea see ***avedeaagara***.

avedeaagara m. Skt. *avedakākāra*, P *avedakākāra*, "the aspect 'there is no one who experiences.'"
instr. sg. *avedeaagareṇa* 11v18.

avhiña see ***avhiñaaśreasuha***.

avhiñaaśreasuha n. Skt. *abhijñāśrayasukha*, P *abhiññāssayasukha* (?), "happiness whose basis is the supernatural knowledges (?)."
nom. sg. *avhiñaaśreasuhe* 11r20.

aśala adj.(?) Skt. *aśalya*, P *asalla*, "(being) without thorns." (noun or bv.)
n.(?) nom. sg. *(*a)[śa]la* 6r5.
See also ***aśalasaña***.

aśalasaña f. Skt. *aśalyasaṃjñā*, P *asallasaññā*, "notion [of being] without thorns."
nom. sg.(?) *aśalasaña* 6r10.

[1]***aśuha*** adj. Skt. *aśubha*, P *asubha*, "unpleasant."
n. nom. sg. *«aśuha»* 4r28, *«(*a)śu[ha]»* 4r28, *aśuha* 11r43, *aśuhe* 11r27 [2×]; acc. sg. *aśuha* 11v9, *aśuhe* 11v5, *aśuho* 11v4; nom. pl. *aśuha* 11v26 [2×].

[2]***aśuha*** n. Skt. *aśubha*, P *asubha*, "unpleasant [state]."
nom. sg. *aśuhe* 11r16; nom. pl. *aśuha* 4r4, 4r11; gen. pl. *aśu[haṇa]* 4r26, *aś(*uhaṇa)* 4v5.

aśpris̱aṇa n. Skt. ~ *asparśana*, BHS *aspṛśana*, P ~ *aphusana*, "discomfort."
gen. pl. *(*a)[śpr](*i)[s̱aṇa]ṇa* 4r27, *aśpris̱a(*ṇa)[ṇa]* 4v7.
Cf. ***śpris̱aṇa***.

aśrea see ***avhiñaaśreasuha***.

as̱a ind. Skt. *atha*, P *atha*, "now, then, (in *atha vā*:) or also."
as̱a 11r17 (uncertain), 11r23 (in *as̱a va*), 11v28 (in *as̱a va*).

asakhada see ***sakhadaasakhada***.

asakhea adj. Skt. *asaṃkhyeya*, P *asaṃkheyya*, "uncountable, innumerable."
m. acc. pl. *as̱akeṃa* 11r35, *asakhea* 11r37.

asagaṇia see ***asagaṇiasuha***.

asagaṇiasuha n. Skt. *asaṃgaṇikāsukha*, P *asaṅgaṇikāsukha*, "happiness of being without company."
nom. sg. *asagaṇia[suh](*e)* 11r20.
Cf. ***sagaṇia***.

asaṃkheda adj. Skt. *saṃkhyāta*, P *asaṃkhāta*, "uncounted, innumerable." (P not in this meaning.)
m. instr. pl. *asaṃkhe[dehi]* 4r15.

as̱atia adj. or n. Skt. *āsaptika* (?), "[group] up to seven (?)."
unclear: *as̱atia* 4v1, 4v9, 4v10, 4v11, *as̱atiade* 4r23, 4v10.

as̱apurus̱a m. Skt. *asatpuruṣa*, P *asappurisa*, "unworthy man."
nom. pl. *«(*as̱apurus̱a)»* 4r5; gen. pl. *as̱apurus̱aṇa* 4r25.
See also ***kamapramuhaas̱apurus̱a***.

asas̱araṇa adj. Skt. *asādhāraṇa*, P *asādhāraṇa*, "uncommon, extraordinary."
f. nom. sg. *asas̱araṇe* 11v2.

as̱iṇa see ***svaas̱iṇasuha***.

as̱ivasida pp. Skt. *adhivāsita*, P *adhivāsita*, "endured, accepted."
n.(?) nom. sg.(?) *[a]s̱ivas̱idae* 4r20 (form uncertain; cf. annotations, p. 174), *as̱ivasidae* 4r20 (form uncertain; cf. annotations).

asuha n. Skt. *asukha*, P *asukha*, "unhappiness."
nom. sg. *asuhe* 11r34.

asti v. Skt. *asti*, P *asti*, "is, exists."
pres. 3rd sg. *asti* 11r25; opt. 3rd sg. *siati* 6r5, 6r6 [2×], *siadi* 6v4 [3×], 6v5, 6v6 [2×], 11r49, *(*siadi)* 6v6; 3rd pl. *siati* 6r5, 6r7.

aspamia adj. Skt. *asvāmika*, P *asāmika*, "not belonging to anyone."
n.(?) nom.(?) sg. *aspami[a]* 6r6.

asvahu see ***ma***-.

aha v. Skt. *āha*, P *āha*, "says."
pres. 3rd sg. *aha* 4r17, 6r8, 6v1, 11r23.

aharea Skt. *āhāraka*, "procuring." (Uncertain; cf. annotations, p. 183.)
unclear: *ahara[e]* 4r25, 11r12, *[a](*hara)e* 4r25, *aharae* 4r25, 4r26 [2×], 11r10, 11r11, 11v6, 11v10, *[a](*harae)* 4r26, *(*a)[ha]rae* 11r9, *(*a)[ha]rea* 4r26, *aharea* 4r27 [3×], 4r28, 4v4 [2×], 4v5, 4v6 [3×], 4v7 [3×], 4v8,

11r22, *(*a)[har](*e)[a]* 4r27, *[aharea]* 4v5, *a(*ha)[re]a* 4v5, *aha[rea]* 4v8.

ahigakṣidava gdv. Skt. *abhikāṅkṣitavya*, P *abhikaṅkhitabba*, "to be desired."
? nom. pl. *[ahi]ga[kṣidave]* 4v3.

ahiṇadidava gdv. Skt. *abhinanditavya*, P *abhinanditabba*, "to be looked forward to, to be rejoiced at." (Reconstruction uncertain but likely.)
mn.(?) nom. pl. *[a] .i + + dave* 4r24 (reconstruct as *[abh]i(*ṇadi)dave*?).

ahivadida pp. Skt. *abhivādita / abhivandita*, P *abhivādita*, "saluted."
mn.(?) nom. pl. *aïvadida* 4v11.

ahivadidava gdv. Skt. *abhivādayitavya*, P *abhivadetabba*, "to be saluted."
mn.(?) nom. pl. *ahivadidava* 4v1, *ahiva⟨*di⟩da[va]* 4v1, *[a](*hiva)didave* 4r24; ? nom. sg. *ahivadidave* 4v3; nom. pl. *ahi(*va)[d](*i)dava* 4r28.

ahu / aho see ***ma-***.

ichadi v. Skt. *icchati*, P *icchati*, "wishes" (pass. "is wished for").
pres. 3rd sg. pass. *ichiadi* 6v8; opt. 3rd sg. pass. *ichiea* 11v3, 11v6.

ichidava gdv. Skt. *icchitavya*, P *icchitabba*, "to be wished for."
n. nom. sg. *ichidava* 6r4, *[ichidava]* 6r7.

ithu ind. Vedic *itthā*, Skt. *ittham*, P *itthaṃ*, "thus, in this way."
⟪ithu⟫ 4r28, *ithu* 6r9, *[ith]u* 6v8.

ithumi ind. Vedic *ittha*, Skt. *iha*, P *idha*, "here, in this existence." (Uncertain, perhaps *ithu* + *mi*, loc. sg.)
[ithumi] 4v8, *ithumi* 4v9, *i[th]umi* 4v12.

ida- dem. pron. Skt. *idam*, P *idaṃ*, "this."
m. nom. pl. *ime* 4r12, 4r18, 11r52, *[i](*m)[e]* 4r18; n. nom. sg. *aya* 11r49 (referring to *suhe*), *io* 4r21 (referring to *ñaṇo*), *ida* 6r3 [6×], 6r4 [2×], 11r50, 11r52, 11v11, 11v25, 11v26, 11v27, *[ida]* 6r2, 6r3, *imo* 4r19 (referring to *ñaṇo*); instr. sg. *imeṇa* 6r7; nom. pl. *ime* 6r1 (referring to *aïdaṇa*); n.(?) instr. pl. *imehi* 11r37.

idara adj. Skt. *itara*, P *itara*, "other." (The gender is uncertain in all instances.)
? nom. sg. *idara* 4r28, *idaro* 4v3; acc.(?) sg. *idara* 4v11; abl. sg. *idarade* 4v10.
See also ***idarasahora***.

idarasahora m. Skt. *itarasaṃhāra/-sambhāra*, P *itarasaṃhāra/-sambhāra* (?), "collection of the other [group]."
nom. sg. *idarasahoro* 4v12.
Cf. ***matrasahora***.

iva ind. Skt. *iva*, P *iva*, "like, as."
iva 11r40, 11v14.

iṣemi ind. Skt. ~ *iha*, P ~ *iha*, "here."
iśemi 4r15, *i(*ṣe)[mi]* 4r17.

uaṇiṣa see ***uaṇiṣasuha***.

uaṇiṣasuha n. BHS *upaniṣatsukha / upaniṣāsukha*, P *upanisāsukha*, "happiness due to a cause."
nom. sg. *[ua]ṇi[ṣa]suhe* 11r26, *u⟨*a⟩ṇiṣa{ṣa}suhe* 11r25–11r26; gen. sg. *uaṇiṣasuhasa* 11v12.

uadae ind. Skt. *upādāya*, P *upādāya*, "(in the phrase *parikalpam upādāya*:) assuming [the hypothetical case]."
uadae 6r1.

uadaṇa n. Skt. *upādāna*, P *upādāna*, "clinging [to existence]."
nom. sg. *uadaṇa* 4r14.

uadi m. Skt. ~ *upadhi*, P *upādi* = *upadhi*, "attachment [to worldly possessions forming a basis for rebirth]."
nom. sg. *uadi* 4r14.

uadiaṇa pres. part. BHS *upādiyāna*, P *upādiyāna*, "clinging."
unclear: *uadiaṇa* 4r13 (m. nom sg. or n. acc. sg. used adverbially), *(*u)[a]diaṇa* 4r13 (m. nom sg. or n. acc. sg. used adverbially).

uadiadi v. Skt. *upādatte*, BHS *upādīyati*, P *upādiyati*, "clings to, holds on to."
opt. 3rd sg. pass. *uadiea* 11r17.

uadiṇa pp. BHS *upādinna*, P *upādinna*, "taken up."
n.(?) nom. sg.(?) *u[adiṇae]* 4r20 (form uncertain; cf. annotations, p. 174).

uayea m. Skt. *upacaya*, P *upacaya*, "increase; (here:) increasing."
gen. sg. *uayeasa* 11r11.
Cf. ***avayea***.

uavati see ***saṃsaraüavatiṇirvaṇaṇaṣadukha-vidimiśasuha***.

ukṣida pp. Skt. *upekṣita*, P *upekkhita*, "looked at with an even mind."
n.(?) nom. sg.(?) *ukṣidae* 4r20 (form uncertain; cf. annotations, p. 174).

uju adj. Skt. *ṛju*, P *uju* (?), "straight, right, honest; (adv.:) in the right manner, correctly (?)." (Uncertain, context missing.)
unclear: *u[j]u* 4v12.

udeṣ̱a see ***sudeṣ̱asuha***.

upajadi v. Skt. *utpadyate*, P *uppajjati*, "arises."
pres. 3rd sg. *upajati* 6v1, *upajadi* 11v1, *[upajadi]* 6r8; opt. 3rd sg. *upajea* 11r29, 11r30, 11r31, 11r32 [2×], 11r33 [3×], 11v4, 11v6, 11v7, 11v14, 11v25, *(*u)pajea* 11r30, *(*upa)[je]a* 11r31, *[upaj](*e)a* 11r32, *upajea[di]* 6v3, *[upaj](*e)[adi]* 6v6; fut. 3rd pl. *upajiśa[ti]* 4v11; abs. *upaje* 11r30, 11r31, *upa[je]* 11r30.

upajidava gdv. Skt. *utpadyitavya*, P *uppajjitabba*, "to arise."
n. nom. sg. *upajidave* 11v11.

upaṇa pp. Skt. *utpanna*, P *uppanna*, "arisen."
n. nom. sg. *upaṇa* 11r29; f. nom. sg. *upaṇa* 11v7, 11v30.

upadidava gdv. Skt. *utpādayitavya*, P *uppadetabba*, "to produce."
n.(?) nom. sg. *upadidave* 4v2.

uṣ̱a see ***śidaüṣ̱adharaṇadukhavidimiśasuha***.

uṣ̱ata pp. ~ Skt. *ucchrita*, BHS *ucchṛta/utsṛta*, P *ussita*; or more probably abs., ~ Skt. *ucchritya*, BHS *ucchritvā/utsṛtvā*, P *ussitvā* (?), "raised, lifted up onto (?)." (Uncertain; cf. annotations, p. 215.)
unclear: *uṣ̱ata* 11r34.

uhae adj. Skt. *ubhaya*, P *ubhaya*, "both."
mn.(?) nom. pl. *«uhae»* 4r23, *[uha]e* 4r24, *uhae* 4v1, 4v4; n. nom. sg. *abhae* 11r8 (read *ubhae*); nom. pl. *uhaa* 11r8 (read *uhae*), *uhae* 11r8.

eka see ***ekakalava***, ***ekadutracadurapaṃcaṣa-yava-sata***.
Cf. ***egagra***.

ekakalava adj. Skt. *ekakālavat*, P *ekakālavat* (?), "having/existing at the same time (?)."
n.(?) nom.(?) sg. *eka[kalava]* 6r7.

ekadutracadurapaṃcaṣa-yava-sata card. Skt. *ekadvitricatuḥpañcaṣaḍ-yāvat-sapta*, P *ekadviticatupañcacha-yāva-satta*, "one, two, three, four, five, six,—up to—seven."
mn.(?) acc.(?) pl. *[e]kadutracadurapa[ṃca]ṣa-yavasata* 4v1; instr. pl. *ekadutracadurepaṃca-ṣahayavasatahi* 4r23.

ekameka adj. Skt. *ekaika*, BHS *ekameka*, P *ekameka*, "one by one, each."
m.(?) gen. sg. *ekamekasa* 4v12.

ega see ***egagra***, ***egagracitasa***.

egagra adj. Skt. *ekāgra*, P *ekagga*, "single-pointed, concentrated."
n. nom. sg. *ega[g](*ra)* 6v6.
See also ***egagracitasa***.

egagracitasa f. Skt. *ekāgracittatā*, P *ekaggacittatā*, "state of a concentrated mind."
nom. sg. *[e]ga[gracitasa]* 6v2, *(*e)[gra]ga-citasa* 6v3.

ecakhaïdava gdv. Skt. *atyākhyāyitavya*, P *accakhāyitabba* (?), "to be explained; to be neglected, ignored (?)."
n. nom. sg. *ecakhaïdave* 11r4.

eda- dem. pron. Skt. *etad*, P *etad*, "this."
m. nom. sg. *eṣ̱a* 11v14; nom. pl. *ed[e]* 6r8; m.(?) nom. pl. *«ede»* 4r23 (m. or n.), *ede* 4v1 (m. or n.); gen. pl. *edeṣ̱a* 11r1, 11r2; n. nom. sg. *edam* 4r21, *eṣ̱a* 6r8 [3×], 11r23, 11r25, 11r26, 11v1, *(*e)ṣ̱a* 6r8; acc. sg. *eṣ̱a* 11v5; instr. sg. *edeṇa* 4r20; n.(?) nom. sg. *eṣ̱a* 11r3; instr. pl. *edehi* 11r4, *e[de]hi* 11r4; nom.(?) pl.(?) *[ete]* 11r6 (uncertain, context missing).
See also ***edapramuha***.

edapramuha adj. Skt. *etatpramukha*, P *etappamukha*, "headed by this."
n. nom. sg. *[eda]pramuhe* 11r48.

evaṇisamartha adj. Skt. *evaṃniḥsāmarthya*, P ~ *evaṃnirattha*, "such useless."
m. loc. sg. *[eva]ṇisamarthami* 6r8.

evadukha adj. Skt. *evaṃduḥkha*, P *evaṃdukkha*, "such painful."
m. loc. sg. *[e]vadukhami* 6r8.

[1]***eva*** ind. Skt. *eva*, P *eva*, "only, exactly."
eva 11r25, 11v24 (in *evam eva*).

[2]***eva*** ind. Skt. *evam*, P *evaṃ*, "thus, in this way; (in *evam eva*:) in the same manner."
eva 11v26, *(*eva)* 11v27, *evam* 11v24 (in *evam eva*).
See also ***evaṇisamartha***, ***evadukha***.

oama see ***sudiṇoama***.

olaïa adj. Skt. *avalagita*, Pkt. *olaggiya*, "fastened, attached [to something]."
n.(?) acc.(?) sg.(?) *ola[ia]* 11v1 (used adverbially?), *ola[i]a* 11v12 (used adverbially?).

osagra m. Skt. *avasarga*, P *vossagga*, "release."
gen. sg. *osagrasa* 11r28.
See also ***osagrasuha***.

osagrasuha n. Skt. *avasargasukha*, P *vossaggasukha*, "happiness of release."
nom. sg. *osagrasuhe* 11r17.

ohoro ind. P ~ *huraṃ* (?), "there, in another existence (?)." (Uncertain, perhaps also corresponding to P *hurāhuraṃ*, "from existence to existence"; cf. annotations, p. 189.)
ohoro 4v8, 4v9, *(*o)h[o]r[o]* 4v9, *[o](*ho)ro* 4v10.

ka ind. Skt. *kam*, "indeed."
ka 11r26.

kaïa adj. Skt. *kāyika*, P *kāyika*, "relating to body."
n. gen. sg. *(*kaï)asa* 11r11.
See also ***kaïacedaṣia***.

kaïacedaṣia adj. Skt. *kāyikacaitasika*, P *kāyikacetasika*, "relating to body and mind."
n. acc. sg. *[kaï]ac[e]daṣia* 4r4 (adv.), *[kaïa]cedaṣia* 4r10–4r11 (adv.).

kaṭava gdv. Skt. *kartavya*, P *kattabba*, "to be done."
m. nom. sg. *kaṭave* 4v12; n. nom. sg. *kaṭava* 6v7 (or pl.), *«kaṭave»* 4r28, *kaṭave* 11r8.

kadhadhaduaïdaṇa n. Skt. *skandhadhātvāyatana*, P *khandhadhātuāyatana*, "aggregates, elements, and sense bases."
nom. pl. *kadhadhaduaïdaṇa* 6r1, 6r7, *kadhadhaduaïdaṇi* 6r5 (read *°aïdaṇa*).

[1]***kama*** see ***kamadhadu***, ***kamabhoyi***, ***kamasuha***.

[2]***kama*** see ***kamapramuhaasapuruṣa***.

kamadhadu f. Skt. *kāmadhātu*, P *kāmadhātu*, "the desire realm."
loc. sg. *kamadhadu* 11v14.

kamapramuhaaṣapuruṣa m. Skt. *kāmapramukhāsatpuruṣa*, P *kāmappamukhāsappurisa*, "unworthy men headed by Kāma [as an epithet of Māra] (?)."
gen. pl. *[kama]pra[mu]haaṣapuru[ṣaṇa]* 4v4.
Cf. ***budhapramuhasapuruṣa***.

kamabhoyi m. Skt. *kāmabhogin*, P *kāmabhogin*, "someone who enjoys sensual pleasures."
nom. sg. *kamabhoyi* 11r24.

kamasuha n. Skt. *kāmasukha*, P *kāmasukha*, "happiness of sensual pleasures."
nom. sg. *kamasuhe* 11r49, 11r50, 11r52; instr. pl. (?) *kamasuhehi* 11r48.

kaya see ***kayadukha***, ***kayadukhacitadukhavidimiśasuha***, ***kayasuha***, ***civarakṣayakayakṣayaamoyaṇakṣayadukhavidimiśasuha***, ***sarvakayadukhavidimiśasuha***.

kayakṣaya see ***civarakṣayakayakṣayaamoyaṇakṣayadukhavidimiśasuha***.

kayadukha n. Skt. *kāyaduḥkha*, P *kāyadukkha*, "suffering of the body."
nom. sg. *kayadukhe* 11r6.
See also ***kayadukhacitadukhavidimiśasuha***.

kayadukhacitadukhavidimiśasuha n. Skt. *kāyaduḥkhacittaduḥkhavyatimiśrasukha*, P *kāyadukkhacittadukkhavītimissasukha*, "happiness mixed with suffering of the body and suffering of the mind."
nom. sg. *[ka]yadukhacitadukhavidimiśasuhe* 11r44.

kayasuha n. Skt. *kāyasukha*, P *kāyasukha*, "happiness of the body."
nom. sg. *kayesuho* 11v7 (read *kayasuho*, or separate into *kaye suho*); loc.(?) sg. *kayasuhe* 11r7.

karaṇa n. Skt. *kāraṇa*, P *kāraṇa*, "reason, cause."
acc. sg. *[karaṇa]* 4r6, *karaṇa* 4r8; instr. sg. *ka[ra](*ṇeṇa)* 4r5, *karaṇeṇa* 11r50, 11v16, 11v23, 11v30, *«karaṇeṇa»* 11v15, *[karaṇe](*ṇa)* Gloss; loc. sg. *(*ka)raṇe* 4r5.

karamaṇa pres. part. Skt. ~ *kurvant*, P ~ *kubbanta*, "doing."
n. nom. sg. *[karamaṇa]* 4r21, *[karama]ṇa* 4r21.

karavida pp. Skt. ~ *kārita*, P *kārāpita*, "caused to be made."
n. nom. sg. *karavidae* 6v4 (compound future tense); f. nom. sg. *karavi[da](*e)* 6v4 (compound future tense).

karitava gdv. Skt. *kārayitavya*, P *kāritabba*. (Meaning unclear; cf. annotations, p. 238.)
n.(?) nom. sg. *karitava* 6r1.

karodi v. Skt. *karoti*, P *karoti*, "does."
opt. 3rd sg. *kareati* 6v6, *k[ar]eadi* 6v5,

kar[e]adi 6v5; fut.(?) 3rd sg. *kahati* 4r24, 4v3, *ka[hati]* 4v3.

karpa m. Skt. *kalpa*, P *kappa*, "eon."
acc. pl. *karpa* 11r35, 11r37; instr. pl. *[ka]rpehi* 4r15.

karma n. Skt. *karman*, P *kamma*, "[good] activity."
gen. pl. *[ka]rmaṇa* 4r27, *karmaṇa* 4v7.
See also ***prahaṇakarma***. Cf. ***akarma***.

karya n. Skt. *kārya*, P *kāriya*, "use, purpose (?)." (Used synonymously with *kica*.)
nom. sg. *kaye* 11r1 (read *karye*?), 11r2 (read *karye*?), *ka[r]ya* 11r48 (read *karye*), *karye* 11r2, 11r27, 11r34, 11r37, 11r49.

kala see ***ekakalava***.

kavalaa m. Skt. *kapālaka*, P *kapālaka*, "[beggar's] bowl."
instr. sg. *kavalaeṇa* 4r19.

kaṣ̱a ind. Skt. *katham*, P *kathaṃ*, "how?"
[ka]sa 11v6, *kaṣ̱a* 6r9, 6v1 [2×], 11v4, *[kaṣ̱a]* 6r8.

[1]***kica*** n. Skt. *kṛtya*, P *kicca*, "things to be done."
nom. sg. *kica* 6v7; gen. pl. *kicaṇa* 4r27, 4v7.

[2]***kica*** noun Skt. *kṛtya*, P *kicca*, "use, purpose (?)." (Used synonymously to *karya*.)
? nom. sg. *kice* 11r3, 11r4.

kicakica n. Skt. *kṛtyākṛtya*, P *kiccākicca*, "what is to be done and what is not to be done."
acc. pl. *kicakica* 6v5.

kici adj. Skt. *kiṃcid*, P *kiñci*, "(with *na*:) nothing."
n. acc. sg. *kic⟨*i⟩* 11v17, *kici* 11v19.

[1]***ki*** interr. pron. Skt. *kim*, P *kiṃ*, "who, what; (instr.:) how."
m. nom. sg. *ko* 4r13, 4r14, 6v9; n. nom. sg. *k[i]* 4r7, *ki* 4r20, *kim* 11r34; instr. sg. *keṇa* 11r12 ("how?"), 11r50, 11v23; n.(?) nom. sg. *ki* 4v10 (uncertain, possibly also m. referring to *aṇuśaśe*; or used in the sense of "how? why?").

[2]***ki*** ind. Skt. *kim*, "[interrogation particle introducing a question]."
ki 4r17, 11r23.

ku ind. Skt. *kū* = *kva*, P *ku*, "(with *na*:) why then?"
[ku] 11v16, *ku* 11v20.

kuḏea adj. Skt. *kūṭa+ka*, P *kūṭa+ka*, cf. *kūṭeyya*, "deceitful." (Uncertain; cf. annotations, p. 256.)
n. acc. sg. *kuḏae* 6v3 (referring to *ñaṇo*, or used adverbially?); n.(?) loc. sg. *kuḏ[e]ami* 6v7 (perhaps referring to *ñaṇo* which is not written).

kuś̱ala adj. Skt. *kuśala*, P *kusala*, "wholesome/good [deed or state (n.)]."
m. gen. pl. *(*kuś̱a)l[aṇa]* 11r5; n. nom. sg. *kuśalo* 4r21; acc. sg.(?) *kuś̱ala* 4r8; instr. sg. *kuś̱aleṇa* 11r1; gen. sg. *kuś̱a[la]s[a]* 6v2; loc. sg. *kuśale* 4r5; nom. pl. *kuśala* 4r11, *kuś̱ala* 4r4; instr. pl. *kuś̱alehi* 11r4; gen. pl. *(*kuś̱a)[laṇa]* 4r26, *kuś̱alaṇa* 4v6; unclear: *kuś̱a(*l).* 11r1–11r2 (instr. sg. or cpd.).
Cf. ***akuś̱ala***.

kuhica see ***kuhicaagamaṇakuhicagamaṇa***.
Cf. ***akuhica***, ***kuhicaagamaṇakuhicagamaṇa***.

kuhicaagamaṇakuhicagamaṇa n. Skt. *kutracid-āgamanakutracidgamana*, P *kuhiñcāgamana-kuhiñcigamana*, "coming from anywhere, going anywhere."
nom. sg. *kuhicaagamaṇa(*ku)[h](*icagamaṇa)* 6r1–6r2.
Cf. ***akuhicaagamaṇaakuhicagamaṇa***.

kerea adj. Skt. *kāryaka*, BHS *keraka*, Pkt. *-keraka/-keraa*, "belonging to (?)."
unclear: *[ka]raï* 4v9, *karae* 4r23, *⟨*ka⟩rae* 4r23, *keraa* 4v9, 4v10, *[ke]rao* 4v1, *kerea* 4v1, *[k]erea* 4v9, *[kere](*a)* 4v10, *k[e]rea* 4v11, *(*k)[e]rea* 4v11, *[ko]* 4v10.

koḍi see ***trikoḏi***.

kṣati f. Skt. *kṣānti*, P *khanti*, "endurance."
nom. sg. *kṣati* 11r51.

kṣaya see ***civarakṣayakayakṣayaamoyaṇakṣaya-dukhavidimiśasuha***, ***puñakṣaya***.

khaïta pp. Skt. ~ *khyāta*, BHS *khyāyita*, P *khāyita*, or abs., Skt. *khyāyitvā*, P *khāyitvā*, "(having been) declared."
n. nom. sg. *khaïta* 11r6 (or abs.), 11v7 (or abs.).
Cf. ***akhaïta***.

khaïti v. Skt. *khyāyate*, P *khāyati*, pass. "is declared."
pres. 3rd sg. pass. *khaï[ti]* 11r1, *khaïti* 11r4.

khaḏea adj. Skt. *khaṇḍaka*, P ~ *khaṇḍa*, "broken."
m. instr. sg. *khaḏaeṇa* 4r19.

khavedi v. BHS *kṣepayati*, P *khepeti*, "spends [time]."
opt. 3rd sg.(?) *khaveati* 11r37.

gaga see ***gagaṇadivalias̱amaloadhadu-***.

gagaṇadivalias̱amaloadhadu f. Skt. *gaṅgānadīvālikāsamalokadhātu*, "world systems as [numerous as] the sands of the river Gaṅgā."
nom.(?) pl. *gagaṇadivalias̱amaloga(*dhadu)* 4r12–4r13 (or acc.), *gagaṇa[diva]lias̱amaloadhadu* 4r13 (or acc.).
See also ***gagaṇadivalias̱amaloadhaduduha***, ***gagaṇadivalias̱amaloadhadusuha***.

gagaṇadivalias̱amaloadhaduduha n. Skt. *gaṅgānadīvālikāsamalokadhātuduḥkha*, "suffering in world systems as [numerous as] the sands of the river Gaṅgā."
nom.(?) pl. *gagaṇadivalias̱amaloadhadu(*d)u(*ha)* 4r13 (or acc.).

gagaṇadivalias̱amaloadhadusuha n. Skt. *gaṅgānadīvālikāsamalokadhātusukha*, "happiness in world systems as [numerous as] the sands of the river Gaṅgā."
nom.(?) pl. *[gaga]⟨*ṇadi⟩[valias̱ama]loadhadusuha* 4r14 (or acc.).

gachadi v. Skt. *gacchati*, P *gacchati*, "goes."
opt. 3rd sg. pass. *gachiea* 11r15.

gaḍa m. Skt. *gaṇḍa*, P *gaṇḍa*, "boil."
instr. sg. *gaḍeṇa* 6r3; nom. pl. *gaḍa* 11v13, 11v26, *[gaḍa]* 11v27 [2×], *gada* 11v25; gen. pl. *gaḍaṇa* 11v14.
See also ***gaḍasagharya***. Cf. ***agaḍa***.

gaḍasagharya n. Skt. *gaṇḍasaṅghārya* (?) = ~ *gaṇḍasaṃharaṇa*, P ~ *gaṇḍasaṅgharaṇa*, "accumulation of boils."
acc. sg. *gaḍa[sagha]rya* 11v22.

gada see ***vivegagada***.

gamaṇa see ***akuhicaagamaṇaakuhicagamaṇa***, ***akuhicaagamaṇaakuhicagamaṇaagara***, ***kuhicaagamaṇakuhicagamaṇa***.

guṇa see ***avarimaṇaguṇavidimiśa***.

gelaña n. Skt. ~ *glāna*, BHS *glānya*, P *gelañña*, "sickness."
gen. pl. *gelañaṇa* 4r28, 4v7.

ca ind. Skt. *ca*, P *ca*, "and."
ca 4r3 [2×], 4r4 [3×], 4r5, 4r8, 4r10 [2×], 4r11, 4r12, 4r14, 4r15 [2×], 4r16 [4×], 4r17 [3×], 4r18 [5×], 4r19 [3×], 4r21 [2×], 4r22 [5×], 4r23 [3×], 4r24 [2×], 4r28 [5×], 4v1 [2×], 4v2 [4×], 4v3 [2×], 4v10, 4v11 [4×], 4v12 [4×], 6r5 [2×], 6r7 [3×], 6r8 [2×], 6r9 [2×], 6r9 ("too"), 6r10 [5×], 6v1 (uncertain, context missing), 6v3, 6v4 [4×], 6v4 ("and indeed"), 6v5, 6v7, 6v8, 6v9 [2×], 11r1 [2×], 11r3, 11r8, 11r9 [2×], 11r10, 11r12 [3×], 11r15, 11r17 [2×], 11r18, 11r26 [2×], 11r28, 11r35 [2×], 11r36, 11r38, 11r49 [2×], 11v4 [3×], 11v5 [4×], 11v9 [2×], 11v10, 11v12, 11v13, 11v15, 11v20, 11v28, *[ca]* 4r3, 4r10 [2×], 4r16 [2×], 4r18, 4r19, 4r23, 6r2 [3×], 6r6 [2×], 6r7, 6r8 [2×], 6r9, 6v3 [2×], 11r26, *c[a]* 6r5, 6v3, *⟪ca⟫* 4r28, 4v4, 4v10, *⟪(*ca)⟫* 4r28, *(*ca)* 6r9, 6r10, 11r3, 11r12, *⟨*ca⟩* 4v9, 11r25, 11v1, 11v9, *[ja]* 6v8, *ya* 4r15 [2×], 4r18, 4r22, 4v11.

cakṣu see ***divacakṣu***.

cadura see ***ekadutracadurapaṃcaṣa-yava-sata***.

caduraguḏiehi adj. (a) Skt. *caturaṅgulika*; (b) Skt. *caturguḍaka*, "(a) four fingers long/broad; (b) four [hot iron] balls." (Uncertain; cf. annotations, p. 216.)
? instr. pl. *caduraguḏiehi* 11r35 (gender uncertain).

caradi v. Skt. *carati*, P *carati*, "goes."
fut. 1st sg. *cariśe* 4r21.

cita n. Skt. *citta*, P *citta*, "thought, mind." (In Skt. only n., in BHS and P also m.)
nom. sg. *cita* 6v6, *cite* 4v2.
See also ***kayadukhacitadukhavidimiśasuha***, ***citadukhavidimiśasuha***, ***citasuha***, ***paracitañaṇa***.

citaṇa n. Skt. *cintana*, P *cintana*, "reflecting upon, contemplation."
nom. sg. *citaṇe* 4r3, 4r9.

citadukha n. Skt. *cittaduḥkha*, P *cittadukkha*, "suffering of the mind."
nom. sg. *ci[ta]dukhe* 11r6.
See also ***kayadukhacitadukhavidimiśasuha***, ***citadukhavidimiśasuha***.

citadukhavidimiśasuha n. Skt. *cittaduḥkhavyatimiśrasukha*, P *cittadukkhavītimissasukha*, "happiness mixed with suffering of the mind."
nom. sg. *citadukhavidimiśasuhe* 11r44–11r45.

citasa see ***avikṣitacitasa***, ***egagracitasa***.

ñaṇa n. Skt. *jñāna*, P *ñāṇa*, "knowledge." nom. sg. *ñaṇe* 4r17, *(*ña)ṇo* 4r19; acc. sg. *[ñaṇo]* 6v3 (uncertain reading); loc. sg. *ñaṇami* 11r8.
See also ***ṇiṣamarthañaṇa***, ***ṇiṣamarthadukhañaṇa***, ***dukhañaṇa***, ***dukhañaṇaṇisamarthañaṇa***, ***paracitañaṇa***, ***bhudañaṇa***, ***suṭhuñaṇa***.

ṭhaṇa n. Skt. *sthāna*, P *ṭhāna*, "possibility." (In the phrase *ṇa ida ṭhaṇo*, "this is not possible.") nom. sg. *ṭhaṇe* 11r50, 11v11, *ṭhaṇo* 11r52, 11v25, 11v26, 11v27.

ṭhavaṇia gdv. Skt. *sthāpanīya*, P *ṭhāpaniya*, "to be established." ? nom. sg. *ṭhavaṇia* 11r24 (context missing).

ṭhidigica adj. Skt. *sthitikṛtya*, P *ṭhitikicca*, "to be done permanently (?)." ? acc. pl. *[ṭhi]digica* 6v5.

ṇa ind. Skt. *na*, P *na*, "not." *ṇa* 4r2, 4r3, 4r4 [3×], 4r5, 4r8, 4r10 [3×], 4r11 [2×], 4r12, 4r14 [2×], 4r16, 4r17 [2×], 4r19 [2×], 4r22 [2×], 4r24 [2×], 4v11, 6r5, 6r6, 6r7, 6v2 [4×], 6v3 [2×], 6v4, 6v6 [2×], 6v7 [2×], 6v8, 6v9, 11r2 (= *ṇ(*e)⟨*vi⟩* ?), 11r5, 11r8, 11r13 [2×], 11r14, 11r24 [2×], 11r26 [3×], 11r27, 11r29, 11r33, 11r34, 11r37, 11r38, 11r39, 11r40, 11r42, 11r43, 11r48, 11r49 [2×], 11r50, 11r52 [2×], 11v3, 11v4, 11v6, 11v8, 11v11, 11v16, 11v17, 11v19, 11v20, 11v25, 11v26, 11v27, *[ṇa]* 4r3, 6r4, 6v1, 11r2 (?), 11r16, 11v16, *⟪(*ṇa)⟫* 4r5, *(*ṇa)* 4r5, 4r11, *ṇ[a]* 6v8.

ṇagaa m. Skt. *nagnaka*, P *naggaka*, "naked [mendicant]." nom. sg. *ṇagao* 4r19.

ṇaṇa see ***ṇaṇaparigrahidia***.

ṇaṇaparigrahidia adj. Skt. *nānāparigṛhītika*, "surrounded (?) by different [kinds of beings]." m. nom. sg. *ṇaṇaparigrahidia* 11r25.

ṇadi see ***gagaṇadivaliaṣamaloadhadu-***.

ṇama adv. Skt. *nāma*, P *nāma* (?), "indeed." (Uncertain; cf. annotations, p. 205.) *ṇame* 11r17 (adv.?).

ṇamasaṇiva see ***sarvaṣatvaṇamasaṇivasuha***.

ṇaṣa see ***saṃsaraüavatiṇirvaṇaṇaṣadukha-vidimiśasuha***.

ṇaśadi v. Skt. *naśyati*, P *nassati*, "perishes." pres. 3rd sg. *ṇaśadi* 11v13.

ṇaśida pp. Skt. *nāśita*, P *nāsita*, "destroyed, ruined; (here:) deprived of … (?)." m.(?) nom.(?) sg. *ṇaśida* 11r36, *ṇaṣida* 11r36 [2×].

ṇaṣea Skt. *nāśaka*, P *nāsaka*, "destroying." (Uncertain; cf. annotations, p. 183.) unclear: *ṇa[ṣa]e* 4r25, *ṇaṣae* 4r25, *ṇaṣ̄ae* 4r25, *ṇaṣe* 4r25, 4r26, 11r9, 11r10, 11r12, 11v5, 11v20, *(*ṇa)[ṣ](*e)* 11r12, *(*ṇaṣe)a* 4r26, *(*ṇaṣ)e[a]* 4r26, *ṇaṣea* 4r27 [2×], 4r28, 4v4 [2×], 4v5 [3×], 4v6 [2×], 4v7 [3×], *(*ṇaṣ)e(*a)* 4r27, *[ṇa]ṣea* 4v5, *ṇaṣe[a]* 4v6, *(*ṇa)ṣea* 4v8, *[ṇa]ṣee* 4r26.

ṇaṣedi v. Skt. *nāśayati*, P *nāseti*, "destroys." opt. 3rd sg.(?) *ṇaṣeati* 11r37 [2×]; opt. 3rd sg. pass. *ṇaṣiea* 11r17.

ṇikhalida pp. Skt. *niṣkālita*, P *nikkhālita*, "removed." f. nom. sg. *ṇikhalida* 11r31.

ṇikhaledi v. Skt. *niṣkālayati*, P *nikkhāleti*, "removes." opt. 3rd sg. *ṇikhalidea* 11r30.

ṇica adj. Skt. *nitya*, P *nicca*, "permanent." n. nom. sg. *ṇi[ca]* 11r26; nom. pl. *ṇi[c]e* 6r1 (uncertain, perhaps also adv.); ? nom. sg.(?) *ṇica* 11v24.
See also ***ṇicasaña***. Cf. ***aṇica***.

ṇicakalo adv. Skt. *nityakālam*, P *niccakālaṃ*, "(neg.:) never." *ṇicakalo* 11r33.

ṇicasaña f. Skt. *nityasaṃjñā*, P *niccasaññā*, "notion of [being] permanent." nom. sg. *ṇicasaña* 6r10.

ṇidaṇa n. Skt. *nidāna*, P *nidāna*, "cause, motive, foundation; (here:) [underlying] theme." nom. sg. *ṇidaṇa* 4r5.

ṇirvaṇa n. Skt. *nirvāṇa*, P *nibbāna*, "extinction." nom. sg. *ṇivaṇ[u]* 11r17.
See also ***saṃsaraüavatiṇirvaṇaṇaṣa-dukhavidimiśasuha***.

ṇirvaṇaṇaṣa see ***saṃsaraüavatiṇirvaṇaṇaṣa-dukhavidimiśasuha***.

ṇiṣaṇa see ***boṣimaḍaṇiṣaṇa***.

ṇiṣamartha adj. Skt. *niḥsāmarthya*, P ~ *nirattha*, "ineffectual, unsuitable, useless." m. nom. sg. *ṇisamartho* 11v14; nom. pl. *ṇisamartha* 6r8; mn. nom. sg. *ṇisamarthe*

4r18; n. nom. sg. *《ṇisamartha》* 4r13, 4r28, *[ṇisa]martha* 11r27, *ṇisamartha* 11r27, *《ṇis̱amarthe》* 4r25, *《ṇ(*i)s̱amarth(*e)》* 4r28, *《(*ṇi)[sama]rthe》* 4r28, *ṇisamarthe* 11r9, *ṇis̱amartho* 4r16; nom.(?) sg. *《ṇi[s̱a](*marthe)》* 4v4; acc. sg. *ṇisamartho* 4r15, *ṇisamarthe* 11v5, *ṇisamartha* 6v9, 11v4, 11v9; instr. sg. *ṇisamartheṇa* 6r7; nom. pl. *(*ṇisamartha)* 11v27 [2×].
See also ***evaṇisamartha***, ***ṇis̱amarthañaṇa***, ***ṇis̱amarthadukhañaṇa***, ***ṇis̱amarthavidimiśasuha***, ***dukhañaṇaṇisamarthañaṇa***.

ṇis̱amarthañaṇa n. Skt. *niḥsāmarthyajñāna*, P ~ *niratthañāṇa*, "knowledge of [what is] useless."
nom.(?) sg. *(*ṇi)[s̱ama]rthañaṇo* 4r19.
See also ***dukhañaṇaṇisamarthañaṇa***.

ṇis̱amarthadukhañaṇa n. Skt. *niḥsāmarthya-duḥkhajñāna*, P ~ *niratthadukkhañāṇa*, "knowledge of [what is] useless and [what is] painful."
nom. sg. *ṇis̱ama(*r)thadukhañaṇo* 4r21.

ṇis̱amarthavidimiśasuha n. Skt. *niḥsāṃarthya-vyatimiśrasukha*, P ~ *niratthavītimissasukha*, "happiness mixed with the useless."
nom. sg. *《ṇis̱amarthavidimiśasuhe》* 11r48.

ṇeva [ṇa + eva] ind. Skt. *naiva*, P *neva*, "neither … nor …."
ṇevi 11r1 [2×], 11r2, 11r3 [2×], *ṇev〈*i〉* 11r2.

[1]***ta-*** dem. pron. Skt. *tad*, P *ta*, "this, that, it."
m. nom. sg. *se* 11r24, *so* 6v5, 11v14; abl. sg. *tasva* 4r18; gen. sg. *tasa* 6v5, 6v6; gen. pl. *tes̱a* 11v13; n. nom. sg. *ta* 4r12, 4r17, 4r18, 6r9, 6v1, 11r1, 11r14, 11r51, 11r52, 11v28, *[ta]* 11v23, *[de]* 6r6 (or perhaps involving sandhi with the preceding *hi* in *aji hi de*; then *ide* for Skt. *idam*), *sa* 4r17; instr. sg. *teṇa* 11r34, 11v30, *[teṇa]* Gloss; abl. sg. *tasva* 6v8, 11r7; gen. pl. *te[s̱a]* 11v25, *tes̱a* 11v26, *[te] (*s̱a)* 11v27; n.(?) nom. sg. *ta* 11r14, *so* 4r18 (related to *bodhimaṇḍa*, either m. or n.) [2×]; f. nom. sg. *[ta]* 11r42 (in *ta vela* = BHS *taṃ velaṃ* instead of *tāṃ velāṃ*); f.(?) nom. sg. *sa* 11r30 (referring to *pridi* f. or *śiṭha* n.) [2×], 11r31; acc. sg. *ta* 11r30 (referring to *pridi* f. or *śiṭha* n.).

[2]***ta*** ind. Skt. *tad*, P *taṃ*, "thus, therefore, then."
ta 4r15, 4r17, 4r20 [2×], 6r7, 6r8, 6v1, 6v3, 6v4, 11r37, 11v4, 11v7, 11v8, *[ta]* 6r8, *(*ta)* 6v3, *te* 4r14 (or pronoun, f. nom. pl.), 4v10, 4v11 [2×], 11r52, *[te]* 4r14 (or pronoun, n. nom. pl.), *t[e]* 6v6; *se* 4r2, 4r15.

tae (Uncertain, perhaps Skt. *tayā* or *taṃ ca*, "thus.")
unclear: *tae* 11v30.

taṇu adj. Skt. *tanu*, P *tanu*, "thin, little, reduced."
n. nom. sg. *taṇu* 6v6.

taṇua adj. Skt. *tanuka*, P *tanuka*, "thin, little, reduced."
f. nom. sg. *taṇua* 6v4; unclear: *taṇua* 6v5 (context missing).

tati f. Skt. *tṛpti*, P *titti*, "satisfaction."
nom. sg. *[tati]* 11r5, *tati* 11r13.

tatra ind. Skt. *tatra*, P *tatra*, "there, then, thereby."
tatra 6v4 [2×], 6v6, 11r43, *ta[tra]* 6v7.

tatva n. Skt. *tattva*, P *tatta*, "truth, true state."
nom. sg. *tatva* 6v2.

taraṇa n. Skt. *taraṇa*, P *taraṇa*, "overcoming." (Uncertain, perhaps also a misspelling for *tīrṇa* as part of a compound future tense construction; cf. annotations, p. 256.)
dat.(?) sg.(?) *[ta]raṇae* 6v4.

taraṇia gdv. Skt. *taraṇīya* (?), P *taraṇīya* (?), "to be crossed (?)." (Form uncertain, either gerund or infinitive; cf. annotations, p. 162.)
f.(?) nom.(?) pl.(?) *[ta]raṇia* 4r13, *ta《[ra]》ṇ{u}ia* 4r13.

tava ind. Skt. *tāvat*, P *tāva*, "now."
tava 4r25, 4v1, 11v16, *《tava》* 11v15.

tas̱e adj. Skt. ~ *tathya*, BHS *tatha*, P *tatha*, "real."
n. nom. sg. *tas̱e* 6r8.

tahi ind. Skt. *tarhi*, P *tarahi*, "then, at that time, in that case."
tahi 6v7.

tu- pers. pron. Skt. *tvam*, P *tvaṃ / tuvaṃ*, "you."
nom. sg. *t[uo]* 6r9.

tuli f. Skt. *tulā*, P *tulā* (?), "balance, beam, stake, pole (?)." (Uncertain; cf. annotations, p. 215.)
unclear: *tulie* 11r34.

tus̱a m. Skt. *tuṣa*, P *thusa*, "husk [of grain]."
nom. sg. *tus̱e* 11r53.

tra see ***ekadutracadurapaṃcaṣa-yava-sata***.

tri card. Skt. *tri*, P *ti*, "three."
m. nom. pl. *trae* 4r3, 4r11, «(*trae)» 4r5; gen. pl. *triṇa* 4r25 [3×], 4v4 [2×], 4v5, 4v8 [2×]; n. nom. pl. *trae* 4r4 [6×], 4r10, 4r11 [4×], «(*trae)» 4r5, *[trae]* 4r10, *tra[e]* 4r11; gen. pl. *triṇa* 4r25 [3×], 4r26 [5×], 4r27 [5×], 4r28, 4v4, 4v5 [5×], 4v6 [4×], 4v7 [7×], *(*triṇa)* 4r26, 4r27, *(*tr)iṇa* 4r27, *(*t)[r](*i)[ṇa]* 4r27, *[tri]ṇa* 4v6; f. nom. pl. *trae* 4r3 [2×], 4r10, *tra[e]* 4r10; gen. pl. *triṇa* 4r25 [2×], 4r26, 4v4 [2×], 4v6, 4v8 [2×]; ? nom. pl. *trae* 4r3, *(*tra)e* 4r10.
See also ***trikoḏi***, ***triboṣa***.

trikoḏi f. Skt. *trikoṭi*, P *tikoṭi*, "three points of time (?)." (Perhaps three points of time with reference to the past, future, and present, or three points of time during the day and at night; cf. annotations, p. 183.)
acc.(?) sg. *trikoḏi* 4r24.

triboṣa m. Skt. *tribodha*, P *tibodha*, "three [kinds of] awakening."
dat. sg. *triboṣae* 4r15.

tredhadua n. Skt. *traidhātuka*, P *tedhātuka*, "triple world [consisting of three planes of existences]."
abl. sg. *tr(*e)dhaduade* 4r9, *(*tredhaduade)* 4r2.

dakṣadi v. Skt. *drakṣyati*, P *dakkhati*, "perceives, considers (?)." (Uncertain; cf. annotations, p. 238.)
fut. 3rd sg. *[dakṣiśati]* 6r1.

daṇa n. Skt. *dāna*, P *dāna*, "giving."
nom. sg. *daṇe* 11r51 [2×].
See also ***amiṣadaṇa***, ***dharmadaṇa***.

darśaṇa see ***sapuruṣadarśaṇa***.

di ind. Skt. *iti*, P *ti*, "thus, hence."
ti 4r19 (uncertain), *di* 11r17 (uncertain), 11r43.

diva see ***divacakṣu***.

divacakṣu n. Skt. *divyacakṣu*, P *dibbacakkhu*, "divine eye."
nom. sg. *divacakṣu* 11r21.

du card. Skt. *dva*, P *dvi*, "two."
m. nom. *due* 11v13; m.(?) nom. *[dum](*e)* 4r24, *dume* 4v4; n. nom. *due* 11r7.
See also ***ekadutracadurapaṃcaṣa-yava-sata***, ***dupadua***.

[1]***dukha*** adj. Skt. *duḥkha*, P *dukkha*, "painful."
m. nom. pl. *dukha* 6r8; mn. nom. sg. *dukhe* 4r18; n. nom. sg. «*dukhe*» 4r28 [2×], *dukho* 4r16; acc. sg. *dukha* 6v9, 11v9, *dukhe* 11v5, *dukho* 4r15, 11v4; nom. pl. *dukha* 11v24, 11v25.

[2]***dukha*** n. Skt. *duḥkha*, P *dukkha*, "suffering, painful [state]."
nom. sg. *dukha* 4r20, 6r6, 11r6, *dukhe* 11r6, *duhe* 4r14; acc. sg. *dukha* 6v5, *[d]ukho* 11v21, *[du]kho* Gloss; acc.(?) sg. *[d]u[kho]* 4r2, *(*dukho)* 4r9; instr. sg. *[dukheṇa]* 6r4, *dukheṇa* 6r4; gen. sg. *dukhasa* 6v5; nom. pl. *dukha* 4r10, 11r7, 11r8, *duha* 4r4; gen. pl. *[d](*u)[khaṇa]* 4r25, *du(*kha)[ṇa]* 4v5.
See also ***avarimaṇadukhavidimiśasuha***, ***evadukha***, ***kayadukhacitadukhavidimiśasuha***, ***gagaṇadivaliaṣamaloadhaduduha***, ***citadukhavidimiśasuha***, ***civarakṣayakaya-kṣayaamoyaṇakṣayadukhavidimiśasuha***, ***cedaṣiadukhavidimiśasuha***, ***jadidukha-yava-maraṇadukha***, ***ṇiṣamarthadukhañaṇa***, ***dukhañaṇa***, ***dukhañaṇaṇisamarthañaṇa***, ***dukhabia***, ***dukhavidimiśasuha***, ***dukha-sagharya***, ***durgadidukhavidimiśasuha***, ***payeladukha***, ***priaviṇabhavaagradukha***, ***bahujaṇasaṣaraṇadukha***, ***viñatidukha-vidimiśasuha***, ***śidaüṣadharaṇadukha-vidimiśasuha***, ***saṃsaraüavatiṇirvaṇaṇaṣa-dukhavidimiśasuha***, ***sarvakayadukha-vidimiśasuha***.

dukhaavaṇaa m. Skt. *duḥkhāpanaya*, P ~ *dukkhāpanayana*, "removal of suffering."
nom. sg. *dukhaavaṇao* 11v8.

dukhañaṇa n. Skt. *duḥkhajñāna*, P *dukkhañāṇa*, "knowledge of [what is] painful."
nom.(?) sg. *(*dukh)[oñaṇo]* 4r19.
See also ***dukhañaṇaṇisamarthañaṇa***.

dukhañaṇaṇisamarthañaṇa n. Skt. *duḥkha-jñānaniḥsāmarthyajñāna*, P ~ *dukkhañāṇa-niratthañāṇa*, "knowledge of [what is] painful and knowledge of [what is] useless."
instr. sg. *dukhañaṇaṇisamarthañaṇeṇa* 4r20.

dukhabia n. Skt. *duḥkhabīja*, P *dukkhabīja*, "seed of suffering."
acc. sg. *dukhabie* 11v22, *dukhabio* 11v21.

dukhavida pp. Skt. *duḥkhāpita*, P *dukkhāpita*, "pained."
m.(?) nom.(?) sg. *dukhavida* 11r35 (or n. acc. sg. used adverbially?).

dukhavidimiśasuha n. Skt. *duḥkhavyatimiśra-sukha*, P *dukkhavītimissasukha*, "happiness mixed with suffering."
nom. sg. *dukhavidimiśa[s]u(*he)* 11r42, *dukhavidimiśasuhe* 11r43.

dukhasagharya n. Skt. *duḥkhasaṅghārya* (?) = ~ *duḥkhasaṃharaṇa*, P ~ *dukkhasaṅgharaṇa*, "accumulation of suffering."
nom. sg. *dukhasagha(*r)ye* 11v23; acc. sg. *dukhasa{r}gharya* 11v22.

dupadua adj. Skt. *dvipadika*, P *dvipadika*, "consisting of two parts."
m. nom. pl. *dupadua* 11v13.

dura see ***sudura***.

durgadi f. Skt. *durgati*, P *duggati*, "bad destination."
acc. sg. *durgadi* 11r15; gen. sg. *droatie* 6r1 (uncertain); nom. pl. *(*durga)[di]* 4r3, *durgadi* 4r10; gen. pl. *dro[ga]diṇa* 4r25, *drogadiṇa* 4v4.
See also ***durgadidukhavidimiśasuha***.

durgadidukha see ***durgadidukhavidimiśasuha***.

durgadidukhavidimiśasuha n. Skt. *durgatiduḥkhavyatimiśrasukha*, P *duggatidukkhavītimissasukha*, "happiness mixed with suffering due to bad destinations."
nom. sg. *d[u]rgadidukhavidimiśasuhe* 11r45.

duśadi v. Skt. *duṣyati*, P *dussati*, "becomes hateful."
pres. 2nd sg. *duśaṣ̱i* 6r9; 3rd sg. pass. *duśiadi* 6v3; 1st pl. *[d]u[ś]ama* 6v8; opt. 3rd sg. pass. *duśi[e]adi* 6v3.

duṣaṇa n. Skt. *dūṣaṇa*, P *dussanā*, "the act of becoming hateful."
nom. sg. *d(*u)ṣaṇa* 6v8.

duha see [2]***dukha***.

deṣ̱a m. Skt. *deśa*, P *desa*, "place."
loc. sg. *deṣ̱e* 11r43; nom. pl. *deṣ̱a* 4r18 [2×].
See also ***añatradeṣ̱a***, ***sarvatradeṣ̱a***.

deṣ̱amaṇa pres. part. Skt. ~ *deśayant*, P ~ *desenta*, "showing."
n. nom. sg. *deṣ̱amaṇa* 4r21.

deśidava gdv. Skt. *deśayitavya*, BHS *deśitavya*, P *desitabba*, "to be shown."
? nom. sg. *deśidavo* 4r17 (context missing).

[1]***doṣ̱a*** m. Skt. *doṣa*, P *dosa*, "fault."
gen. pl. *do(*ṣ̱aṇa)* 4v8, *doṣ̱aṇa* 11v5.
See also ***avarimaṇadoṣ̱a***, ***avarimaṇadoṣ̱aprahaṇa***, ***svadoṣ̱a***.

[2]***doṣ̱a*** m. Skt. *dveṣa*, P *dosa*, "hatred."
nom. sg. *[doṣ̱a]* 6r8.

driṭhadhamia adj. Skt. *dṛṣṭadhārmika*, P *diṭṭha-dhammika*, "relating to present life."
n. acc. sg. *driṭhadhamio* 4r25, *[driṭhadhamia]* 4v5; gen. sg. *driṭhadhamiasa* 11r10.
See also ***driṭhadhamiasaparaïa***.

driṭhadhamiasaparaïa adj. Skt. *dṛṣṭadhārmika-sāmparāyika*, P *diṭṭhadhammikasamparāyika*, "the present life and the next."
n. acc. sg. *[dri]ṭha[dha]mi[a]sapara[ia]* 6r4; gen. sg. *driṭhadhami⟨*a⟩saparaïa[ṣ̱]a* 11v15.

drugaṇa m. Skt. *durgaṇa*, P *duggaṇa*, "bad company."
nom. pl. *⟪(*drugaṇa)⟫* 4r5, *drugaṇa* 4r11.

drujaṇa see ***drudeṣ̱a(*ja)drujaṇasamoṣ̱aṇa***.

drudeṣ̱a see ***drudeṣ̱a(*ja)drujaṇasamoṣ̱aṇa***.

drudeṣ̱a(*ja)drujaṇasamoṣ̱aṇa n. Skt. *durdeśa-(*ja)durjanasamavadhāna*, P *duddesa(*ja)-dujjanasamodhāna*, "meeting bad people (*coming from) bad places." (The reconstruction of *(*ja)* is very uncertain.)
instr. sg. *drude[ṣ̱a](*ja)drujaṇasamoṣ̱aṇeṇa* 6r3–6r4.

droaca n. Skt. *daurgatya*, P *duggacca*, "misery."
nom. sg. *droaca* 6r6; gen. sg. *droacasa* 11r11; loc.(?) sg. *droace* 11r37; gen. pl. *droacaṇa* 11v5.
See also ***sarvadroaca***, ***svadroaca***.

dhaṇaedi v. Skt. *dhanāyati*, P *dhanāyati*, "[denom. to *dhana*] strives after, desires."
abs. *dhaṇaïta* 11v16.

dhadu see ***arupadhadu***, ***kamadhadu***, ***gagaṇadivaliaṣ̱amaloadhadu-***, ***ruvadhadu***.

dharaṇa see ***śidaüṣadharaṇadukhavidimiśasuha***.

dharetra f. Skt. *dhārayitṝ* (*dharitrī*), "earth, ground."
loc. sg. *[dha]retrami* 4r17.

dha(r)ma m. Skt. *dharma*, P *dhamma*, "entity, dharma."
nom. pl. *dhama* 6r8, 11r52; instr. pl. *(*dha)mehi* 11r3; gen. pl. *dharm[a]ṇa* 11r5.
See also ***aparihaṇadhama***.

dharma n. Skt. *dharma*, P *dhamma*, "[Buddhist] doctrine, the Dharma" (In Skt./P usually m.; cf. annotations on 4r21 *dharme*, p. 176.)
nom. sg. *dharme* 4r21.
See also ***dharmadaṇa***, ***budhadharmasagha***.

dharmadaṇa n. Skt. *dharmadāna*, P *dhamma-dāna*, "giving of the Dharma."
nom. sg. *dharmadaṇe* 11r51.

pac̱a adv. Skt. *paścāt*, BHS *pacchā*, P *pacchā*, "later, afterwards."
pac̱a 11r27, *«pa[c̱]a»* 4r28, *«pa(*c̱a)»* 4r28, *pac̱i* 6v8.

paṃca see ***ekadutracadurapaṃcaṣa-yava-sata***.

paḏitiṭhadi v. Skt. *pratitiṣṭhati*, P *patiṭṭhahati*, "establishes oneself."
impv. 2nd sg. *paḏi[ti]ṭha* 4v12.

paḏiladha pp. Skt. *pratilabdha*, P *paṭiladdha*, "obtained."
f. nom. sg. *paḏiladha* 4r16.

paḏhama see ***paḏhamacitupada***.

paḏhamacitupada m. BHS *prathamacittotpāda*, P *paṭhamacittuppāda*, "first resolve [to strive for perfect awakening]."
nom. sg. *paḏhamacitupa[de]* 4r15.

paṃḍida adj. Skt. *paṇḍita*, P *paṇḍita*, "wise."
m. nom. sg. *paḍide* 6v9; gen. pl. *paṃḍidaṇa* 11r7.
See also ***paṃḍidaśriya***.

paṃḍidaśriya f. BHS *paṇḍitaśriyā* (?), "fortunes of the wise (?)."
gen. pl. *paṃḍidaśriyaṇa* 11r21.

patade adv., "on the back[side], on the reverse [side of the scroll]." (Presumably from Skt. **patta-*, "back, behind"; cf. CDIAL s.v. [2]*patta*.)
patade 4r28, 6r11.

pada n. Skt. *pada*, P *pada*, "word."
nom. sg. *pada* 6v7 (or pl.?).

padilabha m. Skt. *pratilambha*, P ~ *paṭilābha*, "obtaining."
nom. sg. *padilabhe* 11v20.

padua see ***dupadua***.

payela see ***payeladukha***.

payeladukha n. (a) Skt. *paryāyaduḥkha*, P *pariyāyadukkha*, "indirect suffering"; (b) Skt. *paryāyaduḥkha*, BHS *peyāladuḥkha*, P *peyyāladukkha*, "all other kinds of suffering." (Uncertain; cf. annotations.)
instr. sg. *payeladukh[e]ṇa* 6r3.

para see ***atvahisaparahisasarvas̱atvahisa-vidimiśasuha***, ***paracitañaṇa***, ***parahida***.

paracita see ***paracitañaṇa***.

paracitañaṇa n. Skt. *paracittajñāna*, P *paracitta-ñāṇa*, "knowledge of others' thoughts."
nom. sg. *paracitañaṇa* 11r21.

parama adj. Skt. *parama*, P *parama*, "highest."
mn.(?) instr. sg. *parameṇa* 11r13, 11r14.

paramida f. Skt. *pāramitā*, P ~ *pāramī*, "perfection."
instr. pl. *paramidehi* 11r2.
See also ***prañaparamida***.

parahida n. Skt. *parahita*, P *parahita*, "welfare for others."
nom. sg. *parahida* 4r22.

parahisa see ***atvahisaparahisasarvas̱atvahisa-vidimiśasuha***.

pariapa m. Skt. *parikalpa*, P *parikappa*, "assumption; (in the phrase *parikalpam upādāya*:) [assuming the] hypothetical case."
acc. sg. *pariapo* 6r1.

parigrahida pp. Skt. *parigr̥hīta*, P *pariggahīta*, "surrounded." (Uncertain; cf. annotations, p. 210.)
m. nom. sg. *parigrahida* 11r24.

parigrahidia see ***ṇaṇaparigrahidia***.

paricaa m. Skt. *parityāga*, P *pariccāga*, "letting go, relinquishment."
nom.(?) sg. *paricae* 11v16 (or opt. 3rd sg.?), 11v17 (or opt. 3rd sg.?); dat. sg. *(*pa)ricaae* 11r10, *paricaea* 11r13; abl. sg. *paricaade* 11v10.

paricaïdava gdv. Skt. ~ *parityaktavya*, BHS *parityajitavya*, P *pariccajitabba*, "to be given up, to be let go."
n. nom. sg. *paricaïdave* 11r5, 11r13, *parica[i](*dav)[e]* 11r13–11r14.

paricata pp. Skt. *parityakta*, P *pariccatta*, "given up, let go."
n. nom. sg. (?) *pa[ri]cata* 4r14; n.(?) nom. sg.(?) *paricatae* 4r20 (form uncertain; cf. annotations, p. 174).

paricayadi v. Skt. *parityajati*, P *pariccajati*, "gives up, lets go."
opt. 3rd sg. *par[ica]e* 6v9 (uncertain but based on context to be read as *paricea*), *par⟨*i⟩cea* 11r14; abs. *paricaïta* 4r12, 11v4, 11v5, 11v6, 11v15, 11v17, 11v19, 11v21, *pari[caïta]* 11v21, *par⟨*i⟩caïta* 11v9, 11v22, 11v23, *[pa]ri(*caïta)* Gloss, *(*pa)ricaïta* Gloss, line2, *paricaeta* 11v6 (read *paricaïta*).

paricean̩a pres. part. Skt. ~ *parityajant*, P *pariccajanta*, "giving up, letting go."
unclear: *[pariceaṇa]* 4r14 (m. nom. sg. or n. acc. sg. used adverbially), *paricea[ṇa]* 4r14 (m. nom. sg. or n. acc. sg. used adverbially).

pariña f. Skt. *parijñā*, P *pariññā*, "thoroughly understanding."
nom. sg. *pariña* 11v28.
See also ***pariñaprahaṇa***, ***pariñapridi***, ***pariñasuha***.

pariñada pp. Skt. *parijñāta*, P *pariññāta*, "thoroughly understood."
n. nom. sg. *[pari]ña[d]*. 4r16 (uncertain).

pariñaprahaṇa n. Skt. *parijñāprahāṇa*, P *pariññāpahāṇa*, "thorough understanding [of suffering] and abandoning [of its origin]."
nom. sg. *pariñaprahaṇa* 11r8.

pariñapridi f. Skt. *parijñāprīti*, P *pariññāpīti*, "joy of thoroughly understanding."
nom. sg. *pa[r]iñapridi* 11v1.

pariñasuha n. Skt. *parijñāsukha*, P *pariññāsukha*, "happiness of thorough understanding."
nom. sg. *pariñasuhe* 11r18.

pariṇirvahida pp. Skt. *parinirvāyita*, P *parinibbāyita*, "reached complete extinction."
m. nom. sg. *par⟨*i⟩ṇirvahi[do]* 4r20.

paripuṇa adj. Skt. *paripūrṇa*, P *paripuṇṇa*, "full of …"
n.(?) nom. sg. *paripuṇa* 6v1 (probably referring to *maṇas̱a*).

paribhaṭha pp. Skt. ~ *paribhāṣita*, BHS *paribhāṣṭa*, P *paribhaṭṭha*, "admonished."
mn.(?) nom. pl. *paribhaṭha* 4v11.

paribhaṣ̱a m. Skt. *paribhāṣa*, P *paribhāsa*, "admonition." (In Sanskrit, *paribhāṣā* f. or *paribhāṣa* m.; in Pali only *paribhāsa* m.)
instr. pl. *paribhaṣ̱ehi* 4r23.

paribhaṣ̱idava gdv. Skt. *paribhāṣitavya*, P *paribhāsitabba*, "to be admonished."
mn.(?) nom. pl. *paribhaṣidav⟨*e⟩* 4v9, *paribhaṣ̱idave* 4v9, 4v10; n.(?) nom. sg. *paribhaṣ̱idave* 4r24.
See also ***suparibhaṣ̱idava***.

paribhujidava gdv. Skt. ~ *paribhoktavya*, BHS *paribhuñjitavya*, P *paribhuñjitabba*, "to be enjoyed."
? nom. pl. *paribhujidave* 4v3.

paribhuta pp. Skt. *paribhukta*, P *paribhutta*, "enjoyed."
n. instr. sg. *parubhuteṇa* 11r39 (read *paribhuteṇa*); gen. sg. *paribhu[ḏ]asa* 11r32.
Cf. ***aparibhuta***.

parimaṇa see ***parimaṇasacea***, ***parimaṇasaceaagara***.

parimaṇasacea adj. Skt. *parimāṇasatyaka*, P *parimāṇasaccaka*, "having truth as the [only] measure."
n.(?) nom.(?) sg. *parimaṇasacea* 6r7.
See also ***parimaṇasaceaagara***.

parimaṇasaceaagara m. Skt. *parimāṇasatyakākāra*, P *parimāṇasaccakākāra*, "the aspect of truth being the [only] measure."
instr. sg. *parimaṇasaceaagareṇa* 11v19.

pariyaṇea gdv. Skt. ~ *parijñeya*, P ~ *pariññeyya*, "to be thoroughly understood."
n. nom. sg. *(*pa)riyaṇeo* 11v29, *pariyaṇeo* 11v29.

parvayida m. Skt. *pravrajita*, P *pabbajita*, "one who has gone forth, a mendicant."
instr. pl. *parvayidehi* 11r31.

palala mn. Skt. *palāla*, P *palāla*, "[stalk of] straw."
nom. sg. *palale* 11r53.

palaśpada pp., "guarded, protected, maintained (?)." (Cf. annotations, p. 187.)
mn.(?) nom. pl. *palaśpada* 4v12.

palaśpidava gdv., "to be guarded, protected, maintained (?)." (Cf. annotations, p. 187.)
mn.(?) nom. pl. *palaśpidave* 4v10, *palaśpidava* 4v2; ? nom. pl. *palaśpidava* 4r28.

palios̱a m. BHS *paligodha*, P *paligedha*, "desire."
nom. sg. *[pa]lios̱e* 4r8; instr. sg. *palios̱eṇa* 6v7.
Cf. ***apalios̱a***.

pava n. Skt. *pāpa*, P *pāpa*, "bad [deed]."
instr. sg. *paveṇa* 4r5.

paśadi v. Skt. *paśyati*, P *passati*, "sees."
abs. *paśita* 11r28.

piala ind. BHS *peyālam*, P *peyyālaṃ*, "(*pialo*:) etc., in short; (in *eva pialo*:) and so on [in this way]; (in *piala yava*:) etc. [up to]."
piala 11r17 (in *piala yava*), *pialo* 4v12 (in *[va] ? pialo*), 11v26 (in *eva pialo*), *(*pi)[a]l(*o)* 11v27 (in *eva pialo*).

picara adj. BHS *pratyarha*, "according to merit."
n. acc. sg. *picara* 4v1 (adv.).

picu ind. Skt. *pretya*, P *pecca*, "after having gone past, after death." (Uncertain; cf. annotations, p. 228.)
picu 11v16.

pidivaṇa (Uncertain; cf. annotations, p. 237.)
unclear: *pidivaṇe* 11v29, *[pidi]vaṇeo* 11v29.

piṣida pp. Skt. ~ *piṣṭa*, P *piṭṭha/pisita*, or abs. Skt. ~ *piṣṭvā*, P rarely *pisitvā*, "crushed."
n. nom. sg. *piṣita* 11r34.

puña n. Skt. *puṇya*, P *puñña*, "merit."
acc. sg. *puña* 11v16.
See also ***puñakṣaya***.

puñakṣaya m. Skt. *puṇyakṣaya*, P *puññakkhaya*, "decay of merit."
nom. sg. *puñakṣae* 4r5.

puyamaṇa pres. part. Skt. ~ *pūjayant*, P ~ *pūjenta*, "honoring."
m. nom. sg. *puyamaṇa* 4r21.

pura ind. Skt. *purā*, P *purā*, "formerly, before."
pura 6v5.

purvagama adj. Skt. *-pūrvagama*, BHS *-pūrvaṃgama*, P *-pubbaṃgama*, "preceded by …"
m. nom. pl. *《? [ma]p[u]rvagama》* 4r5 (reconstruct as *kamapurvagama*?).

purve adv. Skt. *pūrve*, P *pubbe*, "before, earlier."
《purv[e]》 4r28, *《purve》* 4r28, *purve* 6v4 [2×], 11r27, *prove* 6v5.

praïṭhavamaṇa pres. part. Skt. ~ *pratiṣṭhāpayant*, P ~ *patiṭṭhāpenta*, "establishing."
m. nom. pl. *praïṭhavama[ṇa]* 4r22.

praoḍidava gdv. BHS *prachoḍ(ḍ)ayitavya/ prachaḍḍayitavya*, P *pachaḍḍetabba*, "to be thrown away."
n. nom. sg. *praoḍ̱idave* 4r17, 4r19, *[praoḍ̱idave]* 4r19; n.(?) nom. sg. *praoḍ̱idave* 4r16.

pragrida adj. Skt. *prakr̥ta*, P *pakata*, "natural."
n. nom. sg. *[pragri](*de)* 6r8.

pracupaṇa n. Skt. *praytupanna*, P *paccupanna*, "present."
loc. sg. *pracupaṇe* 4v2, *pracu[pa]ṇae* 4r24 (read *pracupaṇe*).
See also ***adidaaṇagadapracupaṇa***.

pracea see ***budhapracea***.

prajahaṇa see ***prajahaṇapridi***.

prajahaṇapridi f. Skt. *prajahanaprīti*, P *pajahanapīti*, "joy of abandoning."
nom. sg. *prajahaṇap[r]i〈*di〉* 11v1.

prajahadi v. Skt. *prajahāti*, P *pajahāti*, "abandons."
pres. 3rd sg. *prajahati* 4r15; abs. *prajahita* 11v29; unclear: *prajaha* 11v29 (reconstruct as *prajahadi* or *prajahidava*).

praña see ***prañaparamida***.

prañaparamida f. Skt. *prajñāpāramitā*, "perfection of insight."
nom. sg. *prañaparamida* 4r16; nom.(?) sg. *pracaparamido* 4r19 (read *prañaparamido*), *[praña](*paramida)* 4r15.

praṇida pp. Skt. *praṇīta*, P *paṇīta*, "superior (?)." (Uncertain; cf. annotations, p. 176.)
unclear: *praṇide* 4r23.

pradigarasuha n. Skt. *pratikārasukha*, P *paṭikāra-sukha*, "happiness due to a remedy."
nom. sg. *pradigarasuhe* 11r25, *pradigara[s](*u)[he]* 11r26; gen. sg. *(*pra)digarasuhasa* 11v12.

pradibhava (Uncertain; cf. annotations, p. 227.)
pradibh[ave] 11v16.

pramuha adj. Skt. *pramukha*, P *pamukha*, (in cpd.:) "headed by …; (adv.:) "first."
n. acc. sg. (?) *pramuha* 11r34 (adv.?).
See also ***edapramuha***, ***kamapramuha-as̱apuruṣ̱a***, ***budhapramuhasapuruṣ̱a***.

praladha pp. Skt. *pralabdha*, P *paladdha*, "seized."
? nom. sg. *[pra]l[adhe]* 4r16 (gender uncertain).

pras̱aṇa see ***prahaṇakarma***.

prahaṇa see ***avarimaṇadoṣ̱aprahaṇa***, ***pariñaprahaṇa***, ***prahaṇakarma***.

prahaṇakarma n. Skt. *prahāṇakarman*, P *pahānakamma*, "act of abandoning."
nom. sg. *prasaṇaka[rmo]* 11r23, *prahaṇakarmo* 11v28.

prahadava gdv. Skt. *prahātavya*, P *pahātabba / pajahitabba*, "to be abandonded."
n. nom. sg. *pajahidava* 11v29, *prahadava* 11v29.

pria see **priaviṇabhavaagradukha**.

priaviṇabhavaagradukha n. Skt. *priyavinābhāvāgraduḥkha*, P *piyavinābhāvāggadukkha*, "suffering due to being separated from loved ones and so on (?)."
instr. sg. *priaviṇabha[vaa]gradukheṇa* 6r3.

pridi f. Skt. *prīti*, P *pīti*, "joy."
nom. sg. *pridi* 11r29, 11r31, 11r32, 11v2 [3×], 11v3 [4×], 11v4 [2×], 11v6, 11v7, 11v9, 11v30, *(*pridi)* 11v9; acc. sg. *pridi* 11r30; nom. pl. *pridi* 4r3, 4r9.
See also **pariñapridi**, **prajahaṇapridi**.

pridisuha n. Skt. *prītisukha*, P *pītisukha*, "happiness of joy."
nom. sg. *pridi[suhe]* 11v1, *pri[dis]uhe* 11v7, *pridisuhe* 11v11, *pridisuha* 11v2.

phaṣadi v. Skt. *spṛśati*, P *phusati / phassati*, "touches."
pres. 3rd sg. *[phaṣa]di* 6v4.

badhaṇa n. Skt. *bandhana*, P *bandhana*, "fetter."
gen. pl. *badhaṇaṇa* 4r25.
See also **saṃsarabadhaṇa**.

bala n. Skt. *bala*, P *bala*, "forceful exertion."
instr. sg. *baleṇa* 6v1.

balava adj. Skt. *balavat*, P *balavat*, "possessed of forceful exertion."
m.(?) nom. sg. *[ba]la[va]* 6v2.

bahira adj. Skt. *bāhira*, P *bāhira*, "outer."
n. nom. pl. *bahira* 11v24–11v25, 11v26, *(*ba)hira* 11v26, *(*bahira)* 11v27, *[bah](*i)[ra]* 11v27.
See also **aȷ̄atvabahira**.

bahu adj. Skt. *bahu*, P *bahu*, "plentiful; (adv.:) for many."
n. acc. sg. *[ba](*hu)* 11r3 (adv.), *bahu* 11r12 (adv.), *baho* 11r1 (adv.); f. nom. sg. *bahu* 6v4.
See also **bahujaṇasasaraṇadukha**.

bahujaṇa see **bahujaṇasasaraṇadukha**.

bahujaṇasasaraṇadukha adj. Skt. *bahujanasādhāraṇaduḥkha*, P *bahujanasādhāraṇadukkha*, "[partaking of the] suffering common to many people."
m. nom. sg. *bahujaṇasasaraṇadukha* 11r25.

bahumaṇa m. Skt. *bahumāna*, P *bahumāna*, "[held in] high esteem."
nom. sg. *bahumaṇa* 6v2; instr. sg. *bahumaṇeṇa* 6v7.

bia see **dukhabia**.

budha m. Skt. *buddha*, P *buddha*, "awakened [one], the Buddha."
gen. sg. *budhe{{hi}}sa* 11r31; gen. pl. *«budhaṇa»* 4r25.
See also **budhadharmasagha**, **budhapracea**, **budhapramuhasapuruṣa**.

budhadharmasagha m. Skt. *buddhadharmasaṃgha*, P *buddhadhammasaṅgha*, "Buddha, Dharma, and Sangha."
nom. sg. *[b](*u)[dhadha]rmasagho* 4r21.

budhapracea adj. Skt. *buddhapratyaya*, P *buddhapaccaya*, "based on [trust in] the Buddha(s)."
m. nom. pl. *«budhapracea»* 4r5, *budhaprac(*e)a* 4r11.

budhapramuha see **budhapramuhasapuruṣa**.

budhapramuhasapuruṣa m. Skt. *buddhapramukhasatpuruṣa*, P *buddhapamukhasappurisa*, "worthy men headed by the Buddha(s)."
gen. pl. *budhapramuhasapuruṣaṇa* 4v4.
Cf. **kamapramuhaasapuruṣa**.

bosa m. Skt. *bodha*, P *bodha*, "awakening."
loc.(?) sg.(?) *bosa* 4r22 (either loc. sg. or first member of a compound).
See also **tribosa**.

bosi f. Skt. *bodhi*, P *bodhi*, "awakening."
nom. sg. *bosi* 11r17.
See also **bosimaḍa**, **bosisatva**.

bosimaḍa mn. Skt. *bodhimaṇḍa*, P *bodhimaṇḍa*, "seat of awakening."
nom. sg. *bosimaḍe* 4r18, *bosimaḍ⟨*e⟩* 4r18; loc. sg. *bosimaḍami* 4r17 [2×].
See also **bosimaḍaṇiṣaṇa**.

bosimaḍaṇiṣaṇa adj. Skt. *bodhimaṇḍanisaṇṇa*, P *bodhimaṇḍanisanna*, "sitting on the seat of awakening."
n. nom. sg. *mosimaḍaṇiṣaṇa* 4r18 (read *bosimaḍaṇiṣaṇa*).

bos̱is̱atva m. Skt. *bodhisattva*, P *bodhisatta*, "aspirant to awakening on the path to buddhahood, bodhisattva."
nom. pl. *bos̱is̱atva* 4r17.

bhaṭarea m. Skt. *bhaṭṭāraka*, "master."
gen. sg. *bhaṭareasa* 6v6.

bhava m. Skt. *bhāva*, P *bhāva*, "existence (BC 6); continuous state (BC 11)."
nom. sg. *[bhava]* 6r2, *bhave* 11r26.
See also ***bhavasaña***. Cf. ***abhava***.

bhavaṇa see ***margabhavaṇa***.

bhavasaña f. Skt. *bhāvasaṃjñā*, P *bhāvasaññā*, "notion of [being of] existence."
nom. sg.(?) *bha[va](*saña)* 6r10.

bhavida Skt. *bhāvita*, P *bhāvita*, "developed." (Uncertain reconstruction.)
unclear: *[bhavid].* 4r6 (context missing).

bhavidava gdv. Skt. *bhāvayitavya*, P *bhāvetabba*, "should come into existence."
n. nom. sg. *bhavidave* 11v8.

bhikṣadi v. Skt. *bhikṣate*, P *bhikkhati*, "begs."
fut. 1st sg. *bhikṣiśe* 4r19.

bhuda adj. Skt. *bhūta*, P *bhūta*, "true."
n. nom. sg. *bhude* 6r8.
See also ***bhudañaṇa***, ***yas̱abhuda***, ***yas̱abhudaaṇuśaśa***. Cf. ***hoda***.

bhudañaṇa n. Skt. *bhūtajñāna*, P *bhūtañāṇa*, "true knowledge."
instr. sg. *bhudañaṇeṇa* 11v17.

bhuyo adv. Skt. *bhūyaḥ*, P *bhiyyo*, "more, again; (here with *na*:) no further, not anew."
bhiu 11r40, *bhio* 11r38, *bhi⟨*o⟩* 11r39, *bhuyo* 4v11.

bhes̱aje n. Skt. *bhaiṣajya*, P *bhesajja*, "medicine."
nom. sg. *bhes̱aje* 11v14.
See also ***bhes̱ajesuha***.

bhes̱ajesuha n. Skt. *bhaiṣajyasukha*, P *bhesajja-sukha*, "happiness due to a remedy."
nom. sg. *bhes̱ajesuhe* 11v13.

bhodi v. Skt. *bhavati*, P *bhavati*, *hoti*, "is; (caus.:) becomes, develops."
pres. 3rd sg. *bhoti* 6v1, 6v2 [2×], 6v3, *[bh](*oti)* 6v1, *[bh](*odi)* 6v7; opt. 3rd sg. *bhavea* 11r52, 11v25, 11v26, 11v27, gloss line1, *[bha]veati* 6r2, *[bhaveadi]* 6r2, *bhaveadi* 6r2; opt. 3rd sg. pass. *[bhavi]{[da]}ea* 11r16 (perhaps read *⟨*aṇu⟩bhavi{da}ea*); impv. 3rd sg. *bhodu* 11v7, 11v8 [2×]; fut. 3rd sg. *hakṣati* 4r2, 4r8, 4r20, *hakṣadi* 4r2, 4r3, 4r9, 4r20 [2×], 4r22 [2×], 4v10, *ha[kṣadi]* 4r5, 4r20, *[hakṣadi]* 4r7, *(*hakṣadi)* 4r9, *ha(*kṣa)[di]* 4r12, *[ha](*kṣa)[di]* 4r22; 3rd sg.(?) *bhaviśadi* 11v24; 3rd pl. *akṣati* 4v11, *hakṣati* 4r3 [2×], 4r4 [5×], 4r10 [4×], 4r11 [5×], 4r12 [2×], 11r8 [2×], *[hakṣa]ti* 4r3, *(*hakṣa)[ti]* 4r3, *[hakṣati]* 4r3, 4r10, *(*hakṣa)ti* 4r4, *⟪hakṣati⟫* 4r5, *⟪(*hakṣati)⟫* 4r5, *[ha]kṣati* 4r5, 4r11, *(*hakṣati)* 4r5, 4r10, *hakṣaṯi* 4r12; 3rd pl.(?) *(*ha)[kṣa]ti* 4r5; abs. *hoita* 4r19.

bhoyi see ***kamabhoyi***.

ma ind. Skt. *mā*, P *mā*, "not."
ma 6v8.

ma- pers. pron., "I, we."
nom. sg. *ahu* 11r14 (cf. BHS *ahu*; see BHSD § 20.7), *[aho]* 6v8 (uncertain, context missing), *[a]h[o]* 6v9 (uncertain, context missing); gen. sg. *mahi* 4r17 (genitive agent), *mah⟨*i⟩* 4r15 (genitive agent), *mama* 4r12, 11r13, *mame* 11v7 [2×], 11v8, 11v9, *me* 4r17, 4r22, 11r14 (or read *cirim eta* instead of *ciri me ta*), *meme* 11v8 (read *mame* or *me*); nom. pl. *mio* 11r14 (cf. P *mayam* = *vayam*); gen. pl. *amahu* 11r39, *amaho* 11r38, *[a]svahu* 11r4, *a[sva]hu* 11r5.

maja n. Skt. *madhya*, P *majjha*, "middle." (Used adverbially in loc. sg., "in the middle.")
loc. sg. *⟪maja⟫* 4r28, *[maja]* 11r27, *maja* 11r27, *⟪maje⟫* 4r25, 4r28, *⟪maj(*e)⟫* 4v4, *[ma]je* 11r9, *⟪[ma](*je)⟫* 4r28, *⟪ma[j](*e)⟫* 4r25.

maṇas̱a n. Skt. *mānasa*, P *mānasa*, "mind, mental action."
nom. sg. *maṇa[s̱a]* 6v1, *maṇas̱a* 6v6.
See also ***mraduamaṇas̱a***, ***saṃthidomaṇas̱a***, ***spuramaṇas̱a***.

matra f. Skt. *mātrā*, P *mattā*, "full measure [of seven]."
nom. sg. *matra* 4r28, *matro* 4v2; acc.(?) sg. *matra* 4v9, 4v11; abl.(?) sg. *⟪matra⟫* 4v10.
See also ***matrasahora***.

matrasahora m. Skt. *mātrāsaṃhāra/-sambhāra*, P *mattāsaṃhāra/-sambhāra* (?), "collection of the full measure [of seven]."
nom. sg. *[ma]tra[sa]horo* 4v12.
Cf. ***idarasahora***.

matredi v. Skt. *mantrayate*, P *manteti*, "says."
opt. 3rd sg. *matreadi* 6v5.

mama* / *mame see ***ma-***

maraṇa see ***jadidukha-yava-maraṇadukha***.

marga see ***margabhavaṇa***, ***margasuha***.

margabhavaṇa f. Skt. *mārgabhāvanā*, P *magga-bhāvanā*, "developing of the path."
nom. sg. *margabhavaṇe* 4r2, *(*ma)r[gabha](*vaṇe)* 4r8–4r9.

margasuha n. Skt. *mārgasukha*, P *maggasukha*, "happiness of the path."
instr. sg. *marga[suhe]ṇa* 11r2.

mahaś̱ie f. Skt. *mahāśrī*, BHS *mahāśriyā*, P *mahāsirī*, "great fortune."
nom. sg. *mahaś̱ie* 11r18, 11r23, *maha[ś̱](*ie)* 11r17.

mahi, ***mio*** see ***ma-***

midha n. Skt. *middha*, P *middha*, "sleepiness."
gen. pl. *midhaṇa* 4v6, *mi(*dhaṇa)* 4r26.

mis̱a adj. Skt. *miśra*, P *missa*, "indiscriminate."
n. acc. sg. *«mis̱o»* 4r23 (adv.), *miṣo* 4v1 (adv.).

mucadi v. Skt./P *muñcati*, "releases" (pass. Skt. *mucyate*, P *muccati*, "is released").
pres. 1st sg. pass. *mucami* 11r38 (perhaps also active = middle; cf. BHSD § 37.16).

muḏea adj. Skt. *mūḍhaka*, P *mūḷhaka*, "perplexed (?)."
unclear: *muḏeasa* 11r29.

me, ***meme*** see ***ma-***

mokṣa m. Skt. *mokṣa*, P *mokkha*, "liberation."
nom. sg. *mokṣa* 11r38, *mokṣe* 11v15; acc. sg. *mokṣo* 11r37; abl. sg. *mokṣade* 11r36; nom. pl. *mokṣa* 4r3; gen. pl. *mokṣaṇa* 4r25, 4v5.
See also ***mokṣasapati***, ***mokṣasuha***.

mokṣasapati f. Skt. *mokṣasampatti*, P *mokkha-sampatti*, "fortune of liberation."
nom. sg. *mokṣasapati* 4r14.

mokṣasuha n. Skt. *mokṣasukha*, P *mokkhasukha*, "happiness / bliss of liberation."
nom. sg. *mokṣasuha* 4r12, *mokṣasuhe* 11r20.

moyea adj. Skt. *mocaka*, "liberating." (Uncertain; cf. annotations, p. 188.)
n. nom. sg. (?) *moyea* 4v4.

mos̱imaḍa see ***bos̱imaḍaṇis̱aṇa***.

mradua see ***mraduamaṇas̱a***.

mraduamaṇas̱a adj. Skt. *mṛdukamānasa*, P *mudukamānasa*, "having a pliant mind."
m. nom. sg. *mraduamaṇas̱a* 6v2.

[1]***ya-*** rel. pron. Skt. *yad*, P *ya*, "who, which."
m. nom. sg. *ya* 11r24, 11v14, *ye* 11r25; n. nom. sg. *ya* 4r12, 4r19 (uncertain), *[ya]* 6v8; acc. sg. *ya* 6v5, *yo* 4r17; mn.(?) nom. sg. *yo* 4r23 [2×]; n.(?) nom. sg. *ya* 11r3; f. acc. sg. *ya* 11r19 (in *ya vela* = BHS *yaṃ velaṃ*), *yo* 11r42 (in *yo vela* = BHS *yaṃ velaṃ*); ? instr. sg. *[yeṇa]* 11v23 (context missing).

[2]***ya*** ind. Skt. *yad*, P *yad*, *yaṃ*, "if, as."
ya 6r9, 6v3 (uncertain if m. or n.), 6v3.

[3]***ya* [in *yam ida*]** rel. pron. Skt. *yad idam*, P *yad idaṃ*, "such as."
n. nom. sg. *yam* 6r3 [6×], 6r4 [2×], *[yam]* 6r2, 6r3.

yaṇa n. Skt. *yāna*, P *yāna*, "vehicle (?)."
nom. sg. *yaṇa* 11r33.

yatra ind. Skt. *yatra*, P *yatra*, "where."
yatra 11r19, 11r43, 11r52, *[ya]tra* 11v23.

yadi ind. Skt. *yadi*, P *yadi*, "if."
yati 11r29, *yadi* 6r8, 6v1, 6v6, 11v3, 11v14 [2×], 11v15, *yidi* 11v6 (read *yadi*).
Cf. ***yahi***.

[1]***yava*** m. Skt. *yava*, P *yava*, "corn."
gen. sg. *yavasa* 11r53.

[2]***yava*** ind. Skt. *yāvat*, P *yāva*, "as far as, up to."
yava 6v7, 11r17, *yavi* 11r36, *[yavi]* 6r4.
See also ***ekadutracadurapaṃcas̱a-yava-sata***, ***jadidukha-yava-maraṇadukha***.

yavade ind. BHS *yāvatā*, P *yāvatā*, "as long as."
yavade 11r8.

yas̱a ind. Skt. *yathā*, P *yathā*, "as; so that (?)."
yas̱a 6r6, 11r5.

yas̱abhuda adj. Skt. *yathābhūta*, P *yathābhūta*, "true, truthful."
n. acc. sg. *yas̱abhuda* 4v1 (adv.); m. instr. pl. *ya⟨*s̱a⟩bhudehi* 4r23, *[yas̱abhude]hi* 4r24, *yas̱abhudehi* 4v2.
See also ***yas̱abhudaaṇuśaśa***.

yas̱abhudaaṇuśaśa m. Skt. *yathābhūtānuśaṃsa*, P *yathābhūtānisaṃsa*, "true benefit."
instr. sg. *yas̱abhudaaṇuśaśeṇa* 4r28.

yaṣave adj. Skt. *yathāvat*, P *yathāva*, *yāthāva*, "as it is."
n. nom. sg. *yaṣa[ve]* 6r8.

yahi ind. Skt. *yarhi*, "when, if."
[ya]hi 6v3, 11v13, *yahi* 6v7 (*yahi* … *tahi*), 11v7.

raga m. Skt. *rāga*, P *rāga*, "passion."
nom. sg. *ra[ga]* 6r8.
Cf. ***viragraaṇuśaśa***, ***virata***, ***vivegaveragrasuha***, ***veragrasuha***, ***suveraa***.

rajaṇa n. Skt. *rañjana*, P *rajjana*, "the act of becoming passionate."
nom. sg. *rajaṇa* 6v8.

rajadi v. Skt. *rajyati*, P *rajjati*, "becomes passionate."
pres. 2nd sg. *rajaṣi* 6r9; 3rd sg. pass. *rajiadi* 6v3, 6v7; 1st pl. *ra[jama]* 6v8; opt. 3rd sg. pass. *ra[ji]eadi* 6v3.

ruva n. Skt. *rūpa*, P *rūpa*, "form."
loc. sg. *ruve* 11r23, 11v28 [2×], 11v30.
See also ***ruvadhadu***, ***ruvaruva***.

ruvadhadu f. Skt. *rūpadhātu*, P *rūpadhātu*, "the form realm."
loc. sg. *ruvadhadu* 11v14.

ruvaruva n. Skt. *rūpārūpa*, P *rūpārūpa*, "form and the formless."
loc.(?) sg. *ruvaruva* 11v28 (context missing).

roa m. Skt. *roga*, P *roga*, "disease."
nom. sg. *gro* 11v13; instr. sg. *[r](*o)[ge](*ṇa)* 6r2 (uncertain reconstruction).
See also ***roasagharya***.

roasagharya n. Skt. *rogasaṅghārya* (?) = ~ *rogasaṃharaṇa*, P ~ *rogasaṅgharaṇa*, "accumulation of disease."
acc. sg. *roasagharya* 11v22.

ladha pp. Skt. *labdha*, P *laddha*, "obtained."
n. nom. sg. *ladhe* 4r17.

labha n. Skt. *lambha*, P ~ *lābha*, "obtaining."
instr. sg. *labheṇa* 11r38.

labhadi see ***lavhadi***.

lavha m. Skt. *lābha*, P *lābha*, "gain."
nom. sg. *lavha* 4r17 (or adverbially used dat. sg. *lābhā* for *lābhāya* as in Pali).

lavhadi v. Skt. *labhate*, P *labhati*, "obtains."
pres. 3rd sg. pass. *labha[di]* 4r18, *labhadi* 11r38, 11r42, 11r43; pres. 3rd pl. *lavheti* 4r17.

lahuṭhaṇa n. Skt. *laghūtthāna*, P *lahuṭṭhāna*, "physical alertness."
gen. pl. *[lah](*u)[ṭhaṇa](*ṇa)* 4r26, *lahuṭhaṇaṇa* 4v6.

likhida pp. Skt. *likhita*, P *likhita*, "written."
n. nom. sg. *likhid[a]* 6r6, *[likh]ide* 6v8.

likhidae adj. BHS *likhitaka*, P *likhitaka*, "written."
n. nom. sg. *likhidae* 6r11.

loadhadu see ***gagaṇadivaliaṣamaloadhadu-***.

loia adj. Skt. *laukika*, P *lokika*, "relating to this world."
n. instr. sg. *«loi[e]ṇa»* 11v15.
Cf. ***aloia***.

loutara adj. Skt. *lokottara*, P *lokuttara*, "superworldly."
n. instr. sg. *loutareṇa* 11v17.

loga m. Skt. *loka*, P *loka*, "[this] world."
abl. sg. *[lo]gado* 4r21.
See also ***loadhadu***.

va ind. Skt. *vā*, P *vā*, "or."
va 6v1, 6v6, 11r21, 11r23, 11v3, 11v6, 11v9, 11v14 [2×], 11v15, 11v28, *(*va)* 11v9, *⟨*va⟩* 11r21.

vacadi v. Skt. ~ *vakti*, P ~ *vatti*, "says, speaks of" (pass. Skt. *ucyate*, P *vuccati*, "is said").
pres. 3rd sg. *vacadi* 11r14 (or read *vucadi*, pass.); pass. *vucadi* 4r18, 6r9, 6v1, 11r1, 11r51, 11v28, *[v](*u)[ca]di* 11v23; fut. 3rd sg. *vaïśadi* 4r6, 4r8, *(*va)[i]śadi* 4r8.

vaṇa ind. Skt. *punar*, P *pana*, "but, on the contrary." (In 4r19, 11r13, and 11r14 used as emphatic particle.)
vaṇa 4r19, 6v3, 11r7, 11r13, 11r14, *[va]ṇa* 11r4.

vatava gdv. Skt. *vaktavya*, P *vattabba*, "to be spoken."
mn.(?) nom. pl. *vatave* 4r24, 4v4.

vada m. Skt. *vāda*, P *vāda*, "statement."
nom. sg. *vado* 4r5.

***vayida* (?)** adj. Skt. *vyayita* (?), "spent."
n. instr. sg. *vayaeṇa* 11r40 (read *vayieṇa* ?).
Cf. ***avayida* (?)**.

varedi v. Skt. *varayati*, P *vāreti*, "choose [for oneself]." (Uncertain, perhaps also Skt. *vārayati*, "prevents, restrains.")
pres. 3rd sg. *varedi* 4r13, *[va]redi* 4r14.

varjamaṇa pres. part. Skt. ~ *varjayavant*, P ~ *vajjenta*, "avoiding."
n. nom. sg. *varjamaṇa* 4r21, 11r6.

varjita pp. Skt. *varjita*, P *vajjita*, "avoided."
mn.(?) nom. pl. *varjida* 4v11; n. nom. sg. *varjita* 11r7 (or abs.).

varjidava gdv. Skt. ~ *varjanīya*, P ~ *vajjanīya* or Skt. *varjayitavya*, P *vajjetabba*, "to be avoided."
mn.(?) nom. pl. *varjidava* 4r24, *«[va]r[jidave]»* 4v9; ? nom. sg. *varjidavo* 4r17 (context missing).

valia see ***gagaṇadivalias̱amaloadhadu-***.

vi ind. Skt. *api*, P *pi*, "also."
vi 4r24, *[vi]* 6v5.

viartha(e) adj. Skt. *vyartha(ka)*, "unprofitable." (Uncertain, perhaps also dat. sg. of *vyartha*, "not for the benefit of …" in both instances.)
n. nom. sg. *viarthae* 6v2, 6v2–6v3.

vijadi v. Skt. *vidyate*, P *vijjati*, pass. "exists." (Only in the phrase *ṇa ida ťhaṇo vijadi*.)
pres. 3rd sg. pass. *vijadi* 11r50, 11r52, 11v11, 11v25.

viñati see ***viñatidukhavidimiśasuha***.

viñatidukhavidimiśasuha n. Skt. *vijñaptiduḥkha-vyatimiśrasukha*, P *viññattidukkhavītimissa-sukha*, "happiness mixed with suffering due to cognition."
nom. sg. *viñatidukhavidimiśasuhe* 11r42.
Cf. ***aviñatisuha***.

viṇabhava see ***priaviṇabhavaagradukha***.

vitra adj. Skt. *vitta*, P *vitta* (?), "acquired (?)."
? nom. sg. *[vitra]e* 6v4 (compound future tense, referent word is missing).
See also ***vitrasua***.

vitrasua n. Skt. *vittasukha*, P *vittasukha* (?), "happiness due to acquired possessions (?)."
nom. sg. *[vi]trasu[a]* 6v4.

vitrea gdv. Skt. *vitārya* (?), "to be gone through (?)." (Form uncertain, either gerund or infinitive; cf. annotations, p. 163.)
n.(?) nom.(?) pl.(?) *(*vitre)[a]* 4r13, *vitrea* 4r14.

vidimiśa see ***atvahisaparahisasarvas̱atva-hisavidimiśasuha***, ***avarimaṇaguṇavidimiśa***, ***avarimaṇadukhavidimiśasuha***, ***kayadukhacitadukhavidimiśasuha***, ***citadukhavidimiśasuha***, ***civarakṣayakaya-kṣayaamoyaṇakṣayadukhavidimiśa-suha***, ***cedas̱iadukhavidimiśasuha***, ***ṇis̱amarthavidimiśasuha***, ***dukhavidimiśasuha***, ***durgadidukhavidimiśasuha***, ***viñatidukhavidimiśasuha***, ***vidimiśasuha***, ***śidaüṣadharaṇadukhavidimiśasuha***, ***saṃsaraüavatiṇirvaṇaṇas̱adukhavidimiśasuha***, ***sarvakayadukhavidimiśasuha***.

vidimiśasuha n. Skt. *vyatimiśrasukha*, P *vītimissa-sukha*, "mixed happiness."
nom. sg. *[vidimiśas]uhe* 11r44.

vipaḏis̱ara n. Skt. *vipratisāra*, P *vippaṭisāra*, "regret." (Used in a phrase where Sanskrit and Pali texts use *vipratisāriṇo* or *vippaṭisārino* respectively.)
nom. sg. *vipaḏis̱ara* 6v8.

vibo(j̄adi) v. Skt. *vibudhyate*, P *vibujjhati*, "becomes aware of, awakens to." (Uncertain reconstruction.)
pres. 3rd sg. *vi[bo]* + + 6v1 (reconstruct as *viboj̄adi*?).

viragra see ***viragraaṇuśaśa***.
Cf. ***vivegaveragrasuha***, ***veragrasuha***.

viragraaṇuśaśa m. BHS *virāgānuśaṃsa*, P *virāgānisaṃsa*, "benefit of dispassion."
loc.(?) sg. *(*viragraaṇuśa)[ś](*e)* 4r2–4r3, *viragraaṇuśaśe* 4r9.

virata pp. Skt. *virakta*, P *viratta*, "dispassionate."
m. gen. sg. *(*viratasa)* 4r2, *viratasa* 4r9.

vivaryaa m. Skt. *viparyăya*, P *vipariyăya*, "opposite, (instr.:) inversely."
instr. sg. *vivaryaeṇa* 4r28.

vivega see ***vivegagada***, ***vivegaveragrasuha***, ***vivegasuha***.

vivegagada m. Skt. *vivekagata*, P *vivekagata*, "[someone who has] gone into solitude."
gen. sg. *vivegagadasa* 11r33.

vivegaveragrasuha n. BHS *vivekavirāgasukha*, P *vivekavirāgasukha*, "happiness of detachment and dispassion."
instr. sg. *vivegaveragrasuhe⟨*ṇa⟩* 11r48–11r49 (uncertain reconstruction of the final *ṇa*).

vivegasuha n. Skt. *vivekasukha*, P *vivekasukha*, "happiness of detachment/seclusion."
nom. sg. *vivegasuhe* 11r20; loc. sg. *vi(*ve)ga-suami* 11r50, *vivegasuhami* 11r49.

viś̱adi card. Skt. *viṃśati*, P *vīsati*, "twenty."
nom. pl. *viś̱adi* 4r3 [2×], 4r9, 4r10.

viṣ̱ajadi v. Skt. *viṣajjate*, P *visajjati* (?), pass. "is attached, adheres to (?)."
abs. *viṣ̱a{ja}[ji]ta* 11v8 (form is uncertain, cf. annotations, p. 226).

vihañadi v. Skt. *vihanyate*, P *vihaññati*, pass. "is distressed, suffers."
pres. 3rd sg. pass. *vihañadi* 11v12 [2×], 11v13.

vucadi see ***vacadi***.

vuta pp. Skt. *ukta*, P *vutta*, "called."
m. nom. sg. *vuto* 11r53.

ve ind. Skt. *vai*, P *vai*, "indeed."
[ve] 4r22.

veragra see ***vivegaveragrasuha***, ***veragrasuha***.

veragrasuha n. BHS *virāgasukha*, P *virāgasukha*, "happiness of dispassion."
loc. sg. *veragrasuhami* 11r49, 11r50.

vela f. Skt. *velā*, P *velā*, "time."
acc. sg. *vela* 11r19, 11r42, *[v]ela* 11r42.

vovaś̱ama m. Skt. *vyupaśama*, P *vūpasama*, "bringing to rest."
nom.(?) sg. *[vovaś̱am]o* 6v6; acc. sg. *vovaś̱amo* 6v6.

vruda pp. Skt. *vr̥ta* for *vr̥tta* (?), "performed (?)." (Uncertain; cf. annotations, p. 168.)
m. nom. sg. *[vr]ud[e]* 4r16.

śaki adj. Skt. *śakya*, P *sakka*, "possible." (Uncertain, perhaps also ind. Skt. *śakyā*, P *sakkā*.)
n. nom. pl. (?) *[śaki]* 4r13, *śaki* 4r14; f. nom. pl. (?) *śaki* 4r13 [2×].

śala n. Skt. *śalya*, P *salla*, "thorn." (MW "anything tormenting or causing pain"; PTSD "often metaphorically of the piercing sting of craving, evil, sorrow etc.")
instr. sg. *[śaleṇa]* 6r3.
See also ***śalasagharya***.

śalasagharya n. Skt. *śalyasaṅghārya* = ~ *śalyasaṃharaṇa*, P ~ *sallasaṅgharaṇa*, "accumulation of thorns."
acc. sg. *(*śalasagharya)* 11v23.

śali m. Skt. *śāli*, P *sāli*, "grain."
nom. sg. *śali* 11r53 [2×].

ś̱aṣ̱idava gdv. Skt. *śaṃsitavya* = *śaṃsanīya*, P *saṃsitabba*, "to be praised, commended."
mn.(?) nom. pl. *ś̱aṣ̱idava* 4v2.

śiṭha n. Skt. *śiṣṭa*, P *siṭṭha*, "the rest."
nom. sg. *śiṭha* 11r29.

śida see ***śidaüṣ̱adharaṇadukhavidimiśasuha***.

śidaüṣ̱adharaṇadukhavidimiśasuha n. Skt. *śītoṣṇadharaṇaduḥkhavyatimiśrasukha*, P *sītuṇhadharaṇadukkhavītimissasukha*, "happiness mixed with suffering due to enduring cold and hot."
nom. sg. *śidaüṣ̱adharaṇadukhavidimiśasuhe* 11r46.

śila n. Skt. *śīla*, P *sīla*, "morality."
nom. sg. *śile* 11r51.

śuña adj. Skt. *śūnya*, P *suñña*, "empty."
m. nom. pl. *śuña* 4r18; mn. nom. sg. *śuñe* 4r18.
See also ***śuñagara***.

śuñagara m. Skt. *śūnyākāra*, P *suññākāra*, "the aspect of [being] empty."
instr. sg. *śuñagareṇa* 11v18.

[1]***śuha*** adj. Skt. *śubha*, P *subha*, "pleasant."
n. nom. sg. *śuhe* 11r20.

[2]***śuha*** n. Skt. *śubha*, P *subha*, "pleasant [state]."
nom. sg. *śuhe* 11r16; nom. pl. *śu[ha]* 4r4, *śuha* 4r11; gen. pl. *śuhaṇa* 4r26, 4v5.

śeṣ̱a mn. Skt. *śeṣa*, P *sesa*, "remainder."
nom. sg. *śeṣ̱a* 6r11; dat.(?) sg. *śeṣ̱ae* 4r28 (or loc.?).

śoa m. Skt. *śoka*, P *soka*, "sorrow."
nom. pl. *śoa* 4r3, 4r10.

śpadima adj. Skt. *smr̥timant*, P *satimant*, "mindful."
n.(?) acc.(?) sg. *śpadimo* 4v3 (adv.?).

śpabhavasa f. Skt. *svabhāvatā*, P *sabhāvatā*, "state of intrinsic nature."
nom. pl. *śpabhavasa* 4v11.

śpaho adv. Skt. *svayam*, P *sayaṃ*, "for oneself."
śpahu 11r3, 11r12, *śpaho* 11r1.

śpriṣ̱aṇa n. Skt. ~ *sparśana*, BHS *spr̥śana*, P *phusana*, "comfort."
gen. pl. *śpriṣ̱aṇaṇa* 4r27, 4v7.
Cf. ***aśpriṣ̱aṇa***.

śriya f. Skt. *śrī*, BHS *śriyā*, P *sirī*, "fortune."
gen. pl. *śriyaṇa* 11r21.
See also ***paṃḍidaśriya***, ***mahaṣ̱ie***.

ṣa card. Skt. *ṣaṣ*, P *cha*, "six."
instr. pl. *ṣ̱ahi* 11r2.
See also ***ekadutracadurapaṃcaṣa-yava-sata***.

ṣada adj. Skt. *ś(r)ānta*, BHS *śāta / sāta*, P *sāta* (?), "content; n. contentment." (Cf. annotations, p. 193.)
n. nom. sg. *ṣade* 11r38, 11r39 [2×], 11r41 [2×], *ṣad(*e)* 11r39–11r40, *«ṣade»* 11v17, *ṣado* 11r14, 11v16; gen. sg. *ṣadasa* 4v12.

ṣadima adj. Skt. *ś(r)āntimant*, P *sātimant* (?), "possessing contentment, being content." (Cf. annotations, p. 202.)
mn.(?) instr. sg. *ṣadimeṇa* 11r13, 11r14.

ṣaṣada adj. Skt. *śāśvata*, P *sassata*, "constant, permanent."
m. dat. sg. *ṣaṣadae* 11r13; n.(?) instr. sg. *ṣaṣadaeṇa* 4v2 (adv.).

saïthida adj. Skt. *svayaṃsthita* (?), "scattered (?)." (Cf. annotations, p. 257.)
n. nom. sg. *saïthida* 6v4.

saṃthida adj. Skt. *saṃsthita*, P *saṇṭhita*, "composed."
m. nom. sg. *sa[ṃ]thido* 6v5 (or n. acc. sg. used adverbially); n. nom. sg. *[saṃ]thidae* 6v5 (compound future tense).
See also ***saṃthidomaṇaṣ̱a***.

saṃthidomaṇaṣ̱a adj. Skt. *saṃsthitamānasa*, P *saṇṭhitamānasa*, "having a composed mind."
m. nom. sg. *[saṃ]thidomaṇaṣ̱a* 6v1, *sa[ṃ]thidomaṇaṣ̱a* 6v6.

saṃsara m. Skt. *saṃsāra*, P *saṃsāra*, "cycle of existence."
nom. sg. *sasaṃra* 11r17.
See also ***saṃsaraüavatiṇirvaṇaṇaṣ̱a-dukhavidimiśasuha***, ***saṃsarabadhaṇa***.

saṃsaraüavatiṇirvaṇaṇaṣ̱adukhavidimiśasuha
n. Skt. *saṃsāropapattinirvāṇanāśaduḥkha-vyatimiśrasukha*, P *saṃsāropapattinibbāna-nāsadukkhavītimissasukha*, "happiness mixed with suffering due to rebirth in the cycle of existence and the destruction of extinction."
nom. sg. *saṃsaraüavatiṇirvaṇa[ṇa]ṣ̱a-[dukhavidi]miśasuhe* 11r45–11r46.

saṃsarabadhaṇa n. Skt. *saṃsārabandhana*, P *saṃsārabandhana*, "fetter to the cycle of existence."
gen. pl. *sa[ṃ]sa[ra]{ra}badhaṇaṇa* 4v4–4v5.

sakṣi (Uncertain, possibly corresponding to Skt. *sākṣin* or *saṃkṣipta* or *sākṣiptam*; cf. annotations, p. 203.)
unclear: *sakṣi* 11r14.

sakṣiteṇa adv. BHS *saṃkṣiptena*, P ~ *saṃkhepato*, "in brief."
sakṣiteṇa 4r12, 4v8, 6r4, 11r22, 11r32, 11r36.

sakhada see ***sakhadaasakhada***.

sakhadaasakhada adj. Skt. *asaṃkhyātāsaṃkhyāta*, P *asaṃkhātāsaṃkhāta*, "enumerated or non-enumerated."
n. gen. sg. *sakhadaasakhadasa* 11r11.

sagaṇia f. Skt. *saṃgaṇikā*, P *saṅgaṇikā*, "society, company."
nom. sg. *sagaṇia* 11r33.
Cf. ***asagaṇiasuha***.

sagha see ***budhadharmasagha***.

sagharya n. Skt. *saṅghārya / saṃhārya* = ~ *saṃharaṇa* (?), P ~ *saṅgharaṇa / saṃharaṇa* (?), "accumulation."
acc.(?) sg. *[sa]gh[arya]* Gloss (context missing); abl. sg. *sagharyade* 11v25, *[sa](*gharyade)* 11v26, *[sagha](*r)[ya]⟨*de⟩* 11v27.
See also ***ak̲h̲adasagharya***, ***gaḍasagharya***, ***dukhasagharya***, ***roasagharya***, ***śalasagharya***.

sacea see ***parimaṇasacea***, ***parimaṇasaceaagara***.

saña f. Skt. *saṃjñā*, P *saññā*, "notion."
nom. sg. *saña* 6v4.
See also ***agaḍasaña***, ***aṇak̲h̲adasaña***, ***atvasaña***, ***arogasaña***, ***aśalasaña***, ***jivasaña***, ***ṇicasaña***, ***bhavasaña***, ***suhasaña***.

sata card. Skt. *sapta*, P *satta*, "seven."
acc.(?) pl. *sata* 4v9, 4v11; instr. pl. *satahi* 4v8, 4v10.
See also ***ekadutracadurapaṃcaṣa-yava-sata***.

satida f. Skt. *saptitā*, P *sattitā*, "sevenness (?)."
instr. pl. *sati[dehi]* 4v12.

satva m. Skt. *sattva*, P *satta*, "living being."
nom. pl. *satva* 4r22; gen. pl. *satvaṇa* 4r21.
See also ***satvahidasuha***. Cf. ***s̱atva***.

s̱atva see ***atvahisaparahisasarvas̱atvahisa-vidimiśasuha***, ***bos̱is̱atva***, ***sarvas̱atva…suha***, ***sarvas̱atvaṇamasaṇivasuha***, ***sarvas̱atvahida***.

satvahida see ***satvahidasuha***.

satvahidasuha n. Skt. *sattvahitasukha*, P *satta-hitasukha*, "happiness of the welfare for [all] beings."
nom. sg. *satvahidasuhe* 11r21.

sadakalo adv. Skt. *sadākālam*, P *sadākalaṃ*, "always."
sadakalo 4v12.

sadriṭhia adj. Skt. *sāṃdṛṣṭika*, P *sandiṭṭhika*, "relating to the present life."
n. acc. sg. *[sadr]iṭhia* 4r10 (adv.), *sadriṭhia* 4v8 (adv.); nom. pl. *sadriṭhia* 4r4; ? nom. pl. *[sadriṭhi]a* 4r3 (context missing).

sapati f. Skt. *sampatti*, P *sampatti*, "fortune."
nom. sg. *sapati* 4r14; acc. sg. *sapati* 11r37; gen. sg. *(*sapatie)* 11r12; gen. pl. *sapatiṇa* 4v8, 11v6, 11v10.
See also ***mokṣasapati***, ***sarvasapati***, ***svasapati***.

saparaïa adj. Skt. *sāmparāyika*, P *samparāyika*, "relating to future/next life."
m. nom. pl. *saparaïa* 4r3; n. acc. sg. *saparaïa* 4v8 (adv.); gen. sg. *(*saparaïasa)* 11r11.
See also ***driṭhadhamiasaparaïa***.

sapurus̱a m. Skt. *satpuruṣa*, P *sappurisa*, "worthy man."
gen. pl. *sapurus̱aṇa* 4r25.
See also ***budhapramuhasapurus̱a***, ***sapurus̱a-darśaṇa***. Cf. ***as̱apurus̱a***.

sapurus̱adarśaṇa n. Skt. *satpuruṣadarśana*, P *sappurisadassana*, "meeting with worthy men."
nom. pl. *《(*sapurus̱a)[da]rśaṇa》* 4r5, *sapurus̱adarśaṇa* 4r11.

sama adj. Skt. *sama*, P *sama*, "same."
m. nom. pl. *same* 4r18; mn. nom. sg. *samo* 4r18; n. nom. sg. *same* 4r18, *samo* 4r17, 4r18, *[sa]mo* 4r18.

s̱ama see ***gagaṇadivalias̱amaloadhadu-***.

samos̱aṇa n. Skt. *samavadhāna*, P *samodhāna*, "meeting, encountering."
instr. sg. *[samos̱a]ṇeṇa* 6r4.
See also ***drudes̱a(*ja)drujaṇasamos̱aṇa***, ***sugadasamos̱aṇasuha***.

sayas̱avi ind. BHS *sayyathāpi*, P *seyyathāpi*, "just as."
sayavisa 11r53 (read *sayas̱avi*).

sarva adj. Skt. *sarva*, P *sabba*, "all, every, each."
m. acc. sg. *sarva* 11r15; n. nom. sg. *sarva* 11r16 [2×], *sarve* 4r20 [2×], 11r16, *[sa]rve* 4r14, *s[a]va* 6v7 (or pl.?); f. nom. sg. *sarva* 4r14.
See also ***atvahisaparahisasarvas̱atvahisa-vidimiśasuha***, ***sarvakayadukhavidimiśasuha***, ***sarvagara***, ***sarvadroaca***, ***sarvarthae***, ***sarvas̱atva***, ***sarvas̱atvaṇamasaṇivasuha***, ***sarvas̱atvahida***, ***sarvasapati***, ***sarvasiṇeha***.

sarvakayadukhavidimiśasuha n., Skt. *sarvakāya-duḥkhavyatimiśrasukha*, P *sabbakāyadukkha-vītimissasukha*, "happiness mixed with suffering of the whole body."
nom. sg. *sarvakayadukhavidimiśasuhe* 11r44.

sarvagara m. Skt. *sarvākāra*, P *sabbākāra*, "every aspect."
instr. sg. *(*sarva)[g̱a]re[ṇa]* 4r21 (uncertain reconstruction).

sarvatra ind. Skt. *sarvatra*, P *sabbattha*, "everywhere, in every case."
《sarvatra》 4r28.
See also ***sarvatrades̱a***.

sarvatradea ind. Skt. *sarvatratāye*, P *sabbattatāya*, "(neg.:) in no way."
sarvatradea 11r32.

sarvatrades̱a m. Skt. *sarvatradeśa*, P *sabbattha-desa*, "(neg.:) nowhere."
instr. pl. *sarvatrades̱ehi* 11r32 (instr. for loc.).

sarvadroaca n. Skt. *sarvadaurgatya*, P *sabba-duggacca*, "every misery."
nom. sg. *sarvadroaca* 4r22; acc. sg. *sarvadroaca* 11r36; abl. sg. *sarvadroacade* 11r38, 11v15; gen. sg. *(*sarvadroacasa)* 11r9, *sarvadroacasa* 11r10, 11r12, *[sarva]-droacasa* 11v20; nom. pl. *(*sarvadroaca)* 4r5, *sarvadroaca* 4r12.

sarvarthae ind. Skt. *sarvārthāya*, P *sabbātthāya(ṃ)*, "in all matters."
sarvarthae 11r53.

sarvas̱atva m. Skt. *sarvasattva*, P *sabbasatta*, "every living being."
instr. pl. *sarvas̱atve[hi]* 11r24.
See also ***atvahisaparahisasarvas̱atvahisa-vidimiśasuha***, ***sarvas̱atva…suha***, ***sarvas̱atvaṇamasaṇivasuha***, ***sarvas̱atvahida***.

sarvas̱atva…suha n. Skt. *sarvasattva…sukha*, P *sabbasatta…sukha*, "happiness … of all beings."
*sa(*r)va[s̱atva].i[ya]ṇ.s(*u)h(*e)* 11r19.

sarvas̱atvaṇamasaṇivasuha n., "happiness … of all beings." (The meaning of *ṇamasaṇiva* is unclear; cf. annotations, p. 207.)
nom. sg. *sarvas̱atvaṇamasaṇivasuhe* 11r19.

sarvas̱atvahida n. Skt. *sarvasattvahita*, P *sabbasattahita*, "welfare for every living being."
nom. sg. *sarvas̱atvahida* 4r22.

sarvas̱atvahisa see ***atvahisaparahisasarvas̱atvahisavidimiśasuha***.

sarvasapati f. Skt. *sarvasampatti*, P *sabbasampatti*, "every fortune."
nom. sg. *(*sa)r[va]sapati* 4r22; acc. sg. *sarvasapati* 11r38; abl. sg. *s[arvasapati]* 11r36 (probably reconstruct as *sarvasapati⟨*e⟩*); gen. sg. *sarpasapatie* 11v20 (read *sarvasapatie*), *sarvasapatie* 11r9, 11r10, *[sa](*r)[va]-(*sa)patie* 11r12; gen.(?) sg. *sarva[sa]patie* 11v15; nom. pl. *sarvasapati* 4r5, 4r12; unclear: *sarvasa(*pati)* 11v16–11v17.

sarvasiṇeha m. Skt. *sarvasneha*, P *sabbasineha*, "every affection."
acc. sg. *sarvasi⟨*ṇe⟩ha* 4r12.

savala adj. Skt. *sabala*, P *sabala*, "with forceful exertion."
m.(?) nom.(?) sg. *saval[o]* 6v1 (or n. acc. sg. used adverbially).

sas̱araṇa see ***bahujaṇasas̱araṇadukha***.

sahora see ***idarasahora***, ***matrasahora***.

siṇeha see ***sarvasiṇeha***.

su see ***sudura***, ***sudes̱asuha***, ***suparibhas̱idava***.

sua see ***vitrasua***. Cf. ***suha***.

sugada see ***sugadasamos̱aṇasuha***.

sugadasamos̱aṇasuha n. Skt. *sugatasamāvadhānasukha*, P *sugatasamodhānasukha*, "happiness due to meeting the 'Sugata' [epithet of the Buddha]."
nom. sg. *su[gadasa]mos̱aṇasuhe* 11r19.

sugadi f. Skt. *sugati*, P *sugati*, "good destination."
nom. pl. *su[gadi]* 4r3, *(*s)u(*gadi)* 4r10; gen. pl. *sugadiṇa* 4r25, 4v4.

suṭhu adj. Skt. *suṣṭhu*, P *suṭṭhu*, "excellent; (here:) proper(ly)."
n. acc. sg. *suṭhu* 6v3 (related to *ñaṇo* or used adverbially).
Cf. ***suṭhuñaṇa***.

suṭhuñaṇa n. Skt. *suṣṭhujñāna*, P *suṭṭhuñāṇa*, "proper knowledge (?)." (Uncertain; cf. annotations, p. 200.)
loc. sg. *suṭhuñaṇami* 11r7 (or *suṭhu* as adv. and *ñaṇami* as loc. sg.).

sudiṇa m. Skt. *svapna*, BHS/P *supina*, "dream."
nom.(?) sg. *su[di](*ṇa)* 6r7.
See also ***sudiṇagara***, ***sudiṇoama***.

sudiṇagara m. Skt. *svapnākāra*, BHS/P *supinākāra*, "the aspect of [being like a] dream."
instr. sg. *sudiṇagar⟨*e⟩ṇa* 11v18.

sudiṇoama adj. Skt. *svapnopama*, P *supinopama*, "like a dream."
n. nom. sg. *sudiṇoamo* 4r16; acc. sg. *sudiṇoamo* 4r15.

sudura adj. Skt. *sudūra*, P *sudūra*, "distant."
n. acc. sg. *s[u]duro* 4r24 (presumably used adverbially, or as first part in compound with *adide*).

sudes̱a see ***sudes̱asuha***.

sudes̱asuha n. Skt. *sudeśasukha*, P *sudesasukha*, "happiness due to a good place."
(Cf. annotations, p. 207.)
nom. sg. *sudes̱asuhe* 11r19.

sudhu adv. P *suddhaṃ*, "only." (Etymology uncertain.)
sudhu 11r14, 11r37, 11v11.

suparibhas̱idava gdv. Skt. *suparibhāṣitavya*, P *suparibhāsitabba*, "to be thoroughly admonished."
mn.(?) nom. pl. *suparibhas̱idavo* 4r23.

suladha pp. Skt. *sulabdha*, P *suladdha*, "easily obtained."
n. nom. sg. *suladha* 4r17.

suveraa n. BHS *suvirāga*, P *suvirāga*, "complete dispassion."
nom. sg. *suverao* 11r5, *《suverao》* 11r32.

suha n. Skt. *sukha*, P *sukha*, "happiness, bliss."
nom. sg. *sue* 11v9, *suhe* 4r20, 11r18, 11r19, 11r21 [3×], 11r42, 11v8, *s(*u)he* 11r19, *s(*u)h(*e)* 11r19, *[s]uhe* 11r23, *suh[e]* 6v4,

Plates

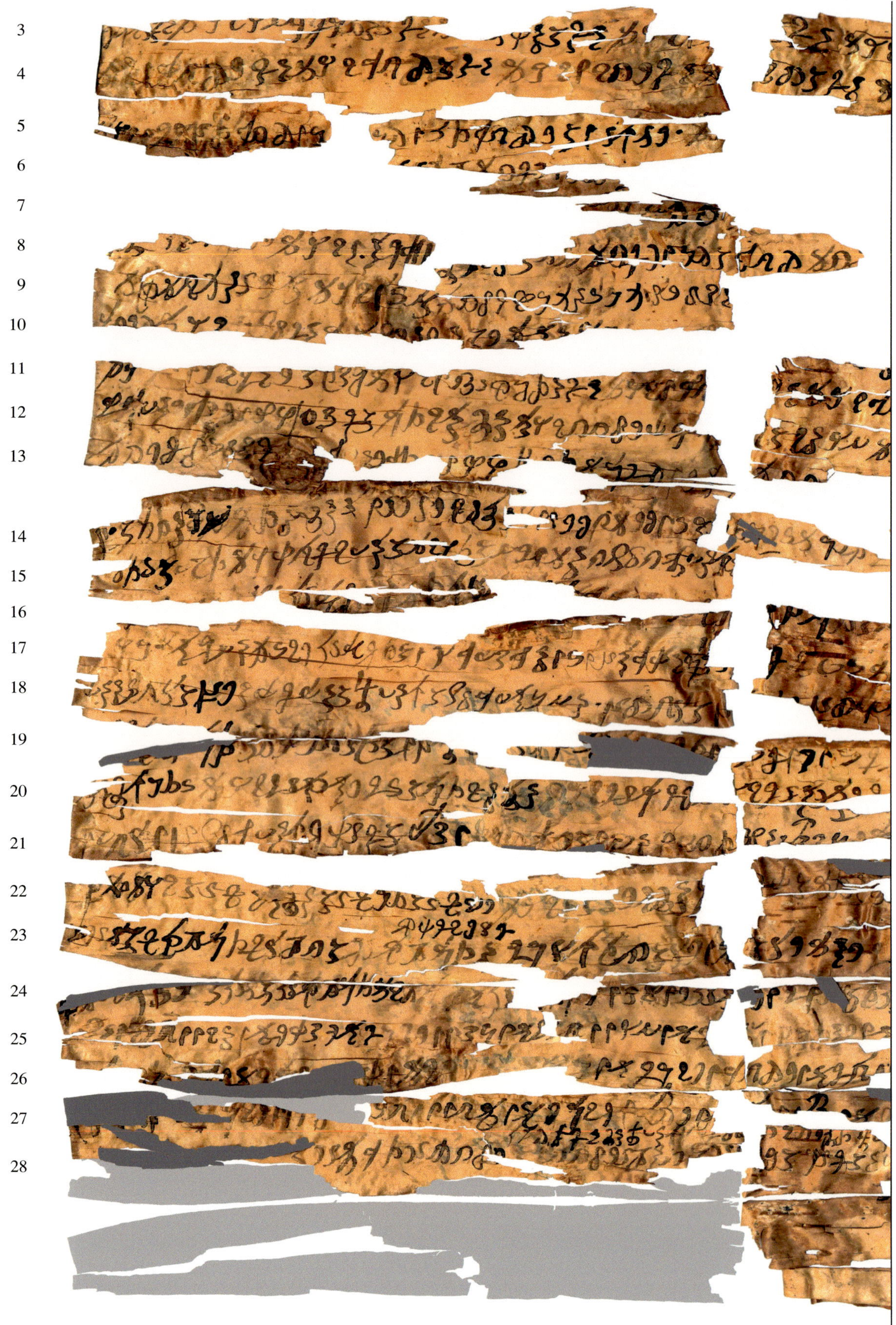

Pl. 1a. BC 4, reconstructed, recto, left half (scale 100 %).

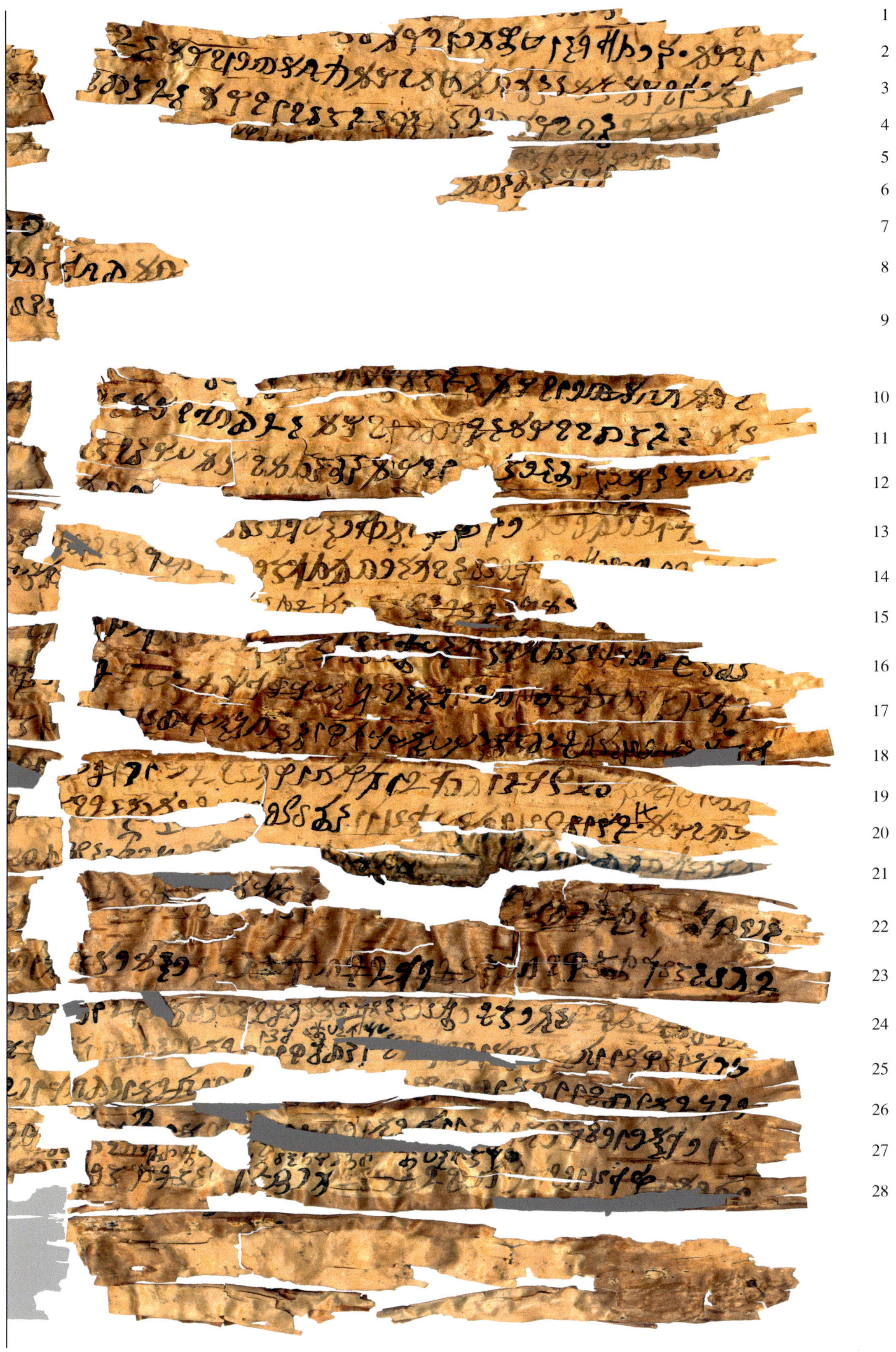

Pl. 1b. BC 4, reconstructed, recto, right half (scale 100 %).

Pl. 2a. BC 4, reconstructed, verso, left half (scale 100 %).

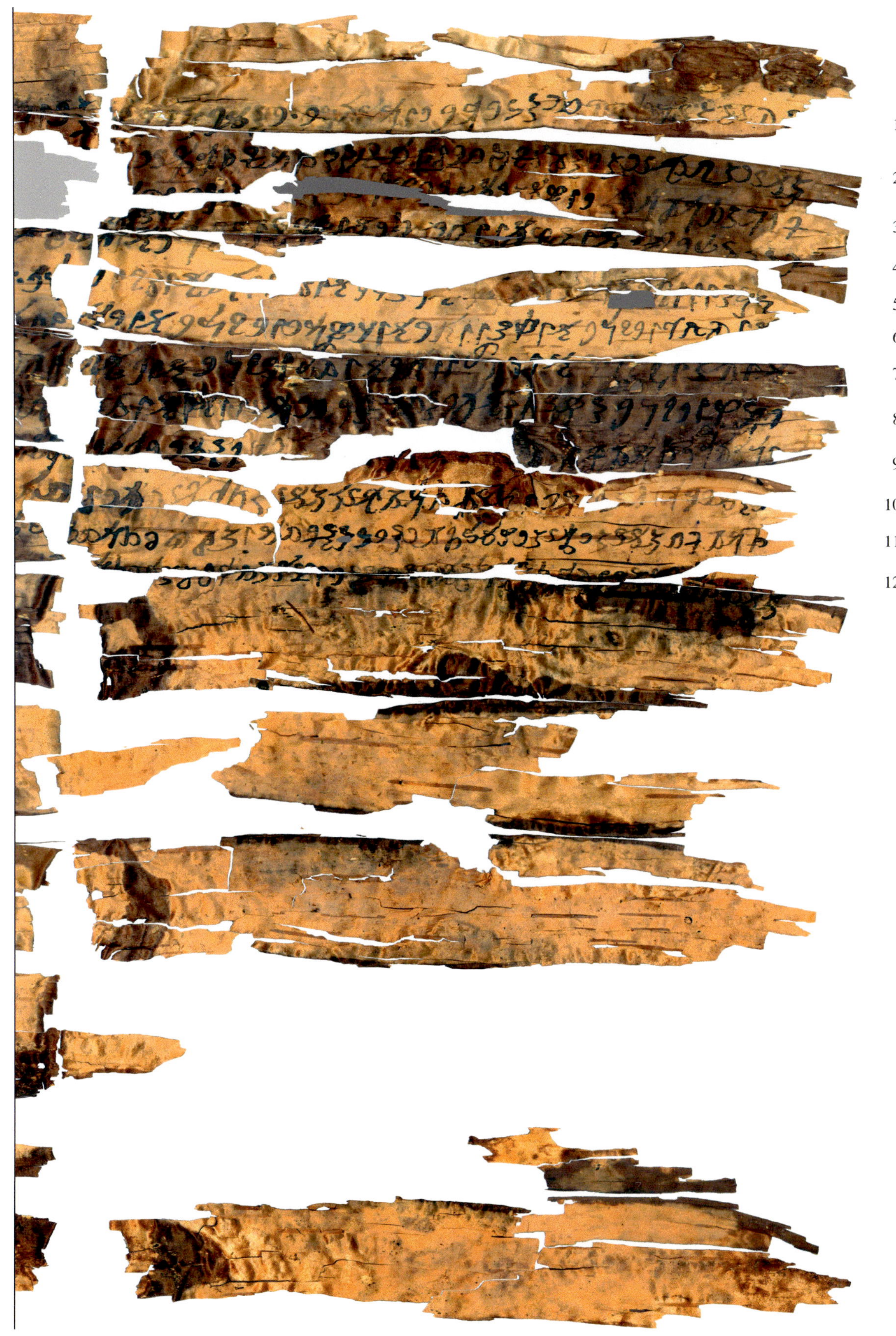

Pl. 2b. BC 4, reconstructed, verso, right half (scale 100 %).

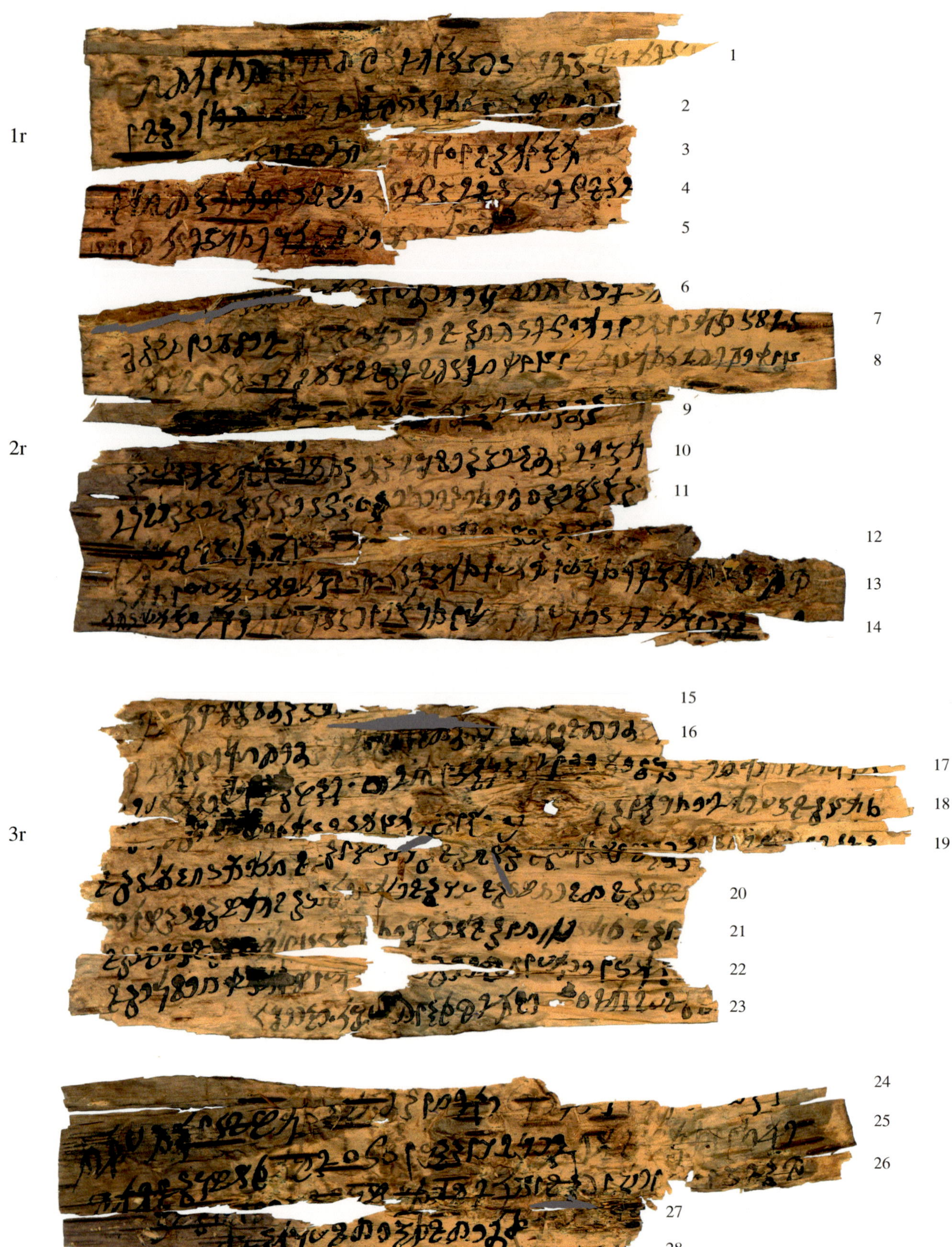

Pl. 3. BC 11, reconstructed, recto, lines 1–26 (scale 100 %).

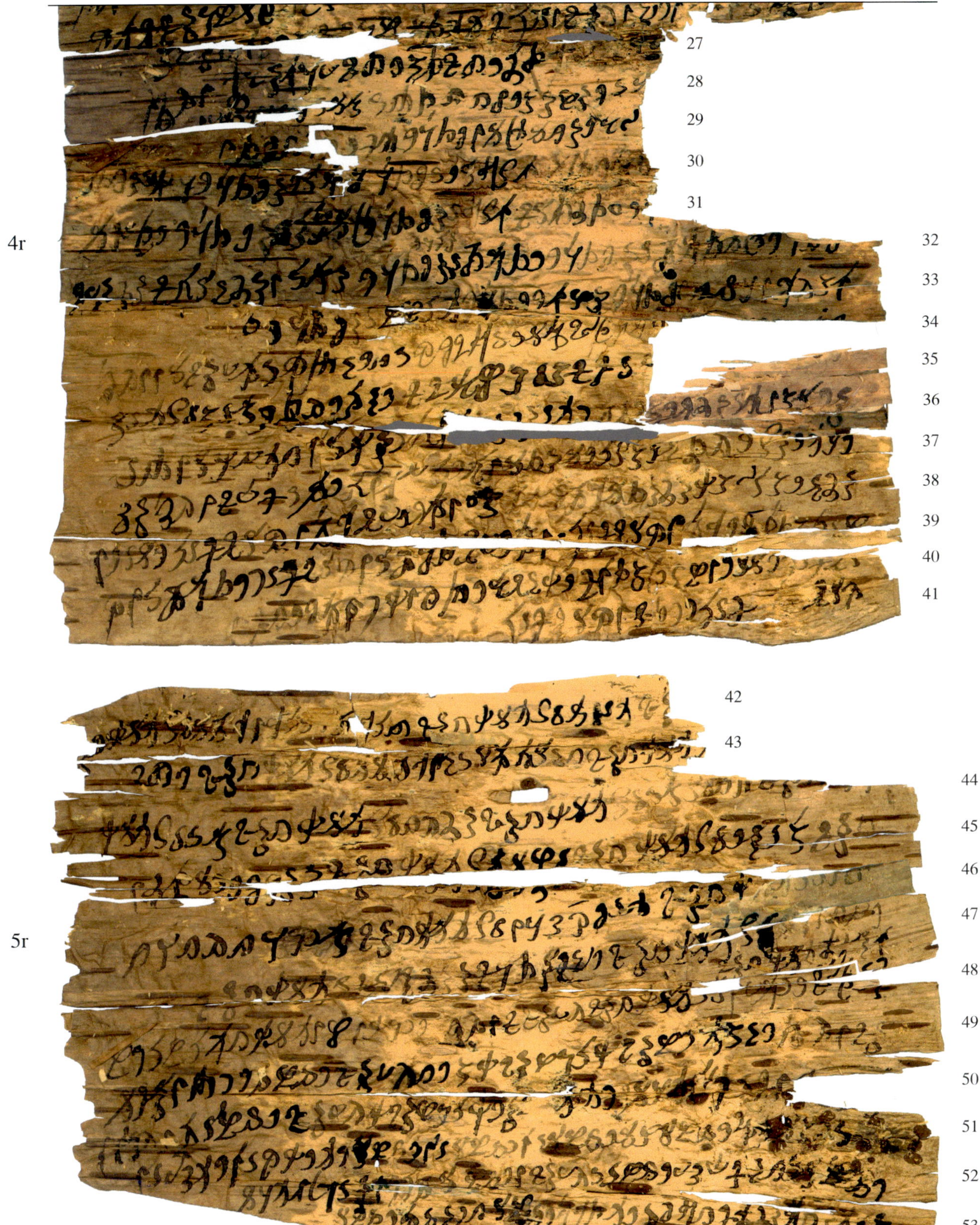

Pl. 4. BC 11, reconstructed, recto, lines 27–53 (scale 100 %).

Pl. 5. BC 11, reconstructed, verso, lines 1–24 (scale 100 %).

Pl. 6. BC 11, reconstructed, verso, lines 25–30 (scale 100 %).

Pl. 7a. BC 6, reconstructed, recto, left half (scale 100 %).

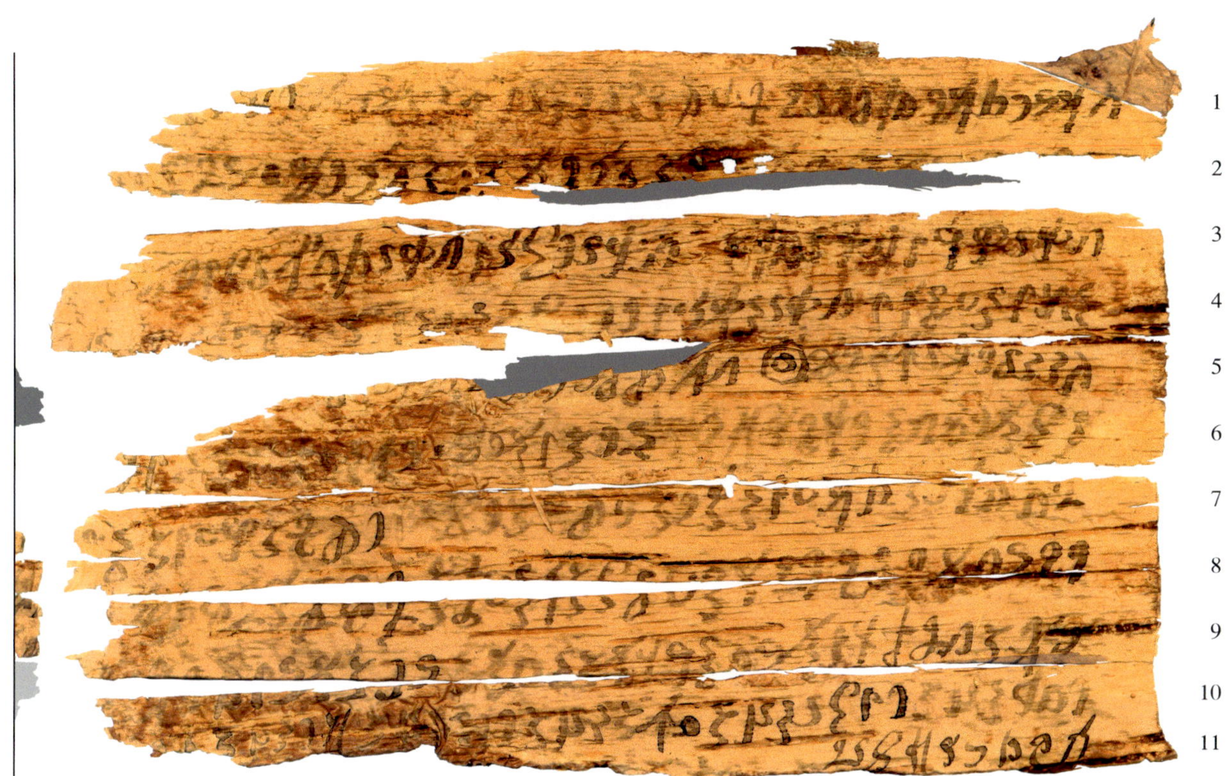

Pl. 7b. BC 6, reconstructed, recto, right half (scale 100 %).

Pl. 8a. BC 6, reconstructed, verso, left half (scale 100 %).

Pl. 8b. BC 6, reconstructed, verso, right half (scale 100 %).

Pl. 9. BC 19, reconstructed, recto (scale 100 %) with presumed width.

Pl. 10. BC 19, reconstructed, verso (scale 100%) with presumed width.